Gard Granerød

Dimensions of Yahwism in the Persian Period

Beihefte zur Zeitschrift
für die alttestamentliche
Wissenschaft

Edited by
John Barton, Reinhard G. Kratz,
and Markus Witte

Volume 488

Gard Granerød

Dimensions of Yahwism in the Persian Period

Studies in the Religion and Society of the Judaean Community at Elephantine

DE GRUYTER

ISBN 978-3-11-045211-2
e-ISBN (PDF) 978-3-11-045431-4
e-ISBN (EPUB) 978-3-11-045317-1
ISSN 0934-2575

Library of Congress Cataloging-in-Publication Data
A CIP catalog record for this book has been applied for at the Library of Congress.

Bibliographic information published by the Deutsche Nationalbibliothek
The Deutsche Nationalbibliothek lists this publication in the Deutsche Nationalbibliografie; detailed bibliographic data are available on the Internet at http://dnb.dnb.de.

Typesetting: Konrad Triltsch, Print und digitale Medien GmbH, Ochsenfurt
Printing and binding: CPI books GmbH, Leck
♾ Printed on acid-free paper
Printed in Germany

MIX
Papier aus verantwortungsvollen Quellen
FSC® C083411

www.degruyter.com

To Prof. Dr Karl William Weyde in gratitude

These people worship God the overseer and creator of all, whom all men worship including ourselves, O King, except that we have a different name. Their name for him is Zeus and Jove. (*Letter of Aristeas*)

Preface

This book is a child that was conceived when I started my postdoctoral research at MF Norwegian School of Theology in August 2010. The idea was to write a monograph about the religion of the Judaeans at Elephantine. My working title was *The Temple of YHW, the God Dwelling in Elephantine: The Non-Biblical Judaism on the Nile Island of Elephantine in the Fifth Century BCE as a Challenge for Biblical Theology.* Now, I have been delivered of the child, which indeed turned out to be a monograph. Throughout the pregnancy, the focus continued to be on the Judaean community at Elephantine in the Achaemenid period. However, as the time lapsed, I found myself emphasising the religio-historical aspects at the cost of the original biblical-theological interest. Therefore, the alternative title jokingly suggested by the PhD student Matthew P. Monger—*The Elephant in the Room: Persian Period Yahwism and the Judaean Community at Elephantine*—does indeed capture some important aspects of the present book. In this volume I do not present any hitherto unknown ancient documents. Instead, what I do offer is a fresh investigation of the so-called Elephantine documents and other relevant sources, working primarily on the basis of texts that already have been published, and focussing particularly on religio-historical questions. I hope to demonstrate that the Yahwism practiced in Elephantine represents a fully-fledged example of Persian-period Judaean religion. In the Persian period, Yahwism had several dimensions, and the historically best-attested one is reflected in the documents from Elephantine. Therefore, my "Bible" is above all the text edition of Bezalel Porten and Ada Yardeni, *Textbook of Aramaic Documents from Ancient Egypt*, vols. I–IV (Jerusalem: The Hebrew University of Jerusalem – Department of the History of the Jewish People, 1986–1999), from which I have also taken the text numbering system—even when I quote translations offered in other text editions than that of Porten and Yardeni, or in a few cases present my own translations. Thus, e.g., A4.1:1–3 refers to Porten and Yardeni, *Textbook of Aramaic Documents from Ancient Egypt*, vol. I, section 4 (which in fact is the so-called Jedaniah communal archive), text no. 1, lines 1–3.

In the preface to *In the Shadow of the Temple: Jewish Influences on Early Christianity* (Downers Grove, IL: InterVarsity Press, 2002), my professor of church history, Prof. Dr Oskar Skarsaune, wrote words I would like to make my own:

> Most authors feel the need for serious disclaimers with regard to books as comprehensive as this one: it simply must contain mistakes of fact, judgement and method. It certainly does. But it lies in the very nature of historical inquiry that "results" are always preliminary and open to revision and improvement. I would very much like to think of a book like this as my contribution to an open-ended conversation going on in the enlightened community of readers.

Others will have to decide to what extent I have succeeded in making this book a fruitful contribution to the ongoing conversation about Persian-period Yahwism and Elephantine. Nevertheless, I am grateful to my wonderful wife, Antone Varhaug Granerød, and our children, Eira, Ansgar and Berge, for supporting (and tolerating) a husband and father who has been pregnant with a book for five years, and who spent the last months of writing it with a DAAD scholarship in Göttingen—leaving the family behind. Moreover, I am grateful to my parents, Grete and Vidar Granerød, for offering our children a second home whenever Antone and I were busy working.

I am grateful to Dr Duncan Burns of Forthcoming Publications for proofreading and copyediting the manuscript and for preparing the indices. I am also grateful to my *alma mater*, MF Norwegian School of Theology, for having shown confidence in me, and to its librarians for their excellent assistance. Moreover, I wish to record the gratitude I feel towards a number of colleagues and research networks: OTSEM, for having given me the opportunity to present papers when I was a postdoc; Prof. John Ma (Oxford) and Prof. Christopher Tuplin (Liverpool), for including me in the project "Communication, Language and Power in the Achaemenid Empire: The Correspondence of the Satrap Arshama"; and Hekhal – The Irish Society for the Study of the Ancient Near East, for hosting conferences at which I was able to present some of my ideas. Furthermore, I am thankful to Dr Martin Hallaschka (Hamburg) for his useful responses to an early draft of Chapter 6, "The Ethical Dimension". My thanks also go to Prof. Dr Reinhard G. Kratz, who gave useful responses at several stages in the writing process. My colleague Prof. Dr Liv Ingeborg Lied gave useful feedback when this work was in its early stages. Furthermore, my colleagues in the Department of Hebrew Bible/Old Testament studies have provided a fine environment for a number of minor and major discussions: the PhD students Ingunn Aadland, Matthew Philip Monger, Håkon Sunde Pedersen (also Asst. Prof., Fjellhaug International University College), Hans-Olav Mørk (The Norwegian Bible Society), Asst Prof. Andrew Wergeland, Prof. Dr Kristin Joachimsen, Prof. Dr Corinna Körting (now University of Hamburg), and—last but not least—Prof. Dr Karl William Weyde. Throughout the entire writing process Prof. Weyde has been mentor, critical reader, and "cheer leader" (although I suspect that he doesn't agree with everything in this book!). I do not exaggerate when I say that I would not have been able to bring this project to completion without his generous support. Therefore, it is an honour to dedicate this book to Prof. Weyde: teacher, *Doktorvater*, colleague and friend.

Stokke (Norway) and Göttingen, Autumn 2015
Gard Granerød

PS:
The lion's share of the book is original work. However, parts of section 5.3, "The Elephantine Judaean Temple Foundation Narrative," builds upon Gard Granerød, "The Former and the Future Temple of YHW in Elephantine: A Traditio-Historical Case Study of Ancient Near Eastern Antiquarianism," *ZAW* 127 (2015): 63–77. Moreover, parts of section 5.4, "Myths about Sacral Kingship," draws upon *idem*, "A Forgotten Reference to Divine Procreation? Psalm 2:6 in Light of Egyptian Royal Ideology," *VT* 60 (2010): 323–336, and *idem*, "'By the Favour of Ahuramazda I Am King': On the Promulgation of a Persian Propaganda Text among Babylonians and Judaeans," *JSJ* 44 (2013): 455–480.

Contents

Abbreviations

ADPV	Abhandlungen des Deutschen Palästina-Vereins
ABD	*Anchor Bible Dictionary*. Edited by David Noel Freedman. 6 vols. New York: Doubleday, 1992
AH	Achaemenid History
AJEC	Ancient Judaism and Early Christianity
AJJS	*Australian Journal of Jewish Studies*
ANET	*Ancient Near Eastern Texts Relating to the Old Testament*. Edited by J. B. Pritchard. 3rd ed. Princeton, 1969
AOAT	Alter Orient und Altes Testament
ATANT	Abhandlungen zur Theologie des Alten und Neuen Testaments
ATD	Das Alte Testament Deutsch
BA	*Biblical Archaeologist*
BAR	*Biblical Archaeology Review*
BASOR	*Bullentin of the Americal School of Oriental Research*
BCSMS	Bullentin of the Canadian Society for Mesopotamian Studies
BEvtThA	Beiträge zur evangelischen Theologie: theologische Abhandlungen
Bib	*Biblica*
BibEnc	Biblical Encyclopedia
BG	Biblische Gestalten
BJSUCSD	Bibical and Judaic Studies from the University of California, San Diego
BN	*Biblische Notizen*
BO	*Bibliotheca Orientalis*
BWANT	Beiträge zur Wissenschaft von Alten Testament und Neuen Testament
BZAW	Beihefte zur Zeitschrift für die alttestamentliche Wissenschaft
CAD	*The Assyrian Dictionary of the Oriental Institute of the University of Chicago*. Chicago: The Oriental Institute of the University of Chicago, 1956–2006
CAL	*Comprehensive Aramaic Lexicon*. Edited by Del Hillers, Joseph Fitzmyer S.J., Stephen A. Kaufman, M. Sokoloff, et al. URL: http://cal1.cn.huc.edu/index.html
CBET	Contributions to Biblical Exegesis and Theology
CBQ	*Catholic Biblical Quarterly*
CBQMS	Catholic Biblical Quarterly Monograph Series
CHANE	Culture and History of the Ancient Near East
CHJ	*Cambridge History of Judaism*. Edited by William D. Davies and Louis Finkelstein. 4 vols. Cambridge: Cambridge University Press, 1984–2006
CII	Corpus Inscriptionum Iranicarum: Part I – Inscriptions of Ancient Iran
COMES	Civitatum Orbis MEditerranei Studia
ConBNT	Coniectanea Biblica: New Testament Series
ConBOT	Coniectanea Biblica: Old Testament Series
COS	*The Context of Scripture*. Edited by W. W. Hallo. 3 vols. Leiden, 1997–2002
CPJ	*Corpus Papyrorum Judaicarum*. Edited by Victor A. Tcherikover. 3 vols. Cambridge: Cambridge University Press, 1957–1964
CUSAS	Cornell University Studies in Assyriology and Sumerology
DB	Darius I's Rock Inscription at Bisitun
DB Aram	The Aramaic version of DB

DB Bab	The Babylonian version of DB
DNa	Darius's inscription from Naqsh-e Rustam (a)
DSe	Darius's inscription from Susa (e)
DSf	Darius's inscription from Susa (f)
DSk	Darius's inscription in Old Persian on mud-baked brick from Susa
DZc	Darius's inscription from the Red Sea Canal (c)
DDD	*Dictionary of Deities and Demons in the Bible*. Edited by Karel van der Toorn, Bob Becking, and Pieter W. van der Horst. Leiden: Brill, 2nd rev. ed. 1999
DM	Demotische Studien
DMOA	Documenta et Monumenta Orientis Antiqui
DNWSI	*Dictionary of the North-West Semitic Inscriptions*. J. Hoftijzer and K. Jongeling. 2 vols. Leiden: Brill, 1995
EBR	*Encylopedia of the Bible and Its Reception*. Edited by Hans-Josef Klauck et al. Berlin: de Gruyter, 2009–
EIr	*Encyclopaedia Iranica*. Edited by Ehsan Yarshater. London: Routledge and Kegan Paul, 1982–
EncJud	*Encyclopaedia Judaica*. Edited by Fred Skolnik and Michael Berenbaum. 2nd rev. ed. 22 vols. Detroit: Macmillan Reference USA, 2007
EvT	*Evangelische Theologie*
FAS	FAS: Publikationen des Fachbereichs Angewandte Sprachwissenschaft der Johannes Gutenberg-Universität Mainz in Germersheim, Reihe A: Abhandlungen und Sammelbände
FAT	Forschungen zum Alten Testament
FGH	F. Jacoby, *Die Fragmente der Griechischen Historiker*. Leiden: Brill, 1954–1964
GOF	Göttinger Orientforschungen
HALOT	Koehler, L., W. Baumgartner, and J. J. Stamm, *The Hebrew and Aramaic Lexicon of the Old Testament*. Translated and edited under the supervision of M. E. J. Richardson. 4 vols. Leiden, 1994–1999
HdO	Handbuch der Orientalistik
HKAO	Hilfsbücher zur Kunde des Alten Orients
HSM	Harvard Semitic Monographs
HTR	*Harvard Theological Review*
IBK	Innsbrucker Beiträge zur Kulturwissenschaft
ILR	*Israel Law Review*
INJ	*Israel Numismatic Journal*
JAOS	*Journal of the American Oriental Society*
JASBC	*Journal of the American Society of Brewing Chemists*
Jastrow	Marcus Jastrow, *Dictionary of the Targumim, the Talmud Babli and Yerushalmi, and the Midrashic Literature*. New York: Title, 2nd ed. 1903
JBL	*Journal of Biblical Literature*
JEA	*Journal of Egyptian Archaeology*
JNES	*Journal of Near Eastern Studies*
JNSL	*Journal of Northwest Semitic Languages*
JQR	*Jewish Quarterly Review*
JRAS	*Journal of the Royal Asiatic Society*
JSHRZ	Jüdische Schriften aus hellenistisch-römischer Zeit
JSJ	*Journal for the Study of Judaism in the Persian, Hellenistic, and Roman Periods*

JSOT	*Journal for the Study of the Old Testament*
JSOTSup	Journal for the Study of the Old Testament Supplement Series
JSS	*Journal of Semitic Studies*
KAI	*Kanaanäische und aramäische Inschriften.* H. Donner and W. Röllig. 2nd ed. Wiesbaden, 1966–1969
Kairós	*Kairós*
KUT	Kohlhammer Urban-Taschenbücher
LÄ	*Lexikon der Ägyptologie.* Edited by Wolfgang Helck, Eberhard Otto, and Wolfhart Westendorf. Wiesbaden: Harrassowitz, 1972–1992
LACTOR	London Association of Classical Teachers – Original Records
LAS	Leipziger Altorientalistische Studien
LCL	Loeb Classical Library
LOS	Lehrbücher orientalischer Sprachen
LSTS	Library of Second Temple Studies
MDAIK	*Mitteilungen des Deutschen Archäologischen Instituts Abteilung Kairo*
MémAIBLIF	*Mémoires présentés par divers savants à l'Académie des inscriptions et belles-lettres de l'Institut de France*
MAIBL	Mémoires de l'Académie des inscriptions et belles-lettres
MCM	Media and Cultural Memory = Medien und kulturelle Erinnerung
MBPF	Münchener Beiträge zur Papyrusforschung und antiken Rechtsgeschichte
MC	Mesopotamian Civilizations
Méditer	*Méditerranées*
Memorie	Memorie. Serie VIII - Classe di scienze morali, storiche e filologiche
MSSSUS	Monografie scientifiche: Serie Scienze umane e sociali
NEA	*Near Eastern Archaeology*
NRSV	New Revised Standard Version
Numen	*Numen: International Review for the History of Religions*
OBO	Orbis Biblicus et Orientalis
OIP	Oriental Institute Publications
OIS	Oriental Institute Seminars
OLA	Orientalia Lovaniensia Analecta
Or	*Orientalia*
OSAD	Oxford Studies in Ancient Documents
OTL	Old Testament Library
OWC	Oxford World's Classics
PF	Persepolis Fortification tablets, published in R. T. Hallock, *Persepolis Fortification Tablets.* OIP 92. Chicago: University of Chicago Press, 1969.
PLO	Porta Linguarum Orientalium
RB	*Revue biblique*
RBL	*Review of Biblical Literature*
RGRW	Religions in the Graeco-Roman World
RlA	*Reallexikon der Assyriologie und vorderasiatischen Archäologie.* Edited by Erich Ebeling et al. Berlin: de Gruyter, 1928–
RSO	*Rivista degli Studi Orientali*
SAOC	Studies in Ancient Oriental Civilizations
SBFCMa	Studium Biblicum Franciscanum, Collectio major
SBLSBS	Society of Biblical Literature Sources for Biblical Study

SBS	Stuttgarter Bibelstudien
Sem	*Semitica*
Semeia	*Semeia*
SemeiaSt	Semeia Studies
SHJPLIMS	Studies in the History of the Jewish People and the Land of Israel Monograph Series
SHR	Studies in the History of Religions
STAR	Studies in Theology and Religion
SymS	Symposium Series
TADAE, I–IV	*Textbook of Aramaic Documents from Ancient Egypt*. Newly Copied, Edited and Translated into Hebrew and English by Bezalel Porten and Ada Yardeni. 4 vols. Jerusalem: The Hebrew University of Jerusalem – Department of the History of the Jewish People, 1986–1999
TB	Theologische Bücherei
TeoT	*Teologisk tidsskrift*
Transeu	*Transeuphratène*
TSAJ	Texte und Studien zum antiken Judentum
TUAT	*Texte aus der Umwelt des Alten Testaments*. Edited by Otto Kaiser. Gütersloh, 1984–
UF	*Ugarit-Forschung*
VT	*Vetus Testamentum*
VTSup	Supplements to Vetus Testamentum
VWGT	Veröffentlichungen der Wissenschaftlichen Gesellschaft für Theologie
WAW	Writings from the Ancient World
WAWSup	Writings from the Ancient World Supplement Series
WiBiLex	*Das wissenschaftliche Bibellexikon im Internet* (*WiBiLex*). Edited by Michaela Bauks and Klaus Koenen. Stuttgart: Deutsche Bibelgesellschaft, 2004–. URL: http://www.bibelwissenschaft.de/wibilex/
WUNT	Wissenschaftliche Untersuchungen zum Neuen Testament
WZKM	*Wiener Zeitschrift für die Kunde der Morgenlandes*
ZA	*Zeitschrift für Assyriologie*
ZÄS	*Zeitschrift für ägyptische Sprache und Altertumskunde*
ZAW	*Zeitschrift für die alttestamentliche Wissenschaft*
ZPE	*Zeitschrift für Papyrologie und Epigraphik*

1 Introduction

1.1 Problem and Hypotheses

What was Judaean religion in the Persian period like? And is it necessary to use the Bible to give an answer to this question?

Not surprisingly, generations of biblical scholars have not seldom resorted to biblical texts from or relating to the Persian period in order to answer this question and to find a historical scheme in accordance with which one could describe the religious developments. Some of these texts, like Ezra and Nehemiah, contain narratives about incidents that took place in the Persian province of Judah after the return of the Judaeans from Babylon after the exile. Others, like Haggai and Zechariah, contain prophecies addressed to the Judaeans or their leaders in Jerusalem, prophecies that explicitly are spoken in the Persian period. In addition, the question has been informed by biblical texts that biblical scholars date to the Persian period on the basis of the various methods that have developed during the last centuries of biblical criticism (for instance, Isa 56–66, 1–2Chr, and several psalms). The biblical text types in question have different tendencies. An attempt to answer the initial question on the basis of these sources will not give a coherent and univocal result. Nevertheless, I believe that I am on firm ground when stating that any reconstruction of Judaean religion in the Persian period that is made on the basis of the biblical sources *alone* (including both the texts' face value *and* the critical research on the texts) will share certain characteristics. Some of them may be summarised thus:

- In the Persian period the worship of YHWH, and YHWH alone, became normative for the inhabitants of the province of Judah.
- In the Persian period the inhabitants of Judah considered themselves as the true religious heirs of the inhabitants of Israel and Judah of the monarchic period.
- In the Persian period the only true, legitimate cultic centre for the worship of YHWH was the temple of YHWH that had been rebuilt in the reconstructed city of Jerusalem.
- The Babylonian exile was, for better or worse, an epoch-making period in the history of Israelite and Judaean religion(s), and for that reason a number of scholars find no reason to abandon the dichotomy intrinsic in the distinction between the so-called preexilic period and the postexilic period.
- In the Persian period the Torah of YHWH revealed to Moses was about to become a religious source of utmost importance and eventually *the* source of religious authority *par excellence*.

- The Persian period was the formative period for much of the biblical literature. During this period religious texts other than the Torah (such as prophetic books) also gained an increased importance.

However, although the Hebrew Bible is an important source for the history of Judaean religion, the relationship of this collection of ideological and in part propagandistic texts to the religion that was actually lived and practiced by the Judaeans (and their predecessors) is complex. The texts of the Hebrew Bible do indeed offer templates that can be, and often actually are, used when reconstructing the history of Israelite and Judaean religion. Suffice it to mention the idea of the centralisation of the YHWH cult to Jerusalem. But, one should acknowledge that the biblical texts are ideological texts that themselves (or perhaps I should say: their authors) are in (fierce) dialogue with religious developments at the time they were written or edited. So, from a religio-historical perspective the biblical texts are *part* of the history of religion that they at the same time portray.

In this study I seek to approach the initial question concerning Judaean religion in the Persian period in a different way. An assumption that underlies this study is that *religious diversity* was characteristic of the history of Israelite and Judaean religion(s), as has been demonstrated in many recent contributions that are based on the various sources.[1] One particular example of *lived Judaean religion* in the Persian period is reflected in the many Aramaic texts that stem from or attest to the fifth-century BCE Judaean community at the Nile island of Elephantine.[2] This study takes as a point of departure the views

- that the religion practiced in the fifth-century BCE Elephantine community and which is reflected in, *inter alia*, the so-called Elephantine documents as a matter of fact represent a *relatively well-attested* manifestation of *lived Judaean religion* in the Persian period,

1 See, e.g., the contributions in Francesca Stavrakopoulou and John Barton, eds., *Religious Diversity in Ancient Israel and Judah* (London: T&T Clark, 2010). Furthermore, see Erhard S. Gerstenberger, *Israel in the Persian Period: The Fifth and Fourth Centuries B.C.E.*, BibEnc 8 (Atlanta: Society of Biblical Literature, 2011), 136–139.

2 Our sources for the Judaean garrison in Upper Egypt are primarily Aramaic papyri and ostracon inscriptions that have either been found in or assumed to originate from Elephantine. The standard edition of the relevant primary sources is Bezalel Porten and Ada Yardeni, *Textbook of Aramaic Documents from Ancient Egypt*, vols. I–IV (Jerusalem: The Hebrew University of Jerusalem – Department of the History of the Jewish People, 1986–1999). Comprehensive introductions to Elephantine and the documents discussed in this study can be found in, e.g., Alejandro F. Botta, "Elephantine," *EBR* 7: 648–651; and Bezalel Porten, "Elephantine Papyri," *ABD* 2: 445–455.

- that this lived religion can be characterised as a form of *Yahwism*, and
- that this particular form of Yahwism may even function as a *window* into the contemporary, *lived* Yahwism of the province of Judah in the Persian period.

I believe these assumptions are justified by several factors. First, the self-definition of the community in question shows that it considered itself a *Judaean*[3] community. The Judaean [*sic*] community we meet in the Aramaic documents from ancient Egypt refers to itself as "the Judaean garrison" or simply "the Judaeans," although its members also occasionally used the designation "Aramaeans."[4] This self-designation is used both by individuals in private letters and contracts and by the community as a whole in official letters. Moreover, particularly important is a letter sent by the leaders of the Elephantine community to various leading groups in the province of Judah (A4.7/A4.8 [two drafts of one and the same letter]). In the letter sent to the governor of Judah, which refers to a previous letter to "the nobles of Judah/the Judaeans," the leaders of the Elephantine community refer to themselves as "Judaeans," that is, they use the same ethnicon. A student of Judaean religion in the Persian period should take this claim seriously. There is no reason to dismiss the community's definition of itself as being Judaean, although the question of the origin of the community remains obscure.[5] Quite to the contrary, an unbiased approach will have to regard the community and its members in accordance with their own self-definition: as Ju-

3 In the present study the English term "Judaean," and not "Jewish," will render the Aramaic word *yhwdy* which is used in the fifth-century BCE textual sources for the Judaean [*sic*] community at Elephantine. First, when used in the texts in question the term *yhwdy* is often used in the same context as other ethnicity/geographical designations such as "Egyptian" (*mṣry*), "Caspian" (*kspy*), "Babylonian" (*bbly*), cf., e.g., B2.2. Second, the leaders of the Elephantine community in question describe themselves as *yhwdyʾ* of Elephantine in a letter addressing i.a. the governor of *yhwd* ("Judah," Aramaic: "Yehud") and in which they refer to a previous letter written to i.a. the high priest of Jerusalem and the nobles of *yhwdyʾ* ("the Judaeans," alternatively "the Yehudites"), cf. A4.7:1, 18 – 19, 22 and the parallel text in A4.8. The use of one and the same ethnicity designation suggests that the community of Yahwists at Elephantine identified itself with the inhabitants of Jerusalem and Judah—regardless whether or not this was a "historically correct" designation in light of the origin of the community. Consequently, in my opinion the term "Judaean" is a more appropriate rendition of the Aramaic *yhwdy* than is the English "Jewish."

4 In her recently published study, Angela Rohrmoser solves the problem by referring to the Yahwists at the southern border of Egypt as "the Judaeo-Aramaeans of Elephantine," cf. Angela Rohrmoser, *Götter, Tempel und Kult der Judäo-Aramäer von Elephantine: Archäologische und schriftliche Zeugnisse aus dem perserzeitlichen Ägypten*, AOAT 396 (Münster: Ugarit-Verlag, 2014), 6 – 8, 70 – 73.

5 For a recent overview of various conjectures about the origin of the group and the date of its arrival at Elephantine, see Rohrmoser, *Götter, Tempel und Kult*, 73 – 81.

daeans, who admittedly happen to be living in Upper Egypt, but who in spite of that call themselves Judaeans, and for that reason have to be treated as such.

Second, that it is appropriate to characterise the religion reflected in the Elephantine documents as Yahwism is justified in several ways. The centre of the community's religious life was the temple of YHW in Elephantine, YHW being the god who is sometimes called"the god who dwells in Elephantine." Etymologically, there is no doubt that YHW is identical with the biblical god YHWH, the main god of the people of Israel and Judah in the monarchic period and the god that the Judaeans (and the Samaritans) worshipped in the Persian period. This overall impression is not threatened by the fact that several documents clearly show that Judaeans in Elephantine were by no means "monotheists" or even "monolatrists," to use modern and probably also anachronistic terms.[6] Even if one may speak about a Judaean pantheon at Elephantine,[7] the personal names from Elephantine also justify that the lived religion was a form of Yahwism. The divine name used in the theophoric names of the individuals associated with the Elephantine community is YHW.

Third, the Elephantine community stood in contact with Jerusalem. Although Elephantine was located on the traditional southern border of Egypt, it was not an isolated outpost on the fringe of the world. The Nile was navigable all the way from the Nile delta to Elephantine. A journey from Elephantine to Jerusalem might take approximately one month.[8] In comparison, according to the Bible it took Ezra around *four months* to travel from Babylon to Jerusalem. In terms of travel time, the Judaeans in Elephantine were much closer to Jerusalem than was the priest-scribe who is often accorded great importance in the (re-)formation of Judaean religion in the Persian period. Whereas this may indicate potential contact and demonstrate that the historical-geographical conditions for travelling between Elephantine and Jerusalem were more favourable than those between Babylon and Jerusalem, it is also evidenced by documents from Elephantine that there was actually a two-way contact between Jerusalem and Judah (and Samaria). Not only did the Judaeans in Elephantine know the names of the tenuring governors of Judah and Samaria (in this case, even the names of the sons of the governor) and the high priest in Jerusalem (cf. A4.7 par.), they also wrote letters to them and even got a reply (although the Judaeans

---

6 For a discussion of the idea of monotheism and the use of it in (modern, post-enlightenment) Europe, see Nathan MacDonald, *Deuteronomy and the Meaning of "Monotheism"*, 2nd ed., FAT 2. Reihe 1 (Tübingen: Mohr Siebeck, 2012), 5–58.

7 See, e.g., Gard Granerød, "'By the Favour of Ahuramazda I Am King': On the Promulgation of a Persian Propaganda Text among Babylonians and Judaeans," *JSJ* 44 (2013): 455–480 (476).

8 See Section 1.1.1. below, Excursus: The Distance between Elephantine and Jerusalem.

in Elephantine regret that the Jerusalem high priest and his colleagues did not respond to their initial letter).

Fourth, the Elephantine documents are contemporary sources and probably even more representative of the lived and practiced Yahwism of the Persian period than are the biblical texts. Any source, whether it is a biblical or an epigraphic one, has a certain tendency to reflect the author's biases, regardless of whether or not this was intentional. It is a crucial part of a historical hermeneutics to try to understand a given source in light of the (historical, cultural, religious etc.) context of its author. A position often found in biblical scholarship is that it was the priestly circles of Judah that provided the main environment for the literary culture of the Persian period. Against this assumption it can be claimed that we simply do not know in what niches of the Israelite-Judaean society the biblical traditions were nourished before they were eventually codified.[9] A prerequisite for scribal activity was an economical surplus, and as far as Jerusalem is concerned the temple itself may or may not have been the primary employer of literary scribes. Notwithstanding, even on economic grounds alone it is not likely that all segments of the population took part in the literary culture that fostered what we today know as the received biblical traditions. As far as the biblical sources for the Persian period are concerned, they all reflect a Jerusalem centrism in the sense that they all somehow relate to the temple of YHWH there. On the one hand, the books of Ezra and Nehemiah reveal an enthusiasm towards its rebuilding. On the other hand, Malachi offers terse criticism of the priesthood connected to the Jerusalem temple. In either case, the biblical sources are centred around the Jerusalem temple. They presuppose a centralisation of the cult of YHWH, or to put it differently, they seem to take a form of mono-Yahwism as the norm. This kind of mono-Yahwism centred around the temple in Jerusalem has also quite often in the scholarship been taken to be the default manifestation of Yahwism in this particular period. However, from a historical perspective the big question is to what extent the biblical sources reflect Judaean religion beyond the milieus of the authors and the milieu of those who passed on the biblical tradition.[10]

---

9 Reinhard Gregor Kratz, "Zwischen Elephantine und Qumran: das Alte Testament im Rahmen des antiken Judentums," in *Congress Volume Ljubljana 2007*, ed. André Lemaire, VTSup 133 (Leiden: Brill, 2010): 129–146 (144), and Gard Granerød, *Abraham and Melchizedek: Scribal Activity of Second Temple Times in Genesis 14 and Psalm 110*, BZAW 406 (Berlin: de Gruyter, 2010), 253–254.

10 Recently Erhard S. Gerstenberger has argued correctly that we should regard the emergence of a Scripture-based type of Yahwism as a local form of belief in YHWH that was anchored in Palestine and Mesopotamia, whereas other Judaean communities (such as Elephantine) were

The biblical sources have a complicated, and often obscure, literary history. When, how and why did someone compose them? In most cases the texts do not tell and the answers have to be ferreted out. In light of this, then, it should come as no surprise that there is no scholarly consensus about the literary history of the biblical texts. Despite the fact that the Bible has been studied from a historical-critical perspective for many centuries, a number of historical questions pertaining to the Hebrew Bible remains to be solved: the extent of the redactional reworking of the texts, the guiding principles that underlie these reworkings, in what (geographical, social, religious) environments the biblical texts started being promulgated as normative texts, and so on.[11]

Epigraphic material like the Elephantine papyri is by no means exempt from critical-hermeneutical questions. Such texts also have to be interpreted in light of their provenance, their genre, the setting in which they assumedly functioned at the outset, and so on. Nevertheless, the provenance of the Elephantine papyri is much easier to discern than that of the biblical texts. The Elephantine papyri are in most cases either written by the members of the Judaean community at Elephantine themselves or by professional scribes hired by them. In other words, considered as historical sources for Yahwism in the Persian period, they are closer to the experiences and everyday lives of the people that they narrate of than are the biblical texts.

In sum, I will argue that the religion reflected in the Elephantine documents offers a historically well-attested manifestation of one form of lived Yahwism in the Persian period. The Elephantine documents show that poly-Yahwism did not cease in connection with, say, the religious reforms of the Judaean king Josiah in the seventh century BCE (provided that 2Kgs 22–23 render a historically accurate core). The Elephantine documents give the opportunity to focus on one particular dimension of the diverse Persian-period Yahwism practiced among Judaeans in Judah and in the diaspora, namely the one followed at Elephantine.

1.1.1 Excursus: The Distance between Elephantine and Jerusalem

In the ancient world, most communication between Egypt and Palestine went through Pelusium and Gaza. Pelusium (probably identical with Migdol mentioned in A3.3:4) was a main seaport located in the eastern part of the Nile

far less bound to the norms formed in the fixed, emerging canonical literature. See Gerstenberger, *Israel in the Persian Period*, 136–139.

11 See, e.g., Granerød, *Abraham and Melchizedek*, 249–260 and additional references there.

delta. In addition, it was located along the so-called "Great Trunk Route," the main artery between Asia and Africa that went along the northern part of the Sinai peninsula.[12] The Egyptians referred to this road as "the Way of Horus"[13] and the Romans as "Via Maris." In the Bible it was called "the way of the land of the Philistines" (Exod 13:17). This route followed the coast of Palestine and connected Egypt with Mesopotamia. After the Persian conquest of Egypt in 525 BCE, the route along the coast of northern Sinai was even more tightly organised with forts, way stations and landing facilities. The stations along the coastal route became nuclei for a network that continued to the Byzantine period.[14]

When travelling from Pelusium to Gaza one basically faced two options. Either one could follow the land route, or, if the seasonal winds and the economy allowed it, one could sail between the Nile delta and Gaza. By foot, the distance across the northern shore of Sinai is approximately two hundred and forty kilometres. In the ancient world a person travelling by foot would average between twenty-seven and thirty-seven kilometres a day, depending on several factors such as the person's physical condition, the purpose of the travel, the standard of the roads, and the season.[15] In other words, an individual travelling from Pelusium on "the Way of Horus" covering an average of twenty-seven kilometres a day would be able to reach Gaza in nine days. If his physical condition and the standard of the roads allowed it—and that is likely after the Persian conquest of

12 See Yohanan Aharoni and Anson F. Rainey, *The Land of the Bible: A Historical Geography* (Philadelphia: Westminster, 1979), 45–48, and Barry J. Beitzel, "Roads and Highways (Pre-Roman)," *ABD* 5: 776–782 (778).

13 See, e.g., "The Story of Si-nuhe," translated by John A. Wilson (*ANET*, 18–22 [21]), "The Instructions for King Meri-ka-re," translated by John A. Wilson (*ANET*, 414–418 [416]), and "A Satirical Letter," translated by John A. Wilson (*ANET*, 475–479 [478]).

14 Eliezer Oren, "Sinai," in *The Oxford Encyclopedia of Archaeology in the Near East*, ed. Eric M. Meyers (Oxford: Oxford University Press, 1997), 41–47 (43). Moreover, the Madaba mosaic map (from the sixth century CE) demonstrates that the default route for Christian pilgrims from Egypt to the Holy Land followed the route along the northern part of Sinai, cf. Pau Figueras, "The Road Linking Palestine and Egypt along the Sinai Coast," in *The Madaba Map Centenary 1897–1997: Travelling Through the Byzantine Umayyad Period: Proceedings of the International Conference Held in Amman, 7–9 April 1997*, ed. Michele Piccirillo, SBFCMa 40 (Jerusalem: Franciscan Printing Press, 1999): 121–124.

15 Barry J. Beitzel, "Travel and Communications (OT World)," *ABD* 6: 644–648 (646). However, the march rates for an army were somewhat slower. For instance, it took the army headed by Alexander the Great twenty days to cover the three hundred and seventy kilometres distance from Babylon to Susa, a route without any major topographic obstacles, giving an average daily headway of eighteen and a half kilometres. See Arrian and Peter Astbury Brunt, *Anabasis Alexandri*, vol. 1: Books 1–4, LCL 236 (Cambridge, MA: Harvard University Press, 1976), 492.

Egypt in 525 BCE—the same distance could be covered faster. Moreover, if he *sailed* from Pelusium to Gaza, he could arrive in Gaza even more swiftly.[16] After arriving in Gaza, the traveller would have had to move on to Jerusalem. The distance as the crow flies between Gaza and Jerusalem is around a hundred kilometres. Providing that the traveller could cover about twenty-seven kilometres a day, he would assumedly not need more than four days to get from Gaza to Jerusalem. Consequently, when all these estimates are taken into account, an individual would take some thirteen days or fewer to get from Pelusium, located in the western extremes of the Nile delta, to Jerusalem.

What about the distance from Pelusium to Elephantine? Following the Nile's course, the distance between Pelusium and Elephantine is approximately a thousand kilometres. An individual who travelled on foot at an average of twenty-seven kilometres a day would need thirty-seven days to cover the distance. If his daily average was thirty-seven kilometres, he would need twenty-seven days. However, the main artery for travel and communication in ancient Egypt was no doubt the Nile. We can assume that most trips from Pelusium to Elephantine would have been made on a riverboat.

The daily average distance covered by riverboats on the Nile was between forty and eighty kilometres, depending on conditions such as the wind speed, the velocity of the Nile waters, and whether the voyage went up- or downriver.[17] A voyage from Pelusium to Elephantine would by necessity mean that the boat

16 I am not aware of any ancient travel account enumerating how many days one usually needed to sail from Pelusium (Migdol) to Gaza. In general, in the ancient world one usually sailed along the coast and avoided sailing during the night. However, in the Roman period a journey from Alexandria (which is located in the western extremes of the Nile delta, ca. two hundred and fifty kilometres west of Migdol/Pelusium when following the shoreline) to Palestine by boat could take between five and seven days, cf. Harold W. Hoehner, *Herod Antipas* (Grand Rapids: Zondervan, 1980), 36 note 5.

17 According to calculations of the speed of ancient ships, the best speed a vessel could make working through islands or coastal waters, with favourable winds, was four knots, cf. Alan Edouard Samuel, *Ptolemaic Chronology*, MBPF 43 (Munich: Beck, 1962), 7. On the Nile, the navigation was at least as difficult as in coastal waters, and a ship could hardly make more than 4 knots. Sailing only took place during daylight hours on the Nile, and a ship could make up to eighty kilometres a day. Moreover, a Ptolemaic letter, namely P. Ord. Ptol. 29, shows that individuals from anywhere in Upper Egypt ("beyond Naukratis") were expected to reach Alexandria within twenty days, cf. Roger S. Bagnall and Peter Derow, *Greek Historical Documents: The Hellenistic Period*, SBLSBS 16 (Missoula, MT: Scholars Press, 1981), 221 (no. 133). Thanks to Meron M. Piotrkowski (Hebrew University of Jerusalem) for directing my attention to these texts (in a personal communication). Herodotus offers many accounts of the travel speed on the Nile, cf. references in Rolf Krauss, "Reisegeschwindigkeit," *LÄ* 5: 222–223. In these accounts the average speed varies between forty and eighty kilometres a day.

had to sail upstream. Such a journey was possible due to the meteorological conditions of Egypt, which is characterised by northern winds. These winds are especially strong in the summer. The hot air above the desert rises, causing cooler air from the Mediterranean to blow southward (the Etesian winds). The winds from the north would have propelled ships upstream, enabling two-way traffic on the Nile. Given the premise that a riverboat with sail hoisted sailing upstream could in fact cover eighty kilometres a day throughout the entire thousand-kilometre-long voyage, the trip could be made in twelve and a half days (i.e. eighty kilometres a day) under favourable conditions. However, taking into consideration the fact that such a voyage had to be done upstream and that the seasonal Etesian winds were not constant throughout the entire day—the winds peak in the afternoon—double that figure is, as far as I can see, more realistic: twenty-five days.

Considering the travel distance between Pelusium and Jerusalem and Pelusium and Elephantine, respectively, the entire journey could be made in between thirty and forty days. Therefore, for all purposes Elephantine was geographically much closer to Judah and Jerusalem than was Babylon. In comparison, it took approximately *four months* to travel from Babylon to Jerusalem. According to Ezra 7:9, Ezra took four months to travel to Jerusalem but according to Ezra 8:31–32, his caravan took only *three and a half months*. However, on the other hand, it was *five months* after Nebuchadnezzar's troops had entered Jerusalem that the prophet Ezekiel, who had been deported to Babylon, received the news from a refugee about the fall of the city (compare Ezek 33:21: "in the tenth month, on the fifth day of the month," and Jer 52:12: "In the fifth month, on the tenth day of the month").[18]

1.2 "Religion," "Dimensions of Religion," and "Religion Here, There, and Anywhere"

The word *dimension* has a double meaning in this study. Not only does it characterise my fundamental assumption, namely that there was indeed diversity within the many forms—or *many dimensions*—of lived and practiced Yahwism in this period (in other words: the phenomenon of poly-Yahwism survived the Assyrian and Babylonian periods). In addition, the word *dimension* foreshadows the way the present study attempts to untangle the question of what Judaean re-

18 See Thomas Willi, *Esra: Der Lehrer Israels*, BG 26 (Leipzig: Evangelische Verlagsanstalt, 2012), 121.

ligion looked like in the Persian period, namely on the basis of an adaption of Ninian Smart's multidimensional model of religion.

However, first a few words about *religion*. To speak of "the religion of society N.N." in the ancient Near East is problematic for many reasons. First, the word *religion* itself is irrevocably a Western term. Second, the modern usage of it has been and is still debated. The history of the study of religion has witnessed various approaches to the concept of religion. Moreover, both previous and recent studies are characterised by a plurality of theories of religion.[19] Third, even if there should be a consensus about its modern meaning, it is highly questionable that there ever was a similar concept in any of the cultures of the ancient Near East. None of the languages of the ancient Near East has a word for religion.

In this study I will cut the Gordian knot of defining religion by building on the following assumptions:

- Religion is a cultural and social system interwoven with other cultural and social systems such as economy and politics. In short, although a cliché it is nevertheless true that religion is a complex phenomenon. This is true for the living religions of today and it is also true for any ancient Near Eastern religion.
- Any manifestation of religion possesses certain recognisable elements that are possible to study. Together these elements make up the complex patchwork of religion.

There are many ways to cut a cake. In order to break down the complex patchwork of Judaean religion (or perhaps I should say the Yahwism in Elephantine) into more manageable elements the author of the present study is *informed* (but not dictated to!) by the multidimensional model of religion coined by Ninian Smart. Smart's taxonomy of religion includes seven dimensions.[20] Principally and methodologically, each one of the dimensions in Smart's scheme is of equal value, and, as far as I read Smart, neither the number of dimensions nor the order of their appearance should be considered canonical. "The cake" (any religion in general or a concrete religion like the Yahwism in Elephantine in particular) may be sliced on the basis of the following pattern, where each

---

19 See, e.g., Michael Stausberg, *Contemporary Theories of Religion: A Critical Companion* (London: Routledge, 2009).

20 Smart proposed his model in Ninian Smart, *The Religious Experience of Mankind* (New York: Scribner, 1969), 15–25. To begin with, the model encompassed six dimensions. Later on Smart added a seventh, the material dimension, cf. Ninian Smart, *Dimensions of the Sacred: An Anatomy of the World's Beliefs* (Berkeley: University of California Press, 1996).

"slice" represents a particular dimension of religion. The following presentation is my more or less free rendition of Smart's anatomy of religion:

- The ritual dimension: A religion usually reflects itself in individual and communal *rites*. For instance, for many Jews today it is an essential part of their religion to observe the Sabbath, as are the daily five prayers essential for Muslims. Characteristic of a rite (as I use the term) is that it is based on formal or informal rules. Because of the rules, the particular rite is not confined to a single individual but may also be adopted by others when they somehow find themselves in analogue circumstances. Therefore, a rite is in principle interpersonal and repeatable.
- The mythological dimension: A religion usually reflects itself in *myths* (widely defined as para-historical narratives, as seen from the perspective of a Western individual) *and narratives*. It has probably been a constant in religions throughout all ages that there have been (religious) ideas about how and for what purpose the cosmos was once created and how it continues to be preserved (cosmogony and cosmology). Other aspects of mundane realities are also typically explained by means of myths and narratives. For instance, how should a human being understand its relation to the other living creatures of the earth? And how should one understand the relationship between men and women? Moreover, especially in the ancient Near Eastern there were many societies that exercised sacral kingship (though for instance in the monarchy Denmark–Norway a semi-divine absolute monarchy was introduced as late as in the seventeenth century CE[21]). The king was claimed to have been elected or even conceived by the god.[22] In order to legitimate the political status quo, there was need for etiological myths and narratives that could anchor the *de facto* power in, say, the god's act of creating the world or

21 In Norway, remnants of a sacred kingship continue to be vaguely present in, i.a., the active involvement of the Church in connection with the so-called *ritual of benediction*, a ceremony that has replaced the coronation ceremony. The ritual of benediction marks the king's accession to the throne, a ceremony during which the crown is present in the Nidaros Cathedral (Trondheim) but not put upon the king's head. (As a point of interest, the Nidaros Cathedral is built over the burial site of Saint Olaf, an eleventh-century king of Norway who became the patron saint of the nation.)

22 See, e.g., Gard Granerød, "A Forgotten Reference to Divine Procreation? Psalm 2:6 in Light of Egyptian Royal Ideology," *VT* 60 (2010): 323–336; Erica Ehrenberg, "*Dieu et Mon Droit:* Kingship in Late Babylonian and Early Persian Times," in *Religion and Power: Divine Kingship in the Ancient World and Beyond*, ed. Nicole Brisch, OIS 4 (Chicago: Oriental Institute of the University of Chicago, 2008): 103–131; and Bruce Lincoln, "The Role of Religion in Achaemenian Imperialism," in *Religion and Power: Divine Kingship in the Ancient World and Beyond*, ed. Nicole Brisch, OIS 4 (Chicago: Oriental Institute of the University of Chicago, 2008): 221–241.

the god's never-ending fight against the (mostly) malicious and threatening powers of chaos. Furthermore, myths and narratives usually play an important role in the legitimation of sacred places like temples, and so on.

- The doctrinal dimension: A religion often reflects itself in *doctrines and philosophical concepts.* A doctrine can be understood as the result of an intellectual clarification of religious belief and experience. This dimension of religion is typically the domain of the religious elite. It is often motivated by the need to define the characteristic features that set the religion of one's own group apart from the religion of other (often neighbouring) groups. Doctrinal and philosophical clarification marks the boundaries of a religion by defining its characteristic features. Moreover, the boundaries do not only separate one's own religion from the religion of "the Others": they can be used internally to separate orthodoxy from heterodoxy.
- The ethical dimension: A religion usually reflects itself in the *ethics* of its adherents. In most, if not all, living religions, there is a connection between religion and ethics. Similarly in the ancient Near East there could be a link between ethics and religion.[23] The Egyptian wisdom literature shows this, as do perhaps more clearly quite a few biblical texts. In ancient Israel, the prophet Micah preached that YHWH had told his people what is good and what he required: "to do justice, and to love kindness, and to walk humbly with your God" (Mic 6:8). Moreover, as far as laws are concerned, the many laws in the Pentateuch have in common that they are portrayed as not only divinely ratified laws but even as *god-given* laws. For instance, in the Pentateuch YHWH is clearly acting as legislator in the context of the Decalogue, cf. Deut 5:5b, 22b: "YHWH said: ... He [YHWH] wrote them on two stone tablets, and gave them to me [Moses]." The legal implications of religion are also evident in ancient Near Eastern oath procedures. In the absence of firm evidence, an oath taken by an individual to his/her god may be accepted by the other party in a legal dispute.
- The social dimension: A religion usually reflects itself in the *organisation* of a particular group or the entire society, and in how the adherents of the religion relate themselves to the surrounding world. Shared religious commitment binds people together. Some religious activities may be connected to a specified sacred time so that a common calendar is required. Moreover, in order to understand a religion it is also important to know how it is financed. Who pays for the sacrifices? Who pays for the religious specialists performing the sacrifices? Who

23 See, e.g., Robert Karl Gnuse, *No Other Gods: Emergent Monotheism in Israel*, JSOTSup 241 (Sheffield: Sheffield Academic, 1997), 249–252.

maintains the temples? And who benefits from the religious duties (e.g., tithes and pilgrimages) that are imposed on the adherents?
- The experiential dimension: A religion reflects itself in *experiences and emotions*. These experiences may be exceptional like Isaiah's response upon seeing YHWH in the temple (cf. Isa 6:5 "Woe is me! I am lost...," although this may also be understood as a stereotypic reaction when a mundane man finds himself in a liminal situation at the threshold of the transcendent world). However, they may also be ordinary, everyday emotions experienced by ordinary people, who may have, for example, experienced that previous prayers have been answered to his/her benefit.
- The material dimension: A religion usually reflects itself in *artefacts, architecture and ideas about sacred places*. A god may be, if not identified with, then at least represented by, an image. The image may be an actual statue or a two-dimensional image that functions as the conventional representation of the deity. The deity's immanence may be represented by certain sacred spaces. This can be a temple, understood as "the house of the god N.N." However, the sacred space can also be certain mountains, rivers, groves, and so on.

Each one of the dimensions is present in any religion, whether it be a living or an ancient one. However, the importance of each one of the dimensions varies from religion to religion, and even from one group within a given religion to another group. For instance, in the living religions of today it is obvious that the doctrinal-philosophical dimension is emphasised much more among Roman Catholic clergy living in the Vatican than it is by hunter-gather societies in the Kalahari Desert.

It can be argued that the multidimensional model of religion as outlined above is essentially synchronic in its approach. It is particularly suitable for describing how a religion exists at one point in time. Consequently, it is less concerned with the way in which one and the same religion has developed and evolved throughout a given period of time (the diachronic aspect). In spite of that I chose to apply the model to the study of a particular ancient Near Eastern religion, the Yahwism in Elephantine in the fifth century BCE. The available sources for the Judaean community at Elephantine all stem from a relatively limited period of time: the fifth century BCE. Although the Elephantine-Judaean community experienced a dramatic incident at the end of the fifth century (their local temple devoted to YHW being destroyed), I nevertheless assume that the sources do not reflect any corresponding dramatic change in their religion. As will be demonstrated, in the sources there are no traces of any call for a drastic reformation of Yahwism on the part of the Judaeans in Elephantine. On the contrary, the documents of the so-called Jedaniah archive (A4.1–10) show that in the wake of the destruction, the Judaean community called for a *restoration* and *continuation* of the status quo prior to the destruction of the temple.[24] In light of this conservatism, but also in light of the fact that the sources chronologically date to a relatively short time period, the synchronic multidimensional model of religion offers a fruitful scheme for the study of this particular manifestation of Yahwism around the middle of the Persian period.

The potential usefulness of any approach (including the multidimensional model of religion) will always be determined by the nature of the primary sources. The sources for the religion of the Judaean community of Elephantine are primarily texts, and secondarily a few archaeological remains that nevertheless have to be interpreted in the light of the textual sources.[25] It is important to keep in mind that field studies are unable to inform the study of an ancient religion. It is not possible to use methods such as observations and interviews of those who practiced the religion in question. The available textual sources represent a collection arbitrary in nature. They were obviously not written in order to draw a comprehensive image of the religion of the Elephantine community for the benefit of the modern student. One should not expect that our sources reflect the Yahwism of the Judaeans in Elephantine in its complex and diverse entirety. Using the taxonomy introduced above, some of the dimensions of their religion have obviously not been reflected in the sources. For instance, we do not really know much about how individual Judaeans in Elephantine practiced their religion within a family setting or what their private, individual religious experiences were really like. Moreover, in the cases where the sources as a matter of fact say something about religious experiences, we cannot really know how representative the sources are with regard to the historical realities. For instance, when

24 See Gard Granerød, "The Former and the Future Temple of YHW in Elephantine: A Traditio-Historical Case Study of Ancient Near Eastern Antiquarianism," *ZAW* 127 (2015): 63–77.

25 A reconstruction of the plan of the ancient town of Elephantine based on archaeology in combination with textual sources sheds light on the location of the temple of YHW in relation to other identifiable archaeological structures, such as the so-called "City of Khnum" and the public thoroughfare called "the street of the king," cf. Cornelius von Pilgrim, "Tempel des Jahu und 'Strasse des Königs': ein Konflikt in der Späten Perserzeit auf Elephantine," in *Egypt: Temple of the Whole World: Studies in Honour of Jan Assmann = Ägypten: Tempel der gesamten Welt*, ed. Sibylle Meyer, SHR 97 (Leiden: Brill, 2003): 303–317 (308). It should nevertheless be stressed that the archaeologists' reconstruction of the neighbourhood of the temple of YHW in the Achaemenid period is highly dependent upon the textual sources. See, e.g., Cornelius von Pilgrim, "Textzeugnis und archäologischer Befund: Zur Topographie von Elephantine in der 27. Dynastie," in *Stationen: Beiträge zur Kulturgeschichte Ägyptens Rainer Stadelmann gewidmet*, ed. Heike Guksch and Daniel Polz (Mainz: von Zabern, 1998): 485–497, and Rohrmoser, *Götter, Tempel und Kult*, 161.

the leaders of the Judaean community wrote to the Persian governor Bagavahya to inform him that the entire community had been fasting for three years since the temple of YHW was destroyed (A4.7:15 "we with our wives and our children"), was that really an accurate description or should it rather be understood as a conventional exaggeration?[26]

Methodologically one could consider a distinction between the religion of the Judaean community on the one hand, and the religion of the Elephantine papyri on the other.[27] After all, we are dealing with textual sources. With this important epistemological point in mind, I nevertheless intend to study the religion of the Judaean community of Elephantine, knowing that our knowledge of it is necessarily confined by the nature of the arbitrary collection of available sources that are made up of texts, and to a limited extend, archaeological findings. This situation is, however, not unique for the Yahwism represented in Elephantine. On the contrary, this is the situation for the study of any ancient Near Eastern religion. The textual sources may be broken and fragmented and the context in which they originated may be unclear. Nevertheless, the goal for the student of the history of religion is to interpret the sources and draw an image of the realities they assumedly reflect.

A potential drawback of the multidimensional model outlined above is that it does not manage to account fully for internal religious diversity within one and the same group. Jonathan Z. Smith has proposed a tripartite, spatial model for religions in the ancient Near East that acknowledges the various spatial spheres in which religion was practiced:

- "religion here,"
- "religion there" and
- "religion anywhere."[28]

---

26 For a concise discussion of the Mesopotamian city-lament genre as a precursor of the laments over the destroyed temple of YHWH and the fallen city of Jerusalem in Lamentations, see Frederick William Dobbs-Allsopp, *Lamentations*, Interpretation, a Bible Commentary for Teaching and Preaching (Louisville, KY: John Knox Press, 2002), 6–12.

27 See the title of the essay by Paul-Eugène Dion, "La religion des papyrus d'Éléphantine: un reflet du Juda d'avant l'exil," in *Kein Land für sich allein: Studien zum Kulturkontakt in Kanaan, Israel/Palästina und Ebirnâri für Manfred Weippert zum 65. Geburtstag*, ed. Ulrich Hübner and Ernst Axel Knauf, OBO 186 (Freiburg [Swizerland] and Göttingen: Universitätsverlag Freiburg Schweiz and Vandenhoeck & Ruprecht, 2002): 243–254. However, to what extent the subtitle is correct, namely that the Elephantine papyri reflect the religion of preexilic Judah, is another question.

28 Jonathan Z. Smith, "Here, There, and Anywhere," in *Prayer, Magic, and the Stars in the Ancient and Late Antique World*, ed. Scott Noegel et al. (University Park: Pennsylvania State University Press, 2003): 21–36.

The first spatial category of Smith's model, the "here" of religion, pertains to the domestic religion whose setting was the extended family. Typically, this kind of "popular religion" has left ambiguous traces such as, for example, clay female pillar figurines—"ambiguous" because one cannot really say exactly what these artefacts represented and what function they fulfilled.[29] The "religion here" did not take place in the temples and is often not reflected in the textual sources, at least the texts written by the elite. However, in general, burial sites and burial practices suggest that this kind of religion was concerned with the ancestors. The extended family also included deceased family members. From Mesopotamia, for example, the practice of funerary offerings and ritual banquets for the deceased (*kispu*) is well attested. To this category one can also add personal gods, who in some cases are reflected in proper names.

The second spatial category, the "there" of religion, is concerned with public, civic and state religion. In the ancient Near East, this kind of religion was for the most part temple-based or at least temple-centred. Smith identifies this category with what most of us think of first when we imagine ancient religion: the dominant deities and their attendant mythologies and liturgies, the impressive constructions associated with temple etc. From the perspective of ordinary people in the ancient Near East, these locales represented some places else, not "here" but "there." The "religion there" was the religion of the elite. It was mostly the king who appointed the religious specialists who served at the temples. In many ancient Near Eastern cultures the kingship was understood in sacral terms. The king claimed to have been elected or even conceived by the god.[30] Politics and economy were important aspects of "religion there."

Finally, according to Smith's tripartite model of religion in the ancient Near East the third spatial category is "religion anywhere." In short, this category is made up of a rich diversity of religious formations "that occupied an interstitial space between these other two loci,"[31] namely, between the domestic and public religions. To this category Smith allocates a variety of entrepreneurial religious

---

29 See, e.g., Rüdiger Schmitt, "Gab es einen Bildersturm nach dem Exil? – Einige Bemerkungen zur Verwendung von Terrakottafigurinen im nachexilischen Israel," in *Yahwism After the Exile: Perspectives on Israelite Religion in the Persian Era: Papers Read at the First Meeting of the European Association for Biblical Studies, Utrecht, 6–9 August 2000*, ed. Rainer Albertz and Bob Becking, STAR 5 (Assen: Van Gorcum, 2003): 186–198, and Rainer Albertz, "Personal Piety," in *Religious Diversity in Ancient Israel and Judah*, ed. Francesca Stavrakopoulou and John Barton (London: T&T Clark, 2010), 135–146 (especially 142).

30 As for Egypt and Israel, see Granerød, "A Forgotten Reference?," 323–336. Moreover, see Ehrenberg, "Dieu et Mon Droit," 103–131, and Lincoln, "The Role of Religion," 221–241.

31 Smith, "Here, There, and Anywhere," 21–36 (23).

figures and practitioners not officially recognised by the centres of religious powers, like prophets and dream readers.

Smith's tripartite, spatial model of religion enriches Smart's multidimensional model. First of all, it reminds the student of the Yahwism in Elephantine that a Judaean individual practiced religion in various loci. He/she was a member of both a household and an ethnically/religiously defined community located in a multiethnical/-religious environment. In addition, he/she was a subject of an empire that claimed to derive its authority and legitimacy from the god Ahuramazda.[32]

When studying the Yahwism practiced in Elephantine, which most likely was ignorant of any concept of a Torah and whose practitioners most probably did not possess any sort of "Bible,"[33] Smart's multidimensional model of religion has a heuristic value. It offers an approach to describe the religion in question *without* using concepts and ideas borrowed from and dependent upon the Bible. Moreover, Smith's tripartite model has a particular heuristic value because it raises important questions. Obviously, the "religion here" of the Judaeans of Elephantine was religion as it was practiced within the household. However, it is less clear what represented the public, official religion (Smith's "religion there") from the perspective of an ordinary Judaean individual at Elephantine. Was it the temple of YHW at Elephantine? Was it the temple of YHWH in Jerusalem? Was it the temple of Khnum and the other Egyptian gods in Elephantine? Or was it perhaps the local manifestations in Egypt of the official Achaemenid ideology, whatever guise such manifestations may have taken?[34] Finally, what about the "anywhere" of the religion of the Judaeans in Upper Egypt? Were they aware of the phenomenon of prophecy and did someone function as proph-

---

32 Granerød, "'By the Favour of Ahuramazda'," 455–480.

33 See Ernst Axel Knauf, "Elephantine und das vor-biblische Judentum," in *Religion und Religionskontakte im Zeitalter der Achämeniden*, ed. Reinhard Gregor Kratz, VWGT 22 (Gütersloh: Gütersloher Verlagshaus, 2002): 179–188 (187): "Es gibt im Judentum von Elephantine nicht nur keinerlei Hinweis auf die Existenz einer 'Bibel', es gibt im Gegenteil deutliche Hinweise auf die Nicht-Existenz einer Bibel." Similar positions are also found in, e.g., Kratz, "Zwischen Elephantine und Qumran," 129–146 (133 note 8); Lester L. Grabbe, "Elephantine and the Torah," in *In the Shadow of Bezalel: Aramaic, Biblical, and Ancient Near Eastern Studies in Honor of Bezalel Porten*, ed. Alejandro F. Botta, CHANE 60 (Leiden: Brill, 2013): 125–136, and Reinhard Gregor Kratz, *Historisches und biblisches Israel: Drei Überblicke zum Alten Testament* (Tübingen: Mohr Siebeck, 2013), 274–283.

34 See, e.g., Gard Granerød, "The Passover and the Temple of YHW: On the Interaction between the Authorities and the Judaean Community at Elephantine as Reflected in the Jedaniah Archive," in *Arshama and Egypt: The World of an Achaemenid Prince*, ed. Christopher Tuplin and John Ma, OSAD (Oxford: Oxford University Press, forthcoming).

ets in Elephantine? Or did adherents of the various religious groups evidently present in Achaemenid Egypt share religious mavericks even across the boundaries of their religions, regardless whether the boundaries were drawn on the basis of doctrinal considerations or ethnicity? Smith's tripartite, spatial model offers templates against which the Yahwism of Elephantine can be studied.

1.3 The Present Study in the Context of Positions in the History of Research

A question that arose when the great discoveries of the Elephantine papyri were made more than a century ago was how to relate the Judaean community at Elephantine, and in particular their religion, to the general history of Israelite and Judaean religion. In my view, two, in part contrasting, typical approaches can be found in the history of research. One the one hand, many scholars argue that the Achaemenid-period Judaean community at Elephantine offers a window into Judaean religion as it was practiced in the Assyrian and Babylonian periods. On the other hand, some argue that the Achaemenid-period Judaean community at Elephantine gives a view of contemporary Judaean religion in the period in question. The wider context of these considerations is how to assess the role of the Bible in the reconstruction of Israelite and Judaean religion(s).

1.3.1 A Relic from the Preexilic Period?

Just a few years after the discoveries of the documents of the Jedaniah communal archive, Julius Wellhausen characterised the community as a "merkwürdige[r] Überrest des vorgesetzlichen Hebraismus."[35] In his view, the community located at the border between Egypt and Nubia adhered to its "altes Wesen." Wellhausen regarded the Judaeans in Elephantine to be standing "noch auf der vorgesetzlichen Stufe," in contrast to the elite of postexilic Judah. In his view, the Judaean community at Elephantine represented a "fossile[r] Überrest des unreformierten Judentums."

Moreover, Bezalel Porten has taken a comparable view in his discussions of the religious life of the Elephantine community. All the evidence for the religion of the Judaeans at Elephantine, Porten contends, points to a "devotion to their ancestral deity YHW." The temple of YHW at Elephantine indicated his presence

35 Julius Wellhausen, *Israelitische und jüdische Geschichte* (Berlin: de Gruyter, 1921), 176–178

and, according to Porten, the observance of "His [i.e. YHW's] Sabbath and the celebration of the Passover marked attachment to his covenant community." Moreover, the theophorous names borne by most Judaeans "demonstrated their personal faith in YHW's saving power."[36] Porten is aware of and regrets that no sacred writings have been uncovered at Elephantine.[37] Nevertheless, in spite of this he has frequently made use of biblical texts to fill in gaps. An example of such a gap is the lacunae in the so-called Passover letter (A4.1), and here Porten uses biblical Passover regulations, especially from Exod 12, to reconstruct the text of the papyrus.[38] This is done, as far as I can see, without really discussing the literary history of the biblical text. In any case, at the same time as the Judaeans in Elephantine were devoted to their "ancestral deity" YHW, Porten nevertheless finds indications in the sources of an "attachment to deities other than YHW." These "pagan contacts"[39] are to a large degree explained as a result of the fact that "Jews and Arameans" lived in close proximity at Egypt's southern border. Both groups had temples devoted to their respective deities (the Hermopolis papyri show that there were several temples in Syene devoted to Aramaic deities) and each exerted a certain influence on the other through intermarriage, among other things.[40] In short, according to Porten, the cult of the Elephantine Jews (which is the term he uses) was more oriented towards the monarchic period. The religion of the Judaeans in Elephantine was conservative and was not influenced by the theological renewal movements of the exilic/postexilic period, contrary to the situation in their homeland.[41]

Finally, a similar position is also taken by Paul-Eugéne Dion, among others. Dion argues that the religion reflected in the Elephantine papyri is in fact a reflection of preexilic Judaean religion. From what we know about the origins of this community, he argues, it is reasonable to assume that it still practiced the kind of religion that its first members brought with them from Judah in the preexilic period.[42]

---

36 Bezalel Porten, *Archives from Elephantine: The Life of an Ancient Jewish Military Colony* (Berkeley: University of California Press, 1968), 150.

37 Porten, *Archives from Elephantine*, 106.

38 See, e.g., Bezalel Porten et al., eds., *The Elephantine Papyri in English: Three Millennia of Cross-Cultural Continuity and Change*, 2nd rev. ed., DMOA 22 (Atlanta: Society of Biblical Literature, 2011), 126–127 notes 17, 19, 22, 24–25.

39 Porten, *Archives from Elephantine*, 150.

40 See Bezalel Porten, "The Religion of the Jews of Elephantine in Light of the Hermopolis Papyri," *JNES* 28 (1969): 116–121 (121).

41 Bezalel Porten, "The Jews in Egypt," *CHJ* 1: 372–400 (374, 385).

42 Dion, "La religion des papyrus," 243–254 (252).

1.3.2 Typical or Contemporary Judaean Religion?

A fundamentally different approach to the question is evident in the works of, for example, Reinhard Gregor Kratz.[43] Kratz introduces a distinction between "biblical Judaism" and "non-biblical Judaism," arguing that both types are attested in the postexilic period. The religion of the Elephantine community is an example of the latter "non-biblical Judaism." Kratz elaborates on this view through a comparison with another manifestation of postexilic Yahwism, namely the "Judentum" of the later Yaḥad at Qumran. Kratz argues that the earlier Elephantine papyri on the one hand and later texts from Qumran on the other represent two completely different types of archives. These archives are diametrically opposed to each other with regard to their attitude towards the biblical traditions. The later Qumran community represents the one pole. The members of the Yaḥad were rigorous ambassadors of a biblical Judaism ("Judentum"). The community there identified itself with the true biblical Israel.[44] The Qumran texts show that the Yaḥad attempted to live in accordance with what it considered to be the correct interpretation of the biblical traditions. The other pole is represented by the chronologically earlier documents from Elephantine. The Judaeans we meet in the Elephantine papyri called themselves Judaeans. Yet, they seem to have been completely ignorant of the biblical texts that played a pivotal role in the life of the later community in Qumran. According to Kratz's distinction, the Judaism of the Elephantine community was not biblical but, on the contrary, *non-biblical.*[45] Kratz suggests that the so-called non-biblical "Judentum" of the Elephantine community was not the exception but on the contrary the rule also in contemporary Judah at the end of the fifth century BCE.[46]

---

43 Most recently, Kratz, *Historisches und biblisches Israel*, 274–283. To a certain degree, though not with a similarly long argumentation, Gerstenberger is open to the understanding that the Yahwism in Elephantine represents a window into the normal situation among YHW worshippers of the Persian period, cf. Gerstenberger, *Israel in the Persian Period*, 126–139.

44 Kratz, "Zwischen Elephantine und Qumran," 129–146 (133 note 8), and Kratz, *Historisches und biblisches Israel*, 274–283.

45 Kratz refers to Knauf, "Elephantine und das vor-biblische Judentum," 179–188, cf. Kratz, "Zwischen Elephantine und Qumran," 129–146 (133 note 8). Without saying it explicitly, it nevertheless seems that Kratz subscribes to one of Knauf's conclusions: "Es gibt im Judentum von Elephantlne nicht nur keinerlei Hinweis auf die Existenz einer 'Bibel', es gibt im Gegenteil deutliche Hinweise auf die Nicht-Existenz einer Bibel." Knauf, "Elephantine und das vor-biblische Judentum," 179–188 (187).

46 Kratz, "Zwischen Elephantine und Qumran," 129–146 (134).

1.3.3 Elephantine As an Archive Challenging the Canon

The title of this study (*Dimensions of Yahwism…*) is intended to serve a double purpose:

- First, the word *dimension* is meant to evoke Smart's taxonomy of religion. Smart's "dimensions of religion" has informed the method of this study and has clearly had an impact on the outline of the present book.
- Second, the title is also a statement incorporating a fundamental assumption, namely that *religious diversity* was characteristic of Yahwism in the Persian period also, namely, that Yahwism had many dimensions in this period.

It is argued that poly-Yahwism is one of the characteristics of Yahwism in the Persian period. One particular dimension of Yahwism is found reflected in the religious practice of the fifth-century BCE Judaean community in Elephantine. Another dimension of Yahwism may be found reflected in, say, the literary world of the biblical texts, such as Ezra and Nehemiah, and yet other dimensions of Persian-period Yahwism may also be added (suffice it to mention Samaria).

The view that the Judaeans in Elephantine practiced an archaic type of Judaean religion which reflected a situation prior to the assumed centralisation of the cult undertaken by King Josiah (cf. 2Kgs 22–23) is problematic for several reasons:

- It is guided by the Deuteronomistic concept of the history of Israelite and Judaean religion(s).
- More important, it presupposes that the Judaean community in Elephantine was in fact a kind of cabinet of curiosities or a living museum.

A religio-historical approach to Yahwism in the Persian period should not allow itself to be "brainwashed by the Deuteronomists," to put it somewhat coarsely. The programme of the centralisation of the YHWH cult—associated with the highly ideological texts of the Deuteronomistic History and having Jerusalem as the centre of any legitimate YHWH worship—should not guide a religio-historical enquiry. As far as Yahwism in the Persian period is concerned, the (Judaean) temple in Elephantine devoted to YHW, "the god dwelling in Elephantine," is of equal importance to the religious historian as the temple in Jerusalem devoted to YHWH.

For that reason, Kratz's terminology for describing the Judaeans in Elephantine may *potentially* turn out to be problematic, as admittedly Kratz himself also observes.[47] Although I subscribe to his overall approach to the Judaean commun-

47 See his discussion of the nomenclature in Kratz, *Historisches und biblisches Israel*, xiii–xvii.

ity, I nevertheless find his term "non-biblical" (as a characterisation of the Elephantine community) as less appropriate, at least if the effect is that the religious practice of the Judaeans in Elephantine is measured with the biblical texts as the backdrop. For, by using a negated form of "biblical" ("non-biblical") there is a danger of letting the Bible and the biblical scholarship determine "the rules of the game," including by letting concepts from the biblical tradition and biblical scholarship define the Yahwism practiced at Elephantine, even if it happens by means of a negation. If any form of "Bible" (or a proto-version thereof) was foreign to the fifth-century BCE Judaean community at Elephantine, as argued by Kratz and others,[48] then the term "biblical" is potentially anachronistic—at least if it leads the focus away from what can be positively said about the *lived and practiced* Yahwism of the Elephantine community. To be sure, it must be stated that this is not the case with Kratz's discussion, which indeed includes the things that can be *positively* said about the religion of the Judaeans at Elephantine.[49]

Summing up, the present study argues that Yahwism in the Persian period was manifold, or to put it differently, it had many dimensions. One of them was the Yahwism of Elephantine. Moreover, the present study will attempt to treat this particular form of Yahwism on an equal footing with any other form of contemporary, lived Yahwism, and not view it as an exotic but marginal phenomenon in comparison to the "Jerusalem centeredness" that has become a somewhat canonised part of traditional histories of Judaean religion. Measured up against the Jerusalem-centred and canonised image of Judaean religion, the documents from Elephantine have the potential of correcting the canonised presuppositions reflected in discussions on the history of the Judaean religion of the Persian period—or even revising it somewhat by showing that the worship of the god YHW(H) indeed was possible outside of and even without Jerusalem as its centre. In my view, Elephantine is a textbook example illustrating very well the idea put forward by Aleida Assmann in her seminal essay "Canon and Archive," namely that an archive can revise the canon.[50]

---

48 Knauf, "Elephantine und das vor-biblische Judentum," 179 – 188 (187); Kratz, "Zwischen Elephantine und Qumran," 129 – 146 (133 note 8); and Grabbe, "Elephantine and the Torah," 125 – 136.

49 Kratz, *Historisches und biblisches Israel*, 186 – 203.

50 Aleida Assmann, "Canon and Archive," in *Cultural Memory Studies: An International and Interdisciplinary Handbook*, ed. Astrid Erll and Ansgar Nünning, MCM 8 (Berlin: de Gruyter, 2008): 97 – 107.

1.4 Outline of the Book

As hinted at several times already, Ninian Smart's taxonomy of religion has left an impact on the outline of the present study. The following core chapters reflect more or less the dimensions of religion suggested by Smart. However, my primary sources, a collection of various Aramaic texts and a few archaeological remains that have in common that they are both old and of an arbitrary nature, do not allow me to say much about that which Smart refers to as the doctrinal or philosophical dimension and the experiential or emotional dimension. Consequently, these dimensions do not have corresponding chapters in the present study.

As I see it, Smart's model can to a certain degree be compared to the corolla of a flower. The entire corolla is, as a unity, comparable to religion. In the corolla, each one of the petals represents a dimension of religion. When pursuing this metaphor, it turns out to be difficult if not even possible to pose a hierarchy between the petals, for instance in terms of which one (of the petals/dimensions) is most important or in terms of the order of their appearance. Moreover, to a certain degree, in some corollas there might be an overlap between the petals (at least when they are located next to each other). Thus, it is possible that some readers will detect issues discussed under one heading that they would have preferred to see under another.

In any case, this present work is a *book* and not a corolla. Therefore, as its author I have had to organise the chapters in a *linear* way, reflecting the format of a book. Therefore, the "petals of the Yahwism in Elephantine" will appear in the following sequence:

- The social dimension
- The material dimension
- The ritual dimension
- The mythic and narrative dimension
- The ethical dimension.

2 The Social Dimension

To my lords Yedanyah, Uriyah and the priests of the God YHW, Mattan son of Yeshobyah, Berekyah son of [..., from] your servant Mauzyah. [May the God of heaven] bless my lords richly at all times, and may the God of heaven be merciful to you. When commander Vidranga arrived in Abydos, he had me arrested on a charge relating to a stolen rhinestone(?) that was found in the hands of the merchants (A4.3:1–4)[1]

2.1 "The Judaean Garrison"

The Judaean community centred around Elephantine was, as far as we can see on the basis of the sources, primarily made up of soldiers and their families. Two documents refer explicitly to "the Judaean garrison" (*ḥyl' yhwdy'*): the letter from Hananiah (A4.1) and the so-called Collection Account (C3.15). The basic unit was the detachment (*dgl*). A *dgl* was subdivided into centuries (singular: *m'h*). In addition to the Judaean garrison, there was also a garrison in the neighbouring Syene named "the Syenian garrison" (*ḥyl' swnkny'*, C3.14:32).[2]

The world of the Judaeans in Upper Egypt was multicultural, multiethnic and multireligious.[3] As far as the international flavour of the military is concerned, a few lines from a contract from 402 BCE can serve as but one of dozens of examples: "(In the) month of Thoth, year 4 of Artaxerxes the king, then in Syene the fortress, said Anani son of Haggai son of Meshullam, a Jew [*yhwdy*, G.G.: 'Judaean'] of the detachment of Nabukudurri, to Pakhnum son of Besa, an Aramaean of Syene of that detachment likewise, saying..." (B3.13:1–2)[4] The Judaean named Anani made business with his Aramaean brother-in-arm Besa.

1 Quoted from James M. Lindenberger, *Ancient Aramaic and Hebrew Letters*, 2nd ed., WAW 14 (Atlanta: Society of Biblical Literature, 2003), 68 (no. 31).

2 Bezalel Porten, "Settlement of the Jews at Elephantine and the Arameans at Syene," in *Judah and the Judeans in the Neo-Babylonian Period*, ed. Oded Lipschits and Joseph Blenkinsopp (Winona Lake, IN: Eisenbrauns, 2003): 451–470 (456)

3 See Janet H. Johnson, "Ethnic Considerations in Persian Period Egypt," in *Gold of Praise: Studies on Ancient Egypt in Honor of Edward F. Wente*, ed. Emily Teeter and John A. Larson, SAOC 58 (Chicago: Oriental Institute of the University of Chicago, 1999): 211–222, and J. D. Ray, "Jews and Other Immigrants in Late Period Egypt," in *Life in a Multi-Cultural Society Egypt from Cambyses to Constantine and Beyond*, ed. Janet H. Johnson, SAOC 51 (Chicago: Oriental Institute of the University of Chicago, 1992): 273–274 (273).

4 Quoted from Bezalel Porten et al., eds., *The Elephantine Papyri in English: Three Millennia of Cross-Cultural Continuity and Change*, 2nd rev. ed., DMOA 22 (Atlanta: Society of Biblical Literature, 2011), 251.

Both were part of a military unit (*dgl*) whose commanding officer had a Babylonian name. Ultimately, they were all under Persian command.

There have been several attempts to estimate the size of the Judaean population on and around Elephantine. A somewhat moderate figure has been offered by Peter Bedford. On the basis of the Collection Account (C3.15) he has suggested that a round figure of one hundred and fifty was the adult population of the Judaean community.[5] With slaves and children the total Judaean population would have been between approximately five hundred and seven hundred.[6]

However, a problem with this calculation is that it presupposes that the Collection Account actually lists the heads of all of the economical units within the Judaean community. As Bob Becking has shown, this is unlikely. Not all people in a society are mentioned in the textual evidence reflecting their social lives.[7] Instead, Ernst Axel Knauf[8] and later on Becking have suggested that the size of the Judaean population on Elephantine may be calculated on the basis of the military organisation of the garrison. Knauf argues that the Judaean garrison was subdivided into four, later three detachments (*dgln*). Each detachment was made up of at least two centuries. A century could comprise between seventy and eighty, sometimes as few as fifty soldiers. Consequently, a detachment would consist of between one hundred and twenty and two hundred soldiers. Multiplied by three detachments, the total number of soldiers that comprised the Judaean garrison would have been five hundred to six hundred. Moreover, Knauf proposes that each soldier could be multiplied with the factor five in order to take women, children and slaves into consideration. Consequently, the entire population of the Judaean garrison including family members and slaves would be between two thousand five hundred and three thousand. What is more, Becking contends that Knauf’s calculation is a conservative one and opens up the possibility that the number of Judaeans living around Elephantine was even higher.[9]

If we, as Angela Rohrmoser has also done, compare these figures with the demographic data for the Persian province Judah, the relative size of the Elephantine population emerges. In recent years, several quantitative analyses of the archaeological data from Persian-period Judah have shown that the number

5 Peter Ross Bedford, “Jews at Elephantine,” *AJJS* 13 (1999): 6 – 23 (8).

6 Compare “Kalkulation 1” in Ernst Axel Knauf, “Elephantine und das vor-biblische Judentum,” in *Religion und Religionskontakte im Zeitalter der Achämeniden*, ed. Reinhard Gregor Kratz, VWGT 22 (Gütersloh: Gütersloher Verlagshaus, 2002): 179 – 188 (181).

7 Bob Becking, “Temple, *marzēaḥ*, and Power at Elephantine,” *Transeu* 29 (2005): 37 – 47 (43).

8 Knauf, “Elephantine und das vor-biblische Judentum,” 179 – 188 (181 [“Kalkulation 2”]).

9 Becking, “Temple, *marzēaḥ*, and Power at Elephantine,” 37 – 47 (43 – 44).

of inhabitants was relatively small, perhaps as few as thirty thousand.[10] Thus, the size of the Judaean community on Elephantine may have been ten percent of the population of the Persian province of Judah.[11]

The point of origin of the Judaean community in Upper Egypt remains uncertain as does the question of the date of the community's migration to Upper Egypt. The sources from Elephantine are silent—that is with two exceptions. First, in my opinion their self-designation "Judaean" points in the direction of Judah. Second, the Judaeans claimed that their temple devoted to YHW had been built by their fathers before Cambyses's conquest of Egypt (A4.7:13–14), which took place in 525 BCE.

In 1955 Cyrus H. Gordon suggested that they came from a Judaean enclave in Aram such as the one which according to 2Chr 8 King Solomon established to secure his empire.[12] In Gordon's view this explains why the community neither used Hebrew nor seemed to have been influenced by any of the religious reforms the biblical texts claim took place in Judah in the monarchic period. Gordon argued that the term *yhwdy* in the Elephantine papyri might have applied to the Zincirli area near Cilicia, the ancient region on the coast of southeastern Asia Minor. In native inscriptions this area was called *y'dy*, and Gordon contended that the *aleph* was a dialectic variation of *he*.

Another variant of the idea of the ultimate place of origin being somewhere other than Judah has been proposed by Karel van der Toorn. Following van der Toorn, the Judaeans (van der Toorn: "Jews") of Elephantine originated predominantly from Northern Israel, to which Aramaeans had migrated in the eighth century BCE. Van der Toorn builds his argumentation on the assumption that the divine name AnathYHW should be regarded as an Aramaean creation. Consequently, the Judaean ("Jewish") character of the Elephantine community is secondary, in part being the result of the Judaean transit of the Israelite colonists on their way to Egypt, and in part by a secondary influx of actual Judaeans.[13]

---

10 See Lester L. Grabbe, *A History of the Jews and Judaism in the Second Temple Period*, vol. 1: Yehud: A History of the Persian Province of Judah, LSTS 47 (London: T&T Clark, 2004), 199–202. Thirty thousand inhabitants is a significantly smaller number than the size of the population that can be extrapolated from the data given in Ezra 2:64–67 and Neh 7:66–69 (approximately between one hundred and fifty thousand and two hundred thousand individuals).

11 Angela Rohrmoser, *Götter, Tempel und Kult der Judäo-Aramäer von Elephantine: Archäologische und schriftliche Zeugnisse aus dem perserzeitlichen Ägypten*, AOAT 396 (Münster: Ugarit-Verlag, 2014), 81–82.

12 Cyrus H. Gordon, "The Origin of the Jews in Elephantine," *JNES* 14, no. 1 (1955): 56–58.

13 Karel van der Toorn, "Anat-Yahu, Some Other Deities, and the Jews of Elephantine," *Numen* 39 (1992): 80–101.

However, in Bezalel Porten's view the most likely scenario is that the migration took place from Judah during the reign of Manasseh. In 667 BCE the king of Judah contributed a contingent of troops to the Assyrian king Ashurbanipal when the latter campaigned against Egypt. In Egypt, Ashurbanipal "made the garrisons stronger than before," and Porten conjectures that the Judaean garrison in Elephantine might stem from one of them.[14]

In my view, fascinating and intriguing as the question of the historical origin of the Elephantine Judaeans is—and other suggestions have been made in addition to the ones mentioned here[15]—it nevertheless is important to state that any suggestion will have to be tentative because of the lack of data. Also, as Rohrmoser among others points out, it is likely that the Judaeans had come to Elephantine as the result of several migration waves.[16] No matter what the origin was, the designation "Judaean" was an important designation for the community in the period that is the scope of this study (the Persian period). In the fifth century BCE, they were Judaeans—and should be treated as such. Moreover, according to their own collective memory, their "fathers" were already living in Egypt when the period of Persian domination started.

On the basis of the fact that the community at times is referred to as a *ḥyl* ("garrison") and the fact that Elephantine was a garrison on Egypt's traditional southern border, we should assume that the community's daily life included military tasks, law enforcement and so on. However, the sources say relatively little about the military duties of the community. For instance, there are only a few hints of any military campaigns or battles and such hints are found indirectly in potential sources. For instance, the *Letter of Aristeas*, which dates to the Ptolemaic period at the earliest, relates that two waves of Judaean troops had entered Egypt before the Ptolemaic period. One came "with the Persians," cf. *Let. Aris.* 13, which give 525 BCE as terminus. Moreover, the letter also relates that another group of Judaean soldiers fought under the command of the Egyptian king Psammetichus against the king of the Ethiopians (cf. *Let. Aris.* 13), that is, under the Twenty-Sixth, Saite Dynasty.[17] Perhaps the Elephantine Judaeans of the Persian time were referring to the Judaean auxiliaries of Psammetichus when they spoke of their "fathers" who had built the temple of YHW "before Cambyses came to Egypt."

14 Porten, "Settlement of the Jews," 451–470 (459–560), cf. "Campaigns against Egypt, Syria, and Palestine," translated by A. Leo Oppenheim (*ANET*, 294–297).

15 See Rohrmoser, *Götter, Tempel und Kult*, 73–81.

16 Rohrmoser, *Götter, Tempel und Kult*, 80.

17 See also Johnson, "Ethnic Considerations," 211–222 (214).

In any case, in light of the information in *Let. Aris.* 13 (and indirectly also in other sources[18]), it is likely that one of the important tasks of the garrisons in Elephantine and in the neighbouring Syene was to protect Egypt's southern border.

In addition to border protection the garrison was also part of the Achaemenid rulers' apparatus to uphold and protect the inner stability of the Persian satrapy. A hint of this aspect of the Judaeans' duties can be seen in a fragmented letter, which might be a draft petition for the reconstruction of the destroyed temple of YHW (A4.5). There, the Judaeans relate that "the detachments of the Egyptians rebelled" (*dgln zy mṣry mrdw*) whereas "we did not leave our posts" (*ʾnḥnh mnṭrtn lʾ šbqn*, A4.5:1).[19] Rebellions within the Egyptian satrapy (in some cases with "the Egyptians" as the agents) are also mentioned in the correspondence of the satrap Arshama,[20] though Judeans are not specifically identified as being among the satrap's loyal troops.[21]

We can also assume that Judaean soldiers were involved in tasks such as protecting and escorting commodities between treasuries. For instance, in B4.4 we read that the two soldiers Hosea son of Hodaviah and Ahiab son of Gemariah were personally responsible for transporting goods, in this case barley, between one treasury and another.[22] According to another document (A3.3 = P. Padua 1), it seems that Shelomam, a person who appears to have been a YHW-worshipping Judaean soldier, was often on the move between Migdol in Lower Egypt and places further south (Memphis, Elephantine).

In addition, the region of Syene was famous for its many stone quarries where above all the famous reddish Aswan granite was cut. Perhaps some Judaeans worked there.[23]

---

18 See Ashurbanipal's account of his campaigns against Egypt, Syria and Palestine in *ANET*, 294–297.

19 A4.5:2 continues *mḥbl lʾ ʾštkḥ ln*, which may be rendered "We were not found to be at fault," cf. Lindenberger, *Ancient Aramaic and Hebrew Letters*, 78 note j. In that case, the Elephantine Judaeans articulate their loyalty (in contrast to the rioting Egyptian troops).

20 A6.7:6; A6.10:1,4; A6.11:2, cf. Porten et al., *The Elephantine Papyri in English*, 136 note 3.

21 Nevertheless, in my view there are good reasons for assuming that it was an important aspect of the self-image of the Elephantine Judaeans that they were the loyal soldiers of the Achaemenids, and when all is said and done, of Ahuramazda, the dynasty god of the ruling Achaemenid kings. See Gard Granerød, "Ahuramazdas lojale judeiske soldater: Om Elefantine-judeernes selvbilde," *TeoT* 3 (2014): 288–303 (298–300).

22 They would be held liable for any loss, cf. B4.4:13–17.

23 Thus also Rohrmoser, *Götter, Tempel und Kult*, 71.

2.2 Judaean Identity in Elephantine

A banal yet important question deals with the characteristics that set the Judaeans apart from other groups in Upper Egypt. What were the factors that coined the identity of the members of the Judaean community?

The question of identity may be discussed both in essentialist terms through the concept of ethnicity and through relational aspects. As for the former, an ethnos can be defined as "a named human population with myths of common ancestry, shared historical memories, one or more elements of common culture, a link with a homeland, and a sense of solidarity among at least some of its members."[24] However, as Magnar Kartveit points out by referring to the Norwegian social anthropologist Fredrik Barth's works, such a definition approaches ethnicity in *essentialist* terms and should be accompanied by *relational* aspects: "an ethnos receives identity also through identification of its friends and enemies."[25]

A prerequisite for this question is that the Judaeans in fact experienced themselves as belonging to a distinct group. Was there a Judaean "we" distinct from other groups in Upper Egypt?

A passage in a letter from Mauziah son of Nathan (A4.3) suggests that this was the case.[26] The undated letter, written sometime during the final decades of the fifth century BCE, which was a troublesome time for Judaeans, gives one example of an individual Judaean who distinguished between "them" and "us." Mauziah writes, "For you it is known that Khnum[27] is against us since Hananiah is/has been in Egypt until now" (A4.3:7). Around 419 BCE Hananiah came and (among other things) imparted to the Judaeans the decree of King Darius II dealing with the Festival of Unleavened Bread and perhaps the Passover (cf. A4.1). What is relevant here is the pronoun "us," expressed in the phrase *ḥnwm hw ʿlyn*. Mauziah clearly referred to Judaeans when he wrote about "us." Among Judaeans there was a comprehension that enabled Mauziah to speak of a collective "we."

---

24 John Hutchinson and Anthony D. Smith, "Introduction," in *Ethnicity*, ed. John Hutchinson and Anthony D. Smith (Oxford: Oxford University Press, 1996): 3–14 (6), cf. Magnar Kartveit, "Samaritan Self-Consciousness in the First Half of the Second Century B.C.E. in Light of the Inscriptions from Mount Gerizim and Delos," *JSJ* 45 (2014): 449–470.

25 Kartveit, "Samaritan Self-Consciousness," 449–470.

26 See also Johnson, "Ethnic Considerations," 211–222 (216): "There is an 'us (Jews) against them (Egyptians)' feeling found repeatedly in documents from the Jewish garrison at Elephantine."

27 Here "Khnum" probably represents the priests of Khnum, cf. A4.5:3, 8 et al.

On the basis of what criteria could Mauziah, and ultimately all other members of his groups, speak of "us" as a group distinct from "them"? Obviously, there were several factors that defined the identity of the Judaean community. On factor could be that the group and its members identified themselves as Judaeans by using the designation *yhwdy.* This is partly but not entirely true. To be sure, individuals used the designation, as is attested by its appearance in several contracts (e.g. B2.9:2, 3–4; B3.1:3; B3.6:2). The designation was also used in communication with officials. For instance, in the letter to Bagavahya the governor of Judah the phrase *yhwdy' kl'*, "all Judaeans," occurs, referring to the "citizens" (plural of *b'l*) of the Elephantine Judaean community (A4.8:22). However, there is evidence to suggest that the term *yhwdy* was not the only factor that defined the group. In the legal documents one and the same individual, Mahseiah son of Jedaniah, is sometimes called "a Judaean of Elephantine" (B2.2:3; B2.4:2), other times called "an Aramaean of Syene" (B2.6:2; B2:7:2) and other times again "Judaean, hereditary property holder in Elephantine" (B2.3:2).[28] Moreover, a group of Elephantine leaders writing to an official referred to themselves as "Syenians" who controlled land at Elephantine (A4.10:6). Therefore, Judaean identity does not seem to have been shaped by the use of the designation *yhwdy* alone.

Another factor that defined the Judaean community was the god YHW, "the god dwelling in Elephantine," and the temple devoted to him. Writing to an Achaemenid official ("our lord") about the rebuilding of the temple of YHW, leading Judaeans refer to YHW as "YHW, the god of ours" (*yhw 'lh' zyln*, A4.10:8). In the many examples of theophoric names borne by individuals affiliated with the Judaean garrison the divine element is exclusively *yhw* or the abbreviated form *yw.*[29] The chief deity of the members of the Judaean community was YHW. Yet, the textual evidence shows that YHW in reality was not the only deity venerated and perhaps even worshipped by the Judaeans. Oaths were sworn by AnathYHW and perhaps the god Ḥerem (?) (B7.3:3), by the Egyptian goddess Sati (B2.8:5) and by Ḥerembethel[30] (B7.2:7).[31] In this regard, the previous case illustrates the problem of defining a Judaean at Elephantine. An individual

28 See the discussion on double designations in Porten et al., *The Elephantine Papyri in English*, 155 note 4, and Johnson, "Ethnic Considerations," 211–222 (216–217).

29 For a discussion of onomastics, see Porten et al., *The Elephantine Papyri in English*, 85–89.

30 Karel van der Toorn has previously argued that this is *not* a compound divine name but refers to "the sacred property of [the god] Bethel," cf. Karel van der Toorn, "Herem-Bethel and Elephantine Oath Procedure," *ZAW* 98 (1986): 282–285 (283), and Toorn, "Anat-Yahu, Some Other Deities, and the Jews of Elephantine," 80–101.

31 See also the ostracon D7.30, where a certain Jarḥu blesses his brother Haggai by "Bel and Nabu, Shamash and Nergal."

who calls himself "Malchiah son of Jashobiah, an Aramaean, hereditary property holder in Elephantine" (B7.2:2–3) had been accused of an unlawful entry/acquisition of a house by someone called Artafrada who was a member of another detachment. In the document, Malchiah, who clearly has a theophoric name with YHW as the divine element, expressed his willingness to declare loudly in the presence of Ḥerembethel that he was not guilty of the accusation (B7.2:7). Moreover, the so-called Collection Account (C3.15) lists the "names of the Judaean garrison who gave silver to YHW the god" (C3.15:1). What continues to perplex scholars is that the list also accounts for the contributions to Eshembethel and Anathbethel (who probably are gods, C3.15:127–128). Furthermore, the servant Giddel blessed his lord Micaiah (cf. the element YHW) "by YHH and Khnum" (D7.21:3). Therefore, also the worship and veneration of YHW did not function alone as the main criteria for defining the Judaean community.

Yet another factor that must have contributed to the shaping of the identity of the Judaean community was the common obligation to observe particular religious festivals. The letter that Hananiah wrote around 419 BCE concerning the Festival of Unleavened Bread (and the perhaps the Passover) was addressed to "Jedaniah and his colleagues the Judaean garrison." The many injunctions of the letter are all directed to the garrison as a whole, for example, *ʾntm kn mnw*, "you [plural] count thus!" (A4.1:3), and *dkyn hww*, "(you [plural], be pure!" (A4.1:5).

Moreover, the conflict that took place in the last decades of the fifth century BCE must inevitably have strengthened the identity of the community as Judaean with YHW as chief god. The textual evidence offers only the version of the Judaeans. No traces of the other party's version of the conflict have been left in the sources.[32] As far as the Judaean community is concerned, the temple of

32 The one-sided nature of the account of the Judaeans has been pointed out by Pierre Briant. Moreover, he has also suggested that one of the reasons behind the conflict between the priests of Khnum and the temple of YHW centred around "The Street of the King." The thesis proposed by Briant and further developed by von Pilgrim and Rohrmoser is that the south-eastern temenos wall of the first temple of YHW may have been *unlawfully* built upon "The Street of the King." As a consequence of the Judaean community's building upon such common land, the passage between the temenos wall of the first temple of YHW and the wall of the Town of Khnum may only have been a half metre wide. This was not enough for carts. During the period of the first temple, carts, pedestrians and possibly also religious processions had to make a detour north-west of the temple of YHW in order to get through, cf. Pierre Briant, *From Cyrus to Alexander: A History of the Persian Empire* (Winona Lake, IN: Eisenbrauns, 2002), 603–607; Cornelius von Pilgrim, "Tempel des Jahu und 'Strasse des Königs': ein Konflikt in der Späten Perserzeit auf Elephantine," in *Egypt: Temple of the Whole World: Studies in Honour of Jan Assmann*

YHW was razed to the ground. Also the well the Judaeans used in Elephantine was stopped up (A4.5:6–8). According to the Judaeans' version, the aggressors were originally the Egyptian priests of Khnum who bribed the local Persian frataraka Vidranga (A4.5:2–4; A4.7:5).

Finally, the community's orientation towards Jerusalem and Judah suggests that the community considered itself affiliated with Jerusalem and Judah, perhaps as a diaspora community. At least two official letters written to Judah and Jerusalem are known. One is explicitly attested: the letter to Bagavahya the governor of Judah (of which two drafts are known, A4.7 and A4.8). Another earlier letter sent to the Jerusalem priesthood, the nobility of Judah and Bagavahya is indirectly attested (A4.7:18–19). The letters to Jerusalem and Judah were written against the background of the conflict with the Egyptian priests of Khnum and the local Persian administration in Upper Egypt. Assumedly, the conflict about the temple of YHW sharpened the community's identity as Judaeans by providing an impetus to reconfirm its ties with the homeland, Judah. However, regardless of whether this was the case or not, the Elephantine Judaeans did not only orientate themselves towards Judah and Jerusalem; they also maintained contact with the Sanballat dynasty in Samaria (A4.7:29 par.). The Elephantine Judaeans received assistance from Samaria by means of a statement. The statement was given by a representative of the Sanballat dynasty in Samaria together with the governor of Judah (A4.9). Regardless of what implications this cooperation between Samaria and Judah may have for the political history of the provinces of Judah and Samaria, the point here is that the Elephantine Judaeans, by also orienting themselves towards Samaria thus displayed a special relationship with Samaria, a relationship that in turn seems to have been confirmed by the ruling dynasty in Samaria.

Summing up, the Elephantine Judaean identity was based on several factors, both essential and relational ones, that were present to various degrees. Judaean identity was constituted by several factors, of which religion was important but not an exclusive characteristic.

2.3 The Leaders of the Judaean Community

Our sources for the internal organisation of the Judaean community are primarily found in the documents of the Jedaniah communal archive. On the basis of the

---

= *Ägypten: Tempel der gesamten Welt*, ed. Sibylle Meyer, SHR 97 (Leiden: Brill, 2003): 303–317 (315); and Rohrmoser, *Götter, Tempel und Kult*, 178.

addresses of the letters written in the last decades of the fifth century BCE it is possible to single out leading individuals and groups. However, the nature of their function within the matrix of the Judaean society in Elephantine is not entirely clear.

2.3.1 Jedaniah and the Priests of YHW

In the last decades of the fifth century BCE, a person named Jedaniah son of Gemariah (A4.4:7; A4.10:1) stood at the head of the community (A4.1; A4.2; A4.3; A4.7; A4.8; A4.10). In the communal letters that are either written to or written by the community, his name appears first in the list of addressees or senders respectively. Only on one occasion is Jedaniah given a title. In a letter to an anonymous superior (the satrap Arshama?) Jedaniah and four other named individuals are called "Syenians who are *mhḥsnn* ['hereditary property holders'[33]] in Elephantine." Except for this, it is not known whether Jedaniah bore other titles.

In the letter to Bagavahya the Persian governor of Judah, Jedaniah appears together with "his colleagues the priests who are in the fortress of Elephantine" (*khny' zy byb byrt'*, A4.7:1). Moreover, when another leading figure called Mauziah son of Nathan wrote in connection with his imprisonment in Abydos, he addressed his letter to "my lords Jedaniah, Uriah and the priests of YHW the God, Mattan son of Jashobiah (and) Berechiah son of [...]" (A4.3:1, cf. A4.10:2). This raises the question: Was Jedaniah himself a priest also? A potential clue might be the sought in the term "colleague" ("Jedaniah and his colleagues [*knwth*] the priests..." (A4.7:1). However, this is not a conclusive argument in favour of Jedaniah being a priest. Some years earlier Hananiah addressed his letter to "Jedaniah and his colleagues the Judaean garrison" (A4.1:1), obviously having an inclusive understanding of the concept of collegiality. A detail in the second draft of the petition that the Judaean community sent to Bagavahya (A4.8) does perhaps shed more light on the question. There, Jedaniah and his colleagues the priests promise Bagavahya that they will offer sacrifices in Bagavahya's name, provided that the temple of YHW is eventually rebuilt: "And the meal-offer, and the incense and the burnt-offering we shall offer [*nqrb*] on the altar of YHW the god in your name..." (A4.8:24–25). In the second draft of the petition, the verb is *nqrb* (first plural), which is a correction to the wording of the first draft (A4.7:25 *yqrbwn:* third masculine plural: "they will offer"). The "we" of the sec-

33 See Section 2.3.3 below.

ond draft includes Jedaniah. Provided that only priests were allowed to offer sacrifices, then it follows from the verb form *nqrb* that Jedaniah was a priest, too.

To be sure, Jedaniah is not explicitly called "priest" in any known source. Therefore, the question whether Jedaniah was a priest, and consequently, the Judaean community of Elephantine was a community led by a priest, must remain unanswered. In any case, Jedaniah and the priests of YHW (in some instances also other named individuals: A4.2:1; A4.3:1) had the authority to both speak and to be contacted on behalf of the Judaean community.

2.3.2 Hananiah

Another leading figure was Hananiah who wrote the so-called Passover letter around 419 BCE to the Judaean garrison. His status vis-à-vis the garrison is somewhat ambiguous. On the one hand he refers to Jedaniah and the Judaean garrison in amicable terms (A4.1:1, 10 "my brothers," "your brother Hananiah"). On the other hand, the contents of the partly broken text of the letter opens up the possibility that he de facto was in a position to impose injunctions concerning a religious festival on the community. We can identify the instructions in the letter on the basis of the inflected verb forms. Each one of the injunctions is represented by either an imperative or a negated jussive. Although there is a lacuna in Hananiah's letter and the wording of the royal decree is lost, it nevertheless seems clear that King Darius II was involved in the regulation of a religious festival celebrated by the Jewish garrison, and that Hananiah stood somewhere in the middle, between the king and the Judaean garrison. Who was this Hananiah, then, and what was his role with regard to the Persian authorities and the Jewish garrison?

Besides being the sender of the so-called Passover letter, Hananiah is also mentioned in one additional text, namely the letter that Mauziah son of Nathan wrote to Jedaniah, Uriah and the priests of YHW and the other leaders of the Judaean community in Elephantine after his imprisonment in Abydos (A4.3). Mauziah puts the ongoing conflict with the Egyptian priests of Khnum in connection with Hananiah's arrival in Egypt (A4.3:7). By combining the two documents mentioning him (A4.1 and A4.3) we can extract some pieces of information about Hananiah:

a. He came from somewhere outside Egypt (A4.3:7),
b. his arrival took place around King Darius II's fifth regnal year (419/418 BCE, A4.1:2),
c. one of his tasks was to impart to the Judeans and the satrap Arshama a royal decree (A4.1:2–8),

d. his coming to Egypt provoked the priests of the Egyptian god Khnum (A4.3:7), and
e. the contents of the royal instruction was probably connected to the date of a religious feast, probably the Festival of Unleavened Bread and perhaps the Passover (A4.1:3 – 9).

We can say more about Hananiah's role and status by focussing on his servant Ḥor. In Mauziah's letter to the Judaean leaders a servant with this name occurs in two contexts. In the last occurrence Mauziah wrote that "Ḥor is a servant of Hananiah" (A4.3:8). However, a few lines above Mauziah had written that Ḥor was one of Anani's servants (A4.3:4). Provided that Mauziah speaks of one and the same person, the chronology is somewhat unclear. Was Ḥor the servant of both Hananiah and Anani at the same time, or did one of them for some reason succeed the other as Ḥor's master? In any case, provided that Mauziah speaks of one and the same servant, Ḥor played an important role in the release of Mauziah. Mauziah had been imprisoned in Abydos by the garrison commander (*rbḥyl'*) Vidranga (A4.3:3). Mauziah wrote that the servants Ḥor and Ṣeḥa "intervened" (*'štdrw*) with Vidranga (and Ḥornufi) "with the help of the god of heaven" until they "rescued me" (*šzbwny*, A4.3:4 – 5). The verb *šdr* seems to denote the activity of reversing a judicial process or a verdict. The verb also occurs once in Biblical Aramaic, and that in a comparable situation. According to Dan 6:15 [ET 6:14] "King Darius the Mede [cf. Dan 6:1 (ET: 5:31)] ... made every effort [*hăwā' mištaddar*] to rescue" Daniel from the lion's den. In the case of Mauziah's imprisonment, it seems that the servant Ḥor was in a position that allowed him to intervene vis-à-vis Vidranga on behalf of Mauziah. Extrapolating from this, it is possible that Hananiah, who had been or still was Ḥor's superior, had an even more superior position as compared with the garrison commander Vidranga. Hananiah was in a position to interfere in Vidranga's business through the servant Ḥor.

Ingo Kottsieper has suggested that Hananiah's role was to regulate Judaean matters in Egypt in the capacity of a Persian official or commissioner, or at least in agreement with and supported by the Achaemenid central administration. According to Kottsieper, Hananiah's mission implied an official recognition by the Achaemenid authorities of the Judaean community as a religious community in Egypt, something which it officially did not have until then.[34] He has tentatively

34 Ingo Kottsieper, "Die Religionspolitik der Achämeniden und die Juden von Elephantine," in *Religion und Religionskontakte im Zeitalter der Achämeniden*, ed. Reinhard Gregor Kratz, VWGT 22 (Gütersloh: Gütersloher Verlagshaus, 2002), 150 – 178 (157 – 158), cf. Reinhard Gregor Kratz, "Judean Ambassadors and the Making of Jewish Identity: The Case of Hananiah, Ezra,

suggested that the change of status is reflected in the designation *ḥyl' yhwdy'*, "the Judaean garrison," a designation Hananiah himself used in his letter (A4.1). On the other side, Pierre Briant has suggested that the initiative for Hananiah's mission came from the authorities in Jerusalem "who wanted to unify ritual throughout the diaspora."[35]

Both the suggestion of Kottsieper and that of Briant are conjectures. Nevertheless, an important argument in favour of Kottsieper's theory is its explanatory force. The theory that Hananiah's coming to Egypt brought with it a change to the official status of the Judaean community would explain the hostility of the Khnum priests. According to the Judaeans, the hostility coincided with Hananiah's arrival in Egypt (see A4.3:7).

Be that as it may, Hananiah did definitely operate in the role of a royal envoy of some kind.[36] Therefore, his role may be compared to that of another, perhaps more famous envoy, namely Udjahorresnet. In order to compare Hananiah and Udjahorresnet I will have to treat the latter in detail. The autobiography of Udjahorresnet is attested in a hieroglyphic inscription on his statue, which was found in Susa in Elam but one may assume originally was erected in the temple of Osiris in Sais. In the autobiography, Udjahorresnet boasted of several things.[37] One thing he emphasised was his close relationship with Cambyses, the Persian king who conquered Egypt, and later on, with his successor King Darius I. During the Twenty-Sixth, Saite Dynasty, Udjahorresnet served as commander of the king's navy. When Cambyses conquered Egypt in 525 BCE, his loyalty turned towards the new king. Cambyses gave him the office as the king's chief physician and "friend," and Udjahorresnet himself claimed that he composed Cambyses's titulatory, "King of Upper and Lower Egypt, Mesutire ['offspring of Re']."

Moreover, Udjahorresnet also boasted of being the one who caused Cambyses to recognise the greatness of Sais, which had been the capital of the last indigenous Egyptian dynasty and was "the seat of Neith-the-Great, the mother who

and Nehemiah," in *Judah and the Judeans in the Achaemenid Period: Negotiating Identity in an International Context*, ed. Oded Lipschits et al. (Winona Lake, IN: Eisenbrauns, 2011), 421–444 (430).

35 Briant, *From Cyrus to Alexander*, 586.

36 Kratz: "ambassador," cf. Reinhard Gregor Kratz, "Judäische Gesandte im Achämenidenreich: Hananja, Esra und Nehemia," in *From Daēnā to Dîn: Religion, Kultur und Sprache in der iranischen Welt: Festschrift für Philip Kreyenbroek zum 60. Geburtstag*, ed. Christine Allison (Wiesbaden: Harrassowitz, 2009): 377–395, and Kratz, "Judean Ambassadors," 421–444 (424–426).

37 For annotated translations, see Amélie Kuhrt, *The Persian Empire: A Corpus of Sources from the Achaemenid Period* (London: Routledge, 2007), 117–122 (no. 4.11), and Maria Brosius, *The Persian Empire from Cyrus II to Artaxerxes I*, LACTOR 16 (London: London Association of Classical Teachers, 2000), 15–16, 47–48 (nos. 20 and 54).

bore Re." The Egyptian goddess Neith was worshipped by Egyptian kings because she provided protection for them.

Furthermore, yet another thing that Udjahorresnet boasted of was his role with regard to Cambyses's religious policy in Egypt. Although Udjahorresnet spoke warmly of Cambyses, it nevertheless shines through the autobiography that the Persian occupation was accompanied by troubles. Udjahorresnet wrote that he petitioned Cambyses about "all the foreigners who had settled themselves down." He asked the king to have them expelled from the temple in Sais so that it should once more be in all its splendour "as it had been earlier." According to the chief physician, Cambyses responded to his petition: "His Majesty commanded to purify the temple of Neith and to restore to it all its people." Moreover, Cambyses commanded that offerings should be given to Neith and the other gods in Sais, "as it was earlier." He commanded that all festivals and all processions should be organised "as it was done earlier." Later on, Cambyses came to Sais himself in order to show reverence to Neith "as every king had done."

After the demise of Cambyses Udjahorresnet served Darius I, who also bore the title "King of Upper and Lower Egypt." When Darius was in Elam, he ordered his chief physician Udjahorresnet to travel on a mission to Egypt. According to Udjahorresnet, who apparently served as a special adviser to the Persian government on Egyptian affairs, the purpose of his mission from Elam to Egypt was "to set to rights the office of the House of Life," which apparently had been neglected for some time.[38]

The information Udjahorresnet gives in his autobiography must be interpreted in light of the fact that he was an Egyptian who collaborated with the Persians. He may have been a special adviser to the Persian government on Egyptian affairs. Hananiah did perhaps have had a comparable role. In the sources there are no traces of Hananiah having been engaged in the everyday administration of the Judaean community. Most likely he did not stay in Egypt for long. Assumedly, he arrived in Egypt around 49/418 BCE and returned before the temple of YHW was destroyed around 410 BCE. When Mauziah wrote his letter to the other Elephantine leaders concerning the imprisonment in Abydos (A4.3), Hananiah had probably already left Egypt.[39]

---

38 On Udjahorresnet's mission to Egypt, see Joseph Blenkinsopp, "The Mission of Udjahorresnet and Those of Ezra and Nehemiah," *JBL* 106 (1987): 409–421.

39 The problem is how to translate *mn zy ḥnnyh bmṣryn ʿd kʿn* (A4.3:7). In Kottsieper's view, Hananiah is no longer in Egypt ("seit Ḥananja in Ägypten war bis jetzt"), Kottsieper, "Die Religionspolitik der Achämeniden," 150–178 (154). Also Porten opens up for Kottsieper's reading, cf. Porten et al., *The Elephantine Papyri in English*, 133 note 32.

2.3.3 The Group of Five Syenians Who Were "Hereditary Property Holders" (*mhḥsnn*) in Elephantine

On one occasion in the Elephantine papyri a group of five individuals appears as the leaders of the Judaean community: Jedaniah son of Gemariah, Mauzi son of Nathan, Shemaiah son of Haggai, Hosea son of Jathom and Hosea son of Nattun (A4.10.1–5). It seems that the five-strong group negotiated with an official whose name is not given in the documents. The purpose was to achieve permission to rebuild "the temple of YHW the god of ours ... as it was built formerly" (A4.10:8–9). It is possible that the letter was addressed to Arshama, the Persian governor of Egypt. What is remarkable is that the five leaders neither present themselves as "Judaeans" nor use any religious titles. On the contrary, they are "Syenians" (*swnknn*) who are *mhḥsnn* (plural participle of *ḥsn* in the *haphel* stem) in Elephantine (A4.10:6).

The question therefore arises: What did it mean to be a *mhḥsn?* The background of the term was the legal institution of hereditary leases in Achaemenid-period Egypt. Acquisition of property could occur in one of three ways: 1. sale, 2. personal gift or state allocation, or 3. inheritance.[40] In the Aramaic documents from ancient Egypt there are examples of pieces of land having being allocated by the satrap to individuals as leases. A built-in feature evident in these cases is that the heir would assume all rights and obligations under the terms of the original lease. Consequently, a person who took over his father's lease according to the terms of the original agreement between the lessor and the lessee, would be referred to by the technical term *mhḥsn* that can be rendered "hereditary property holder."[41] An authorisation of boat repair issued by the satrap Arshama shows that boats could also be held on hereditary lease (A6.2:3).

An illustration of the mechanisms of this system—and its tendency of micromanagement—is found in a letter from the satrap Arshama to the official Nakhtḥor and the accountant Kenzasirma and his colleagues (A6.11:1, 7).[42] The background of the letter was a situation where a lease had not been transferred to an heir upon the death of the lessee. In the letter, Arshama quoted from a request put forward by one of his servants called Peṭosiri. Peṭosiri had related that his father Pamun previously had held an estate (*bg*) as *mhḥsn.*[43] Due to unrest in

40 Zvi Henri Szubin and Bezalel Porten, "'Ancestral Estates' in Aramaic Contracts: The Legal Significance of the term *mhḥsn*," *JRAS* (1982): 3–9 (4).

41 Szubin and Porten, "'Ancestral Estates' in Aramaic Contracts," 3–9, and Zvi Henri Szubin and Bezalel Porten, "Hereditary Leases in Aramaic Letters," *BO* 42 (1985): 283–288.

42 See Szubin and Porten, "Hereditary Leases in Aramaic Letters," 283–288.

43 A6.11:2: *hwh mhḥsn.*

Egypt Pamun and all the household personnel had "perished" (*ʾbd*). As a consequence of that, the estate had been abandoned (*ʾštbq*). Peṭosiri claimed that his father's estate had not been given to him after his father's demise. Therefore Peṭosiri asked Arshama that the estate be given to him so that he could hold it as heir.[44] On the back of this request Arshama asked Nakhtḥor and Kenzasirma to verify the accuracy of Peṭosiri's account. Provided that the satrapal administration had not allocated the estate to another person in the meantime, Arshama ordered that Peṭosiri should hold the estate as hereditary property holder (A6.11:5 *yhḥsn*[45]) under the same conditions as his father Pamun (A6.11:5–6). The satrap's inclination towards micromanagement is evident in the relatively modest size of the estate. It is said that it had a capacity of thirty ardabs[46] of seed, and provided that this was per year, the estate had the capacity to produce 838.8 litres per year. This would only suffice to supply two workmen or soldiers with the standard daily ration of flour.[47]

The circumstances of Arshama's recognition of Peṭosiri as hereditary property holder were probably untypical. The chain of hereditary succession had been broken by unrest in Egypt. The term *mhḥsn* also occurs in legal contracts that involve members of the Judaean community. In a contract between Mahseiah son of Jedaniah and Jedaniah's daughter Mibtahiah, dated in the sixth year of

---

44 A6.11:3: *ʾhḥsn* (first person singular imperfectum of *ḥsn* in *haphel* stem).

45 Imperfect third masculine singular *ḥsn* in *haphel* stem; Bezalel Porten and Ada Yardeni, *Textbook of Aramaic Documents from Ancient Egypt. Newly Copied, Edited and Translated into Hebrew and English*, vol. I: Letters. Appendix: Aramaic Letters from the Bible (Jerusalem: The Hebrew University of Jerusalem – Department of the History of the Jewish People, 1986), 118: "Let him hold-(it)-as-heir."

46 An ardab is a dry measure. The exact correspondence in the kilometric system of one ardab (Aramaic: *ʾrdb*) is unknown. What is certain is that one ardab (Elamite *irtabe*, Greek: *artabē*) = three *grīw* (Aramaic: *sʾh*; Elamite: BAR) = thirty handfuls (Aramaic: *ḥpn*), cf. Bezalel Porten, *Archives from Elephantine: The Life of an Ancient Jewish Military Colony* (Berkeley: University of California Press, 1968), 70–72, and A. D. H. Bivar, "Weights and Measures: i. Pre-Islamic Period," *EIr* (2010): online edition, available at http://www.iranicaonline.org/articles/weights-measures-i. In the Achaemenid period, one ardab may have equalled 27.96 litres so that, in turn, one handful equalled 0.932 litre, cf. Bivar, "Weights and Measures: i. Pre-Islamic Period," online edition, available at http://www.iranicaonline.org/articles/weights-measures-i.

47 One handful (*ḥpn*) constituted the standard daily ration of flour for a soldier or a worker, cf. Godfrey Rolles Driver, *Aramaic Documents of the Fifth Century B.C.* (Oxford: Clarendon, 1954), 22, 60. This is particularly evident in the document Arshama issued to his official Nakhtḥor, authorizing him to travel along a specified route and giving him the right to receive rations for himself and his company. In the document it is specified that Nakhtḥor's servants should each receive one handful of flour per day (A6.9:4).

Artaxerxes (I, i.e. around 459 BCE), Mahseiah is described as "a Judaean, a *mhḥsn* in the fortress of Elephantine" (B2.3:1–2; 23–26).

In the case of the letter from the five Syenians seeking permission to rebuild the temple of "YHW the god of ours" and to resume the offering of sacrifices (A4.10), the purpose of presenting themselves as *mhḥsnn* in Elephantine may probably have been to present themselves as burghers, or freeholders,[48] who were reliable men of means.[49]

That the five *mhḥsnn* in fact were reliable men of means is evident in their conditional offer to their anonymous superior ("our lord"). If[50] "our lord" should make a statement (assumedly concerning the rebuilding of the temple of YHW), then the five *mhḥsnn* in return would offer a considerable payment to "the house of our lord." The conditional payment comprised silver and one thousand ardabs of barley.

To put the offered conditional payment in perspective, the amount of barley that the five Syenians offered "to our lord" can be compared with the ration of barley that a garrison stationed in Syene received. According to an account of disbursement (C3.14:26–31), the fifty-four-strong garrison received one hundred ardabs of barley, which probably was meant to cover a month.[51] Provided that this is correct, the amount of barley that the Elephantine leaders offered to "the house of our lord" could feed five hundred and forty men for a period of one month.[52]

---

48 Thus Szubin and Porten, "'Ancestral Estates' in Aramaic Contracts," 3–9 (8).

49 Porten et al., *The Elephantine Papyri in English*, 153 note 9.

50 In my view, there is a conditional sentence in the last three fragmented lines (A4.10:12–14). The condition (protasis) is not marked formally but may be recognised on the basis of the general context: *wmrʾn ʾwdys yʿb[d]* ...., "And should our lord make a statement ..."

51 According to the account, twenty-two men received one ardab each, two men received one and a half ardabs each and thirty received two and a half ardabs each. The period it was meant to cover is not specified. However, I believe it was a monthly ration, because one arbad = three *gr̄w* (seah) = thirty handfuls, cf. Porten, *Archives from Elephantine*, 70–72, and Bivar, "Weights and Measures: i. Pre-Islamic Period," online edition, available at http://www.iranicaonline.org/articles/weights-measures-i. My proposal is based on the premise that one handful equalled the minimum daily ration for a soldier or workman, cf. Driver, *Aramaic Documents*, 22, 60, and A6.9:4.

52 Any Achaemenid official would probably be interested in enhancing his revenue. Hospitality and generosity was not only a virtue but also one of the (expensive) mechanisms through which Achaemenid kings and officials exercised power and influence (see, e.g., Neh 5:14–18). Administrative documents show that Arshama owned several estates throughout the Persian empire (e.g., A6.9). This did not prevent him from wanting more. For instance, he accused his servant Nakhtḥor of not enhancing his estate (cf. A6.10:9–10). For a thorough discussion of (royal)

The sources do not allow us to tell whether there were other Judaean hereditary property holders in Elephantine who were contemporaneous with the five mentioned in A4.10. In any case, in a time of crisis for the temple of YHW at Elephantine it was the five named hereditary property holders who functioned as spokesmen on behalf of the community that reckoned YHW as "the god of ours" (cf. A4.10:8). Although it cannot be proved, this probably reflected a special situation conditioned by the extraordinary circumstances of the temple of YHW lying in ruins. Nevertheless, the action of the five-strong "hereditary property holders in Elephantine" gives an insight into the *de facto* hierarchy of power within the Judaean community.

2.3.4 The Political and Religious Leaders of Judah and Samaria

After the temple of YHW was destroyed in 410 BCE, Jedaniah and his colleagues the priests sent letters to the political and religious leaders of Jerusalem, Judah and Samaria (A4.7:17–19, 29 par.). The first request addressed to the religious and political leaders of Jerusalem and Judah (including "our lord," i.e. the governor Bagavahya) was never answered:

> Moreover, before this, at the time that this evil was done to us, a letter we sent (to) our lord, and to Jehohanan the High Priest and his colleagues the priests who are in Jerusalem, and to Ostanes the brother of Anani and the nobles of the Jews [*wḥry yhwdy'*, "and the nobles of the Judaeans," G.G.]. A letter they did not send us. (A4.7:17–19 par.)[53]

It was the second letter addressed to the governors of Judah and Samaria (A4:7:1, 29 par.) that provoked a response from the two governors. The response took the form of a joint statement (A4.9). The contact between Elephantine, Judah and Samaria raises several questions regarding the formal/informal relationship between Elephantine, Judah/Jerusalem and Samaria and the relationship within Judah/Jerusalem:

- What was the relationship between Judah and Samaria like?
- Did the governors in Judah and Samaria have any sort of extraterritorial jurisdiction, say, over Elephantine?
- What do the (repeated) letters from Elephantine to Jerusalem say about the Elephantine Judaeans' *own* understanding of their relation to Judah?

---

gifts, see, e.g., Briant, *From Cyrus to Alexander*, 302–323, and Lindsay Allen, *The Persian Empire: A History* (London: British Museum, 2005), 119.

53 Quoted from Porten et al., *The Elephantine Papyri in English*, 144.

The memorandum of the joint statement of Bagavahya the governor of Judah and Delaiah, son of the Samaritan governor Sanballat (A4.9), suggests that there was an amicable relationship between Judah and Samaria in the last decade of the fifth century BCE. The political history of the province of Judah in the Persian period is not entirely clear.[54] One theory is that Judah was originally part of the province of Samaria. At one point it was separated from Samaria and made a province on its own. According to another theory Judah was a separate province throughout the entire Persian period. In light of the available sources the question will have to remain unanswered. Nevertheless, nothing in the memorandum (A4.9) points in the direction of a schism or antagonism between Jerusalem and Samaria at the end of the fifth century BCE.[55]

The first (and unanswered) letter from Elephantine to Judah and Jerusalem had multiple addressees. It was addressed to both the political leader of Judah as well as to the religious leaders, headed by the high priest. As André Lemaire has argued, this suggests that there was a kind of diarchy at the head of Judah at the end of the fifth century BCE.[56] Later numismatic material from Judah dated to the last decades of the Persian period suggests the same. Two almost contemporary coins have the following Hebrew inscriptions respectively: *yḥzqyh hpḥh*, "Yeḥizqiyah the governor," and *ywḥnn hkhn*, "Yôhanan the priest." The fact that the latter, probably the high priest Yôhanan/Yehôhanan/Jehohanan II,[57] also struck

54 See Herbert Donner, *Geschichte des Volkes Israel und seiner Nachbarn in Grundzügen*, 2nd, rev. ed., vol. 2: Von der Königszeit bis zur Alexander dem Großen: Mit einem Ausblick auf die Geschichte des Judentums bis Bar Kochba, ATD Ergänzungsreihe 4/2 (Göttingen: Vandenhoeck & Ruprecht, 1995), 434–435; Grabbe, *History of the Jews, Volume 1*, 1: Yehud: A History of the Persian Province of Judah, 140–142; Erhard S. Gerstenberger, *Israel in the Persian Period: The Fifth and Fourth Centuries B.C.E.*, BibEnc 8 (Atlanta: Society of Biblical Literature, 2011), 87; and Reinhard Gregor Kratz, *Historisches und biblisches Israel: Drei Überblicke zum Alten Testament* (Tübingen: Mohr Siebeck, 2013), 250–251.

55 See Magnar Kartveit, *The Origin of the Samaritans*, VTSup 128 (Leiden: Brill, 2009), 351–362. A completely different image of the relationship between Judah and Samaria is drawn in the biblical books of Ezra and Nehemiah. There, a certain Sanballat the Horonite plays the role as Jerusalem's main enemy (Neh 2:10, 19; Ezra 4; 6). On the basis of epigraphic sources (the Wadi ed-Daliyeh papyri) three Samarian governors with this name are known. The Wadi ed-Daliyeh papyri demonstrate the practice of papponomy (naming the grandson after the grandfather); the name Sanballat was used three times over a period of five generations in Achaemenid Samaria. See Frank Moore Cross, "The Discovery of the Samaria Papyri," *BA* 26, no. 4 (1963): 110–121 (121).

56 So André Lemaire, "Das Achämenidische Juda und seine Nachbarn im Lichte der Epigraphie," in *Religion und Religionskontakte im Zeitalter der Achämeniden*, ed. Reinhard Gregor Kratz, VWGT 22 (Gütersloh: Gütersloher Verlagshaus, 2002), 210–230 (218).

57 Kratz, *Historisches und biblisches Israel*, 251–252.

coins (and not only the governor) suggests that he had not only a religious role but a political one, too.[58]

Did the governors of Judah and Samaria, and possibly also the Jerusalem priesthood, have any extraterritorial jurisdiction in Elephantine? Did the two governors' joint statement (A4.10) have any *formal* authority in Egypt, or was its status more like a, say, letter of recommendation?

If the leaders of Judah and Samaria actually had a formal authority over the Judaeans in Upper Egypt, it had to be delegated to them from someone. A vague analogy can be seen in Ezra 7:11–28 (the so-called Artaxerxes firman). In this account, the Persian king is depicted as the patron of the worship of the god of Ezra and his people, known as "the god of Jerusalem" (Ezra 7:19) and "the god of heaven" (Ezra 7:21). One of the things that the Persian king commissioned Ezra to do was to appoint magistrates and judges "who may judge all the people in [the satrapy] Beyond the River, [i. e.] everyone who does not know the laws of your God" (*dātê ʾĕlāhāk*, Ezra 7:25). No doubt, the exact nature of Ezra's mission can be discussed.[59] And, to be sure, Ezra's mission was limited to but one satrapy, which nevertheless consisted of several traditional political entities. Still, independently of the Elephantine letters, the Artaxerxes firman offers an example of extraterritoriality. According to it, an Achaemenid king delegated to Ezra the jurisdiction in question pertaining to the Judaean god and entitled him to operate across traditional political boundaries in provinces with different legal practices.

In my view, it is possible that the leaders of Judah and Samaria as a matter of fact had some sort of authority over the satrap of Egypt, at least in questions pertaining to the worship of the god YHW.[60] Obviously, they were not in a position to

---

58 Lemaire, "Das Achämenidische Juda," 210–230 (216–218), cf. Dan Barag, "Some Notes on a Silver Coin of Johanan the High Priest," *BA* 48 (1985): 166–168, and Dan Barag, "A Silver Coin of Yohanan the High Priest and the Coinage of Judea in the Fourth Century B.C.," *INJ* 9 (1988): 4–21 + Plate 1. However, Fried dates the silver coin minted by *yhḥnn* approximately thirty years earlier and suggests that it was minted between 378 and 368 BCE by the high priest Yôhanan/Yehôhanan/Jehohanan I (*yhwḥnn*), who is also mentioned as high priest in A4.7:18 (from 410 BCE), cf. Lisbeth S. Fried, "A Silver Coin of Yohanan Hakkôhen (Pls II-V)," *Transeu* 26 (2003): 65–85 (85). Fried interprets the fact that the high priest minted coins as a sign of Johanan having obtained secular control for the priesthood. However, in her view, the secular control did not outlast Johanan himself.

59 For a discussion of this, see various contributions in James W. Watts, ed., *Persia and Torah: The Theory of Imperial Authorization of the Pentateuch*, SymS 17 (Atlanta: Society of Biblical Literature, 2001).

60 Porten argues that the governors did not have any authority over the satrap of Egypt. Consequently, in his view the letter that the Elephantine Judaeans asked Bagavahya (and the gov-

bring about the rebuilding of the temple in Elephantine.[61] However, in the capacity of being *Persian* officials, we should assume that the governors of Judah and Samaria were well versed in the political procedures of the Achaemenid empire. Although it is not explicitly stated anywhere, it cannot be excluded that the Achaemenid king had commissioned them with some sort of formal extraterritorial authority as well.

Nevertheless, in light of the letter written by the five *mhḥsnn* ("hereditary property holders") in Elephantine (A4.10), it seems that the Elephantine leaders in the end considered that the power to grant a reconstruction of the temple of YHW lay in the hands of the one they called "our lord" (*mrʾn*, A4.10:7, 12). In light of A4.9 (the memorandum of the joint statement of Bagavahya and Delaiah) the one whom the five-strong group entitled "our lord" was probably none other than the satrap Arshama himself (cf. A4.9:3). Still, by the very act of involving the Jerusalem priesthood and the governors of Judah and Samaria, the Elephantine Judaeans at the same time showed that they considered them to be their leaders also, in one way or another. The Elephantine Judaeans obviously assumed that the leaders of Judah and Samaria had some sort of influence over the rebuilding of the temple of YHW, regardless whether the power they ascribed to them was thought to be of a formal or informal nature.

Addressing Bagavahya, the Elephantine Judaeans requested that he would take care of "your obligees [*bʿly ṭbtk*] and your friends [*rḥmyk*]" who were "here in Egypt"[62] (A4.7:23–24 par.). As Porten notes, the precise nuance of the phrase *bʿly ṭbtk* eludes us. James M. Lindenberger translates "loyal clients"[63] and Arthur Ernest Cowley "well-wishers."[64] In Akkadian a *bēl ṭābti* was a benefactor.[65] Regardless what it *exactly* meant to be a *bʿl ṭbtʾ* of Bagavahya, the context of the letter makes it clear that there was a relationship between the governor and the Elephantine Judaeans. Although the relationship was probably not equal, it was nevertheless still based on reciprocity. The Elephantine Judaeans who were "here in Egypt" offered their friendship. In return they now expected Bagavahya's help with the rebuilding of the temple.

---

ernor of Samaria) to send (A4.7:24, 29 par.), was nothing but a strong letter of recommendation. Thus Porten et al., *The Elephantine Papyri in English*, 145 note 79.

61 Peter Frei, "Persian Imperial Authorization: A Summary," in *Persia and Torah: The Theory of Imperial Authorization of the Pentateuch*, ed. James W. Watts, SymS 17 (Atlanta: Society of Biblical Literature, 2001): 5–40 (34).

62 Quoted from Porten et al., *The Elephantine Papyri in English*, 145.

63 Lindenberger, *Ancient Aramaic and Hebrew Letters*, 76.

64 Arthur Ernest Cowley, *Aramaic Papyri of the Fifth Century B.C.* (Oxford: Oxford University Press, 1923), 114. Similarly *DNWSI* 1:182–184, s.v. $b\text{ʿ}l_2$.

65 See *HALOT* 1:142–144 (143), s.v. *baʿal* I.

2.4 Law

The sources for the Judaean community at Elephantine give plenty of examples of how private law was practiced, dealing with matters such as marriage, property and inheritance. In addition, there are also examples of what we today would call criminal law (theft and violence). Terminologically, "law" was referred to by the noun *dyn*.[66] In two marriage contracts (in Aramaic this type of document is called *spr ʾntw*, "document of wifehood"), the phrase "the law of this document" (*dyn sprʾ znh*) refers to the decision that the contractual partners have agreed upon (B2.6:31; B3.8:32). The Aramaic documents from ancient Egypt never mention any legal code as a source or basis for the judges' rulings. Nor do they contain traces of divine or divinely sanctioned law, in the sense of laws that are either revealed or approved by a god. In my view, judged on the basis of the actual evidence, Elephantine jurisprudence seems at first sight to have been mundane.[67]

2.4.1 Oath Procedures, Courts, and Judges

The legal practice the Elephantine Judaeans took part in was not secular in the modern sense of the word. Several documents attest to the practice of taking oaths in the name of a god. Legal oaths sworn by an individual by his/her god were a universally accepted substitution for firm evidence in cases where the latter was lacking.

One example is a document of withdrawal (Aramaic: *spr mrḥq*) written by Dargamana, a Khwarezmian,[68] for Mahseiah son of Jedaniah, a Judaean living in Elephantine (B2.2, dated 464 BCE). The background was a dispute about the boundaries of a piece of land. Dargamana had complained against Mahseiah

66 The noun *dt*, i.e. the Persian loanword found in, e.g., the Artaxerxes firman (Ezra 7:25 "the laws of your God [*dātê ʾĕlāhāk*]"), does not occur in the Elephantine papyri. However, it appears in the noun *dtbr* (D3.45:6), a word denoting some sort of judicial official. Tavernier renders the latter word "he who carries the law, judge," cf. Jan Tavernier, *Iranica in the Achaemenid Period (ca. 550–330 B.C.): Linguistic Study of Old Iranian Proper Names and Loanwords, Attested in Non-Iranian Texts*, OLA 158 (Leuven: Peeters, 2007), 418–419, s.v. *Dātabara-.

67 For a thorough discussion of the legal traditions at Elephantine, see Alejandro F. Botta, *The Aramaic and Egyptian Legal Traditions at Elephantine: An Egyptological Approach* (London: T&T Clark, 2009).

68 Khwarezm/Chorasmia was a region in Central Asia and one of the satrapies of the Achaemenid empire (cf. Herotodus, *Hist.* 1.93).

before a certain Damidata and his colleagues "the judges" (*dyny*ʾ, B2.2:6). They had adjured Mahseiah to swear an oath by YHW for Dargamana on account of the disputed piece of land in order to establish his title to it.[69] Moreover, according to the document Dargamana eventually confirmed that Mahseiah had acted in compliance with the ruling of the judges. The document quotes Dargamana saying to Mahseiah: "You swore to me by YHW and satisfied my heart about that land" (B2.2:11–12).[70] Because Dargamana was satisfied with Mahseiah's oath he withdrew his claim on the piece of land and waived all future claims connected to the piece of land in question.

The document of withdrawal that Dargamana issued Mahseiah with sheds light on the milieu that the Judaeans were living in. Both parties of the dispute recognised the jurisdiction of Damidata and his colleagues the judges. It is important to pay attention to the fact that the judges within the multiethnic and multicultural environment, who most probably were not Judaeans themselves, requested that a Judaean to swear by YHW. What is more, it is important that the other, non-Judaean party of the conflict actually accepted an oath sworn by the god YHW.

The document of withdrawal written by Dargamana was evidently important for Mahseiah, too. Later on Mahseiah wrote an inheritance document to his daughter Mibtahiah (also spelled Miptahiah; B2.3, dated 459 BCE). In the inheritance document he explicitly mentioned that she had received the earlier document of withdrawal issued by Dargamana. The document of withdrawal would offer Mibtahiah legal security connected to the ownership of the piece of land in question: "If tomorrow or the next day Dargamana or son of his bring (suit) about that house, that document [i.e. the document of withdrawal, G.G.] take out and in accordance with it make suit with him" (B2.3:26–27).[71]

The Judaean woman Mibtahiah daughter of Mahseiah also made an oath (B2.8, dated 440 BCE). The context of Mibtahiah's oath was a litigation with an Egyptian builder named Peu about chattel and about a document of wifehood. In the document of withdrawal that Peu issued Mibtahiah with, he confirmed her title to the disputed chattel. What is intriguing is how Mibtahiah established her title to it, namely by swearing an oath by the Egyptian goddess

69 The document quotes Dargamana saying "and they adjured you to swear for me an oath by YHW on account of that land" (B2.2:6: *wṭʿnwk ly mwmʾh lmwmʾ byhw ʿldbr ʾrqʾ zk*).
70 Quoted from Porten et al., *The Elephantine Papyri in English*, 162–163.
71 Quoted from Porten et al., *The Elephantine Papyri in English*, 171.

Sati.[72] As a consequence of Mibtahiah's oath Peu withdrew all his claims and waived any future suits against Mibtahiah.

Furthermore, around 401 BCE Malchiah son of Jashobiah was accused of having unlawfully broken into the house of another, struck the man's wife and taken away property (B7.2). On the basis of this allegation Malchiah was interrogated and imposed to swear an oath to *ʿl ḥrmbytʾl ʾlhʾ*, "to Ḥerembethel the god" (B7.2:7–9) in order to establish his innocence.

There are no traces of any autonomous Judaean legal courts in Elephantine. On the contrary, it seems that the Judaeans (voluntarily or not) turned to Persian officials in legal matters that involved only members of the Judaean community. This may be illustrated by yet another document of withdrawal (B2.10). In the presence of Vidranga the troop commander (*rbḥylʾ*) of Syene, Jedaniah son of Hoshaiah son of Uriah affirmed that Jedaniah son of Nathan and the latter's brother Mahseiah son of Jedaniah from now on had the title to a particular house (B2.10:2–4). In this case, it seems that Vidranga functioned as a kind of public notary. It appears that he had this role also in connection with the adoption of a slave undertaken by Uriah son of Mahseiah (B3.9). In both cases, the legally binding actions took place "before" (*qdm*) the Persian official.

If lawsuits were filed against Judaeans or other groups in Upper Egypt, the complainant could address the *sgn* ("prefect"[73]), the *dyn* ("judge"), or the *mrʾ* ("lord," cf. B2.3:13; B3.2:5–6; B3.12:28).

In criminal cases the Judaeans were also under the jurisdiction of Persian officials. In the last part of the fifth century BCE—a turbulent period for the Judaean community—Vidranga put the Judaean Mauziah in prison in connection with a case involving theft (A4.3:3–4). It is not clear whether Mauziah was charged with the theft himself, or whether the reason for the imprisonment was that he, say, in his capacity as caravan escort, was guilty of malfeasance.[74] If the latter was the case, Vidranga's juridical role could perhaps be explained as an example of exercising military law.

---

72 Sati (or Satis) was a goddess worshipped at Elephantine and considered to be the god Khnum's consort, cf. Siegfried Morenz, *Egyptian Religion* (Ithaca: Cornell University Press, 1973), 53, 268.

73 In this context, a *sgn* seems to have a judicial function, cf. Raymond A. Bowman, *Aramaic Ritual Texts from Persepolis*, OIP 91 (Chicago: University of Chicago Press, 1970), 26. However, the *sgn* also occurs in Aramaic administrative texts from Persepolis. There, it seems that a *sgn* had an administrative role over workers employed by the Achaemenid administration, cf. Briant, *From Cyrus to Alexander*, 433.

74 On Judaeans as caravan escorts, see A3.3 and B4.4. The latter also regulates the penalties given in cases of malfeasance.

Moreover, in extreme situations it was possible to appeal to the satrap or perhaps even the Persian king himself. In a fragmentary letter the Judaeans wrote, "If inquiry be made from the judges, police and hearers who are appointed in the province of Tshetres, it would be [*known*] to our lord in accordance with this which we say" (A4.5:8–10).[75] The text is broken and the recipient of the letter is unknown. Was it addressed to the satrap or to the king? Two of the enumerated types of officials, "the police" (*typty'*) and "the hearers" (*gwšky'*), appear in other sources as officials who are appointed by either the satrap or the king himself. "The police" appear in Dan 3:2–3 (NRSV: "magistrates") on a list of officials appointed by King Nebuchadnezzar. "The hearers" (*typty'*) have been associated with a corps of Persian spies that ancient Greek historians called "the king's ear" and "the king's eye," intelligence officers appointed by the king or his agent, and not the satrap.[76] However, Pierre Briant regards them as "satrapal inspectors." In any case, the receiver of the letter A4.5 was apparently in a position to launch an investigation (A4.5:8 *'zd*).

Regardless under whose command "the police" and "the hearers" were (i.e., the king or the satrap), the Judaeans claimed that a *dwškrt* had taken place in Elephantine. The term *dwškrt* is a Persian loanword meaning "crime, evil act."[77] The alleged act of crime was that a royal barley house (*ywdn' zy mlk'*) had been destroyed (A4.5:5), that a wall had been unlawfully built in the middle of the fortress (A4.5:5) and that the well supplying the garrison stationed there with water had been stopped up (A4.5:6–8). The last part of the document is badly broken. However, there is enough extant text to conclude that it contained an account of the destruction of the temple of YHW and possibly also a petition concerning the rebuilding of it (A4.5:11–24).[78] Thus, according to the extant text, the Judaeans presented the alleged criminal acts primarily as a crime against the crown (a royal storehouse and the water supplies of the garrison being destroyed), and possibly secondarily as a crime against the temple of the god of the Judaeans (A4.5:23 "the [temple] of ours that they demolished").

---

75 Quoted from Porten et al., *The Elephantine Papyri in English*, 138.

76 Thus Lisbeth S. Fried, "'You Shall Appoint Judges': Ezra's Mission and the Rescript of Artaxerxes," in *Persia and Torah: The Theory of Imperial Authorization of the Pentateuch*, ed. James W. Watts, SymS 17 (Atlanta: Society of Biblical Literature, 2001): 63–89 (67), and Lisbeth S. Fried, *The Priest and the Great King: Temple–Palace Relations in the Persian Empire*, BJSUCSD 10 (Winona Lake, IN: Eisenbrauns, 2004), 91.

77 Tavernier, *Iranica in the Achaemenid Period*, 418: from Old Persian *Duškṛta-.

78 The highly fragmented text on the verso of the papyrus contains several references to the temple of YHW: A4.5:14 "meal-offering," A4.5:15 "YHW," A4.5:17 "brazier(?)," A4.5:18 "fittings," and A4.5:24 "the [temple] of ours that they demolished."

According to the Judaeans writing the letter, the culprits of the criminal act were the priests of Khnum, the Egyptian god who was worshipped in Elephantine. They undertook their actions "in agreement with" (*hmwnyt*[79]) the Persian local official (*prtrk*) Vidranga. However, the joint Egyptian–Persian agreement involved a bribe; the priests of Khnum gave Vidranga "silver and goods" (A4.5:4, cf. A4.7:5). Thus, in the end, by claiming that they had destroyed royal property, the Judaeans accused them of treason.

In sum, the intervention of the Persian authorities in civil and private judicial affairs is frequently attested in the textual sources for the Elephantine Judaean community. There are no traces of divine or divinely sanctioned laws and there are no references to any codified laws. However, the jurisprudence was not secular in the modern meaning of the word. Legal oaths sworn by YHW and other gods were accepted as evidence that could replace firm evidence.

2.4.2 Marriage and Inheritance

Marriage contracts from Elephantine offer information about the legal aspects of marriage. On the basis of them, it seems that the Elephantine Judaeans did *not* interpret marriage in religious terms. On the contrary, the contracts leave the impression that marriage was an agreement between two parties, the one being the bridegroom and the other being either the bride's father (B2.6), her brother (B3.8) or her owner (B3.3). As a contractual relationship, a marriage involved mutual responsibilities and rights. The groom paid the bride price (*mhr*) to the wife's father and the wife brought dowry into the marriage. Moreover, it is clear that the Judaeans practised and thus accepted intermarriage.

The marriage contracts seem to echo a formula that may have been pronounced orally by the groom in connection with the investiture of the marriage: *hy ʾntty wʾnh bʿlh mn ywm znh wʿd ʿlm*, "She is my wife and I am her husband from this day and forever." (B2.6:4; B3.3:3–4; B3.8:4).

Even though the marriage was meant to last until one of the spouses died, divorce was possible. It is noteworthy that a wife had the same right to divorce as her husband. The marriage contracts seem to reflect a ritual that accompanied a divorce. The technical term for divorce was "to hate" (*śnʾ*).[80] The marriage con-

---

79 Tavernier, *Iranica in the Achaemenid Period*, 418: from Old Persian *Hamaunitā.

80 So Alejandro F. Botta, "Hated by the Gods and your Spouse: Legal Use of *śnʾ* in Elephantine and its Ancient Near Eastern Context," in *Law and Religion in the Eastern Mediterranean: From Antiquity to Early Islam*, ed. Anselm C. Hagedorn and Reinhard Gregor Kratz (Oxford: Oxford University Press, 2013): 105–128, and Hélène Nutkowicz, "Concerning the Verb *śnʾ* in Ju-

tract between the Egyptian builder Esḥor and Mahseiah, the father of Mibtahiah (B2.6) illustrates the procedure that would have taken place in connection with a dissolution of a marriage:

> Tomorrow o[r] (the) next day, should Miptahiah stand up in an assembly and say: "I hated Esḥor my husband," silver of hatred is on her head. She shall PLACE UPON the balance-scale and weigh out to Esḥor silver, 6[+1] (= 7) shekels, 2 q(uarters), and all that she brought in in her hand she shall take out, from straw to string, and go away wherever she desires, without suit or without process. Tomorrow or (the) next day, should Esḥor stand up in an assembly and say: "I hated my [wif]e Miptahiah," her *mohar* [will be] lost and all that she brought in in her hand she shall take out, from straw to string, on one day in one stroke, and go away wherever she desires, without suit or without process. (B2.6:22–29)[81]

Similar divorce procedures are described in the marriage contracts between Ananiah son of Haggai and Zaccur son of Meshullam, the brother of lady Jehoishma (B3.8:21–28), and between Ananiah son of Azariah and Meshullam son of Zaccur, the owner of the maidservant Tamet (B3.3:7–10).

A divorce should be pronounced *bʿdh*, "in the assembly." The nature and status of the assembly in question is unclear. In light of the fact that some of the marriage contracts involved non-Judaeans, it was probably not a proprietary *Judaean* institution.[82] Hélène Nutkowicz hypothesises that "the assembly" referred to a traditional local Egyptian court (a *kenbet*). An implication of this hypothesis is that marriages were organised in accordance with traditional Egyptian laws. Egyptian rituals and customs had been absorbed and were followed by all ethnic groups living in Elephantine and the neighbouring Syene, regardless of the cultural and geographical origins of these groups.[83] However, as far as I can see, this hypothesis is not unproblematic. To my knowledge the possible juridical institution *ʿdh* only occurs in the three mentioned marriage contracts

daeo-Aramaic Contracts from Elephantine," *JSS* 52 (2007): 211–225, who argue against the view expressed in Bezalel Porten and Zvi Henri Szubin, "The Status of the Handmaiden Tamet: A New Interpretation of Kraeling 2 (TAD B3.3)," *ILR* 29 (1995): 43–64.

81 Quoted from Porten et al., *The Elephantine Papyri in English*, 182–183.

82 Contrary Christopher Tuplin, "The Administration of the Achaemenid Empire," in *Coinage and Administration in the Athenian and Persian Empires: The Ninth Oxford Symposium on Coinage and Monetary History*, ed. Ian Carradice, BAR International Series 34 (Oxford: British Archaeological Reports, 1987): 109–158 (111), who assumes that the *ʿdh* was a "Jewish community assembly."

83 Hélène Nutkowicz, "Note sur une institution juridique à Éléphantine, *ʿdh*, la « cour »," *Transeu* 27 (2004): 181–185.

(B2.6; B3.3; B3.8). In addition, it is a Semitic word (some even understand it as a Hebrew loanword[84]) that renders the possibly Egyptian institution *kenbet*.

Be as it may, a divorce was a public affair, and the marriage contracts gave the divorcing women considerable legal and economical protection. Marriage contracts regulated questions pertaining to inheritance. In the marriage between Esḥor and Mibtahiah, the husband had the right to inherit (*yrt*) the property of his wife in the case of the latter's demise (B2.6:20–22). However, on the other hand, if Esḥor died Mibtahiah would only have the legal right to control (*šlyṭh*) his property (B2.6:18), not own it. Likewise, in the marriage between Ananiah and the woman Jehoishma, the latter did not explicitly inherit from her husband if he died; she would only *ʾḥdth*, "hold on to him"[85] in regard to his belongings (B3.8:29).

2.5 Judaean and Non-Judaean Religious Specialists

The Judaean community in Elephantine had its own religious specialists and interacted with other religious specialists, Judaean as well as non-Judaean ones.

2.5.1 "Priest" (*khn*) and "Priest" (*kmr*)

Within the Judaean community in Elephantine, the most important religious specialists were the group of *khnyʾ*, "priests." The identity of the deity they served is evident in the letter that Mauziah sent. It was addressed to "my lords Jedaniah, Uriah and the priests of YHW the God, Mattan son of Jashobiah (and) Berechiah son of [...]" (A4.1:1). Moreover, the "priests of YHW the god" (*khnyʾ zy yhw ʾlhʾ*) could also be referred to as "the priests who are in the fortress of Elephantine" (*khnyʾ zy byb byrtʾ*, A4.7:1), or simply "the priests" (*khnyʾ*, A4.3:12).

The sources are silent about how the priests of YHW in Elephantine were organised (e.g. whether there was any distinction between first- and second-tier priests).[86] Yet, on the basis of epistolographic salutations we can surmise that the priests were probably headed by a certain Jedaniah in the last decades of the fifth century BCE,[87] regardless of whether he was a priest himself or not. According to epistolographic conventions, the senders and addressees of a letter

84 Cowley, *Aramaic Papyri*, 49; Porten et al., *The Elephantine Papyri in English*, 182 note 41.
85 Thus Porten et al., *The Elephantine Papyri in English*, 230.
86 In contrast to, e.g., 1Chr 23–25.
87 See A4.1:1,10; A4.7:1,4.22 par.; A4.10:1.

were not listed arbitrarily but in order of descending importance: *ʾl mrn bgwhy pḥt yhwd ʿbdyk ydnyh wknwth khnyʾ zy byb byrtʾ*, "To our lord Bagavahya governor of Judah, your servants Jedaniah and his colleagues the priests who are in Elephantine the fortress" (A4.7:1).[88]

Elephantine was a multicultural, multiethnical and multireligious society. Therefore, what was the self-consciousness of the priests of YHW in relation to "the others"? We can get a glimpse of the contours of their self-identity by paying attention to how they related themselves to other groups of religious specialists. The petition to the governor of Judah is particularly informative (A4.7/A4.8). It presents the priests (*khnyʾ*) of YHW in Elephantine in relation to two other, clearly defined groups of religious specialists. On the one hand, the priests of YHW in Elephantine interacted with "the priests (*kmryʾ*) of Khnum the god." On the other hand, they interacted with "Jehohanan the high priest and his colleagues the priests who are in Jerusalem" (*yhwḥnn khnʾ rbʾ wknwth khny zy byrwšlm*).

It seems that the Elephantine Judaeans used the term *khn* exclusively for denoting a kind of religious specialist ("priests") who served the god YHW. The shared terminology expressed that they attached themselves to the religious specialists in Jerusalem. The simple fact that the YHW priests of Elephantine called for the assistance of the YHW(H) priests in Jerusalem when they attempted to rebuild the temple of YHW in Elephantine also points in the same direction. By using one and the same technical term (*khn*), the Elephantine priests demonstrated that they, according to their own self-understanding, were colleagues of the priests in Jerusalem. Although the priests in Jerusalem were geographically remote from Elephantine, they were nevertheless regarded as belonging to the same category of religious specialists, the *khnn*.

This assumption is supported by another fact. In the petition to Bagavahya, Jedaniah and the Elephantine priests of YHW also related themselves *negatively* to another group of religious specialists, "the priests of Khnum the god who are in Elephantine the fortress" (A4.7:5). It is noteworthy that another technical term is used. The Egyptian religious specialists were designated *kmrn*, not *khnn*. The distance between the religious specialists of the gods YHW and Khnum respectively was marked terminologically.

The use of the term *kmr* (and *khn!*) must be viewed in light of other occurrences of the term *kmr* in the Aramaic documents from Egypt. In a fragmentary letter we read about a certain Thotomous (an Egyptian name) who was entitled "a priest" (*kmr*, A5.4:2). The surrounding text is badly damaged. Therefore, it is not possible to say whether it was Thotomous himself who used the term *kmr*

88 Quoted from Porten et al., *The Elephantine Papyri in English*, 141.

as a self-designation when writing (and speaking) in Aramaic. Moreover, the term also occurs in a deed of conveyance in which the Judaean Mahseiah transferred the title of his house to his daughter (B2.7). The boundaries of the house in question are described by a reference to the house of a certain "Ḥarwodj son of Palṭu, priest [*kmr*] of K[hnum] the god" (B2.7:15). The document is conventionally formulated, and the term *kmr* is not used with any kind of negative connotations. In addition, the witnesses of the legal transaction are international (one Mithrasarah son of Mithrasarah, apparently a Persian, and two individuals identified as Caspians, cf. B2.7:18–19).

The term is also found in Aramaic inscriptions on sarcophagi found in South Saqqarah. One of them illustrates that *kmr* was a designation that the bearer himself accepted: *lš'yl kmr' zy nbw ytb tqm' bswn*, "(Belonging) to Sheil the priest of Nabu, residing everlastingly [OR: (in the) eternal shrine] in Syene" (D18.1, cf. D18.2).[89]

Finally, the term occurs in the inscription on a memorial stela of a priest of Baal found in Memphis:[90] *l'nn br 'lyš kmr' zy b'l b'l'nwt*, "(Belonging) to 'Anan son of 'Eliash the priest of Baal husband/citizen of Anoth" (D21.17).[91]

In light of the latter examples, it appears that the term *kmr* was used as a commonplace and neutral designation for a particular type of religious specialist in Aramaic documents from Egypt, regardless whether he served an Egyptian god (e.g. Khnum) or was associated with a temple of one of the non-Egyptian gods in Egypt (like Nabu and Baal).[92] Therefore, when Jedaniah and the other Judaeans wrote to Bagavahya and mentioned "the priests (*kmry'*) of Khnum," this was not meant as an insult.[93] To put it differently, the Elephantine Judaeans did

89 Quoted from Bezalel Porten and Ada Yardeni, *Textbook of Aramaic Documents from Ancient Egypt: Newly Copied, Edited and Translated into Hebrew and English*, vol. IV: Ostraca & Assorted Inscriptions (Jerusalem: The Hebrew University of Jerusalem – Department of the History of the Jewish People, 1999), 239.

90 URL: http://www.trismegistos.org/ate/detail.php?tm=91178 (accessed on 30 March 2015).

91 Quoted from Porten and Yardeni, *TADAE*, IV: Ostraca & Assorted Inscriptions, 265.

92 As for the Canaanite-Babylonian (Horn: "Asiatic") gods in Egypt, see Siegfried H. Horn, "Foreign Gods in Ancient Egypt," in *Studies in Honor of John A. Wilson September 12, 1969*. SAOC 35 (Chicago: University of Chicago Press, 1969): 37–42.

93 Paul-Eugène Dion, "La religion des papyrus d'Éléphantine: un reflet du Juda d'avant l'exil," in *Kein Land für sich allein: Studien zum Kulturkontakt in Kanaan, Israel/Palästina und Ebirnâri für Manfred Weippert zum 65. Geburtstag*, ed. Ulrich Hübner and Ernst Axel Knauf, OBO 186 (Freiburg (Swizerland) and Göttingen: Universitätsverlag Freiburg Schweiz and Vandenhoeck & Ruprecht, 2002): 243–254 (247).

not use *kmr* as a derogatory term;[94] rather, they were simply using an ordinary Aramaic word.[95]

All textual remains of the Elephantine Judaeans are written in Aramaic. Aramaic was used for all known kinds of written communication, within the Judaean community of Elephantine and between Elephantine and Judah/Samaria. In light of this, then, it is more striking that they did not use the technical term *kmr* for their own religious specialists, the functionaries of the temple of YHW in Elephantine. On the contrary, they used a terminology that connected them with functionaries of the Jerusalem temple: *khn*.

2.5.1.1 Who Became Priests of YHW in Elephantine, and How?

How did the priests of YHW in Elephantine come into office? The Elephantine papyri do not account for the necessary qualifications for becoming a priest of YHW. Did he inherit the office from his father? Was he elected or appointed, and if so, by whom? Was the priestly tenure a lifelong commitment, or was it a position held for a limited time period?

We are left to take recourse to parallels from the indigenous Egyptian community in Elephantine. The Eskhnumpemet papers[96] from the first decade of the fifth century BCE give an example of the struggle about who had the prerogative to appoint priests. The Demotic documents are letters written between the *wab*-priests of Khnum on the one hand, and the Persian satrap Pherendates on the

---

94 The Hebrew Bible uses the term *kmr* exclusively for a religious specialist devoted to a god other than YHWH, the god of Israel. In a biblical context, a *kmr* is distinct from a *khn*. In all the three occurrences in the Bible, it has a negative, derogatory connotation that justifies a rendition like that of the NRSV: "idolatrous priest" (2Kgs 23:5; Hos 10:5; Zeph 1:4). Moreover, a sidelong glance at Amos 7 suggests that the term *khn* was in particular associated with the cult of YHWH, regardless of where the cult took place. There, Amaziah is called *khn* even though he served in an Israelite shrine in Bethel during the reign of the Israelite king Jeroboam. Although Amaziah is the antagonist of the prophet Amos, his right to the designation *khn* is not renounced.

95 An example of another text that underscores this is the trilingual inscription from Xanthus in Asia Minor. This inscription is about the founding of a new cult and the appointment of a priest. The Aramaic text uses the term *kmr*. For a discussion of the Aramaic text, see Javier Teixidor, "The Aramaic Text in the Trilingual Stele from Xanthus," *JNES* 37 (1978): 181–185, cf. Kuhrt, *The Persian Empire*, 859–863, and Fried, *The Priest and the Great King*, 141–155.

96 An introduction to and a translation of the texts are found in Porten et al., *The Elephantine Papyri in English*, 288–294. See also Kuhrt, *The Persian Empire*, 852–854. Moreover, a brief discussion of the texts is also found in Heike Sternberg-el Hotabi, "Die persische Herrschaft in Ägypten," in *Religion und Religionskontakte im Zeitalter der Achämeniden*, ed. Reinhard Gregor Kratz, VWGT 22 (Gütersloh: Gütersloher Verlagshaus, 2002): 111–149 (123–125).

other. The *wab*-priests (literally: "pure") were the main body of priests, the group of temple servants of low category who assisted the higher ranked temple specialists.

The chronological earliest letter of the Eskhnumpemet papers was written by the *wab*-priests to Pherendates in 493 BCE (P. Berlin 13539). The priests informed the satrap that they had some four months earlier appointed a new so-called *lesonis* priest: "In year 29, Pharmouthi, the time for selecting a successor to the *lesonis*, we replaced Petikhnum son of Haaibre who was *lesonis*. We caused Eskhnumpemet son of Horkheb to follow him as *lesonis*. He will cause to be carried (and) he will cause burnt-offerings to be made before Khnum."[97]

The *lesonis* priest was the administrative head of the temple business and was appointed annually.[98] Among the tasks of the *lesonis* were administrative responsibilities in connection with the collection of the harvest-tax.[99] As it is clear in the letter, the body that had already appointed Eskhnumpemet was the group of *wab*-priests.

However, some four months after the letter from the *wab*-priests was dated, the satrap Pherendates wrote a response (P. Berlin 13540). In the letter to "all the *wab*-priests of Khnum, the lord of Elephantine," Pherendates stipulated the necessary qualifications for a suitable *lesonis* priest. The *lesonis* priest to be elected had to be a *wab*-priest without any previous blemish in his career. Moreover, he could not be a servant of another man. However, most important is that the satrap Pherendates reserved the privilege to appoint the new *lesonis* priest for himself:

> Now, the *wab*-priest whom is suitable to make lesonis is (a) great man whom, it will happen, I will cause to carry out his functions,... Now, the *wab*-priest who will be selected to be made *lesonis* is like this. The one who will be selected, he is to be brought in accordance with that which Darius (the) Pharaoh has ordered.[100]

Pherendates made it clear that he did not accept the procedures the *wab*-priests had followed in connection with the appointment of Eskhnumpemet as new *lesonis*. The latter had *already* been appointed by the *wab*-priests, who had merely sent notification about the result of their election to the satrap. However, the sa-

97 Quoted from Porten et al., *The Elephantine Papyri in English*, 289.
98 Peter Ross Bedford, "The So-Called 'Codification' of Egyptian Law under Darius I," in *Persia and Torah: The Theory of Imperial Authorization of the Pentateuch*, ed. James W. Watts, SymS 17 (Atlanta: Society of Biblical Literature, 2001), 135–159 (156), and Porten et al., *The Elephantine Papyri in English*, 289.
99 Porten et al., *The Elephantine Papyri in English*, 278.
100 Quoted from Porten et al., *The Elephantine Papyri in English*, 292.

trap referred to King Darius's order and demanded that the candidate of the *wab*-priests should be brought to him for his ratification.

We should assume that the Persian administration's grasp on the appointment of the *lesonis* priest was due to the importance of the *lesonis*, in particular in connection to the economical aspects of the Khnum temple in Elephantine. The satrap's control over the appointment of temple personnel could be expressed in other ways, too. A newly appointed *lesonis* was liable to pay an induction fee.[101] Moreover, lower ranked temple personnel also had to pay induction fees. A fragmentary Demotic document dated 487 BCE[102] shows that an Egyptian who had been appointed "second *wab*-priest" had paid silver to a treasury controlled by the Persian official Farnava. Favarna was at one and the same time governor of the province of Thetres and garrison commander of Syene.

As far as the priests of YHW are concerned, the question is whether the Persians treated them in a comparable way as the Persians treated the personnel of the temple of Khnum. In light of the available sources, this cannot be said for sure. On the one hand, provided that the temple of YHW did not have any significant economical role in Upper Egypt, it may be conjectured that the Persians were less concerned with it than they were with the temple of Khnum, "the lord of Elephantine."[103] If that was the case, the Judaeans in Elephantine were themselves responsible for how the priests of YHW came into office, regardless of whether the priests inherited their offices or whether they were appointed by the Judaeans. However, on the other hand, Pherendates based his critique of the *wab*-priests' appointment of the new *lesonis* priest on a royal order issued by Darius I. Some decades later, Hananiah sent a letter to Jedaniah and the Judaean garrison in which calendar issues were regulated on the basis of a decree issued by Darius II (= the so-called Passover letter, A4.1). The Persian king's attempt to micromanage such a (one may assume) minor issue as the dates of a religious festival opens up for the possibility that the appointment of the priests of YHW in Elephantine were among the tasks that needed the satrap's approval.

101 Direct evidence for an induction fee that had to be paid in return for being appointed *lesonis* is found in a chronologically much later document (P. Berlin 13543, from the Ptolemaic period). In the letter written by Eskhnumpemet son of Esnebankh to Herakleides, the governor of the province of Thetres, in 219 BCE, Eskhnumpemet promises to give money to the governor, provided that the appointment is accepted. See Porten et al., *The Elephantine Papyri in English*, 310–311.

102 P. Berlin 13582. See Porten et al., *The Elephantine Papyri in English*, 373–374.

103 See Section 2.6 below.

2.5.2 "Servitor" (*lḥn*), "Servant" (*ʿbd*), and "Gardener" (*gnn*)

In Elephantine there was possibly another kind of religious specialist who was related to YHW besides the priests: *lḥn*, "servitor." In the Aramaic texts that can be connected to Elephantine, two persons bear this title: Ananiah (variant spelling: Anani) son of Azariah, and Azariah. Ananiah is presented using this title in various legal documents, whereas Azariah is only mentioned twice in one and the same document.[104] In principle it should probably be sufficient to identify him by his patronymic, i.e. as son of Azariah. The fact that the title *lḥn* sometimes appears in addition to the patronymic suggests that it was his occupation or office to be a *lḥn* of YHW and, correspondingly, that his contemporaries recognised him as such.

Sometimes Ananiah is called "a servitor" (*lḥn*) without emphasis: "Ananiah ... a servitor of YHH the god who is in Elephantine the fortress" (B3.3:2). Other times he is called "the servitor" (*lḥnʾ*), for example, "Anani son of Azariah, the servitor of YHW the god" (B3.10:23).

This tiny grammatical nuance raises the question: Could only one person hold the office as *lḥn* of YHW at any one time? The sources do not give any answer. Also in the sources the female *lḥnh* is found once, when used to describe Ananiah's wife Tapemet (B3.12:2) in a context where her husband Ananiah is called *lḥn*.[105] Later on in the document in question the couple is mentioned again. In that connection Tapemet (now written Tapememet) only appears as Ananiah's wife, whereas her husband Ananiah continues to be called "a servitor of YHW" (B3.12:33). Therefore, it is a likely conjecture that to be a *lḥnh* (female of *lḥn*) only implied being married to a *lḥn*, and that a *lḥnh* did not hold any office independently of her husband, the *lḥn*.

Unfortunately, the sources give little information about what functions a *lḥn* in general had. In the corpus of Aramaic documents from ancient Egypt the feminine form is found once in the *Words of Aḥiqar*. There, it occurs in the context of a saying on discipline for slaves and is used together with the terms *ʿlym*, "servant, slave" and *ʿbdn*, "slaves" (C1.1:178).[106]

The sources do not indicate what particular functions a *lḥn* of YHW served. The only available approach is via etymology and the use of cognate terms in comparable contexts. Cognate terms are found in Ugaritic and Assyrian. In Ugar-

104 C3.13:45, 48.

105 Judging from her name, Tapemet was an Egyptian woman. However, Ananiah and Tapemet had a daughter with a typical Judaean name: Jehoishma (B3.7:2–3).

106 In later Jewish Aramaic, *ləḥēnâ* could mean "maidservant," cf. Jastrow 2:703, s.v. *ləḥēnâ*/*ləḥênâ*.

itic the term occurs in cultic contexts as well as in the personal name *ylḥn*.[107] In Old, Middle and Neo-Assyrian texts the term *alaḫḫinu*, typically in the phrase "the *alaḫḫinu* of [name of deity: Ashur, Sin, Ishtar, Nabu]," designates an administrative official at a temple.[108] It has been conjectured, albeit without any firm evidence, that a *lḥn* was a kind of Levite, using a biblical analogy.[109]

The corpus of Aramaic texts mentions two further titles that may have denoted other types of religious specialists. First, a court record written in Memphis in 431 BCE mentions a "[PN] servant of Nabu the god."[110] Similarly, one of the neighbours of Ananiah the *lḥn* of YHW was an Egyptian named Ḥor, who is described as a "servant (*ʿbd*) of Kh[num the god]."[111] Second, Ananiah also referred to Ḥor in two other documents. In both cases the latter is presented as "Ḥor the son of Peṭeisi/Peṭeese, a gardener (*gnn*) of Khnum the god."[112] However, as far as YHW is concerned, the sources do not reflect anything similar. If YHW, the god who dwelt in Elephantine next to Khnum, had any servants and/or gardeners in the Achaemenid period, the arbitrary nature of our sources have caused their names to fade into oblivion.

2.6 The Economy of the Temple of YHW

Sacrifices were offered in the temple of YHW. The necessary sacrifices, and the fuel for them, had to be provided for. The temple of YHW also needed regular maintenance. The religious specialists required vestments, and cultic activities meant that the vessels, altars and so on had to be in good condition, repaired and, when necessary, replaced. This raises questions regarding the economy of the temple of YHW. Who paid for all these things? How was the cult of YHW financed? What was the revenue of the temple? Who paid for the first temple of YHW in Elephantine, which was destroyed in 410 BCE, and who paid for the rebuilding of the second temple sometime after 407 BCE? And who paid for the sacrifices to YHW, the god whose dwelling was in Elephantine, according to the statements of the Judaeans themselves?

---

107 Gordon, "The Origin of the Jews in Elephantine," 56–58 (57): "Servitor (of the gods)."
108 Porten, *Archives from Elephantine*, 200, and *CAD* 1.1:294–296, s.v. *alaḫḫinu*.
109 Stephen G. Rosenberg, "The Jewish Temple at Elephantine," *NEA* 67, no. 1 (2004): 4–13 (6).
110 B8.4:7: *ʿbd nbw ʾlh*. The text is broken and the servant's name is unknown.
111 See, e.g., B3.7:8.
112 B3.10:10; B3.11:6.

In the following I will hypothesise the following answer to these questions: The temple of YHW was funded by the members of the Judaean garrison stationed in Elephantine in the Achaemenid period. The temple was *tolerated* by the Persian occupants, if not for another reason, then at least because it would be unwise to oppose it. After all, the Judaean garrison was a *Persian* garrison,[113] and a separate temple devoted to the Judaean chief god could fulfil the religious needs of the Judaean soldiers at the same time as it enhanced the inner stability of the Judaean garrison. However, the sources do not suggest that the temple of YHW ever received economic support from the Persians through direct or indirect benefits. What is more, the sources are silent about any form of economic support from Yahwistic communities in Judah and Samaria. On the contrary, the positive evidence, which is scant and to some extent enigmatic as in the case of the Collection Account (C3.15), suggests that the burden of financing the temple of YHW in Elephantine had to be carried by the Judaeans in Elephantine themselves.

In order to substantiate the hypothesis, I will survey various texts/text groups dealing with temple–palace relationships in the Persian period, or in some cases the relationship between a temple and the satrapal court. In many cases, the historical accuracy of the selected texts has been questioned. I do not, however, claim that the surveyed texts are historically accurate. On the contrary, my purpose of using them is to let them illustrate the various ways a temple could receive direct or indirect economic support in the Persian period. Thus, although the sources may not relate the history accurately, they nevertheless relate *potential historical realities*. Then, in turn, the sources for the temple of YHW in Elephantine will be examined in light of the results of the survey. Using the result of the survey as a grid, I will ask whether there are traces of any kinds of direct or indirect economic support benefitting the temple of YHW and, moreover, what kinds of economic support of the YHW temple the sources are silent about.

2.6.1 Direct and Indirect Economic Support of Cults: A Survey

2.6.1.1 Concession Lands

One way a temple could benefit from economic support was through *land allotments* granted by the king. From the point of view of royal Achaemenid ideology,

113 See, e.g., Gard Granerød, "'By the Favour of Ahuramazda I Am King': On the Promulgation of a Persian Propaganda Text among Babylonians and Judaeans," *JSJ* 44 (2013): 455–480.

"conquered land without exception came under royal control."[114] A text illustrating this is a decree ascribed to King Cambyses, the Persian conqueror of Egypt. The decree is found in a column on the verso of the so-called *Demotic Chronicle*,[115] and it provides a glimpse of the Persian kings' financial administration of the Egyptian temples. The provenance of the papyrus is unknown. However, according to Amélie Kuhrt, the palaeography in the *Chronicle* and its references to Macedonian rule point to the latter half of the third century BCE (i.e., the Ptolemaic period) as the date of its composition.

Presumably, the decree of Cambyses describes the saving measures that Cambyses declared for all the Egyptian temples with the exception of three temples (the temple of Memphis, the temple of *Wn-khm*, and the temple of Perapis):

> Building wood, firewood, flax and shrubs, which used to be given to the sanctuaries of the gods, in the time of Pharaoh ... Amasis ... with the exception of the temple of Memphis, the temple of *Wn-khm* and the temple of Perapis ... (?) those sanctuaries—Cambyses ordered the following: "Do not permit that one gives them as much as (?)... They should be given a place in the copse of the Southern Land and it shall be permitted that building wood and firewood come from there and that they bring it to the gods!' The copse of the three sanctuaries above, Cambyses ordered this, i.e. "They shall receive this as before."
> The cattle, which used to be given to the sanctuaries of the gods, in the time of Pharaoh ... Amasis ... with the exception of the three sanctuaries above—Cambyses ordered the following: "Their share is what they are given." What was given to them, (i.e.) the three sanctuaries above, this was ordered: "It shall continue to be given to them."[116]

The decree offers a few more regulations that curtail the traditional incomes of silver, cattle, birds, cereals, and other benefits of the Egyptian temples ("which used to be given ... in the time of Pharaoh Amasis"[117]), at the same time as the three mentioned temples are favoured. For the remaining, non-favoured temples, it appears that Cambyses commanded that the priests *themselves* should get the animals and things that were necessary for keeping the temples running: "The priests will obtain them ... and they will give them to the gods."

The decree is not a contemporary source for the *Persian* period financial administration of the Egyptian temples. Moreover, it seems to render a negative image of Cambyses's kingship, perhaps comparable to the negative portrayal

114 Briant, *From Cyrus to Alexander*, 415.

115 Wilhelm Spiegelberg, *Die Sogenannte Demotische Chronik des Pap. 215 der Bibliothèque Nationale zu Paris nebst den auf der Rückseite des Papyrus stehenden Texten*, DM 7 (Leipzig: Hinrichs, 1914), 32–33; Brosius, *The Persian Empire*, 19–20 (no. 24), and Kuhrt, *The Persian Empire*, 124–127 (no. 4.14).

116 Quoted from Kuhrt, *The Persian Empire*, 125–126 (no. 4.14).

117 Amasis was the last Egyptian pharaoh before Cambyses's conquest in 525 BCE.

of him given by Herodotus[118] and other classical Greek and Latin historiographers.[119] After the Persian domination of Egypt ended, an anti-Persian king may have wanted to portray Cambyses negatively and, by doing that, present himself as a positive contrast—i.e., as a king who *restored* the temple incomes as they used to be at the time of Amasis, the last Egyptian pharaoh before Cambyses's conquest.[120]

In spite of the possible anti-Persian tendency, we should nevertheless assume that the decree of Cambyses offers a glimpse of aspects of the financial administration in Egypt before and after the Persian occupation. The image of Cambyses gets its negative contour against the background of that which is presented as the *normal* situation—that is, how it apparently used to be. Before Cambyses, the normal situation was supposedly that the Egyptian temples received the necessary incomes from the king and after Cambyses's conquest, this privilege was restricted to only the three mentioned temples.[121] As far as the remaining (non-favoured) temples are concerned, their respective priests allegedly bore a greater responsibility for the incomes of their temples under Cambyses than they had previously when the Egyptian pharaohs ruled.

A qualified guess is that the priests of the Egyptian temples as a rule of thumb were themselves responsible for the incomes of their temples during the Persian period. The decree suggests that funding from the royal treasury was cut as a consequence of Cambyses's ruling. However, it seems that the non-favoured temples were given *other* (and perhaps *inferior*) land allotments as concessions (cf. "They should be given a place in the copse of the Southern Land and it shall be permitted that building wood and firewood come from there and that they bring it to the gods!").

---

118 See, e.g., Herodotus's horror stories about Cambyses's behaviour in Egypt in *Hist.* 3.16; 3.27–29 and 3.37–38.

119 See further references in Edda Bresciani, "The Diaspora: C. Egypt, Persian Satrapy," *CHJ* 1: 358–372 (359).

120 Spiegelberg, *Die Sogenannte Demotische Chronik des Pap. 215 der Bibliothèque Nationale zu Paris nebst den auf der Rückseite des Papyrus stehenden Texten*, 33.

121 According to Bresciani, "The Diaspora: C. Egypt, Persian Satrapy," 358–372 (360), the decree may have been a wise economic measure, reducing the enormous financial expenditure introduced by Amasis, the Pharaoh defeated by Cambyses.

2.6.1.2 Direct Payments from the Royal/Satrapal Treasuries

Another way cults could be financed was through direct payments from the state treasuries. This kind of economic support can be illustrated by two types of sources: administrative texts from Persepolis and the books of Ezra and Nehemiah.

2.6.1.2.1 The Persepolis Tablets and the Persepolis Pantheon

The financial administration of cultic activities is at issue in the archive of clay tablets that were deposited in Persepolis, the city built by Darius I.[122] A substantial number of the Persepolis Fortification texts—which date to the reigns of Darius I, Xerxes I, and Artaxerxes I—deal with the allocation of sacrificial commodities for various gods. Specifically, the direct payments were meant for the so-called *lan* offerings and other types of offerings. The gods who are mentioned as recipients, however, are always members of the *de facto* official Persepolis pantheon. The tablets only refer to cult funding for deities with either an Iranian or Elamite background, not any other "foreign" gods.[123] On the basis of the frequency of mentions, the god Humban appears to have been far more popular than Ahuramazda. The exclusivity of the Persepolis pantheon is striking in light of the fact that there were diaspora communities in Persepolis at that time, yet the texts never mention any payments to the gods of the foreign residents.[124] However, the purpose of noting the Persepolis administrative texts is that they illustrate the following—that direct payments from the state treasury were a way in which a cult potentially could be financed. The bureaucratic procedure of delivery of sacrificial commodities can be illustrated by PF 339: "5 *marriš* 7 QA[125] wine, supplied by Ushaya, Turkama the 'priest' received: 7 QA for the god Auramazda, 2 *marriš* for the god Humban, 1 *marriš* for/at the river

122 The tablets were found at two locations: in the royal treasury—i. e., the Persepolis Treasury Tablets, cf. George G. Cameron, *Persepolis Treasury Tablets*, OIP 65 (Chicago: University of Chicago Press, 1948)—and in a fortification wall—i. e., the Persepolis Fortification Tablets, cf. Richard Treadwell Hallock, *Persepolis Fortification Tablets*, OIP 92 (Chicago: University of Chicago Press, 1969).

123 Wouter F. M. Henkelman, *The Other Gods Who Are: Studies in Elamite–Iranian Acculturation Based on the Persepolis Fortification Texts*, AH 14 (Leiden: Nederlands Instituut voor het Nabije Oosten, 2008), 337.

124 According to Henkelman, the cultic policy in Fars should be explained neither as a consequence of the Achaemenid rejecting foreign gods nor as chauvinism. On the contrary, it was the consequence of the simple logic of indigenous vs. expatriate god, cf. Henkelman, *The Other Gods Who Are*, 342.

125 1 *marriš* = 10 QA = approximately 10 quarts = approximately 10 litres, cf. Hallock, *Persepolis Fortification Tablets*, 72, and Kuhrt, *The Persian Empire*, 224 note 2.

Huputish, 1 *marriš* for/at the river Rannakarra, 1 *marriš* for/at the river Shaushanush. He used it for the gods."[126]

2.6.1.2.2 Ezra–Nehemiah and the Jerusalem Temple

The books of Ezra and Nehemiah hint at *direct payments* from state treasuries as a way of funnelling means to certain cults. Even if the historical accuracy of the accounts in question may be doubted, these biblical books nevertheless illustrate how the official cult funding was *idealised* in the *historical memory* of Yahwists in the Second Temple period.

First, according to a decree that King Cyrus allegedly once issued and that allegedly was found again later at the time of King Darius, the rebuilding of the Jerusalem temple was an official affair. Ezra 6:8 relates that the costs of the rebuilding should be paid in full from *Persian* treasuries: "Moreover I make a decree regarding what you shall do for these elders of the Jews for the rebuilding of this house of God: the cost is to be paid to these people, in full and without delay, from the royal revenue, the tribute of the province Beyond the River" (Ezra 6:8 NRSV). Moreover, the costs of the offerings and sacrifices should be given to the Judaeans "day by day without fail," apparently in this case also from the satrapal treasury (Ezra 6:9 – 10).

Second, according to Neh 2:7 – 8 King Artaxerxes sent a letter to his official Asaph, "the keeper of the king's forest." In the letter the king granted Nehemiah timber in order to make, among other things, "beams for the gates of the temple fortress" (thus the MT).

2.6.1.3 Indirect Economic Support

A cult could also be financed through *indirect* economic support.

2.6.1.3.1 Tax Exemption

According to Ezra 7:21 Artaxerxes commanded that "all the treasurers in the province Beyond the River" (*gizzabrayyāʾ dî baʿăbar nahărâ*) should exempt the religious specialists of the Jerusalem temple from all kinds of taxes. According to Ezra 7:24 (cf. v. 21) the priests, Levites, singers, doorkeepers, temple servants,

126 Quoted from Kuhrt, *The Persian Empire*, 557 (no 11.41), cf. Hallock, *Persepolis Fortification Tablets*, 72.

and other servants should not pay "tribute, custom, or toll" (*midnâ bəlô wahălāk*).

2.6.1.3.2 Privilege to Levy Taxes and the Exemption from Corvée Labour

This kind of indirect support can be illustrated by means of the book of Nehemiah and the so-called Gadatas inscription. According to Neh 1, Nehemiah was given a royal authorisation to go back to Jerusalem and rebuild it. Later on in the book, he appears with the title "governor" (Neh 5:14). The book does not explicitly state that the king granted the personnel of the Jerusalem temple the privilege to levy religious taxes on the Judaean population. However, the book refers to a "firm agreement" (*'ămānâ*, Neh 9:38) that the Israelites [*sic*] made. The sealed document was allegedly signed by the officials (*śārênû*), the Levites, and the priests. The first name on the list of those who signed is Nehemiah the governor (Neh 10:1). Among the things they agreed upon was that the temple personnel would have the authority to levy religious taxes, such as the annual temple tax ("one-thirds shekel," Neh 10:32), the first fruits, the firstborn, and the tithes (Neh 10:35 – 39). Consequently, because Nehemiah the governor was part of the "firm agreement," the account creates the impression that the religious taxes were *de facto* state sanctioned.

Moreover, tax exemption and the exemption from corvée labour are at issue in the Gadatas inscription. The inscription claims to contain a letter from King Darius to a certain Gadatas:

> The King of Kings, Darius ... speaks to Gadatas, his slave, thus: "I find that you are not completely obedient concerning my orders. ... because my religious dispositions are nullified by you, I shall give you, unless you make a change, proof of a wronged (king's) anger. For the gardeners sacred to Apollo have been made to pay tribute to you; and land which is profane they have dug up at your command. You are ignorant of my ancestors' attitude to the god, who told the Persians all the truth ..."[127]

The letter to Gadatas is known through a Greek inscription dating to the first decades of the second century CE. Therefore, its authenticity is disputed; P. Briant, for example, argues that it is a Roman-period forgery.[128] Moreover, the role and

127 Quoted from Brosius, *The Persian Empire*, 93 (no. 198).

128 Pierre Briant, "Histoire et archéologie d'un texte. La *Lettre de Darius à Gadatas* entre Perses, Grecs et Romains," in *Licia e Lidia prima dell'ellenizzazione: Atti del Convegno internazionale, Roma, 11 – 12 ottobre 1999*, ed. Mauro Giorgieri et al., MSSSUS (Rome: Consiglio Nazionale delle Ricerche, 2003): 107 – 144, referred to by Kuhrt, *The Persian Empire*, 85 note 1. However, in Briant, *From Cyrus to Alexander*, 491, he writes that "[t]he authenticity of the document is no

status of Gadatas in relation to Darius is not explicitly stated. He is presented as Darius's *slave* (δουλος) and may perhaps have been the satrap of Ionia. Even if the Greek inscription actually *is* a Roman-period forgery and not an authentic Achaemenid letter, it nevertheless *illustrates* the mechanisms of a state-sanctioned tax exemption. In this particular case the local authorities had allegedly violated the royal decree. Gadatas seems to have defied the decree and stubbornly imposed a tax upon the gardeners[129] of the temple of Apollo in Magnesia. What is more, Gadatas had even imposed corvée labour upon them.

2.6.2 Aspects of the Economic Structures in Achaemenid Egypt

What do the sources from Achaemenid Egypt tell us about taxes and duties in Egypt? I will attempt to give some aspects of the economic structures of Egypt under Achaemenid domination. In particular I will emphasise the question of temple economy in the vicinity of Elephantine.

All the treasuries mentioned in the Aramaic and Demotic sources from the Achaemenid period were controlled by either the king or the satrap. One treasury mentioned in the documents from Elephantine is "the treasury of the king" (*'wṣr' zy mlk'*)/"the royal barley-house" (*ywdn' zy mlk'*).[130] It has been possible to identify its exact location in the urban plan of Elephantine: it was close to the temple of Khnum, the temple of YHW and the residential area where many of the Judaeans were living (B3.4:9; B3.7:7; B3.11:4; cf. B3.13:4).

Moreover, the taxes and duties mentioned in the Achaemenid-period sources have only one addressee: "the king's house." For instance, a customs account possibly drawn up in 475 BCE offers an insight into the maritime trade and the Achaemenid system for collecting taxes on incoming ships and imported goods. The scribes have diligently drawn up the Ionian and Phoenician ships

longer really challenged." For a discussion of the text, see Lester L. Grabbe, "The Law of Moses in the Ezra Tradition: More Virtual Than Real?," in *Persia and Torah: The Theory of Imperial Authorization of the Pentateuch*, ed. James W. Watts, SymS 17 (Atlanta: Society of Biblical Literature, 2001): 91–113 (107–108), Gregor Ahn, "»Toleranz« und Reglement: Die Signifikanz achaimenidischer Religionspolitik für den jüdisch-persischen Kulturkontakt," in *Religion und Religionskontakte im Zeitalter der Achämeniden*, ed. Reinhard Gregor Kratz, VWGT 22 (Gütersloh: Gütersloher Verlagshaus, 2002): 191–209 (192–193), and Fried, *The Priest and the Great King*, 108–119.

129 Fried, *The Priest and the Great King*, 109: "gardener priests."

130 It was "the royal barley-house" the Elephantine Judaeans accused the priests of Khnum of having destroyed in connection with the turmoil in the last decades of the fifth century BCE (A4.5:5).

and the cargo they were loaded with. From each one of the ships taxes were collected (*gby*) and "turned over" (*'byd*) to "the royal treasury" (*byt mlk'*).[131] The central treasury in Egypt was in Memphis.[132]

Furthermore, a demotic document written in 487 BCE illustrates that newly appointed Egyptian religious specialists had to pay an initiation tax (introductory fee) to the Achaemenid administration.[133] In this particular case Djedhor paid a certain amount of silver to the Persian official Farnava on his appointment to the position of second *wab*-priest. Farnava was both the governor of Tshetres (one of the provinces of Upper Egypt) and the garrison commander of Syene.[134]

It is difficult to draw a clear-cut demarcation line between the economy of the *satrap* and the economy of the *king*. A substantial number of the Aramaic documents from Achaemenid Egypt show that the satrap in fact controlled treasuries too. The satrap's private businesses seem to have been mixed with the official economy. For instance, on one occasion Arshama issued a travel authorisation to his official Nakhtḥor who was about to travel back to Egypt. In this authorisation Arshama ordered several named officials located at various places in the Fertile Crescent to give Nakhtḥor's company the necessary daily rations (A6.9). The rations should be given from *Arshama's* estates (*byt' zyly*, A6.9:2) in the provinces of the respective officials. Moreover, Arshama's estates *within* Egypt are at issue in other documents (e.g., in A6.10 where Arshama warns his official Nakhtḥor against causing any decrease in his estates in Egypt).

Moreover, the official documents pertaining to the satrap Arshama suggest that he was inclined to micromanagement. For instance, on one occasion the satrap authorised "the accountants of the treasury" of a boatyard (A6.2:4) to obtain the materials that were necessary in order to repair a boat. Furthermore, he ordered them to collect the worn-out parts. The document also shows that the boat was owned by Arshama and leased to two persons of Carian origin (A6.2:2–3).

Another such example appears in a document describing Arshama's personal involvement in the transfer of a plot of concession land from a deceased father to his son (A6.11).[135] The satrap's inclination to micromanagement is evident in

---

131 Ada Yardeni, "Maritime Trade and Royal Accountancy in an Erased Costums Cccount from 475 B.C.E. on the Aḥiqar Scroll from Elephantine," *BASOR* 293 (1994): 67–78, and Oren Tal, "On the Identification of the Ships of *kzd/ry* in the Erased Customs Account from Elephantine," *JNES* 68 (2009): 1–8.

132 Bresciani, "The Diaspora: C. Egypt, Persian Satrapy," 358–372 (366).

133 P. Berlin 13582, cf. Porten et al., *The Elephantine Papyri in English*, 373–374.

134 Similar fees are attested in the Ptolemaic period too, cf. Porten et al., *The Elephantine Papyri in English*, 310–311 (no. C11).

135 See Szubin and Porten, "Hereditary Leases in Aramaic Letters," 283–288.

the fact that the size of the plot was probably modest. According to B. Porten's interpretation, it had a capacity of thirty ardabs[136] of seed, and provided that this was per year, the plot had the capacity to produce 838.8 litres per year. Arshama granted the son the right to inherit the plot as concession land. One of the conditions was that the new concessionaire paid the same "land tax/tribute" (*hlk'*, A6.11:5) to his estate (*byt' zyly*) as previously.

In short, in the Achaemenid period the economic life of Egypt was under tight Persian control. The Persian rulers founded an economic system based on an exploitation of the Egyptian resources. The satrap and the Persian aristocracy[137] controlled agricultural production and the trading routes. They shared among themselves the high positions in the court, in the army and in the satrapy.[138]

2.6.3 The Temple of YHW

Was the temple of YHW ever granted concession land? Did it benefit from direct payments from official treasuries? Or did it (or its personnel) receive indirect economic support in the form of exemption from taxes or have the authority to levy religious taxes? In short, how was the temple of YHW financed?

To be sure, the sources for the Judaean community and the temple of YHW in Elephantine in the Achaemenid period are, to a large degree, *silent* about these questions. However, in some cases they *do* give some positive information. In addition, when there is a silence about these issues in the documents in contexts where we should expect to that find this kind of information, the silence can be used as an indication.

2.6.3.1 Arguments from (Loud) Silence

Let us start with the arguments from silence. The official documents drawn up around 407 BCE, a few years after the temple of YHW was destroyed (A4.7–

136 See Porten and Yardeni, *TADAE*, I: Letters. Appendix: Aramaic Letters from the Bible, 118. Cf. note 46, above.
137 Briant: the "ethno-classe dominante," i. e., the class recruited from the Persian aristocracy and the social strata around the Great King, cf. Pierre Briant, "Ethno-classe dominante et populations soumises dans l'Empire achéménide: le cas de l'Égypte," in *Method and Theory: Proceedings of the London 1985 Achaemenid History Workshop*, ed. Amélie Kuhrt and Heleen Sancisi-Weerdenburg, AH 3 (Leiden: Nederlands Instituut voor het Nabije Oosten, 1988): 137 – 173.
138 Sternberg-el Hotabi, "Die persische Herrschaft in Ägypten," 111 – 149 (115 – 25, 128).

10), are especially relevant in this regard. These are *official* because they were either written *by* the leaders of the Judaean community or *addressed to* the leaders of the community.

The earliest is the letter written to Bagavahya, the Persian governor of Judah (A4.7/A4.8). An addendum relates that the Elephantine community had sent a similar letter to the house of the governor of the neighbouring province of Samaria (A4.7:29 par.). The Elephantine leaders requested Bagavahya to write a letter of recommendation concerning the rebuilding of the temple of YHW. It seems clear they believed a recommendation would help them to get permission to rebuild the temple of YHW, which at that time was lying in ruins. An important part of their argumentative strategy to convince Bagavahya was to highlight the alleged former privileged status of the temple. They claimed that it was erected before the Persian king Cambyses conquered Egypt in 525 BCE. In addition, the alleged status came to the fore through the religious policy of Cambyses towards the Egyptian temples. Whereas he allegedly overthrew all of the *Egyptian* temples, he *spared* the temple of YHW (A4.7:13–14 par.). In short, the Elephantine leaders sought help to re-establish the temple and the cult as it used to be.

In my view, this is the place we should expect to find potential traces of the Persian financial administration of the temple of YHW. If the temple had ever been granted direct or indirect economic support by the Persians, this would have been the place to mention it. However, the letter is silent about that. Therefore, we should assume that the temple of YHW did *not* get financial help from the state treasury. The temple did not control land concessions. We never learn of a "gardener of YHW." This is in striking contrast to the fact that several of the legal documents drawn up by the Elephantine Judaeans mention an Egyptian named Ḥor. In some documents Ḥor is designated as "a gardener [*gnn*] of Khnum the god."[139] Moreover, the temple of YHW did not receive direct payments from any official treasury. Nor was it exempted from taxes or granted the privilege to levy any sorts of (religious) taxes.

Furthermore, a *loud silence* about economic issues also characterises the *answer* from the governors of Judah and Samaria (A4.9). The governors neither addressed the question of how the rebuilt temple should be financed nor hinted at who they thought should pay for the sacrificial materials in the re-established cult. Therefore, we should also exclude the possibility that the Elephantine Judaeans received any kind of economic support from their co-religionists in Judah and Samaria.

---

139 B3.10:10; B3.11:6. He is also called "a servant (*ʿbd*) of Khnum the god" in B3.7:8.

However, it is remarkable that the image is somewhat *different* in the presumably latest of these official documents dealing with the issue of the rebuilding of the temple: A4.10. In A4.10 the leading figures of the Yahwist community in Elephantine addressed an anonymous official of higher rank than themselves. The one they called "our lord" (*mr'n*) *may* have been the satrap Arshama himself. To be sure, in the address to "our lord" the question of economy is at issue. The document does not name who should pay for the rebuilding and the cult. On the contrary, the economic question is connected to a payment *to* the addressee ("our lord"). The Elephantine leaders promised to hand over a conditional payment if he approved the rebuilding. The payment they would "give to the house of our lord" (*ntn ʿl byt mr'n*, A4.10:13) included silver and one thousand ardabs of barley. It has been proposed to interpret the payment as a kind of bribe (*baksheesh*).[140]

2.6.3.2 Positive Arguments

In contrast to the overall silence of the Elephantine sources discussed so far, there is one particular document that stands out: the so-called Collection Account (C3.15). The account opens with the date "on the 3rd of Phamenoth, year 5" and the heading: "This is (= these are) the names of the Jewish garrison who gave silver to YHW the God each person silver, [2] sh(ekels)." Then, the account lists one hundred and twenty-eight male and female individuals. Each entry is formulated according to a stereotypic syntagm:

> PN1 son/daughter of PN2 [sometimes also: son of PN3], 2 shekel silver [sometimes also: to him/for him-/herself (*lh*)]

The list closes with the grand total:

> The silver which stood that day in the hand of Jedaniah son of Gemariah in the month of Phamenoth: silver, 31 karsh, 8 shekels. Herein: for YHW 12 k., 6 sh.; for Eshembethel, 7 karsh; for Anathbethel, silver, 12 karsh. (C3.15:123 – 28)[141]

140 Max Vogelstein, "Bakshish for Bagoas?," *JQR* 33 (1942): 89 – 92.

141 Quoted from Bezalel Porten and Ada Yardeni, *Textbook of Aramaic Documents from Ancient Egypt. Newly Copied, Edited and Translated into Hebrew and English*, vol. III: Literature, Accounts, Lists (Jerusalem: The Hebrew University of Jerusalem – Department of the History of the Jewish People, 1993), 234.

For some reason, there is an arithmetic problem, which I do not intend to pursue.[142] Moreover, I will also leave aside the question of the identification of Eshembethel and Anathbethel and their position in the pantheon of the Elephantine Judaeans.[143]

The list is dated to the fifth regnal year, but it does not mention the name of the king. Two kings have been suggested: Darius II and Amyrtaeus, the first and only king of the twenty-eighth Egyptian dynasty. If "year 5" refers to the fifth regnal year of Darius II, then the account was drawn up in 419 BCE. However, if "year 5" refers to the fifth regnal year of Amyrtaeus, then it was written in 400 BCE.

The question of the *purpose* of the Collection Account is partially connected to the question of the date. In the history of research several suggestions have been proposed. According to Cowley, "year 5" refers to the fifth regnal year or Darius II (= 419 BCE). This implies that the Collection Account was written in the same year that Hananiah imparted his *instructions connected to the Festival of Unleavened Bread* (and perhaps the Passover) to the Judaean garrison (cf. A4.1). According to Cowley, the collection of the silver may have been connected to the mission of Hananiah in one way or another. Cowley conjectured that the silver may have been needed for the sacrifices that accompanied Hananiah's reinstitution of the Festival of Unleavened Bread (and the Passover).[144]

According to B. Porten, however, it is more probable that the unnamed king is Amyrtaeus. Amyrtaeus ruled between 404 and 399 BCE. Consequently, the Collection Account was drawn up in 400 BCE,[145] shortly after the end of the "first Persian domination" (= the Twenty-Seventh Dynasty). The arguments in favour of the late date are based on palaeography and onomastics.[146] According to Porten, the Egyptian month of Phamenoth paralleled the Babylonian/biblical month

---

142 For an unknown reason, there is a difference of two shekels between the 318 shekels entrusted to Jedaniah and the following account of the distribution of the silver between YHW, Eshembethel, and Anathbethel.

143 According to Porten, they were deities subordinate to or hypostatic YHW forms, cf. Porten, *Archives from Elephantine*, 164. B. Becking, however, understands them as "protective deities of the *marzēaḥ*," cf. Becking, "Temple, *marzēaḥ*, and Power at Elephantine," 37 – 47 (46 – 47); Bob Becking, "Yehudite Identity in Elephantine," in *Judah and the Judeans in the Achaemenid Period: Negotiating Identity in an International Context*, ed. Oded Lipschits et al. (Winona Lake, IN: Eisenbrauns, 2011): 403 – 419 (414); and Toorn, "Anat-Yahu, Some Other Deities, and the Jews of Elephantine," 80 – 101.

144 Cowley, *Aramaic Papyri*, 66.

145 Porten, *Archives from Elephantine*, 162, and Porten and Yardeni, *TADAE*, III: Literature, Accounts, Lists, 226.

146 Porten, *Archives from Elephantine*, 160 – 164.

of Sivan in this period (regardless of whether it was written in 400 BCE or 419 BCE). Calendric calculations enable him to suggest that the collection of the silver was made *around the time of the Feast of Weeks* (*Shavuot*), the festival observed seven weeks after the Passover, according to biblical calendars. As Porten writes, the exact date of the Feast of Weeks is uncertain and was a matter of controversy in rabbinic literature.[147] Therefore, Porten does not make any definite conclusion as to whether the silver in the Collection Account was collected *in anticipation* of the Feast of Weeks or *on* the day it started. In any case, he suggests the contributions of silver were "somehow related to the communal celebration of the Feast of Weeks."[148]

Porten's connection of the Collection Account with the Feast of Weeks has been contested by B. Becking.[149] One of Becking's arguments against Porten's proposal is that the biblical prescriptions rule that there should be an offering of *new grain* to YHWH in connection with the Feast of Weeks. The Collection Account, however, only mentions *silver*. Moreover, Becking's other main argument is that there is no clear references from the Persian period to the celebration of the Feast of Weeks, except for in Lev 23. Becking points to the calendar in Ezek 45:18 – 25 where the feast is lacking.[150] Instead Becking proposes that the silver of the Collection Account was meant for a *marzēaḥ* of YHW in Elephantine. The argument in support of this is based on a short ostracon inscription (D7.29) referring to "the silver of the *marzēaḥ*": "To Haggai. I said (= spoke) to Ashian about the silver of the *marzeah*. Thus he said to me, saying: 'There isn't (any). Now, I shall give it to Haggai or Igdal.' Get to him that he may give it to you" (D7.29).[151]

According to Becking, the institution of *marzēaḥ* is known from various inscriptions in Syria and Palestine from both the second and the first millennium BCE. In some cases it was a funerary banquet held in honour of a deceased

147 The uncertainty is due to discrepancies in the biblical festival calendars. According to the festival calendar in Deut 16, the Israelites should begin to count the seven weeks "from the time the sickle is first put to the standing grain" and then observe the Feast of Weeks (Deut 16:9 – 10). However, according to the calendar in Lev 23, the Israelites should count seven full weeks "from the morrow of the Sabbath [*mimmāḥŏrat haššabbāt*], from the day that you brought the sheaf of the wave offering" (Lev 23:15 – 6). Within the context of early Judaism, four different days have been considered to be the "morrow of the Sabbath," cf. Porten, *Archives from Elephantine*, 162.
148 Porten, *Archives from Elephantine*, 163.
149 Becking, "Temple, *marzēaḥ*, and Power at Elephantine," 37 – 47 (41 – 42).
150 "It is only in later traditions, in Qumran, in the Book of Jubilees and in the New Testament that the feast on the 50th day becomes of a pivotal relevance," Becking, "Temple, *marzēaḥ*, and Power at Elephantine," 37 – 47 (42).
151 Quoted from Porten and Yardeni, *TADAE*, IV: Ostraca & Assorted Inscriptions, 177.

ancestor.[152] In other cases it seems that the *marzēaḥ* was held as a communal meal without any reference to a deceased ancestor.

In my view, Becking's argumentation against Porten's proposal does not hit the mark. Moreover, I find his arguments for linking the Collection Account to the institution of *marzēaḥ* unconvincing,[153] for in the end the Collection Account does not account for the purpose of the collection, except for the two notions in the heading and the grand total, respectively. The silver that was collected was meant for "YHW the god" (C3.15:1) and/or "for YHW, Eshembethel and Anathbethel" (C3.15:123–128).

In any case, we may ask whether silver for the god YHW could have been collected *without* in one way or another involving a temple of YWH, "the god living in Elephantine." If "year 5" is 419 BCE, then the temple was definitely a reality. If "year 5" is 400 BCE, then the temple had presumably already been rebuilt (it may have been rebuilt around 402 BCE). Therefore, in the last resort it is likely it was the *temple of YHW that benefitted from the collected silver* accounted for in the Collection Account.

Consequently, I find it tempting to compare it to Neh 10:32–3 (NRSV):

> We also lay on ourselves the obligation to charge ourselves yearly one-third of a shekel for the service of the house of our God: for the rows of bread, the regular grain offering, the regular burnt offering, the sabbaths, the new moons, the appointed festivals, the sacred

---

152 This kind of *marzēaḥ* corresponds to the *kispum* rite known from Mesopotamia. The rite of *kispum* ("remembrance ritual, funerary offering") was a communal meal in which the living and dead came together. The term *kispum* is used generically by scholars for similar practices elsewhere in the ancient Near East, cf. Nicolas Wyatt, "After Death Has Us Parted: Encounters between the Living and the Dead in the Ancient Semitic World," in *The Perfumes of Seven Tamarisks: Studies in Honour of Wilfred G. E. Watson*, ed. Gregorio del Olmo Lete et al., AOAT 394 (Münster: Ugarit-Verlag 2012): 259–292 (260). The story of Saul's necromancy at En-dor (1Sam 28) may reflect a case of a *kispum* rite in the Bible, cf. Nicolas Wyatt, "Royal Religion in Ancient Israel," in *Religious Diversity in Ancient Israel and Judah*, ed. Francesca Stavrakopoulou and John Barton (London: T&T Clark, 2010): 61–81 (74–75). The term *mirzaḥ* appears in Amos 6:7 (NRSV "revelry") and Jer 16:5 speaks about *bêt marzēaḥ* (NRSV "house of mourning"), cf. T. J. Lewis, "Dead," *DDD:* 223–231 (230).

153 Having said that, there are substantial weaknesses connected to Becking's use of the biblical (and *textual*) calendars in reconstructing the actual, *lived* religious practice in the Persian period. First, Becking does not even mention the calendar in Deut 16. Even if one dated this deuteronomistic calendar to, say, the time of King Josiah, there is still a possibility that it continued to be used somehow also in the Persian period. Second, a more fundamental objection to both Becking—and Porten as well—is connected to how they deal with the very complex relationship between the collection of ideological, and in part propagandistic, texts of the Bible to the religion that was actually lived by the Judaeans in the Persian period.

donations, and the sin offerings to make atonement for Israel, and for all the work of the house of our God.

Many of the questions modern students of the Yahwism of Elephantine may have are left unanswered by the Collection Account. We do not know whether the listed individuals represented every single Judaean household in Elephantine. We do not know whether the Judaeans gave the silver voluntarily or not. However, in respect of my questions connected to the funding of the temple of YHW in Elephantine, the important point is made already in the heading: *znh šmht ḥyl' yhwdy' zy yhb ksp lyhw 'lh' lgbr lgbr ksp*, "This is (= these are) the names of the Judaean garrison who gave silver to YHW the god each person silver" (C3.15:1).[154] The contributors were presented as *individuals* belonging to the *Judaean garrison.*

2.6.4 The Economy: Conclusion

How was the temple of YHW in Elephantine financed? In my view, it was most probably funded by the *members of the Judaean garrison.* The temple was *tolerated* by the Persian overlords in Egypt, if not for another reason, then at least because it would be unwise to do otherwise. After all, the Judaean garrison was a *Persian* garrison, and a temple devoted to the Judaean chief god could fulfil the religious needs of the Judaean soldiers. At the same time it enhanced the inner stability within the Judaean garrison. However, the sources do not suggest that the Persians supported the temple economically through the concession of land plots, direct payments from the state treasuries, or indirect economic support in the form of exemption from taxes. Furthermore, we never hear of any kind of economic support from the Yahwistic communities in Judah and Samaria. On the contrary, as far as the economy of the temple of YHW is concerned, the only positive evidence is the scant, and to some extent enigmatic, Collection Account. Regardless of whether it was drawn up in 419 or 400 BCE, the account suggests that the burden of financing the temple of YHW had to be carried by the Judaeans in Elephantine themselves.

154 Quoted from Porten and Yardeni, *TADAE*, III: Literature, Accounts, Lists, 228.

2.6.5 Where Did the Elephantine Judaeans Get Their Means?

Provided that the Judaeans were themselves responsible for financing the temple of YHW, the question of the economy of the temple is closely connected to the question of the economy of the Elephantine Judaeans as such. The Judaean community was a garrison community. Classical Greek sources do not give a consistent image of how Persian garrisons were organised.[155] According to Xenophon both the military commander within a satrapy and the satrap himself were appointed by the king. Xenophon presents *two* main types of Persian garrisons. One was comprised of soldiers paid by the king. The other garrison type was made up of soldiers paid by the satrap. However, no other Greek sources confirm the organisation outlined by Xenophon.

The organisation of Persian garrisons is reflected in other types of sources, among them the Aramaic documents from Achaemenid Egypt. However, according to Christopher Tuplin these non-Greek sources are not conclusive. They give neither evidence for royal appointment of garrison commanders nor do they support the assumption that the satrap had the authority of all aspects of the military and administrative system of his province, including the garrisons. As Tuplin briefly remarks, the economic support of the Elephantine garrison was a mixture of direct payments in kind and cash plus arguably "'colonial' land grants."[156]

Several Aramaic texts relate that the soldiers of the garrisons in Elephantine and Syene were given payments in kind and in silver. An example of payment in kind is found in a contract between Anani son of Haggai son of Meshullam, a Judaean of the detachment of Nabukudurri, and Pakhnum son of Besa, an Aramaean from Syene of the same detachment (B3.13). Anani had borrowed emmer from Pakhnum. Consequently, he was obliged to pay back the loan by means of his *ration* (*ptp*) of emmer. These rations would be given to him "from the treasury of the king" (*mn ʾwṣr mlkʾ*, B3.13:4). Moreover, the procedures connected to the transfer of barley to be used as rations from one of the royal treasuries to the local treasury of the garrison in Syene may be glimpsed in B4.4 (cf. C3.14). The two (Judaean) soldiers who escorted the shipment, Hosea son of Hodaviah and Ahiab son of Gemariah, were personally responsible for bringing the rations safely to their final destination. In the case that all of the barley did *not* arrive at

155 In the following, see Christopher Tuplin, "Persian Garrisons in Xenophon and Other Sources," in *Method and Theory: Proceedings of the London 1985 Achaemenid History Workshop*, ed. Amélie Kuhrt and Heleen Sancisi-Weerdenburg, AH 3 (Leiden: Nederlands Instituut voor het Nabije Oosten, 1988): 67 – 70 and the references there.
156 Tuplin, "Persian Garrisons," 67 – 70 (70).

the destination, the two protection escorts were liable to incur harsh penalties to be paid in silver (B4.4:13–17).

Moreover, an example of payment in silver is found in a (draft?) contract drawn up between Gemariah son of Aḥio and [PN] son of Jathma (B4.2). The former had borrowed silver from the latter. In the contract, Gemariah committed himself to repay the loan "month by month from my allotment [*prs*] which they will give me from the treasury" (B4.2:5–6). The context suggests that Gemariah got a (monthly?) allotment in silver. Further, it obviously caused problems when the allotments were not paid. A letter written in Migdol in Lower Egypt by a father to his son illustrates that such a problem would affect the extended family (A3.3). Osea wrote to his son Shelomam (both being Yahwists) about the bureaucratic maze he had to go through in order to get hold of his son's legitimate allotment (*prs*): "[And when] we complained to the OFFICIALS about your allotment here in Migdol, thus was said to us, saying: 'About this, [*you, complain* before] the scribes and it will be given to you'" (A3.3:4–5).[157]

We may surmise that for most of the Judaean population in the vicinity of Elephantine (like other foreign soldiers), the monthly rations and allotments were the primary source of income.

It appears that at least *some* Judaeans also had an additional source of income. Some leased concession land, probably from members of the Persian aristocracy. These "hereditary property holders" (*mhḥsnn*)[158] were clearly in a position to accrue a surplus of harvest. In A4.10, the presumably latest official document written as part of the campaign to rebuild the temple of YHW, the five leading Yahwists informed "our lord" (Arshama?) about the size of the payment they would give him (as a *baksheesh?*): *one thousand ardabs of barley* (A4.10:14).

2.7 The Organisation of Time

In any civilisation, the organisation of time is based upon two main factors: *nature* and *culture* – in this particular order of appearance.

First a few words about the natural factors for organising time. Fundamental is the mechanics of planet Earth's orbit around the Sun. The Earth rotates around its own axis, the Moon orbits around the Earth, and the Earth–Moon system or-

---

157 Quoted from Porten et al., *The Elephantine Papyri in English*, 109.

158 Szubin and Porten, "'Ancestral Estates' in Aramaic Contracts," 3–9, and Szubin and Porten, "Hereditary Leases in Aramaic Letters," 283–288.

bits around the Sun. Due to the Earth's rotation one can differentiate between *day* and *night*. However, because the axial tilt (the obliquity) of the Earth's rotation to the perpendicular of its orbital plane is 23 degrees, the length of day and night is a correlate of the latitude of the observer and the position of the Earth in its orbit around the Sun. The closer the observer gets to the equator, the more similar the length of day and night will become. Correspondingly, the more distant one gets from the equator, the greater the difference in length between day and night. In any case, regardless of the latitude of the observer, it is the Earth's rotation that constitutes day and night as basic units of time measurement, and the time the Earth uses to complete an orbit around the Sun (the *solar year*) equals ca. 365.25 days. The Earth's axial tilt and its constantly changing position in its orbit around the Sun causes the orderly change between the *seasons* (regardless of how we divide and name them). The Moon's orbit around the Earth is completed in approximately 27.32 days (the sidereal month). However, due to the Earth's orbit the "experienced" lunar month for a terrestrial observer will be the synodic month, which is about 29.53 days. In other words, for an observer on Earth it takes 29.53 days for the Moon to complete a cycle of moon phases. Therefore, nature has provided humans with several time intervals: the shift between day and night, the solar year and the change of seasons, and the lunar month. A common feature of all of them is that they are regularly repeated and thus cyclical.

Historically humans have used the cycles of nature in order to get a grip on time. Humans' "use" of time has taken place within a number of spheres and has tended to materialise in the form of *calendars*. In the sphere of agriculture calendars have helped people to calculate the appropriate seasons for sowing and harvesting, and by doing so planning and securing their livelihood. In the sphere of business and law calendars have made it possible to establish legally binding chronological fix points, points that have been important to uphold order, stability and in the last resort, public trust. In the sphere of religion calendars have become important in order to separate sacred time from ordinary time, for instance to demarcate periods particularly favourable for praying to the gods or periods that are set aside because the gods have said so. Obviously, there are many other examples of settings where calendars are important.

Throughout history there have been a number of examples of societies with several calendars serving different purposes.[159] What was the situation within

159 For example, in the modern, Western world the civic society uses the Gregorian, solar calendar. However, at the same time and within one and the same Western society there are (religious) groups that are using their own, distinct calendar for religious purposes. The Islamic calendar is a lunar calendar consisting of twelve months and 354 or 355 days and starts with the

the Judaean community in Elephantine in the fifth century BCE, then? The many legal documents that can be associated in one way or another to the members of the Judaean society there demonstrate clearly that the Judaeans no doubt used the calendars of their surrounding society. The legal documents of the Mibtahiah family archive[160] and the Ananiah family archive[161] are either dated according to an Egyptian calendar,[162] or they have (for the most part) been given a synchronous Babylonian and Egyptian month dating.[163] So, in the fifth century BCE the Judaeans in Elephantine were exposed to and used two calendar systems: an indigenous Egyptian calendar and a Babylonian one.[164] The chronological distribution of the use of these calendars differs, and the use of only Egyptian month names (without the synchronous Babylonian date) is almost entirely confined to the beginning and the end of the fifth century BCE.[165] In some cases only a Babylonian date has been used. Moreover, in addition to the specific day of the month and the month name, the same documents clearly attest to the practice of using the regnal year of the ruling king as the chronological fix point. When dated, the documents were dated in year X of king Z, regardless of whether the king was Egyptian or Persian.

This way of organising time was used not only when Elephantine Judaeans wrote letters to or made contracts with non-Judaeans but was even used in legal documents where all the parties were Judaeans. Therefore, the inner-Judaean organisation of time did not differ from that of the surrounding society—at least when business and legal matters were at issue.

But did the Elephantine Judaeans follow any particular religious calendar in addition? This question will also be discussed in Chapter 4, particularly focussing on the possible observance of the Passover, the Festival of Unleavened Bread and the Sabbath. Here, I will limit myself to a few introductory observations. Relatively little is known about the details of how the religion of the Ele-

---

year of Muhammad's Hijra in 622 CE. The (modern) Jewish calendar is lunisolar (a lunar framework adapted to the solar year) consisting of twelve months (and a thirteenth, intercalary month in leap years in order to synchronise the calendar with the cycle of seasons), and starts from the creation, allegedly in 3761 BCE.

160 B2.1–11.

161 B3.1–13.

162 For example B3.11:1.

163 For example B3.7:1.

164 Sacha Stern, "The Babylonian Calendar at Elephantine," *ZPE* 130 (2000): 159–171.

165 Porten et al., *The Elephantine Papyri in English*, 82, and Bezalel Porten, "The Calendar of Aramaic Texts from Achaemenid and Ptolemaic Egypt," in *Irano-Judaica II: Studies Relating to Jewish Contacts with Persian Culture Throughout the Ages*, ed. Shaul Shaked and Amnon Netzer (Jerusalem: Ben-Zvi Institute 1990): 13–32 (16).

phantine Judaeans was reflected in their organisation of time (i.e. the possible "religious calendar of the Elephantine Judaeans"). For example, the use of both an Egyptian and a Babylonian calendar complicates the question of whether they had the concept of a week, and in particular its length. The Egyptian year was made up of twelve months that were divided into three weeks of ten days each ("decades"). In addition, five days were added each year (the epagomenal days), giving the total of 365 days a year.[166] The Babylonian calendar was lunisolar. Each of the twelve months started when a new moon crescent was spotted. In order to synchronize it with the seasons an additional intercalary month was regularly added. Each Babylonian month seems to have been divided into halves. The first half was termed *šapattu mahrītu* and the second *šapattu arkītu*. Moreover, the halves seem to have been divided into seven-day units.[167] Therefore, provided that the Aramaic term *šbh*, which at times is found in the texts from Elephantine, actually corresponded terminologically to the biblical *šbt*, then the question arises: What kind of Sabbath did the Judaeans there know?

It is uncertain to what extent the possible religious calendar of the Elephantine Judaeans was in accordance with the religious calendars of the Bible, calendars that for their part are primarily written texts and that were not necessarily operative in the Persian period. Yet it is obvious that the Elephantine Judaeans had a notion of sacred time. This can be demonstrated in several ways. For instance, a popular personal name in Elephantine was Haggai (*ḥgy*), which is a derivation of the noun *ḥg*, "festival."[168] The name may have been given to a boy child born on the "festival,"[169] or should we perhaps say, on a day that was considered as sacred and set aside from the other days. Having said that we do not know what particular festival(s) the name Haggai refers to.

The existence of a concept of sacred time in Elephantine also appears in another way. In the communal petition to Bagavahya the governor of Judah, the Elephantine Judaeans stated that they had been wearing sackcloth, fasting, praying to YHW and performing other rites (of mourning) ever since the temple of YHW was destroyed. The post-destruction period as a whole was a *période exceptionnelle* in which the Judaeans devoted themselves to YHW in an exceptional way (so at least according to the rhetoric of the communal petition A4.7/A.4.8). Although it had happened against their will, the post-destruction period

166 Francesca Rochberg-Halton, "Calendars: Ancient Near East," *ABD* 1: 810–814 (813).
167 Rochberg-Halton, "Calendars: Ancient Near East," 810–814 (812).
168 A4.4:7; B2.7:19; B2.11:16; B3.8:1; B3.10:26, cf. Porten et al., *The Elephantine Papyri in English*, 270.
169 Porten et al., *The Elephantine Papyri in English*, 86.

was set aside and so in a sense sacred, a special period not characterised by "business as usual."

Summing up, there is no doubt that religion manifested itself socially in the organisation of time for the Judaean community at Elephantine. However, the relatively few concrete cases that are potentially relevant for the question of a distinct Elephantine Judaean religious calendar will be discussed in a separate chapter.

2.8 Chapter Summary

This chapter has focused on aspects of the social dimension of the religion of the Judaean community in Elephantine. Starting with a first presentation of "the Judaean garrison," its possible size, origin and migration to Egypt, and everyday duties in its capacity as a Persian garrison, the chapter moved onto a discussion of some of the factors that seem to have coined the identity of the community. On the basis of the sources it is possible to argue that there in fact was a characteristic Elephantine Judaean "we," distinct from other groups. A feature that apparently set the Judaeans apart from others groups in Upper Egypt in the Achaemenid period was their affiliation to YHW as their chief god. Nevertheless, the community was part of a multiethnic and multicultural society, and the identity was pragmatic and plastic. The individuals affiliated with the Judaean garrison *presented* themselves in different ways in different contexts. The term "Judaean(s)" was used both by themselves (both in documents written to fellow Elephantine Judaeans and in documents written to addressees in the province of Judah/Yehud) and by others when referring to them. Nevertheless, other terms were also used to characterise the group and individuals belonging to it, such as "Aramaean(s)," "Syenians" and "hereditary property holders."

The power structures of the community have also been discussed, focussing on formal and informal leaders of the community in the form of hierarchies headed by individuals such as Jedaniah and the priests of YHW, Hananiah, the group of Judaeans referring to themselves as Syenians and hereditary property holders (*mhḥsnn*) in Elephantine, as well as the political and religious leaders of the provinces of Judah and Samaria.

Furthermore, as religion may reflect itself socially through various kinds of laws, the chapter has discussed some of the legal aspects of the Elephantine Judaean society. Although no written legal code from the community is known (be it "divinely sanctioned" or "secular" laws), the legal practice of the Elephantine Judaeans was not secular; oaths could be made using YHW and other gods as guarantors of validity and trustworthiness. In short, in questions of a legal matter it seems that the practice of the Elephantine Judaeans did not differ from that of their non-Judaean neighbours. Litigations and lawsuits could be made in front of Persian officials, and it may even have been possible to appeal to high-ranked officials such as the satrap. Moreover, questions pertaining to family law were regulated by means of contracts between the bridegroom and the bride-giver (the father, the bride's brother or even her owner). Although it seems that a marriage was meant to last until the death of one of the spouses it nevertheless was possible for both to request a divorce; marriage contracts from Elephantine suggest that the wife had a relatively high degree of legal protection, also in economic issues.

The best-attested religious specialists of the Judaean community are the priests of YHW. It is a characteristic feature that the technical term *khn* seems to have been reserved for the Yahwistic communities of Elephantine and Jerusalem whereas a religious specialists of other gods was called a *kmr*. The exact tasks of the priests of YHW and the procedures for becoming a priests elude us. However, if Egyptian, contemporary documents give at least a hint about the interaction between the local cults and the Persian authorities, then it seems that the Persian satrap claimed to have the privilege to approve the appointment of at least high-ranked religious specialists. Moreover, the Elephantine Judaeans were aware of other kinds of religious specialists besides the priest: "servitor [*lḥn*] of YHW" (whose tasks elude us), "servant [*ʿbd*] of Khnum," and "gardener [*gnn*] of Khnum" (we never learn about any gardener of YHW).

Another question relevant for a discussion of the social dimension of a religion is the question how the religious practice was financed. Various ways of financing temples and cults in the ancient Near East have been surveyed in order to provide a template against which the question of the economy of the temple of YHW can be discussed. On the basis of the explicit information from the sources for the Elephantine community—and partly the *lack thereof* in contexts where we should expect to find such information—the following proposal has been made: The temple of YHW was financed by neither the Persians nor the Yahwistic co-religionists of Judah and Samaria, but by the members of the Elephantine Judaeans themselves. Their income was made up of regular allotments from the Persians—after all, they were a Persian garrison—and in the case of at least some of the Judaeans, surplus accrued from land they leased as concessionaires.

The social dimension of a religion is also reflected in the organisation of time. The Elephantine Judaeans used partly an Egyptian and partly a Babylonian calendar—and in many cases both at one and the same time—and the chronological fix points for dating the year was usually the regnal year of the ruling king. The question of a distinct Judaean religious calendar remains open (the questions of Sabbath, Passover and the Feast of Unleavened Bread will be discussed in more detail in Chapter 4) but it is clear that the community had a notion of sacred time, that is, time set aside and/or distinct from ordinary time.

3 The Material Dimension

Our ancestors built that temple in Fort Elephantine back during the time of the kings of Egypt, and when Cambyses came into Egypt, he found it already built. They pulled down the temples of the Egyptian gods, but no one damaged anything in that temple. (A4.7:13 – 14 par.)[1]

When it comes to the question of how the religion of the Judaeans in Elephantine reflected itself materially, the available textual and archaeological sources suggest that it is but one "thing" that should be the focal point, namely the temple of YHW. The main topic of this chapter, therefore, will be a discussion of this particular Yahwistic sanctuary in Upper Egypt.

Our main sources for the religion of the Judaeans in Elephantine are made up of texts. However, in light of the recent excavations in the vicinity of the Khnum temple on the southern tip of the Elephantine island (undertaken by the German Archaeological Institute, Cairo Department and the Schweizerisches Institut für Ägyptische Bauforschung und Altertumskunde in Cairo) the textual sources can be brought into dialogue with the material remains. The stratification of these remains, namely wall structures and floors, suggests that they stem from the time of the Twenty-Sixth and Twenty-Seventh Dynasties, that is, the Saitic Dynasty and the period of Persian rule over Egypt (525 – 402 BCE).

The archaeological situation regarding the remains of the first temple of YHW contrasts with the textual situation. Whereas the petition to Bagavahya from 407 BCE (A4.7/A4.8)—one of the main textual sources—describes the *first* temple that was assumedly built before Cambyses's conquest of Egypt in 525 BCE, only a few archaeological remains can be ascribed to this first temple. Paradoxically, the archaeologically best described temple of YHW is probably the *second*, rebuilt temple. The textual sources do not describe the latter, except for the fact that the Judaeans in 407 BCE wanted to rebuild it on the very same spot on which the first temple of YHW once stood before it was demolished in 410 BCE (cf. A4.7:23 – 25/A4.8:22 – 24).

3.1 The Temple of YHW in the Textual Sources

The textual references to the temple of YHW in Elephantine are found in various kinds of Aramaic documents from ancient Egypt: in legal documents, in private

1 Quoted from James M. Lindenberger, *Ancient Aramaic and Hebrew Letters*, 2nd ed., WAW 14 (Atlanta: Society of Biblical Literature, 2003), 75 (no. 34).

letters and in official letters written on behalf of the Judaean community in Elephantine.

3.1.1 Legal Documents

When the legal documents refer to the temple of YHW, it is always in connection with real property. The legal documents use the temple of YHW as one of several fix points for describing and delimiting house plots. An example of this is found in a deed of conveyance (B2.7, from 446 BCE). In this document Mahseiah son of Jedaniah transferred the title to his house to his daughter Mibtahiah in exchange for goods that she had already given him. The document describes the boundaries of the house in a way that is typical of legal documents pertaining to real properties (cf. B2.2–3; B2.10; B3.4–5; B3.7; B3.10–12). The boundaries of the property in question are identified and delimited by means of the adjoining houses and/or structures on its four sides, that is "above," "below," "east" and "west," for example:[2]

> Moreover, behold these are the boundaries of that house: above it is the house of Jaush son of Penuliah; below it is the Temple of YHH (the) God; east of it is the house of Gaddul son of Osea and the street is between them; west of it is the house of Ḥarwodj son of Palṭu, priest of Ḥ•[•]• the god. That house – I gave it to you and withdrew from it. Yours it is forever and to whomever you desire give it. (B2.7:13–16)[3]

In the conveyance quoted above "the temple of YHH (the) god" (*ʾgwrʾ zy yhh ʾlh*) functioned as a fix point accepted by all parties, namely, both the grantor and the grantee, who in this particular case were both Judaeans. It is noteworthy that the house of the Egyptian priest Ḥarwodj was situated in close proximity to the temple of YHW. What is more, as will be shown later the temple of YHW did not only have the house of an Egyptian priest in its vicinity. On its eastern/southeastern side there was a large complex belonging to the temple of the Egyptian god Khnum. The neighbourhood of the Judaeans was densely populated by deities.

---

2 On the question of the geographical directions in the relevant sources, see Cornelius von Pilgrim, "Textzeugnis und archäologischer Befund: Zur Topographie von Elephantine in der 27. Dynastie," in *Stationen: Beitäge zur Kulturgeschichte Ägyptens Rainer Stadelmann gewidmet*, ed. Heike Guksch and Daniel Polz (Mainz: von Zabern, 1998): 485–497 (486–487).

3 Quoted from Bezalel Porten et al., eds., *The Elephantine Papyri in English: Three Millennia of Cross-Cultural Continuity and Change*, 2nd rev. ed., DMOA 22 (Atlanta: Society of Biblical Literature, 2011), 187–188.

Other legal documents mention "the temple of YHW the god" in ways comparable to how it was done in B2.7, that is, as a fix point in relation to other plots:

- B3.4:9 – 10 (*'gwr yhw 'lh'*, a contract on the sale of an abandoned house; the house was conveyed from a Caspian couple to Ananiah son of Azariah, a servitor to YHW, dated 437 BCE),
- B3.5:10 (*'gwr' zy yhw 'lh'*, bequest of apartment to wife, from Anaiah "a servitor of YHW the God in Elephantine the fortress" to his wife lady Tamet, dated 434 BCE),
- B2.10:6 (*'gwr' zy yhw 'lh'*, a document in which one Jedaniah son of Hoshiah son of Uriah confirmed to the brothers Jedaniah and Mahseiah sons of Nathan that he had withdrawn from any claims to a particular house, dated 416 BCE), and
- B3.12:18 – 19 (*'gwr' zy yhw*, sale of apartment to a son-in-law, from Anani the servitor of YHW and Tapemet/Tapememet to Anani, dated 402 BCE).

This kind of use of the temple of YHW as a fix point in legal documents is not confined to documents written within the Judaean community. As demonstrated in B3.4 (mentioned above), members of other groups (here: a Caspian couple) also used the temple as a fix point in sales contracts. What is more, in the document issued by the Caspian couple YHW is acknowledged as a god just like the (indigenous) Egyptian god Khnum. For, the Caspians recorded that "the town/way of Khnum the god" (*tmy zy ḥnwm 'lh'*, B3.4:8) was located "below" the house they were about to sell. In this context they also recorded that "the temple of YHW the god[4]" (*'gwr yhw 'lh'*) was located to the west. Both deities, Khnum and YHW, were specified as "gods."

In other words, in the Achaemenid period, the temple of YHW was a physical reality in Elephantine, located in the immediate vicinity of another temple, namely the temple of Khnum.

3.1.2 Private Correspondence

Letters represent the other category of Aramaic documents containing references to the temple of YHW. One subgroup is made up of private letters, of which but one is relevant in this context: A3.3, a letter written by Osea (*'wš'*) to his son[5]

4 The noun *'lh'* was secondarily added above the line to *yhw*.

5 The writer uses a double, contradictory set of designations for the relationship between himself and Shelomam. In the internal address, he writes "To my son Shelomam from your brother Osea" (A3.3:1), and in the external address he writes "To my brother Shelomam son of Osea,

Shelomam (*šlmm*), and that stems from the first quarter of the fifth century BCE. Apparently writing from Migdol in Lower Egypt, Osea opened his letter to Shelomam by greeting the temple of YHW in Elephantine:

> [*šlm b*]*yt yhw byb*
>
> [Greetings], the [T]emple of YHW in Elephantine. (A3.3:1)[6]

In light of other Aramaic letters from Egypt from the same general period (the so-called Hermopolis letters, A2.1–7[7]) this opening phrase seems to have been part of the conventions of Aramaic epistolography in Egypt. In a number of letters that were found in Hermopolis but written to individuals living in Syene, the city on the shore of the Nile just to the east of the island of Elephantine, one can observe similar salutations. For instance, when Nabushezib/Nabusha wrote to his sister Nanaiḥem, he opened with the following line:

> *šlm byt bt'l wbyt mlkt šmyn*
>
> Greetings, Temple of Bethel and Temple of the Queen of Heaven. (A2.1:1)[8]

Similarly, when writing to his sister Tashi, Makkibanit opened by greeting the temple of Banit in Syene (*šlm byt bnt bswn*, A2.2:1), and when writing to another sister (Reia), the same Makkibanit saluted the temple of Nabu (*šlm byt nbw*, A2.3:1). Finally, when writing to his lord Psami, Makkibanit greeted the temple of Banit in Syene (*šlm byt bnt bswn*, A2.4:1). "These letters," Joseph A. Fitzmyer contends, "seem to begin with an invocation of the deity honored in the place

your brother Osea" (A3.3:14). However, in light of the contents it is clear that "brother" is used figuratively here.

6 Quoted from Porten et al., *The Elephantine Papyri in English*, 108.

7 See Edda Bresciani and Murad Kamil, "Le lettere aramaiche di Hermopoli," in *Atti della Accademia Nazionale dei Lincei*. Memorie 12 (Rome: L'Accademia, 1966): 361–428; Bezalel Porten, *Archives from Elephantine: The Life of an Ancient Jewish Military Colony* (Berkeley: University of California Press, 1968), 264–272; Joseph A. Fitzmyer, "Some Notes on Aramaic Epistolography," *JBL* 93 (1974): 201–225; Philip S. Alexander, "Remarks on Aramaic Epistolography in the Persian Period," *JSS* 23 (1978): 155–170; Joseph A. Fitzmyer, "Aramaic Epistolography," *Semeia* 22 (1981): 25–57; Paul-Eugène Dion, "The Aramaic 'Family Letter' and Related Epistolary Forms in Other Oriental Languages and in Hellenistic Greek," *Semeia* 22 (1982): 59–76; Frederick Mario Fales, "Aramaic Letters and Neo-Assyrian Letters: Philological and Methodological Notes," *JAOS* 107 (1987): 451–469; Dirk Schwiderski, *Handbuch des nordwestsemitischen Briefformulars: ein Beitrag zur Echtheitsfrage der aramäischen Briefe des Esrabuches*, BZAW 295 (Berlin; New York: de Gruyter, 2000), 146–149; Lindenberger, *Ancient Aramaic and Hebrew Letters*, 25–36; and Porten et al., *The Elephantine Papyri in English*, 7, 74–77, 89–105.

8 Quoted from Porten et al., *The Elephantine Papyri in English*, 90.

where the addressee is found. ... As far as epistolographic style is concerned, it is a salutation distinct from the initial greeting expressed to the addressee and is indicative of the piety of the writer of the letter."[9]

However, Frederick Mario Fales has suggested another interpretation. In his view, the formula *šlm* + NAME OF TEMPLE should be read together with the greeting that comes immediately after. Consequently, according to Fales *šlm* should be understood as "well-being" in an optative sense. Consequently, Fales renders the initial lines of the letter from Shelomam to Osea (A3.3) thus: "The well-being of the temple of YHW in Yeb to my son Salomam, from your brother Osea."[10]

No matter what the exact function of the greeting was and how we should interpret it, in this context it suffices to say that the letter A3.3 from Osea to Shelomam confirms *that* there was a temple of YHW in Elephantine, just as the Hermopolis letters confirm that there also were temples of the gods Bethel, the Queen of Heaven, Banit and Nabu in the neighbouring Syene, and, moreover, that these temples played a role in one way or another for individuals who found themselves geographically at a distance from them.

3.1.3 Official Correspondence

The other subgroup of Aramaic letters referring to the temple of YHW in Elephantine are several documents belonging to the so-called Jedaniah communal archive, named after the leading personality of the Judaean community in Elephantine at the end of the fifth century BCE. These documents are official and communal because most of them are either written by or addressed to the leaders of the Judaean community in Elephantine, headed by Jedaniah. Some of the documents are addressed to Persian officials or relate the same officials' response to the Elephantine community. Not all of these documents are letters in a strict sense. However, in some of the cases the documents are no doubt letters, in the sense of a written communication between two parties who were in different locales.

---

9 Fitzmyer, "Some Notes on Aramaic Epistolography," 201 – 225 (212), cf. Alexander, "Remarks on Aramaic Epistolography," 155 – 170 (163).

10 Fales, "Aramaic Letters and Neo-Assyrian Letters," 451 – 469 (455 – 456). See also Takamitsu Muraoka, *An Introduction to Egyptian Aramaic*, LOS III 1 (Münster: Ugarit-Verlag, 2012), 91.

3.1.3.1 A4.5

One of these letters, A4.5, is so broken that one cannot tell for sure to whom it was written. The Judaean community in Elephantine addressed someone who was entitled to launch an investigation of the events that had taken place in connection with the destruction of the temple of YHW (cf. A4.5:8 – 9). This someone must have been a Persian official.[11] This is also evident in the appellation "our lord" that they use when they address the addressee directly (*mrʾn*, A4.5:19 – 22). In this letter, the Judaeans of Elephantine describe the "evil act, crime" (*dwškrtʾ*) that the priests of Khnum the god did in the fortress in agreement with the Persian official Vidranga (Vidranga is given the title *frataraka* [*prtrk*], A4.5:3 – 4). The crimes that the Judaeans accused the priests of Khnum of having done included having destroyed parts of a royal storage building, stopped up a well (A4.5:5 – 8) and having "destroyed" (A4.5:24 *ndšw*) something that, although the text is fragmented, must likely must have been the temple of YHW. There are scattered references to *mnḥh* ("meal–offering," A4.5:14), *ʾtrwdn* ("brazier,"[12] A4.5:17) and *ʾšrnʾ* ("fittings, carpentry work,"[13] A4.5:18). All of these can be associated with the temple of YHW. The word *ʾšrnʾ* ("fittings, carpentry work") also reoccurs in another description of the destruction of the first temple of YHW (A4.7:11 and A4.8:10).

3.1.3.2 A4.7 and A4.8

Additional official letters referring to the temple of YHW are A4.7 and A4.8. These two documents are drafts of one and the same letter, dated in the seventeenth regnal year of Darius II, namely, 407 BCE. The drafts were addressed to Bagavahya the governor of Judah and written by Jedaniah and his colleagues the priests in Elephantine. In an addendum Jedaniah and his colleagues informed Bagavahya that they had also sent a similar letter to Delaiah and Shelemiah sons of Sanballat the governor of Samaria. In the letter, the Elephantine leaders requested Bagavahya to write a letter of recommendation. To whom they want him to send the requested recommendation is not uncertain. In any case, it is clear that they believed it would help them to get permission to rebuild the temple of YHW that had been laying destroyed for three years (since the fourteenth

11 See, e.g., Lindenberger, *Ancient Aramaic and Hebrew Letters*, 63.

12 According to Jan Tavernier, *Iranica in the Achaemenid Period (ca. 550 – 330 B.C.): Linguistic Study of Old Iranian Proper Names and Loanwords, Attested in Non-Iranian Texts*, OLA 158 (Leuven: Peeters, 2007), 461 from Old Persian *Ātr̥vadana-, "brazier, fan to fan the fire."

13 According to Tavernier, *Iranica in the Achaemenid Period*, 437 from Old Persian *Āčarna-, "furniture, equipment."

year of Darius). Although the text of the first draft (A4.7) is best preserved, the second draft (A4.8) is likely to represent a version that is closer to (if not identical with) the final version that eventually was submitted to Bagavahya. The scribe who wrote the second draft made almost fifty stylistic corrections as compared to the first draft, all aimed at achieving greater precision and clarity.[14]

3.1.3.3 A4.9 and A4.10

Two further official documents belonging to the Jedaniah communal archive deal with the temple of YHW: A4.9 and A4.10. A4.9 is not a letter according to the definition above. The document is explicitly characterised as a memorandum (*zkrn*) of what Bagavahya and Delaiah "said to me." In other words, A4.9 is basically a written record of the oral communications of the governors of Judah and Samaria. The document's topic is the rebuilding of what the governors refer to as "the altar-house [*byt mdbḥ'*] of the god of heavens which is in Elephantine the fortress" (A4.9:3). The memorandum obviously renders the joint response that the governors of Judah and Samaria gave to the previous request concerning the rebuilding of the temple of YHW in Elephantine and which is reflected in A4.7/A4.8. According to the memorandum, the words that Bagavahya and Delaiah said should be said "in Egypt, before Arshama" (A4.9:2–3). In other words, the memorandum contains a diplomatic statement, namely the message of the governors of Judah and Samaria to the Persian satrap of Egypt.[15]

Eventually, the last document of the Jedaniah communal archive is A4.10. This text, having no *praescriptio*, is also a draft. The Elephantine community leaders addressed an otherwise unnamed—and for us anonymous—person. They referred to the addressee as "our lord." Although the preserved text does not say so, he is definitely a Persian official, perhaps even the satrap Arshama himself. In A4.10 it seems that the Judaean leaders were in fact negotiating with the unnamed official. This is evident in (probably) two conditional clauses, A4.10:7–11 and A4.10:12–14.[16] First, if "the temple of YHW the god of ours" (*'gwr' zy yhw 'lh' zyln*, A4.10:8) in were to be rebuilt (i.e., as a result of the unnamed official approving it), then the Judaeans of Elephantine were willing to refrain from any further burnt-offerings. Instead, in the future they would offer only in-

14 Porten et al., *The Elephantine Papyri in English*, 147.
15 The two governors' endorsement of the initial request from the Judaeans in Elephantine was not without important reservations. The memorandum is silent about the requested resumption of the offering of burnt-offerings (holocaust) in Elephantine.
16 See Gard Granerød, "The Former and the Future Temple of YHW in Elephantine: A Traditio-Historical Case Study of Ancient Near Eastern Antiquarianism," *ZAW* 127 (2015): 63–77 (72).

cense and meal-offerings. Moreover, if the recipient of the letter (the satrap himself?) in the end would make a positive statement allowing "the temple of YHW the god of ours" to be rebuilt, then Jedaniah and the other leaders would give—probably as a "fee" or a bribe—considerable amounts of silver and barley to "the house of our lord" (A4.10:12–14).

3.1.4 Milestones in the History of the Temple

The texts leave no doubt about the presence of a temple of YHW in Elephantine in the fifth century BCE. And, as I will show below, this is also confirmed by archaeological excavations. If we follow the testimony of the leaders of the community it is possible to single out some important milestones in the history of the temple.

3.1.4.1 The Origin: Before 525 BCE

The foundation of the temple of YHW dates back to a time before the Persian conquest of Egypt under Cambyses: *wmn ywmy mlk mṣryn ʾbhyn bnw ʾgwrʾ zk byb byrtʾ wkzy knbwzy ʿl lmṣryn ʾgwrʾ zk bnh hškḥh*, "And from the days of the king(s) of Egypt our fathers had built that Temple in Elephantine the fortress and when Cambyses entered Egypt—that Temple, built he found it" (A4.7:13–14).[17]

Moreover, also A4.9:4–5 states that the temple (literally "the altar-house") "was built formerly before Cambyses" (*bnh hwh mn qdmn qdm knbwzy*). This information implies that the *terminus ad quem* of the construction of the temple of YHW in Upper Egypt was 525 BCE. The Egyptian historian Manetho (third century BCE), who divided the succession of the rulers of Egypt into thirty dynasties, regarded the first period of Persian rule of Egypt as the Twenty-Seventh Dynasty (525–402 BCE). Consequently, according to the Judaeans of Elephantine them-

17 Quoted from Porten et al., *The Elephantine Papyri in English*, 143–144. The parallel text in A4.8:12 reads *wmn ywm mlky mṣryn ʾbhyn bnw ʾgwrʾ zk*. The adverbial phrase introduced by the preposition *mn* clearly denotes time. However, one may wonder why the writer did not rather use the preposition *b* like in the phrase *bywmyk*, "in your days" (C1.1:86). In 1986 Porten translated "during the days of," cf. Bezalel Porten and Ada Yardeni, *Textbook of Aramaic Documents from Ancient Egypt: Newly Copied, Edited and Translated into Hebrew and English*, vol. I: Letters. Appendix: Aramaic Letters from the Bible (Jerusalem: The Hebrew University of Jerusalem – Department of the History of the Jewish People, 1986), 71. Lindenberger renders the phrase "back during the time of the Egyptian kings," cf. Lindenberger, *Ancient Aramaic and Hebrew Letters*, 75.

selves, the temple of YHW was built sometimes in the Twenty-Sixth Dynasty (ca. 685 – 525 BCE) at the latest, if not even earlier.

Moreover, the reference to "the day(s) of the king(s) of Egypt" (A4.7:13; A4.8:12) may also reflect a sensibility toward historical and political questions. The Judaeans in Elephantine were obviously aware of the fact that there had been a time when the Egyptians ruled Egypt. According to Manetho's succession of Egyptian dynasties, the Twenty-Sixth Dynasty was a native dynasty, with the Egyptian rulers of Egypt having their residence in Sais in the Nile delta. The rulers of the preceding Twenty-Fifth Dynasty (ca. 760 – 656 BCE) originated from the Nubian kingdom of Kush. In light of the fact that the Judaeans actually distinguished between Egyptian and non-Egyptian kings (the Persian kings being representative of the latter group), it is tempting to assume that they distinguished in the same way between the Egyptian and non-Egyptian kings of earlier times as well. Following this train of thought, the Judaean leaders probably did *not* include the kings of the Twenty-Fifth Nubian Dynasty when they referred to the days of the kings of Egypt.

All things considered, the questions when and why the temple of YHW was built in Elephantine cannot be (fully) answered. The temple's prehistory remains unknown. The only dateable milestone in its history prior to the period of the Achaemenid domination of Egypt is 525 BCE. When Cambyses entered Egypt, the Judaean leaders underscored in their letter to Bagavahya, he found the temple already built (A4.7:13 – 14 par.).

3.1.4.2 The Destruction: Ca. 410 BCE

The sources do not offer any information about any particular historical incidents that took place in the history of the temple after the Persian conquest in the last part of the sixth century BCE. Perhaps it was "business as usual" and therefore not worthy of any further explication. Or perhaps the silence is due to the accidental nature of our available sources. In any case, in their letter to Bagavahya, the Elephantine community leaders informed the Judaean governor that the temple of YHW in Elephantine had been destroyed in the fourteenth regnal year of King Darius (A4.7:10). This information is accompanied by two additional pieces of information. First, it is said that Arshama had "departed (from Egypt) and gone to the king" (A4.7:4 – 5). In other words, the Persian satrap had left his satrapy for one reason or another—probably he was simply visiting Susa in Elam in order to pay homage to the Persian king—and was therefore unaware of the incident that took place in the garrison on Egypt's southern border. Second, the Elephantine leaders told the governor of Judah that the Egyptian priests of Khnum had conspired with Vidranga against the temple of YHW

(A4.7:5–6). Vidranga, whom they called "(the) *frataraka* there" (*prtrk tnh*), had issued an order to his son Naphaina. Naphaina was at that time the commander (*rbḥyl*) of the garrison in the neighbouring Syene. Acting upon this order Naphaina led a contingent consisting of his own and Egyptian troops which, according to the Judaean leaders, entered the temple of YHW "with their weapons ... and destroyed it to the ground" (A4.7:8–9).[18]

3.1.4.3 Still in Ruins: 407 BCE

The letter the Elephantine leaders wrote to Bagavahya the governor of Judah (A4.7 par.) and to Delaiah and Shelemiah sons of Sanballat governor of Samaria (cf. A4.7:29 par.) was dated "20 Marcheshvan, year 17 of King Darius" (A4.7:30 par.). Therefore, the temple of YHW was laying in ruins when they wrote the letter in 407 BCE.

3.1.4.4 Rebuilt around 402 BCE?

The textual sources do not reveal to us exactly what happened after the community leaders of Elephantine wrote to the governors of Judah and Samaria (A4.7; A4.8; A4.9). Nor do they account for the outcome of the negotiations with the unnamed official (the satrap Arshama?; A4.10). We do not possess any report about the possible rebuilding of the temple, a rebuilding that could have taken place sometimes after 407 BCE at the earliest.

However, there is one Aramaic document from Elephantine that seems to suggest that the temple of YHW eventually *was* rebuilt: B3.12. The document in question is a legal document stipulating the details that the parties had agreed upon in connection with the sale of a property. It is dated on the twelfth of the (Egyptian) month of Thoth, in the fourth year of Artaxerxes [II], which equals 13 December 402 BCE (B3.12:1).[19] Although this document was written more than eight years *after* the destruction of the temple of YHW, it nevertheless contains a boundary description referring to "the temple of YHW" (B3.12:18–20). The boundaries of the house in question were routinely described according to its adjacent plots. As for the house in question the document states that the temple of YHW was laying on its western side: *mʿrb šmš lh ʾgwrʾ zy yhw wšwq mlkʾ bynyhn*, "West of it is the temple of YHW and the street of the king is between them"

---

18 The one-sided nature of the account of the Judaeans has been pointed out by Pierre Briant. Cf. Chapter 2, note 32.

19 See Porten et al., *The Elephantine Papyri in English*, 245.

(B3.12:18–19).[20] This tiny piece of information *may* imply one out of two. Either had the temple already been rebuilt (possibly: was being rebuilt) in year 402 BCE, or the statement is merely reflecting a conventional practice for boundary description that continued for many years after the destruction of the temple.

The latter alternative seems unlikely. If the statement reflects a "frozen" practice, the parties of the legal transaction would have been using a no longer existing architectonic structure as a fix point when describing the boundaries of a real property. After all, the very purpose of such a legal document was to describe the boundaries as accurately as possible. Moreover, the statement's distinction between "the street of the king" and "the temple of YHW" suggests that the latter was *not* an empty and barren piece of ground when the document was written in 402 BCE. If we are to believe the report of the Elephantine leaders to Bagavahya, the temple was demolished "to the ground" (A4.7:9 par.). Moreover, originally the temple had gateways of hewn stone that were destroyed and all flammable building materials were burnt down (A4.7:9–12 par.). In light of this, then, the likeliest explanation is that the temple of YHW was again a physical reality in 402 BCE.

This explanation is further supported by the designation given to the couple presented as sellers in the above-mentioned contract. The two sellers are described as "Anani son of Azariah, a servitor of YHW and lady Tapemet his wife, a servitoress of YHW the god (who is) dwelling (in) Elephantine the fortress" (B3.12:1–2). In year 402 Anani and his wife Tapemet still found it appropriate to use the titles "servitor/servitoress" (*lḥn*/*lḥnh*) of YHW.

Furthermore, the epithet given to YHW in the above-mentioned document also suggests that the temple had been (or was being) rebuilt. For, YHW was presented as *yhw ʾlhʾ škn yb brtʾ*, "the god dwelling in Elephantine the fortress" (B3.12:2). The epithet reveals that YHW was believed to be immanent in Elephantine even in 402 BCE. In light of ancient Near Eastern temple concepts, a temple was conceived of as a place where the deity had its dwelling. As, for example, Michael B. Hundley has shown, peoples throughout the entire ancient Near East conceived of their temple as a house of god, conceptually as well as terminologically.[21] Mostly the divine presence materialised itself in divine cult images such as statues and standing stones. The cult images functioned as the terrestrial locus of divine presence.[22] As far as Elephantine is concerned, the

20 Quoted from Porten et al., *The Elephantine Papyri in English*, 248.

21 Michael B. Hundley, *Gods in Dwellings: Temples and Divine Presence in the Ancient Near East*, WAWSup 3 (Atlanta: Society of Biblical Literature, 2013), 7–10, 118, 131–136.

22 Hundley, *Gods in Dwellings*, 139–152, 363–371.

YHW's epithet, "the god dwelling in Elephantine the fortress," would not make sense if a rebuilt temple of YHW was not a reality in the year 402 BCE.

This conclusion is supported by two other legal documents written by the above-mentioned Anani son of Azariah, the servitor of YHW: B3.10 and B3.11. The chronologically earliest one of these two has both a Babylonian and an Egyptian date: "On the 24th of Marcheshvan, that is day 29 of Mesore, year 1 of Artaxerxes the king" (B3.10:1).[23] In other words, already on 25 November[24] 404 BCE Azariah presented himself as a "servitor" (*lḥn*) of YHW. Moreover, in the chronologically later document B3.11, dated 9 March 402 BCE,[25] Azariah used the same title again.

Finally, yet another document *may* perhaps indirectly suggest that the temple was eventually rebuilt: the so-called Collection Account (C3.15) that may be dated to the fifth year of an unnamed king. The account opens with a date and an explanatory note: "On the 3rd of Phamenoth, year 5. This is (= these are) the names of the Jewish garrison who gave silver to YHW the God, each person silver, [2] sh(ekels)" (C3.15:1).[26] As far as the question of the rebuilding of the temple of YHW is concerned, one key question is whose regnal years "year 5" was intended to refer to. Provided that it was Amyrtaeus, the native Egyptian pharaoh of the Twenty-Eighth Dynasty, the account stems from around 400 BCE.[27] The other question is whether or not Judaeans in Elephantine could have collected silver for YHW even if there was *not* an institution like the temple of YHW there. I believe that the answer is no.

3.1.5 The Textual Evidence for the Inventory and the Architecture

It is an irony of fate that the most illuminating description of what the temple of YHW looked like is the description of how it was destroyed. Addressing Bagavahya the governor of Judah, the Elephantine leaders wrote that it was the commander (*rbḥyl*) Nephaina son of Vidranga who in 410 BCE led the platoon that destroyed the temple of YHW (A4.7:8–9 par.). After this information the El-

23 Quoted from Porten et al., *The Elephantine Papyri in English*, 236.

24 Porten et al., *The Elephantine Papyri in English*, 236.

25 Porten et al., *The Elephantine Papyri in English*, 241.

26 Quoted from Bezalel Porten and Ada Yardeni, *Textbook of Aramaic Documents from Ancient Egypt: Newly Copied, Edited and Translated into Hebrew and English*, vol. III: Literature, Accounts, Lists (Jerusalem: The Hebrew University of Jerusalem – Department of the History of the Jewish People, 1993), 228.

27 See 2.6.3.2 above, Positive Arguments.

ephantine leaders continued their report by specifying particular architectonic features and parts of the inventory that were destroyed or looted in connection with the assault (A4.7:9–13 par.). On the basis of the above-mentioned report of the sacrileges it is possible to get a few glimpses of the temple of YHW as it appeared prior to its destruction.

The report makes it clear that the temple had *ʿmwdyʾ zy ʾbnʾ*, "columns/pillars of stone." The number is not specified (there must have been at least two, cf. the plural); in any case the intruders "smashed them" (*ḥbrw hmw*). Moreover, the report reveals that the temple had five "great gateways" (*trʿn rbrbn*) made of hewn stone (*pslḥ zy ʾbn*), structures that the intruders destroyed (*ndšw*). Furthermore, the report contends that the temple structure also contained several wooden parts, all of which were set on fire by the intruders. In each one of the gateways there was a standing door (*dšyhm qymn*) that was attached to the doorpost with bronze hinges (A4.7:10–11). The temple also had a cedar wood roof (A4.8:10 *wmṭll ʾgwrʾ zk klʾ ʿqhn z[y] ʾrz*, "and the roof of that temple, all wood o[f] cedar"). In addition to these wooden building materials, the report also mentions additional parts subsumed under the term *ʾšrn*, a Persian loanword meaning "furniture, equipment."[28]

According to the Elephantine leaders' report, Nephaina and his troops also looted the temple of YHW (*lqḥw wlnpšhwm ʿbdw*, "they took and made their own" A4.7:12–13). Their loot was "anything which was in that temple," though specific mention is made of the "bowls" or "basins" (*mzrqyʾ*) of gold and silver (A4.8:11).

There was also an altar in the temple. The Elephantine leaders reported only a single altar: "the altar of YHW the god" (*mdbḥʾ zy yhw ʾlhʾ*, A4.7:26 par.). Similarly, the memorandum of the joint statement of the governors of Judah and Samaria referred to offerings made "on that altar" (and A4.9:9–10: *ʿl mdbḥʾ zk*). Grammatically, in both cases the noun *mdbḥʾ* is in the singular and emphatic state. Perhaps there was but *one* altar used for all kinds of offerings. The latter seems to be the implication of the memorandum A4.9, which dealt with the rebuilding of the destroyed temple of YHW. Regarding the location of the altar of YHW within the temple precincts, the texts do not give any hints about this. However, when animals were slaughtered and sacrificed in the temple of YHW before

---

28 See Tavernier, *Iranica in the Achaemenid Period*, 418. The noun also occurs in the shipyard jargon evident in another Aramaic document from ancient Egypt, namely the Achaemenid administrative document A6.2. There the word refers to the materials that were required in connection with the repair of a boat. In this administrative document building materials subsumed under the category *ʾšrn* included not only wood but also bronze and iron nails (A6.2:9–17).

the destruction in 410 BCE we must assume that there was sufficient space to allow animals to be tethered and slaughtered in a convenient way.[29]

On the basis of the data I have presented so far, we are not able to reconstruct the floor plan of the temple of YHW in Elephantine. However, in my view an undated ostracon inscription (D7.18, dated to the first quarter of the fifth century BCE[30]) offers a tiny piece of information that allows us to say something more about the floor plan of the temple of YHW. In the inscription, the anonymous writer instructs the likewise anonymous recipient of the message about the former's tunic (*ktwny* "my tunic"). Although the inscription is terse, it nevertheless seems that the writer previously had either intentionally or unintentionally left his tunic *byt byt yhh*, "(in) the house of the house of YHH" (D7.18:2–3). At the time of writing the inscription he wanted the recipient to see to it that one Uriah delivered the tunic to the house of one Shalluah.

As far as the question of the floor plan of the temple of YHW is concerned, the question is what was possibly meant by the expression "the house of the house of YHH." It cannot be ruled out that the entire phrase came about due to a dittography, so that the intention was only to refer to "the house of YHW." However, in light of the short message, and in light of the limited amount of space available on the writing surface, it is—if not unthinkable then at least—less likely. Therefore, the inscription opens up for the possibility that "the house of the house of YHH" represented an architectonic structure that was closely connected to, yet distinct from, the more overall term "the house of YHH/YHW."

If that is the case, then, what could "the house of the house of YHH" refer to? One possibility is that "the house of the house of YHH" referred to an auxiliary building of some kind, for instance a kind of "sacristy" where the priests prepared for the rituals and where they stored vestments (like, e.g., a tunic!) and other essential things used in the cult. However, another possibility is that "the house of the house of YHH" referred to the very temple building—the proper temple—set in the courtyard which was surrounded by walls. In the latter case, the phrase "the temple of YHW" designated the entire temple complex, including the courtyard and its outer walls, whereas the phrase "the house of the house

---

29 Therefore, it is likely that the altar was set up in a courtyard, cf. Hundley, *Gods in Dwellings*, 116. Compare, e.g., also the location of the sacrificial altar in the middle of the courtyard of the Iron Age temple in Arad, cf. Ze'ev Herzog et al., "The Israelite Fortress at Arad," *BASOR* 254 (1984): 1–34 (7).

30 See Bezalel Porten and Ada Yardeni, *Textbook of Aramaic Documents from Ancient Egypt: Newly Copied, Edited and Translated into Hebrew and English*, vol. IV: Ostraca & Assorted Inscriptions (Jerusalem: The Hebrew University of Jerusalem – Department of the History of the Jewish People, 1999), 170, and Lindenberger, *Ancient Aramaic and Hebrew Letters*, 49.

of YHH/YHW" designated a smaller building at the heart of the precincts, the sanctuary. As I will show below in connection with the discussion of the archaeological remains of the temple of YHW, the latter possibility as a matter of fact corresponds with the findings. "The house of the house of YHW" may have been a separate building, the sanctuary itself inside of the courtyard.

3.2 The Temple of YHW and the Archaeology of Elephantine

3.2.1 The Continuity of the Urban Fabric

In the fifth century BCE when the Judaean community was present at Elephantine, there had already been an urban settlement on the southern tip of the island for several millennia and the inhabitation of the island continued for a long time after the fifth century BCE. The first known temple on the island was built around 3200 BCE. It was devoted to the goddess Sati who originally was regarded as the mistress of Elephantine. During the following millennia, the temple of Sati was located on the same spot, even though it was rebuilt several times. Around the time of Sesostris I (1908 – 1875 BCE, in the Twelfth Dynasty), a temple devoted to the god Khnum was built in the more elevated centre of the ancient town. The temple of Khnum was expanded and rebuilt several times, but it was always located on the same spot. The last and massive expansion of the temple of Khnum was started by the first pharaohs of the Thirtieth Dynasty (Nektanebos I, 380 – 362 BCE, and Nektanebos II, 360 – 342 BCE) and was continued by the later Ptolemaic and Roman rulers.

As far as the archaeology of the first and the second rebuilt temple of YHW is concerned, it can be said that the above-described continuity of the building activity is a complicating factor. In the Persian period, the place had been in use for millennia and it continued to be used up until approximately the fourteenth century CE. Another complicating factor is that the temple of the Egyptian god Khnum was considerably expanded in the Ptolemaic and Roman periods. The expansion of the Khnum temple took place at the expense of the chronologically earlier architectonic structures. Yet another complicating factor is that parts of the ancient town have in the meantime slipped away (some places the landslip is as tall as twelve metres high), basically as a result of sebakh digging in later periods (see Fig. 1).[31]

31 W. Honroth et al., "Bericht über die Ausgrabungen auf Elephantine in den Jahren 1906 – 1908. Mit 9 Tafeln und 27 Abbildungen," *ZÄS* 46 (1909): 14 – 61 (14 – 15); Bezalel Porten, "Set-

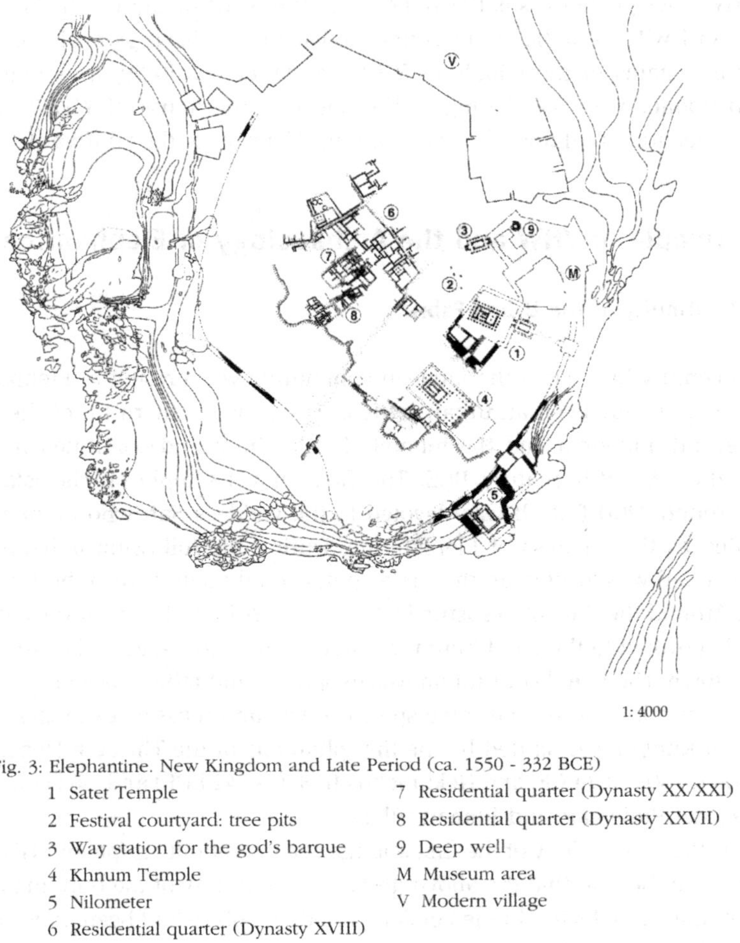
1: 4000
Fig. 3: Elephantine. New Kingdom and Late Period (ca. 1550 - 332 BCE)
1 Satet Temple
2 Festival courtyard: tree pits
3 Way station for the god's barque
4 Khnum Temple
5 Nilometer
6 Residential quarter (Dynasty XVIII)
7 Residential quarter (Dynasty XX/XXI)
8 Residential quarter (Dynasty XXVII)
9 Deep well
M Museum area
V Modern village

Figure 1: Facsimile of plan of the ancient town of Elephantine between ca. 1550 and 332 BCE. From: German Institute of Archaeology (Cairo), *Elephantine: The Ancient Town: Official Guidebook* (Cairo: German Institute of Archaeology, 1998), 15 (Fig. 3). Copyright by the German Institute of Archaeology, Cairo. Reproduced with the kind permission of the copyright owner.

---

tlement of the Jews at Elephantine and the Arameans at Syene," in *Judah and the Judeans in the Neo-Babylonian Period*, ed. Oded Lipschits and Joseph Blenkinsopp (Winona Lake, IN: Eisenbrauns, 2003): 451–470 (453); Cairo German Institute of Archaeology, *Elephantine: The Ancient Town: Official Guidebook* (Cairo: German Institute of Archaeology, Cairo, 1998), 39. Sebakh is decomposed organic material that has accumulated on the top of ruins throughout centuries. Sebakh can be used as both fertiliser and as fuel for fire.

At the beginning of the twentieth century there were French- and German-led archaeological campaigns on the southern tip of the island. Many of the important papyri inscriptions were found at that time, such as, for example, the so-called Jedaniah archive (A4.1–10), named after a leading figure in Judaean society in the last part of the fifth century BCE. However, in retrospect the archaeological methods and the documentation procedures used then have turned out to suffer from deficiencies. In many cases the information about the exact find spot and the stratification was not accurately documented. The excavations that took place more than a hundred years ago have been characterised as "hunt for papyri."

In 1969 the German Archaeological Institute in Cairo in cooperation with colleagues from the Swiss Institute of Architectural and Archaeological Research on Ancient Egypt, Cairo, started annual archaeological campaigns in Elephantine. In the last part of the 1990 s Cornelius von Pilgrim started a systematic search for the temple of YHW. Von Pilgrim actively used the available *textual* sources as well as Porten's reconstruction of the plan of the ancient town. Recently, Angela Rohrmoser has conveniently synthesised the history of the archaeological research in her fine monograph on the Persian period Judaean community in Elephantine and its temple(s) devoted to YHW.[32]

One of the important cornerstones in von Pilgrim's search for the temple was his identification of the so-called "Town of Khnum" (*tmy zy ḥnwm ʾlhʾ*, B3.4:8; B3.5:10). It functions as a fix point in some of the boundary descriptions in the legal documents, for example, B3.4:7–10:

> And behold these are the boundaries of that house which we sold you: above it is the house of Shatibara; below it is *the town/way of Khnum the god [tmy zy ḥnwm ʾlhʾ]* and the *street of the king* is between them; east of it the treasury of the king adjoins it; to the west of it is *the Temple of YHW the God and the street of the king* is between them.[33]

In von Pilgrim's view, the "Town of Khnum" was either the temenos of the Khnum temple or an adjacent and enclosed area that was dedicated to the business activity of the Khnum temple in the Persian period. The other cornerstone in von Pilgrim's search was his identification of "The Street of the King," which

32 See Rohrmoser, *Götter, Tempel und Kult*, 161–185. For the history of research, see also Cornelius von Pilgrim, "'Anyway, We Should Really Dig on Elephantine Some Time': A Short Tour Through the Research History of the Towns along the First Nile Cataract," in *Zwischen den Welten: Grabfunde von Ägyptens Südgrenze = Between Worlds: Finds from Tombs on Egypt's Southern Border*, ed. Ludwig D. Morenz et al. (Rahden, Westphalia: Leidorf, 2011): 85–96.

33 Quoted from Porten et al., *The Elephantine Papyri in English*, 214 (emphasis mine and slightly modified).

similarly functioned as a fix point in the boundary descriptions, with the main thoroughfare in the ancient town and the way that ran along the northwestern side of the "Town of Khnum."

3.2.2 The Second Temple of YHW

Consequently, von Pilgrim could search systematically for the temple of YHW in the area between the "Town of Khnum" (where it was located in the Persian period) and "The Street of the King." In this area, close to the landslides, he made discoveries that stratigraphically could be ascribed to the Persian period. The nature of the findings suggested that they were the remains of a sacral building that could *not* be identified with the Persian period temple of Khnum. Von Pilgrim found remains of a five-metre-wide paved flooring and remains of thick walls (see Fig. 2).[34] The walls were thicker than the walls of the residential houses on the northwestern side. In the eyes of von Pilgrim, the thickness indicated that it was "a building of a special kind" and he interpreted them as the remains of the second temple of YHW, that is, the temple that is not described in the Aramaic documents except for the desire to rebuild it.[35]

Due to the landslides, it is not possible to recover the length of the flooring and the walls. However, the paved flooring was laid upon a fire layer made up of the ashes form burnt grain and wood. Consequently, von Pilgrim interpreted the paved flooring and the walls as the remains of the *second* temple of YHW, namely, the temple that was rebuilt in the last part of the fifth century BCE. The second temple of YHW is not described in the textual sources except for the fact that the Judaeans in 407 BCE wanted to rebuild it on the very same spot on which the first temple of YHW once stood before it was demolished in 410 BCE (cf. A4.7:23–25/A4.8:22–24).

On the northwestern and the southeastern sides of the paved floor there were two carefully built, 1.2 metre (= three bricks) thick walls (= M 419 and M 360[36]). These were probably the outer walls of a building. A third wall (= M 472[37]) at right angles with the outer walls M 419 and M 360 delimited the paved floor on the northeastern side. Moreover, wall M 419 seems to have continued on the northeastern side of the delimiting wall M 472. Therefore, it is possible that further rooms were located on the northeastern (and southwestern) side

---

34 Pilgrim, "Tempel des Jahu und 'Strasse des Königs'," 303–317 (305, 308).

35 Cornelius von Pilgrim, "XII. Der Tempel des Jahwe," *MDAIK* 55 (1999): 142–145 (143).

36 See Rohrmoser, *Götter, Tempel und Kult*, 179.

37 See Rohrmoser, *Götter, Tempel und Kult*, 179–180.

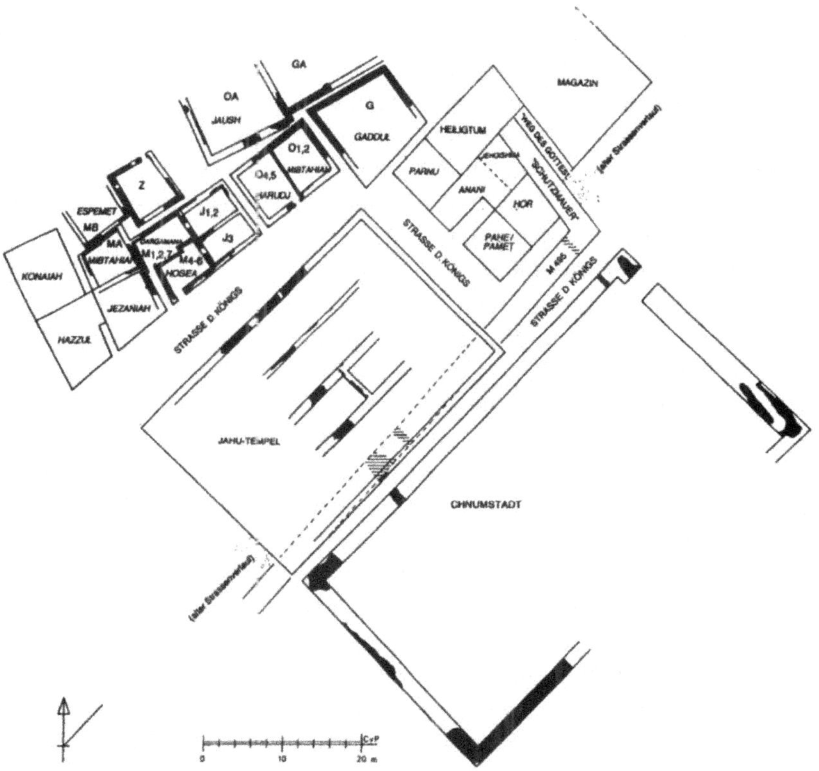

Figure 2: Plan of the second and rebuilt temple of YHW. From: Cornelius von Pilgrim, "Tempel des Jahu und 'Strasse des Königs': ein Konflikt in der späten Perserzeit auf Elephantine," in *Egypt: Temple of the Whole World: Studies in Honour of Jan Assmann = Ägypten: Tempel der gesamten Welt*, ed. Sibylle Meyer, SHR 97 (Leiden: Brill, 2003), 303–317 (308). Copyright by Cornelius von Pilgrim. Reproduced with the kind permission of the copyright owner.

(s) of the paved floor. However, the additional rooms are unrecoverable due to the landslip and the deep foundation pit of the chronologically later Ptolemaic Khnum temple on each sides.[38]

According to von Pilgrim's interpretation, the flooring and the walls were the remains of a temple building that was standing alone in the midst of a courtyard. However, according to Rohrmoser's interpretation it is an open question whether

38 Cornelius von Pilgrim, "VI. Das Aramäische Quartier im Stadtgebiet der 27. Dynastie," *MDAIK* 58 (2002): 192–197 (192).

the room with paved flooring actually was the proper naos of the temple or just an adjacent storeroom.[39] This courtyard was delimited by enclosing walls. One of these enclosing walls was M 355, which was at least fourteen metres long and ran parallel to the outer walls of the assumed temple building (distance between M 355 and M 419: ca. eleven metres).[40] Finally, the courtyard on the western side of the temple building was separated into two distinct zones by an additional wall (= M 491). The separation wall M 491 also parallels the walls enclosing the courtyard and the outer walls of the temple building.[41]

A preliminary conclusion on the basis of von Pilgrim's reports and Rohrmoser's synthesis is that the second temple of YHW consisted of an enclosed courtyard and a separate building. Moreover, a separation wall (M 491) marked off two zones within the courtyard. On the southeastern side of both the enclosing wall M 355 that delimited the temenos from the public street, and the separation wall M 491 that divided the enclosed courtyard into two zones, there was a freestanding building enclosed by outer walls (M 419 and M 360). The building may have had several rooms, and at least one of them had a paved floor. The separate building may have been the proper temple building.

All in all, these structures indicate that the second and *rebuilt* temple of YHW—including its courtyard and the freestanding temple building—as a whole had a *rectangular* structure. The proper temple building ("the house of the house of YHH/YHW") of the second, rebuilt temple—which is not textually but only archaeologically attested—may according to von Pilgrim have been a variant of a direct-axis temple.[42] However, Rohrmoser observes that there is no

39 Rohrmoser argues that the careless paving, which contrasts the carefully made outer walls of the building, supports the suggestion that it was a storeroom, cf. Rohrmoser, *Götter, Tempel und Kult*, 171–172, 179.

40 Rohrmoser, *Götter, Tempel und Kult*, 173, 176–177, 179, and Pilgrim, "XII. Der Tempel des Jahwe," 142–145 (145).

41 Rohrmoser, *Götter, Tempel und Kult*, 173.

42 See Pilgrim, "VI. Das Aramäische Quartier im Stadtgebiet der 27. Dynastie," 192–197 (192): "Bei dem Tempel dürfte es sich damit um ein Gebäude mit langrechteckigem schmalen Grundriß gehandelt haben, der am ehesten dem Typ eines syrischen Langraumtempels bzw. Antentempels entsprochen haben dürfte." See also Hundley, *Gods in Dwellings*, 107–114. However, Rohrmoser, *Götter, Tempel und Kult*, 172, opens up for the possibility that it was a bent-axis temple. For a comparison of several Bronze Age and Iron Age Levant temples from the Levant, see Jens Kamlah, "Temples of the Levant – Comparative Aspects," in *Temple Building and Temple Cult: Architecture and Cultic Paraphernalia of Temples in the Levant (2.–1. Mill. B.C.E.): Proceedings of a Conference on the Occasion of the 50th Anniversary of the Institute of Biblical Archaeology at the University of Tübingen (28–30 May 2010)*, ed. Jens Kamlah and Henrike Michelau, ADPV 41 (Wiesbaden: Harrassowitz, 2012): 507–534, especially pp. 516–520 ("4.2 Architectural Types of Iron Age City Temples").

threshold in the wall that delimits the paved floor on its northeastern side (M 472). Therefore, she prefers the idea that it was a bent-axis temple.[43]

3.2.3 The First Temple of YHW

The archaeological situation regarding the remains of the first temple of YHW contrasts with the textual situation. Whereas the petition to Bagavahya (A4.7/ A4.8) describes the first temple that assumedly was built before Cambyses's conquest of Egypt in 525 BCE, only a few archaeological remains can be ascribed to this first temple (see Fig. 3). One of the remains of the first temple is the northwestern enclosing wall M 355. A second remain is a clay floor (on which the fire layer was found) that is partly framed by a third remain, namely that which must have been one of the outer walls of the freestanding temple building (= M 390).[44] In my opinion, it is possible that it is to this particular building that the ostracon inscription D7.18 refers when it mentions "the house of the house of YHH" (*byt byt yhh*, D7.18:2–3) in which a tunic had been left (cf. discussion above). A possible fourth remain is a southeastern enclosing wall that may stem from the period of the first temple (= M 500).[45]

In contrast to the period of the second temple of YHW, no separation wall has been found in the courtyard of the first temple. In addition, in contrast to the second temple of YHW, the southeastern temenos wall of the first temple was located some one and a half metres further to the southeast in comparison to the corresponding enclosing wall of the second temple. As a result of that, during the period of the first temple there was only a half metre wide passage between the southeastern temenos wall and the northwestern wall of the "Town of Khnum."[46] The proximity between these two walls blocked the old main thoroughfare and caused the main street to make a detour along the northwestern side of the temple of YHW.[47] Finally, during the period of the first temple of YHW, the freestanding temple building seems to have been laying a couple of metres further to the northwest in comparison to its location during the second temple period. During the period of the first temple, when there probably was no

43 See Rohrmoser, *Götter, Tempel und Kult*, 172, 179–180.
44 See Pilgrim, "XII. Der Tempel des Jahwe," 142–145 (145); Rohrmoser, *Götter, Tempel und Kult*, 171.
45 See Rohrmoser, *Götter, Tempel und Kult*, 175.
46 See Rohrmoser, *Götter, Tempel und Kult*, 178.
47 Cf. Chapter 2, note 32.

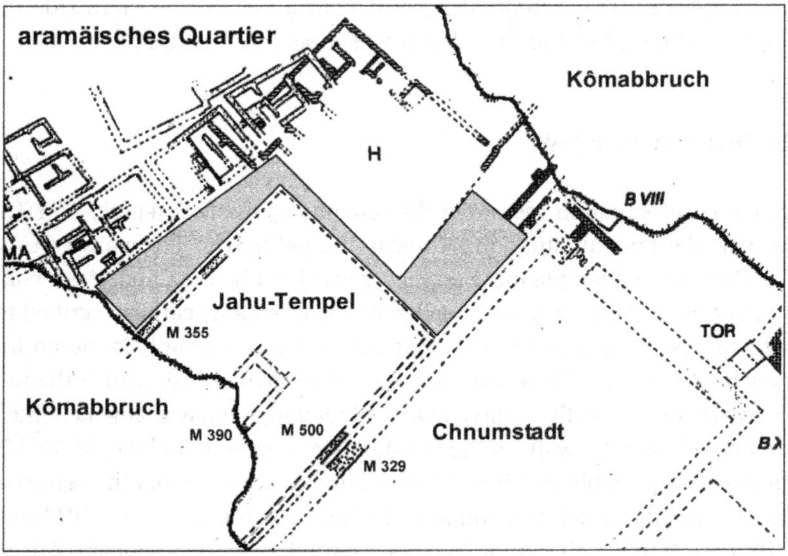

Figure 3: Facsimile of reconstruction of the plan of the first temple of YHW. From: A. Rohrmoser, *Götter, Tempel und Kult der Judäo-Aramäer von Elephantine: Archäologische und schriftliche Zeugnisse aus dem perserzeitlichen Ägypten*, AOAT 396 (Münster: Ugarit-Verlag, 2014), 177 (Fig. 25). Copyright by Ugarit-Verlag. Reproduced with the kind permission of the copyright owner.

separation wall inside of the courtyard, the temple building seems to have been lying in the midst of the courtyard.[48]

3.2.4 Stephen G. Rosenberg's Reconstruction

Building upon the publications of von Pilgrim and the German Archaeological Institute, Stephen G. Rosenberg has also discussed the architecture of the temple of YHW and offered a tentative artistic reconstruction of what apparently is the first phase of the temple.[49] According to Rosenberg's reconstruction the temenos consisted of a separate temple building (the temple itself, the sanctuary) and a courtyard enclosed by outer walls. The temple building itself, which probably stood off-centre within the courtyard, was only six metres wide, Rosenberg indi-

48 See Rohrmoser, *Götter, Tempel und Kult*, 180.
49 Stephen G. Rosenberg, "The Jewish Temple at Elephantine," *NEA* 67, no. 1 (2004): 4–13.

cates. Remnants of a dividing wall inside of the assumed temple building suggest that it had two chambers. Because of the landslip on the southwestern side it is not possible to tell for sure how long the walls surrounding the courtyard were. Rosenberg nevertheless suggests that the courtyard may have been as long as forty metres whereas the temple building was sixteen metres long (see Fig. 4).[50]

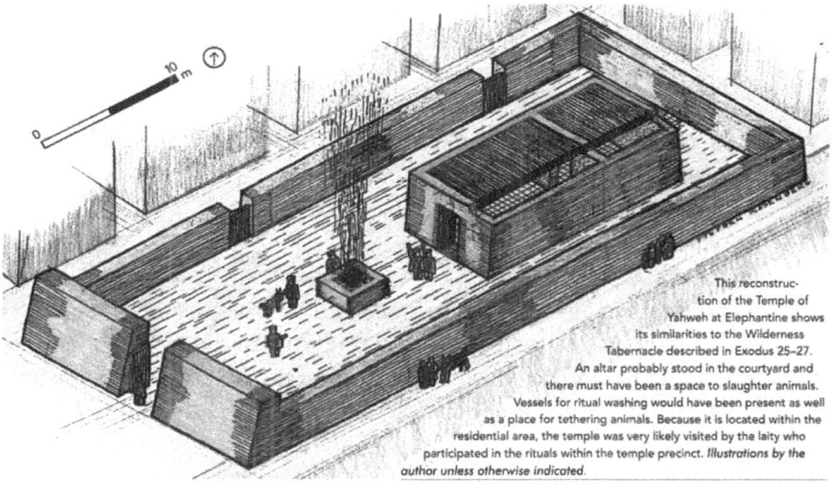
0
10 m
This reconstruction of the Temple of Yahweh at Elephantine shows its similarities to the Wilderness Tabernacle described in Exodus 25–27. An altar probably stood in the courtyard and there must have been a space to slaughter animals. Vessels for ritual washing would have been present as well as a place for tethering animals. Because it is located within the residential area, the temple was very likely visited by the laity who participated in the rituals within the temple precinct. *Illustrations by the author unless otherwise indicated.*

Figure 4: Facsimile of Stephen G. Rosenberg's reconstruction of the (first) temple of YHW. From: Stephen G. Rosenberg, "The Jewish Temple at Elephantine," *NEA* 67.1 (2004): 4–13 (4). Copyright by Stephen G. Rosenberg. Reproduced with the kind permission of the copyright owner.

Neither the written nor the archaeological sources give any hints about the location of the altar. However, Rosenberg has assumed that it was located in the courtyard and that there must have been sufficient space there for vessels for ritual washing and for the tethering and slaughtering of animals.

In contrast to Porten, Rosenberg holds that the temple of YHW in Elephantine was unlike the Solomonic temple as described in 1Kgs 6 and 2Chr 3.[51] Rather, he considers that the relatively small shrine set in an assumed large courtyard bears a closer resemblance to the Tabernacle described in Exod 25–27.

50 Rosenberg, "The Jewish Temple at Elephantine," 4–13 (10).

51 In other words, Rosenberg argues against the implication of Porten's assessment that the measures of the Elephantine temple were reminiscent of that of Solomon's temple, cf. Porten, *Archives from Elephantine*, 110.

The texts mention five great gateways. It is explicitly mentioned that the gateways were built of hewn stone (A4.7:9–10 par.). However, archaeologists have not found traces of any of the gates of the assumed temple of YHW. What the archaeological evidence suggests is that wall constructions were in mud-brick. Rosenberg's artistic reconstruction implies that three of the gateways were part of the wall enclosing the courtyard whereas the remaining two were part of the smaller two-chambered shrine located in the courtyard. This is, as far as I understand, within the bounds of possibility, even though it should be stated that the exact location of the mentioned five gateways remains unknown.

3.3 Aspects of a "Elephantine Temple Theology" in Light of the Material Dimension

3.3.1 A Real Temple?

So far, I have not problematised the use of the word "temple" as the designation of the institution in question. Is the English term fitting in the light of the function it had according to the textual sources? Or does the function of the institution and/or the Aramaic terms used for describing it suggest that other English terms should be used?

On the basis of the textual sources alone, it is clear that there was an area that was cut off from its surroundings and set aside especially for the god YHW. The sources mention five gates of hewn stone, although we cannot say anything about where they were located. Nevertheless, the basic function of any gate is to serve as an entrance to or exit from one spatially demarcated area to another.

Although the sources never explicitly contend that the especially designated area was *holy* (the word *qdš* is missing in the sources), it is nevertheless clear that the spatially demarcated area was not for common use. Rather, it served as the space where the deity *met* his worshippers and vice versa. Moreover, the fact that this especially designated area was well suited as a *meeting place* is evident in the names that were used for the area in question:

- "the house of YHW" (*byt yhw*),
- "the temple of YHW" (*ʾgwrʾ zy yhw*),
- "the altar house" (*byt mdbḥʾ*), and
- perhaps "the place of prostration" (*msgdʾ*).

The name "the house of YHW/YHH (in Elephantine)" (*byt yhw*, cf. A3.3:1; D7.18:2–3 et al.) conveys the notion of a close relationship between YHW and the designated area ("house") in question. Grammatically, the relationship between YHW and the house is expressed by means of a construct chain. A reasonable interpretation of this is that YHW was considered owner of the house. The deity YHW had his own house *in Elephantine* (cf. A3.3:1 *byt yhw byb*) in the same way that the deities Bethel, the Queen of Heaven, Banit and Nabu had their houses *in the neighbouring Syene*, according to some of the so-called Hermopolis papyri (cf. A2.1:1: *byt bt'l wbyt mlkt šmyn*, “the house of Bethel and the house of Malkatshemayin”; A2.1:1: *byt bnt bswn*, “the house of Banit in Syene”; A2.3:1: *byt nbw*, “the house of Nabu”; A2.4:2: *byt bnt bswn*, “the house of Banit in Syene”). As Michael B. Hundley shows, peoples throughout the entire ancient Near East conceived of their temple as a house of god, conceptually as well as terminologically.[52] This was also the case in the Judaean community in Elephantine. In this context, the term *byt* conveyed the notion of being a *dwelling place*. This is supported by a legal document from the end of the fifth century BCE (B3.12, dated 402 BCE). There, YHW was referred to as “YHW the god dwelling (in) Elephantine the fortress” (*yhw 'lh' škn yb brt'*, B3.12:1–2).[53] Consequently, if we borrow a much later (and perhaps anachronistic) rabbinic term, then we may argue that the Judaeans in Elephantine believed the *Shekinah* (“dwelling”) of YHW was in his temple in Elephantine. If this single occurrence is read isolated from the other material, one may get the impression that it confined YHW to but one place of dwelling, his house in Elephantine. However, against such a narrow reading it one must point to other epithets connected to YHW, showing that the deity was thought to transcend the physical building. In a letter to the leaders of the Elephantine Judaean community, fellow Judaean Mauziah referred to “the god of heaven” (*'lh šmy'*, A4.3:2–3, 5). This god, whom the writer of the letter in question apparently thought was protecting him against false accusations, was not explicitly identified. However, in the petition to Bagavahya the governor of Judah, the appellation “the god of heavens” was explicitly identified with YHW (*yhw 'lh šmy'*, A4.7:27–28 par.).[54] So, for the Elephantine community YHW may have been dwelling in his house. However, they also regarded him as a celestial being *not* limited to but one single place.

Moreover, another designation used frequently in different documents was *'gwr' zy yhw*. More interesting than the etymology of the noun *'gwr* is how it ac-

52 Hundley, *Gods in Dwellings*, 7–10, 118, 131–136.

53 Grammatically, the participle *škn* (singular, masculine) refers to YHW, and not the two individuals Azariah and Tapemet mentioned earlier in the clause. In other words, it was primarily YHW who was described as the one living in Elephantine.

54 See also A4.7:15 par. *yhw mr' šmy'*.” For a discussion of the epithet, see Gard Granerød, “‘By the Favour of Ahuramazda I Am King’: On the Promulgation of a Persian Propaganda Text among Babylonians and Judaeans,” *JSJ* 44 (2013): 455–480 (477–478).

tually functioned. It is worthwhile noting that the Judaeans of Elephantine—within one and the same letter—used the noun not only as a designation of the holy place of their own god YHW but also as a common name for all Egyptian holy places. In the petition to Bagavahya, the leaders of the Judaeans in Elephantine also referred to the alleged destruction of all of "the temples of the gods of Egypt" (*ʾgwry ʾlhy mṣryn*) at the time of Cambyses (A4.7:14 par.). In the same letter, the place of worship of YHW was equally referred to by the noun *ʾgwrʾ* ("the temple"). On the basis of the shared terminology, it is evident that they contended that the *ʾgwr* ("temple") of the god of the Judaeans functionally corresponded to the *ʾgwrn* ("temples") of the gods of the Egyptians.

In Imperial Aramaic, the noun *ʾgwr* is to my knowledge only attested in the Aramaic documents from ancient Egypt. Etymologically, the word is mostly understood as a borrowing from Akkadian *ekurru*, which in turn is a borrowing from the Sumerian *e.kur*, "mountain house." In these languages the noun denoted a temple or a shrine. In light of the importance of the Assyrian empire for the promulgation of Aramaic as a lingua franca, we can surmise that the Aramaic word *ʾgwr* carried a similar meaning. In practical usage, a *ʾgwr* was one of the default terms for an area or a building especially designated for a particular deity, or to set it straight, one of the default terms for a temple. Thus, etymologically *ʾgwr* once encompassed a notion of the deity's dwelling.

Two alternative explanations of the etymology and meaning of the phrase *ʾgwrʾ zy yhw* have been proposed by Diether and Mechthild Kellermann.[55] One explanation is that the noun *ʾgwr* is a nominal derivation of the verbal root *ʾgr* with the meaning "to gather, pile up." In Biblical Hebrew the root is attested with this meaning three times (Deut 28:39; Prov 6:8; 10:5). Moreover, according to Kellermann and Kellermann it may also be considered that the Aramaic *ʾgwr* was a borrowing from the Greek ἀγορά. In later rabbinic Aramaic texts, there are examples of the Greek word having been borrowed with the meaning "market-place, court session, court."[56] Kellermann and Kellermann consider it possible that the Egyptian Aramaic borrowed the Greek word with the meaning "place of assembly." The implication of both of these proposals, proposals with quite different etymologies, would be that the phrase *ʾgwrʾ zy yhw* should be rendered "YHW's place of assembly."

---

55 Diether Kellermann and Mechthild Kellermann, "YHW-Tempel und Sabbatsfeier auf Elephantine?," in *Festgabe für Hans-Rudolf Singer zum 65. Geburtstag am 6. April 1990 überreicht von seinen Freunden und Kollegen*, ed. Martin Forstner, FAS 13 (Frankfurt am Main: Peter Lang, 1991): 433–452.

56 See Jastrow 1:12, s.v. *ʾăgôrāʾ* II.

However, in my view none of these proposals are likely. That Akkadian in fact had an impact on the religious terminology of other Semitic languages is also attested in the Biblical Hebrew noun *hêkāl*, which is used to designate the temple of YHWH in Shilo (e.g., 1Sam 1:9), the temple in Jerusalem (e.g., 2Kgs 18:16) or one of the rooms of the temple of Jerusalem (e.g., 1Kgs 6:5). The Hebrew word is originally borrowed from Akkadian *ēkallu*, which again is borrowed from Sumerian *e-gal*, "large house."[57] However, the most important argument against it is that the etymological explanation(s) is not as important as the description of the *function* of the *ʾgwr* of YHW: from the perspective of the Judaeans in Elephantine it *functioned* similarly to the *ʾgwrn* of the gods of Egypt.

As far as the *function* of the *ʾgwr* of YHW is concerned, an additional designation found in the corpus from Egypt is relevant: *byt mdbḥʾ zy ʾlh šmyʾ zy byb*, "the altar-house of the god of heaven in Elephantine." The name of the holy place devoted to YHW in Elephantine is only attested once: A4.9:3–4. Those who used the designation in A4.9:3–4 were not residents of Elephantine but were living in Jerusalem and Samaria, namely the governor of Judah and Delaiah of the Sanballat Dynasty. One of the key subjects of the document in question is what kinds of offerings and sacrifices could and should take place in the future in the rebuilt "altar-house" in Elephantine. It seems clear that all Yahwistic parties involved in the discussion concerning the future of the Yahwistic sanctuary in Elephantine agreed about one thing: even in the future offerings would take place within the area especially designated to the cult of the god YHW.[58]

In short, the area in Elephantine set aside for the god YHW was a *temple* in all meanings of the word:

- it was a place where YHW's immanence was thought to be found so that we may cautiously borrow a much later (and perhaps anachronistic) rabbinic term and say that the Judaeans in Elephantine believed the *Shekinah* ("dwelling") of YHW was in his temple in Elephantine (cf. B3.12:2), and
- it was a place where it was also possible for humans to communicate and interact with YHW by means of sacrifices.

Consequently, in terms of etymology and function it was by no means simply a holy place comparable to a biblical "high place" (*bāmâ*)[59] but a *fully fledged temple* that was *self-contained*. Its existence was connected to the fact that YHW was dwelling and accessible there. Moreover, the importance that the Judaeans in El-

57 See *HALOT* 1:224–245, s.v. *hêkāl*.
58 A separate problem is *what kind* of offerings, cf. also A4.10.
59 So Kellermann and Kellermann, "YHW-Tempel," 433–452 (442).

ephantine conferred to the temple as a place of meeting between the immanent world and the transcendent realms of YHW was further evident in the time of the uttermost crisis for the temple of YHW. When it was destroyed in 410 BCE, it was of such importance for the Judaean community there that it was rebuilt so that they could resume their former religious practice (cf. A4.7–10).

A possibly fourth name referring to the temple of YHW, or parts thereof, is *msgd*ʾ. The noun occurs once in what appears to be a court record of an oath taken or imposed in connection with a litigation over the title to a she-ass (B7.3:3). The gods that were (or were to be) invoked in connection with the oath functioned as heavenly guarantors,[60] probably in the absence of firm evidence. One Menahem son of Shallum swore (or would swear) to one Meshullam son of Nathan. Unfortunately, the name of one of the deities involved is unclear. Porten conjectures that the lacuna in line 3 may be restored *bḥ*[*rm ʾlh*]ʾ *bmsgd*ʾ *wbʿntyhw*, "by Ḥ[*erem*] *the* [*god*] in/by the place of prostration and by AnathYHW."[61] Nevertheless, regardless of whether Porten's reconstruction is correct or not, it is still not clear whether there is any connection between *msgd*ʾ and the temple of YHW at all, and if there is, what the nature of this of connection is. A (weak) link is that the oath had to be taken (also) *bʿntyhw*, "by AnathYHW." In any case, it seems likely that the noun *msgd* is a derivation of the verb *sgd*, "to bow down," so that the derivation means something like "place of prostration." This meagre piece of information opens up for the possibility that the temple of YHW in Elephantine, or at least parts of it, could be referred to as "a place of prostration." This, in turn, may suggest that (parts of) the temple also functioned as a place of prostration, or to use an etymologically related word from contemporary language, as a *mosque*.[62]

60 Bob Becking, "Die Gottheiten der Juden in Elephantine," in *Der eine Gott und die Götter: Polytheismus und Monotheismus im antiken Israel*, ed. Manfred Oeming and Konrad Schmid, ATANT 82 (Zurich: TVZ, 2003): 203–226 (219–220).

61 Bezalel Porten, "Aramaic Papyri and Parchments: A New Look," *BA* 42, no. 2 (1979): 74–104 (102). See also Porten et al., *The Elephantine Papyri in English*, 265 note 6.

62 From an etymological viewpoint, the Aramaic *msgd* and Arabic *masgid* ("mosque") are comparable if not identical nominal derivations. See Arthur Ungnad, *Aramäische Papyrus aus Elephantine: kleine Ausgabe unter Zugrundelegung von Eduard Sachau's Erstausgabe*, HKAO 4 (Leipzig: Hinrichs, 1911), 50, and Kellermann and Kellermann, "YHW-Tempel," 433–452 (445).

3.3.2 "The Pillars of Stone" (*ʿmwdyʾ zy ʾbnʾ*): *maṣṣəbôt* or Entry Pillars?

Regardless of whether we should to follow Rosenberg's reconstruction or not, the question of the function and role of the stone pillars (*ʿmwdyʾ zy ʾbnʾ*) is potentially important. Did the pillars primarily have a religious function, namely, to represent one or several deities? Or alternatively, did they primarily function as entry pillars? In short, two mutually exclusive interpretations are possible.

The first alternative would imply that the Elephantine community used the noun *ʿmwd* to denote what in Biblical Hebrew is referred to by the noun *maṣṣēbâ*, a nominal derivation of the verb *nṣb* "to stand." No surprise that similar nominal derivations (e.g., *nṣb* and *mṣb*) are also found in other Semitic languages.[63] Another term that seems to have been used for the same type of sacred stones—steles with a religious function—is *bytʾl*, which was rendered βαίτυλος (*betyl*) in later Greek inscriptions from Syria and Mesopotamia.[64] In the first century CE Philo of Byblos referred to them as "animated stones" (λίθους ἐμψύχους).[65]

From an archaeological point of view, it is not always clear what was considered to be a *maṣṣēbâ*. Since most potential candidates have no inscription, the interpretation of its original function must be informed by the archaeological context in which they have been found. At times, the potential *maṣṣəbôt* have been found in religious contexts such as temples and shrines. Consequently, a usual interpretation of the many "standing stones" attested in the ancient Near East is that they had a *religious* function.[66] When found in clear cultic contexts they may have been regarded as markers of sacred space where one could contact the god or even as representations of the god.[67]

---

63 See *HALOT* 2:620–621, s.v. *maṣṣēbâ*, and *DNWSI* 2:675–676, s.v. *mṣb*, and op. cit., 676–677, s.v. *mṣbh*.

64 George Athas, *The Tel Dan Inscription: A Reappraisal and a New Interpretation*, JSOTSup 360 (London: JSOT Press, 2003), 310, and Hundley, *Gods in Dwellings*, 347–349, 356–358.

65 Hundley, *Gods in Dwellings*, 357.

66 The Jacob narratives are particularly instructive as to the nature and function of "standing stones" (*maṣṣəbôt*). For instance, in Gen 28:18–22 Jacob explicitly connects the noun *maṣṣēbâ* and the word *bêt ʾēl*. Moreover, see Tryggve N. D. Mettinger, *No Graven Image? Israelite Aniconism in Its Ancient Near Eastern Context*, ConBOT 42 (Lund: Gleerup, 1995), 115–134, 135–197, and Aaron A. Burke, "The Archaeology of Ritual and Religion in Ancient Israel and the Levant, and the Origins of Judaism," in *Oxford Handbook of the Archaeology of Ritual and Religion*, ed. Timothy Insoll (Oxford: Oxford University Press, 2011): 895–907.

67 Hundley, *Gods in Dwellings*, 349.

A good example of a *maṣṣēbâ* with a clearly *religious* function is the carefully shaped stele found in the Iron Age II temple at Arad in Judah.[68] In Arad a *maṣṣēbâ* stood in a cubicle niche.[69] The niche was elevated above the ground level of the broadroom in front of it and accessed by steps. Functionally, the niche was the adyton, corresponding to, for example, "the holy of holies" of the Tabernacle described in Exod 25–27 (cf. Exod 26:33) as well as other comparable sanctuaries of the symmetrical, direct-axis type. Traces of red paint have been found on the Arad stele. In addition, two incense altars stood immediately on the steps in front of it.[70] Tryggve Mettinger holds that the *maṣṣəbôt* in general were part of an aniconic cult type predating the emergence of Israel. In his view, the aniconic cult was a religious feature that Israel shared with its neighbours, at least until the emergence of the Israelite iconoclasm that eventually even led to a veto on the aniconic *maṣṣəbôt.*[71]

As far as Elephantine is concerned, an implication of this line of thought could be that the stone pillars (*ʿmwdyʾ zy ʾbnʾ*) as a matter of fact referred to the same phenomenon, namely an aniconic cult with each one of the standing stones representing a deity. Mettinger, in passing, assumes that YHW was represented by a *maṣṣēbâ* in the temple of YHW in Elephantine.[72] However, one should note that the Elephantine leaders employed the word *ʿmwd* in the plural. Independent upon Mettinger but nevertheless obviously paying attention to the fact that the word occurs in the plural in the Elephantine documents, George Athas speculates whether "the pillars of stone" in the YHW temple were "sacred Bethel-stones representing the five deities" mentioned specifically as revered by the Judaean community in Elephantine.[73]

---

68 Herzog et al., "The Israelite Fortress at Arad," 1–34.

69 Matthias Köckert, "YHWH in the Northern and Southern Kingdom," in *One God – One Cult – One Nation: Archaeological and Biblical Perspectives*, ed. Reinhard Gregor Kratz et al., BZAW 405 (Berlin: de Gruyter, 2010): 357–394 (377–378), who maintains that but one *maṣṣēbâ* was in use. See, however, Amihai Mazar, "Temples of the Middle and Late Bronze Ages and the Iron Age," in *The Architecture of Ancient Israel: From the Prehistoric to the Persian Periods: In Memory of Immanuel (Munya) Dunayevsky*, ed. Immanuel Dunayevsky et al. (Jerusalem: Israel Exploration Society, 1992): 161–187 (186) who reckons with two *maṣṣəbôt.*

70 Dale W. Manor, "Massabah," *ABD* 4: 602, and Mettinger, *No Graven Image?*, 143–149.

71 Mettinger, *No Graven Image?*, 195–196.

72 Mettinger, *No Graven Image?*, 131, 141.

73 Athas, *The Tel Dan Inscription*, 315. According to Athas, the five gods were YHW, Anathbethel, Eshembethel, Ḥerembethel and Bethel.

According to the second alternative interpretation, the stone pillars of the temple of YHW at Elephantine were in fact an architectural structural feature.[74] Pillars (or: columns) were an important part of temple buildings in the ancient Near East in general, including in the geographical, cultural and religious vicinity of the Yahwistic communities in Judah and Israel, which in turn were communities that the Judaeans in Elephantine associated themselves with (cf. A4.7 par. and A4.9). For example, the Iron Age temples of Tell Taʿyinat (in Turkey) and ʿAin Daraʿ (in northwestern Syria) had pillars at the entrance. Regardless of whether or not they had any carrying function,[75] the pillars in these temples definitely had a symbolic function. To the spectator the entry pillars conveyed to the viewer the notion of a limen. When passing the pillars one made a passage into an area separated from the outside, mundane world. This is visible in particular in the case of the ʿAin Daraʿ temple. The ʿAin Daraʿ temple was decorated with oversized footprints (ca. one metre long) impressed into the floor. The direction of movement indicated by the left and right footprints (the last one found at the threshold of the sanctuary) was presumably intended to signify that the deity (whose identity is not known in this particular case) had made his/her presence in the sanctuary. Moreover, the fact that there are no return footprints presumably created the impression that he/she had not left the abode since.[76] Consequently, the pillars signified to the ancient Near Easterners that the temple was a place set off from the outside by its divine presence.[77]

In 1961, Porten in passing proposed an even simpler and more functional interpretation of the stone pillars mentioned in A4.7:9 par. Building on a proposal by Emil Kraeling, Porten considered the possibility that the function of the pillars was to support the cedarwood roofbeams. According to this suggestion, a row of stone pillars crossed the temple building lengthwise and divided the span of the beams in two.[78] However, in light of the recent archaeological inter-

---

74 Rohrmoser, *Götter, Tempel und Kult*, 158, suggests that they formed a kind of colonnade surrounding the sanctuary.

75 According to John Monson, "The New Ain Dara Temple: Closest Solomonic Parallel," *BAR* 26, no. 3 (2000): 20–35, 67 (31–33), the pillars of the temple of ʿAin Daraʿ were probably load-bearing.

76 Hundley, *Gods in Dwellings*, 110–112, 128.

77 Also the temple of Solomon, which is only attested textually, had entry pillars. According to 1Kgs 7, King Solomon ordered that two pillars of bronze should be made (*šənê hāʿammûdîm nəḥōšet*), each eighteen cubits high and twelve cubits in circumference. The two pillars, named Jachin and Boaz, were set up at the vestibule or porch (*ʾûlām*) of the temple (1Kgs 7:15–22).

78 See Bezalel Porten, "The Structure and Orientation of the Jewish Temple at Elephantine—A Revised Plan of the Jewish District," *JAOS* 81 (1961): 38–42 (42 note 12).

pretations of von Pilgrim and Rosenberg, according to which the temple building itself was ca. six metres wide, the proposed interpretation is possible but not necessary. As far as I am concerned, cedarwood beams with a length of six metres would not need any support additional to the walls that carried them.

The question of the interpretation of what "the pillars of stone" (*ʿmwdyʾ zy ʾbnʾ*) referred to— *maṣṣəbôt* or entry pillars—has a bearing on our understanding of the religion of the Elephantine Judaean community. If the phrase *ʿmwdyʾ zy ʾbnʾ* in fact referred to standing stones like the *maṣṣəbôt* of the Bible and the standing stones attested in ancient Near Eastern archaeology, the Judaean community practiced a type of aniconic cult attested in, e.g., Arad.

However, in my view it is not likely that the "pillars of stone" were *maṣṣəbôt*, in the sense of sacred standing stones/religious steles with an aniconic divine representation. I find the second alternative to be likelier, namely that the stone pillars represented an architectural structural feature of the temple of YHW. My argument is connected to the literary micro-context in which the "pillars of stone" in question occur. The Elephantine leaders mentioned them in the context of the *other* architectural structural features that Nephaina and his soldiers destroyed. According to the résumé in the letter to Bagavahya, Nephaina's men destroyed (in order of appearance): the *temple*, the *pillars of stone*, the five great *gateways of stone* and their *doors*, and finally, the *roof of cedarwood* (A4.7:8 – 12 par.). At the end of this list they mention what most modern readers would characterise as cultic, religious artefacts in a narrow sense: the *basins* or *bowls* of silver and gold. Unlike the things just mentioned, the basins were not destroyed but unlawfully taken by Nephaina's men (A4.7:12 – 13).

Exactly what architectural function the mentioned pillars of stone had eludes us. It is, however, by analogy, quite possible that they functioned symbolically, as entry pillars. We may ask: Were they located at the entrances from the public streets to the courtyard the temple of YHW? Or were they perhaps located inside the courtyard at the entrance to the outer chamber of the temple building proper (i.e., what I propose was called "the house of the house of YHW")?

Although "the pillars of stone" in A4.7:9 probably referred to entry pillars and not any cult objects like standing stones, this does not exclude the possibility that there could have been standing stones inside of the temple of YHW, for example, in the inner chamber. It is noteworthy that the petition to Bagavahya does not say anything about its possible destruction (provided that my identification of *ʿmwdyʾ zy ʾbnʾ* is correct). Nor does the petition mention the destruction of any other cult image. Therefore, in the end it appears that the cult of YHW in Elephantine was aniconic because the description of its destruction does not mention any sacred focal point such as a (anthropomorphic or theriomorphic) cult statue or any other cult image or symbol.

3.3.3 Concentric Circles of Sanctity

Any attempt to reconstruct the temple of YHW at Elephantine must primarily be based on a combination of the scant textual sources about its floor plan, and the scant archaeological data. In addition, it is inevitable that any reconstruction will need to be informed by how other temples were built in the ancient Near East. Rosenberg's proposal that the Elephantine temple bore resemblances with the Wilderness Tabernacle described in Exod 25–27 may be correct. However, the general floor plan of the Tabernacle was in accordance with the so-called symmetrical, direct-axis temple type. This temple type was common in the Syro-Palestine area in the second and first millennia BCE.[79] Despite varying forms, the differences between the different attestations of the temple type were superficial.[80] A symmetrical, direct-axis temple was characterised by a series of enclosures or rooms with diminishing sanctity as one moved along the temple axis from the adyton (the immediate locus of divine presence, i.e. "the holy of holies") outwards, or—borrowing M. B. Hundley's terminology—from the "primary space" (the inner sanctuary and the immediate locus of divine presence), via the secondary, third spaces, and so on. In many temples the adyton was elevated above ground level and accessed by steps (compare the above-mentioned temples of Arad, ʿAin Daraʿ and Tell Taʿyinat).

According to a passage in the Elephantine papyri, the Judaeans in Elephantine conceived of YHW as a god *dwelling* (*škn*) in Elephantine (B3.12:2). We can assume that YHW's place of dwelling par excellence was thought to be the inner chamber of the sanctuary, that is, the building situated in the courtyard of both the first and the second, rebuilt temple. As mentioned, the proper temple building, which may have been two-chambered,[81] was perhaps distinguished terminologically from the entire temple of YHW.[82] The ostracon inscription about the tunic that Uriah should deliver to the house of Shalluah (D7.18) mentioned to "the house of the house of YHH" (D7.18:2–3 *byt byt yhh*). As discussed above, we can consider the possibility that "the temple" (*ʾgwrʾ*) or "house" (*byt*) of YHW referred to the entire precinct enclosed by the outer walls. In contrast, the two-chambered building set on the courtyard inside of the precinct may have been called the "the house of the house of YHW." If this was the

79 Hundley, *Gods in Dwellings*, 107–114. See also Kamlah, "Temples of the Levant," 507–534 (514–520).

80 Hundley, *Gods in Dwellings*, 111.

81 However, see Rohrmoser, *Götter, Tempel und Kult*, 184, who opens up for the possibility that it was a bent-axis temple.

82 See Section 3.1.5.

case, the inner chamber of "the house of the house of YHH/YHW" was more holy than the outer chamber, which in turn was more holy than the enclosed courtyard.

3.3.4 "The Five Great Gateways," the Proximity to the Residential Areas and the Possible Participation of the Laity in the Cult

The outer enclosures of the temple of YHW were located next to a residential area on the one side, and the temple of Khnum on the other. The temple was separated from them by public streets only. Needless to say, it was not a remote and isolated sanctuary only accessible to the few who would and could travel to it. On the contrary, the temple was located in the very heart of a densely populated area.

Many of the inhabitants of the neighbouring residential area (the so-called Aramaic quarter) were at the same time members of the Judaean community (cf. the legal documents of real estate). This basic fact suggests that the temple of YHW played a role in the everyday life of the Judaeans.

A tiny detail that Jedaniah and the other leaders give in their written petition to Bagavahya may indicate that the temple of YHW was somehow open to the laity. They informed Bagavahya that the *five great gateways* and the *doors* hinged to them were destroyed in connection with the destruction of the temple.

The number of entrances connected to the temple of YHW opens up for speculations about their location. If we follow Rosenberg's tentative reconstruction, then we may surmise that the two-chambered temple building in the courtyard—that is, the building I propose was called "the house of the house of YHW"—had two gateways. Assumedly, one of the gateways functioned as the entrance to the inner chamber (the adyton), whereas the other one, which *perhaps* was flanked by stone pillars, functioned as the entrance to the outer chamber. The remaining three gateways, then, would be part of the outer wall that separated the courtyard from the public streets.

The exact location of the three remaining gateways of the first temple of YHW are neither textually nor archaeologically attested. However, if Rosenberg's reconstruction should prove to render the overall floor plan correctly, then one of the remaining gateways was along the axis that led to the outer and inner chamber of the very sanctuary ("the house of the house of YHW"). Other ancient Near Eastern direct-axis temples may serve as analogies. When one stood at the threshold of the main entry to the temple precinct, one could potentially see the sanctuary or even the adyton itself.

However, even with three of the five gateways accounted for along the axis of the temple complex, there are still two gateways unaccounted for. According to Rosenberg's conjecture, the remaining two gateways led to the street that separated the walls of the temple courtyard from the residential area.

On the basis of the proximity to the residential area, and probably also on the basis of the conjecture that there were three entrances to the courtyard, Rosenberg surmises that the laity participated in the rituals that took place within the temple precinct.[83] The example he gives as comparison to laity participation in the temple rituals is taken from the Bible, namely the narrative about Hannah's prayer for a son in the temple of YHWH in Shiloah (1Sam 1:12). In my view, the validity of this example is rather dubious, for several reasons. According to the Hebrew Bible, Hannah is said to "have risen" (*wattāqām ḥannâ*) whereas Eli the priest is presented as sitting on his chair beside the doorpost of the temple (*hêkal*) of YHWH, cf. 1Sam 1:9. More illuminating is perhaps the Greek translation, which adds that Hannah rose "and stood (or: presented herself) before the Lord" (κατέστη ἐνώπιον κυρίου). Yet there is a great distance between the Shiloah temple and the Elephantine temple—in many ways. Besides the questions pertaining to the textual criticism of the biblical text, the fact that Hannah is said to be praying to YHWH at an otherwise unidentified location inside or outside of the temple in Shiloah does not contribute much to the question of whether and how the laity participated in the rituals of the temple of YHW in Elephantine.

A better hint at the participation of the laity in the cult of YHW in the temple of YHW in Elephantine is found in the draft letter from the Judaean community there to Bagavahya the governor of Judah. The draft comes in two versions: A4.7 and A4.8. In the letter, the Judaeans of Elephantine promise that meal-offering, incense and burnt offering will be offered in Bagavahya's name if the destroyed temple is rebuilt (A4.7:25–26; A4.8:24–25). However, as far as the grammatical subject of the offering is concerned, there is a difference between these two versions. In the latest draft the verb *qrb* is in the first person plural: "we will offer" (*nqrb*).[84] The question, then, arises: Who was included in the pronoun "we"? The subsequent clause contains a stylistically similar promise, namely that "we shall pray" (*nṣlh*) for Bagavahya at all times if the destroyed temple of YHW is rebuilt. Immediately after this promise there is a clarification as to who are meant by

83 Rosenberg, "The Jewish Temple at Elephantine," 4–13 (4, 12).

84 Note that this is the corrected draft. The first draft originally reads *yhqrbwn*. In the first draft the verb form was secondarily corrected to *yqrbwn*, "they shall offer" (A4.7:25).

"we," namely "we and our wives and our children and the Judaeans, all who are here" (A4.7:26–27; A4.8:25–26).

Did the extended "we" only relate to the prayers for Bagavahya? Or was the performing of the sacrifices also included, so as to say that in principle every member of the Judaean community in Elephantine was entitled to offer sacrifices to YHW? Or did "the priests" (*khny'*) of YHW (cf. A4.7:1 et al.) have an exclusive privilege to offer sacrifices?[85]

When everything is taken into consideration, we simply do not know. Nevertheless, several factors support the general notion of laity participation in the temple of YHW in Elephantine. First, as Rosenberg points out, there was a physical proximity between the residential area where many of the Judaeans were living, and the temple of YHW. Second, the written evidence opens up for it.

3.3.5 (Sacred) Orientation toward Jerusalem?

In 1961 Bezalel Porten published an article in which he reconstructed the plan of the Persian period temple of YHW in Elephantine and its environs. Porten was able to sketch the plan on the basis of the boundary descriptions in the many legal documents from fifth-century BCE Elephantine (contracts, conveyances etc.). He refined suggestions made already in 1953 by Emil G. Kraeling. Kraeling had proposed that the Aramaic relational terms "above" and "below," terms that occur together with "east" and "west" in the legal documents, meant north and south respectively, contrary to the traditional view at that time.[86] As I have already shown above, in some of the legal documents the phrase *'gwr' zy yhw 'lh'* ("the temple of the god YHW") functions as one of several geographic fix points that the boundaries of the land plot in question are described in relation to. Porten's 1961 plan of the temple of YHW was accompanied by an interpretation with far-reaching consequences for the history of Israelite religion. Porten noticed that the temple of YHW was oriented in a direction approximately toward Jerusalem.[87] In Porten's view, the temple of YHW was intentionally oriented to-

85 This seems to be Porten's view, as he explains the first person plural verb form in A4.8 as an attempt to align with the following "we shall pray." See Porten et al., *The Elephantine Papyri in English*, 145 note 81, 149 note 21.

86 Emil Gottlieb Heinrich Kraeling, *The Brooklyn Museum Aramaic Papyri: New Documents of the Fifth Century B.C. from the Jewish Colony at Elephantine*, Publications of the Department of Egyptian Art (New Haven: Yale University Press, 1953), 81.

87 Porten, "The Structure and Orientation," 38–42 (42), cf. Bezalel Porten, "Boundary Descriptions in the Bible and in Conveyances from Egypt and the Judean Desert," in *Dead Sea Scrolls:*

ward Jerusalem. What is more, Porten argued that the orientation toward Jerusalem expressed the relationship of the Judaeans in Elephantine with Jerusalem. The physical orientation of the temple of YHW reflected the Elephantine Judaean community's "sacred orientation."[88]

Already in the 1961 article Porten argued that the temple of YHW in Elephantine was the chronologically earliest archaeological evidence for a sacred orientation toward Jerusalem. In the 1961 article he contended that the earliest *written* evidence for the orientation of prayer toward Jerusalem is Dan 6:11 [ET 6:10]. In a narrative set in the Babylonian diaspora and narrated in a book dating from the middle of the second century BCE,[89] the main character Daniel is said to have defied King Darius's prohibition to pray to anyone other than the Persian king: "[Daniel] continued to go to his house, which had windows in its upper room open towards Jerusalem, and to get down on his knees three times a day to pray to his God and praise him, just as he had done previously" (Dan 6:11 [6:10], NRSV). In later publications Porten developed the theory of the orientation of the temple of YHW. In 1968 he suggested that the building of the (first) temple of YHW in Elephantine may have been done at the time of King Manasseh under the inspiration of the prophecy in Isa 19:19, and in the same book Porten argued that the orientation of the temple was inspired by King Solomon's prayer at the dedication of the temple in Jerusalem (1Kgs 8:12–53).[90] In the prayer Solomon gave expression to the practice of directing one's prayers toward Jerusalem when outside of the land, e.g.:

> If your people go out to battle against their enemy, by whatever way you shall send them, and they pray to the LORD toward the city that you have chosen and the house that I have built for your name, then hear in heaven their prayer and their plea, and maintain their cause. ... if they repent with all their heart and soul in the land of their enemies, who took them captive, and pray to you toward their land, which you gave to their ancestors, the city that you have chosen, and the house that I have built for your name; then hear in heaven your dwelling place their prayer and their plea, maintain their cause ... (1Kgs 8:44–5.48–9 NRSV)

On the basis of the biblical texts quoted above, Porten concluded: "If His [= YHWH's] attention could be called to a momentary need by prayer directed to

---

Fifty Years After Their Discovery: Proceedings of the Jerusalem Congress, July 20–25, 1997, ed. Lawrence H. Schiffman et al. (Jerusalem: Israel Exploration Society in Cooperation with The Shrine of the Book, Israel Museum, 2000): 852–861.

88 Porten, "The Structure and Orientation," 38–42 (42).

89 Porten, "The Structure and Orientation," 38–42 (42).

90 Porten, *Archives from Elephantine*, 119–121, cf. also Porten, "The Structure and Orientation," 38–42 (42 note 15).

the site of His Temple in Jerusalem ..., then His presence could be permanently assured by the erection of a shrine [in Elephantine, G.G.] oriented toward Jerusalem."[91]

To my knowledge, Porten's theory has never really been discussed in the history of research. The only exception I am aware of is an article by Jörg Frey, who subscribes to Porten's interpretation. According to Frey, we can deduce from the physical orientation of the temple of YHW to the "spiritual orientation" of the Judaeans in Elephantine: "[W]e might conclude that this was also the basic spiritual orientation of the Jewish community from the very beginning of its cult, probably before the Persian conquest of Egypt in 525 BCE."[92]

Porten's theory is also reflected in the second, revised edition of *The Elephantine Papyri in English* from 2011 (see Fig. 5).[93]

As I have shown above, in the meantime German and Swiss archaeologists have excavated the area in the ancient town where Porten located the temple of YHW. To a large extent, their results *confirm* the sketch of the plan of the YHW temple that Porten made already in 1961—at that time only on the basis of the boundary descriptions found in the legal documents.

However, is Porten's thesis likely, namely that the temple of YHW was oriented toward Jerusalem and that the orientation reflected the spiritual orientation of the Judaean community? In the following I will argue that the thesis is unlikely for several reasons:

- The biblical texts used by Porten to interpret the Judaean community in Elephantine are alien to the latter and therefore not relevant.
- Moreover, it was the general orientation of the urban fabric of the ancient town of Elephantine—above all the course of the main thoroughfare "The Street of the King"—that was the determining factor for the orientation of the temple of YHW.
- In addition, the temple theology of the Judaeans in Elephantine did not need the temple of YHW to be oriented toward a remote holy place such as Jeru-

91 Porten, *Archives from Elephantine*, 121.

92 Jörg Frey, "Temple and Rival Temple: The Cases of Elephantine, Mt. Gerizim, and Leontopolis," in *Gemeinde ohne Tempel: zur Substituierung und Transformation des Jerusalemer Tempels und seines Kults im Alten Testament, antiken Judentum und frühen Christentum = Community without Temple*, ed. Beate Ego et al., WUNT 118 (Tübingen: Mohr Siebeck, 1999): 171–203 (179, 196).

93 The book reproduces a plan of the temple of YHW and its surroundings, describing it as a "Disposition of houses with [the] Temple of YHW oriented toward Jerusalem," cf. Porten et al., *The Elephantine Papyri in English*, 151.

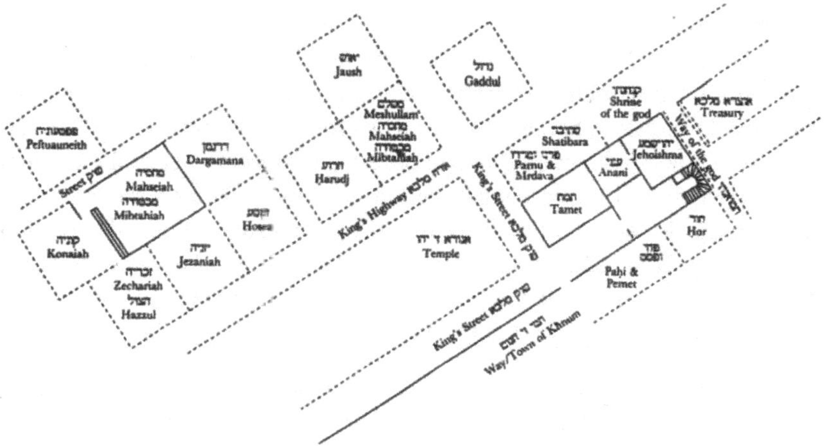

Figure 5: Facsimile of Bezalel Porten's plan of the temple of YHW, with the interpretation that it was oriented toward Jerusalem. From: Bezalel Porten et al. (eds.), *The Elephantine Papyri in English: Three Millennia of Cross-Cultural Continuity and Change*, DMOA 22 (Atlanta: Society of Biblical Literature, 2nd rev. ed., 2011), 151 (Fig. 1). Copyright by Bezalel Porten. Reproduced with the kind permission of the copyright owner.

salem. On the contrary, the Elephantine temple theology seems to speak against any idea of an orientation toward Jerusalem.

3.3.5.1 The Concept of Sacred Direction in Yahwistic Textual Sources

A working definition of a "sacred direction" could be presented as follows: The idea of a sacred direction is present when the following two conditions are fulfilled:

- An individual or a society located in place X is directing his/her/its religious devotions to a (in his/her/its view) holy place located in place Y.
- Geographically, there is a (short or long) distance between place X and place Y.

Understood in this way, the concept of sacred direction is clearly attested in the rabbinic literature from the first millennium CE where the custom of facing Jerusalem (*mizraḥ*) was normative for prayers.[94] At some point in history the con-

94 See, e.g., m. Ber. 4:5. The Talmud (b. Ber. 30a) demands the orientation toward Jerusalem

cept of sacred direction also became normative for synagogue architecture; ideally, the Holy Ark should be placed on the side facing Jerusalem.[95]

Do we find *textual evidence* demonstrating that Judaeans in the Persian period in general were acquainted with the concept of sacred direction? Using this working definition, then a handful of narratives from the Hebrew Bible/Old Testament and the Apocrypha can be said to reflect the concept of sacred direction. These narratives are set in the Persian period or even in earlier periods.

One example is Daniel 6 (mentioned above), a narrative set in the Persian period, and one of the texts also referred to by Porten in his 1961 article. A second example of prayers conducted outside the land but directed toward Jerusalem is found in 1Esd 4, also in a narrative set in the Persian period:

> When the young man went out, he lifted up his face to heaven toward Jerusalem, and praised the King of heaven, saying, "From you comes the victory; from you comes wisdom, and yours is the glory. I am your servant. Blessed are you, who have given me wisdom; I give you thanks, O Lord of our ancestors." (1Esd 4:58–60 NRSV)

A third example probably reflecting a similar concept can be found in Tob 3:11. The narrative in the book of Tobit is set in eighth-century BCE Mesopotamia, after the deportation of Israel by the Assyrians. A fourth example has also already been mentioned because of Porten's use of it in his argumentation: King Solomon's prayer at the dedication of the temple in Jerusalem (1Kgs 8:12–53). Solomon's prayer also gives voice to the concept of sacred direction. Solomon urges YHWH to give ear to the prayers that the Israelites direct toward Jerusalem from outside of the land.

However, there is a general problem connected to the use of these texts as evidence for the existence of a notion of a sacred direction. In all of these cases there are reasons to assume that the time of the narrative is *not* identical with the time of the narrator.

The book of Daniel is usually believed to have been written in the Hellenistic period (as Porten admittedly acknowledges). Moreover, 1Esdras is usually dated to the last century BCE or the first century CE.[96] Furthermore, according to a conservative estimation, Tobit dates to the last part of the Persian period or a little

---

for the Amidah. For further references, see Michael Berenbaum and Fred Skolnik, "Mizraḥ," *EncJud* 14: 392–393.

95 See, e.g., Louis Isaac Rabinowitz et al., "Synagogue," *EncJud* 19: 352–383 (362, 364–366). In his dissertation on the origin of the synagogue, Anders Runesson does not single out the question of the orientation of the synagogues as a separate issue, cf. Anders Runesson, *The Origins of the Synagogue: A Socio-Historical Study*, ConBNT 37 (Lund: Gleerup, 2001).

96 See William R. Goodman, "Esdras, First Book of," *ABD* 2: 609–611 (610).

bit later.[97] However, there are also those who date it to the last part of the third century or the first part of the second century BCE.[98] Finally, King Solomon's prayer is part of the so-called Deuteronomistic History and clearly bears the hallmarks of Deuteronomistic theology (cf. "the city that you have chosen and the house that I have built for your name" and the Deuteronomistic concept of cult centralisation in general). Gary N. Knoppers, who argues for the literary unity of 1Kgs 8, interprets it as a late preexilic Deuteronomistic propaganda text, that is, a text from the sixth century BCE (the Babylonian period). The purpose was to promote the central role of the Jerusalem temple in the everyday life of the king, the land and the people.[99] However, Thomas Römer argues that 1Kgs 8 has been subject to redactional growth. In his view, three Deuteronomistic redactions can be found in the text of Solomon's prayer, ranging from the time of King Josiah to the Persian period. One of them (including vv. 46–56) makes Solomon predict the exile and hint at a cult *without* a temple.[100]

Again, do we find *textual evidence* demonstrating that Judaeans/Jews in the Persian period in general were acquainted with the concept of sacred direction? The answer is a *conditional yes*. The prayer of Solomon at the dedication of the temple *may* indicate that such a concept was actually known within Israelite religion already in the Persian period. However, I must hasten to add that the evidence discussed here stems from the literature of the Deuteronomistic school.[101] Its primary characteristic feature was the centralisation of the legitimate YHWH worship to Jerusalem, in opposition to other cult places of YHWH.

The preliminary conclusion above is at the same time my first objection to Porten's theory about the sacred orientation of the temple of YHW. Porten's theory presupposes a model of Israelite religion that builds upon the great idea of the Deuteronomistic school. For the Deuteronomists Jerusalem was *the* place that YHWH had chosen as dwelling place for his name. For the Deuteronomistic theological school the Jerusalem temple was the very landmark (taken literally as

---

97 See James C. VanderKam, *An Introduction to Early Judaism* (Grand Rapids: Eerdmans, 2001), 70.

98 See Carey A. Moore, "Tobit, Book of," *ABD* 6: 585–594 (591).

99 Gary N. Knoppers, "Prayer and Propaganda: Solomon's Dedication of the Temple and the Deuteronomist's Program," *CBQ* 57 (1995): 229–254.

100 Thomas Römer, "Redaction Criticism: 1 Kings 8 and the Deuteronomists," in *Method Matters: Essays on the Interpretation of the Hebrew Bible in Honor of David L. Petersen*, ed. Joel M. LeMon and Kent Harold Richards, RBS 56 (Atlanta: Society of Biblical Literature, 2009): 63–76. See also John Gray, *I & II Kings: A Commentary*, OTL (London: SCM Press, 1977), 203–204, 228.

101 Yet another expression of this *Deuteronomistic* concept of sacred direction can be found in the book of Jeremiah: "Remember YHWH in a distant land, and let Jerusalem come into your mind" (Jer 51:50b).

well as figuratively) in a legitimate religious practice. However, it is methodologically problematic to let the Deuteronomistic theologians bias or even "brainwash" a presentation of the history of Yahwism. The great ideas of the Deuteronomists should rather be understood as biased presentations in an internal debate among Yahwists. This debate, which may have started already in the Babylonian period and continued in the subsequent Persian and Hellenistic period, was, among other things, about the question of YHWH's transcendence and immanence and about the legitimate centre(s) of worship.

There is nothing in the Aramaic sources from Elephantine suggesting that the Judaeans there were familiar with and adhered to the ideology of the Deuteronomistic school. Therefore, we should not use sources that are alien to the Elephantine Judaean community (such as the biblical texts are) in order to interpret the community.

3.3.5.2 The Longitudinal Orientation of the Temple in the Light of the General Orientation of the Ancient Town

Porten's thesis implies that the axes of the second and first temples of YHW were *intentionally* oriented toward Jerusalem. In my opinion, this is not likely.

One has to keep in mind that the plan of the ancient town of Elephantine was characterised by continuity throughout centuries and even millennia. One of the things that directed this continuity was the main thoroughfare called "The Street of the King." This street went from the harbour bay on the northeastern side of the ancient town toward the centre of the ancient town to the southwest. The archaeology of Elephantine shows that most urban developments in the ancient town took place along this street.

The course of the main thoroughfare, "The Street of the King," was determined by the fact that it had originally been a wadi. In the earliest phases of Elephantine the settlements were on the "isles" on the northwestern and southeastern sides of the wadi.[102] In the second millennium BCE the depression was filled in and was turned into the ancient town's main thoroughfare. The former wadi ended up lying above water level, even when the Nile flooded its banks.[103] The street retained its function as the main street until the Roman period.[104] Moreover, the temples of the indigenous Egyptian deities, above all

---

102 See German Institute of Archaeology, *Elephantine: The Ancient Town*, 10–11.

103 Rohrmoser, *Götter, Tempel und Kult*, 168, cf. German Institute of Archaeology, *Elephantine: The Ancient Town*, 12, 39, 60.

104 See Pilgrim, "Tempel des Jahu und 'Strasse des Königs'," 303–317 (315), and German Institute of Archaeology, *Elephantine: The Ancient Town*, 42, 53–54.

Sati, Khnum and Heqaib (who had originally been a governor of Elephantine), all remained on the same plot, although they were improved and even expanded several times throughout history.[105]

As far as the orientation of the first and the second temple of YHW is concerned, the longitudinal axis of the temenoi and buildings of both phases simply concurs with the longitudinal axis of the former wadi that was filled in and turned into the main street and a processional way for the Egyptians.

True, the axis of the former wadi and subsequent public streets concurs with the direction toward Jerusalem. However, this is a coincidence. Therefore, it is a more likely explanation that the orientation of the temple of YHW was the result of the general orientation of the main street of the ancient town of Elephantine. From an archaeological point of view, the orientation of the temple of YHW is most probably *not* the architectonic expression of the spiritual orientation of the YHW worshippers in Elephantine. The main street constituted the central axis—as a matter of fact the *only* unhindered[106] connection from north to south—along which the developments in the urban fabric of the ancient town of Elephantine took place.[107]

3.3.5.3 Conclusion

Was the temple of YHW in Elephantine intentionally directed toward Jerusalem, and did the orientation convey the notion of a sacred direction among the Judaean community there in the Persian period? In my opinion, the answer to both questions is a negative one.

First, the very idea of a community of YHW(H) worshippers outside of the land of Israel and Judah directing its prayers toward Jerusalem reflects a Deuteronomistic perspective. Admittedly, in the history of Israelite religion there are texts, even biblical ones, that give voice to such a concept. Probably the earliest attestation is found in King Solomon's prayer at the dedication of the (first) temple of YHWH in Jerusalem (1Kgs 8). However, Solomon's prayer is clearly a piece of Deuteronomistic theology and dates to the late so-called preexilic period at the earliest. A religio-historical enquiry should treat the examples of Deuteronomistic Jerusalem-centeredness as biased presentations in an internal debate in

105 See, e.g., Dieter Arnold, *The Encyclopaedia of Ancient Egyptian Architecture*, trans. Sabine H. Gardiner and Helen Strudwick (London: Tauris, 2003), 80–82.

106 Taken as a whole, the possible blocking of the street caused by the southeastern temenos wall of the first temple of YHW was just but a passing episode in the history of the ancient town of Elephantine.

107 See Pilgrim, "Textzeugnis und archäologischer Befund," 485–497 (490–491).

the Persian period among the Israelites about YHWH's transcendence and immanence.

Second, the archaeological excavations have verified one of Porten's findings from 1961, namely that the temple(s) of YHW was/were (a) rectangular structure(s) built between the residential area (the so-called Aramaic quarter) and the "Town of Khnum," and that "The Street of the King" separated the temenos wall of the temple(s) of YHW from the latter. However, as far as I can see, the archaeological excavations do not offer evidence for Porten's *theological interpretation*, namely that the temple was oriented toward Jerusalem on purpose. In my opinion, a much more sound interpretation of the archaeology of the ancient town is that the longitudinal axes of both the first and the second, rebuilt temple of YHW was determined by the general orientation of the main street, "The Street of the King." At the outset, it was the wadi that was gradually filled in and turned into a public thoroughfare that gave it its course.

Third, as I have already in part elaborated upon above, from the perspective of the inner-Elephantine temple theology the temple of YHW was probably understood as independent and "self-contained." Its existence was connected to the belief that YHW was dwelling and accessible there, in *his* "house." Although this aspect of the Elephantine temple theology apparently did not hinder the Judaeans in Elephantine to accept that the god YHW(H) also—simultaneously—was dwelling in Jerusalem, their efforts to rebuild the temple of YHW testify to how important they thought it was to re-establish a house for YHW and thus a place where they could access him through prayers and offerings.

The idea that the orientation of the Elephantine temple reflected a concept of sacred orientation found among the Judaeans of Elephantine in the Persian period is unlikely. Rather, in my opinion it is a projection of later—and biblical—concepts onto the past and onto the form of Yahwism that was practised in Elephantine in the Persian period.

3.3.6 Rival, Succeeding, or Complementary?

In the history of Yahwism, there have been several temples devoted to YHWH. These temples include both real ones that were actually built but also conceptual ones that were never realised, such as the temple described in the book of Ezekiel. Yet, at the same time most religio-historical studies presuppose that at one point, at least from the Persian period onwards, the temple of YHWH in Jerusalem had a privileged status. The relationship between this temple and the *other* temples devoted to YHWH can be understood by means of three words: rival, succeeding and complementary. These other temples were either *rival* temples, *succeeding* temples, or *complementary* temples.

A clear example of a rival temple is mentioned by Josephus: the temple in the Egyptian chora of Heliopolis (*B.J.* 7.420–436; *Ant.* 13.62–73).[108] According to the sources, this temple was set up by a runaway Zadokite priest named Onias. Josephus informs that his aim was "to rival the Jews at Jerusalem" (*B.J.* 7.431). On the basis of the scant evidence it nevertheless seems that the Oniad temple was intended to install a new religious tradition separating itself from Jerusalem. Something similar can perhaps be said about the temple on Mount Gerizim.[109] At least at one point in history this temple was regarded as a rival to the temple in Jerusalem (cf., e.g., Joh 4:20).[110]

Within the context of Yahwism one can find (at least) two examples of succeeding temples. One is the so-called Second temple, built by Zerubbabel after the return from the Babylonian exile and that was conceived to succeed the first temple of YHWH in Jerusalem, namely, King Solomon's temple. Another example is the second, rebuilt temple of YHW in Elephantine. The Judaeans there clearly conceived of this temple as one that should succeed the first one, which was razed to the ground. The second, rebuilt temple of YHW should be built "on its site" in accordance with how it used to be before the first temple of YHW was destroyed.[111]

On the basis of the Aramaic documents from Egypt there is no reason to suggest that the Judaeans in Elephantine regarded their temple of YHW as a rival or a succeeding temple in relation to the temple in Jerusalem. Rather, it is likely that was they regarded the temple of YHW in Elephantine as a *complementary temple*. Its very existence by no means implied that the Judaeans in Elephantine

---

108 See e.g. Frey, "Temple and Rival Temple," 171–203 (186–194).

109 A recent discussion on Mount Gerizim is offered in Jürgen K. Zangenberg, "The Sanctuary on Mount Gerizim: Observations on the Results of 20 Years of Excavation"," in *Temple Building and Temple Cult: Architecture and Cultic Paraphernalia of Temples in the Levant (2.–1. Mill. B.C.E.): Proceedings of a Conference on the Occasion of the 50th Anniversary of the Institute of Biblical Archaeology at the University of Tübingen (28–30 May 2010)*, ed. Jens Kamlah and Henrike Michelau, ADPV 41 (Wiesbaden: Harrassowitz, 2012): 399–418.

110 For a discussion on how the rivalry may have been visible in the later, Hellenistic period, see Magnar Kartveit, "Samaritan Self-Consciousness in the First Half of the Second Century B.C.E. in Light of the Inscriptions from Mount Gerizim and Delos," *JSJ* 45 (2014): 449–470.

111 See Granerød, "The Former and the Future Temple," 63–77 (71–76), and Section 5.3 below. Similar concepts are also found in the New Testament. According to Heb 8:2, the meeting tent and the sanctuary prescribed in the Torah was set up by mortals, whereas the (succeeding) "true tent" by the Lord. On the use of typology as an exegetical tool in Hebrews, see, e.g., Gard Granerød, "Melchizedek in Hebrews 7," *Bib* 90 (2009): 188–202 (191–194).

regarded the Jerusalem temple as an illegal place to worship the god YHW/YHWH. Moreover, conversely, nothing in the documents suggests that the Judaeans in Elephantine ever expected or feared that their fellow Yahwists in Judah and Jerusalem would regard the temple of YHW in Elephantine as a rival or succeeding temple of the Jerusalem temple.

3.4 Chapter Summary

The focus of the chapter is how the religion of the Judaeans on Elephantine reflected itself materially. The chapter builds on the premise that the most important aspect of the material dimension of the Yahwism in Elephantine was the temple of YHW.

The chapter started with a presentation and discussion of the *textual* sources for the temple of YHW organised on the basis of the different types of documents of the so-called Elephantine papyri (the legal documents, the private and the official correspondence). Besides giving us information about the approximate location of the first temple of YHW in the urban fabric of Elephantine, the textual sources also give some key information about the milestones in its history (allegedly built before 525 BCE, destroyed in 410 BCE, attempted rebuild in 407 BCE and probably rebuilt around 402 BCE). Moreover, the textual sources give information about the first temple's inventory and architecture, paradoxically in a description of how it was destroyed. On the basis of the documents it is clear that the temple was a real temple in all meanings of the word.

Moreover, the chapter has also offered a discussion of the *archaeology* of the first and the second, rebuilt temple of YHW. This has been done with a view to the archaeology of the ancient town of Elephantine, which was characterised by continuity in the urban fabric. Building upon above all the archaeological reports of C. von Pilgrim and the recent monograph of A. Rohrmoser an attempt has been made to show how paradoxical the situation is. The second, rebuilt temple of YHW is the archaeologically best attested but textually least attested phase. Vice versa, the textually best described phase (the first temple of YHW) is, archaeologically speaking, less attested.

In a separate section aspects of the theology of the Elephantine temple have been discussed. It has been argued that the temple was perceived as a fully fledged temple where—borrowing a later and potentially anachronistic rabbinic term—YHW's *Shekinah* was thought to be present. Moreover, the location and function of the pillars of stone and the five great gateways have been discussed. In addition, in a separate section the thesis of B. Porten, namely that the physical orientation of the temple of YHW reflected a concept of sacred direction, is critically scrutinised. It has also been argued that the Judaeans in Elephantine did neither conceive of the temple of YHW as a rival nor a successor to the temple of YHWH in Jerusalem. On the contrary, it was regarded as a complementary temple.

4 The Ritual Dimension

If the flour for your bread has been ground, make up a small portion of dough to last until their mother gets there. Let me know when you will be celebrating Passover. Tell me how the baby is doing! (D7.6:6 – 11)[1]

4.1 Rituals: Repeatable, Interpersonal and Purpose-Driven

Any culture and religion is permeated with rituals, in a wide sense of the word. However, most of us do not interpret our own rituals—for instance, why do Westerners shake hands when they meet?—but only those of others. Mostly it is the rituals of others we need to understand, not our own. According to the way I understand the term "(religious) ritual" here, it has at least three characteristic aspects: it is repeatable, interpersonal and purpose-driven.

First, a ritual is *repeatable* in one way or another. For instance, a religious festival celebrating the harvest is typically determined by the cycle of seasons. However, the repeatability of rituals does not limit itself to the cycle of calendars and seasons. A ritual may also be repeatable in terms of being conducted at the same stage in different individuals' life cycles. Rituals of this kind include typical rites of passage such as, for example, the initiation of an infant into the (religious) community. Although rites of passage usually take place only once in a lifetime, they are nevertheless repeated on a community level. Moreover, religious rituals may also be repeatable from one situation to another, more or less similar one. For instance, rituals conducted in connection with (and with the purpose of bringing an end to) extraordinary situations such as drought, starvation and the outbreak of war and epidemics may be repeated each time similar situations are looming.

Second, as a logical consequence of the regularity of a given ritual, it also tends to be *interpersonal*. A ritual "belongs" to a community, regardless of whether it is an individual or a communal ritual. A ritual performed by one individual on some specific occasion can be repeated by another individual on a similar occasion.

Third, a ritual is usually originally *purpose-driven*. Presumably, a ritual is conducted in order to achieve something. For instance, this "something" can be to wake up and get the attention of a particular god so that he/she in turn

1 Quoted from James M. Lindenberger, *Ancient Aramaic and Hebrew Letters*, 2nd ed., WAW 14 (Atlanta: Society of Biblical Literature, 2003), 48 (no. 19).

can solve a particular problem in the life of the petitioner or his community. This "something" can also be to establish a new reality. For instance, in a modern Western wedding ceremony (religious and civil alike) the minister or civil servant pronounces the couple husband and wife. By doing so the status of the couple changes. Another example of a performative ritual is found in Lev 13. There, a person with a potential skin disease shall be brought to a priest. Thereupon the priest shall pronounce the person "clean" (Lev 13:17 *ṭhr* [*piel*]) or "unclean" (Lev 13:3 *ṭm'* [*piel*]), depending on the symptoms. The status of the sick person is totally dependent upon the priest's performative utterance.

However, the purpose of a ritual is quite often (and in particular in ancient Near Eastern sources) *not* given. Not seldom the purpose of the ritual eludes the interpreter. We should even assume that the purpose of an ancient Near Eastern religious ritual eluded the ancient Near Easterners themselves, in a way comparable to how many of the purposes of modern rituals elude Westerners. Why, for instance, do some Christians put their hands together when they pray? When studying the ritual dimension of an ancient Near Eastern religion such as Elephantine Yahwism on the basis of textual sources, the challenge is that, while we do observe in the written evidence hints at, references to and even descriptions of the rituals, unfortunately quite often we are left to figure out ourselves *why* the rites were performed. In written sources, explicit explanations accounting for the raisons d'être of the rituals are rare. What was once common knowledge about the nature and function of the ritual in the society that produced the textual sources is now the subject of scholarly investigation and conjectures.

With these methodological reservations in mind I will approach the question of how Yahwism in Persian-period Elephantine manifested itself in rituals. The following discussion will focus on the sacrificial cult, individual and communal rites such as mourning and prayer, the Festival of Unleavened Bread, the Passover and the Sabbath.

4.2 Sacrifices

When the Persian and Egyptian troops destroyed the temple of YHW in Elephantine "in the month of Tammuz in the fourteenth year of Darius" (A4.7:4 par.), that is in 410 BCE, the destruction resulted in the cessation of the offering of sacrifices to YHW. Jedaniah and the priests of YHW related this when they wrote to Bagavahya the governor of Judah more than three years after their tragedy. In their petition they portrayed the miserable situation connected to the cessation of the offerings as perhaps the main problem: "Moreover, from that (time) until (this) day, year 17 of Darius the king, meal-offering, and ince[n]se and burnt-offering they did not make in that Temple" (A4.7:21–22 par.).[2]

By writing to Bagavahya, the Elephantine leaders obviously hoped to get help to overcome the obstacles that hindered them from rebuilding the temple. It is evident that the Elephantine leaders intended to resume the sacrificial cult in the rebuilt temple. If Bagavahya helped them and the temple eventually was rebuilt, they promised that meal offerings, incense and burnt offerings should be offered "on the altar of YHW the god in your name" (A4.7:25–26). In other words, they wanted everything to return to the way it had been prior to the destruction, just as it was "formerly" (A4.7:25 par.: *qdmyn*).[3]

On the basis of the information provided in the petition to Bagavahya, it seems that three types of sacrifices were normally offered in the temple of YHW:
- meal-offering (*mnḥh*),
- incense (*lbwnh*), and
- burnt offering, "holocaust" (*ʿlwh*).[4]

The Judaeans in Elephantine also used the term *mqlw*, apparently with a meaning more or less identical with the noun *ʿlwh*, "burnt offering" (A4.10:10). They also employed the general term *dbḥn*, "sacrifices" (A4.7:28 par., cf. Clermont-

2 Quoted from Bezalel Porten et al., eds., *The Elephantine Papyri in English: Three Millennia of Cross-Cultural Continuity and Change*, 2nd rev. ed., DMOA 22 (Atlanta: Society of Biblical Literature, 2011), 145.

3 As to the notion of antiquarianism, see Section 5.3.5 below, and Gard Granerød, "The Former and the Future Temple of YHW in Elephantine: A Traditio-Historical Case Study of Ancient Near Eastern Antiquarianism," *ZAW* 127 (2015): 63–77 (73–76).

4 See Angela Rohrmoser, *Götter, Tempel und Kult der Judäo-Aramäer von Elephantine: Archäologische und schriftliche Zeugnisse aus dem perserzeitlichen Ägypten*, AOAT 396 (Münster: Ugarit-Verlag, 2014), 200–209. Moreover, Rohrmoser also points to a bone depository ("Knochendeponie") that was found in 1988 in a basement of a house within the residential area on the northwestern side of the temple of YHW, the so-called "Aramaic quarter," cf. Rohrmoser, *Götter, Tempel und Kult*, 94–97, 209–211. The depository is dated to the Twenty-Fifth or Twenty-Sixth Dynasty, i.e. no later than the sixth century BCE. According to the archaeological report, the nature of the deposit is striking. The deposit included bones of cattle (four calves or young animals), goats, a donkey, and fish, but the donkey and fish bones may have been secondarily put there as waste. The nature of the calf and goat bones suggests that they were cooked. Moreover, the size of the goat and the fact that some of them were without horns may indicate that they were not of the ordinary Egyptian type but imported from Palestine, although these characteristics can also be explained as the result of castration. According to Rohrmoser, the fact that the bones were deposited suggests that they did not stem from a profane slaughtering but from a sacrifice. Moreover, because the depository is located closer to the temple of YHW than the temple of Khnum Rohrmoser opens up for the possibility that the bones can be connected with the cult of the (first) temple of YHW.

Ganneau 17cv4: *dbḥ'*, "the sacrifice"[5]). Moreover, in the available texts the Judaeans in Elephantine use two technical terms for denoting the ritual activity of offering sacrifices. One is *'bd* (*peal* "to make," cf. A4.7:22 par.; A4.10:10). The other is *qrb* (*pael* "to bring near, to offer," cf. A4.7:25).[6] To the above mentioned terminology of sacrifice we may also add the terminology occurring in the so-called Collection Account (C3.15). In this document someone accounted for the silver that the one hundred and twenty-eight named members of the Judaean garrison gave to YHW, "each person 2 sh[ekels]." The term used here to denote the activity is *yhb*, "to give."

It seems that the Judaeans in Elephantine benefitted from their petition to the governors of Judah and Samaria (cf. A4.7:29 par.). According to the memorandum of the joint response of Bagavahya and Delaiah (A4.9), the governors of Judah and Samaria supported the attempts of the Elephantine community to rebuild the temple of YHW and to resume the sacrificial cult of YHW. According to the memorandum, the envoy was authorised to impart to Arshama, the Persian satrap in Egypt, the two governors' approval of the rebuilding.

However, the memorandum of the joint response of Bagavahya and Delaiah refers to only two out of the originally three types of offerings. The Judaeans around Elephantine should "offer" (*qrb*) the meal offering (*mnḥt'*) and the incense (*lbwnt'*) "on that altar" (*'l mdbḥ' zk*), as it used to be done previously. No mention was made of the third type, the burnt offering (*'lwh*).

The lack of any reference to the burnt offering in A4.9 was most likely no mistake. In A4.10, the presumably latest document in the story of the bureaucratic and diplomatic efforts of the Judaean community to rebuild the temple, the Judaeans in Elephantine explicitly refrained from offering animals such as sheep, oxen and goats as burnt offering (this time using the noun *mqlw*). The addressee of the document A4.10 is not stated. However, it must have been an official, and it was probably no other than the satrap Arshama himself. The leading figures of the Judaeans in Elephantine explicitly stated that they intended only to resume the offering of meal offerings (*mnḥh*) and incense (*lbwnh*) in the prospective rebuilt temple of "YHW our god" (A4.10:8 – 10).

---

5 Hélène Lozachmeur, *La collection Clermont-Ganneau: ostraca, épigraphes sur jarre, étiquettes de bois*, 2 vols., MAIBL Nouvelle série 35 (Paris: Boccard, 2006), 189 – 190.

6 This term is also used in Clermont-Ganneau 103cv2: *zy yqrb 'l yh*[*h*], "that he will offer to YH [H]," cf. Lozachmeur, *La collection Clermont-Ganneau*, 259 – 260.

4.2.1 The Agents and Beneficiaries of the Sacrifices

Who performed the sacrifices in the temple of YHW at Elephantine? The written evidence makes it clear that there were religious specialists connected to the temple. However, the texts are at the same time inconsistent as to who actually made the sacrifices. In some cases, a passive verb form is used. In A4.10, assumedly written to Arshama, the Elephantine leaders wrote that animals "will not be made" (*l' ytʿbd*, A4.10:10) as burnt offering. Here, *ytʿbd* is a passive (*ithpeel* or possibly *ithpaal*[7]), probably with *mqlw* "burnt offering" as grammatical subject. The expression does not identify the agent of the sacrificial verb, so we cannot say whether the agent was a religious specialist like a priest or, say, a *pater familias*.

However, the second and improved draft of the letter styled to Bagavahya—namely A4.8—is potentially more illuminating. Here, the verb form *nqrb* is employed, that is, imperfect first person plural "we shall offer" (A4.8:25).[8] The grammatical subject of the offering is therefore the group included in the English pronoun "we." The key question is who the writers of the petition to Bagavahya meant by "we." The letter opening made it clear that the letter was written by Jedaniah and his colleagues the priests who were in the fortress of Elephantine (cf. A4.7:1 par.). Therefore, the priests of YHW and Jedaniah must obviously have been included in "we." However, immediately after the verb *nqrb* there is another verb in imperfect first person plural, too: *wnṣlh*, "and we shall pray for you [i.e. Bagavahya]" (A4.8:25). Particularly important for our purposes is what comes after. For, after the verb *nṣlh* the writers of the petition accounted in detail for who were included in this particular "we": "we, and our wives, and our sons, and all Judaeans who are here" (A4.7:26–27 par.).

The latter clarification suggests that the writers of the petition to Bagavahya—i.e. Jedaniah and his colleagues the priests—reckoned with two types of "we" in connection with cultic activities. One was an "exclusive we" that only represented the writers of the petition. It was the "exclusive we" that performed the sacrifices. However, they also operated with an "inclusive we," to which every male and female Judaean living in Elephantine belonged.

7 Because the text it unvocalised, it is difficult to determine exactly what stem the verb *ytʿbd* is to be assigned, cf., e.g., Takamitsu Muraoka, *An Introduction to Egyptian Aramaic*, LOS III 1 (Münster: Ugarit-Verlag, 2012), §14a.

8 A4.8 is a corrected draft vis-à-vis the first draft A4.7, cf. Porten et al., *The Elephantine Papyri in English*, 147. Originally A4.7 contained the verb form *yhqrbwn*, presumably *haphel* of *qrb*. This form was secondarily corrected to *yqrbwn*, third person plural *pael*, "they shall offer" (A4.7:25).

Why did the Judaeans in Elephantine offer, who benefitted from the offerings in the temple of YHW and how did they benefit? These questions pertain to the question of the nature and function of the sacrifices. To be sure, as is mostly the case with ancient Near Eastern sources this type of question cannot be solved once and for all. No ancient Near Eastern text really discusses the epistemology of sacrifices, even though several manuals and tracts on the *modus operandi* of various kinds of sacrifices are known. As James W. Watts comments with particular reference to the Bible, ritual texts like those in Lev 1–7 and 16, and sermons in Deuteronomy, or votive inscriptions from the ancient world are more likely to describe and commend a ritual than to explain it.[9]

As is also the case in other ancient Near Eastern sources, the written sources for the Judaean community in Upper Egypt do not give a clear-cut answer to the question why offerings were made. The emphasis was more on the ritual practice, not on the ritual interpretation. The Hebrew Bible, the definitely largest corpus of sources for the worship of YHWH, undoubtedly reflects anthropomorphic ideas associated with sacrifices. In some cases, the sacrifices have been referred to as YHWH's food (cf. Lev 3:11; 21:21–22; Num 28:2). Correspondingly, the altar upon which the sacrifices are made has sometimes been called YHWH's table (*šulḥān*, cf. Ezek 41:22; 44:16; Mal 1:7, 12). The smoke of the sacrifices burnt on the altar was understood to be a pleasing odour (*rêaḥ nîḥôaḥ*) before YHWH (Gen 8:21; Lev 1:9 et al.).[10] As far as the Judaeans of Elephantine are concerned, a highly fragmentary papyri seems to articulate explicitly to whom the offerings were made, just in case there was any doubt: they were made "to YHW" (*lyhw*, A4.5:15).

Because YHW was the addressee of the sacrifices, one may surmise that the Judaeans thought that he somehow needed the sacrifices. Having said that, it is obvious that they did not consider YHW to be totally dependent upon the sacrifices they offered to him. For, even during the religious state of emergency that took place after the destruction of the temple of YHW in 410 BCE the Judaeans in Elephantine continued to attempt to influence YHW by methods other than the offering of sacrifices (prayers and rites of mourning, cf. A4.7:15–17 par.). Thus, the Judaeans did not believe that their deity YHW had died or ceased to exist even though the locus of his divine presence was no longer available to them.

---

9 James W. Watts, "The Rhetoric of Sacrifice," in *Ritual and Metaphor: Sacrifice in the Bible*, ed. Christian A. Eberhart, RBS 68 (Atlanta: Society of Biblical Literature, 2011): 3–16 (8).

10 On the burning rite as an essential element of sacrifice, see Christian A. Eberhart, "Sacrifice? Holy Smokes! Reflections on Cult Terminology for Understanding Sacrifice in the Hebrew Bible," in *Ritual and Metaphor: Sacrifice in the Bible*, ed. Christian A. Eberhart, RBS 68 (Atlanta: Society of Biblical Literature, 2011): 3–16.

In other words, the destruction of the temple and the cessation of the sacrificial cult of YHW did not imply that YHW had become totally inaccessible.

It may be that one of the original intentions for offering sacrifices was to provide sustenance for YHW on a regular basis, although there is no evidence for any regular cultic care and feeding.[11] However, the Judaeans in Elephantine nevertheless believed that YHW of Elephantine survived—in spite of the fact that sacrifices were no longer brought to him after YHW's place of dwelling in Elephantine had been destroyed. Therefore, the question why the Judaeans offered to YHW cannot be confined only to the potential needs of the deity. On the contrary, as I will attempt to show below, the sources suggest that the Judaeans in Elephantine offered sacrifices to YHW in order to achieve something—either for their own benefit or for the benefit of the person in whose name the sacrifices were offered. In other words, they did not only offer sacrifices on account of an altruistic concern for the sustenance of their deity but also out of consideration for themselves.

4.2.1.1 Excursus: Sacrifice as Atonement?

A brief note should be made to the fragmentary ostracon inscription Clermont-Ganneau J8 which perhaps contains theologically loaded terminology of sacrifice.[12] Within one and the same inscription we find the words *kpr* ("to atone"?) and *qrb*, albeit without a clear connection and within an inscription characterised by the lack of a clear context. Judging from the swearing in J8cc6 (*ḥy lyhh*) and the other mentions of the name *yhh* (cc9, cv7), the writer was apparently a YHW worshipper. For some reason the writer referred to the day he would die ("the day I will die," *ywm zy ʾmwt*, J8cc8). According to Hélène Lozachmeur's interpretation, the lines immediately after, namely Clermont-Ganneau J8cc9 – 12, read:

> *y/w/k]blky yhh ṣbʾt*
> *kprt stryh*

11 From the Syro-Palestinian region there only a few sources that indirectly attest to such a practice. In the Ugarit literature (which predates the Elephantine documents by seven to eight centuries), the gods could become hungry and thirsty. Moreover, in the Bible there are several references to "the bread of Presence" that was carried into the sanctuary and left in YHWH's presence on a specially dedicated table (e.g., Exod 25:30; Num 4:7), cf. Michael B. Hundley, *Gods in Dwellings: Temples and Divine Presence in the Ancient Near East*, WAWSup 3 (Atlanta: Society of Biblical Literature, 2013), 353 – 354.

12 See Lozachmeur, *La collection Clermont-Ganneau*, 447 – 448 and Plates 322 – 323.

w kprt kl
ʾnth

These lines can be perhaps be translated as the following:

YHH ṢBʾT *has tied* you (fem.) up[13]/*has brought you* (fem.)[14]/and YHH ṢBʾT *has made* you (fem.) *worn out* (= sterile?)[15]
I have forgiven Setariah
and I have forgiven all
women

Moreover, the convex side offers an enigmatic clause where YHH may be the subject. According to Lozachmeur, the lines in question, namely Clermont-Ganneau J8cv7–8, read:

]*kʿn ʿd hʾth lky w/yhh*
] . *qrb*

A possible translation of these two lines may be like the following:

…] Now, until YHH (?) has brought to you (fem.)
…] and he has approached/come near/offered (a sacrifice)[16]

No doubt, the context is far from clear. However, it is tempting to speculate: Did the Judaeans in Elephantine have a concept of atonement associated with some of their sacrifices? Unfortunately, the above ostracon inscription is so fragmentary and confusing that no clear answer can be given, especially with respect to the question of any conceptual connection between the act of forgiving (*kpr*) and any potential sacrifice (cf. *qrb*).

13 Provided that the word is *kbl*, "to tie up," cf. *CAL*, s.v. *kbl* (accessed 21 April 2015).
14 Provided that the word is *ybl*, "to bring," cf. *CAL*, s.v. *ybl* (accessed 21 April 2015).
15 Provided that the word is *wblky*, i.e. the conjunction waw plus a perfect of the verb *bly*, "to be worn out," cf. *CAL*, s.v. *bly* (accessed 21 April 2015).
16 Compare the translation in Lozachmeur, *La collection Clermont-Ganneau*, 447:

] maintenant jusqu'à ce qu'il te (à toi, *fém.*) l'ait apporté, Yahô [
…] il s'est approché / il a offert (en sacrifice) / il a approché / un proche ?

4.2.2 Sacrifices as Measurable and Assessable Commodities

Many aspects of the historical and political situation behind the petition to Bagavahya are obscure. For instance, why did the Judaeans in Elephantine address a petition to the governors of Judah and Samaria, and not directly to the satrap Arshama? Whatever the reasons for this bureaucratic detour were (from Elephantine on Egypt's southernmost border, via Judah and Samaria, and back to Arshama, whose satrapal residence was in Memphis in Egypt), the petition clearly attests to the attempts to influence the governor. The Elephantine community offered Bagavahya spiritual bribes.

The petition contains a report of the things that had taken place in Elephantine in the previous years before it was sent. In the absence of the Persian satrap Arshama, the Persian commander Vidranga had, in cooperation with the Egyptian priests of the god Khnum, attacked the temple of YHW (A4.7:4–12). The time after the demolition of the temple of YHW had been, the Judaeans in Elephantine reported, a time of mourning (A4.7:13–21). Since then, the sacrifices had ceased to be brought to YHW (A4.7:21–22). At this point in the petition Jedaniah and his colleagues, "burghers of Elephantine" (A4.7:22), addressed the governor Bagavahya directly on behalf of the Judaean community:

> If to our lord it is good, take thought of that Temple to (re)build (it) since they do not let us [*lʾ šbqw ln*] (re)build it. Regard your obligees and your friends [*bʿly ṭbtk wrḥmyk*[17]] who are here in Egypt. May a letter from you be sent to them about the Temple of YHW the God to (re)build it in Elephantine the fortress just as it had been built formerly. (A4.7:23–25 par.)[18]

The Elephantine leaders asked for Bagavahya's sympathy and consideration (cf. A4.7:23 par.: *ḥzy*, "see"). However, they also requested concrete action, in the form of a letter of recommendation that should be sent "to them." The Elephantine leaders referred to themselves in the third person plural in the clauses before and after this request. Therefore, the phrase "to them" as the addressees of the letter presumably referred to the very same members of the Elephantine Judaean community. Presumably they would themselves bring the requested letter of recommendation to the appropriate person(s) in Egypt.

In any case, the Judaeans in Elephantine had something to offer the governor of Judah in exchange for the coveted letter of recommendation: prospective

---

17 Probably the Akkadian loanword *bēl ṭābti* with the Aramaic *rḥm* having been added as an explanatory gloss, cf. Muraoka, *An Introduction to Egyptian Aramaic*, 107. Lindenberger, *Ancient Aramaic and Hebrew Letters*, 76: "your loyal clients and friends."

18 Quoted from Porten et al., *The Elephantine Papyri in English*, 145.

sacrifices in Bagavahya's name and the prayers of the entire Elephantine community (A4.7:25–26). In the event that the temple would be eventually rebuilt, the Judaeans in Elephantine would offer[19] meal offerings, incense and burnt offerings on the altar of YHW the god in Bagavahya's name (*bšmk*, "in your name," A4.7:26 par.). Moreover, they would all—the leaders of the community, their wives, their children and all the Judaeans in Elephantine—pray for Bagavahya constantly (*bkl ʿdn*, "at all times," A4.7:26 par.).

The chronological aspect here is relevant. The prospective sacrifices could not be offered in Bagavahya's name as long as the temple of YHW was laying in ruins. Only after it had been rebuilt could the prospective sacrifices be carried out. At the time when the petition was written the temple had been destroyed more than three years before, and the sacrifices brought to YHW there had stopped since. The prospective offer was dependent on a successful rebuilding.

Jedaniah and his colleagues the priests were inferior to the governor of Judah. Despite this, they presented the prospective sacrifices and their constant intercession as an offer he could not refuse. This they did not by threatening him but, on the contrary, by pointing out the incredible value of the prospective sacrifices in Bagavahya' name. Important here is the conditional clause that follows immediately after the spiritual bribe (A4.7:27–28):

> *hn kn ʿbdw ʿd zy ʾgwrʾ zk ytbnh wṣdqh yhwh lk qdm yhw ʾlh šmyʾ mn gbr zy yqrb lh ʿlwh wdbḥn dmn kdmy ksp knkryn 1 lp wʿl zhb*

Our understanding of this passage is complicated by the fact that the second draft (A4.8) differs slightly from the first one (A4.7).[20] Consequently, in the second and presumably most final draft of the petition the prospective sacrifices offered in Bagavahya's name are closely connected with Bagavahya's future actions. Using the text of the first draft A4.7 to restore the lacunas, the corresponding passage in A4.8 can be translated thus:

---

19 The second draft reads *nqrb* (first person plural "we will offer," A4.8:25). The final text of the first draft has *yqrbwn* (third person plural "they will offer," A4.7:25).

20 In the first draft of the letter, the verb is *ʿbdw* (perfect third person plural, cf. A4.7:27). The second draft reads *tʿbd* (imperfect second person singular, cf. A4.8:26). The reading of the first draft is possible per se; in Aramaic the third masculine plural can express an impersonal subject, so that the translation could be "If one does thus," cf. Franz Rosenthal, *A Grammar of Biblical Aramaic*, PLO 5 (Wiesbaden: Harrassowitz, 1983), §181. Moreover, in the second draft the order of the particles *zy ʿd* have been changed to *ʿd zy* (A4.8:26 *hn tʿbd zy ʿd ʾgwrʾ zk*). Here, the particle phrase *zy ʿd* presumably introduces a subordinate clause with a final connotation, cf. Rosenthal, *A Grammar of Biblical Aramaic*, §86, cf. however Muraoka, *An Introduction to Egyptian Aramaic*, §9 h.

> If you do thus, so that that temple will be rebuilt, then[21] it[22] will be a merit [ṣdqh] for you before YHW (the) god of heavens exceeding[23] (i.e. the merit of) a man who offers to him burnt offering and sacrifices (with) a value like the value of one thousand talents of silver, and gold. (A4.8.26–27)

The spiritual bribe is part of a conditional clause. The protasis is marked by the particle *hn*. The apodosis is probably marked by a waw of apodosis. In other words, on the condition that Bagavahya would help out by writing a letter of recommendation, then it would be regarded as a *ṣdqh* for Bagavahya before YHW.

Here Jedaniah and his colleagues the priests of YHW disclose some aspects of their theology of sacrifice. They connected the prospective *ṣdqh*[24] to the temple rebuilding and the resumption of the offering of sacrifices to YHW. Bagavahya's actions in this regard would potentially produce a spiritual surplus. And, what is more, the spiritual surplus could be measured.

As mentioned, nowhere in the sources do we find any epistemological treatment of the Elephantine community's theology of sacrifice. Nevertheless, the petition to Bagavahya gives us a glimpse of the community's operational theology of sacrifice. The community obviously offered sacrifices to YHW with the expectation that he would give something to them in return. In this particular case, however, the community would offer on behalf of someone else than itself, namely on behalf of Bagavahya. This implies a notion that the deity's return favour could be readdressed, from the offering community to their (mundane) benefactor Bagavahya.

In Elephantine as elsewhere in the ancient Near East offering sacrifices was one of the techniques that was available for communicating with and even influencing a god. The petition to Bagavahya (A4.7 par.) suggests that the Elephantine community made offerings in accordance with the principle *do ut des*, "I give so that you [i.e. YHW] give."

Presumably this was not the sole guiding idea associated with sacrifices in the temple of YHW, even though the sources do not tell much. However, absence of evidence is only proof that evidence is absent. By analogy we must expect that the Judaeans in Elephantine also offered sacrifices such as, for example, those of

21 The conjunction *w* functions as a waw of apodosis.

22 The grammatical subject of the verb *yhwh* (imperfect third person masculine singular) is not *ṣdqh* (feminine singular) but Bagavahya's potential actions as such, cf. Muraoka, *An Introduction to Egyptian Aramaic*, 108.

23 The preposition *mn* introduced the phrase that the noun *ṣdqh* is compared with, cf. Muraoka, *An Introduction to Egyptian Aramaic*, §28c.

24 Lindenberger, *Ancient Aramaic and Hebrew Letters*, 76 (no. 34) renders *ṣdqh*, "righteous deed."

thanksgiving, or, to reformulate, that some of their sacrifices were offered in accordance with the principle *do quia dedisti*, "I give because you have given." Provided that sacrifices of thanksgiving were also part of the repertoire, such sacrifices were motivated by various religious traditions involving YHW, traditions that—alas!—elude us in the Elephantine documents. Unfortunately we cannot tell whether YHW was celebrated as the giver of the harvest (i.e. as a god of fertility) or as a god who once brought (political and military) redemption to the forefathers of the Judaeans living at Elephantine.[25]

It appears that the leaders of the Judaean community attempted to bribe Bagavahya. In exchange for assistance to acquire permission to rebuild the temple the Elephantine community promised it would offer sacrifices in Bagavahya's name when the temple was eventually rebuilt. From the perspective of the modern reader, a bribe in the form of sacrifices seems to be somewhat odd. After all, a Westerner may reply, it is hardly possible to change sacrifices offered in one's own name in a distant and remote temple into tangible goods or money.

However, what appears as odd to the modern reader was clearly not odd in the eyes of Jedaniah and his contemporaries. According to the petition, the merit Bagavahya would potentially have before YHW was measurable and assessable. The Elephantine leaders measured Bagavahya's prospective merit by comparing it to a large sacrifice. The prospective merit would exceed the merit a man would achieve if he offered burnt offerings and sacrifices (*ʿlwh wdbḥn*, A4.7:28 par.) to the tune of one thousand talents of silver.

The weight measure "talent" (*knkr*) is only rarely used in the Aramaic documents from Achaemenid Egypt. Therefore, the exact value of one thousand talents of silver eludes us. We can approximate the value by calculating the weight on the basis of data drawn from the Bible. According to Exod 38:25–26 there were three thousand shekels to the talent.[26] Provided that these measures applied to Elephantine also, one thousand talents of silver equalled three million shekels. Moreover, provided that one Elephantine shekel equalled 8.76 grams,[27] one thousand silver talents equalled 26,280 kilograms of silver.[28]

---

25 Compare how the Passover sacrifice is offered as a sacrifice of thanksgiving, commemorating the exodus out of Egypt, in Deut 16.

26 R. B. Y. Scott, "Weights and Measures of the Bible," *BA* 22, no. 2 (1959): 22–40 (32).

27 Lindenberger, *Ancient Aramaic and Hebrew Letters*, 172.

28 However, if the petition to Bagavahya was referring to a Babylonian talent, which equalled 30.25 kg, the value would equal 30,250 kg of silver, cf. A. D. H. Bivar, "Weights and Measures: i. Pre-Islamic Period," *EIr* (2010): online edition, available at http://www.iranicaonline.org/articles/weights-measures-i.

The astronomical figure suggests that Jedaniah and his colleagues exaggerated on purpose. The grandiose amount of silver value was probably intended to function as a signal to Bagavahya that the text should not be taken at face value. The hyperbole was presumably used as a rhetorical device in order to underscore how treasured Bagavahya's help would be.

However, even if used as a rhetorical device, the statement nevertheless reveals a fundamental element of the operational theology of sacrifice in Elephantine: the value of a sacrifice could be measured and assessed. The degree of merit one achieved before YHW when offering to him was a function of the value of the sacrifice one offered to him.[29]

4.2.3 Resumption of Cereal Offerings, Cessation of Burnt Offerings

As I pointed out above, one can observe a change in the sacrificial cult of YHW from A4.7 par., via A4.9 to A4.10. In the petition to Bagavahya the Judaeans of Elephantine explicitly named three types of sacrifices they used to offer to YHW: the meal offering, the incense and the burnt offering (cf. A4.7:21–22, 25–26 par.). However, in their response the governors of Judah and Samaria only mentioned two types (meal offerings and incense), omitting burnt offerings (A4.9). And, as the leading figures of the Judaean community explicitly stated in a document presumably addressed to the satrap Arshama (?), animals such as sheep, oxen and goats would not be made as burnt offering (*mqlw*) in the to-be rebuilt temple, only incense and meal offerings (A4.10:10–11).

The explicit cessation of burnt offerings is only attested in the document the leading figures of the Judaean community in Elephantine wrote to the satrap (A4.10). The memorandum of the joint statement of the governor of Judah and the representatives of the Sanballat Dynasty in Samaria (A4.9) did not explicitly forbid the resumption of burnt offerings. However, it is unlikely that the Judaeans in Elephantine imposed the restrictions upon themselves on their own initiative. Quite the contrary, the origin of the restriction should presumably be sought elsewhere. In the light of the available evidence, the most likely place to look for the origin of the restriction would be in the courts of the governors of Judah and Samaria, who failed to mention burnt offering where we should expect to find it.

Nevertheless, still nothing is said about what reasons the governors of Judah and Samaria may have had for curtailing the sacrificial cult of their "obligees

29 Compare in contrast the poor widow's offering in Mark 12:41–44 par.

and friends" in Egypt (cf. A4.7:23–24 par.). Why did Bagavahya and Delaiah impose restrictions on the sacrifices offered to YHW in Elephantine?

Ingo Kottsieper has outlined three types of explanations put forward in the history of research.[30] All three have in common that the prohibition of burnt offerings in the Elephantine temple was intended to protect someone. The restriction on the sacrificial cult was either imposed in order to safeguard someone's religious feelings or in order to protect someone's religious privileges.

One type of interpretation seeks to ground the explanation for the prohibition in the Jerusalem priesthood. Accordingly, burnt sacrifices were forbidden in the temple of YHW because the Jerusalem priesthood vetoed against it. In turn, the veto of the governors of Judah and Samaria was ultimately a reflex of the development towards a centralisation of the cult of YHWH. Textually, this tendency is reflected in the Bible in Deut 12 and other texts that may be influenced by Deuteronomistic theology.

According to another type of interpretation the continuation of animal sacrifices in the rebuilt temple of YHW was prohibited out of consideration for the Egyptian priests of Khnum. The god Khnum, whose main cultic centres were in Elephantine and Esna further north along the Nile, was usually depicted with the head of a ram. Consequently, the priests of Khnum would presumably have been offended by bloody sacrifices involving sheep.

Finally, the third type of interpretation attempts to anchor the rationale of the ban on further burnt offerings in Achaemenid religion. This type of interpretation is based on two variants. According to the first variant, the Persians allegedly abhorred blood sacrifices. They tolerated them only as long as they had been practiced earlier so that there was a precedent for it. However, the Persians did not permit the initiation of any new bloody sacrificial cults. According to the second variant, the Persians considered fire as sacred. Consequently, dead ani-

---

30 Ingo Kottsieper, "Die Religionspolitik der Achämeniden und die Juden von Elephantine," in *Religion und Religionskontakte im Zeitalter der Achämeniden*, ed. Reinhard Gregor Kratz, VWGT 22 (Gütersloh: Gütersloher Verlagshaus, 2002): 150–178 (169–175), cf. Reinhard Gregor Kratz, "The Second Temple of Jeb and of Jerusalem," in *Judah and the Judeans in the Persian Period*, ed. Oded Lipschits and Manfred Oeming (Winona Lake, IN: Eisenbrauns, 2006): 247–264 (261–262); Reinhard Gregor Kratz, *Historisches und biblisches Israel: Drei Überblicke zum Alten Testament* (Tübingen: Mohr Siebeck, 2013), 192 note 15; Arthur Ernest Cowley, *Aramaic Papyri of the Fifth Century B.C.* (Oxford: Oxford University Press, 1923), 126; Heidemarie Koch, "Iranische Religion im achaimenidischen Zeitalter," in *Religion und Religionskontakte im Zeitalter der Achämeniden*, ed. Reinhard Gregor Kratz, VWGT 22 (Gütersloh: Gütersloher Verlagshaus, 2002): 11–26 (14); and Hélène Nutkowicz, "Eléphantine, ultime tragédie," *Transeu* 40 (2011): 185–198 (197). Moreover, as to various hypotheses that scholars have suggested to explain the veto on burnt offerings, see also Rohrmoser, *Götter, Tempel und Kult*, 214–218.

mal bodies would defile fire and was thus an offence against Zoroastrian teaching.

4.2.3.1 A Veto Out of Consideration for Persian Theological Concepts?

In my view, the third type of explanation is improbable, if for no other reason than because it builds upon multiple unverifiable factors. As far as the theory of a possible Persian abhorrence of blood sacrifices is concerned, this theory presupposes that the Achaemenids in fact were Zoroastrians. However, there is no consensus among scholars over the question how, and if so, in what way, Zarathustrianism/Zoroastrianism influenced the Achaemenid kings.[31] Moreover, although Iranologists argue that there are many grammatical features in the Gathas of the Old Avesta that hint at a date of composition in the first millennium BCE,[32] the presumably oral composition was first written down around the middle of the first millennium CE at the earliest.[33] Therefore, as far as I can see it is problematic from a methodological point of view to retroject the Avestan texts of Zoroastrianism back into the Achaemenid period or even earlier. In addition, recent studies suggest that cults officially supported by the Achaemenids in fact could involve animal sacrifices.[34]

4.2.3.2 A Veto out of Consideration for the Priests of Khnum?

As far as the possible concern for the Egyptian priests of the (ram-headed) god Khnum is concerned, then why would the priests of Khnum have been offended if animals other than rams were sacrificed as burnt offerings? In the letter to Ar-

---

31 William W. Malandra, "Zoroastrianism i. Historical Review up to the Arab Conquest," *EIr* (2005): online edition, available at http://www.iranicaonline.org/articles/zoroastrianism-i-historical-review, and Wouter F. M. Henkelman, "Animal Sacrifice and 'External' Exchange in the Persepolis Fortification Tablets," in *Approaching the Babylonian Economy: Proceedings of the start Project Symposium Held in Vienna, 1–3 July 2004*, ed. H. D. Baker and M. Jursa, AOAT 330 (Münster: Ugarit-Verlag, 2005): 137–165 (141–143).

32 Prods Oktor Skjærvø, *The Spirit of Zoroastrianism* (New Haven: Yale University Press, 2011), 2–3.

33 Malandra, "Zoroastrianism i. Historical Review up to the Arab Conquest," online edition, available at http://www.iranicaonline.org/articles/zoroastrianism-i-historical-review, and Prods Oktor Skjærvø, *Zarathustras sanger: de eldste iranske skriftene*, Verdens hellige skrifter 22 (Oslo: De norske bokklubbene, 2003), xxxv–xxxvi.

34 Wouter F. M. Henkelman, *The Other Gods Who Are: Studies in Elamite-Iranian Acculturation Based on the Persepolis Fortification Texts*, AH 14 (Leiden: Nederlands Instituut voor het Nabije Oosten, 2008), vi, and Henkelman, "Animal Sacrifice," 137–165 (142–145).

shama, the leading figures of the Judaean community of Elephantine also include oxen among the animals that would not be offered as burnt offerings (A4.10:10). Why should the possible reverence of the priests of Khnum for the ram have affected all kinds of animal sacrifices?

Also the priests of Khnum brought forth burnt offerings. A letter written in Demotic in 493 BCE, that is some eighty-five years before the letter from the Judaeans of Elephantine to Bagavahya, may shed light on the question of why restrictions were imposed upon the sacrificial cult of YHW in Elephantine.[35] The letter was written by the *wab*-priests of Khnum, that is, a group of second-tier priests, to the Persian satrap Pherendates. The topic of the letter is about the appointment of a new *lesonis*, the chief priest who administered and organised the temple service. The *wab*-priests informed Pherendates that they had appointed a new *lesonis*. The letter gives the job description for a *lesonis:* "He will cause to be carried (and) he will cause burnt-offering to be made before Khnum."[36]

The letter from the *wab*-priests of Khnum suggests that it was the prerogative of a *lesonis* to administer the sacrifice of burnt offerings in the temple of Khnum. Admittedly, the burnt offering mentioned in this letter was sacrificed to Khnum, definitely not YHW. However, it is tempting to speculate whether one of the reasons for the ban on animal offerings in the temple of YHW could be sought here. The Achaemenid authorities—represented by the governors of Judah and Samaria and the satrap Arshama alike—may have been reluctant to approve any sacrificial rite (i. e. animal sacrifices) that the indigenous Egyptian priests of Khnum historically had the privilege to perform.

4.2.3.3 A Veto out of Consideration for the Privileges of the Jerusalem Temple?

Did the veto of Bagavahya and Delaiah (A4.9; A4.10) reflect the aspirations of the Jerusalem priesthood that their temple should be the only legal cultic centre of YHWH? Beguiling as it seems at first sight to explain the ban upon burnt offerings in A4.10 (and the lack of reference in A4.9) as the practical realisation of Deut 12 and its laws on the centralisation of the cult of YHWH to his "chosen place," this explanation is not without difficulties. To be sure, there are good reasons to assume that the composition of Deuteronomy (or at least the so-called

---

35 Papyrus Berlin 13539. Annotated translations are offered in Amélie Kuhrt, *The Persian Empire: A Corpus of Sources from the Achaemenid Period* (London: Routledge, 2007), 852–853 (no. 17.30), and Porten et al., *The Elephantine Papyri in English*, 289–290 (translated by Cary J. Martin).

36 Quoted from Porten et al., *The Elephantine Papyri in English*, 289.

Deuteronomic Code in Deut 12–26) predates the documents from the Elephantine community by several centuries. Biblical scholars assume that it was a reality when King Josiah reigned over Judah in the last half of the seventh century BCE, and some even argue for an origin in the Northern Kingdom, which fell at the hands of the Assyrians in 722 BCE.[37] Therefore, in terms of chronology the explanation is possible per se.

However, for one Deut 12 itself does not specify YHWH's chosen place, although texts influenced by Deuteronomistic theology and reflecting a Judaean perspective no doubt equated it with Jerusalem.[38] Moreover, this explanation presupposes that the Deuteronomic Code was in use not only in the priestly milieu of Jerusalem but also in the (Achaemenid) administration of both Judah and Samaria. In other words, the explanation presupposes that the Deuteronomic Code was applied and used in the civic societies of Judah and Samaria, and in the last resort, of Elephantine.

One of the greatest challenges affiliated with this model is how one should explain the involvement of Delaiah son of Sanballat, the governor of Samaria (cf. A4.9:1). Is it likely that a member of the Sanballat Dynasty sanctioned a veto that ultimately protected the privileges of Jerusalem?

When attempting to answer this question it is easy to fall into the trap of being biased by the presentation of Samaria in the biblical books of Ezra and Nehemiah. Delaiah's involvement attested by the memorandum A4.9 suggests that there was no schism between Jerusalem and Samaria at the end of the fifth century BCE. The memorandum gives the impression that there was a non-hostile relationship between the governors of Judah and Samaria respectively in the last decade of the fifth century BCE. This complies with the results of Magnar Kartveit's investigation of the origins of the Samaritans. According to Kartveit, the moment of birth of the Samaritans as a distinguished group coincided with the construction of the temple on Mount Gerizim. In contrast to the account of Josephus, who relates that the Mount Gerizim temple was founded at the time of Alexander the Great at the beginning of the Hellenistic period,[39] Kartveit cautiously dates the beginning of the temple-building project back to the first part of the fourth century BCE (the last part of the Persian period).[40]

---

37 See, e.g., Jeffrey H. Tigay, *Deuteronomy* (Philadelphia: Jewish Publication Society, 1996), xix–xxiv.

38 For instance 1Kgs 11:36.

39 Josephus, *Ant.* 11.302–347, in particular 11.324–325.

40 Magnar Kartveit, *The Origin of the Samaritans*, VTSup 128 (Leiden: Brill, 2009), 351–362, cf. also Jörg Frey, "Temple and Rival Temple: The Cases of Elephantine, Mt. Gerizim, and Leontopolis," in *Gemeinde ohne Tempel: zur Substituierung und Transformation des Jerusalemer Tem-*

The non-hostile relationship between Bagavahya and Sanballat's son Delaiah evident in their joint statement (A4.9) stands in sharp contrast with the presentation of Sanballat the Horonite in the Bible. The books of Ezra and Nehemiah present Sanballat as one of Jerusalem's chief enemies (Neh 2:10, 19; Ezra 4; 6). Presumably, the Sanballat mentioned in Nehemiah and Ezra referred to one of the Achaemenid governors of Samaria, this name known from epigraphic inscriptions such as the Elephantine documents (cf. A4.7:29 par.; A4.9:1) and the Wadi ed-Daliyeh papyri. The Wadi ed-Daliyeh papyri attest to the phenomenon of papponomy: within the Sanballat Dynasty the name Sanballat was used three times over a period of five generations.[41] In the light of "the facts on the ground," that is, the apparently non-hostile relationship between Judah and Samaria reflected in the Elephantine documents, we should subscribe to Kartveit's notion that the books of Ezra and Nehemiah probably belong "to the period following the amicable relations between Jerusalem and Samaria."[42]

In other words, the books of Ezra and Nehemiah should not automatically hinder us from imagining that even a governor of Samaria could make a decision that in the last resort promoted the interests of the temple of YHWH in Jerusalem and its priesthood. However, whether Bagavahya and Delaiah themselves had any knowledge of Deut 12, and if so, whether this part of the so-called Deuteronomic Code was part of their preparatory proceedings before they announced publicly their joint statement, eludes the modern religious historian.

4.2.3.4 Suggestion: A Veto out of Consideration for the Satrap Arshama

Summing up the explanations for the ban against burnt offerings mentioned above, we cannot know exactly what reasons Bagavahya and Delaiah had for being involved in a veto on burnt offerings in the temple of YHW in Elephantine. Nevertheless, their statement (A4.9) and the statement of the Judaeans in Ele-

---

pels und seines Kults im Alten Testament, antiken Judentum und frühen Christentum = Community without Temple, ed. Beate Ego, et al., WUNT 118 (Tübingen: Mohr Siebeck, 1999): 171–203 (184). Yitzhak Magen, however, dates the foundation of the temple on Mount Gerizim even earlier, i.e. to around 450 BCE, cf. Jürgen K. Zangenberg, "The Sanctuary on Mount Gerizim: Observations on the Results of 20 Years of Excavation," in *Temple Building and Temple Cult: Architecture and Cultic Paraphernalia of Temples in the Levant (2.–1. Mill. B.C.E.): Proceedings of a Conference on the Occasion of the 50th Anniversary of the Institute of Biblical Archaeology at the University of Tübingen (28–30 May 2010)*, ed. Jens Kamlah and Henrike Michelau, ADPV 41 (Wiesbaden: Harrassowitz, 2012): 399–418 (404–409).

41 Frank Moore Cross, "The Discovery of the Samaria Papyri," *BA* 26, no. 4 (1963): 110–121 (121).

42 Kartveit, *The Origin of the Samaritans*, 351–362.

phantine (A4.10) appear to tally with the interests of the Jerusalem priesthood to centralise the cult of YHW to Jerusalem. Whatever the reason they had, it is conceivable that the earliest epigraphic source reflecting the centralisation of the YHWH cult to Jerusalem is in fact the memorandum A4.9 from the last decade of the fifth century BCE.

However, even if the claim made by the Jerusalem temple to be the sole focal point of the worship of YHWH should happen to be part of the explanation, the decision of the governors of Judah and Samaria may at one and the same time also have been guided by other considerations.

Even though Bagavahya and Delaiah were governors in Judah and Samaria respectively, they may nevertheless—or exactly because of that—for one reason or another have been interested in "downsizing" the temple of YHW in Elephantine. One possibility for this could be that it was in their own interests as governors not to have (yet) another YHW temple outside of their territories.

However, I would like to suggest another explanation that can be combined with all three mentioned above. The governors of Judah and Samaria may have vetoed against the resumption of burnt offerings in the rebuilt temple of YHW in Elephantine out of consideration for the inner stability of the multicultural Elephantine and—ultimately—out of concern for Arshama, the Achaemenid satrap of Egypt.

The two minor governors of Judah and Samaria had to be on good terms with Arshama, who was a player on the political scene of the Achaemenid Empire. Achaemenid administrative letters from Egypt (e.g., A6.1–16) as well as Demotic and even Old Persian, Babylonian (including documents from the Murashu archive) and Greek sources refer to him.[43] Some of these texts suggest that he had great economic interests spread out throughout the entire fertile crescent. This is perhaps particularly visible in the travel authorisation Arshama issued to his official Nakhtḥor, who was about to travel from the Mesopotamia region to Egypt.[44] In the travel authorisation Arshama addressed several named officials in locations such as Arbel, Salam and Damascus, ordering them to supply the above-mentioned Nakhtḥor's company with daily rations:

---

43 For a fuller presentation of the sources referring to Arshama, see Christopher Tuplin, "Arshama: Prince and Satrap," in *The Arshama Letters from the Bodleian Library*, vol. 1: Introduction, ed. John Ma et al., OSAD (Oxford: 2013): 5–44.

44 See, e.g., Pierre Briant, *From Cyrus to Alexander: A History of the Persian Empire* (Winona Lake, IN: Eisenbrauns, 2002), 364–365, who describes this kind of Persian administrative document as a travel voucher (Elamite name: *halmi*, "sealed document"), and Lindsay Allen, *The Persian Empire: A History* (London: British Museum, 2005), 117.

> And n[o]w, [behol]d (one) named Nakhtḥor, m[y] official, [is] g[oing] to Egypt. You, give [him ra]tions from my estate which is in your province(s), day by day: ... And to his servants, ten per[s]ons, to each per day: ... Give them this ration, each official in turn, according to the route which is from province to province until he reaches Egypt. And if he be in one place more than one day then for those days do not given them extra rations. Bagasrava knows this order. Rashta is the scribe. (A6.9:2–3, 5–6)[45]

Admittedly, neither Judah nor Samaria are mentioned as stations along the route of Nakhtḥor's company. Nevertheless, the travel authorisation illustrates the breadth of Arshama's economic interests, and from a geographical perspective. Arshama had a series of estates also outside of Egypt, also in the—literally speaking—neighbourhood of Judah and Samaria (cf. Damascus).

In my view, it is not beyond possibility that it was in Arshama's interest that the rebuilt temple of YHW in Elephantine was somehow reduced and downsized in comparison to the earlier phase. One reason for this could be the inner stability of Elephantine. Another reason could be related to Arshama's interest in the economic surplus. A fully fledged sacrificial cult also in the rebuilt temple of YHW (including its need for animals) could potentially drain the economic surplus of the Judaean community in Elephantine, and ultimately of the satrap himself.

Provided that my thesis should turn out to be correct, namely that Arshama in fact was eager to downsize the cult in the rebuilt temple of YHW, and, moreover, that his wish at one and the same time concurred with the interests of the Jerusalem priesthood and even the interests of the governors of Judah and Samaria, it was probably no difficult decision to make for Bagavahya and Delaiah to veto against burnt offerings.

4.2.4 Why and How Could the Elephantine Community Theologically Legitimate the Veto on Burnt Offerings?

Having discussed the question of the possible reasons for the veto against burnt offerings in the rebuilt temple I will now turn my attention toward Elephantine.

---

45 Quoted from Bezalel Porten and Ada Yardeni, *Textbook of Aramaic Documents from Ancient Egypt: Newly Copied, Edited and Translated into Hebrew and English*, vol. I: Letters. Appendix: Aramaic Letters from the Bible (Jerusalem: The Hebrew University of Jerusalem – Department of the History of the Jewish People, 1986), 114. Annotated translations are offered in Maria Brosius, *The Persian Empire from Cyrus II to Artaxerxes I*, LACTOR 16 (London: London Association of Classical Teachers, 2000), 87–88 (no. 184), and Kuhrt, *The Persian Empire*, 739–740 (no. 15.4). The latter also includes a sketch map of the route taken by Nakhḥtor.

Why could the Elephantine community accept the (for them: newly imposed) ban on burnt offerings? And how could the community theologically legitimate a reestablished cult without burnt offerings? The first question—why—is probably the easiest one to answer. The Judaeans in Elephantine accepted the imposed restrictions because they had to. Presumably, they had no other choice than to accept the veto of the two governors of Judah and Samaria as a necessary condition for achieving support for the reconstruction of the temple.

Less easily answered is the question how they could reconcile the new and trimmed sacrificial cult with their previous religious practice and the corresponding articulated or unarticulated theology of sacrifice. As mentioned, no written source from Elephantine discusses the community's theology of sacrifice. This does not come as a surprise. Not only is our knowledge of the Elephantine community determined by the accidental nature of the sources available. What is more, even in the case of highly literate cultures such as ancient Roman society animal offerings were central rites, yet in spite of this, it seems that Roman thinkers did not reflect upon why animals were offered.[46]

As a matter of fact, some of the best-known descriptions of sacrifices in the entire ancient Near East come from the Hebrew Bible.[47] Within the Bible the description of sacrifices found in Lev 1–7 is definitely the most comprehensive. Therefore, in order to approximate the Elephantine community's thinking it is worthwhile taking a detour to this particular (Priestly) text.

In Lev 1–7 it is neither the slaughtering of the animal nor the animal's vicarious representation of the offerer before YHWH that is the constitutive element of the sacrifice. In my view, Christian A. Eberhart has convincingly drawn attention to a neglected feature of sacrifice, namely the burning rite.[48] It is the burning of the sacrificial material on the altar that determines whether any cultic ritual qualifies as a *qorbān*, an "offering" to YHWH.

Eberhart's proposal is made on the background of a scholarly debate where there are "almost as many theories on sacrifice as there are scholars studying the subject."[49] In biblical scholarship an influential theory has been put forward by Hartmut Gese, which focusses on the concept of atonement (*kpr*) and describes

46 Watts, "The Rhetoric of Sacrifice," 3–16 (8).
47 Watts, "The Rhetoric of Sacrifice," 3–16 (8).
48 Christian A. Eberhart, "A Neglected Feature of Sacrifice in the Hebrew Bible: Remarks on the Burning Rite on the Altar," *HTR* 97 (2004): 485–493, and Eberhart, "Sacrifice? Holy Smokes!," 3–16.
49 Eberhart, "A Neglected Feature," 485–493 (486).

sacrifice as a vicarious process.[50] According to Gese, the offerer identified himself with the sacrificial animal by placing his hand on it. The animal was then vicariously killed. Through the vicariously killed animal's blood the sacrifice of atonement provided for the offerer a vicarious encounter with YHWH.

However, as Eberhart shows, this model does not prove correct when tested against the account of sacrifices in Lev 1–7. The account there mentions five main types of sacrifice:

- the burnt offering (*ʿōlâ*, cf. Lev 1:1–17; 6:1–6),
- the grain offering (*minḥâ*, cf. Lev 2:1–16; 6:7–16),
- the communion sacrifice (NRSV "sacrifice of well-being," *zebaḥ šəlāmîm*, cf. Lev 3:1–17; 7:11–34),
- the sin offering (*ḥaṭṭāt*, cf. Lev 4:1–5:13; 6:17–23), and
- the guilt offering (*ʾāšām*, cf. Lev 5:14–26; 7:1–17).

Each one of the main types is described as an "offering" (*qorbān*) to YHWH. As Eberhart points out, only four of these five types of sacrifices involve the slaughtering of an animal. However, this is not the case with the *minḥâ* (NRSV: "grain offering"), even though Lev 5:11–13 state that this cereal offering can replace the sin offering (*ḥaṭṭāt*).

Focussing in particular on how the grain offering functions, Eberhart asks what its climax was and why the (Priestly) theologian could call it an offering (*qorbān*, cf. Lev 5:11), just like any of the other types of sacrifice. Eberhart points to a feature shared by all five types of sacrifice in Lev 1–7: the burning of the sacrificial material on the altar. As Eberhart points out, the account in Lev 1–7 uses three technical terms to describe the ritual. The first is the hiphil stem of the verb *qṭr* ("to cause to go up in smoke"[51]); the second is the noun *ʾiššê* ("offerings made by fire"[52]); the third is the phrase *rêaḥ nîḥôaḥ* ("pleasing odour"), which alludes to the anthropomorphic idea that YHWH actually smelled the smoke.

As Eberhart shows, a sacrifice was a communicative act. In Lev 1–7 it seems that it was the fire on the altar that transformed the offering and transported it up to the divine sphere. Consequently, in the Priestly text it was the burning rite that constituted the sacrifice and made it transform into an "offering" (*qorbān*).

Back to Elephantine: How could the Judaean community theologically legitimate the new sacrificial cult without animal sacrifices? I propose to use Lev 1–7

50 Hartmut Gese, "Die Sühne," in *Zur biblischen Theologie: alttestamentliche Vorträge*. BEvtThA 78 (Munich: Kaiser, 1977): 85–106.

51 *HALOT* 3:1094–1095, s.v. *qṭr* I.

52 *HALOT* 1:93–94, s.v. *ʾiššê*.

as an analogy: The Judaeans at Elephantine could theologically legitimate the new sacrificial cult in the rebuilt temple because it was the burning rite that in the last resort constituted the sacrifice, not the killing of the animal. The book of Leviticus may also potentially give us a glimpse of the theology of sacrifice of the Elephantine Judaeans, not only because the Priestly theologians behind Leviticus and the Judaeans in Elephantine alike were YHW(H) worshippers, but because Lev 1–7 is one of the most comprehensive descriptions of sacrifice from the entire ancient Near East. When the leading figures of the Elephantine community wrote to Arshama (?) that "sheep and ox and goat shall not be made there as burnt offering, only incense and meal offering" (A4.10:10–11), this was obviously the second-best option, from their perspective. Nevertheless, even though it was a compromise, it was a theologically acceptable compromise. Although the sacrificial cult was trimmed in comparison to how it was prior to the destruction of the temple of YHW, the new and trimmed sacrificial cult without animal sacrifices would continue to assure the community's communication with YHW, the god dwelling in Elephantine.[53]

4.3 Communal Rites of Mourning

In addition to the offering of sacrifices, other methods of communication with and influencing YHW were also available for the Elephantine community. Among them were a group of rites I summarise under the rubric rites of mourning, even though the Aramaic verb *'bl*, "to mourn" is only attested as the nominal derivation *'bwlh*, "the mourning" in an ostracon inscription in a very fragmentary context.[54]

Again, our best source is the petition Jedaniah and his colleagues the priests wrote to Bagavahya the governor of Judah (A4.7 and A4.8), with a copy also sent to his counterparts Delaiah and Shelemiah, the sons of Sanballat the governor of Samaria (A4.7:29 par.). In the petition the Judaeans in Elephantine related that they had experienced a state of emergency since the day the temple of YHW was destroyed in the fourteenth regnal year of Darius (A4.7:4 par.). In the petition they referred twice to the rites they had been performing since then. According to

53 Compare B3.12:2 *yhw 'lh' škn yb brt'*.

54 However, H. Lozachmeur also opens up for the reading *'kwlh*, "meal," cf. Lozachmeur, *La collection Clermont-Ganneau*, 352–353, and André Lemaire, "Judean Identity in Elephantine: Everyday Life according to the Ostraca," in *Judah and the Judeans in the Achaemenid Period: Negotiating Identity in an International Context*, ed. Oded Lipschits et al. (Winona Lake, IN: Eisenbrauns, 2011): 365–373 (371).

the first reference, "we with our wives and children have been wearing sackcloth, and fasting and praying to YHW the lord of heavens."[55] In the second reference, Jedaniah and his colleagues also added other rites. Their wives had been "made like widow(s)" (*nšy' zyln k'rmlh 'bydyn*).[56] In addition, ever since the temple was destroyed they did "not anoint [themselves with] oil" (*mšḥ l' mšḥyn*), and did "not drink wine" (*ḥmr l' štyn*).

The phrase "wives made like widows" presumably referenced one of the ways to express the grief caused by the destruction of the temple, just like the reference to sackcloths did. Porten speculates whether it could be a poetic image that husbands refrained from sexual activities with their wives.[57] However, rather than three and a half years of total abnegation of sexual activities, I think that the phrase should be understood as an idiom reflecting the common ancient Near Eastern notion that mourning is the specialism of women, and in particular widowed women.[58]

Moreover, Porten points to the fact that abstinence from drink and anointing were part of the fasting and mourning procedure, as suggested by passages in the Bible.[59]

If the humans practiced abstinence from wine as a sign of mourning, it is by analogy reasonable to conjecture that libations had ceased to be made to YHW in the same period. An ostracon inscription (D7.9, from the first quarter of the fifth century BCE[60]) suggests that the Judaeans in Elephantine in fact offered libations. In the inscription the anonymous writer gave instructions about, inter alia, the *ḥnt'*, presumably "the gift," that one Uriah had given him "for the liba-

---

55 A4.7:15 and A4.8:14. Moreover, the noun *ṣwm'*, "the fast" is mentioned in a fragmentary context in Clermont-Ganneau 200cc3, cf. Lozachmeur, *La collection Clermont-Ganneau*, 349, and Lemaire, "Judean Identity in Elephantine," 365–373 (371).

56 A4.7:19–21 and A4.8:18–20. A separate, grammatical question is why there is a disagreement in gender between *nšy'*, "the women" (feminine plural determined state) and *'bydyn* (participle *peal* passive [= *peil*] masculine plural) and, moreover, in number and determination between *nšy'* and *'rmlh* (feminine singular absolute state)? As for the former question, Murakoa conjectures that *'bydyn* may not be a grammatical slip but "stress the suffering borne by the husbands," cf. Muraoka, *An Introduction to Egyptian Aramaic*, 107.

57 Porten et al., *The Elephantine Papyri in English*, 145 note 67.

58 See, e.g., Marjo Christina Annette Korpel and Johannes Cornelis de Moor, *The Silent God* (Leiden: Brill, 2011), 131–132.

59 2Sam 12:20; 14:2; Dan 10 3, cf. Porten et al., *The Elephantine Papyri in English*, 145 note 68.

60 Bezalel Porten and Ada Yardeni, *Textbook of Aramaic Documents from Ancient Egypt: Newly Copied, Edited and Translated into Hebrew and English*, vol. IV: Ostraca & Assorted Inscriptions (Jerusalem: The Hebrew University of Jerusalem – Department of the History of the Jewish People, 1999), 161–162.

tion" (*lnsk*ʾ). The anonymous receiver was told to give the gift to Gemariah son of Ahio so that the latter could prepare beer from it. The context of the inscription D7.9 is unclear but it seems that this was the beer used for libation in this particular case.

As far as the status of libation in Elephantine is concerned, mention should be made of the *Words of Aḥiqar*, a wisdom text that the Judaeans of Elephantine probably had in their possession.[61] According to *Aḥiqar*, the god Shamash considered it a good thing to "drink the wine and pour it out."[62] In other words, provided that *Aḥiqar* found resonance in the religious life of the Judaean community, this document also attests to the practice of offering libations, although in this particular document to Shamash, not YHW.

Jedaniah and the priests presented the rites of mourning as communal rites. They were performed not only by themselves but also by their wives and their children (cf. A4.7:15 par.). Moreover, given the circumstances, the rites were exceptional, conditioned by the miserable status quo with the temple of YHW laying in ruins. If we take the information given by the leaders of the Elephantine community at face value, the entire Judaean population in Elephantine, including women and children, had been fasting since the temple of YHW was destroyed in the summer season of 410 BCE. The petition to Bagavahya was written some three and a half years later. In the same period the male members of the community presumably continued to serve as soldiers, regularly receiving rations from the Persian authorities.

It is hardly likely that an entire population could have been fasting for more than three years. No doubt, their cultic activities were affected by the destruction of the temple of YHW. However, the entire community connected to the temple cannot have ceased to take food for such a long period. Therefore, it should be understood as an exaggeration when Jedaniah and the priests wrote that the entire community had been fasting ever since the temple was destroyed. Consequently, as an exaggeration the statement of Jedaniah and his fellow Judaeans resembles another, perhaps more famous exaggeration ascribed to another ancient Near Easterner: King David. According to Ps 132:2–5 he swore to YHWH that he would neither enter his house, get into his bed, give sleep to his eyes, nor give slumber to his eyelids until he had found a place (*māqôm*) and a dwelling place (*miškānôt*) for YHWH.

---

61 See 6.5.1 below, *The Words of Aḥiqar* (C1.1).

62 C1.1:187: *š[th] ḥmrʾ wynyqnhy* ..., cf. Bezalel Porten and Ada Yardeni, *Textbook of Aramaic Documents from Ancient Egypt: Newly Copied, Edited and Translated into Hebrew and English*, vol. III: Literature, Accounts, Lists (Jerusalem: The Hebrew University of Jerusalem – Department of the History of the Jewish People, 1993), 49.

This leads to the question of what the purpose of the rites of mourning was. In the light of the exaggeration pertaining to the fast, I suggest that the purpose was in part to impress the addressees of the petition, Bagavahya and the sons of Sanballat. In other words, in the literary discourse of the letter, the mention of the three and a half year fast had a rhetorical role.

However, this clearly does not exclude the possibility that the enumerated rites of mourning also served a religious function. The rites were obviously not only performed in order to impress the governors in the provinces of Judah and Samaria. On the contrary, the primary "addressee" of the rites of mourning was YHW.

Not surprisingly, the writers of the petition did not state what the ultimate purpose of their mourning was. Nevertheless, it is unlikely that they were carried out only for their own sake. On the contrary, one should consider the possibility that the ultimate goal was to prompt YHW's intervention in order to change the miserable status quo. Although the rites that Jedaniah and the priests described were *communal* and exceptional, occasioned by the extraordinary circumstances, they were nevertheless modelled after individual and ordinary rites of mourning. Rites like fasting and wearing sackcloth obviously expressed grief. In the ancient Near East, such rites were part of the repertoire of the human–divine communication. Individuals and communities could address the deities not only by means of songs and prayers, letters written to the deities and by means of magic and sorcery and so on,[63] but also by means of fasting and wearing sackcloth.[64]

In the end, by adopting individual and ordinary rites of mourning, the Judaean community of Elephantine expressed its hope for mercy on the part of YHW. Although the written sources do not say so, the rites presumably expressed a hope comparable to the hope the people of Nineveh was said to have associated with fasting and wearing sackcloth. According to Jonah 3:5–9, the Ninevites said: "Who knows? God may relent and change his mind." (Jonah 3:9). Although not explicitly stated, it is tempting to speculate whether the mourning rites of the Judaeans in Elephantine ultimately hoped to achieve the same outcome: that YHW would change his mind and intervene into their lives. If that was the case, the Elephantine community reckoned with the possibility that YHW in fact could intervene in history.

---

63 Korpel and Moor, *The Silent God*, 111–118.

64 See, e.g., 2Sam 2:16–22; Joel 2:12–14; Ps 35:13–14, cf. Korpel and Moor, *The Silent God*, 268–269.

4.4 Communal and Individual Prayers

That the members of the Judaeans in Elephantine communicate with YHW by means of prayers is beyond doubt. However, the written sources do not tell much about it. Presumably, both individual members and the community as a whole directed prayers to YHW. Again, our best source is the petition written to Bagavahya the governor of Judah (A4.7 and A4.8), with a copy sent to his counterparts Delaiah and Shelemiah, the sons of Sanballat the governor of Samaria (A4.7:29 par.). In the petition the Elephantine leaders referred twice to prayers (A4.7:15, 26 par.). In both cases it was the collective "we" of the Judaean community that performed the prayer. In other words, the two references were to communal prayers. On the basis of the contents it is appropriate to speak of a communal prayer of curse (A4.7:15 par.) and a communal prayer of intercession (A4.7:26 par.) respectively.

4.4.1 A Communal Prayer of Intercession

The ultimate goal of the petition to Bagavahya is found at the end of the document. The Elephantine Judaean leaders, referring to themselves as "your obligees and friends who are here in Egypt," asked the governor of Judah to send a letter concerning the rebuilding of the temple of YHW (A4.7:23–25 par.). As discussed above, Bagavahya would get a conditional spiritual payment if he supported his friends in Egypt.[65] The Judaeans in Elephantine would offer meal-offerings, incense and burnt offering on the altar of YHW in Bagavahya's name (A4.7:25–26 par.).

It is in connection with the prospective offerings in Bagavahya's name that Jedaniah and his co-authors the priests mentioned their communal prayer of intercession. If Bagavahya sent a letter recommending the rebuilding of the temple, then the Elephantine community would advocate for him before YHW: "and we shall pray for you [*nṣlh ʿlyk*] at all times, we, and our wives, and our children, and the Judaeans, everyone here" (A4.7:26 par.).

As far as I can see, it is unclear exactly when the Judaeans would start to pray their prayers of intercession on behalf of Bagavahya. Did prayers of intercession require a temple in order to be conducted properly, as was the case with sacrifices? Or did the Judaean community start to pray for Bagavahya already when the temple of YHW was lying in ruins? In any case, it seems that the Judaeans in

65 See Section 4.2.2 above.

Elephantine took for granted that Bagavahya would assess a continuous prayer of intercession to be something valuable and desirable.

4.4.2 A Communal Prayer of Curse

In the petition to Bagavahya, Jedaniah and the priests of YHW stated twice that the members of the Judaean community had been wearing sackcloth, fasting and praying to YHW the lord of heavens since the temple of YHW was destroyed more than three years earlier (A4.7:15, 19–21 par.). Following immediately after the first of these two references there is a not easily understood passage (A4.7:15–17 par.). Because this passage deals with the role of the Persian commander Vidranga in the destruction of the temple, it is often referred to as "the Vidranga section."[66] For the sake of clarity I render the Vidranga section of the first draft of the letter (A4.7) in context (A4.7:15–17):

> [A4.7:15] *wkzy kznh ʿbyd ʾnḥnh ʿm nšyn wbnyn śqqn lbšn hwyn wṣymyn wmṣlyn lyhw mrʾ šmyʾ*
> [A4.7:16] *zy hḥwyn bwydrng zk klbyʾ hnpqw kblʾ mn rglwhy wkl nksyn zy qnh ʾbdw wkl gbryn*
> [A4.7:17] *zy bʿw bʾyš lʾgwrʾ zk kl qṭylw wḥzyn bhwm …*

There are two main problems with the Vidranga section quoted above. The first one pertains to the meaning of some of the words found there. Probably the most problematic word is *kblʾ* in A4.7:16.[67] No matter what its meaning was, there was obviously a pun between *klbyʾ* ("the dogs") and *kblʾ*. In the history of research, most translators have identified *kblʾ* with a Jewish–Aramaic noun meaning "foot-chain, anklet, fetter."[68] The other main problem pertains to the syntax of the verbs. In the history of interpretation, the dominating view has been that the verbs in perfect (suffix conjugation) are used indicatively, referring to actions that have taken place in the past. Porten's 2011 translation is representative of these assumptions:

---

66 James M. Lindenberger, "What Ever Happened to Vidranga? A Jewish Liturgy of Cursing from Elephantine," in *World of the Aramaeans III: Studies in Language and Literature in Honour of Paul-Eugène Dion*, ed. P. M. Michèle Daviau et al., JSOTSup 326 (Sheffield: Sheffield Academic, 2001): 134–157.

67 The second draft reads *kblwhy* (A4.8:15).

68 For an overview of the suggestions made in the history of research, see Lindenberger, "What Ever Happened to Vidranga?," 134–157 (139–143). See also Porten et al., *The Elephantine Papyri in English*, 144 note 56.

> [A4.7:15] And when this had been done (to us), we with our wives and our children sackcloth were wearing and fasting and praying to YHW the Lord of Heaven
> [A4.7:16] who let us gloat over that Vidranga, the cur. They removed the fetter from his feet and all goods which he had acquired were lost. And all persons
> [A4.7:17] who sought evil for that Temple, all (of them), were killed and we gazed upon them.[69]

However, the traditional reading is problematic. It implies that Vidranga, as seen from the perspective of the writers of the petition, had already been punished in the past. Moreover, the traditional reading also implies that "all persons" who "sought evil" for the temple of YHW had already been killed by the time the petition was written.

But, if the enemies of the Judaean community in Elephantine were already dead, that would presumably mean that nobody could obstruct the reconstruction of the temple of YHW any longer. If all the evildoers were dead, one should expect that there was no need for assistance in the form of a letter of recommendation from the governor of Judah. In other words, a reading of the Vidranga section presupposing that the main verbs in the passage were referring to actions that already had taken place in the past is difficult to harmonize with the overall thrust of the letter.

Moreover, there is an additional problem with the traditional interpretation of the verbs of the Vidranga section. According to Porten's translation, it appears that Vidranga had already been mutilated by dogs in a public place. Consequently, one should expect that Vidranga was already dead, like the rest of the "people who sought evil" for the temple of YHW. The letter is dated to the seventeenth year of Darius II, i.e. 407 BCE (A4.7:30 par.). In other words, as a consequence of the traditional reading Vidranga should already have met his creator when Jedaniah and the priests wrote the petition to Bagavahya.

However, another Aramaic document (A3.9) provides information about Vidranga that calls the traditional translation of the perfect verbs in the Vidranga section into question. The letter in question stems from 399 BCE.[70] In the document Shewa son of Zechariah reported to his lord Islaḥ the following (A3.9:7):

---

69 Porten et al., *The Elephantine Papyri in English*, 144.

70 The document mentions both Amyrtaeus and king Nepherites. Amyraeus led a successful revolt against the Persians after the death of Darius II and established the Twenty-Eighth Dynasty in 404 BCE. In 399 BCE, however, Nepherites defeated Amyrtaeus and established the Twenty-Ninth Dynasty.

ypṭrwn[ny ʿld]br wydrng.[71] This can be rendered "they will release [*me in the matt*] er of Vidranga" or "[*because*] of Vidranga." Although the text is broken, it nevertheless opens up for the possibility that Vidranga was still alive in 399 BCE. Admittedly, one can neither exclude the possibility that the document from 399 BCE referred to an already old affair nor rule out that it referred to another person called Vidranga. Yet, despite these possibilities the reference to a Vidranga in a document written some eight years after the petition to Bagavahya calls for a reconsideration of the traditional reading of the Vidranga section.

On the basis of the obstacles against the traditional interpretation of the Vidranga section mentioned above, James M. Lindenberger has made another proposal. In Lindenberger's view, the Vidranga section did not account for Vidranga's fate in the past. Quite the contrary, the Vidranga section offers the words the Elephantine community prayed against Vidranga, grammatically speaking in the form of precative perfects.[72] As Lindenberger argues, in the Vidranga section verbs in imperative frame three verbs in the middle in perfect (*ʾbdw*, *hnpqw*, and *qṭylw*):

- *hḥwyn* (A4.7:16, *haphel* imperative[73] masculine singular of *ḥwy*, "to see" + first plural suffix, A4.8:15 *ḥwynʾ*, *pael* imperative[74] masculine singular of *ḥwy*, "to see" + first plural suffix),
- *hnpqw* (A4.7:16, *haphel* perfect third masculine plural of *npq*, "to go out"),
- *ʾbdw* (A4.7:16, *peal* perfect third masculine plural of *ʾbd*, "to be lost, disappear, perish"),
- *qṭylw* (A4.7:17, *peil* perfect third masculine plural of *qṭl*, "to kill"), and
- *ḥzyn* (A4.7:17, *pael* imperative[75] masculine singular of *ḥwy*, "to see" + first plural suffix).

71 Following Porten's reconstruction in Porten and Yardeni, *TADAE*, I: Letters. Appendix: Aramaic Letters from the Bible, 46–47. See Lindenberger, "What Ever Happened to Vidranga?," 134–157 (140–141 and note 18).

72 Lindenberger, "What Ever Happened to Vidranga?," 134–157 (146).

73 Morphologically, the unvocalised form of this Lamed-Yod verb can also be parsed as a *hapfel* perfect third masculine singular + first plural suffix. See Muraoka, *An Introduction to Egyptian Aramaic*, §21.

74 Morphologically, the unvocalised form of this Lamed-Yod verb can also be parsed as a *haphel* perfect third masculine singular + first plural suffix. See Muraoka, *An Introduction to Egyptian Aramaic*, §21.

75 Morphologically, the unvocalised form of this Lamed-Yod verb can also be parsed as a *haphel* perfect third masculine singular + first plural suffix. See Muraoka, *An Introduction to Egyptian Aramaic*, §21.

The Aramaic verb system is not a tempus system. The main distinction between perfect and imperfect is that the former expresses complete action and the latter incomplete action. Whether the action (complete/incomplete) takes place in the past, present or future cannot be determined on the basis of the morphology. In the case of the Vidranga section, Lindenberger suggests that the perfects have been used in a special way: as precative perfects. A precative perfect expresses entreaty or supplication and may also be called "perfect of prayer." As a consequence of Lindenberger's interpretation, the Vidranga section in fact renders a communal prayer of curse. Lindenberger's translation of the prayer of the Elephantine community is as follows:

> After this had been done to us, we with our wives and our children put on sackcloth and fasted and prayed to YHW the lord of heaven: "Show us our revenge[76] on that Vidranga: May the dogs tear his guts out from between his legs! May all the property he got perish! May all the men who plotted evil against that temple—all of them—be killed! And may we watch them!"[77]

Lindenberger's proposal has not gone unnoticed and has been a subject of dispute. In the 2003 grammar of Egyptian Aramaic by Bezalel Porten and Takamitsu Muraoka one reads: "Our idiom [i.e Egyptian Aramaic] does not use the perfect with optative force to indicate a wish. Hence Lindenberger's 'May the dogs tear his guts out from between his legs etc.' for *klbyʾ hnpqw kblʾ mn rglwhy* A4.7:16 is unlikely."[78] Moreover, Porten contends that Lindenberger's attempt to see the whole section as an actual prayer "founders on the past tense of the verbs."[79]

---

76 There are no words in the Aramaic text corresponding to "our revenge." Lindenberger considers the construction (both the *haphel* imperative in A4.7 and the *pael* imperative in A4.8) to be a special case of the so-called doubly transitive construction. Normally the verb would have two objects associated with it, e.g., "They made him [OBJECT 1] king [OBJECT 2]." In this case, however, the second object of the verb *hḥwyn* (A4.7:16)/*ḥwynʾ* (A4.8:15) is implied but not stated. This view is also found in *DNWSI* 1:354, s.v. *ḥwy*$_1$, where however the verb is interpreted as perfect and rendered as an indicative past tense: "he let us behold (our desire) on W. (i.e. he has revenged us on W.)." In my view the clause *hḥwyn bwydrng zk* should be rendered "Cause us to look upon that Vidranga!" This sort of hostile, triumphant act of looking at one's enemies is attested elsewhere in cognate languages. For instance, in a mid-ninth-century inscription King Mesha of Moab claimed that the god Chemosh *hrʾny bkl śnʾy*, "caused me to look upon my enemies" (*KAI* 181:4). Moreover, according to Ps 59:11b (ET 59:10b), Elohim let the triumphant psalmist look on his enemies (*ʾĕlōhîm yarʾēnî bəšōrərāy*, cf. NRSV "my God will let me look in triumph on my enemies").

77 Lindenberger, *Ancient Aramaic and Hebrew Letters*, 75, cf. Lindenberger, "What Ever Happened to Vidranga?," 134–157 (154).

78 Takamitsu Muraoka and Bezalel Porten, *A Grammar of Egyptian Aramaic*, 2nd rev. ed., HdO 32 (Leiden: Brill, 2003), §51e.

In my view, the arguments against Lindenberger's proposal do not convince. From a grammatical point of view, it should be noted that scholars argue to have found cases of precative perfect in Phoenician[80] and Ugaritic.[81] The best attested examples of "perfect of prayer" are found in Biblical Hebrew.[82] As far as Biblical Hebrew is concerned—the most intensively studied and probably best described Northwest Semitic language—Bruce K. Waltke and Michael Patrick O'Connor consider the precative perfect ("perfect of prayer") to be a distinct use of the irreal perfect. The precative can be used with reference to situations the speaker prays for and expects to be realized. Unfortunately, the perfect precative can only be recognised contextually. Nevertheless, it is "invariably found alternating with the imperfect or the imperative; it is by this outward sign that the precative perfect may unfailingly be identified."[83] According to the estimation of Waltke and O'Connor, the form occurs some twenty times in the book of Psalms (e.g. Pss 22:22 ET 22:21; 31:5–6 ET 31:4–5; and 4:2 ET 4:1):

bəqorʾî ʿănēnî ʾĕlōhê ṣidqî baṣṣār hirḥabtā lî ḥānnēnî ûšəmaʿ təpillātî

When I cry out, answer me, O my righteous God. In [my] distress, bring me relief. Be gracious to me and hear my prayer. (Ps 4:2 [ET 4:1])

As it is to be expected, the examples of precative perfect in Biblical Hebrew are found in poetical-liturgical contexts, in texts typically addressing the deity.[84] However, as far as Egyptian Aramaic is concerned, the documents written in this idiom contain very few poetical-liturgical texts. Therefore, one should not be surprised that there are few examples of the "perfect of prayer" either. Contrary to the assessment of Muraoka and Porten, we cannot completely rule out

79 Porten et al., *The Elephantine Papyri in English*, 144 note 58.

80 Michael L. Barré, "An Unrecognized Precative Construction in Phoenician and Hebrew," *Bib* 64 (1983): 411–422.

81 Iain W. Provan, "Past, Present and Future in Lamentations 3:52–66: The Case for a Precative Perfect Re-Examined," *VT* 41 (1991): 164–175 (165–166).

82 Lindenberger, "What Ever Happened to Vidranga?," 134–157 (146–147). See Bruce K. Waltke and Michael Patrick O'Connor, *An Introduction to Biblical Hebrew Syntax* (Winona Lake, IN: Eisenbrauns, 1990), 494–495.

83 Waltke and O'Connor, *An Introduction to Biblical Hebrew Syntax*, 494–495, quoting from Moses Buttenwieser, *The Psalms: Chronologically Treated with a New Translation* (Chicago: University of Chicago Press, 1938), 21. Waltke and O'Connor express discontent over the fact that several modern Bible translations ignore this point or waffle on it.

84 Moreover, it has also been suggested that the "perfect of prayer" is characteristic of Lam 3:55–63 (56–61), cf. Frederick William Dobbs-Allsopp, *Lamentations*, Interpretation, a Bible Commentary for Teaching and Preaching (Louisville, KY: John Knox Press, 2002), 126–127.

the possibility that the precative perfect existed as a prayer form in Egyptian Aramaic. Lindenberger admits that the precative perfect is not very frequent in Aramaic. Nevertheless, there are good reasons to subscribe to him and consider the Vidranga section to be "virtually a textbook case" of precative perfects in Egyptian Aramaic.[85]

The very intention of the letter to Bagavahya was to get help. The backdrop of the letter seems to have been that the adversaries were still active. In the light of this, it is difficult to understand how the Vidranga section could be referring to the death of Vidranga and the other enemies. Historically, Vidranga may have been alive many years after the letter to Bagavahya was written. Therefore, as Lindenberger states, it is a mistake to read the section as a factual narrative. All of the clauses in the passage can be read as volitives, that is, as a series of imprecatory wishes.[86]

Summing up, the sources mention two types of communal prayers. One is a prayer of intercession for Bagavahya. The other one is a prayer of curse for Vidranga, the one who played an important role in the destruction of the temple of YHW. In the petition to Bagavahya, the communal prayer of intercession was presented as a conditional offer to him. Moreover, in the petition, the communal prayer of curse is presented as a prayer that has accompanied the community's rites of morning since the temple was destroyed. We should expect that the community's repertoire of communal prayers exceeded the two discussed here. However the sources are silent about any other types of communal prayers.

4.4.3 Individual Prayers

If we define "prayer" as a solemn request for help or expression of thanksgiving addressed to YHW or another deity, there are no quotations or references to individual prayers in the documents that give us access to the Elephantine Judaean community. Nevertheless, there are indirect references to individual prayer practice. They fall into two groups:

- epistolary salutations
- proper names

85 Lindenberger, "What Ever Happened to Vidranga?," 134–157 (146).
86 Lindenberger, "What Ever Happened to Vidranga?," 134–157 (152).

As I will show below, it is questionable if and to what extent these indirect references have any value as sources for the individual prayers of the Judaeans in Elephantine.

4.4.3.1 Epistolary Salutations

In Aramaic letters, the salutation is typically found at the very beginning, following immediately after the address. The degree of elaboration varies.[87]

A simple form of greeting can be illustrated by the so-called Passover ostracon D7.6. Following immediately after the address ("To Hoshaiah") there comes a brief greeting: *šlmk* (D7.6:2 "Your welfare"). This brief greeting is likely to be an abbreviation of the longer salutation formula. An example of a longer greeting is found in a letter written from Hosea to lady Shalwah (A3.7). Coming immediately after the address, the salutation reads *ʾlhyʾ kl yšʾlw šlmky bkl ʿdn*, "may all the gods seek after your welfare at all times" (A3.7:1). Here the plural of the verb (*yšʾlw*) underscores that the plural of the noun *ʾlhyʾ* in fact denotes "gods" in plural and not a majestic plural. However, in other texts the same type of greeting appears with a grammatical agent in the singular. For instance, when Hoshaiah son of Nathan wrote to his brother Pilti (A3.6), he opened the letter with the following wish:

> [... *šlmk ʾl*]*h šmyʾ* [*y*]*šʾl bkl ʿdn*
>
> [... May the Go]d of Heaven seek after [your welfare] at all times. (A3.6:1)[88]

Epistolary salutations of this type only expressed a wish that "the gods"/"the god" would seek after the welfare (*šlm*) of the receiver of the letter. Formally, the wish is manifested in a jussive form, either in plural (*yšʾlw*) or in singular (*yšʾl*). Therefore, the epistolary salutations are not prayers in the sense of a solemn request for help or an expression of thanksgiving addressed to a deity.

---

87 On the question of Aramaic epistolography, see Philip S. Alexander, "Remarks on Aramaic Epistolography in the Persian Period," *JSS* 23 (1978): 155–170; Joseph A. Fitzmyer, "Some Notes on Aramaic Epistolography," *JBL* 93 (1974): 201–225; Joseph A. Fitzmyer, "Aramaic Epistolography," *Semeia* 22 (1981): 25–57; Paul-Eugène Dion, "Aramaic Words for 'Letter'," *Semeia* 22 (1981): 77–88, Paul-Eugène Dion et al., "La lettre araméenne passe-partout et ses sous-espèces," *RB* 89 (1982): 528–575; and above all, Dirk Schwiderski, *Handbuch des nordwestsemitischen Briefformulars: ein Beitrag zur Echtheitsfrage der aramäischen Briefe des Esrabuches*, BZAW 295 (Berlin; New York: de Gruyter, 2000), 115–126.

88 In the official letter written by the leaders of the Judaean community at Elephantine to Bagavahya the governor of Judah we can observe a highly elaborated greeting of the same type (A4.7:1–3 par.).

A formally different epistolary salutation is the formula "I have blessed you by [DIVINE NAME] that he may let me see your face in peace." In the so-called Hermepolis papyri[89] the divine name is Ptah.[90] A slightly variant form can be seen in the letter to Shelomam from his father Osea (A3.3). Here, a participle of *brk* is used and the divine name is presumably YHW (A3.3:2–3).[91] Moreover, in an ostracon inscription that Giddel sent to his lord Micaiah, he wrote that he had blessed him "by YHH and Khnum" (*brktk lyhh wlḥnwm*, D7.21:3). In general, salutations of this type encompass the notion that the deity is acting as protector and source of welfare.

The salutations attested in the letters that can be associated with the Judaean community are commonplace in Aramaic epistolography. In other words, the epistolary salutations are conventional. Still, even though they are conventional, the salutation formulas indirectly attest to the practice of invoking one or several deities for the benefit of others.

4.4.3.2 Proper Names

Proper names represent the other type of source that potentially sheds light on the subject of individual prayers in the Judaean community. Particularly relevant are theophoric names formed as verbal sentences with an explicitly articulated theophorous element. From an etymological perspective, such names can be understood as terse prayers. These names can be divided into three groups: a) statements of thanksgiving in the perfect tense, b) petitions in the imperfect (functioning as jussive) and c) commands in the imperative.[92] As examples of a) we can list names such as *ʿnnyh*/Ananiah ("YH has answered me"), *qwnyh*/

---

89 Admittedly, the so-called Hermopolis papyri, i.e. a parcel of family letters discovered at Hermopolis and that date back to the late sixth/early fifth century BCE, are not of Judaean but of Aramaean provenance, written by (Aramaean) individuals connected to the Aramaean garrison in Elephantine's twin town Syene. Nevertheless, they offer, among other things, valuable information about the cultural and religious context the Judaean garrison in Elephantine was part of. See, e.g., Bezalel Porten, *Archives from Elephantine: The Life of an Ancient Jewish Military Colony* (Berkeley: University of California Press, 1968), 264–272; Porten et al., *The Elephantine Papyri in English*, 7, 75–78, 90–107; and Lindenberger, *Ancient Aramaic and Hebrew Letters*, 25–36.

90 *brktky*/*brktk lptḥ*, cf. Schwiderski, *Handbuch des nordwestsemitischen Briefformulars*, 126–128.

91 The text is broken, but in the light of the initial greeting to the temple of YHW in Elephantine (A3.3:1) this is a likely conjecture.

92 Porten et al., *The Elephantine Papyri in English*, 87–88.

Konaiah[93] ("YH has acquired") and *ḥnnyh*/Hananiah ("YH has shown mercy"). Moreover, the name *yhwyšmʿ*/Jehoishma ("may YHW hear!") can serve as an example of b). Finally, an example of c) is *ʾwšʿyh*/Oshaiah, alternatively *hwšʿyh*/ Hoshaiah ("Save, O YH!").[94]

The potential sources of error are many when using a proper name uncritically as a source for individual prayers.

First, the modern identification of the assumed verbal root may be wrong.

Second, the practice of giving names with the theophorous element YHW/ YHH/YH can be explained as something more of a cultural phenomenon reflecting the heritage of the Judaean community in Elephantine than as a deliberate expression of their belief. Presumably also factors other than theological deliberations guided the choice of name for a newborn. Genealogies made on the basis of the many legal documents show that the practice of papponomy, that is the naming of a grandson after his grandfather, was an established practice in the Judaean community, as it was elsewhere in its cultural and religious vicinity.[95] Just to give but one example, we can trace the line of decent of a certain Jezaniah son of Penuliah (*yznyh br pnwlyh*). In a legal document from 416 BCE (from the ninth year of King Darius II, B2.10:1) he appeared as one of the legal witnesses in the case of a transfer of ownership of a house (B2.10:19). In a marriage contract written some thirty-three years earlier (in the sixteenth regnal year of Artaxerxes I, B2.6:1), a person who probably was Jezaniah's father witnessed to a marriage contract. Here, Penuliah was presented as the son of Jezaniah (B2.6:38). Thus, the grandson seems to have been named after his paternal grandfather.

Third, even if we can account for the etymology of a given name with some certainty, it is still difficult to account fully for the religious ideas the Judaeans in Elephantine possibly associated with the names. For instance, provided that the Judaeans actually understood the name *qwnyh* (Konaiah) as a statement of thanksgiving meaning "YH has acquired," we cannot tell what particular reli-

---

93 See B2.2:8–9 where Konaiah son of Zadak is given the ethnicon Judaean and B2.1:2 where presumably the same Konaiah son of Zadak is called an Aramean.

94 The name Oshaiah/Hoshaiah occurs much more frequently in its hypocoristic form Osea/ Hosea, cf. Porten et al., *The Elephantine Papyri in English*, 88.

95 For a presentation of selected genealogies, see Michael H. Silverman, *Religious Values in the Jewish Proper Names at Elephantine*, AOAT 217 (Neukirchen-Vluyn: Neukirchener Verlag, 1985), 291–293. Moreover, the phenomenon of papponomy is also attested in other textual corpora from the same general period. For instance, the Wadi ed-Daliyeh papyri demonstrate that the name Sanballat was used three times within five generations within the Sanballat Dynasty of Achaemenid Samaria. See Cross, "The Discovery of the Samaria Papyri," 110–121 (121).

gious connotations the concept of YHW's acquisition may have had in Elephantine. For instance, did the Judaeans think of it in terms of creation?[96]

4.4.3.3 Profane Swearing

Profane swearing may not be a religious ritual according to an ordinary understanding of the term ritual. However, when the swearing involves the name of a deity it is inevitably an indirect reflex of the ritual dimension of everyday religion.

In fifth-century BCE ostraca from Elephantine the swearing phrase *ḥy lyhh*[97] occurs ten times in everyday contexts.[98] An example is D7.16 (= Clermont-Ganneau 152) where the writer of the inscription urged Islaḥ to meet him, apparently to take care of the vegetables he is bringing by boat. The swearing underscores the importance:

> *lmh hn yʾbd ḥy lyhhhn lʾ npšk[y] ʾlqḥ*
>
> Lest, if they get lost, by the life of YHH, if not (= surely) yo[ur] life I shall take. (D7.16:3–4)[99]

As André Dupont-Sommer has emphasised, the ostraca suggest that such swearing was used in everyday conversation. The Yahwists of Elephantine did not have any taboos connected to the pronunciation of the name YHH/YHW comparable to the avoidance of pronouncing the name YHWH evident in (the textual tradition of) the received Bible. In a way, the Judaeans' swearing was a tribute to their god YHW.[100]

---

96 See the discussion of the epithet "creator of heaven and earth" (*qōnê šāmayim wāʾāreṣ*) found in Gen 14:19, in Gard Granerød, *Abraham and Melchizedek: Scribal Activity of Second Temple Times in Genesis 14 and Psalm 110*, BZAW 406 (Berlin: de Gruyter, 2010), 161–163.
97 Porten and Yardeni, *TADAE*, IV: Ostraca & Assorted Inscriptions, 169: "by the life of YHH"; Lindenberger, *Ancient Aramaic and Hebrew Letters*, 50 (no. 22): "I swear to God"; and Muraoka, *An Introduction to Egyptian Aramaic*, 131: "good heavens!"
98 According to Lemaire, "Judean Identity in Elephantine," 365–373 (366), the phrase is found in Clermont-Ganneau ostraca nos. 14, 20, 41, 56, 152 [= D7.16], 174, 185, 214 (possibly), X16, and J8, cf. Lozachmeur, *La collection Clermont-Ganneau*.
99 Quoted from Porten and Yardeni, *TADAE*, IV: Ostraca & Assorted Inscriptions, 168–169.
100 After A. Dupont-Sommer, quoted in Lemaire, "Judean Identity in Elephantine," 365–373 (366).

4.4.4 Summary

The destruction of the temple of YHW brought the offering of sacrifices to YHW to an end. However, the destruction did not stop the community from praying to YHW. In the available source for the Elephantine community the communal prayers are best attested (prayers of intercession and prayers of curse).

Unfortunately, only little can be said about individual prayer in the Judaean community. By analogy with other Yahwistic communities, and on the basis of the proper names formed as prayers to YHW, we should expect that individual Judaeans also prayed to YHW. Judging from the etymology of the proper names, the contents of the individual prayers included both prayers of thanksgiving where YHW was thanked for things he had already done, and various forms of prayers with a present and/or future horizon.

4.5 The Passover and the Festival of Unleavened Bread

4.5.1 A Potential Terminological Pitfall

The Yahwistic community in Elephantine observed Passover and presumably also the Festival of Unleavened Bread. However, the textual evidence (two ostraca inscriptions, D7.6 and D7.24 and a fragmentary letter, A4.1, often called "the Passover letter") for this is limited and fragmented. In short, the texts open up for many speculations. In the history of research much of the discussion has been guided by biblical scholarship. The Passover (with or without the Festival of Unleavened Bread) has an important position in the festival calendars and the many narratives of the Hebrew Bible. There, it is connected to one of Israel's founding myths, the tradition about the exodus out of Egypt. In short, the discussions of biblical scholarship have also coined the discussion about the Passover in Elephantine. Quite often, the texts of the Hebrew Bible have supplied the interpretative framework for understanding the Passover (and the Festival of Unleavened Bread) in Elephantine.

There are only two ostracon inscriptions (D7.6 and D7.24) that contain the term *psḥʾ*,[101] a term commonly rendered "the Passover." Already here in connec-

101 In addition, according to H. Lozachmeur, Clermont-Ganneau 62cv4 reads *lm psḥḥnty qdmy*, which she translates "ainsi: mon cadeau de pâque/pascal ? (est/était) premier/devant moi," "thus: 'my Passover gift is/was my first/in front of me'," cf. Lozachmeur, *La collection Clermont-Ganneau*, 229 – 230 and Plates 134 – 135, and Lemaire, "Judean Identity in Elephantine," 365 – 373 [370]).

tion with the choice of terminology one can detect the influence of biblical studies, because the term "the Passover" is coined by the Hebrew Bible, in particular the reception of Exod 12. In Exod 12 YHWH says that he will *pasāḥ ʿal* the houses of the Israelites where the doorposts had been smeared with blood (cf. Exod 12:13, 23, 27). The English translation "pass over" can be traced back to the Vulgate's Latin rendition of the verb *psḥ*, namely that YHWH, upon seeing the blood, would "transibo vos," i.e. "pass over you." However, the Hebrew verb *psḥ* originally meant "to spare, to have compassion, to protect."[102] In any case, Exod 12 is referring to a kind of apotropaic rite providing protection against YHWH's destroyer (*hammašḥît*, Exod 12:23), and the entire procedure is placed in the context of the narrative about YHWH's rescuing of the Israelites out of Egypt. Therefore, the term Passover is potentially a theologically biased concept because it is often coined by the biblical texts as well as the later reception of them in Judaism and Christianity. In spite of that, in the following I will retain the traditional rendition for the sake of simplicity by letting "the Passover" render the Aramaic *psḥʾ*.[103] The relevant texts will be discussed in chronological order, with the earliest ones (the ostraca inscriptions) first and the so-called Passover letter (A4.1) thereafter.

4.5.2 D7.24 "On the Passover" and D7.6 "Inform Me When You Will Make the Passover!"

The Passover ostraca inscriptions contain no date but have been dated to the beginning of the fifth century BCE. One of the ostraca (D7.24) offers information supporting this by mentioning a certain Rauk (*rwk*, D7.24:15). He may be identical with the garrison commander named Rauk who otherwise appears in a contract dated in 495 BCE (*rwk rbḥylʾ*, B5.1:3). The date of the other ostracon (D7.6) is more disputed. The commonly held opinion is to date it to the same general period as D7.24.[104] However, others suggest that it was written sometime between 440 and 430 BCE.[105]

---

102 Tigay, *Deuteronomy*, 153.

103 For a presentation of the biblical Passover, see, e.g., Karl William Weyde, "Passa (AT)," *WiBiLex:* available online at http://www.bibelwissenschaft.de/stichwort/30031/, and Menahem Haran, *Temples and Temple-Service in Ancient Israel: An Inquiry into the Character of Cult Phenomena and the Historical Setting of the Priestly School* (Winona Lake, IN: Eisenbrauns, 1985), 317–348.

104 So, e.g., Porten, *Archives from Elephantine*, 131: "beginning of the fifth century," cf. Porten and Yardeni, *TADAE*, IV: Ostraca & Assorted Inscriptions, 174.

D7.24 is the most perplexing of the two inscriptions. The context seems to be that the writer was announcing that he would arrive at Syene by boat (cf. D7.24:2–3). Moreover, it seems that he gave the recipient various instructions. One of these instructions suggests that the brief letter was sent in connection with business; the recipient (?) was given the order to "examine his vessels!" (*wm'nhy bḥn*, D7.24:7).[106] One of the broken lines (D7.24:5) contains the phrase *bpsḥ'*, "on the Passover" and two proper names connect the ostracon to the Yahwistic community at Elephantine: Hosea (*hwšʿ*) and Micaiah (*mykyh*) (D7:24,13, 17).

As far as the question of the Passover is concerned, the inscription reveals relatively little information. Above all, it only attests that the term *psḥ'* was known in Judaean circles in Upper Egypt at the beginning of the fifth century. Moreover, the preposition *b* in the phrase *bpsḥ'* may perhaps give a hint about the length of the Passover. The phrase can be compared to phrases denoting time such as *bšbh* "on the Sabbath" (D7.16:2; D28.4; D7.48:5) and the way dates are indicated in letters and legal documents.

D7.6 is more legible and therefore also more informative.[107] The inscription is a short letter written to Hoshaiah by an anonymous writer. Hoshaiah was apparently babysitting because the writer instructed him to look after "the children" (*ynqy'*) until a certain Aḥutab arrived. Hoshaiah was told not to entrust them to anyone else (D7.6:2–5). Moreover, he was told to knead bread for the children until their mother came (D7.6:6–8). The writer concluded by asking about news about "the child" (singular: *ynq'*, D7.6:10–11).

It is within the context of babysitting and concern for the children that the anonymous writer asked about the Passover: *šlḥ ly 'mt tʿbdn psḥ'*, "Inform me when you will make Passover!" (D7.6:8–10). The technical term for observing the Passover used here is the verb *ʿbd*. Strictly speaking, *tʿbdn* is the imperfect second plural feminine. However, there is no doubt that Hoshaiah was a man (cf. the pronominal suffix *šlmk* in D7.6:2 and the inflected verbs with Hoshaiah as subject, as for instance the imperative *šlḥ* in the request about the date of

---

105 Kottsieper, "Die Religionspolitik der Achämeniden," 150–178 (151 note 5, referring to a suggestion made by Pierre Grelot).

106 In my view, it is unlikely that the ostracon links the term *psḥ'* with inspecting vessels, as Simeon Chavel tentatively suggests. Simeon Chavel, "The Second Passover, Pilgrimage, and the Centralized Cult," *HTR* 102 (2009): 1–24 (24 note 97).

107 Besides the translation in Porten and Yardeni, *TADAE*, IV: Ostraca & Assorted Inscriptions, 158, annotated translations are found in, e.g., Lindenberger, *Ancient Aramaic and Hebrew Letters*, 48 (no. 19), and *COS* 3.87 A:208–209 (translated by Bezalel Porten).

the Passover). Therefore, it is presumably a scribal error for *tʿbdwn* (second masculine plural).

The value of the inscription as a source for the Passover in Elephantine is threefold. First, nothing in D7.6 suggests that the addressee Hoshaiah was unfamiliar with the Passover. On the contrary, the plain question about when Hoshaiah and the other would "do the Passover" presupposed that both the writer and the addressee already knew it. The writer obviously presupposed that Hoshaiah understood what *psḥʾ* was referring to. Second, the writer's inquiry suggests that there was no fixed date for the Passover. The conjunction *ʾmt* ("when") clearly shows that there was an uncertainty about the date, at least on the part of the one who wrote the inscription. Third, the inscription is clearly not official writing. On the contrary, the reference to babysitting (and what is more, by a male babysitter!), the writer's concern for the child's security and nourishment, and the writer's wish to hear news about "the child" irrefutably puts the Passover in the context of the family. According to Jonathan Z. Smith's spatial model of religion, the inscription demonstrates that the Passover was part of the "religion here." It pertained to domestic religion whose setting was the extended family.[108]

D7.6 suggests that the Passover observance was a family concern in the fifth century BCE. Having said that, the inscription D7.24 and D7.6 give neither any description of the rites that presumably were performed on the Passover, nor reveal any information about why the Judaeans in Elephantine observed it in the first part of the fifth century BCE. We are only left to speculation. Did the Passover in Elephantine include, say, apotropaic rites similar to those reflected in Exod 12? And did the Judaeans connect the Passover to a religious myth, such as, for example, Israel's origin narrative according to the book of Exodus?

4.5.3 The Festival(s) According to A4.1 (the So-Called Passover Letter)

In the fifth regnal year of King Darius II (419/418 BCE) a certain Hananiah wrote to Jedaniah and his colleagues, subsumed under "the Judaean garrison" (*ḥylʾ yhwdyʾ*). The designation Hananiah used in the address (A4.1:1, 10 "to my broth-

108 Jonathan Z. Smith, "Here, There, and Anywhere," in *Prayer, Magic, and the Stars in the Ancient and Late Antique World*, ed. Scott Noegel et al. (University Park: Pennsylvania State University Press, 2003): 21–36, cf. also Section 1.2 above.

ers," "your brother Hananiah") suggests that Hananiah was neither subordinate nor superior to them in rank but on an equal footing with the addressees.[109]

The body of the letter is only partially intact. There, Hananiah referred to a decree or letter that King Darius had sent to Arshama (A4.1:2). Unfortunately the wording of the royal decree is lost in a lacuna. In the light of the assumed width of the papyrus the lacuna has been estimated to have consisted of some ten words or thirty-seven characters.[110] The lines of extant text immediately after the lacuna contain several injunctions imposed upon the Judaean community (A4.1:3–8).

The (partially broken) reference to a royal decree issued to the satrap Arshama suggests that royal authority in one way or another had been lent to the instructions Hananiah communicated. Either formally or in reality, the Persian king stood behind them.

No formal title is ascribed to Hananiah. However, by analogy to the roles that Ezra and Nehemiah played according the Hebrew Bible, it has been proposed that he was an ambassador[111] or a "minister of state for Jewish affairs."[112] Another figure that may shed light on the question of Hananiah's role is the Egyptian Udjahorresnet.[113] Udjahorresnet was originally an Egyptian navy commander. After Cambyses conquered Egypt Udjahorresnet became a collaborator in the new king's service. His autobiography suggests that there were two phases in his new career.[114] First, he played an important role in the restoration of the cult of the dynastic sanctuary of Neith in Sais. Then, when Darius I had acceded to the throne, he played an important role in the reorganisation of the institutions of scribalism and religious learning in Egypt. In both phases, he served the Persian government as a special adviser on Egyptian affairs.

---

109 A case of non-equality in terms of the social status of the writers and the addressee respectively is evident in the petition that the leaders of the Elephantine community sent to Bagavahya the governor of Judah (cf. A4.7:1–3, 22, 24).

110 See Porten et al., *The Elephantine Papyri in English*, 127 note 13, and Kottsieper, "Die Religionspolitik der Achämeniden," 150–178 (151).

111 Reinhard Gregor Kratz, "Judäische Gesandte im Achämenidenreich: Hananja, Esra und Nehemia," in *From Daēnā to Dīn: Religion, Kultur und Sprache in der iranischen Welt: Festschrift für Philip Kreyenbroek zum 60. Geburtstag*, ed. Christine Allison (Wiesbaden: Harrassowitz, 2009): 377–395, and Reinhard Gregor Kratz, "Judean Ambassadors and the Making of Jewish Identity: The Case of Hananiah, Ezra, and Nehemiah," in *Judah and the Judeans in the Achaemenid Period: Negotiating Identity in an International Context*, ed. Oded Lipschits et al. (Winona Lake, IN: Eisenbrauns, 2011): 421–444.

112 Lindenberger, *Ancient Aramaic and Hebrew Letters*, 61.

113 See Section 2.3.2.

114 An annotated translation can be found in Kuhrt, *The Persian Empire*, 117–122 (no. 4.11).

Even though the instructions in the so-called Passover letter seem to have a royal authority, the overall communicative situation is unclear. Was it sent from the king as a response to a foregoing letter sent by the Elephantine community? Was it an answer to a request from the satrap Arshama? Or did the king order Hananiah to send it without any previous requests from Egypt?

In any case, we can identify the instructions in the letter on the basis of the inflected verb forms. Each one of the injunctions is represented by either an imperative or a negated jussive.

In the surviving text it is possible to identify the following injunctions. First, the Judaean community (*'ntm*, "you," referring to the entire Judaean garrison) was instructed to "count" (*mnw*, A4.1:3). The object governed by the imperative *mnw* is only partially intact: *'rb...*, "four..." The following line (A4.1:4) contains the phrase "from the fifteenth day until the twenty-first day of ..." Therefore, it is likely that Jedaniah and his colleagues are instructed to count days. Moreover, the next intact injunctions come in A4.1:5 and are represented by the two imperatives "be pure!" (*dkyn hww*) and "beware!"/"take care!" (*'zdhrw*, *ithpeel* of *zhr*). Following immediately after these two commands the extant text reads *'bydh '* [*l*...], "work no[t ...](?)." Furthermore, the next extant injunction comes in the form of a negated jussive: "do not drink" (*'l tštw*, A4.1:6). Finally, the last two extant injunctions are:

> [... *h*]*n'lw btwnykm wḥtmw byn ywmy*
>
> [... b]ring into your chambers and seal off between the days (A4.1:8)

Since German archaeologists discovered the document in Elephantine in 1907 the commonly held opinion has been that the letter contains instructions about the Passover and the Festival of Unleavened Bread, two religious festivals attested above all in the Bible. As a consequence of that, the letter has since then mostly been referred to as the Passover letter,[115] although the word *psḥ'* is paradoxically not found in the extant text.

4.5.3.1 Rather a Letter on the Festival of Unleavened Bread?

Why was the letter given the name the Passover letter in the first place? The background for this interpretative name should above all be found in the letter's calendric references and other loaded terms. The week between the fifteenth and

115 So already William R. Arnold, "The Passover Papyrus from Elephantine," *JBL* 31 (1912): 1–33.

the twenty-first day of Nisan attested in A4.1:4, 7 is partially paralleled by the instructions concerning the Passover and the Festival of Unleavened Bread in the Bible, in particular in Exod 12:1–28 but also in Lev 23:5–8 and Deut 16:1–8. According to Exod 12:18, the people of Israel were commanded to eat unleavened bread "in the first month, from the evening of the fourteenth day until the evening of the twenty-first day."

The letter from Hananiah does not explicitly mention the Festival of Unleavened Bread, which is referred to as *ḥag hammaṣṣôt* (Lev 23:6 et al.) or simply *hammaṣṣôt* (Exod 12:17 et al.) in the Bible. There is also, though, a terminological correspondence with the biblical texts, apart from the calendric parallels outlined above (cf. Exod 12:15, 19 et al.), namely the Aramaic noun *ḥmyr*. In the rabbinic literature the word denotes "leaven, leavened bread." For instance, the Targums on Exod 12:15 use the Aramaic *ḥămîr/ḥămîrâ* where the Hebrew text has the noun *śəʾōr*, "leaven." In other words, Aramaic texts dating from later periods used the word *ḥămîr* to denote "leaven." Therefore, there are reasons to assume that the word had the same meaning in the Aramaic letter from Hananiah to the Judaean garrison, too.[116]

Furthermore, one of the only partially extant sentences in Hananiah's letter finds a possible parallel in the biblical regulations on the Passover and the Festival of Unleavened Bread:

> *ʿbydh* ʾ[*l*...]
>
> work no[t ...](?) (A4.1:5)

According to Exod 12:16, the people of Israel should not work (*kol məlākâ lōʾ yēʿāśê*) on either the first or the seventh day of the week of eating unleavened bread. Instead, they should hold a "solemn assembly" (*miqrâ qōdeš*). Leviticus 23:7–8 also offer prohibitions against work on the first and last day of the Festival of Unleavened Bread.

In other words, the commonly accepted conjecture that Hananiah's letter was about the Festival of Unleavened Bread and perhaps also about the Passover is a probable point of departure for further inquiries into the letter.

---

116 Erasmus Gass problematises the conventional understanding of the word *ḥmyr*. In his view, it is poorly attested in Northwest Semitic languages. Besides, it can also be explained as a derivation of other words (cf. *DNWSI* 1:382, s.v. *ḥmr*$_3$ "wrath," or *DNWSI* 1:382 *ḥmr*$_5$, cf.), cf. Erasmus Gass, "Der Passa-Papyrus (Cowl 21) – Mythos oder Realität?," *BN* 99 (1999): 55–68 (58 note 18).

4.5.3.2 Should a Restoration Be Made on the Basis of the Bible?

In Hananiah's letter the word *ḥmyr* occurs once. The context is a prohibition of drinking an otherwise unidentified beverage:

> [...]*ʾl tštw wkl mndʿm zy ḥmyr ʾl*[...]
>
> [...] do not drink, and anything leavened not [...] (A4.1:6)

The extant text does not contain the verb that presumably governed the phrase *wkl mndʿm zy ḥmyr*. However, on the basis of analogy with other legible passages of the letter, it is highly probable that the phrase is governed by a negated jussive, of which only the negation *ʾl* has survived in the extant text. The verbal root is lost. Nevertheless, the preceding verb ("do not drink") calls for symmetry. A reasonable conjecture based on inner-textual considerations is that the verb that originally governed the phrase in question was *ʾkl*, "to eat."

The inner-textual conjecture is in accordance with the biblical prescriptions concerning the Festival of Unleavened Bread. According to Exod 12:15, the people of Israel should remove leaven (Hebrew: *śəʾōr*; cf. Targ. Exod 12:15 *ḥămîr*) from their houses on the first day of the week of eating unleavened bread.

A century ago William R. Arnold published the subsequent scholarly research on the letter:

> It is perfectly clear that we have here a letter of instruction to the Jewish community at Elephantine, with directions for the punctilious observance of a feast to which the seven days extending from the fifteenth to the twenty-first day of the month Nisan sustain some essential relation; a feast which, moreover, requires abstinence from labour during at least a part of its continuance. This can be none other than the Passover—employing the term in the looser sense, of the Passover and feast of Unleavened Bread combined. And with this much assured, we need not hesitate to find in the suspended words of line 7 a reference to the banishing of leaven from every nook and corner of the houses of the faithful.[117]

Indeed, there are parallels between the extant text of the letter and the Bible. Arnold, and many after him, have therefore used the biblical instructions on the Passover and the Festival of Unleavened Bread as a source for restoring the many lacunas in the letter from Hananiah.

Yet despite the parallels between Hananiah's letter and the biblical regulations, there are also differences. Lindenberger has pointed out three features without any clear parallels in the biblical instructions:[118]

---

117 Arnold, "The Passover Papyrus from Elephantine," 1–33 (7).

118 See Lindenberger, *Ancient Aramaic and Hebrew Letters*, 62.

1. The last two extant injunctions, "bring into your chambers [probably referring to *ḥmyr*] and seal off" (A4.1:8),
2. the command "do not drink" (A4.1:6), and
3. the command "be pure and take care" (A4.1:5).

In addition to the differences enumerated by Lindenberger, there are additional ones:

4. Hananiah used the (Babylonian) month name Nisan, the first month of the year according to the Babylonian calendar.[119] Exodus 12:1 referred to "the first month of the year," and Deut 16:1 to "the month of Abib" (or alternatively: "the new moon of [the season of] abib).
5. In the Bible, the Passover and the Festival of Unleavened Bread were closely connected to the tradition about the exodus of the Israelites out of Egypt. For instance, according to Exod 12:17 the reason why the Festival of Unleavened Bread should be observed is that YHWH brought the Israelites out of Egypt "on this day" (i. e. the first day of the week of eating unleavened bread). Likewise, also Deut 16:1–4 has connected the Passover and the Festival of Unleavened Bread. There, the eating of unleavened bread, which is also called "the bread of affliction," is a sort of reenactment of the speedy exodus out of Egypt. However, Hananiah's letter does not contain any traces of a similar exodus tradition.

Porten has briefly suggested that the injunction to bring the leaven into chambers and seal off (A4.1:8) was an attempt to resolve a logical conflict found in the biblical material.[120] On the one hand, Exod 12:19 required that no leaven should be found (*lōʾ yimmāṣēʾ*) in the houses of the Israelites. On the other, Exod 13:7 required that no leaven should be seen (*lōʾ yērāʾê*). This contradiction was apparently noticed by the rabbis, too. A tradition that the Talmud ascribes to Rabbi Akiva puts an end to it by stating that there is no other way to remove leaven except by burning (b. Pesaḥ 5b).

The proposal outlined above would imply that Hananiah's letter as a matter of fact reflected some sort of early biblical and/or rabbinic exegesis. If so, its goal was to harmonise contradicting biblical regulations. The model assumes that Hananiah's letter ultimately reflects one or another version of the Pentateuch. Porten's proposal implies that Hananiah's letter is comparable to the biblical book of

119 See Esth 3:7 and Sacha Stern, "The Babylonian Calendar at Elephantine," *ZPE* 130 (2000): 159–171.
120 See Porten et al., *The Elephantine Papyri in English*, 127 notes 25, 27, and *COS* 3.46:117 note 28.

Chronicles and its attempts to reconcile contradictions in its *Vorlage*. As far as the Passover is concerned, the account of Josiah's Passover offered in 2Chr 35:1–19 is clearly a synthesis of conflicting biblical traditions. This is particularly clear in connection with how the Passover lamb was prepared: "They boiled [*waybaššəlû*] the passover lamb [*happesaḥ*] with fire [*bāʾēš*] according to the ordinance" (2Chr 35:13a).

This description presumably attempted to combine Exod 12:8–9 with Deut 16:7. According to Exod 12:8–9, the flesh of the lamb should be "roasted over the fire" (*ṣəlî ʾēš*) and not eaten "raw or boiled in water" (*nāʾ ûbāšēl məbušāl bammāyim*). However, according to Deut 16:7 the Israelites were commanded to boil (verb: *bšl*) the passover sacrifice at the place chosen by YHWH as his dwelling place.

Against the idea of making Hananiah's letter an early example of halachic exegesis I will argue that another model is more likely. In the Persian period there were several contrasting, and in part competing legislations on the Festival of Unleavened Bread and the Passover.[121] Most of them are reflected in the received text of the Hebrew Bible. Suffice it so mention the differences between Exod 12 and Deut 16. According to Exod 12 the Passover and Festival of Unleavened Bread constitute a combined festival that should be celebrated by each household. Each family should slaughter a lamb (Exod 12:3–6). However, according to Deut 16:5–6 the passover sacrifice (termed *happesaḥ*) should be offered only in the temple, the place chosen by YHWH as a dwelling for his name. In my view, the instructions in Hananiah's letter added but yet another voice into this choir of disharmonious legislations about the Festival of Unleavened Bread and the Passover evident in Yahwistic communities. It is not necessary to explain Hananiah's letter as an attempt to harmonise contradictions in the Bible.

In my view, the other differences I have enumerated above also point in the same direction. The extant text of Hananiah's letter does not identify the beverage the Judaeans in Elephantine were commanded not to drink. However, on the basis of a Mishnah passage it has been argued that it was a fermented drink. According to m. Pesaḥ 3:1, "Egyptian barley beer" is among the beverages that shall be removed at Passover.[122] Nevertheless, whatever drink Hananiah's letter originally prohibited, there is no biblical parallel to the prohibition. Moreover, as far

121 Compare, e.g., Exod 12:1–26; 23:14–15; 34:18–21; Lev 23:5–8; Deut 16:1–8. For an overview, see, e.g., Weyde, "Passa (AT)," available online at http://www.bibelwissenschaft.de/stichwort/30031/, and Karl William Weyde, "Mazzen/Mazzotfest," *WiBiLex:* available online at http://www.bibelwissenschaft.de/stichwort/25696/.

122 Quoted from Jacob Neusner, *The Mishnah: A New Translation* (New Haven: Yale University Press, 1988), 233.

as the injunction on purity (A4.1:5: "be pure and take care") is concerned, none of the legal texts of the Bible offer any rulings concerning purity in connection with the celebration of the mentioned festivals. The closest parallel is found in a narrative passage in Ezra 6:20. There it is related that the priests and the Levites "had purified themselves [*ṭhr* in the *hitpael* stem]; all of them were clean [*kullām ṭəhôrîm*]," when they slaughtered the passover offering (*happesaḥ*) for all the returned exiles, for their fellow priests and for themselves.

Summing up so far, there are arguments in favour of the view that Hananiah's letter imparted regulations concerning the Festival of Unleavened Bread and probably also the Passover to the Elephantine community. However the differences between Hananiah's letter and the biblical texts do not favour the idea that there is a genetic relationship between them, as if Hananiah's letter presupposed and reflected any of the Passover injunctions offered in the various regulations that we (today) find in the received biblical texts. On the contrary, independently of each other Hananiah's letter (A4.1) on the one hand, and the biblical texts on the other, attest to the characteristic diversity of the question of how to observe the Passover and the Festival of Unleavened Bread in the last half of the first millennium BCE. Some of this diversity is reflected in the received Bible, some is reflected in Hananiah's letter.

4.5.3.3 Any References to the Passover and the Passover Sacrifice?

The surviving part of Hananiah's letter does not contain any irrefutable references to the Passover/the Passover sacrifice. However, the majority of scholars have restored A4.1:3–4 on the assumption that it actually referred to the Passover. Arthur E. Cowley restored the lacuna as follows:

> *mnw ʾrb[ʿt ʿśr ywmn lyrḥ nysn psḥʾ ʿb]dw*
>
> Count fo[urteen days of the month Nisan and kee]p [the Passover][123]

Bezalel Porten's restoration differs slightly from Cowley's but nevertheless builds on the same assumption:

> *mnw ʾrb[ʿt ʿśr ywmn lnysn wb 14 byn šmšʾ psḥʾ ʿb]dw*
>
> Count four[teen days in Nisan and on the 14th at twilight ob]serve [the Passover][124]

123 Cowley, *Aramaic Papyri*, 62–64.
124 Porten and Yardeni, *TADAE*, I: Letters. Appendix: Aramaic Letters from the Bible, 54–55, and Porten et al., *The Elephantine Papyri in English*, 127.

However, on the other hand Ingo Kottsieper has argued that the letter originally lacked any references to *psḥ'* whatsoever. He suggested that A4.1:3–4 could be restored as the following:

> *mnw 'rb['t 'śr ywmn lnysn w'd 14 lnysn kl 'bydh 'b]dw*
>
> Count fo[urteen days with regard to Nisan and until 14 Nisan d]o [any work][125]

As long as no other version of the letter is known, any attempts to fill in the gaps will be conjectural. The phrase "to do ['*bd*] Passover" is admittedly found in the ostraca inscription D7.6 but not in Hananiah's letter. But, even if there can be given good reasons for filling in the gaps of Hananiah's letter with the word *psḥ*, it is in my view too loosely founded to be used as a basis upon which to discuss how the Passover was to be observed, according to the letter.[126] Did it include the slaughtering of an animal at all? If so, was the blood used for apotropaic purposes? Was the possible Passover sacrifice made in the temple of YHW (compare Deut 16:5–6; cf. 2Kgs 23:21–23) or in the context of the households (compare Exod 12:3–6)? The lacunas prevent us from knowing for sure.

4.5.3.4 Did the Letter Signal a Change of the Social Sphere of the Festival(s)?

The questions arising from Hananiah's letter are legio and open up for many, often contradicting answers. Nevertheless, some things concerning the ritual aspect can positively be said. In Hananiah's letter all of the inflected volitive verbs are in the second person plural. Paired with the fact that the letter is addressed to "Jedaniah and his colleagues the Judaean garrison" (A4.1:1, 10), it is plausible to claim that the verbs denote communal rites. All of the Judaeans in Elephantine were expected to take part in them. Moreover, the official tenor of the letter and its communicative situation emphasise that it was an official matter. Therefore, in my view the temple was the locus for the communal rite.

So, Hananiah's letter may have signalled a change in the social sphere the Passover was observed in. In the earlier Passover ostracon D7.6 the context was the family. However, Hananiah's letter clearly (?) puts the Festival of Unleavened Bread (and perhaps the Passover) in an official context. This is not only proved by the prescribed rites being addressed to a collective "you" (cf. A4.1:1, 10 "to Jedaniah and his colleagues the Judaean garrison"); what is more, the in-

---

125 Kottsieper, "Die Religionspolitik der Achämeniden," 150–178 (151 and notes 3–4).
126 Porten et al., *The Elephantine Papyri in English*, 127 note 18.

structions are somehow anchored in the Achaemenid bureaucracy. The legal basis was a royal decree issued by King Darius and sent to Arshama, the satrap of Egypt:

> *wk'ṭ šnt' z' šnt 2+3 drywhwš mlk' mn mlk' šlyḥ 'l 'rš[m]*
>
> And now, this year, year 5 of Darius the king, from the king it has been sent to Arsha[ma] (A4.1:2)[127]

Borrowing the terminology of the spatial model of religion used by Jonathan Z. Smith, we should consequently understand the Passover described in the ostracon inscription D7.6 as part of "religion here," that is, the domestic religion set in the family. In contrast, the religious festivals described in Hananiah's letter definitely give the impression of being part of a public, if not even state, religion. Using Smith's terminology, the communal rite described in Hananiah's letter was part of "religion there," that is, the public, civic and state religion, typically the religion of the elite.

Therefore, Hananiah's letter reflects an attempt to take control over and regulate parts of the religious life of the Judaeans. Religious rituals that originally were practiced within a family sphere were turned into a public matter, affecting the Judaean community's communal organisation of time.

4.5.3.5 The Purpose of Hananiah's Letter: Not to Introduce but to Fix the Date

The references to the Passover found in D7.24 and D7.6, the two ostraca from the first quarter of the fifth century BCE (however, D7.6 may be later[128]), imply that the Passover was already known in Elephantine. Whatever the purpose of Hananiah's letter from 419 BCE was, it was not to introduce a new festival to the Judaean community there.

Although the evidence is scant, it is nevertheless tempting to read Hananiah's letter on the background of D7.6:8–10. There, the question was not whether or not the Passover should be celebrated but *when*. The writer asked Hoshaiah, who decidedly belonged to the same extended family, to inform him (or her?) *when* he and the other ones would "make Passover."

---

127 Quoted from Porten et al., *The Elephantine Papyri in English*, 127 (slightly modified).
128 Kottsieper, "Die Religionspolitik der Achämeniden," 150–178 (151 note 5, referring to Pierre Grelot).

When Hananiah wrote his letter more than a half century later, he also presumably focussed on when (the Passover and) the Festival of Unleavened Bread should be observed. However, whereas the ostracon written to Hoshaiah seemed to presuppose a fluctuating date, Hananiah's letter referred to a fixed date, using the Babylonian calendar.

Therefore, provided that Hananiah's letter was about the Passover and the Festival of Unleavened Bread, its purpose was presumably to fix the date. In the last part of the fifth century BCE someone (the king, Hananiah himself, or perhaps someone else?) considered it necessary to regulate the (religious) calendar of the Judaean community in Elephantine.

4.5.3.6 The Purpose of Hananiah's Letter: To Regulate out of Consideration for the Economy and the Stability?

In general, it is difficult to account for the purpose of a religious ritual. One problem is that various subgroups within one and the same religious group may observe identical rituals but for different reasons. Several examples of this are known from biblical scholarship, such as the various motivations for the Sabbath reflected in the two versions of the Decalogue[129] and the different theories concerning the historical origins of the Passover and the Festival of Unleavened Bread on the one hand, and the assumed secondary combination of them on the other.[130]

Moreover, a second problem is the limitation of the sources. If it is not possible to interview and observe the practitioners in situ (which always is the case when studying religions of ancient times), then we have to rely on textual sources and/or archaeological artefacts. However, such sources never offer every as-

129 According to Exod 20:8–11, the reason for remembering the Sabbath day and keeping it holy is that YHWH made heaven and earth in six days but rested on the seventh day. In contrast, according to Deut 5:12–15 the reason for observing the Sabbath day and keeping it holy is related to the exodus from Egypt. The Israelites are urged to remember that they were slaves in Egypt and that YHWH brought them out from there "with a mighty and an outstretched arm" (Deut 5:15).

130 It is reasonable that the Festival of Unleavened Bread originally was an agricultural festival because it presupposed a sedentary population, cf. Weyde, "Mazzen/Mazzotfest," available online at http://www.bibelwissenschaft.de/stichwort/25696/. The Passover, in contrast, has often been regarded as a festival with a nomadic origin, cf. Haran, *Temples and Temple-Service*, 318–323, whereas others, pointing to the mentioning of lintels and doorposts in, e.g., Exod 12:1–10, 21–23, have argued that the Passover was a ritual that originated among the inhabitants of a cultivated land, cf. Weyde, "Passa (AT)," available online at http://www.bibelwissenschaft.de/stichwort/30031/.

pect of a given subject matter. As far as the religious rituals of the Judaeans in Elephantine are concerned, the things that were once presumably common knowledge among them are no longer known to us.

Did the Judaeans in Elephantine celebrate and reenact YHWH's salvation of the people of Israel and the exodus out of Egypt? Or did they celebrate the Passover as an apotropaic ritual that protected against demons such as the Destroyer of YHWH (cf. Exod 12:23)? All things considered, no definite answer can be given. We do not know for what purpose they kept the Passover and the festival of unleavened bread.

On the positive side, the unfortunate silence of the sources regarding the motivations of the Judaeans at Elephantine for observing the Passover and the Festival of Unleavened Bread opens up for conjectures. It is possible to approach the question of the purpose of the combined festival in Elephantine in a different way, focussing on:

- the communicative situation evident particularly in Hananiah's letter (A4.1): a royal, Persian decree communicated through an envoy to a Judaean garrison under Persian command stationed at the southwestern border of the Persian empire, and
- in particular the question of who would potentially benefit/suffer from the Passover and the Festival of Unleavened Bread.

In my view, it is possible to point out at least three groups that potentially would have been affected positively or negatively by the (combined) festival described in Hananiah's letter.

One possible group may have been the priests of Khnum and the indigenous Egyptians in general. If we surmise that the Judaeans in Elephantine actually connected the festivals with a religious narrative about YHW's rescue of the people of Israel from the hands of Pharaoh—an assumption that neither can be verified nor falsified but nevertheless suffices as a working hypothesis—then the combined festival would potentially have an anti-Egyptian tendency. According the biblical version of the exodus narrative, the Egyptians had the role as oppressors whereas the Israelites were the victims of the hardship. Moreover, the biblical exodus narrative portrays the god of the Israelites as by far more powerful than the Egyptian gods: "For I will pass through the land of Egypt that night, and I will strike down every firstborn in the land of Egypt, both human beings and animals; on all the gods of Egypt I will execute judgments: I am the LORD" (Exod 12:12 NRSV).

Correspondingly, upon hearing "of all that God had done for Moses and for his people Israel, how the LORD had brought Israel out of Egypt" (Exod 18:1 NRSV), Jethro, Moses' father-in-law, proclaimed: "Now I know that the LORD is greater than all gods, because he delivered the people from the Egyptians, when they dealt arrogantly with them" (Exod 18:11 NRSV). Provided that the Judaeans in Elephantine actually commemorated and reenacted a religious tradition comparable to (or even related to) the narrative found in the book of Exodus, such a celebration could potentially cause anti-Judaean reactions among the Egyptians, and vice versa, an anti-Egyptian reaction among the Judaeans. No one would benefit from such a latent ethnic-religious conflict, in particular not the Persians.

Such a scenario could potentially explain why the Persian administration was concerned with the festival. On the one hand, the royal decree reflected in Hananiah's letter permitted the Judaeans to celebrate. However, on the other hand, it also placed boundaries on when and how to celebrate.

A second group possibly affected by the Judaeans' celebration of the festivals was the Persian administration itself. As soldiers, the Judaeans provided law-enforcement and security for the Persians, and a celebration of the Passover and Festival of Unleavened Bread would probably imply absence from such military duties. The text of Hananiah's letter is badly damaged, but the extant text definitely contains injunctions calling for ritual purity and most probably also an injunction prohibiting against work (A4.1:5). If the Passover and the Festival of Unleavened Bread entailed that the Judaeans would be unable to fulfil their military duties for a certain period, it was necessary for the Persian administration to regulate the necessary leave of absence.[131]

Finally, a third group that possibly may have been affected were those involved in the production and trade of foodstuff. The Festival of Unleavened Bread implies that the Judaeans ceased to demand leavened products for a period. The extant text of Hananiah's letter contains injunctions concerning food consumption:

> [...]*ʾl tštw wkl mndʿm zy ḥmyr ʾl*[...]
>
> [...] do not drink, and anything leavened not [...] (A4.1:6)

In the extant text, the noun governed by the negated verb "do not drink" (*ʾl tštw*) is missing, as is also the verb governing the nominal phrase "and anything of leaven" (*wkl mndʿm zy ḥmyr*). Nevertheless, in the light of the context, in particular the verb "drink," the verb in the lacuna is likely to have been "eat" (Porten reconstructs the jussive *tʾklw*, which parallels the verb *tštw*[132]). Moreover, the

131 Thus already Arnold, "The Passover Papyrus from Elephantine," 1–33 (15–16).

132 Porten and Yardeni, *TADAE*, I: Letters. Appendix: Aramaic Letters from the Bible, 54–55.

drink that according to the injunction should not be drunk was probably a fermented beverage, corresponding to the prohibition to eat anything leaven.

Admittedly, it is not clear to what extent the economic life in the areas where the Judaeans were settled was affected by their festivals. After all, the Festival of Unleavened Bread was not a festival of fasting. The Judaeans replaced their ordinary bread (which typically was leavened) with bread that was not leavened. The difference was that it should not be made by sourdough and/or yeast. However, flour was still needed for making the unleavened bread which is called *maṣṣâ* in Biblical Hebrew. Presumably, the total quantity of the Judaeans' demand for grain used for making bread was not affected by the festival.

The presumably fermented beverage that should not be drunk during the festival was probably beer. Loaves of bread made from a richly yeasted dough were the basis for beer brewing in Egypt.[133] The loaves were lightly baked and the resulting bread was crumbled and strained through a sieve with water. The dissolved bread (which may have been enriched by dates and extra yeast) was then fermented in large vats before being tapped into jars that were sealed. The result was a highly nutritious beverage that was used on a daily basis both for refreshment and for sustenance. In ancient Egypt, beer was of utmost importance. Together with bread, it was a staple item of the diet, for poor as well as rich, and for children as well as for adults.[134] A passage from the "Instruction of Any," a wisdom text written sometimes in the second millennium BCE, illustrates the importance of beer in the Egyptian diet. The father instructs his son to take care of his mother: "Double the food your mother gave you, Support her as she supported you; ... When she sent you to school, And you were taught to write, She kept watching over you daily, With bread and beer in her house."[135]

Beer was so valuable in the economic life of Egypt that beer jars were often used as a measurement of values.[136] Beer was closely connected to the production and distribution of grain. Cereal products formed the basis of the economy and political organisation of the ancient Egyptian society.[137]

---

133 Wolfgang Helck, "Bier," *LÄ* 1: 789–792.
134 Rosemarie Drenkhahn, "Brot," *LÄ* 1: 871, and Wolfgang Helck, "Getränke," *LÄ* 2: 586.
135 "Instruction of Any," translated by Miriam Lichtheim (*COS* 1.46:110–115[113]), cf. also *ANET*, 420–421.
136 Compare, e.g., the fragmentary account C3.11:1–3: "The [silver] which stands in year 6: silver, [x] karsh, [y shekels. Herein]: 1 [... of] beer (amounting) to silver, 1 karsh, 4 shekels; 1 [... of] *ṭyq* bread (amounting) to silver, 1 karsh." Quoted from Porten and Yardeni, *TADAE*, III: Literature, Accounts, Lists, 209.
137 Wolfgang Helck, "Getreide," *LÄ* 2: 586–589.

Therefore, in the light of the pivotal position of beer brewing in the economy of Egypt, a religious festival requiring that a group abstained from the economically central commodity would potentially cause disturbance, as it could cause economic losses. For the Persians, who themselves were highly involved in the economic life of Egypt,[138] but at the same time dependent upon non-Egyptian soldiers like those in the Judaean garrison in Elephantine, there may have been the need to regulate the religious festival of the Judaeans out of consideration for the economy.

4.6 The Sabbath in Elephantine

4.6.1 The Sabbath as an Identity Marker in the Last Half of the First Millennium BCE in Biblical and Intertestamental Literature

In the last half of the first millennium BCE the Sabbath, meaning the seventh day of the seven-day week, gradually became an important identity marker of Yahwism, which developed into Judaism in the same period.[139] Yahwistic, or in this case more precisely, Jewish texts from the last centuries BCE, seem to reflect an ongoing discussion about the Sabbath, in particular the rules regulating what one was allowed or not allowed to do on the Sabbath, and the dilemmas such regulations caused.

The dilemmas caused by the Sabbath can be illustrated by a narrative set in the second century BCE at the time of Antiochus Epiphanes. According to 1Macc 2:31–41, a group of pious Israelites led by the priest Mattathias had fled from the persecutions of Antiochus. Mattathias and his followers were unwilling to comply with the king's blasphemous commands. Some of the Israelites belonging to Mattathias's group were attacked by the king's soldiers on the Sabbath day. In

---

138 Compare how inclined the satrap Arshama was to economical micromanagement in, e.g., A6.2 (Arshama being involved in the repair of a boat leased to two Carians).

139 For a recent discussion of the characteristics of Judaism/the Jewish religion(s) of the so-called postexilic period in contrast to Israelite–Judaean religion and the biblical traditions, see Kratz, *Historisches und biblisches Israel*, 62–78. For an overview of the Sabbath in the Hebrew Bible, see Corinna Körting, "Sabbat (AT)," *WiBiLex:* available online at http://www.bibelwissenschaft.de/stichwort/25732/. The following discussion is also partly indebted to the fine discussion in Bob Becking, "Sabbath at Elephantine: A Short Episode in the Construction of Jewish Identity," in *Empsychoi logoi—Religious Innovations in Antiquity: Studies in Honour of Pieter Willem van der Horst*, ed. Alberdina Houtman et al., AJEC 73 (Leiden: Brill, 2008): 177–189, reprinted in *Ezra, Nehemiah, and the Construction of Early Jewish Identity*, FAT 80 (Tübingen: Mohr Siebeck, 2011): 118–127.

order not to profane the Sabbath the group of pious Israelites chose not to defend themselves. The result of the Sabbath observance was the death of a thousand men, women, and children. However, later on, when Mattathias and his friends heard about this, they realised the dilemma. Therefore, they made the following decision: "Let us fight against anyone who comes to attack us on the sabbath day; let us not all die as our kindred died in their hiding places" (1Macc 2:41 NRSV).

The question of the observance/lack of observance of the Sabbath as a day of rest is also a topic in biblical narratives set in earlier periods. An example is the book of Nehemiah, set in the Persian period. Nehemiah 8 relates that the scribe Ezra brought "the book of the law of Moses which YHWH had given to Israel" before the entire people of Israel and read it in public (v. 1ff.). After having heard the words of the book, the Israelites "separated themselves from all foreigners, and stood and confessed their sins and the iniquities of their ancestors" (Neh 9:2). After the communal confession, the people made "a firm agreement in writing," a sealed document signed by the officials of the people, the Levites and the priests (Neh 9:38). The people were apparently headed by the governor Nehemiah (cf. Neh 10:1 [ET 10:2]). One of the things that the Israelites promised to do, according to the written document, was connected to the Sabbath: "If the peoples of the land bring in merchandise or any grain on the sabbath day to sell, we will not buy it from them on the Sabbath or on a holy day" (Neh 10.32 [ET 10:31] NRSV).

However, later on in the book, Nehemiah the governor reports that he himself witnessed a breach of the Sabbath halacha, admonished the wrongdoers and imposed measures in Jerusalem by posting Levites as guards at the gates to keep the Sabbath holy (Neh 13:15–22).

The theological importance ascribed to the Sabbath in the book of Nehemiah is particularly evident in two statements at the book's conclusion. First, in his admonition of the Judaeans who had violated the Sabbath regulations, the governor Nehemiah referred to the past. His (theological) interpretation of Israel's history comes close to explaining the fall of the kingdom of Judah and the city of Jerusalem, the Babylonian exile and the present situation after the exile as a consequence of the ancestors' profaning of the Sabbath (Neh 13:18, cf. Neh 9). Second, according to Neh 13:22 Nehemiah addressed God directly: "Remember this also in my favor, O my God, and spare me according to the greatness of your steadfast love" (Neh

13:22b NRSV). The thing Nehemiah boasted of in the presence of God and adjured him to remember was his measures to keep the Sabbath holy.[140]

The importance of the Sabbath is not confined to the biblical narratives. It is also an important subject in the laws of the Hebrew Bible. For instance, both versions of the Decalogue prescribe that the Sabbath shall be a day of rest. Although the motivations for keeping the Sabbath differ between the two versions (Exod 20:11: reference to God's creation of the world in six days and Deut 5:15: reference to the exodus from Egypt), both agree in that no human or animal in the households of the Israelites shall do any work on that day. Moreover, both versions agree in defining the Sabbath as the seventh and last day of the week.

Another example somewhat isolated from its narrative context is the law on the Sabbath given in Exod 35:1–3. It states that no work shall be done on the seventh day because this day shall be "a holy Sabbath of solemn rest to YHWH." He who violates the prohibition on work shall be put to death.

Further, the idea of keeping every seventh day as a day of rest is also found in other biblical laws such as, for example, Exod 23:12 (part of the Covenant Code) and Exod 34:21. It should be noted that the term "Sabbath" does not appear in any of these two cases. Exodus 23:12 occurs in the context of various laws that YHWH gave the Israelites. These laws clearly protect the rights of the *persona miserae* such as foreigners and the poor. The seventh day as a day of rest is closely connected to the law on fallow years that is found immediately before it. YHWH commanded the Israelites to let their agricultural land rest and lie fallow every seventh year "so that the poor of your people may eat" (Exod 23:10–11). Moreover, the reference to the seventh day in Exod 34:21 comes in the context of the statutes YHWH prescribed in connection with the renewal of the covenant after the Israelites' apostasy in connection with the golden calf (cf. Exod 32). Within the context of other calendar issues connected to the covenant renewal, YWHW also commanded the Israelites to rest on the seventh day, even during ploughing time and harvest.

140 For a discussion of Nehemiah's (self-boasting) invocation of YHWH and the so-called *Gedächtnismotiv*, see Blenkinsopp, "The Mission of Udjahorresnet," 409–421 (414–421).

4.6.2 What Kind of Sabbath: A Lunar Sabbath or the Seventh Day of a Seven-Day Week?

Some of the biblical texts mentioned above were no doubt composed in the Persian period or in the Hellenistic period. Others, above all the legal texts, are more difficult to date and biblical scholars consequently disagree about their literary history. This is not the place to discuss the literary history of the biblical texts. Neither is it the place to discuss each and every religio-historical aspect of the Sabbath, understood as the divinely prescribed day of rest that the Israelites kept holy on the last day of the seven-day week. Nevertheless, there are a handful of biblical passages that seem to portray the Sabbath in a way that differs distinctively from the biblical passages mentioned above: 2Kgs 4:22–23; Amos 8:5; Hos 2:13 [ET 2:11] and Isa 1:13. Common for all of these four texts is that the noun "Sabbath" (*šabbāt*) appears together with the "new moon" (*ḥōdeš*).

For example, in 2Kgs 4:22–23 (part of the story about the woman from Shunem, her son and Elisha) the woman's husband asked: "Why go to him [i. e. Elisha, the man of God] today? It is neither new moon nor Sabbath." In this case and in the other three texts mentioned above, the "new moon" presumably represented the opposite of the "Sabbath." In other words, in these texts, the Sabbath presumably designated the day of the full moon.

Since Johannes Meinhold's seminal publications on the origin of the biblical Sabbath, scholars have mostly understood the references to the Sabbath found in the presumed early biblical texts from the monarchic period as the day of the full moon.[141] Moreover, in addition to the four presumably preexilic texts mentioned above, there is also another type of argument for tracing the origin of the Sabbath to a monthly day of full moon: the Akkadian term *šapattu*. In several Akkadian inscriptions, the word *šapattu* was the name of the fifteenth day of the month or the day of the full moon, which fell on the fifteenth day of the month.[142]

From a religio-historical viewpoint, the literary history of the Hebrew Bible suggests that there was a development in the way the Sabbath was understood. The four text passages mentioned above presumably reflect the typical situation in the monarchic period of Israel and Judah. At that time the Sabbath was observed on the day of the full moon, and this a day that took place once a month. However, the majority of the biblical texts (and definitely their reception

141 See, e.g., Johannes Meinhold, "Die Entstehung des Sabbats," *ZAW* 29 (1909): 81–112.
142 See M. J. Geller, "šapattu," *RlA* 12: 25–27, and Erica Reiner et al., "šapattu," *CAD* 17: 449–450. Moreover, see Alexandra Grund, *Die Entstehung des Sabbats: seine Bedeutung für Israels Zeitkonzept und Erinnerungskultur*, FAT 75 (Tübingen: Mohr Siebeck, 2011), 106–117.

history) reflect an understanding of the Sabbath as, first, a day of rest that, second, takes place every seventh day.

In the light of this, then, one of the main questions in the following will be: How did the Achaemenid period Judaeans in Elephantine understand the term Sabbath?

- One problem is connected to the term "Sabbath" as a rendition of the Aramaic *šbh*. Did the Aramaic *šbh* correspond to the Hebrew *šabbāt*[143] and the Akkadian *šapattu?*[144]
- Provided that the Aramaic *šbh* actually corresponded to the Hebrew *šabbāt* and/or the Akkadian *šapattu*, there is the question of the nature and function of the *šbh* in the Judaean community. Was the Sabbath in Elephantine a (religiously motivated) day of rest observed on the last day of a seven-day week, and if so, were there any halachic prescriptions ("rites") that had to be done in connection with it? Or did *šbh* in Elephantine refer to a lunar Sabbath, that is, the fifteenth day of a month and the day of the full moon, corresponding to the Akkadian *šapattu?*
- Closely connected to the questions above is the question about the origin of the *šbh* in Elephantine. Was the Sabbath of the Judaeans in Elephantine part of the Yahwistic heritage that their ancestors brought down with them from Judah? Or was the Sabbath brought to (Upper) Egypt by people from Mesopotamia or influenced by Mesopotamian culture? Or, alternatively, did the *šbh* of the Elephantine Judaean community take up elements from both?

---

143 According to *DNWSI* 2:1107, s.v. *šbh*, *šbh* is a hyper-correct status absolutus derived from the status constructus *šbt*ʾ. An almost similar position is taken in Diether Kellermann and Mechthild Kellermann, "YHW-Tempel und Sabbatsfeier auf Elephantine?," in *Festgabe für Hans-Rudolf Singer zum 65. Geburtstag am 6. April 1990 überreicht von seinen Freunden und Kollegen*, ed. Martin Forstner, FAS 13 (Frankfurt am Main: Peter Lang, 1991): 433–452 (446): the Aramaic form was allegedly created on the basis of the misunderstanding that the Hebrew *šbt* was a feminine status constructus of the status determinativus *šbh*. Finally, according to Muraoka, *An Introduction to Egyptian Aramaic*, 131, the Aramaic noun was created from Hebrew *šbt* by wrongly analysing the final *tav* as the feminine ending. However, according to A. Dupont-Sommer, "Sabbat et Parascève à Eléphantine d'après des ostraca araméens inedits," *MémAIBLIF* 15, no. 1 (1960): 67–88 (75–81), both the Aramaic *šbh* and the Hebrew *šabbāt* were, independently of each other, derivations of the Akkadian *šapattu*.

144 Gerhard F. Hasel, "Sabbath," *ABD* 5: 849–856, argues against the common assumption that there is an etymological connection between the Akkadian term *šapattu* and the Hebrew *šabbāt*. However, this widely accepted assumption is reflected in, e.g., Körting, "Sabbat (AT)," available online at http://www.bibelwissenschaft.de/stichwort/25732/, and, above all, Grund, *Die Entstehung des Sabbats*, 130–133.

Moreover, the personal name Shabbethai (*šbyt*) occurs several times in Aramaic inscriptions from ancient Egypt and opens up for several questions:

- Provided that its etymology can be explained as "the one who belongs to the Sabbath"[145] et al.), it nevertheless remains an open question what the original meaning of "Sabbath" was in the context of a personal name. Was it "Sabbath" meaning "the day of the full moon" that fell on the fifteenth day of the month (cf. Akkadian *šapattu*)? Or was it meant in the sense "the last day of the seven-day week"?
- Closely connected to the questions above is the question of the direction of borrowing. In the cases where presumably non-Judaeans bore the name Shabbethai, is can this be explained as being a response to the growing importance of the Sabbath in the Persian period?[146] Or did non-Judaeans get the name because they were born on the day of the full moon? In other words, did non-Judaeans adopt the name from the Judaeans?[147] Or did people, Judaeans and non-Judaeans alike, borrow the name as a result of the influence of the Babylonian calendar?

4.6.3 The Terminology: Hebrew *šabbāt* and Egyptian Aramaic *šbh*

In the Persian period sources from Egypt the Sabbath is potentially reflected in two terms:

- in the Egyptian Aramaic noun *šbh*, and
- in the personal name *šbty*, "Shabbethai."

Although the Aramaic ostraca containing the noun *šbh* were acquired early in the twentieth century, it took half a century before André Dupont-Sommer proposed *šbh* to be the Aramaic rendition of the Hebrew noun *šabbāt*.[148]

If we leave the biblical material aside, to my knowledge the earliest known potential Hebrew occurrence of the noun *šabbāt* is found in the Yabneh-Yam

145 *HALOT* 4:1412, s.v. *šabbətay*.

146 So Albert Vincent, *La religion des judéo-araméens d'Eléphantine* (Paris: Geuthner, 1937), 414, and several others after him.

147 So, e.g., Porten et al., *The Elephantine Papyri in English*, 234 note 22, and Bezalel Porten, "The Religion of the Jews of Elephantine in Light of the Hermopolis Papyri," *JNES* 28 (1969): 116–121.

148 See Lutz Doering, *Schabbat: Sabbathalacha und -praxis im antiken Judentum und Urchristentum*, TSAJ 78 (Tübingen: Mohr Siebeck, 1999), 23–24.

(Meṣad Ḥashavyahu) ostracon from the late seventh century BCE.[149] A servant complained to his superior (line 1: *'dny hšr*, "my lord the commander") about a certain Hoshaiah son of Shobai who had taken his garment. In lines 3–8 there is a passage where the servant describes this situation:

[3] *qṣr hyh'bdk bḥ*
[4] *ṣr 'sm wyqṣr 'bdk*
[5] *wykl w'sm kymm lpny šb*
[6] *t k'šr kl ['ʿ]bdk 't qṣr w'*
[7] *sm kymm wyb' hwšʿyhw bn šb*
[8] *y wyqḥ 't bgd ʿbdk ...*

[3] Your servant is a harvester in Ḥa-
[4] zarasam. And your servant harvested
[5] and he finished and he stored (it) a few days[150] before šb
[6] t. As your [se]rvant had finished his harvest, he st-
[7] ored (it) a few days. And Hoshiah son of Shob-
[8] i came and he took your servant's garment ...

In this context, the interesting question is obviously what was meant by the phrase *lpny šbt*. William F. Albright proposed to read "before the Sabbath." On the other hand, James M. Lindenberger has interpreted it as "before stopping," i.e. "Your servant finished his harvest and stored it a few days before stopping" (lines 4b–6a).[151] From a philological as well as a religio-historical viewpoint both alternatives are possible. Provided that the phrase *lpny šbt* actually means "before the Sabbath," it cannot be said what kind of Sabbath the Yabneh-Yam ostracon referred to.

As far as the history of Yahwism is concerned, there was indeed an idea of the Sabbath even before the Babylonian exile, as is evident in texts such as 2Kgs 4:22–23, Amos 8:5, Hos 2:13 [ET 2:11] and Isa 1:13. However, these texts by no means prove that the noun *šbt* designated a weekly day of rest during the monar-

---

149 For the Hebrew text, see Graham I. Davies et al., *Ancient Hebrew Inscriptions: Corpus and Concordance* (Cambridge: Cambridge University Press, 1991), 76 (no. 7.001), and Lindenberger, *Ancient Aramaic and Hebrew Letters*, 109–110 (no. 50). For English translations and commentaries, see, e.g., *ANET*, 568 (by W. F. Albright) and Lindenberger, *Ancient Aramaic and Hebrew Letters*, 110.

150 Albright translates *kymm* "usually," giving the clause "as they finished the storage of grain, *as usual before the Sabbath*," cf. *ANET*, 586 (my emphasis).

151 Lindenberger, *Ancient Aramaic and Hebrew Letters*, 109–110 (no. 50), thus also Dennis Pardee in *COS* 3.41:77–78 ("before stopping [work]"). However, in a footnote Lindenberger opens up for the possibility of translating "before Sabbath," cf. Lindenberger, *Ancient Aramaic and Hebrew Letters*, 110.

chic period of Israel and Judah. In each one of these texts it seems that the Sabbath occurred in a pair with the term *ḥdš*, "new moon." Moreover, 2Kgs 4:22–23 seem to suggest that the Sabbath and the new moon were considered to be particularly favourable days for visiting a holy man. Amos 8:5 seems to imply that there was a taboo connected to the trading of agricultural products on the Sabbath and the new moon. In other words, in the light of both epigraphic material (the Yabneh-Yam ostracon) and the biblical material, the term *šbt* ("Sabbath") can be traced back to the Yahwism of the period before the Persian period. Therefore, it is possible that the concept of Sabbath—in one way or another—was part of the heritage that the Judaeans in Elephantine had taken over from their ancestors from Judah.

However, strictly speaking the noun *šbt* (*šabbāt*) is not found in Egyptian Aramaic sources. Instead, the word used was *šbh*. From an etymological viewpoint it is probable that the Egyptian Aramaic *šbh* corresponds to the Hebrew *šabbāt*.[152] The noun *šbh* is used in later Aramaic dialects, too,[153] and the form *šbh* found in the sources from Elephantine consequently represents the earliest Aramaic attestation of the form. Nevertheless, the question arises: Why did the Judaeans in Elephantine use the noun *šbh*, and why did they not continue to use the Hebrew form *šabbāt?*

In order to seek an answer to this question, one needs to take as a point of departure the language shift that occurred in the Judaean community in Elephantine at some point before our sources were written. The mother tongue of the ancestors of the Judaeans in Elephantine was presumably Hebrew when they still lived in Judah.[154] However, irrespective of when the Judaean community migrated to Elephantine (and how), the mother tongue was about to become or had already become Aramaic in the fifth century BCE, even when writing to Judah (cf. A4.7 and A4.8).[155] If for no other reasons, this was convenient in the light of the fact that the Judaeans in Elephantine served in the Persian army, and Aramaic had become an important lingua franca in the Persian empire.

---

152 So, e.g., also Lemaire, "Judean Identity in Elephantine," 365–373 (370).
153 The word *šbh* is used for "Sabbath" in, i.a., Palestinian Aramaic. The phrase *qdm šbh* is attested in the Bar Kokhba Letters (second century CE), cf. P.Yadin 50:5–6 = 5/6Ḥev 50:5–6, in Yigael Yadin and Hannah Cotton, *The Documents from the Bar Kokhba Period in the Cave of Letters: Hebrew, Aramaic and Nabatean-Aramaic Papyri*, JDS 3 (Jerusalem: Israel Exploration Society, 2002).
154 The only explicit reference to the ancestors is found in A4.7:13 par.
155 For a brief discussion of the language shift from Hebrew to Aramaic, see William M. Schniedewind, "Aramaic, the Death of Written Hebrew, and Language Shift in the Persian Period," in *Margins of Writing, Origins of Cultures*, ed. Seth L. Sanders, OIS 2 (Chicago: Oriental Institute of the University of Chicago, 2006): 141–151.

It has been proposed that the transition from Hebrew *šabbāt* to Aramaic *šbh* represented a hyper-correct status absolutus derived of the status constructus *šbt*[156] or a misunderstanding where the final *tav* in the Hebrew *šabbāt* was wrongly analysed as the feminine ending.[157]

Kellermann and Kellermann have pointed to an implication of these explanations that is relevant for the history of religion of the Judaeans in Elephantine. Provided that the Aramaic *šbh* in fact was a secondary neologism (regardless whether it is due to an error or a hypercorrection), then any traces of a possible etymological connection between the Hebrew noun *šabbāt* and the Hebrew verb *šbt*, "to rest," has disappeared (see below).[158]

Theoretically, two alternatives are possible. According to the first one, the Aramaic-speaking Judaeans accepted the loss of the etymological connection between the Hebrew verb *šbt*, "to rest," and the Hebrew noun *šabbāt* when they took on the "new" form *šbh*. This alternative implies that the Judaeans in Elephantine had abandoned a supposedly theologically important aspect of the "original" Sabbath theology. According to the second alternative, the Aramaic speaking Judaeans of Elephantine had never at any point in their prehistory been aware of an etymological connection between the verb *šbt* and the noun *šabbāt*. The second alternative suggests that such a connection had not yet been made when the ancestors of the Elephantine Judaeans left Judah and migrated to Egypt. Furthermore, the second alternative also implies that the Judaeans had never been exposed to such an etymology with theological implications later on either.[159]

In my view, the second alternative—that the Judaeans in Elephantine were unaware of any etymological connection between the Hebrew noun *šabbāt* and the verb *šbt*, "to rest"—is much more likely than the first one. The etymological connection was first made relatively late in the history of Yahwism, as can be glimpsed via the literary history of the Hebrew Bible, in particular the Pentateuch.

A popular etymological connection between the noun *šabbāt*, "Sabbath" and the verb *šbt*, "to rest," is definitely evident in the late, so-called Priestly texts of the Pentateuch. According to the Priestly creation account, God "rested [*wayyišbōt*] on the seventh day" of the creation week (Gen 2:2). Although the noun *šabbāt* ("Sabbath") does not occur in the context of the Priestly creation account, there is nevertheless no doubt that "the seventh day" referred to the

156 *DNWSI* 2:1107, s.v. *šbh*.
157 Muraoka, *An Introduction to Egyptian Aramaic*, 131.
158 Kellermann and Kellermann, "YHW-Tempel," 433–452 (446).
159 Kellermann and Kellermann, "YHW-Tempel," 433–452 (446).

Sabbath. Moreover, this has been made perfectly clear in another Priestly text, the Priestly version of the Decalogue:

> Remember the sabbath day [*yôm haššabbāt*], and keep it holy. Six days you shall labor and do all your work. But the seventh day is a sabbath [*šabbāt*] to the LORD your God; you shall not do any work—you, your son or your daughter, your male or female slave, your livestock, or the alien resident in your towns. For in six days the LORD made heaven and earth, the sea, and all that is in them, but rested [*wayyānaḥ*] the seventh day; therefore the LORD blessed the sabbath day and consecrated it. (Exod 20:8–11 NRSV)

Admittedly, the Hebrew text of the Decalogue in Exod 20 employs the verb *nwḥ*, and not the verb *šbt*. Yet, the two mentioned lexemes belong to the same semantic field with overlapping meaning. This is proved by the so-called Covenant Code's command to rest on the seventh day:

> Six days you shall do your work, but on the seventh day you shall rest [root: *šbt*], so that your ox and your donkey may have relief [root: *nwḥ*], and your homeborn slave and the resident alien may be refreshed. (Exod 23:12 NRSV)

Regardless of how the Covenant Code and the Pentateuch's Priestly texts should be dated, their theological concept of the Sabbath as a day of rest seems to have been totally unknown to the Judaeans in Elephantine in the fifth century BCE. Below I will show that the occurrences of *šbh* in the relevant Aramaic sources do not suggest that the Sabbath was understood in Elephantine as a day of rest that fell on the last day of a seven-day week.

4.6.4 *šbh:* The Sources

A handful of ostraca, all from Elephantine,[160] mention the word *šbh:* D7.10 (= Clermont-Ganneau 44), D7.12 (= Sachau 80,6 [Plate 67/6]), D7.16 (= Clermont-Ganneau 152), D7.28 (= Berlin, Ägyptisches Museum P. 17818), D7.35 (= Clermont-Ganneau 186), D7.48 (= Berlin, Ägyptisches Museum P. 11372) and Clermont-Ganneau 49.[161] In addition, it has been proposed that both D7.8 (= Sachau

160 See Porten and Yardeni, *TADAE*, IV: Ostraca & Assorted Inscriptions, vi.

161 According to A. Lemaire, the rendition of Clermont-Ganneau 49cc8 offered in Lozachmeur, *La collection Clermont-Ganneau*, 219–220, should be corrected so that the line reads the phrase *ywm šbh*, cf. Lemaire, "Judean Identity in Elephantine," 365–373 (370). However, regardless of whether Lemaire's correction should prove to be correct or not, the context is so broken that I will not discuss it here.

76,1 [Plate 63,1]) and Clermont-Ganneau 204 indirectly refer to the day of preparation for the Sabbath, the Sabbath eve.[162] All eight ostraca were written in the first quarter of the fifth century BCE.[163] Even though some of them are more complete than others, none are entirely legible. In the case of each mention of *šbh* the context is unclear. The most legible ones are formally speaking short letters.

4.6.4.1 The Fragmentary Reference to *šbh* in D7.10; D7.12; D7.28; D7.35; and D7.48

D7.10 is described by Porten as a sarcastic request for provisions[164] and as a report of imprisonment by Lindenberger.[165] Being written to one Jedaniah (*šlm ydnyh*, D7.10:1) it contains a series of requests or instructions. The context of the mention of *šbh* is unclear. Nevertheless, one possibility is that *šbh* was a particular day the writer assumed the reader to be already familiar with:

> [... *y*]*wm šbh*
>
> [... d]ay of (the) Sabbath(?) (D7.10:5)

However, another interpretation is also possible. In the light of the rest of the inscription one may understand *šbh* here as an infinitive of the verb *šby*, "to take captive." The imprisonment motif is evident in D7.10:2 ("I put [in] the stocks/confinement"[166]) and in D7.10:6 ("Now, if they did not capture Nathan there"[167]). Therefore, it is also possible—or perhaps even likelier—to understand *ywm šbh* as "day of capturing."

D7.12 contains the words *šbh ʾth* (D7.12:9). This can be translated "(the) Sabbath came/comes." However, the ostracon is broken and it is also possible that *šbh* is not the subject of the verb *ʾth*.

In D7.28 the noun occurs in an isolated prepositional phrase: *bšbh*, "on (the) Sabbath" (D7.28:4).

---

162 For Clermont-Ganneau 204, see Lozachmeur, *La collection Clermont-Ganneau*, 352–353 and Plate 229. Lozachmeur offers the reading of André Dupont-Sommer as well as her own.
163 See Porten and Yardeni, *TADAE*, IV: Ostraca & Assorted Inscriptions, 151. However, as for Clermont-Ganneau 204, André Dupont-Sommer has dated it more openly to the fifth century BCE, cf. Dupont-Sommer, "Sabbat et Parascève," 67–88 (68).
164 Porten and Yardeni, *TADAE*, IV: Ostraca & Assorted Inscriptions.
165 Lindenberger, *Ancient Aramaic and Hebrew Letters*, 44 (no. 14).
166 Quoted from Porten and Yardeni, *TADAE*, IV: Ostraca & Assorted Inscriptions, 162.
167 Quoted from Porten and Yardeni, *TADAE*, IV: Ostraca & Assorted Inscriptions, 162.

In the case of D7.35 it is clear that the religious milieu the inscription originated in was a Yahwistic one. The writer wished that the god YHH should seek after the welfare of the addressee at all times (D7.35:1–2).[168] Still, the inscription shows that business was made with persons with non-Yahwistic names (cf. the Egyptian name Waḥpre in D7.35:3). The name of the addressee is lost, but he apparently had a theophoric name with YHW as the theophorous element (cf. D7.35:1). D7.35:7 reads *ʿd ywm šbh*, "until the Sabbath day."

Finally, in the case of D7.48 the top of the pot sherd is broken off. Consequently, the names of those involved in the communication is unknown. The extant text shows that the writer, among other things, instructed the receiver to send him commodities such as foodstuff. It is possible that there is a mention of the Sabbath in D7.48:4–5:

> *wkʿnt hytyw ly bš•tʾ*
>
> And now, bring (OR: they brought) to me on the Sabbath (D7.48:4–5)[169]

Regardless whether *hytyw* should be read as an imperative or a perfect, the inscription suggests that goods were transported on the Sabbath. This interpretation presupposes that *bš•tʾ* is actually a determined form of *šbh*. However, this is uncertain. First, this identification presupposes that the illegible letter between *shin* and *tav* is a *bet*. Second, the noun *šbh* does not appear in the determined state elsewhere in our sources from Elephantine.

4.6.4.2 D7.16

In the secondary literature, the interpretation of D7.16 differs in terms of how *šbh* has been understood. The pot sherd inscription is a letter written to the woman Islaḥ. The writer informed her that he intended to send vegetables the day after ("tomorrow") and gave her instructions in connection with that (D7.16:1–4):

> *šlm yslḥ kʿnt hʾ bqlʾ ʾwš*
> *r mḥr ʿrqy ʾlpʾ mḥr bšbh*

168 It has been conjectured that the inscription once, when it was complete, assigned the epithet *ṣbʿt* to YHH in line 2. Thus, e. g., Porten and Yardeni, *TADAE*, IV: Ostraca & Assorted Inscriptions, 180, and Doering, *Schabbat*, 32. The argument in favour of this is, as far as I can see, merely built on the basis of the assumed original length of the first part of the line, which is now lost. The phrase *yhw ṣbʾt* occurs in three ostraca of the Clermont-Ganneau collection: Clermont-Ganneau 167cc1, and probably in Clermont-Ganneau 186cc1–2 and Clermont-Ganneau 175 = Clermont-Ganneau J8cc,9, cf. Lemaire, "Judean Identity in Elephantine," 365–373 (369).
169 Quoted from Porten and Yardeni, *TADAE*, IV: Ostraca & Assorted Inscriptions, 187.

lmh hn y'bd ḥy lyhhhn l' npk[y]
'lqḥ 'l ttkly 'l mšlmt

Lindenberger's translation is relatively free:

> Greetings, Yislah! Look, I'm sending you the vegetables tomorrow. Get there before the boat comes in—on account of the Sabbath—so they won't be spoiled. I swear to God, if you don't I'll kill you! Don't trust Meshullemet ...[170]

An implication of this kind of translation is that the Sabbath was the very reason for the instructions to Islaḥ. She had to get to the landing place early in order to avoid the vegetables decaying during the Sabbath. In other words, according to this interpretation the writer and Islaḥ were observing the Sabbath by not doing business on it.[171]

In my view, there are two major problems with Lindenberger's translation of D7.16. First, it is difficult to find support in the Aramaic text for the English temporal adverb "before." The Aramaic *mḥr* occurs twice in D7.16:2. It seems that Lindenberger lets the first occurrence be rendered "tomorrow" and the second "before." However, the latter translation is, as far as I am concerned, not likely; in no other Aramaic text does *mḥr* mean "before," and nothing in the syntax of the clause *mḥr 'rqy 'lp' mḥr bšbh* suggests such an idiomatic expression. Second, Lindenberger renders the preposition *b* in the phrase *bšhb* with a causal expression: "on the account of the Sabbath." Isolated, this could perhaps be considered as a potential function of the preposition. However, a few lines below, the inscription probably offers but yet another causal construction: *'l dbr tqbḥ*, "because of *tqbḥ*" (D7.16:9).[172] Although not impossible, it nevertheless seems strange that such a short text would employ two different expressions for one

170 Lindenberger, *Ancient Aramaic and Hebrew Letters*, 50 (no. 22).
171 Also André Dupont-Sommer, who was the first to publish Clermont-Ganneau 152 = D7.16, translated the first three lines in a way that made it reflect a Sabbath observance: "Voici, je n'enverrai pas de cruche demain. Attache le boeuf demain, au Sabbat, de peur qu'il ne s'égare," "Behold, I will not send (any) jar tomorrow. Tie the ox tomorrow, on the Sabbath, lest it gets lost," A. Dupont-Sommer, "L'ostracon araméen du Sabbat (Collection Clermont-Ganneau No 152)," *Sem* 2 (1949): 29–39 (31). However, there are two problems with this translation. First, the reading *bql'*, "vegetables" is more likely than *bq l'*, "jar not." Second, *'lp'* should be rendered "the ship," not "the ox." Consequently, the ostracon does not reflect any Sabbath observance. On the contrary, it reflects business on the Sabbath! See Doering, *Schabbat*, 24–25.
172 The meaning of *tqbḥ* is not known. On the causal construction *'l dbr*, see Granerød, *Abraham and Melchizedek*, 201–203.

and the same thing, namely a causal expression. In sum, it seems that Lindenberger stretches the meaning of the text so as to make it give the impression of a Sabbath observance.

Therefore, in my view it is more plausible to render *mḥr bšbh* "tomorrow on the Sabbath":[173]

> Shalom, Islaḥ! Now look, I will send the vegetables tomorrow. Meet the boat tomorrow on the Sabbath! (D7.16:1–2)

As a consequence of this reading, it appears that the Sabbath was but a point in time, a chronological fix point that all involved parties were familiar with. The inscription does not suggest that the Sabbath was accompanied by any religious rites.

4.6.4.3 D7.8 and Clermont-Ganneau 204

The term *ʿrwbh* occurs a few times in ostraca from Elephantine. One occurrence is in D7.8, which in fact contains two separate messages. One of them is addressed to Uriah (D7.8:1–12a) and the second one to Aḥutab (D7.8:12b–16). In the latter message the writer gave Aḥutab instructions about a certain bread that should be eaten *ʿd mḥr ʿrwbh*, "until tomorrow, *ʿrwbh*" (D7:8:14–15). Moreover, a second occurrence is in Clermont-Ganneau 204cv4–5: *wʾnh ʾzl wlʾ ʾth ʿd ʿrwbh*, "I will go and I will not come [root: *ʾty*] until *ʿrwbh*."

Although the noun *šbh* does not occur in any of the two ostraca, André Dupont-Sommer suggested that *ʿrwbh* was a reference to the day of preparation before the Sabbath, the Sabbath eve, comparable to the παρασκευή in Matt 27:62 et al.[174] In the rabbinic literature *ʿrwbh* is the name of Sabbath eve and sometimes also the eve of Yom Kippur.[175] More recently, Héléne Lozachmeur has followed this line of thought by translating Clermont-Ganneau 204cv4–5 "et moi, allant et n'arrivant pas (jusqu') au soir/avant le soir (= vendredi ?)."[176] Moreover, James M. Lindenberger renders the *ʿd ʿrwbh* in D7:8:14–15 "by tomorrow,

173 Similarly Porten and Yardeni, *TADAE*, IV: Ostraca & Assorted Inscriptions, 168–169, cf. Kellermann and Kellermann "YHW-Tempel," 433–452 (447–448): "Komm zum (begegne dem) Schiff morgen, am Sabbat, damit es (das Gemüse) nicht verdirbt!"

174 Dupont-Sommer, "Sabbat et Parascève," 67–88 (67–71), cf. Kellermann and Kellermann, "YHW-Tempel," 433–452 (448–449), and Lozachmeur, *La collection Clermont-Ganneau*, 352–353.

175 Jastrow 2:1114, s.v. *ʿărûbətāʾ* III, *ʿărûbāʾ*.

176 Lozachmeur, *La collection Clermont-Ganneau*, 353.

(Friday),"[177] nevertheless admitting that this technical usage is otherwise attested only in much later texts so that the phrase could simply be rendered "by tomorrow evening."[178]

In my view, Dupont-Sommer's interpretation is not very likely. The rest of the data, which admittedly is meager, does not give the impression that the Judaeans in Elephantine observed the Sabbath as a day of rest. Therefore, it is more plausible that *ʿrwbh* in this context has the ordinary temporal meaning "evening," and not a technical meaning alluding to a Sabbath observance on the part of the Judaeans in Elephantine. What is more, it is this general meaning that the noun has in the *Words of Aḥiqar*, where the form *ʿrb* has been used: *wbʿrb*, "and in the evening" (C1.1:119).

4.6.5 The Personal Names *šbty* and *šbtyt*

The names *šbty* (Shabbethai) and the female *šbtyt* (Shabbethit) occur several times in Aramaic texts from ancient Egypt. The masculine Shabbethai is found in inscriptions from the early phase of the period of Persian occupation of Egypt until the Ptolemaic period, whereas the female *šbtyt* is only attested in texts from the Ptolemaic period.[179]

4.6.5.1 A2.1 (Late Sixth/Early Fifth Century BCE): "Greetings (to) Shabbethai Son of Shug"

Perhaps the earliest attestation of *šbty* is found in A2.1:10. The document in question is one of the so-called Hermopolis papyri. The contents of the letter, in particular the conventional epistolary greetings, suggest that it was written by a member of the Aramaean community to a fellow Aramaean. The address tells us that the addressee was a resident of Syene (cf. A2.1:15). In the last half of the letter, the writer has a series of greetings, formulated by means of the syntagm *šlm* plus a personal name. One of them is relevant here: "Greetings (to) Shabbethai [*šbty*] son of Shug" (A2.1:10).

---

177 Lindenberger, *Ancient Aramaic and Hebrew Letters*, 45 (no. 16).

178 Lindenberger, *Ancient Aramaic and Hebrew Letters*, 56 note f. Similarly, Porten and Yardeni, *TADAE*, IV: Ostraca & Assorted Inscriptions, 160, translates "until tomorrow evening."

179 The following occurrences are found in *TADAE: šbty:* A2.1:10; B3.9:10; B4.4:21; C3.15:40; C3.28:73, 86, 100, 101; D1.7:3; D7.56:2; D8.3:6; D8.5:3; D8.9:11, 12; D11.26:2; D18.18:1, and *šbtyt:* C3.28:81; D8.4:19. The names do not appear in any of the ostraca inscriptions of the Clermont-Ganneau collection, cf. Lozachmeur, *La collection Clermont-Ganneau*, 539.

Obviously, there is no waterproof method for establishing the ethnic/religious identity of the above-mentioned Shabbethai. Yet, it is relevant that the name Shabbethai appears alongside personal names of Aramaean and Egyptian origin (e.g., A2.1:3, 9 Bethelnathan and A2.1:15 Peṭekhnum, the father of the one who wrote the letter). All things considered, the personal names suggest that Syene was an ethnic melting pot in the time shortly after the Persian conquest of Egypt in 525 BCE. As far as the mentioned Shabbethai is concerned, it is possible that he was a Judaean. However, it is equally likely that he was a member of one of the other groups that made up Syene in the period shortly after the Persian conquest.[180]

4.6.5.2 B4.4 (483 BCE): The Witness Shabbethai son of Kibda/Kibra

The name Shabbethai occurs in yet another document dating back to the early part of the fifth century BCE: B4.4. The document was written in the third year of King Xerxes, i.e. 483 BCE, and is found in two copies (B4.3 and B4.4). Here, Hosea son of Hodaviah and Ahiab son of Gemariah (cf. B4.4:1, 18, 22) attested that they had received certain amounts of barley and lentils. Moreover, they confirmed that they, as protection escorts, were responsible for the transport of it all to the royal treasury in Syene (cf. B4.3:9; B4.4:12, 14). The document stipulates the penalty that the two escorts were liable to pay in the event that they failed to bring the entire amount of grain to the treasury (B4.4:14–17). It is in this context one Shabbethai was one of the approximately nine witnesses:

> The witnesses: Kaya son of Eskaishu; Nushkuidri son of N[abenathan; PN son of PN]; Rochel son of Abihu; Shuri son of Kurz; Attaidri son of [PN; Bagadata son of Psamshek]; Arvaratha son of Jeh(o)nathan; Shabbethai son of Kibda/Kibra [*kbd'/kbr'*]. (B4.4:19–21, cf. the corresponding lines in the other draft of the same document, B4.3:22–24)[181]

In this case also the religious/ethnic identity of the Shabbethai in question is unknown. The fathers of both of the protection escorts bore theophoric names with YHW as the theophorous element (B4.4:2 Hodaviah and Gemariah). This observa-

180 Edda Bresciani and Murad Kamil, "Le lettere aramaiche di Hermopoli," in *Atti della Accademia Nazionale dei Lincei.* Memorie 12 (Rome: L'Accademia, 1966), 361–428 (402).
181 Quoted from Bezalel Porten and Ada Yardeni, *Textbook of Aramaic Documents from Ancient Egypt: Newly Copied, Edited and Translated into Hebrew and English*, vol. II: Contracts (Jerusalem: The Hebrew University of Jerusalem – Department of the History of the Jewish People, 1989), 111.

tion, however, only hints at the possibility of the escorts Hosea and Ahiab having been attached to the community of YHW worshippers, not whether the witness Shabbethai son of Kibda/Kibra was a YHW worshipping Judaean. As a matter of fact, the name and the patronymic of the second-last witness demonstrate the difficulty of using proper names as a source for ethnic and/or religious identity. Arvaratha son of Jehonathan (*ʾrwrt br yhntn*, B4.4:21) apparently bore a Persian name. His father, however, had a Yahwistic name.[182]

4.6.5.3 B3.9 (416 BCE): The Witness Sinkishir Son of Shabbethai

The name Shabbethai occurs again in a legal document on adoption (B3.9) from King Darius II's eighth regnal year, that is, 416 BCE. Uriah son of Mahseiah declared to Zaccur son of Meshullam that he would adopt the latter's boy (*ʿlym*) called Jedaniah son of Takhoi and make him his own son (B3.9:5). Uriah affirmed Jedaniah's new legal status by declaring that no one should have the right to brand him and make him a slave (B3.9:5–6).

The emancipation and adoption of Jedaniah took place in the presence of the Persian official Vidranga (B3.9:2), apparently in the fortress of Syene. The whole ceremony was certified by eight witnesses of whom the second was a certain Sinkishir son of Shabbethai (*snkšr br šbty*, B3.9:10). Sinkishir was a Babylonian name.[183] Among the other witnesses there were people with Aramaic and Persian names. Even though Uriah son of Mahseiah bore a Yahwistic name he nevertheless referred to himself as an Aramaean of Syene.

Also in this case the question of the ethnic/religious identity of Sinkishir and his father Shabbethai remains open. The possibility that they were YHW worshippers and members of the Judaean community can neither be ascertained nor excluded.

4.6.5.4 D18.18 (Elephantine Museum 2605): A Sarcophagus from Aswan with Aramaic Inscription

In 1963 three sandstone sarcophagi were excavated less than two hundred metres from the temple of Isis in Syene. The sarcophagi were human-shaped and

---

182 See Lisbeth S. Fried, "'You Shall Appoint Judges': Ezra's Mission and the Rescript of Artaxerxes," in *Persia and Torah: The Theory of Imperial Authorization of the Pentateuch*, ed. James W. Watts, SymS 17 (Atlanta: Society of Biblical Literature, 2001): 63–89 (66 note 13).

183 See Joseph A. Fitzmyer, "Aramaic Kephāʾ and Peter's Name in the New Testament," in *To Advance the Gospel: New Testament Studies* (Grand Rapids: Eerdmans, 1998): 112–124 (116).

featured iconographic as well as textual inscriptions, that is, names written in Aramaic as well as hieroglyphics.[184]

On one of the sarcophagi (Elephantine Museum inventory number 2605, cf. D18.18) there is a depiction of Apis on the base. Moreover, on each side there is a depiction of a snake, and close to the base on one of the sides there is a depiction of Anubis, the god of mummification. On the base there is a ca. 17.5 cm × 9.5 cm inscription reading *šbty*, "Shabbethai." Furthermore, the corresponding Aramaic inscriptions on the other two remaining sarcophagi inscriptions feature the names *ʾbwty*/*ʾbrty brt šmšnwry*, "Abutai[185]/Abarti[186] daughter of Shamashnuri" (Aswan Museum inventory number 2607, cf. D18.16) and *ḥwr*, "Ḥor" (Elephantine Museum inventory number 2606, cf. D18.17), respectively.

These inscriptions were first published by Walter Kornfeld. On the basis of the find spot and the Aramaic inscriptions, Kornfeld argued that the sarcophagi no doubt were used by members of the "Jewish military colony on Elephantine."[187] Moreover, in Kornfeld's view, the choice of a burial place in the immediate proximity of the Isis temple and the use of sarcophagi with "emblems from the religion of Egypt"[188] proved how separated ("getrennt") the members of the colony were from Yahwism. Furthermore, Kornfeld concluded that the greatest significance of the sarcophagi is that they provide an additional insight (besides the Aramaic papyri) into the life of the "Jewish–Aramaic colony on Elephantine" in the fifth century BCE. In his opinion, the sarcophagi made it possible for the first time to prove the syncretistic religion of the Judaeans in their burial practice.[189]

In my view, Kornfeld's interpretation of the sarcophagi with regard to the religion of the Judaeans cannot be retained. Admittedly, it is possible to claim that the religion of the Judaeans had "syncretistic traits" (to use a normative and evaluative term) insofar as various textual sources demonstrate they were not monotheists.[190] However, the name Shabbethai does not prove that the one who once was buried in the sarcophagus was a Judaean. Having that said, the sarcophagi with Aramaic inscriptions do indeed shed light on the religious en-

---

184 For descriptions and photographs of the three sarcophagi, see the *editio princeps* in Walter Kornfeld, "Aramäische Sarkophage in Assuan," *WZKM* 61 (1967): 9–16.
185 So according to the reading of Porten and Yardeni, cf. Porten and Yardeni, *TADAE*, IV: Ostraca & Assorted Inscriptions, 247.
186 So according to Kornfeld's reading, cf. Kornfeld, "Aramäische Sarkophage in Assuan," 9–16 (13).
187 Kornfeld, "Aramäische Sarkophage in Assuan," 9–16 (14).
188 Kornfeld, "Aramäische Sarkophage in Assuan," 9–16 (14).
189 Kornfeld, "Aramäische Sarkophage in Assuan," 9–16 (16).
190 See Section 5.5 below.

vironment of Syene and Elephantine. The use of Aramaic presumably dates them to the period when the Persians ruled Egypt, although the Ptolemaic period cannot be excluded. In any case, they indicate that originally Egyptian burial practices could in fact be adopted by non-Egyptian inhabitants of Egypt, regardless of whether they were Judaeans or not.

4.6.5.5 The Remaining Occurrences

With one possible exception, the highly fragmentary ostracon inscription D1.7 which possibly is a writing exercise from the fifth century BCE, all of the remaining occurrences of the name *šbty* in the Aramaic documents from Egypt stem from the Ptolemaic period, as do the references to the female name *šbtyt* also.

4.6.5.6 Is the Name Shabbethai a Relevant Source?

As I have partially hinted at above, there have been attempts to make religio-historical statements about the Sabbath in Elephantine on the basis of the name Shabbethai.

According to Albert Vincent, the name Shabbethai indicated a growing importance of the Sabbath observance in the Persian period.[191] Similarly, in Bezalel Porten's view, expressed in 1969, the references to the Sabbath (*šbh*) and the presence of the name Shabbethai "clearly indicate an awareness of the Sabbath."[192] At the same time, Porten realised that the name also causes some problems because we do not know for sure that "all four of the Elephantine–Syene Shabbethais were Jews."[193] Porten pondered over the possibility that the Shabbethai son of Shug mentioned in A2.1 may have been a proselyte and that Sinkishir son of Shabbethai a Jew named after a "pagan grandfather."[194] However, against this view he noted the "non-Jewish context in which their

191 Vincent, *La religion des judéo-araméens d'Eléphantine*, 414.

192 Porten, "The Religion of the Jews of Elephantine," 116 – 121 (117).

193 The "four Elephantine–Syene Shabbethais" Porten referred to were C 2:21 [= B4.4:21], 58:3 [= D1.7:3]; K 8:10 [=B3.9:10]; and BK 4:10 [= A2.1:10], cf. Porten, "The Religion of the Jews of Elephantine," 116 – 121 (117). In his 1969 article, Porten did not discuss the Aramaic sarcophagi from Aswan, which were published too late to be considered there, cf. Porten, "The Religion of the Jews of Elephantine," 116 – 121 (121).

194 Porten, "The Religion of the Jews of Elephantine," 116 – 121 (117), cf. Porten, *Archives from Elephantine*, 127.

names occur." The context suggests that they were "neither Jews nor proselytes but sons of Arameans or Babylonians attracted by Sabbath observance."[195]

In his study of Sabbath halakah and Sabbath practice, Lutz Doering has also argued that the name Shabbethai points to the significance of the Sabbath since the Babylonian exile and that the name could be adopted by non-Judaeans, too. In Doering's view, it is unlikely that the name was an independent formation based on the Akkadian word *šapattu*, contrary to what was proposed by Edda Bresciani and Murad Kamil.[196] In connection with the first publication of the Hermopolis papyri in 1966, Bresciani and Kamil commented (in connection with the name Shabbethai son of Shug, A2.1:10) that the name Shabbethai is not necessarily of a Jewish origin but may be associated with the Babylonian day of the full moon, *šapattu*.[197] In contrast, in Doering's view the name was originally a Judaean name. Moreover, Doering argued that the name reflected a "Wahrnehmung des Sabbats bei den jüdischen Militärkolonie,"[198] but at the same time he underscored that one cannot know what Judaean Sabbath observance was like on the basis of the name.

One can understand the opinion of Porten and Doering, especially since the only three occurrences of the name Shabbethai in the Bible are found in narratives that, like the Aramaic documents from Egypt, are set in the Persian period (Ezra 10:15; Neh 8:7; 11:16). Moreover, later on in the Hellenistic period, there are several examples of non-Judaeans having been attracted by and even observing the Sabbath as a day of rest on the last of the seven-day week.[199]

However, in my view, the proposal already made by Bresciani and Kamil is more probable, namely that the name Shabbethai that appears in the vicinity of Elephantine should be explained as a Babylonian name, formed on the basis of the word *šapattu*, the Akkadian name of the day of the full moon.

When discussing the name Shabbethai, one should also take into consideration that the name is attested in a Babylonian context, as well. The name occurs

---

195 Porten, "The Religion of the Jews of Elephantine," 116 – 121 (117). Similarly also Bezalel Porten, "The Jews in Egypt," *CHJ* 1: 372 – 400 (387 – 388), and Porten et al., *The Elephantine Papyri in English*, 234 note 22.

196 Bresciani and Kamil, "Le lettere aramaiche di Hermopoli," 361 – 428 (402).

197 Bresciani and Kamil, "Le lettere aramaiche di Hermopoli," 361 – 428 (402): "Ma bisogna ricordare che *šapattu* in babilonese, è il giorno della luna piena … e quindi il nome, … non è necessariamente giudaico."

198 Doering, *Schabbat*, 36 – 39 [39].

199 Compare, e.g., the many Jews and non-Jews bearing the name Sambathion in Egyptian papyri dating from the Hellenistic and Roman periods, giving testimony to the great respect given the Sabbath among the Egyptians then, cf. *CPJ* 3.43 – 87 (43 – 56, 84) etc.

in documents from the so-called Murashu archive as well as in one of the so-called Āl-Yāḫūdu ("Judahtown") documents.

As far as the Murashu archive is concerned, the evidence from these documents is as equally ambiguous as the Aramaic documents from Persian-period Egypt. Some of the individuals bearing the name Shabbethai may have been Judaeans but not necessarily all of them.[200] The Murashu archive, numbering approximately seven hundred clay tablets mostly written in Akkadian, represents the business archive of the Murashu family of Nippur. In the last part of the fifth century BCE the Murashus were businessmen involved in land lease and loans in Babylonia. In other words, the Murashu archive is contemporary with the Aramaic documents from ancient Egypt. (As a matter of fact, one person is mentioned in both corpora: Arshama. Arshama was the Persian satrap of Egypt where he also had economic interests,[201] but he had economic interests in Babylonia, too.[202]) Of the many personal names occurring in the Murashu documents, some of them have been tentatively identified as Judaeans on the assumption that a theophoric name with the divine element YHW indicates a Judaean name. Among the names, four occur with the theophorous element YHW prefixed, whereas more than twenty names occur with the theophorous element YW suffixed.[203] Moreover, approximately nine individuals who bore the name Shabbethai are known from the Murashu documents.[204] According to Michael David Coogan, two of these individuals "can be identified as Hebrews" for genealogical reasons.[205] One of them had a father named *gadalyaw* (Gedaliah), whereas the other one had a father called *ʾabiyaw.* In the remaining cases, it is not possible to identify whether the Shabbethais in question were members of the Judaean diaspora or not on the basis of the patronymic or the name of other family members.[206]

---

200 Contrary to Ran Zadok, *The Jews in Babylonia During the Chaldean and Achaemenian Periods: According to the Babylonian Sources*, SHJPLIMS 3 (Haifa: University of Haifa, 1979), 22–23, who argues that Shabbethai is a "typical Jewish name" in the Murashu documents.

201 See A6.1–16.

202 See, e.g., A6.9 and additional references in Tuplin, "Arshama: Prince and Satrap," 5–44.

203 Michael David Coogan, *West Semitic Personal Names in the Murašû Documents*, HSM 7 (Missoula, MT: Published by Scholars Press for Harvard Semitic Museum, 1976), 49–53.

204 Coogan, *West Semitic Personal Names*, 34–35.

205 Coogan, *West Semitic Personal Names*, 84.

206 One Shabbethai had a son named *Ḥaggay* whereas another one had a brother called *Minyamin* (a West Semitic name) and a father called [Id]EN.AD.URÙ, cf. Coogan, *West Semitic Personal Names*, 35.

As mentioned, one of the documents from the Āl-Yāḫūdu archive also refers to an individual bearing the name Shabbethai: CUSAS 28, no. 42.[207] The document in question, which dates back to 509 BCE and thus represents a chronologically earlier attestation of the name than those from Egypt and the Murashu archive, is a receipt for barley and a voiding of previous records. The name Shabbethai occurs in the list of the debtors:

> [1] (This is concerning) the promissory note for three kor of dates, [2] owed to Nanâ-ultaraḫ, slave woman of [3] [...], which were owed by [4] Kīnâ, son of Aḫu, [5] Šabbatāia, son of Banā-Yāma, [6] and Natinā, son of Raḫī-il: ...[208]

In the receipt, the creditor Nanâ-ultaraḫ confirmed that she had received her outstanding amount of dates (cf. lines 9–15). In the case of the attestation in the Āl-Yāḫūdu documents, Shabbethai (= Šabbatāia[209]) had a father with a theophorous Yahwistic name: "Šabbatāia, son of Banā-Yāma." In the Āl-Yāḫūdu archive (as well as other Babylonian sources), one frequent way of expressing the name of the deity YHWH in Yahwistic theophoric names was by means of Yāma.[210]

Unfortunately, neither the occurrences of the name Shabbethai in the Murashu archive nor the single mention of it in the Āl-Yāḫūdu archive are conclusive as far as the questions here are concerned. It seems pretty clear that some of the Shabbethais were Judaeans (provided that a Yahwistic patronymic is an indication of that). However, not all Shabbethais were Judaeans. Moreover, the question of the exact nature of the particular Sabbath that the name alluded to still remains open for discussion.

Nevertheless, according to the Babylonian calendar the *šapattu* was the fifteenth day of the month and the day of the full moon.[211] In my view, even in the light of the attestations in the Murashu and Āl-Yāḫūdu archives it is still possible to explain the name Shabbethai as a derivation of the Akkadian noun for the day of the full moon, in accordance with, for example, the proposal made already by Bresciani and Kamil. For one, the Babylonian *šapattu* (day of the full moon) was

---

207 Laurie E. Pearce and Cornelia Wunsch, *Documents of Judean Exiles and West Semites in Babylonia in the Collection of David Sofer*, CUSAS 28 (Bethesda, MD: CDL, 2014), 165–166 (no. 42).

208 Quoted from Pearce and Wunsch, *Documents of Judean Exiles*, 165–166 (no. 42).

209 See Pearce and Wunsch, *Documents of Judean Exiles*, 81.

210 Pearce and Wunsch, *Documents of Judean Exiles*, 19: "Although the Yahwistic element can appear either in initial or final position in a name, the element's shape and its position in a name are closely linked: Yāḫû- appears almost exclusively in the initial position, and Yāma in the final."

211 See Geller, "šapattu," 25–27, and Reiner et al., "šapattu," 449–450.

a well-known concept in the sixth and fifth centuries, in contrast to the so-called "biblical" Sabbath (in the sense of a day of rest which reoccurred every seventh day). In addition, the ending -ai may be of Akkadian origin.[212] Thus, if the name Shabbethai originally derived from *šapattu*, the appearance of the name cannot be used as an indication of an attraction of the Sabbath (in the sense of the day of rest that fell on the last day of the seven-day week) on the part of non-Judaeans as early as the Persian period.[213]

4.6.6 The Sabbath: Summary and Conclusion

Was the Sabbath an important identity marker in Elephantine, comparable to how the seventh day of the week became a day of rest in the Judaism of the last centuries BCE and onwards? The result of the investigation of the Sabbath in the Judaean community in Elephantine and its surroundings is a negative one.

The Aramaic documents from Persian period Egypt do not give any hints about the Judaeans in Elephantine observing the Sabbath in a way that would accord with the commandments of the Bible (like the two versions of the Decalogue in Exod 20 and Deut 5; Exod 23:12; 34:21 etc.). The relevant documents simply do not suggest that the Judaeans knew the seven-day week and the Sabbath as a day of rest.[214] Nor do they suggest that the Judaeans refrained from working on that day. As Sacha Stern has pointed out, judging from their dates several documents from Achaemenid Egypt—written by and for Judaeans—must have been written on a Saturday.[215] This should warn us against using biblical and rabbinic concepts about Saturday as the Sabbath and weekly day of rest as a

212 See *HALOT* 4:1412, s.v. *šabbətay*.

213 Later on, however, in the Hellenistic and particularly Roman periods the picture changes. In the Roman period, the name Sambathion was popular in Egypt, among both Jews and people that, judging from the names of their kin, were not Jews. This may be seen as a testimony to the great respect given the Jewish, biblical and "kosher" Sabbath among the Egyptians. See *CPJ* 3.43–87 (43–56). It should be noted that in this period (and in contrast to the Persian period) the biblical canon was more or less established and functioned as a sacred text for various Jewish groups, cf. Kratz, *Historisches und biblisches Israel*, 206–208.

214 Contrary to Doering, who assumes that the Aramaic *šbh* in the ostraca from Elephantine (in particular Clermont-Ganneau 205; D7.12; and D7.10) designated a weekly Sabbath ("Wochensabbat"), cf. Doering, *Schabbat*, 27–28.

215 See Stern, "The Babylonian Calendar at Elephantine," 159–171 (168–169). It should be mentioned that Stern does not at all question whether there was a seven-day week in Elephantine. He takes the existence of a seven-day week in Elephantine for granted, cf. Stern, "The Babylonian Calendar at Elephantine," 159–171 (169).

measuring stick and taking for granted that it was known and observed in Elephantine.[216]

The fact that Judaeans wrote documents on the Saturday (according to the seven-day week) suggests that normal business was carried out that day. As far as I can see, the only possible reference to a period of seven days in Elephantine can be found in the so-called Passover letter (A4.1). Provided that Porten's reconstruction of the broken text turns out to be correct, then the Festival of Unleavened Bread imposed upon the Judaeans by royal decree and mediated via Hananiah lasted from the fourteenth day of Nisan until the twenty-first.[217] However, even if this proves to be a correct understanding of the passage in question, this particular seven-day-long festival cannot be used as evidence for the hypothesis that time in Elephantine was divided into seven-day weeks. Consequently, the Aramaic documents from Egypt probably do *not* attest to any awareness of a "Wochenrhytmus des Sabbats."[218]

Moreover, provided that the Aramaic noun *šbh* in fact functionally corresponds to the Hebrew *šabbāt*, then the Judaeans in Elephantine cannot have been aware of any (popular) etymological connection between the noun *šbh* and the (Hebrew) verb *šbt*, "to rest."

Furthermore, both the documents from Elephantine and the contemporary Murashu archive in all likelihood show that the name Shabbethai probably was borne by Judaeans and non-Judaeans alike. However, the appearance of the name need not be taken either as an indication of non-Judaeans being attracted by the (weekly) Sabbath (say, as a day of rest) or as a sign of non-Judaeans having converted to Yahwism. On the contrary, the existence of the concept of *šapattu* as the day of the full moon in the Babylonian calendar and the presumably non-Hebrew ending *-ai* in the name point in the direction of a Babylonian origin. Thus, in Elephantine one Shabbethai may very well have been born on the day of the full moon, and not necessarily on a Saturday.

A couple of decades ago Lester L. Grabbe wrote that the Elephantine ostraca with mentions of *šbh* caused the following impression: In Elephantine the Sabbath was known and given a particular designation but not observed in a strict sense. In his view, this fits a transition period within the history of Yahwism/Judaism when the place of the Sabbath was under debate.[219] In my view, it is clear

216 Moreover, according to Stern also the dates of several Jewish documents from the subsequent Ptolemaic and Roman periods show that they were written on a Saturday, cf. Stern, "The Babylonian Calendar at Elephantine," 159–171 (169 note 55).

217 Porten and Yardeni, *TADAE*, I: Letters. Appendix: Aramaic Letters from the Bible, 54–55.

218 Contrary to Doering, *Schabbat*, 42.

219 Lester L. Grabbe, *Judaism from Cyrus to Hadrian* (Minneapolis: Fortress Press, 1992), 221.

that the Sabbath was known in Elephantine. However, it is far from clear what kind of Sabbath the Judaeans knew: the lunar Sabbath (the day of the full moon) or the Sabbath of the seven-day week. As far as I can see, the Aramaic documents from Persian-period Egypt do not reflect any debates over the nature and observation of the Sabbath whatsoever. The meagre evidence suggests that the Sabbath referred to a particular day, but still a day where business could be done as usual.

4.7 Chapter Summary

A religion reflects itself in various kinds of rituals whose characteristics are that they may be repeated, that they are interpersonal and that they might be done for the sake of a purpose.

A separate section of this chapter has been devoted to the (operational) theology of sacrifices in Elephantine. After a discussion of the different types of sacrifices found in the sources, the chapter continued with a discussion of who performed the sacrifices in the temple of YHW (only religious specialists or other persons?). Another question discussed is why the Judaeans made offerings, who benefitted from the sacrifices and in what way. I have argued that the Judaeans, among other reasons, offered in order to *achieve* something, either for their own sake or for the sake of the one in whose name the sacrifice was made. I have attempted to argue that the value of a sacrifice could be measured and assessed, so that the degree of merit (*ṣdqh*) one achieved before the god YHW when offering to him was a function of the value of the sacrifice offered to him.

Moreover, the official correspondence reflecting the attempts to get permission to rebuild the (second) temple of YHW after it was destroyed in 410 BCE (A4.7–10) show that the Judaeans of Elephantine accepted the ban on animal offerings in the rebuilt temple. Explanations for this proposed in the secondary literature are briefly discussed, and I tentatively conclude by favouring the explanation that the ban on animal offerings may ultimately have been motivated by the interests of the satrap Arshama to downsize the second, rebuilt temple of YHW, perhaps for the sake of the inner stability of Elephantine or because of his wish to influence things that drained the economic surplus (such as animal offerings). However, at the same time the veto against animal offerings seems to have tallied with the interests of the Jerusalem priesthood (in fact, A4.9 may be the earliest epigraphic source reflecting the centralisation of the YHWH cult to Jerusalem). Therefore, one should perhaps not seek a single explanation. Regardless of what the reasons for the veto may have been, I have attempted to discuss the questions *why* and *how* the Judaeans in Elephantine could theologically legitimate the veto. Using an observation made by Christian A. Eberhart as a point of departure (namely, that it is the *burning* of the sacrificial material on the altar that constituted a sacrifice in Lev 1–7—an account which in fact is perhaps *the* most comprehensive descriptions of sacrifices from the entire ancient Near East) I have argued that it was possible for the Judaeans at Elephantine to accept a future sacrificial cult theologically *without* sacrificing animals because it ultimately was the burning rite that was most important.

Yet another ritual of the Judaeans discussed in the present chapter is subsumed under the topic of communal rites of mourning. Among the questions discussed is the purpose of the rites of mourning. It is conjectured that such communal rites, modelled after individual and ordinary rites of mourning, may have been attempts to compel YHW to intervene in history.

Next, a separate section is dedicated to communal and individual prayers. It has been argued that we learn about two communal prayers: a prayer of intercession for Bagavahya the governor of Judah, and a communal prayer of curse against the allegedly corrupt Persian official Vidranga. Following James M. Lindenberger I argue that the latter is evident in the so-called Vidranga section in the petition to Bagavahya and that it is formally expressed by means of so-called precative perfects ("perfect of prayer"). Moreover, direct and, above all, indirect examples of individual prayers are discussed on the basis of epistolary salutations, proper names and profane swearing. However, the value of proper names as sources for the prayers of the Judaeans at Elephantine is limited due to the fact that they seemed to have been practising papponomy.

In a lengthy section I have discussed the existence and nature of the religious festivals of Passover and the Festival of Unleavened Bread on the basis of A4.1, D7.6 and D7.24. The term Passover (Aramaic *psḥ'*) is only found in the last two ostraca inscriptions from the fifth century BCE. It is argued that the Passover was known by the Judaeans but that we cannot know for what purpose it was observed and what religious narrative/myth it was connected with. Moreover, at the beginning of the fifth century it did not have any fixed date. This, however, may have been changed at the end of the fifth century BCE as a consequence of the letter from Hananiah who seems to have operated with some sort of royal approval (A4.1). Although the letter does not mention the term *psḥ'* it is a probable point of departure that the letter was about both the Passover and the Festival of Unleavened Bread. The methodological difficulties connected to the use of the Hebrew Bible in order to "fill in the gaps" are discussed. I argue that Hananiah's letter on the one hand, and the biblical testimonies on how to observe the Passover and the Festival of Unleavened Bread on the other, *together* attest to the religio-historical *diversity* that characterised the observation of these festivals in the Persian period. Hananiah's letter may also signal a change of the social sphere of the festival(s), from being part of "religion here" (domestic religion) to becoming part of "religion there" (public religion), using a spatial model of religion coined by Jonathan Z. Smith. As far as the question of the purpose of Hananiah's letter is concerned, I argue that a partial answer may be found in the need to *regulate* the Passover and Festival of Unleavened Bread out of consideration for the economy and stability of Elephantine. In the event that the Judaeans in Elephantine observed the festival(s) as a religious reenactment of a tradition comparable to or even identical with the biblical exodus narrative, the festival(s) may potentially have caused anti-Judaean reactions among the Egyptians. Moreover, if the Judaeans did not drink any fermented beverages during the festival period, then this may have had economic consequences. After all, beer, which was made from loaves of bread that was made from richly yeasted dough, was a staple item of the Egyptian diet for all kinds of people. Therefore, in short, the Elephantine documents perhaps reflect a development in the way the Passover functioned as a ritual. In the first half of the fifth century BCE it was located within the sphere of domestic religion. However, provided that Hananiah's letter (A4.1) actually referred to the Passover, the Passover became a ritual that was part of public religion in the last decades of the fifth century BCE.

The chapter concludes with a section devoted to the question of the Sabbath in Elephantine. After a prelude offering a selection of texts from the Persian and Hellenistic periods characterised by the observance of the Sabbath as an identity marker for YHWH worshippers, it is asked what kind of Sabbath the Judaeans in Elephantine knew: a lunar Sabbath (i.e., the day of the full moon, as opposed to the new moon) or the Sabbath as the seventh day of a seven-day week? It is observed that if the Egyptian Aramaic *šbh* actually refers to the same word as the Biblical Hebrew *šabbāt*, then one should conclude that the Judaeans were unaware of any etymological connection between the (Hebrew) noun *šabbāt* and the (Hebrew) verb *šbt*, "to rest," a connection important in the legitimation and explanation of the Sabbath institution in the (Priestly parts of the) Hebrew Bible. It is argued that the Judaeans did not understand *šbh* ("Sabbath") as a day of rest that fell on the last day of a seven-day week. The existence of the personal name Shabbethai in the corpus of documents does not have any significance with regard to the question of the origin and perception of *šbh* ("Sabbath") in Elephantine. Therefore, in Elephantine the observance of the Sabbath was not a ritual functioning as an identity marker.

5 The Mythic and Narrative Dimension

Proclaims Darius, the king: By the favour of Ahuramazda I am king; upon me Ahuramazda bestowed the kingship. (DB §5 OP)[1]

A great god (is) Ahuramazda, who created this earth, who created yonder heaven, who created man, who created blissful happiness for man, who made Darius king, one king of many, one master of many. (DNa §1)[2]

5.1 Introduction

How did the religion practiced by the Judaeans at Elephantine reflect itself in myths and narratives? What can we say (and not say) about the religious stories that the Judaeans told themselves and were told by others? These are basically the questions that will be in focus in the following.

This chapter will discuss some of the myths and religious narratives

- that the Judaeans in Elephantine evidently told themselves,
- that evidently were told in the neighbourhood of the Judaeans at Elephantine, and
- that we—with a varying degree of certainty—may assume were told because we find traces of them in the sources.

The chapter will start with a discussion of myths of creation, then focus on the Judaean temple foundation narrative and continue with myths about sacral kingship. The last section will be a discussion of the traces of pantheons that we find in the sources and a discussion of the religio-theological strategies the Judaeans may have had for finding a place for YHW in a world of multiple deities.

However, before discussing these questions I will start by indicating how the concepts of myth and narrative are understood here. In general, a narrative typically involves actors, represented by either humans or beings with anthropomorphic characteristics, such as spirits and animated animals or plants.[3] Sometimes

1 Quoted from Rüdiger Schmitt, *The Bisitun Inscriptions of Darius the Great: Old Persian Text*, vol. I: The Old Persian inscriptions: Texts I, CII (London: School of Oriental and African Studies, 1991), 49 (slightly modified).

2 Quoted from Rüdiger Schmitt, *The Old Persian Inscriptions of Naqsh-i Rustam and Persepolis*, vol. I: The Old Persian Inscriptions: Texts II, CII (London: School of Oriental and African Studies, 2000), 30 (slightly modified).

3 For an introduction to (biblical) narratology, see, e.g., Yairah Amit, *Reading Biblical Narratives: Literary Criticism and the Hebrew Bible* (Minneapolis: Fortress Press, 2001).

the narrative focusses on the relationship between the involved actors. At other times the focus is on the developments of the personality of one of the actors of the narrative. Moreover, a narrative typically has a plot. A plot is characterised by a chain of events, with the actors being somewhat part of, involved in or making experiences with these events. Furthermore, a narrative has a narrator, who may be but does not have to be identical with the very author of the text. The voice of the narrator unfolds the narrative and its plot. In some cases, the narrator himself/herself may be part of the narrative. In other cases the narrator is an anonymous, but often omniscient, figure on the edge of or even outside of the narrative.

Whereas it is more or less unproblematic to define narrative, a myth is much more elusive. In his introductory remarks on the concept Ninian Smart approaches the problem by stating that all stories involving the invisible, divine or sacred world are beyond being straightforward stories.[4] In Smart's view they are *parahistorical*. Another way to characterise a myth is by using a term coined by Richard J. Clifford. According to Clifford, such stories are *suprahistoric*.[5] Accordingly, I will understand a myth as a narrative that unfolds a metaphysical pattern which in turn is beyond history and beyond the causal relationships of everyday life. Consequently, one can, like Smart, argue that while all myths are narratives, not all narratives are myths. Moreover, myths typically serve certain functions. One function is to serve as the script for ritual action. Examples of this are the biblical narratives about the exodus of the Israelites out of Egypt and the narrative about the Last Supper. Another function is that a myth attempts to explain origins. For instance, the Babylonian cosmogony *Enuma Elish* explains the origin of the humans as a society that was organised with a view to serving of the gods. Furthermore, the biblical narratives about the primeval history (Gen 1–11) explain cultural and existential features that are characteristic of human society, such as the reasons for life's hardships, the invention of clothes, the multitude of languages and so on. In addition, myths may also depict the eschaton of the world as we know it. And, not to forget, myths may attempt to depict how the gods act in order to deal with humanity. For instance, a deity may choose for himself a particular person or king that he/she in turn uses as an instrument on earth, for example, in order to punish or save other people and their kings.

---

4 Ninian Smart, *Dimensions of the Sacred: An Anatomy of the World's Beliefs* (Berkeley: University of California Press, 1996), 130–131.

5 Richard J. Clifford, *Creation Accounts in the Ancient Near East and in the Bible*, CBQMS 26 (Washington, DC: Catholic Biblical Association of America, 1994), 8.

To characterise a myth as parahistorical or suprahistorical inevitably presupposes the perspective of modern thinking characterised by rational reasoning. This is unavoidable and does not necessarily have to lead to a condescending value-judgment of the myths under debate or an anachronistic assessment of them. On the contrary, it is simply an acknowledgment of the differences between the perspectives.[6] In a discussion focussing particularly on creation myths (cosmogonies), Clifford has outlined four main differences between ancient and modern concepts of creation: the process, the product or emergent, the manner of reporting and the criteria of truth.[7] As for the first difference (*process*), in many ancient Near Eastern cosmogonies creation often involved wills in conflict. The creator god battled with and subdued the forces of chaos. The second difference (*product*) is visible in those ancient Near Eastern cosmogonies that describe the creation (often understood as human society) as serving a purpose, which in turn is often the service of the gods. The third difference (*manner of reporting*) is a result of the involvement of wills in conflict. Typically, such conflicts are described as a narrative with a plot. In other words, creation is presented as a drama. The fourth difference (*criterion of truth*) is evident in how the verisimilitude was measured in ancient times compared to today's criteria of truth. In the ancient Near East a creation drama did not have to explain and verify all of the empirical data. On the contrary, it was possible to focus on single aspects and leave others unaccounted for.

On the background of the discussion of the concept of myth above, a preliminary conclusion is that there are few myths in our sources for the Judaean community at Elephantine. The clearest exception is the Aramaic version of the Bisitun inscription that presents King Darius (both I and II) as the narrator, speaking in the first person.[8] Here there are traces of mythic elements. In this chapter, I build on the premise that a *myth*, besides being presented in the form of a *narrative*, can also be hidden in fragmentary expressions such as divine epithets and other utterances characterised by a high degree of elevated language. Consequently, according to the way I use the term myth, it refers to the *contents* (above all of a parahistorical nature), not the form. Consequently, mythic elements can be found reflected in various types of texts, not only in

6 In Smart's thinking, one of the characteristics of a myth, i.e. the parahistorical thinking, is also part of Marxist history where "the dialectics plays an unseen role behind the scenes and unfolds a metaphysical pattern which gives the Marxist adherent both insight and hope," cf. Smart, *Dimensions of the Sacred*, 131.

7 Clifford, *Creation Accounts*, 7–10.

8 See Section 5.4.3 below.

fully fledged narratives. In light of this, then, one can say that reconstructing the mythology of the Judaeans in Elephantine from the Aramaic documents from Upper Egypt is rather like piecing together the biblical account of the birth of Jesus from a series of Christmas cards and carols.[9] It is possible, although the procedure has several methodological limitations, and there might potentially be great inadequacies with the results.

5.2 Judaean Myths of Creation in Elephantine?

We know several ancient Near Eastern myths and narratives about the creation of the world or parts thereof (cosmogony), about the creation of the gods (theogony) and about the creator gods' continuing struggle with the always threatening powers of chaos to sustain and uphold the creation (divine combat). In his discussion of *the* ancient Near Eastern creation text that no doubt has had the deepest impact on Western culture, namely Gen 1–11, Claus Westermann operates with a taxonomy of creation that includes four elements: creation through birth, creation as the result of battle and victory, creation through actions such as the separation or the forming of things and creation through words and commands.[10]

To be sure, even though we most likely may expect that the Judaeans had ideas about how the world came into being and how it was sustained, unfortunately no particular Elephantine Judaean creation narrative has survived. Although ideas about these things perhaps may be found in theophoric names such as *qwnyh* (Konaiah),[11] the use of personal names as a source is problematic for several reasons. First, to use the name *qwnyh* as an example, we cannot be sure about whether or not the Elephantine Judaeans themselves recognised the verbal element of the theophoric name as a verb of creation. Second, even if they did understand the verbal element as a verb of creation, we still do not have access to the narrative and mythic framework that may be used to interpret the potential verb of creation within. Unfortunately, none of the divine epithets attested in the textual sources from Elephantine give any clear hints about the

9 Borrowing and rephrasing the words of Ian Shaw about describing Egyptian mythology, especially the Osiris myth, cf. Ian Shaw, *Ancient Egypt: A Very Short Introduction* (Oxford: Oxford University Press, 2004), 116.

10 Claus Westermann, *Genesis 1–11: A Continental Commentary* (Minneapolis: Augsburg, 1984), 19–47, cf. Clifford, *Creation Accounts*, 1–10.

11 See B2.1:2; B2.2:8; B2.3:6.

fields of competence the Elephantine Judaeans attributed to the gods they knew of or even worshipped.

Their chief god YHW is occasionally referred to as "YHW the god of heaven." However, the epithet does not necessarily imply that YHW was revered as the creator of the heaven. It is thinkable that the Elephantine Judaeans used the epithet in tandem with the epithet "YHW the god who dwells in Elephantine." If that is the case, the two epithets together reflect an Elephantine Judaean theology of immanence and transcendence. If that is the case, the two epithets in a way counter-balanced each other.[12] However—and I think this is more likely—the use of the epithet "YHW the god of heaven" may reflect an attempt by the Elephantine Judaeans to assimilate their chief god YHW with Ahuramazda, the dynastic god of the Achaemenids.[13] In royal Achaemenid inscriptions Ahuramazda is occasionally presented as the creator of heaven and earth. The belief that Ahuramazda is the source and upholder of order is clearly expressed in one of the inscriptions on Darius I's tomb at Naqsh-e Rustam (DNa). Darius I's tomb inscription may very well have been known in Elephantine because the so-called Aramaic version of the Bisitun inscription contains material from it. The passage in question reads:[14] "A great god (is) Ahuramazda, who created this earth, who created yonder heaven, who created man, who created blissful happiness for man, who made Darius king, one king of many, one master of many" (DNa §1).[15]

Moreover, some of the occurrences of the epithet in native Elephantine Judaean sources suggest that the epithet "(YHW) the god of heaven" was part of the "court style" of Achaemenid officials (cf. the epistolary greeting in A4.7/A4.8 where Bagavahya the governor of Judah is addressed as a Persian official, and the memorandum of the joint statement of the governors of Judah and Samaria in A4.9).

---

12 As an analogy, see how the question of YHWH's immanence and transcendence are balanced in 1Kgs 8.

13 See the discussion in Gard Granerød, "'By the Favour of Ahuramazda I Am King': On the Promulgation of a Persian Propaganda Text among Babylonians and Judaeans," *JSJ* 44 (2013): 455–480 (475–478).

14 See Jonas C. Greenfield and Bezalel Porten, *The Bisitun Inscription of Darius the Great: Aramaic Version*, vol. V The Aramaic Versions of the Achaemenian Inscriptions, etc.; Texts I CII (London: Lund Humphries, 1982), 3–4, and Jan Tavernier, "An Achaemenid Royal Inscription: The Text of Paragraph 13 of the Aramaic Version of the Bisitun Inscription," *JNES* 60 (2001): 161–176 (162–163).

15 Quoted from Schmitt, *The Old Persian Inscriptions of Naqsh-i Rustam and Persepolis*, I The Old Persian Inscriptions: Texts II, 30 (slightly modified), cf. Amélie Kuhrt, *The Persian Empire: A Corpus of Sources from the Achaemenid Period* (London: Routledge, 2007), 502–503 (no. 11.16).

As far as attempts at assimilating YHW(H) with a dynastic god are concerned, there is a remarkable parallel in the chronologically earlier Āl-Yāḫūdu archive. Two documents from the time of Nabonidus (around 550 BCE) refer to one and the same individual. The individual in question is known under two similarly constructed theophorous names. In one of the documents he is presented as Bēl-šar-uṣur ("O Bel, protect the king!," CUSAS 28, no. 3:2, from 552 BCE). What is remarkable is that in another document he is called Yaḫū-šar-uṣur ("O YHW, protect the king!," CUSAS 28, no. 4:2, from 550 BCE). Worthy of note is that the name type itself reflects loyalty to the ruler, in this case the Babylonian Nabonidus, on the part of its Yahwistic/Judaean bearer. What is more, by substituting YHW with the epithet Bel ("lord") that normally pertains to Marduk, the name giver or the name bearer reveals his aspirations on behalf of YHW. Both YHW and Bel are regarded as holding the same (superior) position in the pantheon.[16]

Thus, to call YHW "the god of heaven" may reflect a similar attempt to place YHW in the same position in the pantheon as Ahuramazda. If that is the case, then we may expect that Persian creation concepts originally associated with Ahuramazda may also have been borrowed by the Judaeans and secondarily ascribed to YHW. If the great god Ahuramazda created, heaven and human beings, then the same may have been thought about YHW.

5.3 The Elephantine Judaean Temple Foundation Narrative

The so-called *foundation narratives* also belong to the world of ancient Near Eastern religious myths and narratives. Foundation narratives can deal with the foundation of a particular group such as a people, the foundation of a particular class of religious specialists within a group or the foundation of a particular social institution.

For instance, the Hebrew Bible offers two narratives about the foundation and origin of the people of Israel. These are, in their order of appearance in the biblical canon, the patriarchal narratives (Gen 12–36) and the narrative about the exodus of the Israelites out of Egyptian captivity (Exod 1ff.). In the Pentateuch the two narratives about Israel's origin are connected by the story about Joseph in Egypt (Gen 37–50). A basic idea in the patriarchal narratives is that YHWH founded the people Israel through the election of and calling

16 See Laurie E. Pearce and Cornelia Wunsch, *Documents of Judean Exiles and West Semites in Babylonia in the Collection of David Sofer*, CUSAS 28 (Bethesda, MD: CDL, 2014), 101.

out of Mesopotamia of Abraham, the grandfather of Jacob/Israel and eponym of the people. Moreover, a basic idea in the exodus narrative is that YHWH, via his mediator Moses, redeemed his people from the oppression it suffered in the foreign land of Egypt and brought it to the land of Canaan which they in turn would inherit.

Another example of a foundation narrative can be seen in the so-called *Cyrus Cylinder*. In the inscription Cyrus, who originally was king of Anshan (line 12), claimed that the god (Bel-)Marduk, "king of the gods," chose him out of the rulers of all of the countries and "called his name for the lordship over the whole world" (lines 11–12) in order to install him as "king of the world, great king, mighty king, king of Babylon, king of Sumer and Akkad, king of the four quarters of the world" (line 20).[17] According to the inscription, Marduk accompanied Cyrus (cf. line 15 "like a friend and companion he [i.e. Marduk] walked by his [i.e. Cyrus's] side") when the latter conquered Babylon (line 17) and defeated the (in Marduk's eyes) evil Babylonian king Nabonidus. Nabonidus had neglected the proper cults of Marduk and the other gods but Marduk's chosen one, Cyrus, restored their cults (cf. lines 26, 32–34).

Yet another foundation narrative with mythic elements is found in the royal Achaemenid inscriptions. In the Bisitun inscription of Darius I the king claimed that he restored the kingship of his dynasty, the Achaemenids, and defeated usurpers and rebelling kings in accordance with the will of the god Ahuramazda.[18]

In the sources for the Elephantine Judaean community we do not find any traces of any religious narratives resembling the biblical patriarchal and exodus narratives. However, in my view there are traces of one particular foundation narrative that belonged to the repertoire of religious narratives in Elephantine: *the tradition about the former temple of YHW*, that is, the temple destroyed at the end of the fifth century BCE, and which the Judaeans of Elephantine attempted to rebuild.[19] The primary sources for this tradition are some of the documents

---

17 Maria Brosius, *The Persian Empire from Cyrus II to Artaxerxes I*, LACTOR 16 (London: London Association of Classical Teachers, 2000), 10–11 (no. 12).

18 See Section 5.4 below.

19 Kratz has also analysed the Elephantine temple foundation narrative, cf. Reinhard Gregor Kratz, "The Second Temple of Jeb and of Jerusalem," in *Judah and the Judeans in the Persian Period*, ed. Oded Lipschits and Manfred Oeming (Winona Lake, IN: Eisenbrauns, 2006): 247–264. His analysis highlights two aspects of the religious-political argumentation of A4.7/A4.8: the avowal of political loyalty and the allusion to the earlier conduct of the Persian kings. The wider context of Kratz's analysis is a comparison between the Elephantine temple rebuilding project and the account in Ezra 1–6 about the reconstruction of the Jerusalem temple. He argues that the Elephantine texts give insight into the historical, religious and political back-

of the so-called Jedaniah communal archive. I will also argue that the sources enable us to identify successive stages in the process of its transmission (the *traditio*) and how its content (the *traditum*) was slightly altered throughout the process of transmission. Furthermore, I will argue that the tradition about the former temple of YHW gives an example of how Achaemenid officials took part in the shaping of Judaean religious traditions. Finally, I will argue that the tradition about the former temple of YHW in Elephantine and the desire to rebuild it was modelled on a pattern of antiquarianism often found in the ancient Near East.[20]

5.3.1 Outline of the History of the Temple

The most informative source for the history of the temple of YHW in Elephantine is found in the petition that the leaders of the Judaean garrison wrote in 407 BCE, of which—as mentioned above—two drafts are known: A4.7, and the parallel text in the second draft, A4.8.[21] The addressee of the petition was Bagavahya, the governor of the Persian province of Judah. On the basis of a concluding remark (A4.7:29 par.), it is clear that an identical letter was also sent to Delaiah and Shelemiah, the sons of Sanballat the governor of the province of Samaria. In the petition the leaders, among other things, outlined the history of the temple of YHW.

The leaders of the Judaeans in Elephantine outlined the history of the temple along three chronological fix points. The first one was the Persian king Cambyses's conquest of Egypt (ca. 525 BCE, A4.7:13–14 par.). The Elephantine leaders claimed that their ancestors had built the temple of YHW before this event, during "the days of the Egyptian kings." The second fix point was the date of the

---

ground of both reconstruction projects. Moreover, he argues that Ezra 1–6 as a whole should be seen as a theological reflection on and literary appropriation of what happened, written from a period after the events themselves took place in Jerusalem. Because Ezra 1–6 bear the hallmarks of historical fiction, it is "only with great caution that one can tap this source for historical information on the reconstruction of the Temple in Jerusalem; and any information thus obtained must be checked against authentic material," i.e. such as the Elephantine documents, cf. Kratz, "The Second Temple," 247–264 (264).

20 The following discussion is based upon Gard Granerød, "The Former and the Future Temple of YHW in Elephantine: A Traditio-Historical Case Study of Ancient Near Eastern Antiquarianism," *ZAW* 127 (2015): 63–77 (66–76).

21 A brief introduction to the two draft letters written to the governor of Judah is found in Bezalel Porten et al., eds., *The Elephantine Papyri in English: Three Millennia of Cross-Cultural Continuity and Change*, 2nd rev. ed., DMOA 22 (Atlanta: Society of Biblical Literature, 2011), 141, 147.

destruction of the temple of YHW. Jedaniah and the priests informed Bagavahya that the temple was completely destroyed in the fourteenth regnal year of King Darius (A4.7:10 par.), 410 BCE. The leaders reported to Bagavahya that the Egyptian priests of Khnum conspired with a local Persian official (Vidranga) against the temple of YHW (A4.7:5–6). The official's son (Naphaina) then led the troops that entered the temple of YHW "with their weapons" and "destroyed it to the ground" (A4.7:8–9 par.). The third fix point was the date of the letter to Bagavahya (A4.7:29 par.). At the time of writing the petition to Bagavahya in the seventeenth year of Darius II (407 BCE), the temple of YHW was still lying in ruins.

5.3.2 *Traditum* in the Petition to the Governor of the Persian Province of Judah

The ultimate goal of the letter from the Elephantine Judaeans to Bagavahya, the governor of Judah, was to elicit his support:

> May a letter from you be sent to them about the Temple of YHW the God to (re)build it in Elephantine the fortress just as it had been built formerly. (A4.7:24–25)[22]

I will not discuss whom the Elephantine Judaeans meant by "to them" (e.g., Arshama, the Persian satrap of Egypt and his bureaucrats?) and why the Judaeans in southern Egypt involved the governors of the Persian provinces of Judah and Samaria anyway. Here, I will rather focus on the contents (*traditum*) and the transmission (*traditio*) of the tradition about the former temple of YHW.

The Elephantine community obviously sought to rebuild the temple just as it was built "formerly." The keyword in the concluding request to Bagavahya (A4.7:24–25 par.) is the adverb "formerly" (*qdmyn*). In the context of the letter, the word "formerly" refers to the situation prior to the destruction in 410 BCE. What were the contents of this tradition, then? One important component was its antiquity. According to the foundation narrative, it was erected before the Persian conquest of Egypt. Another important component was that the temple of YHW enjoyed a privileged status at the time of the Persian conquest. When the Persian king Cambyses conquered Egypt, the Elephantine leaders claimed, he overthrew all the indigenous Egyptian temples. However, the Persian conquerors did not destroy anything in the temple of YHW (A4.7:13–14). In other words, the temple of YHW was spared from the sacrileges perpetrated by the invading Persians.

---

22 Quoted from Porten et al., *The Elephantine Papyri in English*, 145.

The historical accuracy of these two pieces of information has been questioned.[23] However, that is not our concern here. What the petition to Bagavahya positively shows is that around 407 BCE, after the destruction of the temple of YHW, the Judaeans in Elephantine had a tradition about the former temple of YHW. At that time, two of the components of its contents (*traditum*) were that the temple of YHW was ancient, antedating the Persian occupation of Egypt, and that the invading Persian king had given it privileged status by sparing it, in contrast to how he treated the Egyptian temples.

Moreover, the petition to Bagavahya shows us that the tradition about the former temple had a third component, too. The third component was made up of the memory that there was a fully fledged cult in the former temple of YHW. In it, the community (or its priest) offered not only cereal offerings but also animal sacrifices.

The petition to Bagavahya refers twice to the latter sacrifices. The first mention is in a negative context (A4.7:21–22 par.). Since the destruction in the fourteenth year of Darius until the petition to Bagavahya was written three years later, no meal-offering, incense or burnt offering ("holocaust") (*mnḥh wlbwnh wʿlwh*) had been offered. The second mention is in a positive context (A4.7:25–26 par.). If the temple was eventually rebuilt in accordance with its pre-destruction phase (A4.7:25 "just as it was formerly built"), then the Elephantine aimed to resume the former sacrificial cult. Specifically, the community promised both cereal offerings and an animal sacrifice (*ʿlwtʾ*, "the burnt offering") *in Bagavahya's name*, on the condition that he send the requested letter in support of the rebuilding:

> And the meal-offering and the incense and the burnt-offering they will offer [cf. the parallel text in A4.8:25: *nqrb*, "we shall offer"] on the altar of YHW the God in your name [*bšmk*] and we shall pray for you at all times—we and our wives and our children and the Jews, all (of them) who are here. (A4.7:25–27, my emphasis)[24]

23 In support of a destruction of temples in the Persian period, a fire layer has been found in two temples, cf. Heike Sternberg-el Hotabi, "Die persische Herrschaft in Ägypten," in *Religion und Religionskontakte im Zeitalter der Achämeniden*, ed. Reinhard Gregor Kratz, VWGT 22 (Gütersloh: Gütersloher Verlagshaus, 2002): 111–149 (114).

24 Quoted from Porten et al., *The Elephantine Papyri in English*, 145.

5.3.3 *Traditio* and *Tradentes* According to the Petition to Bahavahya and the Subsequent Correspondence

How was the tradition about the former temple of YHW transmitted, and who took part in this transmission? In short, who were the *tradentes?* A close reading of the petition written to the governor Bagavahya and the subsequent correspondence shows that several *tradentes* actually took part, or potentially could take part, in the chain of transmission of the tradition about the former temple of YHW. The following actual or potential *tradentes* may be identified:

1. the Judaean leaders in Elephantine (Jedaniah and the priests; A4.7:1 par.),
2. the entire Judaean community in Elephantine ("we and our wives and our children and the Judaeans"; A4.7:15, 20 par.),
3. the Persian governor of Judah (A4.7:1; A4.9:1),
4. the Persian governor of Samaria (the Sanballat dynasty represented by the sons Delaiah and Shelemiah; A4.7:29 par.; A4.9:1),
5. the leading circles of the province of Judah (Jehohanan the high priest, the priests in Jerusalem, Ostanes and "the nobles," A4.7:18–19 par.), and
6. perhaps Arshama, the Persian satrap of Egypt (A4.9:3; A4.10:7, 12–13, cf. A4.7:30 par.).

Jedaniah and the priests of YHW in Elephantine (# 1) were obviously located in the centre of the *traditio.* It is they who sent petitions to the governors of the Persian provinces of Judah and Samaria (# 3–4), asking for a letter of recommendation to rebuild the temple of YHW. Moreover, the Elephantine leaders received a response from the two Persian governors (# 3–4, cf. A4.9). On the basis of this answer, they probably addressed Arshama, the Persian satrap of Egypt (# 6, cf. A4.10).

Furthermore, according to Jedaniah and the priests of YHW in Elephantine, there were also other groups that kept the tradition about the former temple of YHW alive. One such group was the entire Judaean community of Elephantine (# 2). The petition A4.7/A4.8 refers twice to communal rites that the entire Judaean population in Elephantine had been performing since the temple was destroyed three years earlier.[25]

---

25 According to the first reference, "we with our wives and children" had been wearing sackcloth, had been fasting and had been praying "to YHW the lord of heaven" (A4.7:15 par.). According to the second reference to communal rites of mourning, the wives of the Judaean men in Elephantine had been "made like widows." In addition, they had not anointed themselves with oil and had abstained from wine since the temple was destroyed (A4.7:19–21 par.).

Jedaniah and his colleagues, the priests, claimed that the leading circles of the province of Judah (# 5) had already been informed. After the temple of YHW was destroyed in 410 BCE, the Judaeans in Elephantine sent a letter to Jehohanan the high priest, the priests in Jerusalem, Ostanes and “the nobles of Judah” as well as the governor Bagavahya (A4.7:18 – 19 par.). For some unknown reason, the recipients of this letter did not respond. In the second letter, this time to Bagavahya, the Elephantine leaders made the following comment concerning the reaction the first letter caused: “They did not send us a single letter” (A4.7:19 par.).

Regardless of the explanation for the non-response to the first letter, one thing is clear: the Elephantine community included the priesthood connected to the Jerusalem temple of YHWH and the nobles of Judah in the *traditio* of the tradition about the former temple of YHW in Elephantine.

This clearly suggests that the Judaeans in Elephantine did not know of the Jerusalemite claim to have the central and only legitimate temple of the cult of YHWH. The idea about Jerusalem as the only place chosen by YHWH as a dwelling may have existed at the end of the fifth century BCE in certain Judaean circles within or outside the province of Judah. However, the idea of a centralised cult was by no means known in all sections of the community of YHW(H)-worshippers, and even less was it accepted by all adherents of Yahwism.

In sum, the petition to Bagavahya gives a glimpse of those who were involved in the process of transmission of the tradition about the former temple of YHW (the *tradentes*). The group of *tradentes* was not only made up of the members of the Judaean community in Elephantine, it was also made up of external ones (Judaeans and non-Judaeans), as well.

5.3.4 Alteration of the *Traditum* (A4.9 and A4.10)

Why did Jedaniah and the priests of YHW in Elephantine write to Bagavahya the Persian governor of the province of Judah and the sons of Sanballat, the Persian governor of Samaria?

Whatever the answer to this intriguing question might have been, it is nevertheless clear that Bagavahya was addressed as a *Persian* official. The elaborated salutation in A4.7:1 makes this clear:

> To our lord Bagavahya governor of Judah, your servants Jedaniah and his colleagues the priests who are in Elephantine the fortress. The welfare of our lord may the God of Heaven seek after abundantly at all times, favor may He grant you before Darius the king and the

> princes more than now a thousand times, and long life may He give you, and happy and strong may you be at all times. (A4.7:1 par.)[26]

The context of the wish made by Jedaniah and his colleagues the Elephantine priests is that of the Persian royal court. They wished Bagavahya all the best success in his career as the highest-ranked Persian official in Judah. Moreover, at the very end of the letter they wrote that a copy of the same letter had been sent to Bagavahya's colleagues in Samaria:

> Moreover, all the(se) things in a letter we sent in our name to Delaiah and Shelemiah sons of Sanballat governor of Samaria. (A4.7:29 par.)[27]

The petition from Elephantine to the governors of Judah and Samaria delivered results. The results are reflected in a document containing the memorandum of the joint statement of Bagavahya and Delaiah (A4.9). According to the memorandum, the governors of Judah and Samaria supported the attempts to rebuild the temple and to resume the sacrificial cult of YHW in Elephantine. The memorandum seems to contain the words that the two governors spoke to the envoy sent by the Judaean community in Elephantine. The anonymous envoy (Jedaniah?) was authorised to impart to Arshama, the Persian satrap of Egypt, the words of the governors:

> Memorandum. What Bagavahya and Delaiah said to me. Memorandum. Saying: "Let it be for you in Egypt to say before Arsames about the Altar-house of the God of Heaven which in Elephantine the fortress built was formerly before Cambyses (and) which Vidranga, that wicked (man) demolished in year 14 of Darius the king: 'to (re)build it on its site as it was formerly and the meal-offering and the incense upon they may offer upon that altar just as formerly was done.'" (A4.9)[28]

At first sight, it seems that the two governors subscribed completely to the *traditum* of the tradition about the former temple as it was originally presented in the petition. They recommended (or approved[29]) that the temple, which was built before the reign of Cambyses, was to be rebuilt "on its site as it was formerly" (A4.9:8 *bʾtrh kzy hwh lqdmn*). Moreover, they recommended (approved?) that

---

26 Quoted from Porten et al., *The Elephantine Papyri in English*, 141–142.

27 Quoted from Porten et al., *The Elephantine Papyri in English*, 146.

28 Quoted from Porten et al., *The Elephantine Papyri in English*, 150–151.

29 The choice of word is closely dependent upon the question of whether the two governors had any extraterritorial jurisdiction as, say, in cases pertaining to the cult of YHWH, or whether they simply functioned as influential and powerful friends of the Judaeans in Elephantine.

the offerings should be resumed "upon that alter just as formerly was done" (A4.9:8–9 *ʿl mdbḥʾ zk lqbl zy lqdmyn*). However, there is an important difference. They mentioned only two out of the originally three types of offerings: *meal-offering* and *incense*. No reference was made to the third type, the animal sacrifice (*ʿlwtʾ*, "burnt offering").

There is a paradox here. On the one hand the two governors presented their joint statement as a *complete restoration* of the physical temple and the sacrificial cult. This is clear in light of the fact that derivations of the adverb *qdm* with the meaning "before, former(ly)" occur no fewer than four times in the memorandum of their joint statement (A4.9:5 [×2], 8, 10). In other words, it is a *Leitwort* in the text. In addition, they employed the phrase *bʾtrh*, "on its site." However, on the other hand, what they recommended (or approved) was in fact a *reformation*; they failed to mention the resumption of the burnt offering (*ʿlwh*).

It seems that the leading figures of the Elephantine community accepted the alteration of the *traditum*. This seems to be the implication of the last text from the Jedaniah communal archive to be discussed: A4.10. This document is a draft letter written by a five-strong group of leading Judaeans of Elephantine to an anonymous individual they call "our lord." It is likely that the draft letter was written *after* the envoy had returned from his mission to Judah and Samaria with the joint statement of the two Persian governors there (A4.9). If that is the case, the addressee of the draft letter was probably none other than Arshama himself, the Persian satrap of Egypt (cf. A4.9:3).

The text of A4.10 is broken. Nevertheless, in my view, it seems that the leading Judaean figures actually negotiated with their interlocutor (Arshama?). This is evident in the conditional clause in A4.10:7–9. Parts of the condition itself are lost but in my opinion there is enough of the text intact to verify this (A4.10:7–11):

> [A4.7:7] *kn ʾmrn hn mrʾn* [...]
> [A4.7:8] *wʾgwrʾ zy yhw ʾlhʾ zyln ytbnh*
> [A4.7:9] *byb byrtʾ kzy qdm[n b]nh hwh*
> [A4.7:10] *wqn twr ʿnz mqlw [l]ʾ ytʿbd tmh*
> [A4.7:11] *lhn lbwnh mnḥh* [.........]
>
> [A4.7:7] (The five named individuals) say thus: If our lord [...],
> [A4.7:8] and the temple of YHW the god of ours will be built
> [A4.7:9] in Elephantine the fortress just as it used to be forme[rly bu]ilt,
> [A4.7:10] then sheep, ox (and) goat (as) burnt offering shall [no]t be made there,
> [A4.7:11] only incense and meal-offering [.........] (my translation)

In the apodosis, that is, the consequent clause beginning in line 10, the Elephantine leaders refrained from animal sacrifices[30] and stressed that they will only offer cereal offerings.

It is remarkable that the Elephantine leaders did this, although they used the keyword *qdmn* "formerly." Consequently, A4.10 attests to the same paradoxical situation that was evident in A4.9 (the memorandum of the joint statement of the two governors). On the one hand, the Elephantine leaders advocated for a complete rebuilding of the temple of YHW in accordance with how the temple was built formerly. We should expect that the rites in a future temple, rebuilt following the model of a former temple, would closely resemble the rites of the former temple. In other words, we should expect that the future rites would include animal sacrifices. On the other hand, in the letter A4.10 (to Arshama?) the Elephantine leaders explicitly refrained from animal sacrifices.

Why animal sacrifices were not to be conducted in the rebuilt temple of YHW remains unresolved.[31] In my opinion, it is unlikely that the restriction was self-imposed. On the contrary, it was probably Persian officials who imposed it upon the Elephantine Judaeans, and for an unstated reason. In any case, the Elephantine Judaeans accepted the restriction.

Whatever reasons there were for the ban on animal offerings, in the future temple of YHW, which was to be rebuilt just as it was formerly, animal sacrifices were no longer to be offered.

5.3.5 Summary and Perspectives

We cannot tell whether, and possibly to what extent, the Elephantine Judaeans were aware of the religious traditions that we know from the received texts of the Bible. Nevertheless, the Elephantine papyri attest to a particular religious tradition in circulation towards the end of the fifth century BCE: *the tradition about the former temple of YHW.* The tradition had at least three components: the temple was claimed to be an ancient one, its status was claimed to have been privileged by the Persians and it was claimed that there used to be a fully fledged sacrificial cult taking place in the temple of YHW, a cult that included cereal *and* animal sacrifices.

30 The technical term used for "burnt offering" in A4.10:11 is *mqlw*. In light of the petition to Bagavahya it seems probable that *mqlw* is a synonym of *ʿlwh* (cf. A4.7:21, 25, 28 par.).

31 For a discussion of various explanation models, see Section 4.2.3 above.

Furthermore, the sources also give us a glimpse of how Persian officials were involved in the transmission of the tradition about the former temple of YHW. It would appear that their involvement resulted in the Elephantine Judaeans refraining from any further animal offerings.[32]

The tradition about the former temple of YHW in Elephantine reflects a noticeable degree of *antiquarianism*. In order to find templates for their future, the Elephantine Judaeans looked backwards to the past, to the things of old.[33]

The outlook of the Elephantine Judaeans was by no means without precedent in the ancient Near East. According to the Assyriologist Paul-Alain Beaulieu, Mesopotamian civilisation was struck with an epidemic of antiquarianism that culminated in the Neo-Babylonian period, which was the age of antiquarianism *par excellence*.[34] One of the ways in which this antiquarianism manifested itself was in extensive temple rebuilding projects. It was crucial for the Neo-Babylonian monarchs that a temple was rebuilt on the very same foundations which had been laid previously. This was done in order to please the deity and to avoid the deity's wrath and is attested both archaeologically and textually. Archaeological excavations show that later rebuilt temple structures almost always follow the perimeter enclosing the earliest known foundations. Temple-building inscriptions from the Neo-Babylonian period also reflect the same concept.[35]

---

32 Strictly speaking, the memorandum of the joint statement of Bagavahya and Delaiah does not contain any explicit veto on animal sacrifices in the to-be-rebuilt temple of YHW in Elephantine. However, in the light of the available sources the most probable solution is that it was they who issued the veto. Whatever reasons they may have had for doing that, they gave their statement in the capacity as officials of the *Persian* administration.

33 Compare in contrast YHWH's call to the exiled/recently returned Israelites according to Isa 43:18–19: "Do not remember the former things, or consider the things of old. I am about to do a new thing; now it springs forth, do you not perceive it?"

34 See Paul-Alain Beaulieu, "Antiquarianism and the Concern for the Past in the Neo-Babylonian Period," *BCSMS* 28 (1994): 37–42 (41), and the presentation of the antiquarianism practiced by the last Neo-Babylonian king, Nabonidus, also hailed as "the archaeologist on the throne" in Paul-Alain Beaulieu, "Mesopotamian Antiquarianism from Sumer to Babylon," in *World Antiquarianism: Comparative Perspectives*, ed. Alain Schnapp, Issues & Debates (Los Angeles: Getty Research Institute, 2013): 121–139 (132).

35 Beaulieu, "Antiquarianism and the Concern for the Past," 37–42 (39) gives an example from Nebuchadnezzar's rebuilding of Ebabbar, the temple of the sun-god Shamash at Sippar. Nebuchadnezzar undertakes the rebuilding despite the fact that he has not succeeded in finding the *temennu*, i.e. the foundation deposit of the ancient founder. In his own building inscription, Nebuchadnezzar is almost apologetic to the deity for not having found the original temple layout.

However, the antiquarianism of the Neo-Babylonian empire did by no means cease when the Persian king Cyrus dealt a mortal blow to the last Neo-Babylonian king Nabonidus in 539 BCE. The *Cyrus Cylinder* (which judged on the basis of its style and contents in fact is a typical Mesopotamian building text[36]) reflects a comparable antiquarianism. Cyrus boasts of having restored the cult of several sanctuaries and of having restored their gods to their rightful place:

> [30] From (Nineveh), Assur and Susa, [31] from Akkad, Ešunna, Zamban, Meturni, and Der, to the land of Gutium, the cult places on the other side of the Tirgris, whose sanctuaries had been deserted a long time ago, [32] *I returned (their) gods to their (rightful) place*, and let them be housed there forever. I gathered all their former inhabitants and returned them to their houses, [33] and the gods of Sumer and Akkad, whom Nabonidus had brought into Babylon to the wrath of the great lord (*Marduk*), I installed, in the command of Marduk, the great lord, [34] in their sanctuaries as a place of heart's joy. (*Cyrus Cylinder*, lines 30–34)[37]

Other sources also attest to an antiquarianism on the part of the Persian rulers. According to Ezra 5:15 and 6:7, Cyrus decreed that the temple in Jerusalem should be rebuilt "on its site" (*'l 'trh*), using the same phrasing as the governors of the Persian provinces of Judah and Samaria in their joint statement to the envoy from the Judaean community of Elephantine (A4.9:8).

Moreover, an Egyptian source, the so-called autobiography of Udjahorresnet, seems to refer to an antiquarianism on the part of the Persians. Udjahorresnet, the Egyptian admiral who became the personal physician of Cambyses, Cyrus's successor who conquered Egypt, wrote in his autobiography that he petitioned Cambyses about the miserable situation of the temple of the Egyptian goddess Neith. He wanted to see the temple of Neith again "in all its splendour, as it had been in existence since the beginning."[38] Upon his petition, Udjahorresnet claims, Cambyses restored the cult of Neith and all the gods who are in Sais "as it was before ... since antiquity."

Furthermore, the royal inscriptions of the Achaemenid dynasty that succeeded the line of Cyrus may perhaps develop this idea even further. Not only temples but even people in general and, in particular, the royal Achaemenid family, had their respective "proper places." These "proper places" were determined not only

36 Amélie Kuhrt, "The Cyrus Cylinder and Achaemenid Imperial Policy," *JSOT* 25 (1983): 83–97 (88).
37 Quoted from Brosius, *The Persian Empire*, 10–12 (no. 12), my emphasis.
38 Quoted from Brosius, *The Persian Empire*, 15–17 (no. 20).

by referring to historical precedents but were justified ontologically. In King Darius I's so-called Bisitun inscription the concept of "proper place" is crucial:

> Proclaims Darius, the king: The kingship, which had been taken away from our family, that I reinstated; *I put it in its proper place.* Just as (they were) previously, so I made the places of worship, which Gaumata the magus had destroyed; I restored to the people the farmsteads, the livestock, the menials and (together with) the houses, of which Gaumata the magus had despoiled them. *I put the people in its proper place,* Persia as well as Media and the other countries. Just as (it was) previously, so I restored what had been taken away. By the favour of Ahuramazda this I did. I strove, *until I had put our (royal) house in its proper place, just as (it was) previously.* So I strove by the favour of Ahuramazda that Gaumata the magus did not take away our (royal) house. (DB §14)[39]

Also the Judaeans in Elephantine knew this Achaemenid propaganda text.[40] Other Achaemenid royal inscriptions also reflect an ontological concept of "the proper place." According to Darius I's tomb inscription from Naqsh-e Rustam, the god Ahuramazda saw the earth in turmoil and restored it through Darius: "By the favour of Ahuramazda I put it [the world] *in its proper place*" (DNa §4).[41]

In short, in light of the Achaemenid royal inscriptions, but also in light of the iconographic sources from Persepolis, Klaus Koch argues that the Achaemenid empire was built upon the idea of an ontologically legitimated state of nationalities ("die Idee des ontologisch begründeten Nationalitätenstaates").[42]

The antiquity the Elephantine Judaeans attributed to their temple of YHW reflected a trait that apparently was common in the ancient Near East. The letters to the Persian governor of Judah (A4.7/A4.8) and to "our lord" (Arshama?, A4.10) show that the Elephantine Judaeans considered historical references, references to the antiquity of the temple of YHW, to be weighty arguments in favour of a future rebuilding. Likewise, when the two Persian governors of Judah and Samaria recommended to the satrap Arshama that the temple of YHW should be rebuilt "on its site" (A4.9:8), they reverted to a system that was already established in the ancient Near East. Yet, paradoxically, the antiquarianism did not hinder

---

39 Quoted from Schmitt, *The Bisitun Inscriptions of Darius the Great: Old Persian Text*, I The Old Persian inscriptions: Texts I, 53 (my emphasis, slightly modified).

40 See Section 5.4.3 below.

41 Quoted from Schmitt, *The Old Persian Inscriptions of Naqsh-i Rustam and Persepolis*, I The Old Persian Inscriptions: Texts II, 30 (my emphasis, slightly modified).

42 Klaus Koch, "Weltordnung und Reichsidee im alten Iran und ihre Auswirkungen auf die Provinz Jehud," in *Reichsidee und Reichsorganisation im Perserreich*, ed. Peter Frei and Klaus Koch, OBO 55 (Freiburg (Switzerland) and Göttingen: Universitätsverlag Freiburg Schweiz and Vandenhoeck & Ruprecht, 1996): 133–338 (201, 205).

someone, presumably the Persian authorities, from banning future animal sacrifices in the to-be rebuilt temple of YHW in Elephantine.

The Elephantine papyri dealing with the destroyed temple of YHW in Elephantine, and the attempts to rebuild it, offer epigraphic evidence for a traditio-historical process. They illustrate how a Judaean religious tradition functioned in a religious environment that did not have any canon of authoritative, normative religious texts *yet.*[43]

The tradition about the former temple of YHW has the characteristics of a religious narrative with a mythic potential. It has a historical framework and seemingly historical contents (such as what appear to be factual descriptions of occurrences that took place). Its mythic potential refers to a "golden age," namely, the time before the Persian conquest when "our fathers" built the temple and how it was allegedly spared by Cambyses, in contrast to the temples of the Egyptian gods. Moreover, the mythic potential is evident in the antiquarianism it reflects. The realities of the past, the "golden age," should provide a template for the future, the restoration of the golden age.

5.4 Myths about Sacral Kingship

In the literary remains of many, if not most, of the civilisations of the ancient Near East there are traces of myths about the legitimacy of the ruling dynasty. A common feature of these myths is that the kingship of the ruling monarch was due to the will of the gods, as the result of the gods' election, adoption or even procreation. These myths may be loosely described as myths about sacral kingship.

43 The Elephantine papyri reflect Judaean religion before it became Scripture-based and Scripture-oriented, sometime during the last centuries BCE. For a discussion on the promulgation of the Torah in the Persian and Hellenistic periods, see, e.g., Reinhard Gregor Kratz, *Historisches und biblisches Israel: Drei Überblicke zum Alten Testament* (Tübingen: Mohr Siebeck, 2013), 181–291.

5.4.1 The Egyptian and Ancient Near Eastern Context

5.4.1.1 Egyptian Royal Myths

A recurring motif in Egyptian literature dealing with the king is that the Pharaoh was god's son.[44] The perhaps most condensed presentation of the Egyptian royal ideology is the so-called *Myth of the Procreation and Birth of the King*. This myth is most explicitly presented as a pictorial cycle of fifteen reliefs, each representing a scene and accompanied by a text. The relief cycle is found in two Egyptian temples, the first dating to the fifteenth century and the second to about the fourteenth century BCE.[45] The relief cycle begins with a statement that Amon, the king of the gods, decides to procreate a new king, to whom he will give dominance over the entire world. He finds a particular attractive woman, who happens to be the queen. Then, in the guise of the queen's husband, the king, he sleeps with her. According to the accompanying text, the odour of Amon (probably a euphemism for semen) impregnates the queen's limbs. After that, Amon commands the god Khnum to create the child in his (Amon's) likeliness. Khnum was the creator of infants' bodies. He made them at a potter's wheel and placed each one of them in the womb of its mother. After that follow scenes describing how Khnum actually made the child, how the pregnancy was proclaimed to the queen and scenes from the birth, followed by speeches directed to the child itself. Among other things, Amon, addressing the child, acknowledges his fatherhood. Iconographically, the god Amon is presented embracing the newborn child who is sitting on his lap.[46]

The Egyptian myth of the procreation and birth of the king is also found in an important text from the Ramesside period (Nineteenth–Twentieth Dynasties, ca. thirteenth–eleventh centuries BCE) and is attested in five different versions

---

44 The following draws on Gard Granerød, "A Forgotten Reference to Divine Procreation? Psalm 2:6 in Light of Egyptian Royal Ideology," *VT* 60 (2010): 323–336 (325–326 and 329–331).

45 See Hellmut Brunner, *Die Geburt des Gottkönigs: Studien zur Überlieferung eines altägyptischen Mythos* (Wiesbaden: Harrassowitz, 1964). For a translation of the accompanying text and an outline of each scene, see "Der Mythos von der Geburt des Gottkönigs," translated by Heike Sternberg el-Hotabi (*TUAT* 3:991–1005). Moreover, see Jan Assmann, *Ägypten: Theologie und Frömmigkeit einer frühen Hochkultur*, 2nd rev. ed., KUT 366 (Stuttgart: Kohlhammer, 1991); Othmar Keel, *Die Welt der altorientalischen Bildsymbolik und das Alte Testament: am Beispiel der Psalmen*, 5th ed. (Göttingen: Vandenhoeck & Ruprecht, 1996), 224–247; Klaus Koch, *Geschichte der ägyptischen Religion von den Pyramiden bis zu den Mysterien der Isis* (Stuttgart: Kohlhammer, 1993), 264–298; and Klaus Koch, "Der König als Sohn Gottes in Ägypten und Israel," in *"Mein Sohn bist du" (Ps 2,7): Studien zu den Königspsalmen*, ed. Eckart Otto and Erich Zenger, SBS 192 (Stuttgart: Katholisches Bibelwerk, 2002): 1–32.

46 See Keel, *Die Welt der altorientalischen Bildsymbolik*, 229–230 (figs. 338–339).

and usually referred to as the "Decree or Blessing of Ptah upon Ramesses II and III." In the Ramesside period, Ptah, who was originally worshipped as the god of craftsmen in Memphis, had been grouped with Amon and Re. Together, they represented a national and universal divine triad. In the text in question, Ptah addresses King Ramesses II (Pharaoh Ramesses III in later copies). It has been translated by Kenneth A. Kitchen thus:

> *I am your father who begot you among the gods,* / all of your body being from the gods. / Now, I assumed my form as the Ram, Lord of Mendes, / and *I implanted you*[47] in your august mother, / for I knew that you are (my) champion, / and you, indeed, shall perform benefactions for my spirit. / I fashioned you as when Re shines forth, / and I have exalted you before the gods, / O King of S & N Egypt ... (263:5–13)[48]

After having said this, Ptah continues addressing the king by recalling the king's birth and upbringing and by promising him riches, monuments and the submission of all nations.

5.4.1.2 Israelite–Judaean Royal Myths

Israelite/Judaean literature also reflects myths about sacral kingship. One text illustrating this is found in Ps 2. In the text, YHWH and "his anointed" (*məšîḥô*) are presented as a "winning team" against which the (hostile) kings and rulers of the earth take counsel together (Ps 2:2–3, 8–9). Moreover, the king who reigns on Zion is presented as YHWH's son: "You are my son; today I have begotten you" (Ps 2:7). The psalm uses a procreative language in order to describe the father–son relationship between the deity and the king on Zion. The former is the grammatical subject of the verb *yld*. However, the phrase *hayyôm* ("today") in the received text suggests that the verb is used metaphorically, so that the father–son relationship is established through adoption.[49] Moreover, in my opinion, there is also an additional procreative verb in the psalm, namely in the preceding verse

47 Manfred Görg, *Gott-König-Reden in Israel und Ägypten*, BWANT Folge 6 5 (Stuttgart: Kohlhammer, 1975), 237–238 translates this clause "Ich ergoß meinen Samen." Similar also Günther Roeder, *Urkunden zur Religion des alten Ägypten* (Jena: Eugen Diederichs, 1923), 159, and Jan Assmann, "Die Zeugung des Sohnes. Bild, Spiel, Erzählung und das Problem des ägyptischen Mythos," in *Funktionen und Leistungen des Mythos: drei altorientalische Beispiele*, ed. Jan Assmann, et al., OBO 48 (Freiburg: Universitätsverlag, 1982): 13–61 (35).

48 Quoted from Kenneth A. Kitchen, *Ramesside Inscriptions: Translated and Annotated: Translations*, vol. II: Ramesses II, Royal Inscriptions (Oxford: Blackwell, 1996), 102 (my emphasis).

49 See, e.g., Gerhard von Rad, "Das judäische Königsritual," in *Gesammelte Studien zum Alten Testament*, ed. Gerhard von Rad, TB 8 (Munich: Kaiser, 1965): 205–213 (209).

6. The traditional rendition of this verse can be illustrated by the NRSV: "I have set [*nāsaktî*] my king on Zion, my holy hill." (Ps 2:6).

However, in a 2010 article I have, against the traditional understanding, suggested that the verb *nsk* in Ps 2:6 should be understand in accordance with the meaning it has in all other contexts of the Hebrew Bible.[50] Normally, the verb *nsk* denotes the "pouring out" of some kind of fluid. In this particular context this fluid may originally have been thought to have been YHWH's semen, so that the psalm in turn may reflect an (early) concept of YHWH as the procreator of the king on Mount Zion.[51]

Another biblical text reflecting a similar Israelite/Judaean royal myth is Nathan's prophecy concerning the house of David in 2Sam 7. In the narrative context, the point of departure of the prophecy is David's wish to build a house (*bayit*)—a temple—for YHWH. However, according to Nathan, it is YHWH who instead will build a (royal) house (*bayit*)—a dynasty—for David and his offspring (2Sam 7:11). Also in this particular illustration of the Israelite/Judaean royal myths the relationship between the deity and the king is characterised as a father–son relationship (2Sam 7:14, referring to David's son Solomon). However, the house of David came into power as the result of YHWH's election, not because it had any inheritance rights to the royal throne of Israel from the outset. In the prophecy, YHWH states that he "took you from the pasture, from following the sheep to be prince over my people Israel" (2Sam 7:8). Moreover, characteristic of this text reflecting Israelite/Judaean royal myths is the concept that YHWH is "with" (*ʿim*) the king (cf. 2Sam 7:3, 9–11), but at the same time also liable to be held accountable by the dynasty deity for his wrongdoings (2Sam 7:15–16).

5.4.1.3 Mesopotamian Legendary Tales about Ancient Kings

The accession of King Sargon of Akkad (ca. 2300 BCE) and his subjugation of the neighbouring kingdoms with an empire centred around the city of Akkad marked a watershed in Mesopotamian history. As a model of the world conqueror par excellence, King Sargon became the protagonist in many stories and epics in the centuries and millennia after.

---

50 See note 44 above.

51 However, it should be noted that the anthropological depiction of YHWH in Ps 2 was weakened early in the reception history. In the LXX version of Ps 2:6 the verb *nsk* is rendered by καθίστημι, "to set, install," changing the expression into an act of commissioning the king to the royal office.

One of the stories attached to Sargon of Akkad is a legend about his birth. In the *Birth Legend of Sargon* the king himself speaks in first person.[52] He claimed that his mother was a priestess and that his father was unknown. When his mother had given birth to him "in concealment," she put him in a wicker basket that she impregnated and sealed off with bitumen. Furthermore, according to Sargon, his mother threw the basket with the baby into the river. Driven by the stream the basket was eventually rescued by Aqqi, the water-drawer. Aqqi, in turn, brought up Sargon as his adopted son. When Sargon was working as a gardener at Aqqi's place, the goddess Ishtar "did grow fond of me" and (following immediately after a lacuna) Sargon claimed that he reigned as king. In the autobiographic inscription Sargon stated that he ruled over the "black-headed people," ascended all the high mountains and traversed all the foothills, and that he sailed around the sealands "three times." In a direct address to future kings Sargon urged them to repeat these acts.

The date of composition of the birth legend is unknown; it has been characterised as a "pseudonymous royal inscription."[53] Regardless of its origin, it was evidently promoted with great care in the reign of the Neo-Assyrian Sargon II in the late seventh century BCE.[54] The text is known from two fragmentary exemplars. The earlier one stems from seventh-century Neo-Assyrian Nineveh. The later one is a fifth century BCE school-exercise from Babylonia.[55] That Sargon of Akkad was held in high esteem in the Neo-Assyrian period is evident in the choice of throne name by Sargon II (ca. 722–705 BCE), taking the name of the eponymous king when he seized the kingship by force from his brother.

Elements of the birth legend of Sargon of Akkad may also have been reused in the birth legend of Cyrus II that Herodotus offers (*Hist.* 1.107–123, 127–130).[56] Also in the legend told by Herodotus, the king to-be was an exposed boy-child

---

52 For translations, see "The Legend of Sargon," translated by Ephraim Avigdor Speiser (*ANET*, 119); "The Birth Legend of Sargon of Akkad," translated by Benjamin R. Foster (*COS* 1.133:461); and Joan Goodnick Westenholz, *Legends of the Kings of Akkade: The Texts*, MC 7 (Winona Lake, IN: Eisenbrauns, 1997), 36–49.

53 Amélie Kuhrt, "Making History: Sargon of Agade and Cyrus the Great of Persia," in *A Persian Perspective: Essays in Memory of Heleen Sancisi-Weerdenburg*, ed. Wouter F. M. Henkelman and Amélie Kuhrt, AH 13 (Leiden: Nederlands Instituut voor het Nabije Oosten, 2003): 347–361 (350).

54 Kuhrt, "Making History," 347–361 (351–352).

55 Kuhrt, "Making History," 347–361 (350).

56 On the versions about Cyrus's birth legend offered by the Classical Greek sources, see Lindsay Allen, *The Persian Empire: A History* (London: British Museum, 2005), 24–25, and Pierre Briant, *From Cyrus to Alexander: A History of the Persian Empire* (Winona Lake, IN: Eisenbrauns, 2002), 14–16.

who had been raised by other, lowlier parents than his biological ones. However, whereas Sargon of Akkad seemed to have been bound for kingship due to the fact that Ishtar loved him, the future kingship of Cyrus was his destiny and as such possible to foresee by the Magians. The Magians interpreted the dreams of the boy's grandfather Astyages, the king of the Medes. According to their interpretation of one of these dreams, the offspring of Astyages's daughter Mandane (Cyrus) should be king in Astyages's place. As a result of this dream interpretation Astyages ordered his trusted guard Harpagos to bring the newborn child home with him and slay it. However, at home Harpagos was unable to fulfil the old king's wish. Instead, he found a herdsman called Mitradates and his wife Kyno. Harpagos ordered Mitradates to take Mandane's child and place it in the most desolate part of the mountains so that it should die as quickly as possible. However, in the meantime Mitradates's wife had a stillbirth. The couple decided to let the stillborn child change place with Mandane's child. Mitradates and Kyno thus exposed their own, dead child in the mountains and raised the newborn Cyrus as if he were their own.

A variant of the legendary Mesopotamian tale about the birth of a king is also offered by the historian Aelian (late second century CE). According to his *On the Nature of Animals* 12.21, it was the Babylonian king Se/Euecheros who dreamt about his daughter's son taking away his kingdom.[57] Also in this version the child was born in secrecy. The guards, being afraid of the old king, threw it from the citadel. However, before smashing into the ground the child was rescued by an eagle and brought to a garden. The gardener loved the child and brought it up. Later, the child, which was called Gilgamos (= Gilgamesh), became king of the Babylonians. Moreover, in a brief remark at the end of this story Aelian adds, "Indeed, I hear that Achaemenes, the Persian, from whom the Persian nobility is descended, was nursed by an eagle." Consequently, Aelian connects the legend about the king as an exposed child not only to Gilgamesh, the alleged king of the Babylonians, but even to Achaemenes, the eponym of the Achaemenid dynasty that was founded by King Darius I (ca. 522–482 BCE). As Kuhrt remarks, as Achaemenes does not figure before Darius I became king, "it is conceivable that the legend began to circulate after his accession, strengthening his claim to royalty."[58]

---

57 For an English translation, see Kuhrt, *The Persian Empire*, 176–177 (no. 5.18).
58 Kuhrt, *The Persian Empire*, 177 note 7.

5.4.2 Sacral Kingship and the Official Royal Achaemenid Ideology

Whether the Achaemenid kings themselves (the first of whom was Darius I, 522–482 BCE) also explained their claim to the throne by using a variant of the Mesopotamian legend about the birth and exposure of the king is indeed thinkable but—alas—not verifiable. None of the royal Achaemenid inscriptions seem to refer to such a legend. However, even though we cannot know whether Darius I ever claimed that he had been an exposed child who—like Aelian's claim about Achaemenes—had been nursed by an eagle or the like, we know for sure that the Achaemenids indeed had myths legitimating their royalty. The Achaemenid concept of sacral kingship and the official royal myths are formulated in the monumental, royal Achaemenid inscriptions that reflect the official Achaemenid ideology.

One important Achaemenid propaganda text is the Bisitun inscription of Darius I (= DB).[59] Formally, in DB Darius speaks in the first person. Exactly what happened in connection with the death of King Cambyses II and Darius I's subsequent accession to the throne in 522 BCE has troubled historians.[60] What is certain is that Darius I was not a descendant of Cambyses II. However, the (obscure) legitimacy of his claim to the throne is clearly the main subject matter that Darius I addressed in the inscription.

The Bisitun inscription and the many other monumental royal inscriptions Darius I made are characterised by several significant novelties. First, by tracing his ancestry back to a certain Achaemenes, Darius I introduced the term *Achaemenid* as the designation of the subsequent kings in his line (hence it is called *the Achaemenid dynasty*, DB §§1–2). Secondly, Darius I was the first Persian ruler to use Old Persian (Aryan) as (one of) the language(s) in royal inscriptions. Thus he set a pattern for subsequent Achaemenid monumental inscriptions. Thirdly, in the royal Achaemenid inscriptions from the time of Darius I and onwards, it was the god Ahuramazda who was the principal (mostly the only mentioned) god of the Achaemenids. Fourthly, DB offers the earliest (or at least earliest preserved) reference to a *Persian* king (neither Cyrus nor Cambyses called themselves kings of Persia): "I (am) Darius, the great king, king of kings, king in Persia, king of the countries, the son of Hystaspes, the grandson of Arsames, an Achaemenid" (DB §1).[61] Fifthly, at the conclusion of DB (and only in the Old Per-

59 The presentation and discussion of DB is based upon Granerød, "'By the Favour of Ahuramazda'," 455–480 (456–463).

60 See, e.g., Briant, *From Cyrus to Alexander*, 111.

61 Quoted from Schmitt, *The Bisitun Inscriptions of Darius the Great: Old Persian Text*, I The Old Persian inscriptions: Texts I, 49.

sian text[62]) Darius made a propaganda statement revealing some aspects of his policy. The inscription was to be translated into other languages and distributed throughout the world:

> Proclaims Darius, the king: By the favour of Ahuramazda this (is) the form of writing, which I have made, besides, in Aryan. Both on clay tablets and on parchment it has been placed. Besides, I also made the signature; besides, I made the lineage. And it was written down and was read aloud before me. Afterwards I have sent this form of writing everywhere into the countries. The people strove (to use it). (DB §70)[63]

Darius I's claim that the inscription was distributed throughout the entire empire clearly shows that the purpose of the inscription was to promulgate his own dynasty. The inscription was a propaganda inscription intended for dissemination throughout the empire. That this was not merely an empty boast has been archaeologically verified. In addition to the Aramaic version (DB Aram, which presumably was drawn up at the time of Darius II, approximately a century later) fragments of a Babylonian version (= DB Bab) from Babylon is known.[64] Although DB Bab is highly fragmentary it is nevertheless possible to say that the stela on which is was inscribed also included a relief of Darius. In addition, characteristic of DB Bab is that both the inscription itself and the accompanying relief were adapted to local, Babylonian circumstances. Particularly noteworthy is the fact that DB Bab replaced the Persian god Ahuramazda with the Babylonian god Bel-Marduk.

In the original Bisitun inscription in Media, text and relief were closely connected to each other. Its purpose was obviously to be a piece of royal propaganda aimed at the promulgation of Darius as a legitimate king. I have subsumed Darius's rhetoric of self-justification under three headings: legitimacy *de iure* (genealogy), legitimacy *de facto* (power) and legitimacy *de gratia* (providence).

---

62 Elizabeth N. von Voigtlander, *The Bisitun Inscription of Darius the Great: Babylonian Version*, vol. II: The Babylonian Versions of the Achaemenian Inscriptions: Texts I, CII (London: Lund Humphries, 1978), 62.

63 Quoted from Schmitt, *The Bisitun Inscriptions of Darius the Great: Old Persian Text*, I The Old Persian inscriptions: Texts I, 73 – 74 (slightly modified).

64 Ursula Seidl, "Ein Monument Darius' I. aus Babylon," *ZA* 89 (1999): 101 – 114; Ursula Seidl, "Eine Triumphstele Darius' I. aus Babylon," in *Babylon: Focus mesopotamischer Geschichte, Wiege früher Gelehrsamkeit, Mythos in der Moderne: 2. Internationales Colloquium der Deutschen Orient-Gesellschaft, 24.–26. März 1998 in Berlin*, ed. Johannes Renger (Saarbrücken: In Kommission bei SDV, Saarbrücker Druckerei und Verlag, 1999): 297 – 306, and Voigtlander, *The Bisitun Inscription of Darius the Great: Babylonian Version*, II The Babylonian Versions of the Achaemenian Inscriptions: Texts I, 63 – 66.

De iure: Darius opened the inscription by offering his genealogy. However, historians have questioned his family tree. According to Pierre Briant, his autobiography is "highly suspicious."[65] Neither the preceding king Cambyses II nor the intermediate ruler Bardiya left any male offspring.[66] The circumstances around the death of both of them are unclear since the Classical Greek sources and the cuneiform sources give different information. Nevertheless, it seems clear that Darius grasped power in the vacuum that emerged after Cambyses and Bardiya, regardless of his own role in the making of this vacuum. Now as the dynastic chain had been broken, Darius had to establish a link between himself and previous rulers. According to Amélie Kuhrt, Darius had to forge a link between himself and Cyrus II.[67] The link to this famous Persian king was *Čišpiš* (Old Persian)/*Ši-iš-pi-iš* (Babylonian)/*zi-iš-pi-iš* (Elamite)/*Teispes* (Greek), mentioned in DB §2. This person also appears as one of the ancestors of Cyrus II in the *Cyrus Cylinder* (lines 20–21).

Darius's stress on genealogy is comprehensible if one considers the fact that his kingship represented a break in the previous royal succession. Cyrus I was followed by his son Cambyses I, who was followed by his son Cyrus II (who defeated Babylon), who was followed by his son Cambyses II. The events that succeeded this have troubled and continue to trouble historians. Classical sources, above all Herodotus, also give accounts of these events, some of which resemble details in DB, whereas they differ in other respects. According to DB §30, Cambyses was guilty of fratricide by killing Bardiya, who was "of the same mother and the same father as Cambyses." This was kept secret and afterwards Cambyses went on a mission to Egypt. When he was in Egypt, there was a rebellion in Persia, Media and other countries. Afterwards, according to DB §11, Gaumata the magus falsely claimed to be Bardiya, saying, "I am Bardiya the son of Cyrus, the brother of Cambyses." On the background of this unlawful usurper (in Darius's view), Darius appeared as a contrast, a legitimate ruler coming from a royal family (DB §§3–4), claiming that the kingdom had been taken away from his family and that he had re-established it and strove "until I had put (our) royal house in its proper place, just as (it was) previously" (DB §14). Darius gives many chronological details in connection with Bardiya's usurpation. In the context of this, historians find it striking that Darius only mentions the death of Cambyses in passing (DB §11).

---

65 Briant, *From Cyrus to Alexander*, 100. A concise outline of the problem is offered in Brosius, *The Persian Empire*, 31.

66 As for Cambyses, see Herodotus, *Hist.* 3.61–66.

67 Kuhrt, *The Persian Empire*, 137.

The royal titles claimed by Darius in DB represented an innovation. In §1 he presents himself as "the great king, king of kings, king of Persia, king of peoples / countries." In contrast, his famous predecessor Cyrus II did not use the title "king of Persia." Rather, as seen in the *Cyrus Cylinder*, Cyrus presented himself as an Elamite king ("king of Anshan": Anshan and Susa were traditional principal Elamite cities) to whom the kingships of Babylon, Sumer and Akkad were also entrusted by Marduk (*Cyrus Cylinder*, lines 12 and 20 – 21).

De facto: Darius's claim to the throne was not legitimated by genealogy alone. The relief and the lengthy outline of his many victories over rebels at the beginning of his period as king must obviously have communicated a message to subject kings and commoners alike. Some of the rebellions and uprisings even took place in central provinces such as Elam, Media and Persia (cf. DB §21). To potential usurpers and rebels (that is, as seen from Darius's perspective), his rapid response and punishment of the nine named rebels served as an impressive—and deterring—demonstration of power. Darius ends the summary of his first regnal year thus: "These (are) the countries which became rebellious ... Afterwards Ahuramazda put them into my hand. As (was) my desire, so I treated them, as my desire, so I did unto them" (DB §54).[68] The message to potential rebels was clear: You would rather not come into the hands of the Great King.

De gratia: In DB, the phrase "by the favour of Ahuramazda" occurs more than twenty times, such as in §5 "By the favour of Ahuramazda I am king; upon me Ahuramazda bestowed the kingship." Ahuramazda is the only named god in both this inscription as well as in the remaining inscriptions by Darius I.[69] An Old Persian inscription from Susa (DSk), written by Darius I on a baked mud-brick, sheds light on this intimate relationship: "I (am) Darius, the great king, king of kings, king of countries, son of Hystapes, the Achaemenid. King Darius proclaims: Ahuramazda is mine; I am Ahuramazda's; I worshipped Ahuramazda; may Ahuramazda bear me aid" (DSk §§1 – 2).[70]

Ahuramazda never speaks in the first person in the Achaemenid inscriptions. The Great King's will was Ahuramazda's will and vice versa. Yet, the Achaemenid kings did not deify themselves but remained humans, although

68 Quoted after Schmitt, *The Bisitun Inscriptions of Darius the Great: Old Persian Text*, I The Old Persian inscriptions: Texts I, 69 (slightly modified).

69 The *Cyrus Cylinder* is a striking contrast. There, the god Marduk is referred to as "king of the gods" (line 7) and "my [Cyrus's] lord" (line 35). Cyrus boasts about his restoration of the cult of Marduk, which Nabonidus had desecrated (lines 5 – 10). On the background of Nabonidus's abominations, Cyrus claims to have been chosen by Marduk as a just ruler (lines 11 – 12). However, in DB the only named god is Ahuramazda.

70 Quoted from Kuhrt, *The Persian Empire*, 555 (no. 11.38).

kings by the favour of Ahuramazda.[71] The affinity of the Achaemenids with Ahuramazda is further attested iconographically. The winged disc hoovering above the representation of Darius I in the relief of the Bisitun inscription is present in virtually every official iconographic presentation of an Achaemenid king.[72] The winged disc may have represented Ahuramazda. Nevertheless, it must be stressed that none of the Achaemenid kings were monotheists or even monolatrists. The various sources of the Achaemenid kings supplement each other in regard to this question. In the Achaemenid royal inscriptions, Ahuramazda was definitely "the greatest of the gods."[73] However, the Achaemenid administrative texts from Persepolis give terse snippets of the royal administration's practical policy towards cults and religious ceremonies. These glimpses into the Persepolis bureaucracy suggest that the Achaemenid rulers' affinity with Ahuramazda was not seen as a pattern for everyone. An example is Persepolis fortification tablet no. 339 (PF 339), in which the delivery of commodities is registered: "5 *marriš* 7 QA wine, supplied by Ushaya, Turkama the "priest" received: 7 QA for the god Ahuramazda, 2 *marriš* for the god Humban, 1 *marriš* for/at the river Huputish, 1 *marriš* for/at the river Rannakarra, 1 *marriš* for/at the river Shaushanush. He used it for the gods."[74] In the Persepolis fortification tablets that were published by Richard T. Hallock, the god Humban is more frequently mentioned than any other named god, including Ahuramazda.[75] Therefore, there is a discrepancy between the administrative texts and the royal Achaemenid inscriptions. Nevertheless, we can assume that royal inscriptions reflect the (official) ideology of the Achaemenid rulers—an ideology that might not have been identical with the actual administrative practice (cf. the Persepolis tablets). The royal Achaemenid inscriptions suggest that Ahuramazda was the dynastic god of the Achaemenid family. According to Darius himself, he was made king by Ahura-

---

71 Erica Ehrenberg, "*Dieu et Mon Droit:* Kingship in Late Babylonian and Early Persian Times," in *Religion and Power: Divine Kingship in the Ancient World and Beyond*, ed. Nicole Brisch, OIS 4 (Chicago: Oriental Institute of the University of Chicago, 2008): 103–131 (103). An exception is when the Persian king executed the office as a traditional pharaoh, cf., e.g., the inscription on the base of the statue of Darius, written in Egyptian hieroglyphs and in the capacity as Pharaoh, King of Upper and Lower Egypt, in Brosius, *The Persian Empire*, 45 (no. 50).

72 See illustrations in Rüdiger Schmitt, "Bisotun iii. Darius's Inscriptions," *EIr* (2013): online edition, available at http://www.iranicaonline.org/articles/bisotun-iii.

73 Thus DPh §2, quoted from Kuhrt, *The Persian Empire*, 476 (no. 11.1).

74 Quoted from Kuhrt, *The Persian Empire*, 557 (no. 11.41), cf. Richard Treadwell Hallock, *Persepolis Fortification Tablets*, OIP 92 (Chicago: University of Chicago Press, 1969), 151.

75 Hallock, *Persepolis Fortification Tablets*, 18–19.

mazda: "Proclaims Darius, the king: By the favour of Ahuramazda I am king; upon me Ahuramazda bestowed the kingship" (DB §5).[76]

Likewise, in one of Darius's building inscriptions from Susa he states that Ahuramazda "chose me as (his) man in all the earth; he made me king in all the earth."[77] In column 5 of DB,[78] Darius recounts events that took place in the second and third year after he became king: the rebellion in Elam under the leadership of Athamaita, and the subjugation of the Scythians led by Skunkha (§§71–76). In both cases, Darius closely connects rebellion to the absence of worship of Ahuramazda: "Proclaims Darius, the king: Those Elamites were disloyal, and by them Ahuramazda was not worshipped. I (, however,) worshipped Ahuramazda. By the favour of Ahuramazda, as (was) my desire, so I treated them" (DB §72; cf. §75).[79]

This statement (repeated nearly verbatim in §75 with reference to the Scythians) should not be exaggerated, so as to say that it implicates that Darius's objective was to enforce the worship of Ahuramazda throughout the entire empire at the cost of the worship of other gods. Nevertheless, rebellion against the Great King was not in accordance with worship of Ahuramazda. In not so many words, a rebellion against the Great King equalled rebellion against Ahuramazda himself.

For the Achaemenids, Ahuramazda was the source of order and truth among men and people in society, and the entire cosmos. This is partly evident in DB §§71–76 (discussed above) and in the sections in columns 1–4 that deal with Darius's response to the rebellious kings. The belief that Ahuramazda is the source and upholder of order is clearly expressed in one of the inscriptions on Darius I's tomb at Naqsh-e Rustam (DNa): "A great god (is) Ahuramazda, who created this earth, who created yonder heaven, who created man, who created blissful happiness for man, who made Darius king, one king of many, one master of many" (DNa §1).[80]

---

76 Quoted from Schmitt, *The Bisitun Inscriptions of Darius the Great: Old Persian Text*, I The Old Persian inscriptions: Texts I, 49.

77 DSf, 15–18, quoted from Roland G. Kent, *Old Persian: Grammar, Texts, Lexicon* (New Haven: American Oriental Society, 1953), 144.

78 It was added late in the history of the monument's creation and does not have any Elamite or Babylonian parallel. See Schmitt, *The Bisitun Inscriptions of Darius the Great: Old Persian Text*, I The Old Persian inscriptions: Texts I, 21.

79 Quoted from Schmitt, *The Bisitun Inscriptions of Darius the Great: Old Persian Text*, I The Old Persian inscriptions: Texts I, 75.

80 Quoted from Schmitt, *The Old Persian Inscriptions of Naqsh-i Rustam and Persepolis*, I The Old Persian Inscriptions: Texts II, 32, cf. Kuhrt, *The Persian Empire*, 502–503 (no. 11.16).

In DNa §§2–3 Darius continues accounting for his genealogy by numbering all the countries he, by the favour of Ahuramazda, has seized outside Persia. In §4 in particular, the Great King appears as Ahuramazda's ally and deputy in the latter's fight against chaos: "Ahuramazda, when he saw this earth *in turmoil*, after that he bestowed it upon me; me he made king; I am king. *By the favour of Ahuramazda I put it in its proper place.* What I have said to them, that they did, as was my desire" (DNa §4).[81]

Being the creator of the entire cosmos, Ahuramazda was ultimately responsible for political order and stability. His instrument was Darius. Therefore, to rebel against Ahuramazda's chosen one was no less than to rebel against the creator himself. Political disloyalty equalled chaos, which in turn threatened the cosmos. Ahuramazda's well-ordered cosmos also had political and demographic consequences (cf. DB §14).

Like DB, the text and relief illustration on the facade of Darius's tomb inscription at Naqsh-e Rustam correspond. In DNa §4, Darius asks the (future) reader:

> But if you shall think: "How many (are) those countries which Darius the king held?" *look at the sculptured figures which bear the throne platform.* Then you shall perceive, then it shall become known to you: "The spear of the Persian man has gone forth far away," then it shall become known to you: "The Persian man has repulsed the enemy far away from Persia." (DNa §4)[82]

The "sculptured reliefs," that is, the relief that Darius referred to, portray the Great King on a throne that is held up by twenty-eight men, a motif also used on the tomb facades of subsequent Achaemenid kings.[83] Each one of the men who held up the throne was wearing different clothes, indicating that they represent "all races" (cf. DNa §2) that Darius rules over. The well-ordered earth that Ahuramazda had bestowed upon Darius is multicultural and multiethnic, yet with the Persians at the head.

Darius's founding charter from Susa (DSe) expresses the idea that Ahuramazda's ordering of the earth also had bearing on geography. The reason why people lived where they lived was ultimately due to Ahuramazda's decision:

---

81 Quoted from Schmitt, *The Old Persian Inscriptions of Naqsh-i Rustam and Persepolis*, I The Old Persian Inscriptions: Texts II, 32 (my emphasis, slightly modified).
82 Quoted from Schmitt, *The Old Persian Inscriptions of Naqsh-i Rustam and Persepolis*, I The Old Persian Inscriptions: Texts II, 32 (my emphasis, slightly modified).
83 See illustrations in, e.g., Schmitt, "Bisotun iii. Darius's Inscriptions," online edition, available at http://www.iranicaonline.org/articles/bisotun-iii.

> Much which was ill-done, that I made good. Provinces were in commotion; one man was smiting the other. The following I brought about by the favour of Ahuramazda, that the one does not smite the other at all, *each one is in his place*. My law—of that they feel fear, so that the stronger does not smite nor destroy the weak. (DSe §4)[84]

Pax Persica implied that each people was in its place, a place allotted by Ahuramazda as part of his ordering of the cosmos and under the auspices of whom Darius, the Great King, operated. It is in light of this, then, that one should understand the exhortation with which Darius concluded one of his tomb inscriptions at Naqsh-e Rustam. In the Achaemenid inscriptions, there was no "separation of church and state." Political loyalty towards the Great King and religious obedience towards Ahuramazda were two sides of the same coin: "O man, the commandment of Ahuramazda—let not that seem evil to you! Do not leave the right path! Do not be disobedient!" (DNa §6).[85] According to the royal myths of the Achaemenid dynasty, the Achaemenid king was chosen by Ahuramazda. Because Ahuramazda was presented as the creator of heaven and earth and the upholder of political order, we can state that cosmogonic and cosmological ideas were also associated with the royal myths of Achaemenid ideology. As Ahuramazda's chosen one the Achaemenid king was the deity's ally and deputy on earth.

5.4.3 Achaemenid Propaganda and Judaean Myths about Sacral Kingship

As mentioned above, Darius I commanded that the Bisitun inscription should be translated into other languages and distributed throughout the empire (DB §70). That this actually happened is made clear by the fact that fragments of two local copies are known. One of them is the Babylonian version of the Bisitun inscription (DB Bab), which was carved on a stela that may have been placed along the Processional Way in Babylon.[86] Like the original in Bisitun, the Babylonian version contained a relief plus a text. However, the version found in Babylon was a local adaptation of the original. Where DB speaks of Ahuramazda as the Achae-

84 Quoted from Kent, *Old Persian: Grammar, Texts, Lexicon*, 142 (my emphasis).

85 Quoted from Schmitt, *The Old Persian Inscriptions of Naqsh-i Rustam and Persepolis*, I The Old Persian Inscriptions: Texts II, 33.

86 For a presentation and discussion of DB Bab, see Seidl, "Ein Monument Darius' I. aus Babylon," 101–114; Seidl, "Eine Triumphstele Darius' I. aus Babylon," 297–306; Voigtlander, *The Bisitun Inscription of Darius the Great: Babylonian Version*, II The Babylonian Versions of the Achaemenian Inscriptions: Texts I; and Granerød, "'By the Favour of Ahuramazda'," 455–480 (467–470).

menid dynasty god, DB Bab has Bel. Differences in the iconography between the original and the Babylonian version were also observable.

The other local copy of the Bisitun inscription of Darius I is the *Aramaic version of the Bisitun inscription* written on a papyrus scroll found in Elephantine in connection with an archaeological campaign in 1906–1908 (DB Aram = *TAD* C2.1). DB Aram was probably written at the time of Ochus, the great grandson of Darius I. Approximately a century after the reign of Darius I Ochus seized the kingship and took the throne name Darius II. Originally, DB Aram must have consisted of eleven columns. The last two were written on the verso of the papyrus scroll.[87] The Aramaic text of the Bisitun inscription is close to the Babylonian version of the original in Bisitun and is even closer to the fragmentary text of DB Bab. In addition, it contains an Aramaic translation of the last paragraph of the tomb inscription of Darius I.[88]

Important for the question of the provenance of the Aramaic version—and its relevance for the question of myths about sacral kingship in Elephantine—is the text that comes immediately after column 11. The blank space on the verso of the scroll has been used to write down a record of memoranda (C3.13). From a palaeographical point of view, the record of memoranda has been written by hand other than the one that wrote DB Aram. The earliest date in the record is restored to read "year [3+]3[+1] (=7)," i.e., year 417 BCE. (C3.13:34).[89] In C3.13:51 there is another date: "in Epiph, year 13[+?]," i.e., year 411[–?] BCE. Moreover, the fragmentary record found on the verso mentions several members of the Judaean community in Elephantine: Hanan son of Haggai and Jedaniah son of [PN] (C3.13:2), Menahem son of Azariah (C3.13:11), [Menahe]meth / [Meshulle]meth daughter of Zechariah (C3.13:37), Jehoishma son of Haggai (C3.13:40), Azariah the servitor of *śgḋ*ʾ (= the shrine?, C3.13:45, 48), Menahem son of Shallum (C3.13:46) and Je[da]niah son of Osea (C3.13:51). On the basis of the record of memoranda on the verso of the scroll, two conclusions can be drawn:

87 For the most part, the Aramaic translation follows the Babylonian text of DB. Thus, it is possible to reconstruct the many lacunas of the fragmented papyrus scroll. See Greenfield and Porten, *The Bisitun Inscription of Darius the Great: Aramaic Version*, V The Aramaic Versions of the Achaemenian Inscriptions, etc.; Texts I 16, and Tavernier, "An Achaemenid Royal Inscription," 161–176 (162 note 9).

88 Tavernier, "An Achaemenid Royal Inscription," 161–176 (162–163).

89 Greenfield and Porten, *The Bisitun Inscription of Darius the Great: Aramaic Version*, V The Aramaic Versions of the Achaemenian Inscriptions, etc.; Texts I 3, cf. Bezalel Porten and Ada Yardeni, *Textbook of Aramaic Documents from Ancient Egypt. Newly Copied, Edited and Translated into Hebrew and English*, vol. III: Literature, Accounts, Lists (Jerusalem: The Hebrew University of Jerusalem – Department of the History of the Jewish People, 1993), 216, 219.

- Given that DB Aram (C2.1) on the one hand, and the record of memoranda on its verso on the other hand (C3.13), actually stem from approximately the same period, the scroll in question has been copied at the time of King Darius II.
- The many Judaean names mentioned in the record of memoranda on the verso closely connect the scroll offering the text of DB Aram to the Judaean community in Elephantine.

Therefore, it can be stated that the Judaeans in Elephantine most likely were in possession of a propaganda text reflecting the royal myths of Achaemenid ideology.

The question of what purpose the making of an Aramaic copy of the Bisitun inscription fulfilled in the late fifth century BCE, a century after the original was made in Bisitun, is open to debate. One suggestion is that DB Aram was intended to commemorate the one-hundredth anniversary of the accession of Darius I to the throne.[90] This may very well have been the case. However, in my view such a commemoration cannot have been done out of pure historical interest. I have suggested that the intention of such a retrospect at the time of the reign of Darius II to the time of Darius I probably had a contemporary function.[91] DB Aram was intended to legitimate the kingship of Darius II and function as a demonstration, by way of a deterrent, of what kings with the name Darius had been—and still were—capable of. Moreover, Arshama, the satrap of Egypt in the last part of the fifth century BCE, may have been a political and military ally of Ochus when the latter brought an end to the short reign of his half-brother Sogdanios, seized the kingship and took the throne name Darius (II). The occurrences leading to the seizure of the kingship by Ochus/Darius II are told by Ctesias in his fragmentary *Persica*.[92] Ctesias's history involves a certain Arxanes. Arxanes was probably identical with Arshama with whom the Judaean garrison in Elephantine interacted. Therefore, it is a likely conjecture that Arshama (identified with Ctesias's Arxanes), the satrap of Egypt, played an important role in the promulgation of DB Aram in the Judaean garrison in Elephantine.

Consequently, it is likely that the Achaemenid officials in Egypt actively promoted the royal myths of the Achaemenid dynasty in Egypt in general, and in

90 Greenfield and Porten, *The Bisitun Inscription of Darius the Great: Aramaic Version*, V The Aramaic Versions of the Achaemenian Inscriptions, etc.; Texts I 3, and Tavernier, "An Achaemenid Royal Inscription," 161 – 176 (161 – 62).

91 For a discussion of the purpose of DB Aram, see Granerød, "'By the Favour of Ahuramazda'," 455 – 480 (471 – 474).

92 FGH 688 F15 (48 – 50), quoted from Kuhrt, *The Persian Empire*, 332 – 333 (no. 8.20).

Elephantine particularly (cf. DB Aram). We can take for granted that the Judaeans in Elephantine were aware of the theologically loaded claims that the Achaemenid kings made. For, in DB Aram the king repeatedly claims to be king "with the protection of Ahuramazda" (*bṭllh zy ʾhwrmzd*) and that "Ahuramazda helped me" (*ʾhwrmzd sʿdny*).

However, how did the Elephantine Judaeans receive the royal myths? To be sure, we do not have any text that offers the official response of the Elephantine Judaean community to the claims of the Achaemenid ideology and its royal myths. Consequently, we are left to make some qualified conjectures. First, the socio-political reality was that the community was a garrison that was under *Persian* command. What is more, this took place in a country that neither was their own nor the Persians'. In a way, because the community was part of the Achaemenid power structure in Egypt, one can say that the Judaean garrison (along with the other foreign garrisons) represented the tangible presence of the Persian Empire in Upper Egypt, at its southwestern border.[93] And it all took place in a potentially hostile environment. The environment was potentially hostile in two ways. First, Elephantine was a border town and it was indeed a realistic possibility that Nubia would take control. After all, that was the reality during the Twenty-Fifth Dynasty of Egypt (760 – 656 BCE), known as the Nubian Dynasty. Second, the environments were also potentially hostile for the Judaean garrison because the Persians were definitely regarded as foreign rulers by the local Egyptians.[94] It is a reasonable assumption that one of the objectives of military forces led by the Persians was to secure the inner stability in the satrapy of Egypt. This setting probably caused a self-reinforcing dynamic. From the perspective of the Judaeans it was most fitting to remain loyal towards the Persian king and his local representative, the satrap. In the last half of the fifth century BCE the Judaean garrison was part of a colonial administration, and for ancient Near Eastern kings it was "received wisdom" that the best way to control a foreign country was not to recruit local troops but to deploy foreign, non-native

93 See Gard Granerød, "Ahuramazdas lojale judeiske soldater: Om Elefantine-judeernes selvbilde," *TeoT* 3 (2014): 288 – 303 (289).

94 The inscriptions of Darius I show an ambivalence in the king's own understanding as the ruler of Egypt. One the one hand, an inscription of the base of the statue of Darius, written in Egyptian hieroglyphs, presents Darius I with traditional royal titles, cf. text in Brosius, *The Persian Empire*, 45 (no. 50). However, in the so-called Darius inscription from the Red Sea Canal (DZc) Darius, speaking in the first person, explains his kingship as Ahuramazda's gift. Moreover, it is in the capacity as Ahuramazda's chosen he also rules Egypt: "I am a Persian. From Persia I seized Egypt" cf. text in Brosius, *The Persian Empire*, 47 (no. 52).

troops. Foreign, non-native troops were much more likely to remain loyal than locally recruited ones.[95]

Moreover, we do have fragments of texts suggesting that the Judaean garrison actually fulfilled the Achaemenid desire for loyalty. In a fragmentary letter (A4.5) the Judaeans relate about an Egyptian uprising: "detachments of the Egyptians rebelled" (*dgln zy mṣryʾ mrdw*, A4.5:1–2), probably when the satrap Arshama was on an official journey to the court of the Great King (around 410 BCE, A4.5:2–3). However, "We [= the Judaeans] did not leave our posts" (*ʾnḥnh mnṭrtn lʾ šbqn*, A4.5:1). The letter also gives the impression that the Judaeans had confidence in the legal apparatus of the satrapy (A4.5:8–10).

All in all, the Judaean garrison not only knew the Achaemenid royal myths. It is also conceivable that they accepted them, be it of their own free will or be it out of necessity.

5.5 Traces of Judaean and Other Pantheons

The Judaeans knew and recognised not only YHW but also other deities. For instance, when a Judaean swore an oath by a god, then the oath in reality signalled a recognition of that god. This is the case with AnathYHW and perhaps the god Ḥerem (B7.3:3), with the (Egyptian) goddess Sati (B2.8:5) and with Ḥerembethel (B7.2:7).[96] That the word "recognise" is apt is also evident in the cases where deities were qualified as such by the Aramaic word *ʾlhh*, "goddess" (like in the case of Sati mentioned above) or *ʾlh*, "god." The latter applies to the mention of all of "the gods of Egypt" (*ʾlhy mṣryn*, A4.7:14)/"the gods of the Egyptians" (*ʾlhy mṣryʾ*, A4.8:13), "Khnum the god" (*ḥnwb ʾlhʾ*, A4.7:5) and "YHW the god" (*yhw ʾlhʾ*, C3.15:1). The designation shows that these deities were determined as belonging to the class of gods.

---

95 See, e.g., Jacob L. Wright, "Surviving in an Imperial Context: Foreign Military Service and Judean Identity," in *Judah and the Judeans in the Achaemenid Period: Negotiating Identity in an International Context*, ed. Oded Lipschits et al. (Winona Lake, IN: Eisenbrauns, 2011): 505–528 (514).

96 See 2.4.1 above, Oath Procedures, Courts, and Judges. Moreover, see also D7.21:3 where the servant Giddel blesses his lord Micaiah "by YHH and Khnum."

5.5.1 The Egyptian Pantheon

The Judaeans recognised the Egyptian pantheon. In the petition to Bagavahya they referred to it as "the gods of Egypt." To what extent they also were familiar with, recognised and adopted Egyptian religious myths is a question that has to remain unanswered in the light of the absence of evidence in the sources.[97] Perhaps they were most familiar with the Egyptian gods that were worshipped in Elephantine, the "triad of Elephantine," Khnum and the two goddesses Anuket and Sati. In the Persian period, the temple of Sati was located just a stone's throw away from the temple of Khnum, and both had been laying there for centuries. Three kilometres further south there was a temple of Anuket at the Sehel island. The goddess Sati was considered to be Khnum's consort and Anuket their daughter. For the Egyptians Sati was the deification of the floods of the Nile, the "dispenser of cool water coming from Elephantine." Sati and Anuket were the "mistresses of Elephantine."[98] Sati's consort Khnum was the donor of the Nile waters.[99] Both the Egyptians and the Persian officials referred to him as "the lord of Elephantine."[100] In light of the fact that the Judaean garrison was part of the colonial administration,[101] its members must no doubt have been well aware of the local Egyptian myths of Elephantine. Moreover, they must no doubt also have known other Egyptian gods such as Ptah, by whom Aramaeans blessed their family members in the Hermopolis papyri (see, e.g., A4.1:2) and to whom a weight standard connected (cf. B4.2:2), and Horus, the royal god who according to Egyptian royal mythology was incarnated in the king (cf., e.g., the personal name Ḥor in A4.3).[102]

5.5.2 The Pantheons of the Garrisons in Syene and Elephantine

Did the Judaeans also recognise pantheons other than the Egyptian one? The (non-Judaean) Hermopolis papyri show that deities Bethel, the Queen of Heaven, Banit and Nabu had their temples in the neighbouring Syene (cf. A2.1–4), like

97 Though, see 4.6.5.4 above, D18.18 (Elephantine Museum 2605): A Sarcophagus from Aswan with Aramaic Inscription.

98 Siegfried Morenz, *Egyptian Religion* (Ithaca: Cornell University Press, 1973), 53, 268.

99 Morenz, *Egyptian Religion*, 264.

100 See, e.g., the letter from the satrap Pherendates to the *wab*-priests of Khnum (P. Berlin 13540, from 492 BCE) in Porten et al., *The Elephantine Papyri in English*, 292.

101 See Granerød, "Ahuramazdas lojale judeiske soldater," 288–303 (292).

102 Morenz, *Egyptian Religion*, 34.

YHW had his temple in the neighbouring Elephantine. The garrison stationed in Syene—"the Syenian garrison" (*ḥyl' swnkny'*, C3.14:32)—was dominated by Aramaeans, and the above-mentioned gods worshipped in Syene were part of what we perhaps may term an Aramaean pantheon. However, it should be noted that the sources never mention "the gods of the Aramaeans," comparable to how the Egyptian pantheon is referred to as "the gods of Egypt."

In light of the geographical proximity as well as the general interaction between the foreign garrison communities there is no reason to doubt that the Elephantine Judaeans were aware of the temples of the Syenian-Aramaean gods and the religious myths associated with them. However, unfortunately the sources have not left any traces of any such myth. We may take for granted that the Aramaeans (and their Judaean brothers in arms) told stories in which these gods were the protagonists. However, unfortunately we do not know these religious narratives. The same goes with AnathYHW, Ḥerem, Ḥerembethel, Eshembethel and Anathbethel, all potential gods who are only briefly mentioned in the native Elephantine Judaean sources.[103]

A trajectory that potentially may indirectly help us to get closer to the myths involving these gods is to take into account the sapiential work *The Words of Aḥiqar*, of which a fifth century BCE copy has been found in Elephantine.[104] The work has a narrative and a proverbial part. The proverbial part of *Aḥiqar* attests to a pantheon that scholars believe has affinities to the Syro-Canaanite cultural area. The pantheon in *Aḥiqar* consists of an undefined group of "gods" (*'lhn*), El (*'l*), Shamash (*šmš*), "Lord of the Holy Ones" (*bʿl qdšn*) and perhaps Shamayn (*šmyn*). However, as James M. Lindenberger notes there is a discrepancy between the gods listed in *Aḥiqar* on the one hand and the other Aramaic documents from Upper Egypt (i.e., the Hermopolis letters and the [Judaean] documents from Elephantine) on the other.[105] Therefore, the potential usefulness of *Aḥiqar* in the context of a discussion of the pantheons and myths of the garrisons in Syene and Elephantine is limited. Above all, the pantheon of *Aḥiqar* attests to the broad intellectual world of which the Syene-Aramaean pantheon was a part, and moreover, perhaps even the whereabouts of the origin of these gods: the Syro-Canaanite region.

---

103 For a list of the divine names found in the corpus of Aramaic documents from Egypt, see Bezalel Porten and Jerome A. Lund, *Aramaic Documents from Egypt: A Key-Word-in-Context Concordance* (Winona Lake, IN: Eisenbrauns, 2002), 425–427.

104 *Aḥiqar* is also discussed in Chapter 6.

105 James M. Lindenberger, "The Gods of Ahiqar," *UF* 14 (1982): 105–117 (116).

Another trajectory that potentially may help us to approach the myths of the garrison in Syene and Elephantine is to take into account epigraphic sources other than the Aramaic documents from Achaemenid-period Egypt and compare them to the sparse data from the Aramaic documents from Egypt. Focussing on *Aḥiqar*, Herbert Niehr argues that a survey of the references to the gods mentioned in this particular work shows they are comparable to the pantheons one can reconstruct on the basis of Aramaean inscriptions from Syria and Upper Mesopotamia dating to the ninth and eighth centuries BCE.[106] Consequently, Niehr identifies the god "Lord of the Holy Ones" with Hadad, the head of the latter pantheons. In inscriptions from Syria, "The Holy Ones" represented the court of divine beings assembled around Hadad. Moreover, in Syrian inscriptions *ʾl* is a proper name, the deity El. According to a proverbial saying in *Aḥiqar*, the god El is with any individual standing in front of the king (C1.1:91). In another saying a supplicant begs El to raise him up as a righteous one together with him, namely El (C1.1:109). In yet another saying El will "twist the mouth of a twister" (C1.1:156), that is, he will pay a treacherous one back in his own coin. Nevertheless, according to Niehr the role of El in Syrian inscriptions is far from clear and he does not head the pantheon. Also in *Aḥiqar* one finds the god Shamash, a god of justice. Among other things he provides justice for the innocent (C1.1:107–108; cf. C1.1:92, 138, 187–188, 197). In the epigraphic material Shamash has a similar role. Consequently, Niehr reconstructs the structure of the pantheon of the proverbial part of *Aḥiqar* as follows:

Hadad (= "Lord of the Holy Ones)
The Heavenly Court Assembly
("The Holy Ones")

El
Shamash

"The Gods"

It is of course highly relevant that the sayings in *Aḥiqar* about these gods correspond with the data emerging from the Syrian and Upper Mesopotamian sources. However, in my view, it is even more relevant in the context of the present

106 See Herbert Niehr, *Aramäischer Aḥiqar*, JSHRZ Neue Folge 2 (Gütersloh: Gütersloher Verlagshaus, 2007), 18–20; cf. Reinhard Gregor Kratz, "Aḥiqar and Bisitun: Literature of the Judaeans at Elephantine?" (forthcoming).

discussion that *Aḥiqar*, which after all can be connected to the garrisons of Syene and Elephantine, itself offers fragments of the myths that appear to have been associated with the gods in question. Having said that, it is still not possible to tell for sure to what extent the religious practice of the Judaeans actually incorporated the pantheon of *Aḥiqar* and the myths associated with its gods.

What about the other gods mentioned in the sources except for *Aḥiqar?* In a recent monograph Angela Rohrmoser discusses the gods not mentioned in *Aḥiqar* but in the "native" Judaean sources from Elephantine, namely, AnathYHW, Ḥerem, Ḥerembethel, Eshembethel and Anathbethel.[107] Her discussion includes both biblical and epigraphic material from Syria as well as etymological considerations. One premise of Rohrmoser's discussion is that a god called Bethel was worshipped in the milieu of the Judaean community. The main argument is that the word is part of theophoric names such as Bethelnad (A3.2:7), Bethelnur (C3.15:6) and Bethelnathan son of Jehonathan (B6.4:10). According to Rohrmoser, the latter name constellation (Bethelnathan son of Jehonathan) shows that the two gods Bethel and YHW belonged to the same cultic environment.

However, according to Rohrmoser, the word *bt'l/byt'l* probably also had a second, additional meaning in Elephantine when it occurred in name combinations such as Ḥerembethel, Eshembethel and Anathbethel. In these cases, the word may have referred to a *betyl* (Greek: βαίτυλος). A betyl is the kind of holy stone that is attested, for example, in the story about Jacob's ladder (Gen 28, which also offers a popular etymology for the place name Bethel) and by Philo of Byblos. The latter claimed that βαιτύλια were created by Uranus when he created λίθοι ἔμψυοι ("animated stones") that fell down from the heaven, featuring magical power. Consequently, in this sense, the name element "Bethel" may have corresponded to what the Bible refers to as a *maṣṣēbâ*.

As far as the two names Eshembethel and Anathbethel are concerned, Rohrmoser argues that the names in fact meant "the betyl of (the god/goddess) Eshem" and "the betyl of (the goddess) Anat," respectively. A deity (god or goddess) *'ăšîmā'* (NRSV: "Ashima") is reflected in 2Kgs 17:30 and Amos 8:14. Moreover, a Northwest-Semitic goddess Anat is attested in a huge number of inscriptions, such as the eighteenth-century Mari archives, the thirteenth-century BCE texts from Ugarit, Egyptian inscriptions from the Ramesside period and down

---

107 Angela Rohrmoser, *Götter, Tempel und Kult der Judäo-Aramäer von Elephantine: Archäologische und schriftliche Zeugnisse aus dem perserzeitlichen Ägypten*, AOAT 396 (Münster: Ugarit-Verlag, 2014), 126–149.

to Phoenician inscriptions from the fourth century BCE. Anat is for the most part a war goddess.[108]

However, in contrast to the case of Eshem/Ashima/Eshembethel and Anat/Anathbethel, Rohrmoser does not think that there was a god Ḥerem. Consequently, in her view the name Ḥerembethel did not mean "the betyl of (the deity) Ḥerem." This is despite the fact that the element Ḥerem occurs in theophoric names such as Ḥeremnathan (B6.4:9) and Ḥarman (C4.4:2; C3.15:4). In the research, two oath texts have traditionally been understood as referring to a god Ḥerem (B7.2:7–8 and B7.3:1–3). As far as B7.3 is concerned, the word Ḥerem is perhaps attested, occurring together with the word *msgdʾ* and (the deity) AnathYWH:

mwm[ʾh z]y mnḥm br šlwm br
hw[...] ymʾ lmšlm br ntn
bḥ[...]ʾ bmsgdʾ wbʿntyhw

Oa[th whi]ch Menahem son of Shallum son of Ho[...] swears to Meshullam son of Nathan by Ḥ[...] the [...] by *msgd* and by AnathYHW. (B7.3:1–3, my translation)

Bezalel Porten has reconstructed the lacuna in line 3 to read *bḥ[rm ʾlh]ʾ* and translates "by Ḥ[*erem*] *the* [*god*]," thus interpreting the reconstructed word *ʾlhʾ* as a divine determination word.[109] In contrast, Rohrmoser argues that if the reconstruction should prove to be correct, then one should rather render the phrase "by the *ḥerem* of the god," understanding the reconstructed element *ḥrm* as part of a construct chain. Moreover, she identifies the unnamed god in question with YHW. As a consequence, in Rohrmoser's opinion the word *ḥerem* refers to a sort of offering to the god (i. e., YHW). The offering was *consecrated* to the god (YHW), which in turn implies that the word element in question is a derivation of the common verb *ḥrm*, with the meaning "to devote, consecrate."

Rohrmoser's argumentation also builds on the assumption that the word *msgdʾ* referred to a divinised altar in a way comparable to the use of the word in other Semitic inscriptions from the last half of the first millennium BCE and even in pre-Islamic Arabic religion.[110] Consequently, she suggests the translation "bei den Weihgaben des Gottes (Jahu) bei dem geweihten Altar und bei Anat-

108 A fourth century BCE bilingual inscription from Cyprus (*KAI* 42) identifies her with Athene, the Greek war goddess, cf. Rohrmoser, *Götter, Tempel und Kult*, 137.
109 Bezalel Porten, *Archives from Elephantine: The Life of an Ancient Jewish Military Colony* (Berkeley: University of California Press, 1968), 317.
110 Rohrmoser, *Götter, Tempel und Kult*, 147.

Jahu," that is, "by the offerings of the god [YHW] at the consecrated altar and by AnathYHW."[111]

Furthermore, as far as B7.2:7–8 is concerned (the other oath text often understood as referring to a god Ḥerem), Rohrmoser argues that it in fact attests to a betyl. She hypothesises that the betyl stood in the temple of YHW and was the form in which YHW was worshipped. Consequently, she translates the clause *'nh mlkyh 'qr' lk ʿl ḥrmbyt'l 'lh'* as follows: "Ich, Malkijah erkläre vor dir auf den geweihten Betyl des Gottes (Jahu) ..."[112] Thus, as far as both oath texts (B7.2 and B7.3) are concerned, Rohrmoser hypothesises that the generic word "the god" (*'lh'*) was "das gebräuchlichste Titel für Jahu in Elephantine," that is, "the most common title for YHW in Elephantine."[113]

In my opinion, the fact that no god called Ḥerem is known in other relevant sources such as the Bible and epigraphs does not exclude the possibility that a god with this name was known in Elephantine. In my view, Rohrmoser's argumentation in this particular case is not convincing. First, the very name Ḥeremnathan (B6.4:9) speaks against it. It is modelled as a theophorous name in the same manner as, for example, Bethelnathan (a name occurring as a patronymic also in B6.4:9) and Jehonathan (B6.4:10). Moreover, this is an argument Rohrmoser herself uses in support of the assumption that a god Bethel was known by the Judaeans in Elephantine.[114] Second, in my view the assumption that the word *'lh'* simply referred to YHW is weak. As far as I can see, the use of the word *'lh'* in the phrase *ʿl ḥrmbyt'l 'lh'* (B7.2:7–8) should rather be understood in analogy with B2.8:5 ("by Sati the goddess"), A4.7:5 ("Khnum the god) and C3.15:1 ("YHW the god"). In other words, *'lh'* functions as the "divine determination particle" of *ḥrmbyt'l*. Thus, the oath in B7.2:7–8 should be rendered "I, Malchiah, declare for you to Ḥerembethel the god ..."[115]

What about the deity AnathYHW in B7.3:3, then? As mentioned above a goddess Anat was known throughout the entire ancient Near East. However, the question is what the relationship between her and YHW in Elephantine was like. The problem is partly a syntactical one. As far as I can see, a likely interpretation of the phrase *ʿntyhw* is that it is constructed as a construct chain, meaning "Anat of YHW." Consequently, from a syntactic perspective the phrase *ʿntyhw* is

111 Rohrmoser, *Götter, Tempel und Kult*, 148.

112 "I, Malchiah, declare for you on the consecrated betyl of the god (YHW) ...," cf. Rohrmoser, *Götter, Tempel und Kult*, 425, cf. 148–149.

113 Rohrmoser, *Götter, Tempel und Kult*, 149.

114 Rohrmoser, *Götter, Tempel und Kult*, 127.

115 Similarly also Porten et al., *The Elephantine Papyri in English*, 262.

similar to the phrases *yhwh šmrn* and *yhwh htmn* that occur in a couple of inscriptions from Kuntillet ʿAjrud. One of the inscriptions simply reads *lyhwh htmn wlʾšrth,*[116] "By/for YHWH of Teman and by/for his *ʾšrh*." The other inscription relevant here is the one on Pithos B, which includes the following blessing: *brktk lyhwh tmn wlʾšrth,*[117] "I bless you by YHWH of Teman and by his *ʾšrh*." As suggested, the usual renditions of these phrases are "YHWH of Samaria" and "YHWH of Teman." It should, of course, be noted that Samaria and Teman are place names, whereas the Anat of *ʿntyhw* probably is the name of a deity. No matter what, this brings us to the second problem, namely the exact nature of the relation between the god YHW and the goddess Anat in the pantheon of the Judaeans. Could the phrase *ʿntyhw* imply that the Judaeans regarded Anat as YHW's consort?

To be sure, the idea of male and female deities being closely connected is richly attested in Egypt and the ancient Near East. As mentioned above, the Egyptian goddess Sati was considered to be Khnum's consort, and both were worshipped in Elephantine. The blessings from Kuntillet ʿAjrud just mentioned open up for a comparable concept also. In the two mentioned Kuntillet ʿAjrud inscriptions, sole reference is not made to "YHWH of Samaria/Teman." On the contrary, there is also a mention of "his *ʾšrh*."

Exactly what *ʾšrh* refers to is under debate. The term occurs in the Bible. 2Kgs 23 may illustrate the ambiguity. On the one hand, in 2Kgs 23:4 the word *ʾăšērâ* occurs alongside Baal and "the hosts of heaven." This can imply that *ʾăšērâ* should be rendered "Asherah" with a capital A, thus as a reference to a divine being. However, in 2Kgs 23:6, 15 King Josiah is said to have burned *hāʾăšērâ/ʾăšērâ*. This suggests the rendition "(the) asherah." Moreover, Deut 16:21 offers a prohibition against planting any tree as an *ʾăšērâ* (NRSV: "sacred pole") beside the altar of YHWH. It is possible that such an *ʾăšērâ* as the one mentioned in Deut 16:21 is actually depicted in a drawing on pithos A from Kuntillet ʿAjrud. The drawing depicts a tree that in fact may have been thought to represent the tree of life.[118]

One may hypothesise that the Asherah/asherah of both Kuntillet ʿAjrud and the Bible originally referred to an artefact associated with the cult of YHWH (though, an artefact that the theologians behind the Bible deemed as a deviation

---

116 Graham I. Davies et al., *Ancient Hebrew Inscriptions: Corpus and Concordance* (Cambridge: Cambridge University Press, 1991), 80 (no. 8.016).

117 Davies et al., *Ancient Hebrew Inscriptions*, 81 (no. 8.021).

118 For an image of the drawing, see "Asherah as Tree of Life," *Bible Odyssey* (2015): available online at http://bibleodyssey.org/tools/image-gallery/k/kuntillet-ajrud.aspx. Society of Biblical Literature.

from orthodox Yahwism). If *ʾăšērâ* originally was an artefact, it is conceivable that it was *deified* at a later stage in the development of Yahwism, coming to be understood as YHWH's consort.

No matter what *ʾăšērâ* in the Bible and YHWH's *ʾšrh* in Kuntillet ʿAjrud represented, Anat for her part was no cultic artefact but a goddess from the outset. As far as her role in Elephantine is concerned, it is thinkable that she served the role of YHW's consort. However, there are no clear-cut evidence for the hypothesis that the two gods actually were a couple.

Summing up, there are no fully fledged myths in the form of narratives about the non-Egyptian deities worshipped by the Judaean and Aramaean garrison communities in Elephantine and Syene in the Persian period. To be sure, there are indeed *fragments* of myths. However, in order to make conjectures about them one has to make use of comparative material from other sources in order to fill in the gaps. This procedure, however, inevitably weakens the results.

5.5.3 The Relationship between YHW and the Other Gods

The gods of the garrisons of Syene and Elephantine, as well as the gods of the local Egyptians and the gods of the Persian overlords, were revered and worshipped by peoples of different origin who must have mingled with each other. The fact that the Judaeans in Elephantine were part of an environment that we today would call multiethnic, multicultural and multireligious suggests that they must have had some sort of conscious or unconscious theology of religion. Whether they were aware of it themselves or not, the Judaeans must have positioned the god YHW in relation to the other gods. How was this done?

What is certain is that our modern attempts to reconstruct the theology of religion of the Judaeans in Persian-period Elephantine have to deal with several degrees of certainty. The most certain religio-theological statement of the Judaeans is that they did *not* regard YHW to be identical with Khnum or any other of the Egyptian gods (cf. A4.7:5–6, 14 par.). It is also certain that the Judaeans of Elephantine indeed identified their own god ("YHW, the god/lord of heaven" and "the god who dwells in Elephantine," B3.12:2) with YHWH, the god dwelling in Zion and worshipped in Jerusalem by the high priest Jehohanan and his colleagues the priests, Ostanes the brother of Anani and the nobles of the Judaeans (cf. A4.7:18–19 par.), and probably also with the god YHWH worshipped in Samaria (cf. A4.7:29 par.).

5.5.3.1 YHW and Ahuramazda

Moreover, when the Persians promoted the royal Achaemenid ideology they also promoted theologically loaded claims at one and the same time. As discussed above, the *Aramaic version of the Bisitun inscription* (DB Aram) represents a Persian propaganda text that can be closely connected to the Judaean community at Elephantine. In DB Aram, Darius (both I and II) claims to be king "with the protection of Ahuramazda" (*bṭllh zy ʾhwrmzd*) and that "Ahuramazda helped me" (*ʾhwrmzd sʿdny*).

In my view, the Judaeans had to make a conscious or unconscious choice between four strategies in response to these outspoken and theologically loaded claims. One possible strategy could be to *reject* the claims, either by stating that there is no other god than YHW or by stating that YHW is a more superior god than Ahuramazda. Whereas religio-theological statements that one today would call monotheistic are indeed found in other Yahwistic sources (see, e.g., Isa 44:6–8), this is not the case with the sources from Elephantine (see above). They simply do not open up for the suggestion that the Judaeans confronted the claims about Ahuramazda with monotheistic statements presenting YHW as the sole god or presenting YHW as the most powerful god. Therefore, the Judaean strategy cannot have been rejection.

Another potential strategy for the Elephantine Judaeans could be to *ignore* the contents of the claims of Darius concerning Ahuramazda. However, the claims in DB Aram were so outspoken that, once read and heard, they simply could not be ignored. One would expect that it was the purpose of Persian propaganda to promote the official royal Achaemenid ideology. According to the latter, the Achaemenid dynasty was chosen to be kings by Ahuramazda, the creator of heaven and earth. Therefore, the Judaeans—who in addition were part of the Persian power structure in Egypt—simply cannot have been in a position to ignore the claim concerning Ahuramazda.

A third thinkable strategy for the Judaeans could be to *identify* Ahuramazda with YHW. To be sure, the Aramaic documents from Egypt never explicitly do this. However, the Elephantine Judaeans referred to YHW as "the god of heaven" or "the lord of heaven" in communication with a representative of the Persian bureaucracy, Bagavahya the governor of the (Persian province of) Judah (A4.7:15, 27–28 par.). Moreover, in a communication from the governors of the Persian provinces of Samaria and Judah, the Persian officials on their part referred indirectly to YHW as "YHW the god of heaven" (A4.9:3–4). This epithet is never used in connection with Ahuramazda. However, Ahuramazda is elsewhere presented as the creator of, i.a., the heaven. Therefore, it is conceivable that for the Judaeans the epithet "the god/lord of heaven" in reality identified their own supreme god with the supreme god of the Achaemenid dynasty.

A fourth potential strategy for the Judaeans could be to *accept* the claims about Ahuramazda as superior, and *eo ipso*, recognise YHW as an inferior god, although continuing to worship the latter as *their* primary god.

In light of the sources from Egypt, I believe *acceptance* or perhaps *identification* were the strategies most probably consciously or unconsciously followed by the Judaeans in Elephantine. This conclusion is based on fragmented sources —and, in part, on an absence of sources. I have already mentioned above a relevant analogy from the exiled Judaeans in Mesopotamia, reflected in the Āl-Yāḫūdu archive. There, one and the same individual is known under the two names Bēl-šar-uṣur ("O Bel, protect the king!," CUSAS 28, no. 3:2) and Yaḫū-šar-uṣur ("O YHW, protect the king!," CUSAS 28, no. 4:2). By substituting YHW with the epithet Bel ("lord") that normally pertains to Marduk, religio-theological aspirations on behalf of YHW are revealed in that both YHW and Bel are regarded as holding the same (superior) position in the pantheon.[119] Moreover, judged on the basis of the positive evidence of the Aramaic documents from Egypt it remains a fact that the Elephantine Judaeans awarded their god YHW the epithet "god of heaven," or more often referred to him by this epithet alone.[120] This epithet was probably not part of their religious Judaean heritage—no matter what the prehistory of the Judaean garrison was like, from where they once came and when. A side view to the Bible shows that the epithets *ʾĕlāh šəmayyāʾ* (Ezra 5:11; 7:12, 21, 23; Dan 2:18, 37, 44), *ʾĕlōhê haššāmayim* (Gen 24:3, 7; 2Chr 36:23; Ezra 1:2; Neh 1:4–5; 2:4, 20; Jonah 1:9) and *ʾēl haššāmayim* (Ps 136:26) are mostly found in texts from the Persian and Hellenistic periods (cf. also Deut 4:39; Josh 2:11; 2Chr 20:6; Lam 3:41; Dan 2:28). It should also be noted that *Aḥiqar* was probably read in Elephantine. In this book, obedience to the king is presented as a virtue:

> Do not cover (= ignore) the word of a king; let it be healing [for] your hea[rt]. Soft is the speech of a king (yet) it is sharper and mightier than a [double-]edged knife. . . . [More] over, (do) the word of the king with heat/delight of the heart (= eagerly). (C1.1:84, 88)[121]

Obedience to the Achaemenid king would imply *acceptance* of his claim to be under the protection of Ahuramazda.

---

119 See Pearce and Wunsch, *Documents of Judean Exiles*, 101, and Section 5.2 above.
120 See A3.6:1; A4.3:2–3; A4.7:2; A4.8:2.
121 Quoted from Porten and Yardeni, *TADAE*, III: Literature, Accounts, Lists, 37.

5.5.3.2 YHW and the Other Gods

In principle, the four strategies for positioning YHW vis-à-vis Ahuramazda could also be used for studying the relationship between YHW and the other gods known in Elephantine and its surroundings. However, none of the other Aramaic documents from Egypt promulgate the other gods in a way comparable to how DB Aram promulgates Ahuramazda, the Achaemenid dynastic god. Here, only some conjectures can be made regarding the question of the relationship between YHW and the other gods.

YHW's epithet "the god/lord of heaven" may potentially connect YHW to another celestial deity: The Queen of Heaven (*mlkt šmyn*), whose temple was located in Syene (cf. A2.1:1). Was there any relationship between these two gods? Did the Judaeans (or their Aramaean brothers in arms, for that matter) ever couple the two "celestial" gods?

I would like to hypothesise a positive answer to this question. The argumentation is made up of two parts. First, I will draw attention to the connection between Bethel and the Queen of Heaven in Syene. In the sole reference to the Queen of Heaven (A2.1, one of the so-called Hermopolis papyri) there is also a reference to the temple of Bethel, which was also located in Syene: *šlm byt bt'l wbyt mlkt šmyn*, "Greetings to the Temple of Bethel and the Temple of the Queen of Heaven" (A2.1:1).[122] Moreover, the document in question also contains greetings to a number of people. One of them is Bethelnathan (*byt'lntn*, A2.1:3). Together, the reference to the temple of Bethel and the use of Bethel in a theophoric name proves that Bethel was worshipped as a god. Furthermore, the fact that the temples of Bethel and the Queen of Heaven are mentioned together in one and the same letter opening opens up for the possibility that they were regarded as a couple.

But how did YHW "fit in" in this context? This brings us to the second part of the argumentation. In the marriage contract between Hoshaiah and his wife Shalluah (B6.4) one of the witnesses mentioned has a remarkable name and patronymic: *byt'lntn br yhwntn*, "Bethelnathan son of Jehonathan," or in English "Bethel-has-given son of YHW-has-given" (B6.4:10). As Angela Rohrmoser has pointed out, the name constellation shows that the two gods Bethel and YHW belonged to the same cultic environment.[123] So far, I agree. However, I would like to ponder over yet another explanation that the name constellation Bethelnathan son of Jehonathan opens up for: namely, that YHW and Bethel were *identified* as one and the same god. For, the name Bethelnathan son of Jehonathan

122 Quoted from Porten et al., *The Elephantine Papyri in English*, 90.
123 Rohrmoser, *Götter, Tempel und Kult*, 127.

demonstrates that both the god Bethel and the god YHW are accredited for having *given* (presumably a child) within one and the same family, that is, father and son respectively. Therefore, in light of this it is conceivable that Bethel and YHW in fact referred to one and the same deity, albeit with two different names, YHW and Bethel respectively. To be sure, none of the known texts makes an explicit identification between YHW and Bethel. However, if my hypothesis should prove to be correct, then the one deity in question was worshipped under the name YHW in Elephantine and under the name Bethel in the neighbouring Syene.

In Syene, Bethel's consort may have been the Queen of Heaven. In Elephantine, YHW's consort may have been Anat (cf. the name AnathYHW). Provided that YHW and Bethel were identified, we may speculate: Were also Anat and the Queen of Heaven identified? This conjecture also opens up for an alternative to Rohrmoser's interpretation of the name Anathbethel. Instead of meaning "the betyl of [the goddess] Anat," the name Anathbethel could mean something like "(the god) Bethel's (consort) Anat," comparable to AnathYHW, "(the god) YHW's (consort) Anat."

5.5.3.3 An Operational Theology of Religion

Summing up, the Judaeans at Elephantine evidently worshipped YHW with epithets such as "the god of heaven" and "the god who dwells in Elephantine." However, they evidently knew and recognised other gods also. What is more, it is likely that in some cases they identified their "own" YHW with other deities (cf., e. g., the identification with YHWH of Jerusalem and YHWH of Samaria, perhaps with Ahuramazda, and the identification in the Āl-Yāḫūdu archive of YHW and Bel-Marduk). Yet, the exact relationship between YHW and the other gods is far from clear. In the end, what we have are just traces of pantheons. Again, as stated initially, reconstructing the mythology (and pantheon) of the Judaeans in Elephantine can be rather like piecing together the biblical account of the birth of Jesus from a series of Christmas cards and carols. It is possible that the Judaeans in Elephantine would nod approvingly when confronted with the result. However, it is also possible that they would have been appalled at the degree of inaccuracy.

5.6 Chapter Summary

This chapter has been guided by the question of how the religion of the Elephantine Judaeans reflected itself in myths and narratives. According to the working definition of myth and narrative used I have shown that there are few myths in the sources. However, I have argued that there are mythic elements in the material.

As far as myths about creation are concerned, no explicit myth involving YHW is known. However, royal Achaemenid inscriptions were probably known by the Judaean community in Elephantine, as DB Aram exemplifies. One of the components of the royal Achaemenid ideology was that the god Ahuramazda was the creator of heaven and earth.

Moreover, I have shown that one of the best-attested religious narratives is the Elephantine Judaean temple foundation narrative: *the tradition about the former temple of YHW*, that is the temple destroyed at the end of the fifth century BCE that the Judaeans of Elephantine attempted to rebuild. I have shown how the sources enable us to identify successive stages in the process of its transmission (the *traditio*) and how its content (the *traditum*) was slightly altered throughout the process of transmission. Furthermore, I have shown that the tradition about the former temple of YHW illustrates how Achaemenid officials took part in the shaping of Judaean religious traditions. The tradition about the former temple of YHW and its use in the attempts to rebuild it falls into a pattern of antiquarianism characteristic of the ancient Near East in the first millennium BCE.

Moreover, I have focussed on myths about sacral kingship. After an outline of the Egyptian and ancient Near Eastern context, the main thrust has been on sacral kingship of the official Achaemenid ideology. In the royal Achaemenid inscriptions, and in particular in Darius I's Bisitun inscription (DB), the Achaemenid ruler's rhetoric of self-justification included the claim to be a legitimate king *de gratia*. In DB the phrase "by the favour of Ahuramazda" occurs more than twenty times, such as in §5: "By the favour of Ahuramazda I am king; upon me Ahuramazda bestowed the kingship." What is particularly important in the context of this chapter is that the Achaemenids actively promoted the official royal ideology. A copy of the Aramaic version of the Bisitun inscription (DB Aram)—which also contains passages from one of Darius I's tomb inscriptions —can be closely connected to the Elephantine Judaean community. Moreover, the Judaean garrison (along with the other foreign garrisons) represented the tangible presence of the Persian Empire in Upper Egypt, at its southwestern border. Therefore, we may surmise that the Elephantine Judaeans not only knew the Achaemenid royal myths; it is also conceivable that they accepted them, be it of their own free will or be it out of pure necessity.

The last main section of this chapter has been devoted to a discussion of the traces of Judaean and other pantheons in our material. The Elephantine Judaeans knew and recognised several gods and pantheons. The Egyptian gods were subsumed under the heading "the gods of Egypt/the Egyptians." Moreover, the Elephantine Judaeans sources and the other Aramaic documents from the period in question mention additional gods that were known, recognised and worshipped by the garrison communities in the twin cities of Elephantine and Syene. To be sure, no fully fledged myth about any of these gods has survived. However, there are traces of mythic elements. *The Words of Aḥiqar* is useful for two reasons. First, when used together with religio-historical comparative material it gives glimpses of a pantheon headed by The Lord of the Holy Ones (who Niehr identifies with Hadad). Second, it gives a few glimpses of the competencies of some of the deities mentioned. But, most important, *Aḥiqar* gives a glimpse of the intellectual world of the pantheons of the garrison communities of Syene and Elephantine. Moreover, the goddess Anat and the god/goddess Eshem/Ashima were worshipped in Elephantine, together with YHW. In contrast to, for example, Angela Rohrmoser, I am inclined to think that a god called Ḥerem was also worshipped there.

A special challenge is represented by the word *byt'l*, and I follow Rohrmoser's fundamental assumption that it has two meanings in our material. On the one hand it can refer to a god Bethel. On the other hand, however, it may in other contexts refer to a standing stone used in the cults (including the cult of YHW), that is, a betyl.

The chapter concludes with conjectures about the operational theology of religion of the Judaeans at Elephantine, above all how the Judaeans considered the relationship between YHW and the other gods. I first deal with the relationship between Ahuramazda and YHW. I conclude that the Judaeans probably neither rejected nor ignored the theological claims about Ahuramazda, the chief god of the Achaemenid dynasty, in the official royal Achaemenid ideology. Rather, in my view they either identified Ahuramazda with YHW or accepted the inferior position of YHW vis-à-vis him. Moreover, I ponder over the possibility that the garrison communities in Elephantine and Syene as a matter of fact may have identified YHW and Bethel. The Queen of Heaven, the goddess who had a temple in Syene as also did the god Bethel, may in turn have been regarded as identical with Anat.

6 The Ethical Dimension

> *You swore to me by YHW the God in Elephantine the fortress, you and your wife and your son ... about the land of mine on account of which I (= Dargamana) complained against you before Damidata and his colleagues the judges, and they imposed upon you for me the oath to swear by YHW ... that it was not land of Dargamana ...* (B2.2:4–7)[1]

6.1 Introduction

What were the ethical ideals the Judaeans in Elephantine taught among themselves, how was their moral behaviour, that is, their ethical practice, what was the source of their ethics and how was the ethics legitimated? Did the Yahwism of Elephantine reflect itself in the ethics of the Judaeans there, and if so, in what way?

In the following, the aim will primarily be a descriptive one: to reconstruct and describe the ethics of the fifth-century BCE Judaean community in Elephantine. The task is complex for several reasons. First, there is the problem of identifying the relevant sources. Second, a more general problem pertains to the question of taxonomy. Which ethical topics should be highlighted, in what way and why?

6.1.1 The Relevant Sources

The following discussion takes as its point of departure that the sources fall into two main categories:

- The native Judaean sources from Elephantine. These sources, represented by letters and legal documents, are *descriptive* and partially *prescriptive*.
- The non-native, primarily *prescriptive* sources. They are represented by two literary works, namely the Aramaic version of King Darius's Bisitun inscription and the *Words of Aḥiqar*.

1 Quoted from Bezalel Porten et al., eds., *The Elephantine Papyri in English: Three Millennia of Cross-Cultural Continuity and Change*, 2nd rev. ed., DMOA 22 (Atlanta: Society of Biblical Literature, 2011), 161.

6.1.1.1 The Native Judaean Sources from Elephantine

The category of descriptive sources is made up of the many letters and legal documents from Elephantine. The letters and legal documents were either written by, written to or in other ways involve the members of the fifth-century Judaean community in Elephantine. Common for both the letters and the legal documents is that they—in retrospect as seen from the perspective of the modern reader—describe, directly or indirectly, the ethical ideals and the actual moral practice of the Judaeans. From this perspective, also a legal document such as a contract, which originally was intended to *prescribe* the future actions of the parties to the contract, may serve as a *descriptive* source.

Having their original setting in the everyday life of the Judaeans in Elephantine, the letters and legal documents reflect the lived ethics of the Judaeans, be it (fragments of) their actual moral practice or (fragments of) their desired rules of conduct, their maxims of behaviour.

6.1.1.2 The Non-Native Sources

The category is made up of two literary works: the Aramaic version of the Bisitun inscription (= DB Aram, C2.1) and the sapiential work the *Words of Aḥiqar* (= *Aḥiqar*, C1.1), named after its opening line. In both cases, the question of the provenance poses important problems. To be sure, none of them were originally composed in Elephantine by a member of the Judaean community.

The composition of the Bisitun inscription was originally commissioned by King Darius I sometime after 522 BCE. The original, which eventually became trilingual and accompanied by an iconographic presentation of the king subduing the enemies that are mentioned in the inscription, was incised on a rock cliff at the place called Bisitun in the province of Media. The Aramaic translation found in Elephantine probably stems from the time of King Darius II, a century after Darius I. The document can be connected to Achaemenid-period Elephantine for two reasons. First, the find spot was probably [*sic*] Elephantine.[2] Second, the blank space on the verso of the papyrus scroll was secondarily used to write down a record of memoranda (C3.13). The dates found in the record of memoranda, and in particular the Yahwistic names occurring there, suggest

2 The German archaeologists who originally found the papyrus did not document the find spot accurately. Consequently, its provenance is unclear. However, according to Michael Weigl the document was found in Elephantine, cf. Michael Weigl, *Die aramäischen Achikar-Sprüche aus Elephantine und die alttestamentliche Weisheitsliteratur*, BZAW 399 (Berlin: de Gruyter, 2010), 19–21 (20 note 47) and 691–703. See also Section 6.5.2.3 below.

that DB Aram once must have been in the possession of members of the Judaean garrison.

Various problems are connected with the composition of *Aḥiqar*. The work is made up of a frame narrative about the wise scribe Aḥiqar and his nephew Nadin, and a proverbial part made up of gnomic one-liners. Because the narrative frame and the proverbial part seem to reflect different Aramaic dialects[3] it has been proposed that they have different provenances and that the combination of them represents a later stage in the composition of the work. Moreover, it has also been suggested that the pantheon found in the proverbial part sheds light on the place of origin of the proverbial part. In contrast to the frame narrative, which is set at the Assyrian court at the time of Sennacherib and Esarhaddon, the deities in the proverbial part suggest that it originated in one of the Aramaean kingdoms in northern Syria in the first half of the first millennium BCE.[4]

The papyrus scroll that once contained *Aḥiqar* is a palimpsest. It has been shown that the scroll was originally used for writing a customs account (C3.7). A chronological detail recurring in the account is the date "year 11." According to Ada Yardeni and Bezalel Porten, "year 11" referred to the regnal years of King Xerxes, which was in 475 BCE.[5] This in turn is the terminus for the date of the making of this particular copy of *Aḥiqar*. In other words, the copy of *Aḥiqar* from Elephantine was written in the same general period as there was a Judaean community in Elephantine, namely the fifth century BCE.

Both the Aramaic Bisitun inscription and *Aḥiqar* are prescriptive texts. The Bisitun inscription promoted Achaemenid royal ideology.[6] The aim was to legitimate the rule of Darius (both the first and the second bearing the name) and prescribe the proper behaviour of the subject nations towards the Great King whose kingship had been entrusted by the god Ahuramazda. Moreover, *Aḥiqar* offers a series of exhortations promoting, among other things, discipline, diligence and obedience towards the crown. In short, my discussion will be built on the assumption that both the Bisitun inscription (in the Aramaic guise) and

3 See, e.g., James M. Lindenberger, "The Gods of Ahiqar," *UF* 14 (1982): 105–117.

4 See Section 5.5.2 above.

5 Ada Yardeni, "Maritime Trade and Royal Accountancy in an Erased Costums Cccount from 475 B.C.E. on the Aḥiqar Scroll from Elephantine," *BASOR* 293 (1994): 67–78, cf. Bezalel Porten and Ada Yardeni, *Textbook of Aramaic Documents from Ancient Egypt. Newly Copied, Edited and Translated into Hebrew and English*, vol. III: Literature, Accounts, Lists (Jerusalem: The Hebrew University of Jerusalem – Department of the History of the Jewish People, 1993), xx–xxi, 23.

6 See Sections 5.4.2 and 5.4.3 above. See also Gard Granerød, "'By the Favour of Ahuramazda I Am King': On the Promulgation of a Persian Propaganda Text among Babylonians and Judaeans," *JSJ* 44 (2013): 455–480.

Aḥiqar reflected and promulgated a kind of state-sanctioned ethics that the Judaeans in Elephantine were expected to subscribe to—and in the capacity of being Persian soldiers probably also *did*. The presence of the two literary works—the Aramaic Bisitun inscription and *Aḥiqar*—in Elephantine suggests that their contents found a resonance in the ethics of the Judaean community. In short, even though they did not originate within the Judaean community in Elephantine, we should nevertheless regard them as sources in a discussion of the ethical dimension of the religion of the Judaeans in Elephantine.

6.1.2 The Taxonomy

Another initial problem pertains to the question of the taxonomy of the presentation. Which ethical topics should be highlighted, in what way, and why?

There are no hints in the sources allowing us to assume that the Judaeans in Elephantine were aware of any normative texts reflecting or otherwise related to what we today know as the Bible, the Pentateuch, the Torah of Moses, the Covenant Code and so on. Reinhard G. Kratz has suggested characterising the fifth-century BCE Judaeans in Elephantine as representatives of *non-biblical* Judaism ("nicht-biblisches Judentum"), in contrast to the biblical Judaism of the *ioudaioi* of second-century BCE Alexandria, the Yaḥad of Qumran and so on.[7] No traces of the biblical tradition can be found in the Elephantine papyri. The Judaeans in Elephantine were not "non-biblical" by choice. On the contrary, they were so because they were unaware of any of the sacred writings that we today find in the received biblical texts and that presumably were formative for most Yahwists at the beginning of the Christian era.

This—namely that the Judaeans at Elephantine did not have any Bible—is relevant for the scope of the present chapter. An implication is that we cannot use any theological core concept or (biblical) core text as the prism through which we can observe and describe the ethics of the Judaeans in Elephantine. For instance, in contrast to a discussion of the ethics of the Hebrew Bible, it is meaningless to make the ethics of the Judaeans in Elephantine pivot around con-

7 See, e.g., Reinhard Gregor Kratz, "Zwischen Elephantine und Qumran: das Alte Testament im Rahmen des antiken Judentums," in *Congress Volume Ljubljana 2007*, ed. André Lemaire, VTSup 133 (Leiden: Brill, 2010): 129–146, and Reinhard Gregor Kratz, *Historisches und biblisches Israel: Drei Überblicke zum Alten Testament* (Tübingen: Mohr Siebeck, 2013), 274–283. See, though, my remarks regarding the terminology, in Section 1.3.3 above.

cepts such as, for example, the covenant between YHWH and the Israelites[8] as long as neither the term nor the ideas associated with it are present in the documents from Elephantine.

However, even though there is no concept intrinsic to the sources for the Judaeans in Elephantine that may determine the scheme of classification, there is still a need for a principle of organisation. There are, to put it informally, many ways to cut a cake. In the following, I have chosen to discuss the native Judaean as well as the non-Judaean sources from Elephantine on the basis of the following three focal points:

- the human and the deities,
- the human and the other humans, and
- the human and the authorities of the society.

6.2 The Human and the Deities in the Native Sources

Was there any link between the ethics of the Judaeans in Elephantine and their religion? This question is not as self-evident as it appears to be at first sight.

First, modern, Western notions of the function of religion should not necessarily be applied to an ancient Near Eastern religion. In the ancient world piety was not always connected to morality.[9] This can be glimpsed in various "internal," "inner-religious" discourses. For instance, in Plato's dialogue *Euthyphro*, Socrates and his dialogue partner Euthyphro implicitly criticise the Olympian gods because of their cruelty and ethical inconsistency. The gods fight with one another, have dire quarrels and one of them (Cronus) even has his father (Uranus) castrated. In the dialogue, Socrates formulates the so-called Euthyphro dilemma: "Is that which is holy [τὸ ὅσιον] loved by the gods because it is holy, or is it holy because it is loved by the gods?"[10] Moreover, in the prophetic tradition of the Hebrew Bible there are several statements of harsh criticism of religious practice that per se was not illegitimate but that, from the perspective of the prophets, was an abomination when practiced without connection with just

8 See, e.g., Exod 24:7: "Then he [Moses] took the book of the covenant [*sēper habbərît*], and read it in the hearing of the people; and they said, 'All that YHWH has spoken we will do, and we will be obedient.'"

9 See, e.g., Robert Karl Gnuse, *No Other Gods: Emergent Monotheism in Israel*, JSOTSup 241 (Sheffield: Sheffield Academic, 1997), 249–252.

10 Plato, *Euthyphr.* 10a, quoted from Plato et al., *Plato in Twelve Volumes*, vol. 1: Euthyphro, Apology, Crito, Phaedo, Phaedrus, LCL 36 (Cambridge, MA and London: Harvard University Press, 1914), 35.

behaviour.[11] The traditional Olympian religion and the religious practice criticised by the biblical prophets was presumably more concerned with the religious rituals than the morals of the worshippers. Therefore, it cannot a priori be taken for granted that an ancient Near Eastern individual, for example, an Elephantine Judaean, was of the opinion that "religion" had anything to do with ethical behaviour and that the gods were seriously concerned with how humans lived their lives.

Secondly, in the Elephantine documents there are, perhaps with the exception of the Bisitun inscription,[12] no traces of any divine commandments.[13] As far as we know, the Judaeans there did not have anything comparable to the Covenant Code of the Pentateuch, the Deuteronomic Code, the Decalogue or the Holiness Code. Common to all of these biblical collections and compilations is that they seem to presuppose a *covenant* between the deity and his people, Israel.

Therefore, it is justified to question whether the gods of the Judaean pantheon in Elephantine, which clearly also included other deities besides YHW, required a certain behaviour from humans.

6.2.1 The Ethical Aspects of the Oath Practice

The sources for the Judaeans in Elephantine do not offer any cases of a direct communication between the deity and human beings. From a grammatical perspective, there are no examples of verbs in jussive or imperative, spoken by a deity to a human being. Until this day, no prophet has been attested in Elephantine as speaking on behalf of a deity. No person is known to have mediated between the gods and humans in the Judaean community in Elephantine in a way corresponding to, for example, the biblical Moses.

---

11 See, e.g., Isa 1:12–17; Mic 6:8.

12 Within the corpus of documents from Elephantine there is one text that clearly legitimises itself as divine law: the Aramaic version of the Bisitun inscription (DB Aram). In DB Aram King Darius claims more than twenty times that he is king "by the favour of Ahuramazda," cf. Granerød, "'By the Favour of Ahuramazda'," 455–480 (463).

13 An important feature of the literary growth of the biblical laws and narratives towards the Pentateuch, understood as the Torah of YHWH/Moses, is that which Reinhard G. Kratz calls the "theologisation of the law" ("Theologisierung des Rechts"). In Kratz's view, the process started in the seventh century BCE under the influence of the prophetic tradition with the reworking of an earlier collection of *mishpatim* ("legal rulings," Exod 21:1–22:19), which was expanded and became the Book of the Covenant (Exod 24:4–8). Eventually, the process of the "theologisation of the law" resulted in the received Pentateuch, cf. Kratz, *Historisches und biblisches Israel*, 112–113 and additional references there.

Yet, there are traces of the idea of involving a deity in the assessment of the moral behaviour of humans. Above all, this is evident in the oath practice frequently attested in documents from Elephantine.[14]

The oaths are all attested in legal documents, concretely in the noun *mwm'* and the verb *ym'*. In these documents the oath functioned as proof in legal disputes in the absence of firm evidence. It seems that an oath in a deity's name could be sworn unilaterally by one of the parties. However, there are also examples of cases where officials pass a verdict according to which a person was imposed to swear an oath in a god's name.

An informative example of the value of such an oath is found in the document of withdrawal (*spr mrḥq*, B2.2:22) that the Khwarezmian[15] named Dargamana son of Khvarshaina wrote for the Elephantine Judaean Mahseiah son of Jedaniah. The two had a dispute over the title to a piece of land and Dargamana had complained about Mahseiah's claim to the title "before Damidata and his colleagues the judges" (B2.2:5–6). What is remarkable is that these officials (note that Damidata bears a Persian name) thereupon imposed an oath upon Mahseiah: *wṭ'nwk ly mwmh lmwm byhw 'ldbr 'rq' zk*, "and they imposed upon you for me the oath to swear by YHW on account of that land" (B2.2:6–7).[16] The judges' decision was that the Judaean Mahseiah had to swear by YHW that he retained his claim on the title to the land plot in question, and that Dargamana did not own it.

In this respect, it is equally noteworthy how Dargamana assessed the oath Mahseiah had sworn to YHW as a result of the court decision. Dargamana *accepted* the oath as sufficient evidence to settle the land dispute, as is evident in the formulation "You swore to me by YHW and satisfied my heart [*whwṭbt lbby*[17]] about that land" (B2.2:11–12). As a consequence of his acceptance of the oath Dargamana issued the document of withdrawal. There he explicitly refrained from any future claims on the land plot in question, both on behalf of himself and his descendants (B2.2:12–15). In sum, on the basis of the oath by YHW that the (Persian?) officials imposed upon Mahseiah, Dargamana was ready to affirm the former's title to the piece of land: *w'rq' zk 'pm zylk w'nt rḥyq mn kl dyn zy yqblwn 'lyk 'ldbr 'r'' zk*, "and that land is likewise yours and you are with-

14 See Section 2.4.1 above.

15 Khwarerzm (also written Chorasmia) was a province in Central Asia, located south of the Aral Sea.

16 Quoted from Porten et al., *The Elephantine Papyri in English*, 161.

17 For a discussion of the function of the legal expression *ṭyb lbby*, see Yochanan Muffs, *Studies in the Aramaic Legal Papyri from the Elephantine; with Prolegomenon by Baruch A. Levine*, HdO 66 (Leiden: Brill, 2003), 28–29, 30–33, 43–50.

drawn from any suit (in) which they shall complain against you on account of that land" (B2.2:15 – 16).[18] The oath sworn in this particular legal dispute reveals that good moral behaviour was somehow motivated by the god of the oath. In this particular case, the assumption that an oath motivated good moral behaviour was shared not only by the Judaean but also by the judges and even the other party in the dispute, Dargamana.

Even though the oath procedure in this case clearly took place in a legal context, it nevertheless had ethical implications. The document of withdrawal issued by Dargamana to Mahseiah does not say anything about the consequences in the event that Mahseiah had made a false oath. Nevertheless, we can assume that it was an underlying assumption, shared by all involved in the dispute, that the deity would punish anyone who misused his or her name.[19]

In a bequest written some years later Mahseiah transferred the right of ownership of his house to his daughter Mibtahiah (B2.3). In the bequest Mahseiah referred to the oath by YHW that had previously been imposed upon him in connection with the dispute with Dargamana:

> Moreover, there is a document of withdrawal which Dargamana son of Khvarshaina, the Khwarezmian, wrote for me about that land when he brought (suit) about it before the judges and an oath was imposed (upon me) for him and I swore to him that it was mine, and he wrote a document of withdrawal and gave (it) to me. That document – I gave it to you. You, hold-it-as-heir ... (B2.3:23 – 26)[20]

In other words, Mahseiah's bequest of the house issued to his daughter confirms the long-term validity of the oath that Mahseiah once made by YHW.

Moreover, the documents from Elephantine show that the Judaeans there did not only connect their ethics to the god YHW. On the contrary, there are several examples of Judaeans who also swore to gods other than YHW. One example is an oath sworn by Mibtahiah, the daughter of Mahseiah (both were mentioned above). In 440 BCE there was a legal dispute between the above mentioned Mibtahiah and a builder from Syene called Peu son of Paḥe/Pakhoi about "silver and grain and clothing and bronze and iron—all goods and property" (B2.8:3 – 4). The legal document reflecting this dispute (B2.8) illustrates how the ethnic designation of the Judaean community could fluctuate. Whereas Mibtahiah's father Mahseiah was referred to as a Judaean in the document in which he transferred his house to his daughter Mibtahiah (cf. B2.3:2), the very same Mibtahiah is called an

18 Quoted from Porten et al., *The Elephantine Papyri in English*, 164.

19 Compare Deut 5:11 (NRSV), "You shall not make wrongful use of the name of the LORD your God, for the LORD will not acquit anyone who misuses his name."

20 Quoted from Porten et al., *The Elephantine Papyri in English*, 170 – 171.

Aramaean in the document reflecting the dispute with Peu (B2.8:2–3). No matter what Mibtahiah's identity was, the dispute was solved when Mibtahiah swore an oath that Peu accepted: "Then, the oath came upon you and you swore for me about them by Sati the goddess. And my heart was satisfied with that oath which you made for me about those goods and I withdrew from you from this day and forever" (B2.8:4–7).[21] Even though Mibtahiah's oath was taken by the Egyptian goddess Sati, the result was nevertheless the same. The other party in the litigation, the Syenian builder Peu (note the Egyptian name), accepted the validity and truthfulness of her claims and relinquished his title to the goods.

Other legal disputes were also settled by means of oaths in the same ways as reflected in the documents mentioned above. A dispute about alleged stolen fish was solved by an oath by "YHW the god" (B7.1). One Aramaean of Syene called Mahseiah son of Shibah accused another person (whose name is lost) of having stolen fish. The anonymous accused was interrogated, presumably by the judges. In the absence of other evidence, the judges imposed an oath upon the accused, ensuring that he had not stolen the fish from Mahseiah (B7.1:4).

Further, another case of a serious accusation was solved by an oath sworn to the god Ḥerembethel (B7.2). Artafrada accused Malchiah son of Jashoibah of a series of unlawful actions: illegal entry into his house, violence against his wife and theft of goods (B7.2:4.6). Malchiah, who referred to himself as an Aramaean and a hereditary-property-holder (*mhḥsn*) in Elephantine[22] (B7.2:2), denied the serious accusations. Having been interrogated (verb: *š'l*), presumably by the Persian officials, he was forced to swear an oath:

> [I] was interrogated and the call to (the) gods came upon me in the suit. I, Malchiah, shall call for you to Ḥerembethel the god among 4 [OF]FICIALS/[SUP]PORTERS, say[ing]: "By force I did [not] break into your house, (that) wife of yours I did not assault, and goods from your house by force I did not take." (B7.2:6–9)[23]

Unfortunately, because the papyrus breaks off it is not known whether or not Artafrada accepted the oath and refrained from any further law suits.

The last example given here is an oath that seemed to have been sworn by two deities and a cultic place (B7.3). Meshullam son of Nathan had sued Menahem son of Shallum son of PN about the title to a she-ass. As a response, Menahem swore an oath to prove that he was fully entitled to, not the other party: "Your father did not give me a he-ass in exchange for half of it and [he did

21 Quoted from Porten et al., *The Elephantine Papyri in English*, 190.
22 As to the term *mhḥsn* and the interpretation of it, see Section 2.3.3 above.
23 Quoted from Porten et al., *The Elephantine Papyri in English*, 262.

no]t [gi]ve me silver or the value of silver in exchange for h[alf of it]" (B7.3:7–10).[24] The oath Menahem made was probably taken by two deities and a particular cultic place: *bḥ[rm ʾlh]ʾ bmsgdʾ wbʿntyhw*, "by Ḥ[*erem*] *the* [*god*] in/by the place of prostration and by AnathYHW" (B7.3:3).[25]

Summing up, the oaths discussed above were all sworn in legal disputes by one party to the other. In some cases the oath may have been sworn voluntarily and unilaterally. In other cases, the oath was imposed upon the person by the court. In any case, all who were involved shared a common assumption, namely that a person would *not* misuse the name of the deity to swear falsely. Although none of the oath texts indicate what the gods would do in the case of perjury, it was nevertheless obviously something no one would do willingly. In fact, the oath procedures make clear that there *was* a connection between the question of (good) behaviour and the gods. As far as the Judaeans in Elephantine and their neighbours were concerned, they all apparently shared this assumption. Moreover, the case of Mibtahiah, who swore by the goddess Sati, shows that it was not only the god YHW who could function as the ethical guarantor in the environment of the Judaean community.

6.2.2 Ethical Aspects of the So-Called Vidranga Section

In a time of utmost crisis, the Elephantine Judaean community sent a petition to Bagavahya, the governor of the Persian province of Judah (A4.7/A4.8). In the middle of the letter, after the writers had outlined the history of the temple of YHW and described how the corrupt Persian official Vidranga and the priests of Khnum had razed it to the ground, the writers continued with a passage on Vidranga (A4.7:15–17).

Above I have argued that there are good arguments in support of Lindenberger's proposal to read the Vidranga section as the Elephantine community's post-disaster liturgy of curse in the form of a series of *imprecations*, and not as a factual, retrospective narrative:[26]

> After this had been done to us, we with our wives and our children put on sackcloth and fasted and prayed to YHW the lord of heaven: "Show us our revenge on that Vidranga: May the dogs tear his guts out from between his legs! May all the property he got perish! May all

24 Quoted from Porten et al., *The Elephantine Papyri in English*, 266.
25 Quoted from Porten et al., *The Elephantine Papyri in English*, 265.
26 See Section 4.4.2 above.

the men who plotted evil against that temple—all of them—be killed! And may we watch them! (A4.7:15–17)[27]

The context of the liturgy of curse was extraordinary because the Judaean temple of YHW was laying in ruins. Nevertheless, in spite of the extraordinary circumstances, the words of the so-called Vidranga section reveal some aspects of how the Judaeans conceived of the relationship between the god YHW and ethics.

Although the basis is meagre, the Vidranga section indirectly attests to the idea that YHW was a god of justice. The Judaeans in Elephantine prayed and apparently expected that YHW would see to it that the "evil" (*bʾyš*, A4.7:17 par.) done by Vidranga and the priests of Khnum would hit back at the evildoers themselves. The god YHW was—at least for the Judaeans—the antagonist of evil.

This suggests that the Judaeans possibly expected that the judgement of one's actions would take place in the present life as was the case in Babylonian thought, and not in the life to come, which was the case in Egyptian thought.[28] It follows from this that the Judaeans in Elephantine were not hoping for an eschatological judgement.[29] The Judaeans expected unjust behaviour to be punished by YHW *in this life*, not in the hereafter.

An additional point can be mentioned in connection with the petition to Bagavahya. Immediately after the so-called Vidranga section the Elephantine leaders continued with a brief but nevertheless informative remark: *ʾp qdmt znh bʿdn zy zʾ bʾyštʾ ʿbyd ln ʾgrh šlḥn*, "Moreover, before this, at the time that this evil was done to us, a letter we sent" (A4.7:17–18).[30] It is noteworthy that the writers presented *themselves* as the victims of the aggression of the corrupt Vidranga and the priests of Khnum. The "evil" was done "to us" (*ln*), that is, the Judaean community. However, the Judaeans were obviously not the only victims of the aggression, even though they did not say that the evil was done to YHW. For, according to the writers of the petition to Bagavahya, the aggressors agreed on removing the "temple of YHW the god": *ʾgwrʾ zy yhw ʾlhʾ zy byb byrtʾ yhʿdw mn*

27 Quoted from James M. Lindenberger, *Ancient Aramaic and Hebrew Letters*, 2nd ed., WAW 14 (Atlanta: Society of Biblical Literature, 2003), 75, cf. James M. Lindenberger, "What Ever Happened to Vidranga? A Jewish Liturgy of Cursing from Elephantine," in *World of the Aramaeans III: Studies in Language and Literature in Honour of Paul-Eugène Dion*, ed. P. M. Michèle Daviau et al., JSOTSup 326 (Sheffield: Sheffield Academic, 2001), 134–157 (154).

28 Robert B. Y. Scott, "Wisdom, Wisdom Literature," *EncJud* 21: 95–99.

29 Compare, in contrast, Dan 12:1–4. According to this text the final judgement will take place "at the time of the end" (cf. Dan 11:40) and "those who sleep in the dust of the earth shall awake, some to everlasting life, and some to shame and everlasting contempt."

30 Quoted from Porten et al., *The Elephantine Papyri in English*, 144.

tmh, "The temple of YHW the god that/who is in Elephantine the fortress—let one remove from there!" (A4.7:6, my translation). The temple, i.e. the subject of the destruction, did not exist independently of the deity whose dwellings it confined and to whom it belonged. Consequently, the aggression of Vidranga and the Khnum priests was an act of unethical behaviour that affected not only the Judaeans but also their god YHW.

This banal conclusion raises yet another question: Did YHW punish out of consideration for *himself*, either in order to re-establish his broken divine dignity or in order to restore justice in the transcendent spheres? Or was the idea that YHW avenged out of consideration for his *worshippers*, so as from a humanitarian perspective, aiming at the restoration of immanent, worldly justice? The Vidranga section suggests that the Judaeans favoured the latter option. Their prayers for YHW's revenge upon the evildoers would presumably restore their own justice in this world.

It is noteworthy that the destruction of the temple of YHW did not hinder the Judaeans in Elephantine from praying to YHW, even though the latter in a sense was a homeless deity as long as he did not have his own house. The fact that they continued to address their prayers to YHW, even though his temple was laying in ruins, warns us against the temptation of drawing a too naive and immanent picture of the Judaeans' notion of the god YHW. For the Judaeans, YHW was not solely an immanent deity whose presence was dependent upon his tangible and visible house. The fact that the Judaeans expected that he could hear their prayers for revenge upon the evildoers shows that they also had a transcendent notion of him as god. After all, YHW could also be called "the god of heaven" (cf., e.g., A4.9:3–4).

6.3 The Human and the Humans in the Native Sources

6.3.1 The View on Animals as Backdrop of the Anthropology

Unfortunately, we do not have any source that systematically presents the anthropological concepts of the Judaeans in Elephantine, in particular how they conceived of humans in relation to other living creatures. Even though we should expect that they reflected upon such questions, such ideas have not left any traces in the textual sources.[31]

31 Compare, in contrast, the description of the relationship between the animals and the humans in the creation account in Gen 1:1–2:3 and the Eden narrative in Gen 2:4–3:24.

However, it seems clear that the Judaeans clearly considered animals as subordinate to humans. It goes without saying that members of the Judaean community were by no means vegetarians, even though grain and vegetables were definitely the most important foodstuffs. As one would expect for anyone living on the banks of the River Nile, fish was an important dietary item.[32] Moreover, the Judaeans and the other mercenary groups held domestic animals. Judaeans kept asses (B7.3) and they traded with sheep, lamb and goats (A2.2, D7.1, D7.8). They sheared off the wool (D7.8) and, even though not explicitly stated, they presumably ate mutton. In addition, the Judaeans offered sheep, oxen and goats as animal sacrifices in the temple of YHW before it was destroyed in 410.[33]

As is to be expected from such an arbitrary collection of sources, there are no documents that deal particularly with the issue of animal welfare. However, there is nevertheless one hint in an ostracon inscription from the first quarter of the fifth century BCE showing that this aspect of animal rearing was not neglected. In the brief message Uriah was informed that "the ewe which is yours, the big one" (*t't' zy lk rbt'*) had reached the time for shearing. The one who looked after the sheep related: "The wool of hers already is being torn on the thorn(s). Now, come and shear her" (D7.8:4–6).[34]

In light of this, the keeper requested instructions as to whether he should start washing the ewe as a preparation for the shearing, or whether Uriah would do it himself. No doubt, the keeper's concern for the welfare of the livestock was economically motivated. But even economic reasons (i.e., the fear that the wool might get destroyed) may have driven a concern for the welfare of animals.

Moreover, as to the question whether the Judaeans in Elephantine held any particular animals to be unclean, the Vidranga section may reveal that dogs were reckoned as such. Provided that *klby'* in A4.7:16 par. should be understood as "the dogs," the Judaeans prayed to YHW that their enemies should be mutilated by "the dogs." This may presumably have been considered particularly disgraceful.

32 See, e.g., the dispute over the alleged stolen fish in B7.1.

33 See A4.7:21 par., and A4.10:10.

34 Quoted from Bezalel Porten and Ada Yardeni, *Textbook of Aramaic Documents from Ancient Egypt. Newly Copied, Edited and Translated into Hebrew and English*, vol. IV: Ostraca & Assorted Inscriptions (Jerusalem: The Hebrew University of Jerusalem – Department of the History of the Jewish People, 1999), 160. Lindenberger translates somewhat differently: "The one you sent over before is being combed now," cf. Lindenberger, *Ancient Aramaic and Hebrew Letters*, 44–45.

6.3.2 The View on Work

A discussion of the Elephantine Judaeans' perception of work may set against the backdrop of other ancient Near Eastern sources. Hence, we will make a detour to Mesopotamian and biblical narratives.

According to Mesopotamian accounts, the background of the creation of humans was a negative one. As stated in Atrahasis, in the days of old it was the lower rank deities, namely the Igigi, who had to carry the yoke of undertaking the hard labour and toil: "When the gods instead of man / Did the work, bore the loads, / The gods' load was too great, / The work too hard, the trouble too much, / The great Anunnaki made the Igigi / Carry the workload sevenfold."[35] Eventually, the Igigi rebelled: "Every single of us gods declared war, / We had put [a stop] to the digging. / The load is excessive, it is killing us! / So every single one of us gods / Has agreed to complain to Ellil."[36] The rebelling gods found sympathy for their cause from god Ea (so the Standard Babylonian Version)/Enki (the Old Babylonian Version). Ea/Enki turned his attention towards Belet-ili (also called Nintu and Mami), the womb-goddess: "Let her create primeval man / So that he may bear the yoke ... / Let man bear the load of the gods!"[37] At the behest of Ea/Enki, the god Ilawela was slaughtered and Nintu mixed his flesh and blood with clay. The result was man, whose basic aim was to carry out the toil of the gods.

As has often been pointed out, the biblical creation accounts represent a positive counter image to the negative anthropology evident in the Mesopotamian creation myths. The account in Gen 2:4–3:24 admittedly reflects the notion that the purpose of the creation of the human man was to provide workers: "The LORD God took the man and put him in the garden of Eden to till it and keep it" (Gen 2:15 NRSV).[38] Yet, in contrast to, for example, Atrahasis, where the man was

---

35 Quoted from "Atrahasis," Stephanie Dalley, *Myths from Mesopotamia: Creation, the Flood, Gilgamesh, and Others*, 2nd rev. ed., OWC (Oxford: Oxford University Press, 2000), 9.

36 Quoted from "Atrahasis," Dalley, *Myths from Mesopotamia*, 12.

37 Quoted from "Atrahasis," Dalley, *Myths from Mesopotamia*, 14.

38 The question of the chronological order of the creation of the man and the planting of the garden of Eden is not entirely clear. According to common opinion, the man was formed first (cf. Gen 2:7), and the garden of Eden thereafter (cf. Gen 2:8). In support of this, one may, for example, point to the verb *wayyiṭṭaʿ* (root: *nṭʿ*) in Gen 2:8. The *wayyiqtol* form may be understood as that which Alviero Niccacci has described as a "narrative *wayyiqtol*," i.e. the narrative verb form *par excellence* that indicates the main line of communication, cf. Gard Granerød, "Omnipresent in Narratives, Disputed Among Grammarians: Some Contributions to the Understanding of *wayyiqtol* and their Underlying Paradigms," *ZAW* 121 (2009): 418–434 (427–429) and additional references there. However, there are arguments for reversing the order, i.e. considering the plant-

created in order to grant the gods freedom from hard work, the man in the biblical account appeared to have a more elevated position. This is evident, first, in YHWH Elohim's concern for him ("It is not good that the man should be alone; I will make him a helper as his partner," Gen 2:18 NRSV), and secondly, in the man's naming of all the animals (Gen 2:19 – 20) and the naming of the woman (Gen 2:23). The naming can be understood as an act of sovereignty expressing the man's elevated position.

However, also in the Eden narrative work ends up as something negative. When it came to YHWH Elohim's knowledge that the man and the woman had violated his prohibitions by eating the fruit of the tree in the middle of the garden ("the tree of the knowledge of good and evil"), his verdict on the man was a harsh one: "Cursed is the ground because of you; in toil you shall eat of it all the days of your life" (Gen 3:17 NRSV). According to the Eden narrative, every man was predetermined to eat bread "by the sweat of your face" until the day of his death outside of the garden that YHWH Elohim had planted (cf. Gen 3:18 – 19, 23 – 24). However, according to the Eden narrative the negative predetermination was not part of the original creation but the consequence of the man's guilt.

Moreover, the so-called Priestly creation account in Gen 1:1 – 2:3 offers an even more explicitly positive anthropology. There, the creation of humankind is presented as Elohim's own, freely made decision. No circumstances have forced him to do so: "Then God said, 'Let us make humankind in our image, according to our likeness ...' So God created humankind in his image, in the image of God he created them; male and female he created them" (Gen 1:26 – 27 NRSV). The positive anthropology is most clearly evident in God's assessment of his own work: "God saw everything that he had made, and indeed, it was very good" (Gen 1:31 NRSV).

As far as Elephantine is concerned, we cannot say whether or not the Judaeans there were familiar with concepts comparable to those reflected in the Mesopotamian or biblical myths. Of that the sources are silent. We do not

---

ing of the garden to have taken place first, and the forming of the man second. First, from a religio-historical perspective this was clearly the case in the Mesopotamian myths where the very purpose of the creation of man was to grant the lower-rank gods freedom from toil. Second, in the Hebrew text, the phrase *miqqedem* in Gen 2:8 may point in the same direction. Traditionally, it is translated "in the east" (thus, e.g., NRSV). However, the word *qedem* can also have the meaning "ancient times." Consequently, the phrase *miqqedem* may signal something that was *already* a reality when YHWH Elohim formed the man:

> *wayyiṭṭaʿ YHWH ʾĕlōhîm gan bʿēden miqqedem wayyāśem šām ʾet hāʾādām ʾăšer yāṣār*
> And YHWH Elohim had planted a garden in Eden in/from ancient times, and there he put the man whom he had formed. (Gen 2:8, *my translation*)

know what the (theological) anthropology may have looked like. Nevertheless, the sources do show that the Judaeans in Elephantine were working in various sectors: in "the public sector" as well as in "the primary sector," using terminology from the field of political science.

As for the former ("the public sector"), the main source of income for most of the Judaeans was presumably the salary they received as soldiers.[39] Exactly what the everyday tasks of a Judaean soldier were like must be deduced from the sources. At times, or perhaps even quite often, it involved being on the move along the Nile, the artery of ancient Egypt, depending on where one was deployed.

A letter from the first quarter of the fifth century BCE written by a father to his son may give us a glimpse of what it felt like to be a Judaean soldier in Egypt —but also what it felt like to be a relative of a Judaean soldier: A3.3.[40] The letter is written by Osea (*ʾwšʿ*) to his son[41] Shelomam (*šlmm*). Osea was living in Migdol in Lower Egypt together with his wife. On the basis of two clauses in the letter, it is evident that Shelomam had set out on a journey and thus left Migdol: *mn ywm zy ʾzlt bʾrḥʾ zk lbby lʾ ṭyb ʾp ʾmk*, "From the day that you went [second person singular] on that way, my heart is not good. Likewise, your mother" (A3.3:2).[42] The second reference to Shelomam's travel is even more interesting because of the verb used is in the plural:

> Now, from the day that you went [second person plural] out from Egypt,[43] allotment has not been g[iven to *us/you here*. And when] we complained to the OFFICIALS about your allot-

39 See Section 2.6.5 above.

40 The acquisition of the letter A3.3 (= Padua 1) is the earliest known acquisition of an Aramaic document from Persian-period Egypt. It was acquired by Giovan Battista Belzoni between 1815 and 1819. According to Bezalel Porten, the place of acquisition was Elephantine, cf. Bezalel Porten, "Elephantine Papyri," *ABD* 2: 445–455 (446). However, regardless of how likely this is, in particular in light of the initial greeting to the temple of YHW in Elephantine (A3.3:1 *byt yhw byb*), this is a conjecture. The exact provenance of the letter is unknown, cf. Lindenberger, *Ancient Aramaic and Hebrew Letters*, 26, and Margaretha L. Folmer, *The Aramaic Language in the Achaemenid Period: A Study in Linguistic Variation*, OLA 68 (Leuven: Peeters, 1995), 24 note 125. Moreover, see Section 3.1.2 above.

41 The writer uses a double, contradictory set of designations for the relationship between himself and Shelomam. In the internal address, he writes "To my son Shelomam from your brother Osea" (A3.3:1). In the external address he writes "To my brother Shelomam son of Osea, your brother Osea ..." (A3.3:14). However, in light of the contents it is clear that "brother" is used figuratively here.

42 Quoted from Porten et al., *The Elephantine Papyri in English*, 108.

43 That is, Lower Egypt as distinct from Pathros = Upper Egypt, cf. Porten et al., *The Elephantine Papyri in English*, 109 note 11.

> ment here in Migdol, thus was said to us, saying: "About this [*you, complain* before] the scribes and it will be given to you." (A3.3:3 – 5)[44]

Elephantine was probably the final destination of the group Shelomam was part of.[45] According to James M. Lindenberger, the letter may have been dispatched to Elephantine to be held for the son's arrival there. The mention of, first, the missing allotment (*prs*), secondly the officials (*pḥwt'*, "governors"?) that one should complain to and thirdly the scribes, shows that Shelomam was not making a private journey. On the contrary, Shelomam was obviously under command and on an official mission. The mission of his group was presumably to escort a caravan of some kind along the Nile.[46]

At the end of the letter Osea told his son he had heard that Shelomam and, presumably, his comrades would be "released" (*ttpṭrn: ithpeel* imperfect second masculine plural of *pṭr*, A3.3:13). Perhaps the reference was to Shelomam's obligation as a soldier, so that Osea consequently informed his son that he would be released from active duty.[47]

No matter what the precise nuance of the verb *pṭr* that Osea intended to use in this context, the tasks imposed upon Shelomam implied separation from his loved ones. This is evident in both the emotions of the father and mother (A3.3:2) and in the father's instructions to his son: "Be a man. Do not WEEP until you come ..." (A3.3:7).[48] Being a soldier under Persian command did not only imply being stationed at one place. On the contrary, the letter from Osea to Shelomam suggests that the soldiers for better or for worse had a considerable mobility within Egypt.

Moreover, there are also examples of scribes with Yahwistic names, and who thus presumably were Judaeans. The scribes apparently drew up legal documents and letters. In addition, in many cases they figured as witnesses to contracts drawn up by other scribes. The latter point suggests that the role of the scribes was more complex and perhaps comparable to that of a modern public

---

44 Quoted from Porten et al., *The Elephantine Papyri in English*, 109.
45 Lindenberger, *Ancient Aramaic and Hebrew Letters*, 26.
46 Bezalel Porten, *Archives from Elephantine: The Life of an Ancient Jewish Military Colony* (Berkeley: University of California Press, 1968), 42.
47 Porten et al., *The Elephantine Papyri in English*, 110 note 32 makes this conjecture.
48 Quoted from Porten et al., *The Elephantine Papyri in English*, 109, cf. Lindenberger, *Ancient Aramaic and Hebrew Letters*, 37, and Takamitsu Muraoka, *An Introduction to Egyptian Aramaic*, LOS III 1 (Münster: Ugarit-Verlag, 2012), 109.

notary.[49] Moreover, as a rule of the thumb the scribal profession was presumably hereditary. For example, on the basis of, first, the conventional use of patronymics when mentioning the scribe who drew up a contract, and secondly, the dates of the contracts, it has been possible to identify a four-generation scribal family active in Elephantine between 460 and 400 BCE.[50]

One of the presumably Judaean[51] scribes who had most success in his career was one called Anani the scribe. Anani may be a hypocoristic form of Ananiah. Anani appears in an official document (A6.2) sent by Arshama, the Persian satrap of Egypt, to one Waḥpremaḥi, who presumably was the Egyptian storekeeper of the satrapal shipyard. The background was that the two Carians who held a boat in hereditary lease from the satrap requested material from the satrapal (or royal) shipyard in order to repair the boat (A6.2:3). On the grounds of their request Arshama in turn instructed in detail how the repair should be undertaken and what should be done with the replaced materials (A6.2:4–21). Towards the conclusion of the written permission the satrap addressed Waḥpremaḥi:

> *kʿt ʾršm kn ʾmr ʾnt ʿbd lqbl znh zy hmrkryʾ ʾmrn kzy śym ṭʿm ʿnny sprʾ bʿl ṭʿm nbwʿqb ktb*
>
> Now, Arsames thus says: "You, do according to this which the accountants say, as order has been issued." Anani the Scribe is Chancellor. Nabuaqab wrote. (A6.2:22–23)[52]

Here, Anani is presented as "the scribe" (*sprʾ*) even though Nabuaqab was the one who actually drew up the document (cf. also A6.2:28). However, more important than being a scribe alone is that Anani was the *bʿl ṭʿm*, "chancellor," or literally "the lord of (the) order." Consequently Anani was the one who saw to it that the order issued by the satrap (*śym ṭʿm*) was actually executed. In other words, at least one presumably Judaean individual held a high position in the Persian administration of Egypt, whose headquarters was in Memphis.[53]

---

49 Eleonora Cussini, "The Career of Some Elephantine and Murašu Scribes," in *In the Shadow of Bezalel: Aramaic, Biblical, and Ancient Near Eastern Studies in Honor of Bezalel Porten*, ed. Alejandro F. Botta, CHANE 60 (Leiden: Brill, 2013), 39–52 (48).

50 Cussini, "The Career," 39–52 (39–40).

51 However, according to Lindenberger, "the name is not distinctively Jewish," Lindenberger, *Ancient Aramaic and Hebrew Letters*, 84.

52 Quoted from Porten et al., *The Elephantine Papyri in English*, 122.

53 According to Herodotus, *Hist.* 3.128, each satrapy was provided with "royal scribes." Moreover, on the basis of letters written to the satrap Arshama we may assume that there were also a group of scribes known as "the scribes of the province" (*spry mdyntʾ*, A6.1:1, 6), cf. Porten, *Archives from Elephantine*, 51.

Although Anani was an official in the *Persian* administration of Egypt, he may nevertheless have kept his *Judaean* identity. The Anani of the above-mentioned written permission from Arshama may be identical with the influential Anani mentioned in another document: A4.3.[54] The latter document is a letter that Mauziah wrote to Jedaniah, Uriah, the priests of YHW the god and the Judaeans. In the letter Mauziah referred to the coming of Hananiah to Egypt (A4.3:7), which probably took place in 419 BCE (cf. A4.1:1–2). Hananiah was the one who regulated the festivals, presumably the Festival of unleavened bread and perhaps also the Passover. Consequently, the letter A4.3 referred to events that took place in the last decades of the fifth century BCE, a period that was troublesome for the Judaean community in Elephantine. In the letter, Mauziah told the Judaean leaders in Elephantine that he had been imprisoned in Abydos. However, he had been "rescued" as the result of the intervention of two servants of Anani, namely Ṣeḥa and Ḥor (A4.3:5). Perhaps this Anani was the Persian bureaucrat who also had the role of Arshama's chancellor (*bʿl ṭʿm*) according to the written permission A6.2. Admittedly, the document A4.3 does not make explicit Anani's reasons for intervening in the imprisonment of Mauziah. Nevertheless, it is tempting to speculate that it had to do with bonds. Did he feel a particular concern for Mauziah since they were both Judaeans? As far as Anani's professional ethics as satrapal scribe and chancellor are concerned, we may speculate whether his intervention in the imprisonment of Mauziah was perhaps a case of professional misconduct.

The sources tell us that there were other Judaean scribes, too. Using Yahwistic names as a criteria for identifying a Judaean, one can identify several Judaean scribes. The three most productive were Nathan son of Ananiah,[55] his son Mauziah[56] and Haggai son of Shemaiah.[57] Presumably, the scribes ran semi-private businesses, offering their services to less literate Judaeans and Aramaeans in Elephantine and Syene when someone needed to have a legal document or a letter drawn up.

---

54 So, e.g., Porten et al., *The Elephantine Papyri in English*, 122 note 76. However, in Lindenberger's view there are no clear grounds for identifying the Anani of A6.2 with the Anani of A4.3, cf. Lindenberger, *Ancient Aramaic and Hebrew Letters*, 84.

55 Nathan drew up B3.1 (document of debt), B2.7 (grant of house), B2.6 (document of wifehood), and B3.3 (document of wifehood).

56 Mauziah son of Nathan son of Ananiah drew up at least B6.4, B2.9 (document of withdrawal), B2.10 (document of withdrawal), B3.5 ("document of a house"), B7.1 (document of satisfaction concerning oath), and B3.8 (document of wifehood).

57 Haggai drew up at least B4.6, B3.4, B3.6, B3.10, B3.11, and B3.12.

The Elephantine documents do not give any insight into the Elephantine scribes' professional consciousness, in particular how they conceived of their own profession in relation to other professions in and around Elephantine. However, the ancient Egyptian didactic work "The instruction of Dua-khety" (also known as "Satire on the Trades") offers a presumably representative image of how scribes in the ancient world in general viewed their own profession.[58] The work is styled as the instruction Dua-khety gave to his son Pepi before the latter started his training at the school for scribes. According to Dua-khety, who wanted to make Pepi love scribedom, "the greatest of all callings," more than his mother, other professions were unpleasant and disreputable. They take too much pain, make you dirty and smelly, require that you have to rise too early or have to stay up too late, or they make you exposed to insect stings. Therefore, Dua-khety concluded: "See, there's no profession without a boss, / Except for the scribe; he is the boss. / Hence if you know writing, / It will do better for you / Than those professions I've set before you. A peasant is not called a man, / Beware of it!"[59]

Judaeans were also involved in the trade of, and possibly also production of, vegetables. A brief message to the woman Islaḥ written on a potsherd is often mentioned because the ostracon inscription suggests that the Judaeans in Elephantine worked on the sabbath.[60] However, in the context of the present chapter the inscription is also relevant because of its relevance for the question of the Judaeans' view on work. The degree of entrepreneurship on the part of the Judaeans involved is noticeable: "Greetings, Islaḥ. Now, behold, legumes I shall dispatch tomorrow. Meet the boat tomorrow on Sabbath. Lest, if they get lost, by the life of YHH, if not (= surely) yo[ur] life I shall take. Do not rely on Meshullemeth and on Shemaiah. Now, exchange for me (= send in return) barley" (D7.16:1–5).[61]

The details concerning how and where these vegetables were produced elude us. However, in some contexts members of the Judaean community were referred to as *mhḥsn*, "hereditary property-holders."[62] Presumably, the *mhḥsn* leased land from the Persian satrap. We may surmise that Judaeans, in turn, used the leased land to grow food, either by themselves, or by means of hired

58 See, e.g., Horst Dietrich Preuss, *Einführung in die alttestamentliche Weisheitsliteratur* (Stuttgart: Kohlhammer, 1987), 14–15.

59 Quoted from "Dua-khety or the Satire of Trade," translated by Miriam Lichtheim (*COS* 1.48:122–125).

60 See Sections 4.4.3.3 and 4.6.4.2, above.

61 Quoted from Porten and Yardeni, *TADAE*, IV: Ostraca & Assorted Inscriptions, 168–169.

62 See Section 2.3.3 above.

manpower. Moreover, in addition there are several inscriptions suggesting that Judaeans held livestock such as asses (B7.3) and sheep, lamb and goats (A2.2, D7.1, D7.8).

Summing up, although most of the Judaeans in fifth-century Egypt were probably soldiers serving the Persian administration, there are also examples of Judaeans working in other "sectors." Unfortunately, the sources do not allow us to tell what the (articulated or unarticulated) anthropology of the Judaeans in Elephantine was like.

6.3.3 The View on Slaves

As a rule of thumb, the existence of slavery was the rule and not the exception in any society in the ancient world. Such was the case also in the Judaean community in Elephantine.[63] A simple yet adequate definition of a slave is that it is a person who is the legal property of another person and thus under the latter's control. Quite a few of the documents from Elephantine deal with slaves, in one way or another.

Before discussing aspects of the Judaeans' view on slaves, a few words should be made about how someone became a slave. Why were people driven into slavery? In the ancient world, there were generally speaking three main reasons for why someone was a slave. First, prisoners of war could be sold as slaves,[64] secondly poor people could be driven into slavery because of debt[65] and thirdly a person could be made a slave as a consequence of a crime he/she had committed.[66] Moreover, regardless for what reason a woman was a slave, her children were slaves, too, unless they were emancipated.[67] However,

63 Alejandro F. Botta, *The Aramaic and Egyptian Legal Traditions at Elephantine: An Egyptological Approach* (London: T&T Clark, 2009), 33–35.

64 Muhammad A. Dandamaev, "Slavery (ANE)," *ABD* 6: 58–62 (59).

65 So, e.g., the Code of Hammurabi §117, which gave approval for a man to sell his wife or children if an obligation was outstanding against him, cf. "The Laws of Hammurabi," translated by Martha Roth (*COS* 2.131:343). However, after three years they should be given their freedom back. Moreover, see 2Kgs 4:1 and Isa 50:1.

66 See, e.g., the Code of Hammurabi §§53–54 (a man who neglected to strengthen his dyke so that the water consequently destroyed farmland; the man would have to restore the grain whose loss he had caused, and if he was unable to do so, he could himself be sold) and §141 (a wife who neglected her duties with respect to the house and her husband could be turned into a slave woman).

67 According to the Code of Hammurabi §170, the children a slave woman had borne a free man did not have equal status with the children borne by the man's first-ranking wife. Only

according to the Code of Hammurabi §175 a child borne as the result of a marriage between a male slave and the daughter of a free man was not a slave.

As far as Elephantine is concerned, a telling expression of a person's status as slave is found in a legal document dealing with the division of an inheritance. In 410 BCE a document was drawn up in Elephantine at the instruction of two brothers, Mahseiah and Jedaniah sons of Nathan (B2.11), or to be more precise, by Mahseiah for his brother Jedaniah (cf. B2.11:3, 6 "you, Jedaniah ...," and B2.11:5 "I, Mahseiah ..."). The brothers agreed upon the division of two out of four slaves they had inherited from their mother Mibtahiah (B2.11:3): the slave lads (*ʿlymyʾ*, B2.11:13) Peṭosiri and Belle:

> And behold, this is the share which came to you as a share, you, Jedaniah: Peṭosiri by name, his mother (being) Tabi, a slave, *ywr/ywd*,[68] 1, branded on his right hand (with) a brand reading (in) Aramaic like this: "(Belonging) to Mibtahiah." And behold, this is the share which came to me as a share, I, Mahseiah: Belle by name, his mother (being) Tabi, a slave, *ywr/ywd*, 1, branded on his right hand (with) a brand reading (in) Aramaic like this: "(Belonging) to Mibtahiah." (B2.11:3–6)[69]

In the document Mahseiah assured the right of his brother and his descendants to Peṭosiri: "You, Jedaniah, have right to Peṭosiri, that slave who came to you as a share, from this day and forever and (so do) your children after you and to whomever you desire you may give (him)" (B2.11:6–7).[70] Legally, Jedaniah did not only "have the right to" [*šlyṭ b-]* the slave lad Peṭosiri. After the two brothers' division of their mother's inheritance the slave *belonged to* Jedaniah as his share: "Yours shall he be [*lk yhwh*] and your children's after you and to whomever you desire you may give him ..." (B2.11:12).[71]

Moreover, according to the document of division, the two brothers Mahesiah and Jedaniah agreed to postpone the division of the two remaining slaves, namely a third slave lad named Lilu and Tabi, the mother of Peṭosiri:

> Moreover, there is Tabi by name, the mother of these lads, and Lilu her son whom we shall not yet divide (between) us. When (the) time will be [*kzy ʿdn yhwh*], we shall divide them

---

if he called them "My children" would they have equal status. However, if the man did not accept them as equal to the children borne by his first-ranking wife, the slave woman and her children should be given their freedom after the death of the man, cf. §171.

68 The meaning of *ywd/ywr* is uncertain. However, it has been suggested that it means "slave mark," *CAL*, s.v. *ywd* (accessed 6 May 2015).

69 Quoted from Porten et al., *The Elephantine Papyri in English*, 201.

70 Quoted from Porten et al., *The Elephantine Papyri in English*, 201.

71 Quoted from Porten et al., *The Elephantine Papyri in English*, 202.

> (between) us and, (each) person his share, we shall take hereditary possession, and a document of our division we shall write between us, without suit. (B2.11:12–14)[72]

Perhaps Lilu was yet too small to be separated from his mother. In any case, one day they would be separated, and no matter how and when, their owner and his heirs would own them "forever" (*ʿd ʿlm*, B2.11:7).

In light of the view on slaves emerging from the legal document drawn up by Mahseiah and Jedaniah, it comes as no surprise that a slave's value was measurable. Having that said, none of the known Elephantine documents refers to the sale of a slave.[73] Therefore, we do not know what the prices were. However, the price was presumably dependent upon things such as the age, gender, health, skills and so on of the slave in question. On the basis of comparative material from Babylonia, Porten has estimated that an average Judaean household in Elephantine belonging to the Judaean garrison would have to use between two and four months' payment of silver to buy a single slave. In other words, the price of a slave would be somewhere between twenty-four and forty-eight shekels of silver.[74]

The Judaeans' view on slaves is also indirectly attested in B3.1, a document of loan from 456 BCE. In an IOU one Jehoḥen daughter of Meshullach, "lady of Elephantine the fortress," acknowledged her debts to Meshullam son of Zaccur, "a Judaean of the fortress of Elephantine." Jehoḥen accepted the conditions under which she had borrowed the silver. The loan of four shekels of silver Meshullam had given Jehoḥen was meant for a year, and the parties agreed upon a monthly interest of five percent (cf. B3.1:4–7).

Particularly relevant here are the measures that would be taken in the event that Jehoḥen defaulted on the loan. If a second year occurred without Jehoḥen having repaid Meshullam, he (or his children) had as creditor(s) the right to take as pledge anything that belonged to Jehoḥen until she had repaid all the borrowed silver and the accumulated interest. In her IOU Jehoḥen listed her be-

---

72 Quoted from Porten et al., *The Elephantine Papyri in English*, 202.

73 A possible exception is B3.3:13, according to which Meshullam is obliged to pay Ananiah five karsh of silver (= fifty shekels) if he reclaims the slave child Pilti.

74 Noting that we do not know how much the Elephantine soldier received per month in silver, Porten uses an assumed minimal annual income of one hundred and forty-four shekels for a family of three. See Porten, *Archives from Elephantine*, 73–76. According to Muhammad A. Dandamaev, the average price for a slave in Babylonia was a little bit higher. In the Neo-Babylonian period, an adult male slave would cost an average of fifty to sixty shekels and a slave woman a little less. In the Persian period, the prices for slaves gradually rose to about one and a half times their previous level, cf. Dandamaev, "Slavery (ANE)," 58–62 (60).

longings thus: "... house of bricks, silver or gold, bronze or iron, slave or handmaiden, barley, emmer – or any food which you will find (belonging) to me ..." (B3.1:9 – 10).[75] In other words, "slave and handmaiden" (*ʿbd wʾmh*) were considered as her property, together with real estate, chattel and food.

Moreover, according to the IOU, Jehoḥen's children would inherit her debt and the obligation to repay it to Meshullam and his heirs (B3.1:14 – 20). However, in light of the practice of debt enslavement attested elsewhere in the ancient Near East, also another feature is worth noting in the loan contract. The contract does *not* open up for the creditor taking the children of the debtor as pledge.[76] In other words, there is no mention of any possible enslavement of Jehoḥen's children should she default on the loan.

6.3.3.1 The Status of Children Borne by a Slave

A child borne by a female slave would inherit his/her mother's status as slave. This was the case with Peṭosiri, Belle and Lilu, the children of Tabi, who were mentioned in the document of division between the brothers Mahseiah and Jedaniah (B2.11). This was also the case even when the father of the slave child was a free (Judaean) man. Several legal documents from the family archive of Ananiah son of Azariah (B3.1– 13), who was a servitor (*lḥn*) of YHW, show this.

In 449 BCE Ananiah drew up a so-called document of wifehood, that is, a marriage contract, addressing Meshullam son of Zaccur, the owner of the handmaiden Tamet (B3.3).[77] Because Meshullam was her master, he also functioned as the bride-giver in the marriage contract, a position that a father normally would have had if the bride had been a free woman.[78] The contract includes a clause concerning the handmaiden Tamet's son Pilti (*plṭy*):[79] "And I, Meshullam, tomorrow or (the) next day, shall not be able to reclaim Pilti from under your heart unless you expel his mother Tamet. And if I do reclaim him from you I shall give Anani silver 5 karsh" (B3.3:13 – 14).[80] The document does not indicate who Pilti's father was. However, in other (and chronologically later) legal documents drawn up at the order of Ananiah, Ananiah referred to Pilti and his sister

75 Quoted from Porten et al., *The Elephantine Papyri in English*, 204.
76 In contrast to, e. g., the Code of Hammurabi §117, 2Kgs 4:1, and Isa 50:1.
77 In other documents, her name is written Tapemet (daughter of Patou), cf. B3.12:3; B3.6:2, 11, 18, and Tapememet, cf. B3.12:33.
78 This was the case when Mahseiah married his daughter Mibtahiah to the royal builder Esḥor son of Djeḥo, cf. B2.6.
79 In B3.7:11, a document drawn up in 420 BCE, his is called Pelatiah (*plṭyh*).
80 Quoted from Porten et al., *The Elephantine Papyri in English*, 212.

Jehoishma as “my children whom you [i. e. Tamet] bore me” (B3.5:17, 18) or as “Pelatiah my son and [Jehoi]shma my daughter” (B3.7:11). In other words, Pilti was borne out of wedlock but his biological father was no doubt Ananiah, the man who married his mother, the handmaiden Tamet.[81]

In light of this, then, it is noteworthy that Pilti was not borne free but as a slave. Even after Ananiah (his biological father) and Meshullam, the master of the handmaiden Tamet, had agreed upon the conditions of the marriage, the son Pilti remained partly under the control of Meshullam, in spite of the fact that the marriage had been legally formalised. Admittedly, the clause restricted Meshullam's power over the child.[82] Nevertheless, the child would return to his mother's owner in the event that Ananiah sent his mother away; he would not continue to stay with his father.

Moreover, Meshullam's control over his (former) handmaiden Tamet and her children continued even after the former had manumitted the latter. In a so-called document of withdrawal written in 427 BCE, the above-mentioned Judaean, Meshullam son of Zaccur, set up the terms under which his handmaiden Tamet (here: written Tapemet) and her daughter Jehoishma, whom she had borne to Ananiah the servitor of YHW, were to be manumitted (B3.6):

> *ʾnh ʿštt lky bḥyy ʾzt šbqtky bmwty wšbqt lyhyšmʿ šmh brtky zy ylty ly*
>
> I thought of you in my lifetime. (To be) free I released you [i. e. Tapemet/Tamet] at my death and I released Jeh(o)ishma by name your daughter, whom you bo(r)e me. (B3.6:3–5)[83]

Jehoishma's biological father was Ananiah but her mother being a slave with the inscription *lmšlm* (“To Meshullam,” B3.6:3) branded on her right hand resulted in a double set of fathers:

---

81 In B3.12:11, in a document drawn up in 402 BCE, Tamet (written: Tapemet/Tapememet) is referred to as the one who was *prypt zy mšlm br zkwr.* Jan Tavernier understands the word *prypt* as a rendition of the Old Persian *Fryapati-, “chief of the beloved,” cf. Jan Tavernier, *Iranica in the Achaemenid Period (ca. 550–330 B.C.): Linguistic Study of Old Iranian Proper Names and Loanwords, Attested in Non-Iranian Texts*, OLA 158 (Leuven: Peeters, 2007), 422, s.v. *Fryapati-, i.e. according to Bezalel, “chief concubine,” cf. Porten et al., *The Elephantine Papyri in English*, 247 note 23. An Aramaic counterpart of that expression is given later on in the same document. In B3.12:24 she is referred to as *zy hwt gwʾ lmšlm br zkwr.* The noun *gwʾ* is probably a derivation of the adverb *gwʾh*, “inside.” Consequently, Bezalel Porten translates “who was the inner one of Meshullam son of Zaccur.” In either case, it seems clear that Tamet had a special position in Meshullam's household before she was married to Ananiah.

82 In the Aramaic text the clause “And if I do reclaim him from you I shall give Anani silver 5 karsh” has been added above the line.

83 Quoted from Porten et al., *The Elephantine Papyri in English*, 222.

- a biological and to some extent also a legal one (Ananiah), who already some seven years earlier in a legal document spoke of her as his daughter (cf. B3.5:17–18), and in addition
- an adoptive, legal father (Meshullam, the master of her mother).

In any case, in the document B3.6 Meshullam guaranteed that Tapemet and her daughter would be manumitted after his death. The manumission was irrevocable (B3.6:5–7), and Meshullam stipulated an exceptionally high penalty for anyone of his family members or business partners who violated his intention by attempting to re-enslave Tapemet and her daughter (B3.6:7–8). Whoever might "stand up against" Tapemet or her daughter had to pay fifty karsh, that is five hundred shekels, of silver to Tapemet.

Furthermore, Meshullam expressed the act of manumission by means of the following emancipation formulary:

> ... and you are released from the shade to the sun [*w'nty šbyqh mn ṭl' lsmš'*] and (so is) Jeh(o)ishma your daughter and another person does not have right to you and to Jeh(o)ishma your daughter but you are released to God[84] [*w'nty šbyqh l'lh'*]. (B3.6:8–10)[85]

Regardless of what the background of these two expressions was, and moreover, no matter how exactly they functioned,[86] the document of manumission continued with a declaration spoken by the to-be-manumitted persons themselves:

> And said Tapemet and Jeh(o)ishma her daughter: We, he (ERROR FOR: we) shall serve you, (a)s a son or daughter supports his father, in your lifetime. And at your death we shall support Zaccur your single son ... like a son who supports his father, as we shall have been doing for you in your lifetime. (B3.6:11–13)[87]

In other words, in reality the manumission implied that Tapemet and Jehoishma ceased being slaves and instead became Meshullam's adoptive daughters and, consequently, the adoptive sisters of Meshullam's son Zaccur.[88] Therefore, the manumission did not result in the total freedom of Tapemet and Jehoishma. After the death of their former master, they were continuously obliged to serve (*plḥ*) his son in his as well as their own lifetime. In the event that they refused to fulfil their support of Meshullam and his son, they accepted that a severe pen-

84 Or: "the god."
85 Quoted from Porten et al., *The Elephantine Papyri in English*, 222.
86 See the discussion on the emancipation formularies in Section 6.3.3.2 below.
87 Quoted from Porten et al., *The Elephantine Papyri in English*, 223.
88 The sources are silent about Jehoishma's brother Pilti. Was he ever manumitted, too?

alty—the payment of fifty karsh (= five hundred shekels) of silver (B3.6:13 – 15) to their former master or his son—would be imposed upon them.

Yet another document (B3.8, a marriage contract from 420 BCE) clearly demonstrates that Meshullam's son Zaccur as a matter of fact *did* continue to exercise his control over his adoptive sister Jehoishma, probably after his father's death. Formally, the marriage contract is between Zaccur son of Meshullam and one Ananiah son of Haggai (not to be confused with Jehoishma's biological father Ananiah son of Azariah, the servitor of YHW). The latter had asked for the hand of Jehoishma: "I came to y[ou in] your [hou]se and asked you for the lady Jehoishma by name, your sister, for wifehood and you gave her to me. She is my wife and I am [her] husband from this day forever" (B3.8:3 – 4).[89] So, in the marriage contract it was Zaccur who, in the capacity of being Jehoishma's adoptive brother (cf. "Jehoishma ... your sister," B3.8:4 – 5), acted as the bride-giver. This is remarkable given that Jehoishma's biological father must have been alive when she was married to Ananiah son of Haggai. A series of legal documents from the last years of the fifth century BCE demonstrate that the biological father, Ananiah son of Azariah, was alive as late as in the period between 404 and 402 BCE.[90]

In 404 BCE Jehoishma's biological father Ananiah (now written Anani) son of Azariah drew up a will according to which Jehoishma would be bequeathed a part of his house in Elephantine (B3.10). After having described the house, its boundaries and the associated rights that Jehoishma also would inherit (e.g., the right to use a stairway for ascending and descending, cf. B3.10:3 – 15), Ananiah wrote:

> This ... house whose boundaries and measurements are written and whose words are written in this document – I, Anani, gave it to Jehoishma my daughter at my death in love. Just as she supported me while I was old of days – I was unable (to use) my hands and she supported me – also I gave (it) to her at my death. (B3.10:15 – 18)[91]

Jehoishma had already been granted a right to use the property (usufruct) in a document written in 420 BCE (B3.7), but she did not yet have the full title to it. According to the bequest B3.10 drawn up in 404 BCE it belonged to her biological father, but the title would be transferred to her after his death. However, in 402, some two years later, Ananiah undid the stipulations of his will as of 404 BCE and gave Jehoishma the full title to the house "from this day forever"

89 Quoted from Porten et al., *The Elephantine Papyri in English*, 227 – 228.
90 See B3.10 (dated 404 BCE), B3.11, and B3.12 (both dated 402 BCE).
91 Quoted from Porten et al., *The Elephantine Papyri in English*, 238.

(B3.11:16 – 17) as an after-gift for her dowry. Eventually, later the same year, Anani and his wife Tamet (written Tapemet/Tapememet) sold the remaining part of the house to Anani son of Haggai, their son-in-law who was married to Jehoishma (B3.12).

As for the question of the status of the emancipated slave Jehoishma, it is noteworthy that her obligations towards her adoptive family (her former master Meshullam and his son Zaccur) obviously did not restrain her from taking care of her biological father in his old days. The biological father Anani acknowledged that Jehoishma had "supported me" (B3.10:17 *sbltny*), using the same verb that Jehoishma and her mother Tamet used in the declaration they gave in 427 BCE when accepting the terms under which Meshullam manumitted them (cf. B3.6:13 – 14).

6.3.3.2 Manumission and Adoption

We have just seen how the slave Tamet and Jehoishma, the daughter she had with her husband, the free Judaean man Ananiah, were manumitted by their master Meshullam (B3.6, dated 427 BCE). The condition under which they were set free "from the shade to the sun" and were "released to the god" (cf. B3.6:8 – 10) was that they became adoptive children of the master.

Also another document involving Meshullam's family attests to the close connection between manumission and adoption: B3.9 (dated 416 BCE). Formally, the document was drawn up at the behest of one Uriah son of Mahseiah. The document presents itself as the words that Uriah spoke to Zaccur son of Meshullam in the fortress of Syene in the presence of (literally: "before") Vidranga the Guardian of the Seventh, the Troop Commander of Syene (B3.9:1 – 3):

> Jedaniah by name son of Takhoi, [you]r la[d] whom you gave me and a document you wrote for me about him – I shall not be able, I, Uriah, or son or daughter of mine, brother or sister of mine, or man of mine, he (shall not be able) to press him (into) slave(ry). My son he shall be. I, or son or daughter of mine, or man of mine, or another individual do not have right to brand him. I shall not be able – I, or son or daughter of mine, brother or sister of mine, or man of mine – we (shall not be able) to stand up to make him a s[lave] or brand him. (B3.9:3 – 7)[92]

Similar to the manumission of Tamet and Pilti, this document is also silent about any payment that may have led to the manumission. When Uriah mentions "the document you [i.e. Zaccur] wrote for me about him," he may have been referring

92 Quoted from Porten et al., *The Elephantine Papyri in English*, 234.

to a document of withdrawal in which the agreed-upon sum was mentioned. However, the main thrust of Uriah's document was to ensure that neither he nor any of his kin would ever attempt to enslave the "lad" (*ʿlym*ʾ) Jedaniah again. On the contrary, Uriah expressed his adoption of the boy three times in the document:

- "my son he shall be" (*bry yhwh*, B3.9:5),
- "my son shall he be likewise" (*bry yhwh ʾpm*, B3.9:8), and
- "and an individual does not have right to brand him or make him a slave, but my son he shall be" (*wʾnš lʾ šlyṭ lmšnth wlmʿbdh ʿbd lhn bry yhwh*, B3.9:8–9).[93]

The importance of the act of adoption is evident in, at least, two features. First, as mentioned, Uriah's adoption took place under the auspices of the highest-ranked local Persian official. Second, the document was witnessed by no fewer than eight witnesses.

It is not possible to say why the manumission of Jedaniah was apparently a public case, whereas the manumission of Tamet and Jehoishma seemed to have been a private affair. Was the manumission of Jedaniah of a more finite and absolute nature than was the case with Tamet and Jehoishma? After all, in the case of the two women, they were adopted by the one and the same person who manumitted them, Meshullam. In contrast, in the case of the slave lad Jedaniah, the manumitter (Zaccur) was different from the adopter (Uriah).

The slave lad Jedaniah's filiation is indicated by means of metronymics and not patronymics. He is the son of Tahkoi (or: Taḥo/Taḥwa, *tḥw*ʾ[94]). No father is mentioned but the fact that he had a Yahwistic theomorphic name suggests that he was a houseborne slave,[95] reared as a Judaean in Zaccur's household. Strictly speaking, in the document attesting his adoption, his master Zaccur was presented as "an Aramaean of Syene" (B3.9:2–3, cf. also B3.8:2). However, Zaccur's father Meshullam presented himself at least once as "a Judaean of Elephantine the fortress of the detachment of Iddinnabu" (B3.6:2). Neither in the case of the family of Meshullam and Zaccur was there any problem with such a double identity.

---

93 Compare the Code of Hammurabi §170, according to which a father my legally adopt the children his maid servant has borne him by saying thus: "My children."

94 The word *tḥw*ʾ is a feminine Egyptian name, perhaps a variant spelling of *tḥh* (Taḥa), cf. B8.4:16, 20.

95 In the documents B3.11, B3.12, and B3.13 a person called "Nahum the houseborne" (*br byrt*ʾ, literally "son of the house") is listed among the witnesses. The designation and the lack of patronymics suggest that Nahum was an emancipated slave.

Summing up the discussion of the status of children borne by slaves, the documents of the Ananiah family archive discussed above seem to indicate the following: A child borne by a slave woman was automatically a slave. Also a child borne by a slave woman sired by a free Judaean man was automatically a slave. There is nothing in the sources suggesting that the children borne as the result of a sexual union between a(n Egyptian) slave woman and a free Judaean man was not a slave; the case of Pilti/Pelatiah and Jehoishma suggests otherwise. Moreover, a slave could be manumitted. The manumission could be accompanied by an adoption; the former master's family became the adoptive family of the manumitted slave. However, the manumitted slave continued to have special responsibilities towards the adoptive family. Likewise, the former master continued to have certain privileges and responsibilities over his emancipated slave. Consequently, a manumitted slave was not entirely free. On the contrary, he or she held an intermediate status of being neither slave nor entirely free. A manumitted slave continued to be bound by a legal relationship to his/her former master.

It is worth noting that the sources for the Judaeans' view on slaves do not contain any traces of a special religious legislation on slavery. The legal regulation was of a contractual nature between two parties. In the case of Tamet and Jehoishma, the one party to the contract was the manumitter and the other was the to-be-emancipated slaves. However, in the case of the slave lad Jedaniah, the other party to the contract was the adoptive father.

6.3.3.3 The Background of the Emancipation Formularies

The Judaean slave owner Meshullam son of Zaccur released his handmaiden Tamet (who was already married to Ananiah son of Azariah) and her daughter Jehoishma using three formulaic expressions:

- "(to be) free I released you" (*ʾzt šbqtky*, B3.6:4),
- "and you are released from the shade to the sun" (*wʾnty šbyqh mn ṭlʾ lsmšʾ*, B3.6:8–9), and
- "you are released to God/the god" (*wʾnty šbyqh lʾlhʾ*, B3.6:10).

Meshullam's act of manumission followed legal precedents that were not of a particularly Judaean origin. To begin with, in the first formulary he (or strictly speaking: his scribe Haggai, cf. B3.6:15–16) used the Persian loanword *ʾzt*, "free (i.e. not a slave),"[96] perhaps because there was no corresponding term in

96 Tavernier, *Iranica in the Achaemenid Period*, 404, s.v. *Āzāta-.

Aramaic.[97] Moreover, there are examples of Old Babylonian manumission documents with phraseology partly coinciding with the one found in Meshullam's document. An example is a document from the time of Hammurabi about the manumission of Ištar-ummi and Aḫâtâni, the children of the slave woman Innabatum daughter of Pûr-Sin:

> Urkunde. Ištar-ummi und Aḫâtâni sind die Kinder der Innabatum. Innabatum, die Tochter der Pûr-Sin, hat sie dem Šamaš gereinigt. Solange Innabatum lebt, werden Ištar-ummi und Aḫâtâni sie erhalten. Nach dem Tode der Innabatum, ihrer Mutter, hat unter den Kindern des Aḫušina niemand irgendwelche Ansprüche auf sie. Bei Šamaš, Aja, bei Marduk und Abil-Sin schworen sie.[98]

In this document, which is attested by six male witnesses and twelve female witnesses, the scribe referred to Shamash twice. First, the children that should be emancipated after the death of their mother, were—in one way or another—devoted to him ("Innabatum ... hat sie [i.e. the children] dem Šamaš gereinigt," i.e. " Innabatum ... has purified them [i.e. the children] for Shamash"). Second, the manumission was attested by an oath sworn to i.a. Shamash and his consort Aya. Another document from the same period also connects manumission with devotion to Shamash. The girl to be released from slavery was Amat-Ištar daughter of Kunutum:

> Sklavin Amat-Ištar ist die Tochter der Kunutum. Kunutum und Muḫaddi(tum) haben sie gereinigt. Dem Šamaš und der Aja ... haben sie sie geschenkt. Under den Kindern des Šamaš-idinnam, ob männlich, ob weiblich, hat niemand irgendwelche Ansprüche auf Amat-Ištar. Bei Šamaš, Marduk und Sin-muballiṭ schworen sie.[99]

Neither in this case did the children of the former master have any future rights to the manumitted Amat-Ištar. Her mother Kunutum and Muḫaddi(tum) (her father?) had *devoted* her to Shamash and his consort Aya.

Returning to Elephantine, it is reasonable to assume that the emancipation formularies found in Meshullam's document, historically speaking, were deriva-

---

97 Muffs, *Studies in the Aramaic Legal Papyri*, 40 note 1. See also Porten et al., *The Elephantine Papyri in English*, 222 note 9.

98 Quoted from Josef Kohler and Arthur Ungnad, *Hammurabi's Gesetz*, vol. III: Übersetzte Urkunden, Erläuterungen (Leipzig: Pfeiffer, 1909), 12 (no. 27). The document is attested by six male and twelve female witnesses.

99 Quoted from Josef Kohler and Arthur Ungnad, *Hammurabi's Gesetz*, vol. V: Übersetzte Urkunden, Verwaltungsregister, Inventare, Erläuterungen (Leipzig: Pfeiffer, 1911), 4 (no. 1090). The document is attested by five male and four female witnesses. See also Porten, *Archives from Elephantine*, 220 note 59.

tions of chronologically earlier formularies. Reminiscences of the connection between the god Shamash and the emancipation of slaves are found in the phrase "and you are released from the shade to the sun" (*w'nty šbyqh mn ṭl' lsmš'*, B3.6:8–9). However, unlike the indeed much older Mesopotamian manumission documents quoted above, the word *smš'* does not seem to refer to a deity in this particular context since it is contrasted with "the shade" (*ṭl'*). However, in the case of Meshullam's document, the manumission is not entirely "secular." The handmaiden Tamet was indeed released "to God/the god" (B3.6:10).

6.3.3.4 The Function of the Emancipation Formularies

No matter how intriguing the possible historical background of the emancipation formularies are, the historical background does not necessarily have any bearing on how the formularies actually *functioned* in fifth-century BCE Elephantine. The formularies may offer a glimpse of how fifth-century BCE Judaeans conceived of slavery.

I will make a few points. First, at the outset the formularies appear to be examples of performative speech, that is, speech acts, or words that bring about a new reality. It seems that the words in question, at the moment they were spoken, constituted a new legal status for the individuals spoken to by investing them with the status of being free. However, one of the basic terms of the manumissions in Elephantine discussed above was this change of legal status would take place first *after* the death of the manumitter. In light of this, as well as in light of the slaves' obligation to *continue to serve* the son of the manumitter, the manumission formularies were not effecting manumission in the sense of *ex opere operato*. On the contrary, the effect of the formularies were dependent upon the doer (the manumitter) and the prospective emancipated slave, namely, the extent to which they acted in conformity with the obligations imposed upon them.

Second, the particular phrase "from the shade to the sun" signalled how a free man conceived of the slave's status. Irrespective of whether the noun "the sun" historically was reminiscent of chronologically earlier emancipation formularies according to which the to-be-freed slave was devoted "to [the god] Shamash," the formularies suggest that a free Judaean—no surprise—did not hold the existence of being someone's slave in high regard. Being a slave was a "shadowy" life.

Third, although the formularies were performative in the sense that they caused a new reality (though only under certain conditions and with a deferred effect) they nevertheless did *not* point to a religious aspect of the manumission that was clearly distinguishable as *typical Judaean*. Neither do they suggest that the manumission took place in, say, a temple (i.e. the temple of YHW). On the contrary, the manumission of Tamet and her daughter took place in the presence of witnesses (B3.6:16–17), and the adoption of the slave lad Jedaniah (which was probably accompanied by a foregoing manumission) took place in the presence of the local Persian official (B3.9:3). Historically speaking, the manumission formularies were probably descendants of chronologically earlier formularies in which the religious aspect was much more tangible (cf. idea of the emancipated slave being devoted to Shamash). However, emancipation documents from later periods illustrate the persistence of formulaic expressions involving deities. Greek manumission documents from the Roman and Byzantine periods continue to include phrases similar to those found in B3.6. Among the many Oxyrhynchus papyri, there were a handful of Roman-period manumission documents. According to them a slave to be emancipated was manumitted "under the sanction of Zeus, the Earth, the Sun."[100] The (semi-)divine emancipation formularies persisted over several centuries, if not even millennia. This suggests that the (semi-)divine emancipation formularies found in the Greek as well as the Aramaic documents were "frozen relics." Therefore, the emancipation formularies cannot be taken as hints of a "liturgy of manumission" used when a slave was manumitted within the Judaean community at Elephantine.

100 ὑπὸ Δία Γῆν Ἥλιον, thus P. Oxy. IV 722:6 (from 91 or 107 CE), cf. Bernard P. Grenfell and Arthur S. Hunt, *The Oxyrhynchus Papyri*, vol. IV: Edited with Translations and Notes (London: Published for The British Academy by The Egypt Exploration Society, 1904), 199–202 (no. 722), and P. Oxy. III 494:5 (from 156 CE), cf. Bernard P. Grenfell and Arthur S. Hunt, *The Oxyrhynchus Papyri*, vol. III: Edited with Translations and Notes (London: Published for The British Academy by The Egypt Exploration Society, 1903), 201–206 (no. 494), and additional references in Porten et al., *The Elephantine Papyri in English*, 439 note 8. However, in a papyrus from Byzantine-period Elephantine (*Papyrus Edmondstone*, dated 355 CE), the woman Aurelia Terouterou daughter of Pasmes manumitted her slaves *without* referring to Helios, cf. Grenfell and Hunt, *The Oxyrhynchus Papyri*, IV: Edited with Translations and Notes, 202–203, here quoted from Porten, *The Elephantine Papyri in English*, 438–440:

> (I) have released you as free (persons) under [ὑπὸ] earth and sky, in accordance with piety toward t[h]e all-merciful God, from now for all time ...

When the above-quoted manumission document was written Christianity was the dominating religion. This may explain why the sun/Shamash/Helios is no longer present.

6.3.4 The View on Gender and Family Matters

Was it a man's world? From a modern perspective, a society in the ancient world was patriarchal in the sense that it was as a rule of thumb controlled by men. No surprise that this was also the case with the Judaean community in Elephantine. However, the situation was nevertheless much more nuanced. The available legal documents regulating business and family matters show that (free) Elephantine Judaean women were in fact to some degree emancipated (using an anachronistic term) and, to some extent, on equal terms with their male relatives.

When read in isolation from the Elephantine Judaean legal documents, the official letters of the so-called Jedaniah communal archive from the last decades of the fifth century BCE create the impression that the Judaean community in Elephantine indeed was a man's world. The official letters were written either to or by Judaean men of Elephantine. In the so-called Passover letter Hananiah addresses his "brothers Jedaniah and the Judaean garrison" (A4.1:1, 10). Other letters were written to "Jedaniah, Mauziah, Uriah and the garrison" (A4.2), "Jedaniah, Uriah and the priests of YHW the God, Mattan son of Jashobiah (and) Berechiah son of [PN]" (A4.3). Moreover, the official letters sent from the Judaean community were written by men, too. The letter to the governors of Judah and Samaria were written by "Jedaniah and his colleagues the priests" (A4.7 par.). And the draft letter to the anonymous official concerning the offerings in the rebuilt temple of YHW (A4.10) was authored by Jedaniah son of Gemariah, Mauzi son of Nathan, Shemaiah son of Haggai, Hosea son of Jathom, and Hosea son of Nattun, all titled Syenian hereditary-property-holders (*mhḥsn*) in Elephantine.[101]

6.3.4.1 The Marriage

In the above-mentioned texts, women were neither writers nor recipients.[102] However, women and their relationship to their husbands are the focus of attention in a particular type of document: the marriage contract, or as it was called in Aramaic, "document of wifehood" (*spr ʾntw*).[103] Three more or less extant marriage contracts are known, as well as a few fragments:[104]

101 See Section 2.3.3 above.

102 However, in the petition to Bagavahya, the Judaean leaders of Elephantine referred to their wives and children. Since the destruction of the temple of YHW they had participated, together with their husbands, in the rites of mourning (A4.7:15, 20–21 par.).

103 See Botta, *The Aramaic and Egyptian Legal Traditions*, 59–60.

104 B6.4; B6.3; B6.1; and B6.2.

- the contract between Esḥor the royal builder and Mahseiah concerning Mibtahiah, the latter's daughter (B2.6, from 449 BCE),
- the contract between Ananiah son of Azariah, a servitor of YHW and Meshullam son of Zaccur, concerning Tamet, the latter's slave (B3.3, dated 449 BCE), and
- the contract between Ananiah son of Haggai and Zaccur son of Meshullam, concerning Jehoishma, the latter's former slave and current adoptive sister (B3.8, dated 420 BCE).

The contracts have in common that the marriage is understood as a contractual agreement between the groom on the one hand and the bride-giver, that is, the head of the household of the bride, on the other. In none of the legal documents does the bride herself appear to play an active part in the marriage process.

The three marriage contracts mentioned above differ in the sense that the women did not have one and the same legal status when the contract was drawn up. Mibtahiah[105] was a free woman (Mahseiah's daughter [*brh*]), Tamet a handmaiden (*'mh*) and Jehoishma an emancipated slave and now Zaccur's sister (*'ḥh*). Moreover, the differences in terms of socio-economic status between the women is also reflected in the pecuniary aspects of the marriage contracts.[106] Nevertheless, all three documents show that several steps were taken prior to the conclusion of the marriage:[107]

a. the bridegroom's request,
b. the bridegroom's declaration,
c. the payment of the *mohar* (*mhr*), i.e. the bride-price or marriage-price, and
d. the drawing up of a contract.

The bridegroom's request for the bride (*a*) was expressed by means of a more or less standardised formulation, requesting that the named woman would be given as wife. The three contracts offer more or less similar formulations:

'nh [']tyt bytk lmntn ly lbrtk mpṭḥyh l'ntw

105 The name appears in two forms, Mibtahiah and Miptahiah, seemingly referring to the same individual.

106 See B3.3, where the bridegroom did *not* refer to the payment of a *mohar* (bride-price) for the handmaiden Tamet.

107 In the following, cf. Reuven Yaron, *Introduction to the Law of the Aramaic Papyri* (Oxford: Clarendon, 1961), 44–50.

> I [c]ame to your house (and asked you) to give me your daughter Mipta(h)iah for wifehood. (B2.6:3)[108]
>
> *ʾnh ʾtyt ʿlyk lmntn ly ltmt šmh zy ʾmtk lʾntw*
>
> I came to you (and asked you) to give me Tamet by name, who is your handmaiden, for wifehood. (B3.3:3)[109]
>
> *ʾnh ʾtyt ʿlyk bbytk wšʾlt mnk lnšn yhwyšmʿ šmh ʾḥtk lntw*
>
> I came to y[ou in] your [hou]se and asked you for the lady Jehoishma by name, your sister, for wifehood. (B3.8:3)[110]

The bridegroom's declaration (*b*) was also a more or less fixed formulation. On the bottom line, he affirmed that the woman was his wife and that he himself was her husband forever:

> *hy ʾntty wʾnh bʿlh mn ywmʾ znh wʿd ʿlm*
>
> She is my wife and I am her husband from this day and forever. (B2.6:4; B3.3:3–4; B3.8:4)[111]

On the basis of this formal declaration it is evident that the Judaeans considered the marriage to be ideally a lifelong relationship. However, at the same time the contracts had a realistic approach to the subject in question. Each one of the contracts contain detailed regulations to be put into effect in the event that one of the spouses dissolved the marriage by divorcing the partner or by taking a second wife/husband.

The payment of the *mohar*, that is, the bride-price or marriage-price, to the head of the bride's household (*c*) was the next step the bridegroom made. In the case of the woman Mibtahiah, the bridegroom paid five shekels: "I gave you (as) *mohar* for your daughter Miptahiah: [silver], 5 shekels by the stone (-weight)s of [the] king. It came into you and your heart was satisfied herein" (B2.6:4–6).[112]

In the case of the *mohar* Ananiah son of Haggai paid to Zaccur for Jehoishma, who was an emancipated slave and the latter's adoptive sister, the corre-

---

108 Quoted from Porten et al., *The Elephantine Papyri in English*, 179.

109 Quoted from Porten et al., *The Elephantine Papyri in English*, 210.

110 Quoted from Porten et al., *The Elephantine Papyri in English*, 227.

111 Quoted from Porten et al., *The Elephantine Papyri in English*, 179, 210, 228. In the case of B3.8 there is an additional short clause between the bridegroom's request and his declaration: "and you gave her [= Jehoishma] to me [= Ananiah son of Haggai]," B3.8:3–4.

112 Quoted from Porten et al., *The Elephantine Papyri in English*, 179.

sponding sum was slightly higher, one karsh (= ten shekels), cf. B3.8:4.5.[113] However, Ananiah son of Azariah did not mention any payment of *mohar* to Meshullam for the handmaiden Tamet (cf. B3.3:4).

Historically speaking, the *mohar* was probably originally a bride-price in the real sense of the word, that is, a sum the groom paid to his (future) father-in-law as compensation for the latter's loss of his daughter.[114] However, more important than the possible historical background is how the payment of *mohar* actually functioned in Elephantine. For, both in the case of Mibtahiah and Jehoishma it seems clear that he who gave away the bride actually added the *mohar* to the bride's dowry that she brought with her into the marriage. As far as the contract involving Mibtahiah is concerned, the arrangements that were to be put into effect in the event that her husband divorced her (the technical term was *śnʾ*, literally "to hate"[115]) show that the *mohar* in the end belonged to her:

> Tomorrow or (the) next day, should Esḥor stand up in an assembly and say: "I hated my [wif]e Miptahiah," her *mohar* [will be] lost and all that she brought in in her hand she shall take out, from straw to string, on one day in one stroke, and go away wherever she desires, without suit or without process. (B2.6:26–29)[116]

The clause mentions *mhrh*, presumably "her *mohar*,"[117] which the repudiated wife was presumably entitled to keep together with the dowry (literally: "all that she brought in in her hands," *kl zy hnʿlt bydh*, cf. B2.6:6; B3.3:4; B3.8:5).[118]

113 A possible explanation for this is that Miptahiah had already been married before she got married to Esḥor. B2.4 (cf. B2.3) demonstrates that she was married to Jezaniah son of Uriah in 549 BCE, i.e. some ten years before the document B2.6 was drawn up.
114 For instance, the marriage laws in the Code of Hammurabi presuppose that a "bridewealth" (Akkadian: *terḫatum*) was given by the groom to the bride's father, cf. §159–161 in "The Laws of Hammurabi," translated by Martha Roth (*COS* 2.131:345).
115 See Alejandro F. Botta, "Hated by the Gods and your Spouse: Legal Use of *śnʾ* in Elephantine and its Ancient Near Eastern Context," in *Law and Religion in the Eastern Mediterranean: From Antiquity to Early Islam*, ed. Anselm C. Hagedorn and Reinhard Gregor Kratz (Oxford: Oxford University Press, 2013): 105–128, who argues convincingly for the traditional interpretation that *śnʾ* cannot mean anything but divorce. The backdrop is the claim that the verb does not carry the legal meaning of divorce but of demotion in status, cf. Porten et al., *The Elephantine Papyri in English*, 182 note 42, or that the verb "heralds separation, marks a break but not the marriage's dissolution" so that it is "a preliminary stage *before* the separation," cf. Hélène Nutkowicz, "Concerning the Verb *śnʾ* in Judaeo-Aramaic Contracts from Elephantine," *JSS* 52 (2007): 211–225 (225).
116 Quoted from Porten et al., *The Elephantine Papyri in English*, 183.
117 The pronominal suffix *-h* can also denote the third person masculine ("his"). This understanding is reflected in how *mhrh yʾbd* is translated in Muffs, *Studies in the Aramaic Legal Papyri*,

Likewise, the marriage contract involving Jehoishma mentions "her *mohar*." However, in the latter case, the contract stipulates that Jehoishma, in contrast to Mibtahiah, would *lose* her *mohar* were she one day to repudiate her husband:

> *whn yhwyšm*[ʿ] *tśnʾ lbʿlh ʿnnyh wtʾmr lh śnytk lʾ ʾhwh lk ʾntt ksp śnʾh brʾšh mhrh yʾbd*
>
> And if Jehoishm[a] hate her husband Ananiah and say to him: "I hated you; I will not be to you a wife," silver of hatred is on her head (and) her *mohar* will be lost. (B3.8:24–25)[119]

Other marriage contracts and laws on marriage from the ancient Near East point in the same direction; admittedly, the *mohar* was given by the bridegroom to the head of the bride's household, but it was nevertheless returned to the couple via the dowry.[120]

Therefore, for the Judaeans in Elephantine, marriage was not a commercial enterprise in the sense that the bride was merely a commodity that could be sold. Since it would seem that the bride-giver gave the *mohar* to the couple after himself having received it, the entire payment of a *mohar* as part of the conclusion of a marriage may be considered as a fictitious act. It has been suggested that the *mohar* "simply [was] the brideprice which he [= the groom] has nominally paid to her [= the bride's] guardian but which is actually added to her dowry."[121] If that was the case, the *mohar* institution was above all a historical relic, though nevertheless a relic that continued to be practised (at least in connection with marriages where the bride was a free woman or an emancipated slave).

This was, however, not the entire picture. If the marriage was about to be dissolved, the *mohar* changed its status from being a nominal, and perhaps symbolic, payment to becoming a real economic asset that could actually be lost for

---

181: "his *mohar* will be lost, forfeited." However, Anke Joisten-Pruschke's translation of it as a definite article, "... wird er den Mohar verlieren," Anke Joisten-Pruschke, *Das religiöse Leben der Juden von Elephantine in der Achämenidenzeit*, GOF, 3. Reihe: Iranica, Neue Folge 2 (Wiesbaden: Harrassowitz, 2008), 113, is unlikely, especially since the scribe has used an *aleph* to denote the emphatic state elsewhere in the contract.

118 Contrary Porten, who argues that the wife would *lose* the *mohar* regardless of whether she repudiated her husband or her husband repudiated her, cf. Porten et al., *The Elephantine Papyri in English*, 183 notes 47, 53.

119 Quoted from Porten et al., *The Elephantine Papyri in English*, 230.

120 For references, see, e.g., Porten et al., *The Elephantine Papyri in English*, 179 note 12.

121 Harold Louis Ginsberg, quoted in Yaron, *Introduction to the Law of the Aramaic Papyri*, 57. However, Reuven Yaron casts doubt on Ginsberg's view. He suggests that there actually were two payments by the husband, one at the conclusion of the marriage and the other at the time of its dissolution, cf. Yaron, *Introduction to the Law of the Aramaic Papyri*, 58.

one of the spouses and conversely kept solely by the other one after the divorce. Only two out of the three extant marriage contracts from the Judaean community in Elephantine mention the *mohar*, and they give different answers to the question of who should keep the *mohar* in the event of a divorce. If the royal builder Esḥor divorced his wife Mibtahiah, "her *mohar*" would "be lost" (*mhrh y'bd*, B2.6:27)—in his disfavour and presumably in her favour. However, in the event that Jehoishma might one day divorce her husband Ananiah, the contract stipulated that her *mohar* would be lost (B3.8:25) to her disfavour. In other words, on the basis of the limited knowledge that we have, it seems reasonable to assume that the question of which of the spouses should keep the *mohar* was an issue the parties to a marriage contract had to agree upon before drawing up the contract.

The last step taken as part of the conclusion of a marriage was the drawing up of a contract (*d*). The contract was dated and attested by witnesses. The latter shows that marriage was considered to be a question of public interest as well as a question of important legal interest for those involved.[122] Formally, the contract was written in the first person; it was presented as the words that the bridegroom "said [*'mr*] to NN [i.e. the head of the bride's household], by saying [*l'mr*]: ..."

Most of the narrative space of the contract was devoted to the economic and legal aspects of the marriage and its possible future dissolution. Using the contract concerning the marriage of Mibtahiah as an example (B2.6), the scribe only had to use three lines on the papyri to express the first three mentioned steps accompanying the conclusion of a marriage: (*a*) the bridegroom's request, (*b*) his declaration and (*c*) his payment of the *mohar* (B2.6:3–5). In contrast, he had to use some thirty lines to write down the rest of the contract (B2.6:6–30). More or less the remaining part of the contract was concerned with the dowry and the various legal and economic terms and conditions the parties to the contract had agreed would be realised in the event of divorce or polygamy.

In all three contracts, after the steps (*a*), (*b*) and (*c*),[123] there is a detailed enumeration of the chattel the bride "brought into me [= the groom] in her hand." It is noteworthy that immovables never occur in these enumerations. In addition, most of the enumerated items were assessed with their estimated value given in silver. As is to be expected given their different socio-economic backgrounds, the dowry list of the free woman Mibtahiah's is much longer than the dowry list of the handmaiden Tamet. The grand total of Mibtahiah's en-

122 As does the notion that a possible divorce took place "in an assembly," cf., e.g., B2.6:22–23, 26–27.

123 Note that in the case of the handmaiden Tamet (B3.3), the marriage document does not refer to the payment of any *mohar* by the groom to her master Meshullam.

tire dowry is sixty-five shekels of silver (B2.6:14). In addition she also brought with her other unpriced items too (such as a bed, cf. B2.6:15–16). On the other hand, the meagre total of the value of Tamet's dowry was little more than seven shekels (B3.3:6–7), approximately one-tenth of that of Mibtahiah.

The dowry was "brought into" the house of the groom. However, as in the case of the *mohar*, the question of whom really had the title to it became a pressing one if one of the spouses wished to dissolve the marriage. The contract involving Mibtahiah contains some eight lines entirely devoted to the arrangements that would prevail in the event of a divorce (B2.6:22–29). Regardless of which one of the spouses actively wanted to divorce him- or herself from the other one, the dowry remained with the wife. If Mibtahiah divorced Esḥor, she had to pay him some seven shekels of silver as divorce money ("silver of hatred") and take out "all that she brought in in her hand ... from straw to string, and go away wherever she desires" (B2.6:24–25). Likewise, if Esḥor divorced his wife, Mibtahiah took her dowry with her out of the marriage (B2.6:27–29). The contracts involving the handmaiden Tamet and the emancipated handmaiden Jehoishma also contain corresponding phrases. The enumerated chattel that came into the house of the groom, together with the bride, belonged to the woman if the couple split up.

Moreover, both spouses had the equal capacity to dissolve the marriage.[124] However, the spouses were not entirely on equal terms with respect to the question of inheritance. To take the latter first, the contract involving Mibtahiah shows that she had only the "right" (*šlyṭh b-)* to Esḥor's house if she survived him and they had no children, whereas the latter had the right to "inherit" (*yrt*) from her goods and property (B2.6:17–22) if he survived his wife. However, when it came to the right to divorce they were on an equal footing. The wife could dissolve the marriage from the next day:

> Tomorrow o[r] (the) next day, should Mibtahiah stand up in an assembly and say: "I hated Esḥor my husband," silver of hatred is on her head. She shall PLACE UPON the balance-scale and weigh out to Esḥor silver, 6[+1] (= 7) shekels, 2 q(uarters), and all that she brought in in her hand she shall take out, from straw to string, and go away wherever she desires, without suit or without process. (B2.6:22–26)[125]

The reference to the "assembly" (*ʿdh*) shows that marriage and divorce were matters regarded to be of public interest.[126] However, although public there is no

124 See, e.g., Yaron, *Introduction to the Law of the Aramaic Papyri*, 53.

125 Quoted from Porten et al., *The Elephantine Papyri in English*, 182–183.

126 On this possible legal institution and its possible identification with the Egyptian court, the *kenbet*, see Hélène Nutkowicz, "Note sur une institution juridique à Éléphantine, *ʿdh*, la

mention of any judge or official. Quite the contrary, in Mibtahiah's marriage contract the parties explicitly renounce the opportunity to involve external legal institutions. This is the implication of *l' dyn wl'dbb*, "no/without suit and without process." Therefore, again, a marriage was a question of public interest, even though it was an institution whose terms and conditions were regulated under private law.

While all known marriage contracts contain divorce regulations, other regulations are unique to the respective contracts. The contract regulating the handmaiden Tamet's marriage to Ananiah contains a special agreement about her son Pilti that would be put into effect in the event that Ananiah divorced the boy's mother. Furthermore, the contract about Jehoishma's marriage prohibits polygamy. In the event that Jehoishma took another husband besides her husband Ananiah, this would activate the divorce regulations already agreed upon by the parties to the contract (B3.8:33–34). Likewise, if her husband Ananiah took another wife besides her, the contract obliged him to divorce Jehoishma (B3.8:36–37). Finally, the same contract also offers rules concerning the mutual behaviour of the spouses, expressed by means of a rather obscure construction (B3.8:37–40).[127] The passage presumably prescribes the conjugal rights and obligations of the spouses to sexual intercourse.[128] However, it has also been suggested that the phrases should be interpreted as a continuation of the prohibition in the foregoing lines against polygamy.[129] In my view, the passage is so enigmatic that it is not possible to tell for sure what it really expresses.

« cour »," *Transeu* 27 (2004): 181–185. However, Alejandro F. Botta does not think "assembly" had any adjudicatory judicial function, cf. Botta, *The Aramaic and Egyptian Legal Traditions*, 60.

127 The enigmatic text reads:

> *w'p l' ykhl 'nnyh wl y'bd dyn [ḥdh] wtrtyn mn nšy knwth lyhwyšm' 'ntth whn l' y'bd kwt śn'h [hy] y'bd lh dyn śn'h w'p l' tkhl yhwyšm' wl' t'bd dyn ḥd w[t]ryn l'nnyh b'lh whn l' t'bd lh śn'hy*

128 See Yaron, *Introduction to the Law of the Aramaic Papyri*, 61; Porten, *Archives from Elephantine*, 224; and Botta, *The Aramaic and Egyptian Legal Traditions*, 59. Consequently, Porten translates thus in Porten et al., *The Elephantine Papyri in English*, 231:

> And moreover, Ananiah shall not be able not to do the law of [one] or two of his colleagues' wives to Jehoishma his wife. And if he does not do thus, hatred [it is]. He shall do to her the law of hatred. And moreover, Jehoishma shall not be able not to do the law of one or [t]wo (of her colleagues' husbands) to Ananiah her husband. And if she does not do (so) for him, hatr(ed) (it) is. (B3.8:37–40)

129 So Joisten-Pruschke, *Das religiöse Leben*, 117–118, 199–200, who translates:

> Auch ist nicht erlaubt Anania und nicht handelt er nach dem Recht, (wenn) er (eine) oder zwei Frauen (als) Nebenfrauen (neben) Jehoishma seiner Ehefrau (nimmt). Wenn er nicht

6.3.4.1.1 Some Observations Concerning the Marriage

Was there a distinctive understanding of the marriage institution among the YHW worshippers in Elephantine? The answer is presumably no. First, as shown above marriage appears to have been a legal, contractual arrangement. To what extent one can make generalisations on the basis of these three contracts is uncertain. Presumably, some aspects of the marriage may have been taken for granted and thus not reflected in the three known written contracts. Nevertheless, the positive evidence is that the marriage was legally organised, primarily between the bride-giver and the groom and, to some extent, the wife. Second, one of the three extant marriage contracts from the Elephantine Judaean community reflects a case of intermarriage: the marriage between Esḥor and Mibtahiah (B2.6, from 449 BCE). In light of his name (Esḥor), his patronymic (son of Djeḥo[130]) and his profession (royal builder), Esḥor was presumably a free Egyptian man.[131] Therefore, it is likely that the marriage contracts used by the Judaeans in Elephantine did not differ substantially from contemporary marriage contracts involving non-Judaeans. According to Reuven Yaron, the equal capacity of the spouses as far as the dissolution of the marriage is concerned is in striking contrast to the situation which on the whole obtains in the ancient East and in Talmudic law, where the husband *alone* is entitled to dissolve the marriage.[132] Yaron tentatively explains the equality at Elephantine as being caused by the Egyptian environment, inferring that married Egyptian

(dannach) tut, so ist sie geschieden und er wird ihr tun das Recht der Scheidung. Auch Jehoishma ist es nicht erlaubt und nicht handelt sie nach dem Recht, ein (oder zwei Männer) (neben) Anania ihrem Ehemann (zu nehmen). Wenn sie es nicht so macht, dann ist sie geschieden. (B3.8:37–40)

130 B2.6:2, cf. B2.9:3, 20.

131 Though Esḥor later changed his name to Nathan, cf. B2.10:3. Porten conjectures that this came about as the result of a conversion, cf. Porten et al., *The Elephantine Papyri in English*, 178 note 2.

132 Yaron, *Introduction to the Law of the Aramaic Papyri*, 53. See, however, Arndt Meinhold, "Scheidungsrecht bei Frauen im Kontext der jüdischen Militärkolonie von Elephantine im 5. Jh. v. Chr.," in *"Sieben Augen auf einem Stein" (Sach 3,9): Studien zur Literatur des Zweiten Tempels. Festschrift für Ina Willi-Plein zum 65. Geburtstag*, ed. Friedhelm Hartenstein and Michael Pietsch (Neukirchen-Vluyn: Neukirchener Verlag, 2007): 247–259 (258), who ascribes the equal right to divorce to a long West Semitic tradition that has *not* made an impact in the biblical marriage legislation.

women enjoyed a relatively emancipated status within marriage in comparison to contemporary cultures of the ancient world.[133]

None of the marriage contracts reveal any notion of a religious understanding of the marriage. Admittedly, marriage had eternity as its horizon, although divorce was a possible way to dissolve it. Yet, the contracts do not reveal any notion of an Elephantine-Judaean theology of creation, comparable to, for example, Gen 2:20–25 and perhaps Mal 2:13–16.[134] Neither the marriage contracts nor any other Elephantine document offer any explicit aetiology of marriage explaining it as an institution that was originally part of the creation.

6.3.4.2 More on Women's Legal Status

The marriage contracts yield an image of women as legally inferior to men—i. e. capable of being given away as brides by their father, brother or owner—but nevertheless enjoying the same rights as their husband when it comes to dissolving a marriage. Other documents also create an ambiguous image. On the one hand, women do not seem to have served as witnesses to legal documents. Besides, the legal inferiority is also manifested in the right of inheritance. The marriage contracts gave the surviving husband somewhat more control over the property of his deceased wife than the other way round (cf. B2.6). On the other hand, the sources show that women in fact *could do* and *actually did* business, as in the case of the lady Islaḥ who was urged (by her husband?) to do business with vegetables (D7.16).

Perhaps even more important is what can be deduced from legal documents other than marriage contracts, namely that immovables remained the separate property of a wife, in spite of a marriage. For instance, in 459 BCE Mahseiah son of Jedaniah bequeathed a house to his daughter Mibtahiah (B2.3)[135] (who ten years later married the royal builder Esḥor [B2.6, see above]). Yet in 459 BCE Mibtahiah was married to Jezaniah son of Uriah (cf. B2.4). What is noteworthy is that Mahseiah did not bequeath the house to the couple. On the contrary, he explicitly bequeathed it to his daughter Mibtahiah and her children in contemplation of death (B2.3:3, 8, 9–11, 15, 19). On the same day that Mahsehiah wrote the bequest (Aramaic: "document of a house," cf. B2.3:35) he also drew

133 However, it should be noted that references to divorce initiated by the wife are not attested in Egyptian sources from periods earlier than ca. 500 BCE (the Persian period). According to Wolfgang Helck, the notion of the legal equality of the Egyptian woman should be considered a fiction of egyptologists, cf. Wolfgang Helck, "Scheidung," *LÄ* 5: 559–560 (559).

134 Compare also Eph 5:21–33 and Luke 20:34–36.

135 The spelling of the name varies in the documents.

up another document in which he granted his son-in-law Jezaniah usufruct to the house in question (B2.4). Through the grant of usufruct Mahseiah made it explicitly clear to his son-in-law that it was his daughter Mibtahiah to whom he had given (*yhb*) the property:

> *ʾyty ʾrq by 1 zyly mʿrb lbyt zylk zy ʾnh yhbt lmbṭḥyh brty ʾnttk wspr ktbt lh ʾḥrwhy*
>
> There is land of a house of mine, west of the house of yours, which I gave to Mibtahiah my daughter, your wife, and a document I wrote for her concerning it. (B2.4:3–4)[136]

In other words, the transfer of ownership only involved one of the spouses: Mibtahiah, not her husband Jezaniah. However, the fact that Jezaniah and Mibtahiah were married, and the fact that Jezaniah already owned the neighbouring house, necessitated some arrangements. By means of the following words Mahseiah granted his son-in-law usufruct to the house he had bequeathed to his daughter:

> *kʿn ʾnh mḥsyh ʾmrt lk ʾrqʾ zk bny wʿtd bhmyth wtb bgw ʿm ʾnttk*
>
> Now, I, Mahseiah, said to you: That land build (up) and ENRICH IT (OR: PREPARE IN IT HER HOUSE)[137] and dwell herein with your wife. (B2.4:5–6)[138]

The legal restrictions imposed upon Jezaniah's regarding the house were continued even in the event of the death of his wife Mibtahiah. The father-in-law Mahseiah made it clear that only the children Jezaniah had together with Mibtahiah would have the right to the house.

Yet, Jezaniah was not entirely without rights to the house. Mahseiah considered the possibility that the marriage could be dissolved. If Mibtahiah divorced Jezaniah, the legal heirs to the house would continue to be the common children of Mibtahiah and Jezaniah. Moreover, in the case of a divorce the son-in-law Jezaniah had the right to one half of the house "in exchange for" (*ḥlp*) the construction works that he had done on the house (B2.6:11–12).

In short, the documents attest that it was possible for women to have a separate economy independently of their husbands (see also B2.7, dated 446 BCE in which Mahseiah gave Mibtahiah the full title to a [another] house, at a time when she probably was married to Esḥor, cf. B2.6). The IOU B3.1 also points in the same direction, where Jehoḥen daughter of Meshullach accepted her debt

136 Quoted from Porten et al., *The Elephantine Papyri in English*, 174.

137 It is not clear whether there is a *dalet* or a *resh* in the verb. If it is *ʿtr*, the meaning is "enrich." However, if it is *ʿtd* the meaning is "prepare," cf. Porten et al., *The Elephantine Papyri in English*, 174 note 12.

138 Quoted from Porten et al., *The Elephantine Papyri in English*, 174.

to Meshullam son of Zaccur. In the latter case, a woman was not only an independent economic unit;[139] she also took part in a legal settlement as a party on an equal footing with (the man) Meshullam. In other words, Judaean women took part in the economic life of Elephantine.

6.3.4.3 The Household as the Basic Unit of Society

In Elephantine, as elsewhere in the ancient world, the household (*byt*ʾ) was the basic unit of society. This is particularly evident in the inheritance regulations given in several documents. The intention of the one drawing up a bequest (the testator) was to ensure legally that it would be his own children and grandchildren who inherited his properties. As Bob Becking has pointed out, the measures of the many contracts dealing with the distribution of property after the death of its owner are not only important with regard to their legal aspects. For, the inheritance measures "were based on the concept of continuity."[140] Not only did the one initiating the bequest de facto organise the continuation of control over the bequeathed property within the household across generations; in a bequest a testator demonstrated that he expected the descendants to be responsible for the future continuation of the community in its entirety.

Thus, the inheritance regulations illustrate what presumably is an elementary evolutionary principle: a living creature instinctively wants to ensure security his/her offspring. The concern for offspring transcended physical life; a bequest was also intended to affect the life of the descendants *after* the death of the one who drew up the bequest.

The fact that the household was the basic unit of society also has some negative support, at least as seen from the perspective of a debtor and particularly his/her descendants. According to the IOU written by Jehoḥen to Meshullam, it was her children who inherited her possible debts:

> And if I die and have not paid you this silver and its interest it will be my children (who) shall pay you this silver and its interest. And if they not pay this silver and its interest, you, Meshullam, have right to take for yourself any food or security which you will find (belonging) to them until you have full (payment) of your silver and its interest. And they shall not be able to complain against you before prefect or judge while this document is in your

139 Note also how frequently women are mentioned as contributors to the so-called Collection Account ("the names of the Judaean garrison who gave silver to YHW the god," C3.15:1).

140 Bob Becking, "Yehudite Identity in Elephantine," in *Judah and the Judeans in the Achaemenid Period: Negotiating Identity in an International Context*, ed. Oded Lipschits et al. (Winona Lake, IN: Eisenbrauns, 2011): 403–419 (410–411).

hand. Moreover, should they go into a suit, they shall not prevail while this document is in your hand. (B3.1:14 – 20)[141]

The creditor's family inherited the loan (B3.1:8) while the debtor's family inherited the debt.

6.4 The Human and the Authorities of Society in the Native Sources

As is to be expected, the native Judaean sources from Elephantine do not offer any systematic treatment of what the Judaeans regarded as good behaviour towards the authorities of society. Likewise, the sources do not systematically describe what the subjects considered to be good behaviour towards the subjects on the part of society's authorities. However, these are all important issues in the non-Judaean and prescriptive sources, namely, *Aḥiqar* and DB Aram, which will be in focus in the remainder of the present chapter.[142]

It is possible, however, to ferret out some aspects of the ethics of the Judaeans from the native Elephantine Judaean sources, which are both descriptive and in part prescriptive. Such a search should start by focussing on nominal and actual authority. What kind of people and institutions *nominally* functioned as authorities in Elephantine Judaean society? What kind of people and institutions *actually* functioned as authorities and were correspondingly recognised by the Judaeans as such?

Being a garrison community under Persian command, it is to be expected that the Judaean community paid respects to the various local (military and/or civic) officials,[143] the satrap of Egypt,[144] who all were Persians, and not to forget—obviously—the Achaemenid king himself (cf. A4.1; A4.2:14 "at the order of

141 Quoted from Porten et al., *The Elephantine Papyri in English*, 205.

142 See Section 6.5 below.

143 Such as, e.g., "the garrison commander" (*rbḥyl'*), "the chief/governor" (*prtrk'*) and "the Guardian of the Seventh (part of the world/kingdom)" (*hptḥpt'*), cf. Tavernier, *Iranica in the Achaemenid Period*, 425, s.v. *Haptaxvāpāt.

144 Strictly speaking, the Aramaic documents from Egypt do not mention the title "satrap." Egyptian sources from the fifth century written in demotic Egyptian script refer to Arshama's precursor Pherendates as the one "to whom Egypt is entrusted," cf. the correspondence between Pherendates and the priests of Khnum concerning the appointment of a new *lesonis* priest. Introductions to and translations of the texts can be found in Porten et al., *The Elephantine Papyri in English*, 288 – 294, and Amélie Kuhrt, *The Persian Empire: A Corpus of Sources from the Achaemenid Period* (London: Routledge, 2007), 852 – 854 (no. 17.30).

the king"). The Judaeans evidently made use of the service of the Persian officials in private legal matters, such as adoptions, and these officials also played a role in various kinds of litigations and criminal cases (e.g., A4.5:9 "judges, police and hearers who are appointed in the province of Tshetres"). Moreover, the Elephantine Judaean community also regarded the governors of the provinces of Judah and Samaria as authorities (cf. A4.7:23–24 par. "regard your obligees and your friends who are here in Egypt," and A4.9). In addition, they clearly considered the high priest (*khn' rb'*) in Jerusalem and his colleagues the priests there and the nobles (*ḥry'*) of Judah as *de facto* authorities (cf. A4.7:18–19 par.).

The fragmentary letter A4.5 (drawn up shortly after the destruction of the temple of YHW in 410 BCE, cf. A4.5:2) gives a glimpse of the *Arbeitsethos* of the Judaean soldiers, an ethos that implied *loyalty* towards the Persians. Although the context is obscured by the text being broken, it seems clear that the Judaeans remained loyal even though Egyptian garrison troops mutinied, military units that no doubt were supposed to be under Persian command: *dgln zy mṣry' mrdw 'nḥnh mnṭrtn l' šbqn ... mḥbl l' 'štkḥ ln*, "Detachments of the Egyptians rebelled. We, our posts did not leave ... damage was not found in us" (A4.5:1–2).[145]

The local Persian governor (*prtrk'*) Vidranga sided with the Egyptian rebellions. Whether or not Vidranga also had a political motivation for doing this cannot be ruled out; there was a temporarily political vacuum in Egypt since Arshama, the satrap and the superior of the Judaeans ("our lord"), had left the country to see King Darius II (B4.5:2–3), who probably resided in Susa in the region of Elam (cf. A6.12:1). However, according to the Judaean garrison's version of the event reflected in A4.5, Vidranga's motivation was a more prosaic one. According to their retrospective account, he was corrupt. The local Egyptian priests of Khnum did an "evil act," and they did it "in agreement with Vidranga." According to the Judaeans, the agreement included Vidranga receiving gifts from the Egyptian priests:

> *bšnt 10+3+1 drywhwš [ml]k' kzy mr'n 'ršm 'zl 'l mlk' znh dwškrt' zy kmry zy ḥnwb 'lh' ['bd]w byb byrt' hmwnyt 'm wydrng zy prtrk tnh hwh ksp wnksn yhbw lh*
>
> In year 14 of Darius the [ki]ng, when our lord Arsames had gone to the king, this is the evil act which the priests of Khnub the god [di]d in Elephantine the fortress in agreement with Vidranga who was GOVERNOR here: They gave him silver and goods. (A4.5:2–4)[146]

145 Quoted from Porten et al., *The Elephantine Papyri in English*, 136.
146 Quoted from Porten et al., *The Elephantine Papyri in English*, 136–137.

The precise relation between the mutiny of the Egyptian garrisons (A4.5:1–2) and the "evil act" of the Egyptian priests of Khnum (A4.5:2–4) eludes us. Nevertheless, it is tempting to assume that they were somehow connected, perhaps in the way that the Egyptian priests were inspired by the rebelling Egyptian garrisons.

Moreover, according to the Judaeans' account the "evil act" jointly undertaken by the Egyptians and the allegedly corrupt Persian official also included the destruction of royal property. The Judaean garrison reported that the Egyptian priests had destroyed at least three things: a royal treasury in Elephantine, a well located within the fortress, and—although the text is full of lacunas at this point—probably the temple of YHW.

At least the first two items were royal property. The well that the Egyptian priest "stopped up" in collusion with the Persian official Vidranga was reported to have supplied the garrison with water:

> *ʾyty bʾr ḥdh zy bnyh bg[w] b[y]rtʾ wmyn lʾ ḥsrh lhšqyʾ ḥylʾ kzy hn hndyz yhwwn bbrʾ [z]k myʾ štyn*
>
> There is a well which is built with[in] the f[or]tress and water it does not lack to give the troop to drink so that whenever they would be GARRISONED (there), in [th]at well the water they could drink. (A4.5:6–8)[147]

The Persian loanword *hndyz* may be translated "(be) garrisoned,"[148] or, as Lindenberger has suggested, "confined" or "mobilised."[149] At any rate, the well obviously had a strategical importance for the Judaean garrison stationed in the fortress of Elephantine, and ultimately, the king himself. Therefore, the Judaean garrison accused the Egyptians *and* the local Persian official Vidranga of nothing less than high treason. With these serious allegations as a backdrop, the Judaean garrison obviously intended to present themselves as the king's loyal servants when they wrote the report A4.5 to the—alas—anonymous Persian official. The Judaean garrison clearly had confidence in him and the power structure he represented:

> *hn ʾzd ytʿbd mn dynyʾ typtyʾ gwškyʾ zy mmnyn bmdynt tšṭrs yty[dʿ] lmrʾn lqbl znh zy ʾnḥnh ʾmrn*
>
> If inquiry be made from the judges, police and hearers who are appointed in the province of Tshetres, it would be [*known*] to our lord in accordance with this which we say. (A4.5:8–10)[150]

---

147 Quoted from Porten et al., *The Elephantine Papyri in English*, 137.
148 Tavernier, *Iranica in the Achaemenid Period*, 451, s.v. *Handaiza-.
149 Lindenberger, *Ancient Aramaic and Hebrew Letters*, 71, 79 note k.
150 Quoted from Porten et al., *The Elephantine Papyri in English*, 138.

In sum, in the report found in A4.5 the Elephantine Judaean garrison presented itself as a garrison made up of the king's loyal Judaean soldiers.[151]

6.5 The Ethical Instruction of the Non-Native Sources (DB Aram and *Aḥiqar*)

Above I have attempted to describe aspects of the ethics of the Judaeans in Elephantine on the basis of what I have termed native Elephantine Judaean sources from the fifth century BCE (letters and legal documents, written on papyrus or potsherds). Obviously, originally the native sources served various purposes: communication between members of one and the same family, or between groups such as the Judaean garrison and Persian officials within and outside of Egypt, moreover, regulation of various legal matters such as litigations, bequests and conveyances, and so forth.

However, there are two documents from the same period (and place?, see below) that are fundamentally different: the *Words of Aḥiqar* (C1.1) and the Aramaic version of King Darius's Bisitun inscription (DB Aram, C2.1).[152] *Aḥiqar* and DB Aram can be characterised as literary works. The two works are not connected to each other in any way; nevertheless, they share certain features. First, they are both of a much more elaborate literary character than the letters and legal documents from Elephantine. Whereas the above mentioned native sources may be described as occasional and ephemeral texts because they were drawn up on the background of a particular circumstance and, generally speaking, were meant for a limited group of readers, e.g., the recipient(s) of a particular letter or the parties to a legal contract, *Aḥiqar* and DB Aram are planned compositions obviously intended for a broader audience. Unlike the native Judaean sources, the two works were not written ad hoc. Secondly, the two works share a common purpose. When all is said and done, their true goal was to *instruct* the readers as to how they should behave. In other words, the intention of both *Aḥiqar* and DB Aram was to *prescribe* morally good behaviour, according to the norm guiding the composition of the works. They were definitely intended to guide the ethics of their readers. In the following I build on the assumption that they were also in fact regarded as normative by the (primarily) Yahwistic Judaeans in Elephantine.

151 See, e.g., Gard Granerød, "Ahuramazdas lojale judeiske soldater: Om Elefantine-judeernes selvbilde," *TeoT* 3 (2014): 288–303.
152 See Section 5.4.2 above.

6.5.1 The *Words of Aḥiqar* (C1.1)

6.5.1.1 Outline

The original title of the work may have been "These are the words of Aḥiqar [*mly ʾḥyqr*] by name, a wise and skilful scribe, which he taught his son" (C1.1:1). The work is made up of two parts: a narrative about Aḥiqar and a proverbial part with more or less ahistorical sayings. Aḥiqar, the protagonist of the narrative part, is presented as a wise and skilful scribe. He holds the titles "counsellor of Assyria" and "bearer of the seal (of the king)," first King Sennacherib and then his successor King Esarhaddon. In the narrative, the ageing Aḥiqar is childless. However, he adopts his sister's son Nadin and refers to the latter as "my son who is not my son" (C1.1:30). Moreover, Aḥiqar gets the king's approval to let his nephew and protégé Nadin succeed him. However, after a while Nadin betrays his uncle Aḥiqar and causes Esarhaddon to issue a death sentence against him. The one commissioned to execute the capital punishment is a young man called Nabusumiskun. However, it turns out that Aḥiqar had previously rescued Nabusumiskun from an undeserved death. Aḥiqar reminds Nabusumiskun of this, and Nabusumiskun responds by hiding the persecuted wise man. Nabusumiskun orchestrates a cunning plan. In place of Aḥiqar he kills one of his eunuchs. When the king's inspectors see the corpse they report back to the king that Aḥiqar has been put to death. At this point the Aramaic version breaks off. However, on the basis of the reception history of the Aḥiqar tradition it is possible to make conjectures about the rest of the narrative.[153] Later versions relate that the Egyptian king challenges the king of Assyria to send a wise man who can answer a series of riddles. The Assyrian king regrets that he has sentenced Aḥiqar to death. The king's regret, however, provides an opportunity for Nabusumiskun to reveal his secret. Aḥiqar comes forth from his hiding place, and after having been reinstalled, he is sent off to Egypt. There he accomplishes the mission with success and returns to the Assyrian court. The trickster Nadin, however, is severely punished. Before he eventually dies Aḥiqar reproaches him.

The question of the relationship between the narrative part and the proverbial part has not been settled.[154] The proverbs, being ahistorical by nature, lack any reference to historical events and places. Nevertheless, provided that the an-

153 Later versions from the Common Era of the literary work (the lengthiest being the Syriac and Arabic versions) are found in F. C. Conybeare et al., *The Story of Aḥiḳar from the Aramaic, Syriac, Arabic, Armenian, Ethiopic, Old Turkish, Greek and Slavonic Versions* (Cambridge: Cambridge University Press, 1913).

154 Weigl, *Die aramäischen Achikar-Sprüche*, 691–703.

cient title of the work was "the words that Aḥiqar ... taught his son [*ḥkm lbrh*]" (C1.1:1) it is possible that the proverbial part was once presented as part of Nadin's curriculum in his training for succeeding Aḥiqar. This father–son relationship is accordingly presupposed in many of the proverbs. The father often addresses the gnomes directly to the son, as in the following: *br*[*y*] *ʾl tl*[*w*]*ṭ ywmʾ ʿd tḥzh* [*ly*]*lh*, "[My] son, do not d[a]mn the day until you see[*nig*]ht." (C1.1:80).[155]

The method that once guided the arrangement of the short sayings in the proverbial part are elusive and can only be ferreted out. In James M. Lindenberger's eyes, the collection of slightly over a hundred aphorisms, riddles, fables, instructions and so on have been arranged "in a more or less haphazard manner."[156] However, Michael Weigl argues otherwise. One factor is that many proverbs are clearly grouped thematically. What is more, in Weigl's view there are two types of typographic features in the manuscript that no doubt were intended to function as delimiter symbols. One is a horizontal stroke between some lines on the right margin separating groups of proverbs. The other is the more frequent asterisk-like symbol ("a lapidary *aleph*"[157]). The typographic features suggest that there was an intention behind the arrangement.[158] According to Weigl individual proverbs come in series of two and three respectively on the basis of various criteria such as identical syntax, formal similarity, synonymy or antonymy, catchwords, paronomasia, catchwords and so on. Thematic blocks are always treated once (the topic "the king" in Column 6, "education" in Column 12 etc.).[159]

6.5.1.2 Provenance

Nothing suggests that Elephantine or even Egypt was the place of composition of *Aḥiqar*. Whereas the proverbial part is essentially timeless, the narrative part is set at the Assyrian court. A terminus ante quem for the narrative part must be the death of Sennacherib in 681 BCE.

It has also been pointed out that there is a difference in the Aramaic dialects used in the two parts. Whereas the narrative part is written in Official Aramaic,

---

155 Quoted from Porten and Yardeni, *TADAE*, III: Literature, Accounts, Lists, 37.

156 James M. Lindenberger, "Ahikar: A New Translation and Introduction," in *The Old Testament Pseudepigrapha: Expansions of the "Old Testament" and Legends, Wisdom and Philosophical Literature, Prayers, Psalms, and Odes, Fragments of Lost Judeo-Hellenistic Works*, ed. James H. Charlesworth (Garden City, NY: Doubleday, 1985): 479–507 (479).

157 Porten and Yardeni, *TADAE*, III: Literature, Accounts, Lists, xv.

158 Weigl, *Die aramäischen Achikar-Sprüche*, 709–722, especially 713.

159 Weigl, *Die aramäischen Achikar-Sprüche*, 713–715.

the language of the proverbial part is considered more archaic.[160] This suggests that the proverbial part has a different provenance from the narrative part. As for the proverbial part, philological characteristics have been used as an argument for locating its origin to northern Syria.[161] The contents of the proverbial part also point in the same direction. In particular the pantheon of the proverbial part shows affinities to the Syro-Canaanite cultural area.[162] It consists of an undefined group of "gods" (*ʾlhn*, plural of *ʾlh*), El (*ʾl*), Shamash (*šmš*), "lord of the holy ones"[163] (*bʿl qdšn*) and perhaps Shamayn (*šmyn*).[164] It has been suggested to connect the last two, *šmyn* and *bʿl qdšn*, to the deity Baal-shamayn ("the Lord of Heaven") whose popularity increased at the beginning of the first millennium BCE in the Aramaic-speaking regions of Syria.[165] Another proposal is that *bʿl qdšn* in fact represented Hadad.[166]

As it to be expected, the redaction history of the work is also obscure. However, Reinhard G. Kratz has made a likely plea for an intertextual connection between the narrative and the proverbial parts. Some proverbs seem to reflect the bad situation between Aḥiqar and his nephew Nadin:

> [*A person w*]ho does not exalt in the name of his father and in the name of his mother, may [(the)] su[n] (OR: Sham[ash]) not shine [*for him*] for he is a bad person.
> [*From*] my [*hou*]se went out my bad (situation) and (so) with whom shall I win (= be found innocent)? * The son of my belly spied out my house and (so) what shall I say to the strangers?
> [*My son*] was to me a malicious witness and who, then, (will) let me win (= judge me innocent)? * From my house went out my wrath; with whom shall I dispute and BE WEARIED (OR: be firm and FLOURISH)? (C1.1:138–140)[167]

---

160 Herbert Niehr, *Aramäischer Aḥiqar*, JSHRZ Neue Folge 2 (Gütersloh: Gütersloher Verlagshaus, 2007), 10–13.
161 Lindenberger, "Ahikar," 479–507 (482), and Weigl, *Die aramäischen Achikar-Sprüche*, 677–688.
162 See Section 5.5.2 above.
163 C1.1:79, quoted from Porten and Yardeni, *TADAE*, III: Literature, Accounts, Lists, 37, cf. Weigl, *Die aramäischen Achikar-Sprüche*, 73–79. However, Lindenberger renders *bʿl qdšn*, "the Holy Lord," Lindenberger, "Ahikar," 479–507 (479).
164 C1.1:79. So Lindenberger, "Ahikar," 479–507 (499), but Porten and Yardeni, *TADAE*, III: Literature, Accounts, Lists, 37, and Weigl, *Die aramäischen Achikar-Sprüche*, 73 understand "heaven" as a locale, not a deity.
165 See W. Röllig, "Baal-Shamem," *DDD:* 149–151.
166 Niehr, *Aramäischer Aḥiqar*, 18–20.
167 Quoted from Porten and Yardeni, *TADAE*, III: Literature, Accounts, Lists, 43.

As Kratz puts it, there are good reasons to assume that the connection between the narrative about Aḥiqar and Nadin on the one hand and the proverbial part on the other was made or at least stressed during the process of redaction that fused the narrative with the proverbs. During this process, the narrative and proverbial parts were fused.[168]

The route *Ahiqar* took to Egypt and Elephantine is far from clear. The same goes for its concrete use there. Perhaps it was brought there by the Aramaeans who were part of the garrison stationed in Syene or even in Elephantine. And perhaps *Aḥiqar* was promoted by the Persian bureaucracy, having its primary *Sitz im Leben* in Achaemenid Egypt in the administration's scribal schools.

6.5.1.3 The Human and the Deities

6.5.1.3.1 The Gods and Wisdom

The connection between "wisdom" and the gods is thematised in sayings 95–97 (= C1.1:187–189):

> Two things are beautiful and (that) which is three (= the third) is beloved by Shamash: (one who) d[rinks] the wine and POURS IT OUT AS LIBATION (OR: GIVES IT {OUT} TO DRINK); (one who) masters wisdom [*and shares/guards it*];
> and (one who) will hear a thing and will not tell (it). * Behold, this is precious (OR: heavy) [befor]e Shamash: but whoever will drink the wine and not [POUR IT OUT AS LIBATION (OR: GIVE IT {OUT} TO DRINK)]
> and (OR: then) his wisdom is lost and ... who saw. * From heaven the people were ... and [their wi]sdom the gods ... [...] (C1.1:187–189)[169]

In these sayings, the "mastering" (or: "subjugation, taming," *kbš* in *pael* stem, C1.1:187) of "wisdom" (*ḥkmh*) is presented as a virtue in the eyes of the god Shamash. Wisdom is not intrinsic to humankind but can be acquired—and it can be lost (cf. *ʾbdh*, C1.1:189). The exact nature of wisdom is not stated. Nevertheless, the wisdom may have been personified. It seems that the heavenly abodes have been made to be her ultimate dwelling place. The latter seems to be the point in the following saying: "Moreover, to gods she is pre[ci]ous (or: heavy) ... [...] the kingdom. In hea[v]en she is put for the lord of holy ones exalted [*her*]" (C1.1:79).[170]

168 Reinhard Gregor Kratz, "Aḥiqar and Bisitun: Literature of the Judaeans at Elephantine?" (forthcoming).

169 Quoted from Porten and Yardeni, *TADAE*, III: Literature, Accounts, Lists, 49.

170 Quoted from Porten and Yardeni, *TADAE*, III: Literature, Accounts, Lists, 37.

The saying quoted above introduces Column 6 of the original scroll. It is probably the first proper proverbial saying in the extant Aramaic text of *Aḥiqar*. The 1993 edition of *Aḥiqar* by Bezalel Porten and Ada Yardeni presupposes four now lost columns between the last extant part of the narrative about Aḥiqar and the proverbial saying quoted above.[171] Presumably it was in this lacuna that the transition between the Aḥiqar narrative and the sayings of Aḥiqar took place. As the text now appears according to the ordering of the columns by Porten and Yardeni, the reference of the third person feminine singular pronoun *hy* in the first part of C1.1:79 (*ʾp lʾlhn yq*[*y*]*rh hy*) is *not* explicitly given. Therefore, one cannot say with certitude that "she" (*hy*) actually refers to "wisdom," even though there is a tradition for assuming that in the scholarly literature.[172] Never-

---

171 Porten and Yardeni, *TADAE*, III: Literature, Accounts, Lists, 23, 35, and Niehr, *Aramäischer Aḥiqar*, 6–7. It should be noted that the 1993 edition of the Aramaic text of *Aḥiqar* found in Porten and Yardeni, *TADAE*, III: Literature, Accounts, Lists, offers a reconstruction that *differs* from previous editions in terms of how the columns are organised. This has an important impact on the sayings pertaining to the topic "wisdom." The traditional sequence of the columns goes back to Eduard Sachau, *Aramäische Papyrus und Ostraka aus einer jüdischen Militär-Kolonie zu Elephantine altorientalische Sprachdenkmäler des 5. Jahrhunderts vor Chr* (Leipzig: Hinrichs, 1911), Arthur Ungnad, *Aramäische Papyrus aus Elephantine: kleine Ausgabe unter Zugrundelegung von Eduard Sachau's Erstausgabe*, HKAO 4 (Leipzig: Hinrichs, 1911), and Arthur Ernest Cowley, *Aramaic Papyri of the Fifth Century B.C.* (Oxford: Oxford University Press, 1923). It is also found in Lindenberger, "Ahikar," 479–507 (499). What is designated as saying no. 13 in Lindenberger's translation is made up of the last words of one column and the first words of another one. In the following I have attempted to visualise this. The underlined words belong to what Lindenberger has conceived of as Column 6 and the words not underlined belong to Lindenberger's Column 7:

> From heaven the people are favored; / Wisdom is of the gods. / Indeed, she is precious to the gods; / her kingdom is et[er]nal. / She has been established by Shamayn; / yea, the Holy Lord has exalted her.

However, the traditional reading of the text can no longer be sustained. Underneath the Aramaic text of *Aḥiqar* there is an erased text: a customs account from an unknown port. This erased text was deciphered by Ada Yardeni in Yardeni, "Maritime Trade and Royal Accountancy," 67–78, cf. Porten and Yardeni, *TADAE*, III: Literature, Accounts, Lists, 23, and Oren Tal, "On the Identification of the Ships of *kzd/ry* in the Erased Customs Account from Elephantine," *JNES* 68 (2009): 1–8 (1). The accounts on the duty levied upon incoming and outgoing ships were drawn up chronologically, month by month according to the Egyptian calendar. Therefore, the sequence of the columns of *Aḥiqar* offered in Porten and Yardeni, *TADAE*, III: Literature, Accounts, Lists is claimed to be supported by external criteria. Thus, Columns 6–7 in Lindenberger's translation turn out to be Column 12 and Column 6 respectively according to the arrangement of Porten and Yardeni.

172 Niehr, *Aramäischer Aḥiqar*, 42. For the discussion, however, see Weigl, *Die aramäischen Achikar-Sprüche*, 73–79.

theless, the word *yqyrh* that functions as the complement of *hy* in C1.1:79 is found in the context of wisdom in another saying. For, in C1.1:188 it is stated *hʾ znh yqyr [qd]m šmš*, "Behold! This is precious/heavy be[fore] Shamash." Here, the pronoun *znh* probably refers to the three things mentioned in the foregoing line C1.1:187, and one of them is "(one who) masters wisdom" (*kbš ḥkmh*, C1.1:187).

6.5.1.3.2 The Gods and Determinism

In the proverbial part the notion of determinism is also attested, that is, the idea that events and human actions are determined by causes external to the will of humans. So, for example, in C1.1:96–97:

> [*mh y*]*štmr ʾyš ʿm ʾlhn wmh ytnṭr ʿlʾwn gwh* [...]
> [..]*mn* [*d*]*ššy bṭn wzy lʾ ʾl ʿmh mn yhw..ʾnhy*
>
> [*How* can] a man guard himself with (= against) gods and how can he watch himself (relying) on *his inner strength* (OR: against *his inner wickedness*)?
> [...]... [doo]rs of (the) belly, but (him) with whom El is not – who will ... him? (C1.1:96–97)[173]

The saying in C1.1:96 seems to be a parallelism (each clause introduced by the interrogative pronoun *mh*, followed by passive or reflexive stems of the verbs *šmr* and *nṭr* respectively). The phrase *ʿlʾwn gwh* is a crux. *ʿlʾwn* is likely to be the preposition *ʿl* plus *ʾwn*. However, the noun *ʾwn* is not attested elsewhere in Aramaic.[174] In Biblical Hebrew the noun *ʾôn* can describe generative power, physical power or wealth.[175] As for this text, there is a theoretical possibility that *ʾwn* in the context of this work is a Hebraism. However, a more likely option is that the Aramaic text reflects a common northwest Semitic word for power, although it appears not to have been frequently used in Aramaic. Therefore, the phrase *ʿlʾwn gwh* may perhaps be rendered "against the power of his midst." As a consequence of this interpretation, the saying is about the influence of external as well as internal powers upon the man. Perhaps this particular proverb comes close to Paul's discussion on free will in Rom 7:14–24. According to Paul, he is in "slavery under sin" (Rom 7:14); he is not entirely in control and unable to do what he wants. Needless to say that for *Aḥiqar* the concept of sin as a power is not found in the context of this particular saying. Nevertheless, the man seems to be portrayed here as one who does not (completely) determine his own destiny. The answers to the questions ("how can ...?") are not explicitly given. Neverthe-

---

173 Quoted from Porten and Yardeni, *TADAE*, III: Literature, Accounts, Lists, 39.
174 Lindenberger, "Aḥikar," 479–507 (505).
175 See *HALOT* 1:22, s.v. *ʾôn*.

less, we can assume that it was a negative one: a man can neither be guarded against the gods nor can he rely on "the power of his midst." Both "(the) gods" and the "the power of his (= the man's) midst" (whatever it is) are causes *external* to the man's will.

Moreover, determinism tends to become fatalism, as suggested by the following fable:

> * The bear went to [the] lamb[s ...], "...
> I will be silent." The lambs answered and said to him, "Carry (away) what you [will] carry from us. We ...[...]
> for it is not in the hands of the indivi[dual] (to) carry (= lift) their feet and put them down apart fr[om (the) *god*]s. ...[...]
> for it is not in your hands (to) carry (= lift) your foot to put it down. * (C1.1:168 – 171)[176]

Although the bear's[177] message to the lambs is lost, the response of the lambs suggests he wanted one of them in order to be satisfied (cf. C1.1:169 *ʾštq*, "I will be silent"). The lambs, for their part, do not enter into any discussion. On the contrary, they seem to accept the bear as their superior and consider the bear's wish as inevitable: *śʾ lk zy t*[*n*]*śʾ mnn*, "Carry (away) what you [will] carry from us!" (C1.1:169).[178]

The moral of the fable clarifies the real identity of the lambs. The moral, introduced by *ky*, comes in two versions. The first one is in the third person (C1.1:170) and the second one in the second person (C1.1:171). According to the first one, it is not "in the hands of the individual" (*ky lʾ bydy ʾn*[*š*]*ʾ*, C1.1:170) to move his feet without the gods (provided that the end of line 170 originally read *blʿdy ʾlhn*).[179] The second version is presumably addressed directly to the bear: "for it is not in your hands (to) carry (= lift) your foot to put it down" (*ky lʾ bydyk mnśʾ rglk lmnḥtwth*, C1.1:171). A reasonable interpretation of the fable is that a person does not do the slightest thing without the gods' knowledge and consent.

---

176 Quoted from Porten and Yardeni, *TADAE*, III: Literature, Accounts, Lists, 47.

177 The initial letter of the Aramaic phrase here translated "the bear" can be read as a *resh*. If that is the case, the Aramaic word is *rbʾ*, "the master," cf. Sachau, *Aramäische Papyrus und Ostraka*, Plate 46, and Cowley, *Aramaic Papyri*, 216. However, the fact that the saying in question is preceded by animal proverbs in which other animals are reported speaking (C1.1:165 – 168) support the reading of *dbʾ*, "the bear."

178 Quoted from Porten and Yardeni, *TADAE*, III: Literature, Accounts, Lists, 47.

179 This conjecture is made in Cowley, *Aramaic Papyri*, 216, 240, and Porten and Yardeni, *TADAE*, III: Literature, Accounts, Lists, 46 – 47.

6.5.1.3.3 The Gods and Retribution

However, divine determinism is not the final word. The idea could potentially imply that an individual lacks free will and therefore is unaccountable vis-à-vis the gods. However, immediately after the fable about the bear and the lambs (C1:1:168 – 171) comes another saying depicting the individual as accountable:

> * *hn npqh ṭbh mn pm* [*nš*ʾ *ṭb*]
> *whn lḥyh tnpq m*[*n*] *pmhm* ʾ*lhn ylḥwn lhm* *
>
> * If good goes out from the mouth of [the] in[*dividual – good*];
> and if bad goes out fr[om] their mouth, gods will make (it) bad for them. * (C1.1:171 – 172)[180]

A person is made responsible for what "goes out" from his/her mouth, and the gods follow a policy of retribution. Bad things that come out of the individual's mouth are punished in the way that they bring bad things in return or—to be more precise—in the way that the gods bring bad things in return. The agents are the unspecified "gods" (ʾ*lhn*); they will "destroy them" (*ylḥwn lhm*, *peal* imperfect third masculine plural of *lḥy*, "to destroy"[181] + direct object).

Moreover, the same unspecified group of gods also occurs in the role of guarantors of justice in other sayings found in C1.1:126 – 129. The sayings in this passage are arranged according to an ABAB scheme. Common topics and common key words form the basis of the arrangement. In the ABAB scheme there is a pun on the phrases *ḥṭk*, "your arrow" (C1.1:126, 128), *ḥṭ*ʾ, "sin" (C1.1:128) and *ḥnṭt*ʾ, "the wheat" (C1.1:129):

> [ʾ*l tdrg q*]*štk w*ʾ*l thrkb ḥṭk lṣdyq lmh* ʾ*lhy*ʾ *ysgh b*ʿ*drh wyhtybnhy* ʿ*lyk*
> [.....] ʾ*nt yh bry hkṣr kl kṣyr w*ʿ*bd kl* ʿ*bydh* ʾ*dyn t*ʾ*kl wtšb*ʿ *wtntn lbnyk*
> [... *d*]*rgt qštk whrkbt ḥṭk lṣdyq mnk ḥṭ mn* ʾ*lhn hw*
> [.....] ʾ*nt yh bry zp dgn*ʾ *wḥnṭt*ʾ *zy t*ʾ*kl wtšb*ʿ *wtntn lbnyk* ʿ*mk*
>
> [*Do not bend*] your [b]ow and do not mount (= shoot) your arrow at a righteous (man) lest the gods proceed to his help and turn it back against you.
> [...] you, O my son. Harvest any harvest and do any work. Then, you will eat and be satisfied and give to your children.
> [*Why do*] you [b]end your bow and mount (= shoot) your arrow at (one more) righteous than you? It is a sin from (= against) gods.
> [...] you, O my son. Borrow the grain and the wheat that you may eat and be satisfied and give to your children with you. (C1.1:126 – 129)[182]

---

180 Quoted from Porten and Yardeni, *TADAE*, III: Literature, Accounts, Lists, 47.
181 *CAL*, s.v. *lḥy* (accessed 6 May 2015).
182 Quoted from Porten and Yardeni, *TADAE*, III: Literature, Accounts, Lists, 42 – 43.

The arrow (*ḥṭ*) shot at a righteous man (*ṣdyq*) is a sin (*ḥṭʾ*) against the gods. "The gods" (*ʾlhyʾ*) shall make the arrow return (*twb*) against the archer who shot it. In C1.1:126 there is a lack of agreement between the plural "the gods" and the singular verb *ysgh* (*peal* imperfect third masculine singular). The likeliest explanation is that this is due to a scribal error. The plural noun *ʾlhyʾ* may be a scribal error for the singular *ʾlhʾ*, "the god"[183] or the verb may have been erroneously written in singular.[184]

Furthermore, in another saying on the subject of retribution, it is the god Shamash who is seen as the guarantor of justice:

> *hn yʾḥdn ršyʿʾ bknpy lbšk šbq bydh ʾḥr ʾdny lšmš hw*
> *[y]lqḥ zylh wyntn lk*
>
> If the wicked one seizes the corner of your garment, leave (it) in his hand. Then, submit (your case/yourself) to Shamash; he
> [will] take his and give it to you. (C1.1:107–108)[185]

The saying presumably presupposes a situation of debt comparable to, for example, Exod 22:25–28 and Deut 24:10–13.[186] If so, the "wicked one" (*ršyʿʾ*) is a pawnbroker who has lent something to the person spoken to in the second person. The security furnished by the debtor may have been the garment. In the *Aḥiqar* saying, the pawnbroker collects his pledge ("your garment"). However, here the pawnbroker is also characterised as "the wicked." This characterisation suggests that the forfeiture is illegitimate and that the debtor (i.e. the one addressed as "you") has not defaulted on his loans. Alternatively, by seizing the debtor's garment, the pawnbroker is accused of acting inhumanly (cf. Exod 22:27a "[your neighbour's cloak] is his only clothing, the sole covering for his skin. In what else shall he sleep?").

However that may be, the victim of the pawnbroker's action is urged to *ʾdny lšmš*, "appeal to Shamash" (*aphel* imperative singular of *dny*). The saying displays a conviction that the god will secure the debtor's rights. Shamash also appears in the sphere of justice in another (and much more fragmentary) saying (C1.1:197).[187]

---

183 So Takamitsu Muraoka and Bezalel Porten, *A Grammar of Egyptian Aramaic*, 2nd rev. ed., HdO 32 (Leiden: Brill, 2003), §76ch.
184 Niehr, *Aramäischer Aḥiqar*, 46, refers to additional explanations.
185 Quoted from Porten and Yardeni, *TADAE*, III: Literature, Accounts, Lists, 38–39.
186 Weigl, *Die aramäischen Achikar-Sprüche*, 244–247, cf. Niehr, *Aramäischer Aḥiqar*, 45.
187 See also the reference to "the sun" (*smšʾ*) in the formularies of emancipation used in the native Elephantine Judaean sources, discussed in Section 6.3.3.3 above.

6.5.1.4 The Human and the Other Humans

Aḥiqar contains several sayings on human–human relationship, and in particular sayings related to family matters. Most of them are about how a father should discipline his son and how a son should respect his parents. However, it is noteworthy that the text lacks sayings concerning marriage or women,[188] an issue one would expect in such a type of work. Perhaps this was at issue in parts of the text that now are lost. Nevertheless, a son who dishonours his parents is a bad person: "[*A person w*]ho does not exalt in the name of his father and in the name of his mother, may [(the)] su[n] (OR: Sham[ash]) not shine [*for him*] for he is a bad person" (C1.1:138).[189] A son who proves to be disloyal towards his father defames the latter in the eyes of a stranger (C1.1:139 – 140). Moreover, corporeal punishment may be a good means of disciplining a son: "Do not withhold your son from (the) rod. IF NOT, you will not be able to save hi[m ...]. If I strike you, my son, you will not die; but if I leave (you) to your heart (= your own will) [...]" (C1.1:176 – 177, cf. C1.1:175).[190] Correspondingly, there are sayings urging a slave to obey his master (C1.1:191 – 192). Corporeal punishment as a method of teaching is advisable for slaves, too: "A stroke for a slave-lad, a rebuke for a SLAVE-LASS; moreover, for all your slaves discip[line]" (C1.1:178).[191]

In addition, honesty is a virtue, whereas falsehood is a vice. There are proverbs warning against liars and admonishing truth (C.1.1:132 – 135); the "favour" (*ḥn*) of a man is his "trustworthiness" (*hymnw*), cf. C1.1:132. He who illegitimately acquires a fugitive or a stolen slave defames the name of his father (C1.1:179 – 180).

As far as the view on work is concerned, *Aḥiqar* offers a saying on that, too. Addressing his son, the wise says: *hkṣr kl kṣyr wʿbd kl ʿbydh ʾdyn tʾkl wtšbʿ wtntn lbnyk*, "Harvest any harvest and do any work. Then, you will eat and be satisfied and give to your children" (C1.1:127).[192] Although this is the only saying on this topic, it nevertheless suggests that *Aḥiqar* reflects a positive attitude towards manual labour.

Finally, *Aḥiqar* reflects the principle of just retribution in the narrative part. Aḥiqar's virtue comes to the fore narratively in his previous favourable deeds towards Nabusumiskun, who in the meantime had been appointed by the king to be Aḥiqar's executioner. Reminding the latter of the help he had previously given, Aḥiqar addressed him thus:

---

188 Porten and Yardeni, *TADAE*, III: Literature, Accounts, Lists, xv.

189 Quoted from Porten and Yardeni, *TADAE*, III: Literature, Accounts, Lists, 38 – 39.

190 Quoted from Porten and Yardeni, *TADAE*, III: Literature, Accounts, Lists, 49.

191 Quoted from Porten and Yardeni, *TADAE*, III: Literature, Accounts, Lists, 49.

192 Quoted from Porten and Yardeni, *TADAE*, III: Literature, Accounts, Lists, 42 – 43.

> *kʿn ʾnt lqbl zy ʾnh ʿbdt lk kn ʾpw ʿbd ly ʾl tqṭlny blny lb[y]tk ʿ[d] lywmn ʾḥrnn*
>
> Now, you, just as I did for you, so, then, do for me. Do not kill me. Bring me to your ho[u]se un[til] later days. (C1.1:51–52)[193]

This principle of ethical reciprocity is a variant of the Golden Rule. It is explicitly attested as a guiding ethical maxim in one of the fifth-century BCE Hermopolis letters written to Aramaeans living in Syene, opposite Elephantine.[194]

6.5.1.5 The Human and the Authorities of Society

As shown above, obedience is an important virtue in relations between a father and a son and a slave owner and his slave. This concept is also important in other asymmetrical relationships, too, namely the relationship between the king and his subjects. In the extant text of *Aḥiqar* there is a cluster of sayings especially devoted to obedience to the king.

> Do not cover (= ignore) the word of a king; let it be healing [for] your hea[rt]. Soft is the speech of a king (yet) it is sharper and mightier than a [double-]edged knife.
> See before you a hard (= severe) thing: [*against*] the face of a k[in]g do not stand. His rage is swifter than lightning. You, watch yourself.
> Let him not show it (= his rage) because of your sayings (= utterances) and you go (= lest you die) not in your days (= prematurely).
> [*See the go*]od of a king. If (something) is commanded to you, it is a burning fire. Hurry, do it. Do not kindle (it) against you and (do not) cover your palms (= "sit on your hands").
> [*More*]over, (do) the word of the king with heat/delight of the heart (= eagerly). * [*H*]ow can wood contest with fire, flesh with knife, man with k[ing]?
> I have tasted the bitter medlar and the [*taste*] is strong and (= but) there is not (anything) which is more [bi]tter than poverty. Soft is the tongue of a k[*ing*] (OR: A tongue is softer *than* [...])
> but the ribs of a dragon it will break like death which is [n]ot seen. * In an abundance of sons let not your heart rejoice and in their fewness [*do not mourn*].
> A king is like (the) Merciful (OR: indeed merciful); moreover, his voice i[s] high. Who is there who can stand before him (= serve him) but (he) with whom El is?
> Beautiful is the king to see like (the) sun (OR: Shamash) and precious is his glory to (them that) tread the earth (as) *f*[*ree*] men (OR: in tran[*quility*]). (C1.1:84–92)[195]

The sayings about the king are introduced by a single saying (C1.1:84) that combines two topics, namely the antagonistic power of the word of the king, and the

---

193 Quoted from Porten and Yardeni, *TADAE*, III: Literature, Accounts, Lists, 38–39.

194 See A2.3:4–8, cf. Porten, *Archives from Elephantine*, 270–271, cf. Kratz, "Aḥiqar and Bisitun."

195 Quoted from Porten and Yardeni, *TADAE*, III: Literature, Accounts, Lists, 37.

individual's appropriate response to the word of the king. The fact that the clause "soft is the speech of a king" (*rkyk mmll mlk*) in C1.1:84 is repeated almost verbatim at the end of C1.1:89 ("Soft is the tongue of a k[ing]," *rkyk lšn m[lk]*) indicates editorial activity of some kind.

The word of the king is characterised by a dichotomy. On the one it is given positive characteristics. It is "soft" and is even brought in the sphere of healing (*rp'h*, C1.1:84). However, on the other side the word of the king is also described using more threatening metaphors. It is "sharper and mightier than a double-edged knife" and a (royal) command "is a burning fire."

A subject's response to the word of the king can be seen as a logical and natural consequence of the latter. The threefold rhetorical question in C1.1:88 gives a brief comparison: "[H]ow can wood contest with fire, flesh with a knife, man with a k[ing]?" The answer to each of the questions is obviously that fire is stronger than wood, a knife stronger than flesh, and a king stronger than a man (*'yš*).

Moreover, the king is, no surprise, elevated above ordinary people. The king may not be explicitly divine, yet his realm is in the proximity of that of the gods. For a subject who will "stand" in the presence of the king, it is a prerequisite that he enjoys El's assistance (cf. C1.1:91). Furthermore, the king is even compared to the gods. One case of comparison is potentially found at the beginning of C1.1:91: *mlk krḥmn 'p qlh gbh h[w]*, a clause Bezalel Porten translates "A king is like (the) Merciful (OR: indeed merciful)." However, as Herbert Niehr has pointed out, the syntax is disputed. If the particle *k* denotes comparison and *rḥmn* is written correctly in the absolute state, it is a nominal clause: "A king is like Merciful." In this case, the undetermined "Merciful" is a synonym for the god El who figures later in one and the same saying.[196] The comparison of the king to Shamash (*kšmš*) in the following line 92 supports this interpretation. However, the particle *k* can also been interpreted as the so-called *Kaf veritatis* (denoting asseveration), giving the translation "A king is *indeed* merciful."[197] Support for this can be found in the narrative part of *Aḥiqar*. There, Aḥiqar himself utters his confidence in the king's mercifulness in the presence of the executioner Nabusumiskun: "Esarhaddon the King is merciful [*rḥmn*]" (C1.1:53). Moreover, as mentioned there is a comparison between the king's appearance and the god Shamash in the following line: *špyr mlk lmḥzh kšmš*, "Beautiful is the king to see like Shamash" (C1.1:92). In the latter case the noun *šmš* is not in the emphatic state.

196 Niehr, *Aramäischer Aḥiqar*, 43.

197 Muraoka and Porten, *A Grammar of Egyptian Aramaic*, §87 f. For other suggestions, see Niehr, *Aramäischer Aḥiqar*, 43.

This strongly suggests that it does not refer to "(the) sun," but to (the god) Shamash.

6.5.2 The Aramaic Version of the Bisitun Inscription (C2.1)

The Aramaic version of the Bisitun inscription (= DB Aram) is, as the name suggests, an Aramaic version of King Darius I's Bisitun inscription (= DB), probably dating to the time of Darius II, namely, the last decades of the fifth century BCE.[198] Because of the literary connection between DB Aram and DB, and because DB Aram is fragmentary, attention should also be drawn to its *Vorlage*, that is, DB. Originally, DB was inscribed on a rock face at Bisitun, visible from the main road between Susa, one of the traditional principal cities of Elam, and Ecbatana in the province of Media, by King Darius I who acceded to the throne in 522 BCE. The original inscription was trilingual, written in Elamite, Akkadian and Old Persian, and it was accompanied by an iconographic presentation of Darius I defeating several named opponents.

Why, then, is DB Aram relevant as a source particularly in regard to the question of the ethical dimension of the religion of the Judaeans in Elephantine? On the verso of the papyrus scroll used for drawing up DB Aram there was some empty space after the end of the text. This blank space was used to write down a record of memoranda (C3.13). The dates found in the record, and in particular the Yahwistic names occurring there, suggest that DB Aram must once have been in the possession of members of the Judaean garrison. As I have shown above in the discussion about the Achaemenid concept of sacral kingship and the official royal Achaemenid ideology, the purpose of DB and DB Aram—as well as the other royal Achaemenid inscriptions—was to legitimate the Achaemenid dynasty and promulgate its royal ideology.[199] This was done not only in the *Vorlage*, that is, in DB itself. At the end of DB Darius I himself commanded that the Bisitun inscription should be translated into other languages and distributed throughout the empire (cf. DB §70). The promulgation was done by means of contextually adapted copies of the inscriptions such as the ones found in Babylon (DB Bab, with Bel-Marduk as the main god instead of Ahuramazda) and Elephantine (DB Aram). In the discussion above I have argued that King Darius I in DB (and Darius II in DB Aram) pursued a rhetoric of self-justification that

198 For a more extensive discussion of the Bisitun inscription and the promulgation of royal Achaemenid ideology in Babylon and Elephantine, see Granerød, "'By the Favour of Ahuramazda'," 455–480.

199 See Section 5.4.2 above.

can be subsumed under the headings legitimacy *de iure* (genealogy), legitimacy *de facto* (power) and legitimacy *de gratia* (providence). Therefore, DB and DB Aram can be seen as sources for the ethical demands that faced all the subjects of the Persians and that were imposed on them, at least officially.

Unlike *Aḥiqar*, DB is not concerned with inter-human ethics. The question of what DB (and DB Aram) put forward as good moral behaviour between (ordinary) people in the societies that made up the Achaemenid Empire falls outside of the focus of the inscription. It does not offer ethical instruction pertaining to the axis "human and other humans." On the contrary, it is more concerned with the relation between one particular human and one particular deity, namely King Darius and Ahuramazda. In addition, DB is also concerned with the relation between the Achaemenid king and his subjects.

The Achaemenid ideology expressed in DB Aram as well as other royal Achaemenid inscriptions clearly had ethical implications. It included the idea that the Great King was king by the grace of Ahuramazda. Thus, the subjects—including the Judaeans in Elephantine who evidently had a copy of the Aramaic version of the propaganda text—were implicitly expected to accept the idea of the Achaemenid rulers as kings that had been particularly chosen for this task by Ahuramazda. In a sense, from the perspective of the Bisitun inscription, the subjects of the Achaemenid Empire, including the Judaeans, were ethically accountable to Ahuramazda. Moreover, even though the sources for the Judaeans in Elephantine do not offer much information about it, one should nevertheless keep in mind that they were soldiers under Persian command. Also for this reason we should expect that they accepted—or at least were expected to accept—the ethical demands expressed in DB Aram. In the end, to some extent the Judaean garrison in Elephantine (together with, e.g., the Aramaean [?] garrison stationed in Syene) *was* one of the visible and tangible expressions of Persian supremacy over Egypt.

6.5.3 The Relevance of the Non-Native Sources

Neither *Aḥiqar* nor DB Aram was composed by the Judaeans in Elephantine. On the contrary, they both came from "outside," yet with contents that had definite ethical implications for the Judaeans. The Judaeans were exposed to these sources. Therefore they give us a glimpse of the ethical demands that were presumably *state-sanctioned* in the Persian period.

In this context, it is noteworthy that the Judaeans in Elephantine, on several occasions and in various letters, took great pains to express their loyalty to the

Persian officials.[200] Therefore, it is reasonable to assume that virtues of the normative works *Aḥiqar* and DB Aram resonated among the Yahwistic Judaeans at Elephantine.

6.6 Chapter Summary

This chapter has attempted to present the ethics of the Elephantine Judaean community, that is, its ethical virtues and its actual, practiced ethics, on the basis of the native Elephantine Judaean sources and the non-native sources (*The Words of Aḥiqar* and the Aramaic version of King Darius's Bisitun inscription). The discussions of the native (and in part also the non-native) sources in regards to the ethics of the Judaeans has been made with three focal points in mind: *the human and the deities*, *the human and the other humans*, and *the human and the authorities of society.*

In light of parallels elsewhere from the ancient world it is not self-evident that there existed a link between the ethics and the worship of YHW and the other gods. However, on the basis of i.a. the oath practice attested where an oath to a god could function as evidence in the lack of firm evidence, then it is likely that there were, in fact, connections between good behaviour and the gods. Moreover, the so-called Vidranga section, which was probably a liturgy of curse in the form of a series of imprecations, suggests that the Judaeans expected YHW to punish and revenge unjust behaviour in this life, not in the hereafter.

Although no systematic treatment of the anthropology of the Judaeans in Elephantine is known, it is argued that some aspects may be ferreted out of the sources. Unfortunately the sources do not give any explicit view of how work was perceived (cf. in contrast other ancient Near Eastern texts such as Atrahasis and the biblical creation account and the Eden narrative in Gen 1–3). However, we can observe that the Judaeans in fact worked both in the primary sector and the public sector. As for the latter, most of the male Judaeans were probably soldiers (under Persian command). Moreover, some Judaean families were trained scribes, and some may also have been involved with agriculture (the so-called hereditary property holders, *mhḥsnn*). The Judaeans also practiced slavery, understood as the phenomenon where a person was the legal property of another person. Slaves could, however, be manumitted and adopted by the former owner. The sources do not suggest that there was a particular Elephantine Ju-

200 See Section 6.4 above.

daean view of slavery, distinct from that of its surroundings. On the contrary, slavery was legally regulated and the legal regulations were of a contractual nature.

The marriage was also regulated as a contractual agreement, and then between the bride-giver (father, brother or owner) and the bridegroom. The contractual regulation of the marriage suggests that is was considered to be a public affair. However, the sources do not suggest that marriage had any specifically religious character. Even though formulations in the marriage contracts suggest that marriage was ideally meant to last until the death of one of the spouses, it was nevertheless possible to divorce. What is remarkable is that the husband and the wife had equal capacity to dissolve the marriage, and that the wife enjoyed a relatively high degree of economic protection in the event of a divorce.

As for the ethics of the Elephantine Judaeans vis-à-vis the authorities, it is important to acknowledge that the Judaeans in fact made up a *Persian* military garrison. The respect they paid to various Persian officials is evident in several cases, and we may assume that it was important for them to present themselves as loyal to the Persian king and his deputies.

It is further argued that the ethical demands that the Persian administration placed on its subjects (including the Judaean garrison in Elephantine) may be sought in the two non-native sources *The Words of Aḥiqar* and the Aramaic version of King Darius's Bisitun inscription. Among other things, the international sapiential work *Aḥiqar*, which covers a wide range of ethical topics, promoted obedience to the king as a virtue. As far as the Aramaic version of the Bisitun inscription is concerned, it promoted King Darius as the legitimate king (in the case of the original inscription it was Darius I, in the case of the Aramaic version it was Darius II). In addition, it promoted Achaemenid royal ideology, according to which Darius (both I and II) was a legitimate king *de iure*, *de facto* and *de gratia*. As a consequence of the claim that the king had been chosen and reigned "by the favour of Ahuramazda," political disloyalty ultimately meant disloyalty towards the god Ahuramazda himself.

7 Conclusion and Outlook

7.1 The Dimensions of Yahwism in General and in Elephantine in Particular

What was Judaean religion (or "Judaism," for that matter) in the Persian period like? What were its characteristics? And is it necessary to use the Bible in order to discuss such questions? In the Persian period, Yahwism was practised in several different places and in several different contexts. Consequently, we may say it had many *dimensions*. The Yahwism practised by the Judaean community and reflected in the Aramaic documents from Egypt is a fully fledged representative of Judaean religion in the Persian period, not a curiosity on its fringe.

Judaean religion in the Persian period was *diverse* in many ways. In general, the deity YHWH (or YHW as the name was spelled in Elephantine) was the chief god of Judaeans, regardless of whether they lived in the province of Judah or in diaspora communities like the one in Elephantine. I have not even mentioned that there were non-Judaean Yahwists, too, such as the people of Samaria (cf., e.g., the theophoric names of Delaiah and Shelemiah, the sons of Sanballat, the governor of Samaria). However, the religious system we may call Yahwism —the main characteristic of which was that the deity YHWH (or as he was called in Elephantine: YHW/YHH) was worshipped as the most important god—had *many dimensions*. One dimension of Persian-period Yahwism is reflected in the more or less Jerusalem-centred texts of the Bible. This particular dimension of Persian-period Yahwism was oriented towards the temple of YHWH in Jerusalem. Its "sacred orientation"—in both a concrete and a metaphorical sense—was towards Jerusalem. However, as I have shown in this work, the sources for the Judaean community at Elephantine reflect *another dimension* of Yahwism in the Persian period than the one(s) reflected in the Bible. Also for the Judaeans of Elephantine the god YHW was the chief god. However, their "sacred orientation"— understood both literally and metaphorically—was towards the temple of YHW, "the god dwelling in Elephantine" (B3.12:1–2).

The present study has sought to show that the Yahwism practised in Elephantine is a fully legitimate candidate to represent Judaean religion in the Persian period. The so-called Elephantine papyri and the other Aramaic documents from Persian-period Egypt give us "snapshots" of lived, practised Yahwism in a concrete context, that is, in an identifiable historical, cultural and geographic environment. Thus, as religio-historical sources they enable us to say more about the *actual* religious practice of the Elephantine Judaeans than what the (highly edited) texts of the Hebrew Bible reveal about the actual religious practice of the contemporary Yahwistic co-religionists in Judah. To borrow Magnar Kartveit's words concerning the corpus of inscriptions from Mount Gerizim and the Delos inscriptions, "[i]nscriptions are valuable information because they have not been adjusted and updated like literary texts. They may have been mutilated and tampered with, but often the original text can be read or recovered, which is different from literary evidence."[1]

As a consequence, the religio-historical situation emerging from the Aramaic documents from Egypt should neither be deemed as an exception nor as a curiosity. Rather, in my view it is ironically this particular dimension of Yahwism—i.e. the one reflected in the documents in question and practised by a diaspora community of Judaean soldiers serving Persian overlords on Egypt's traditional southern border—that is *the* best attested actual, practiced example of Judaean religion in the Persian period there is.

According to Ninian Smart's religious taxonomy, any given religion reflects itself in several dimensions: a *social*, a *material*, a *ritual*, a *mythic and narrative*, an *ethical*, an *experiential* and a *doctrinal* dimension. In the present study I have applied a modified version of Smart's model on the Yahwism emerging from the Aramaic documents from Achaemenid Egypt. I believe I have been able to demonstrate that the textual and partly archaeological sources enable us to describe quite a few of the dimensions of the religion of the Judaeans in Elephantine, with the exception of the experiential and doctrinal dimensions.

7.2 Contributions and Findings

The present work's most important contributions to the research on Judaean religion include new and alternative methodologies and frameworks for the study of Judaean religion in the Persian period as well as particular factual findings.

7.2.1 Yahwistic Diversity

The first finding that contributes to the framework is definitely not original but nevertheless still important, namely that the Yahwism—that is the worship of YHWH as the most important deity regardless of towards what temple or shrine the worship was directed—of the Persian period was characterised by *diversity*.

1 Magnar Kartveit, "Samaritan Self-Consciousness in the First Half of the Second Century B.C.E. in Light of the Inscriptions from Mount Gerizim and Delos," *JSJ* 45 (2014): 449–470 (470).

The phenomenon of poly-Yahwism continued to exist also in this period, after many of the inhabitants of Judah had been exiled by the Babylonians and after the subsequent rebuilding of the temple of YHWH in Jerusalem.

7.2.2 The Ordinariness of the Yahwism in Elephantine

The second finding contributing to the framework is that the version—i. e. *dimension*—of Yahwism practised in Elephantine should *not* be treated as "the odd man out." In my view, there is no reason to look at the Judaean community in Elephantine as a cabinet of religious curiosities or as a living museum. On the contrary, I will argue that the Yahwism of Elephantine represents an example of Judaean religion that we should regard as an *equally typical* type of Judaean religion as the one emerging from the (late) texts of the Hebrew Bible. In the latter, Yahwism has become "scripturalised."[2] What is more, whereas the exact social, religious, cultural and geographic environment(s) that the biblical texts were written and edited within still remain elusive at the best, in spite of centuries of historical-critical research, the sources for the Yahwism in Elephantine can be connected to a concrete environment. Thus, I argue that they have been underestimated as sources, particularly in comparison to the texts of the Bible. Instead of being exotified they should be brought to the very centre of the discussion of the history of Judaean religion. Thus, when scholars claim that the Elephantine Judaeans were religiously conservative, for instance by reflecting "pre-exilic Judaean religion" untouched by the religious renewals such as the Deuteronomistic movement, then these statements in reality reflect a stereotype within the scholarly guild about the religious development of Yahwism. To be slightly more provocative: The religious practice of the Judaean community in Elephantine and the more famous community in and around Jerusalem have become subjects and victims of an "Orientalism" (cf. Edward Said) that continues to exercise influence on the history of Judaean religion. Elephantine Yahwism has suffered for having been and still being understood on the basis of stereotypes of what "real," "true" Judaean religion in the Persian period was like. Not seldom the Yahwism practiced in Jerusalem and Judah and reflected in biblical texts have provided the templates for these stereotypes.

2 For a discussion of the "scripturalisation" of Yahwism and in particular the concept of torah, see, e.g., Thomas Willi, "'Wie Geschrieben steht' – Schriftbezug und Schrift: Überlegungen zur frühjüdischen Literaturwerdung in perserzeitlichen Kontext," in *Religion und Religionskontakte im Zeitalter der Achämeniden*, ed. Reinhard Gregor Kratz, VWGT 22 (Gütersloh: Gütersloher Verlagshaus, 2002): 257–277.

7.2.3 The Suitability (and Limitations) of Smart's Multi-Dimensional Model of Religion

The third finding pertaining to the framework is that the Yahwism practised in Elephantine represents a religious practice that *can* and *should* be discussed on its own terms, without using terms and concepts drawn from a corpus of (religious) sources alien to it. As far as I can see, there is no reason to assume that the Yahwists in Elephantine had any sacred books.[3] Therefore, any discussion of this example of Yahwism that depends upon biblical concepts and frameworks might prove to be misleading. Concretely, the way I have chosen to study the religion of the Judaeans in Elephantine on its own terms is by using the religious taxonomy of Ninian Smart. To be sure, Smart has never claimed that his multidimensional model of religion should be understood as a canonical approach, and neither do I. Nevertheless, figuratively speaking there are many ways to cut a cake. And, there are many ways to describe and discuss a specific type

---

3 So, e.g., Reinhard Gregor Kratz, *Historisches und biblisches Israel: Drei Überblicke zum Alten Testament* (Tübingen: Mohr Siebeck, 2013), 186–203, 274–283. However, see also Göran Eidevall, "Review of *Historisches Und Biblisches Israel: Drei Überblicke Zum Alten Testament*, by Reinhard Gregor Kratz," *RBL* 8 (2014): online edition, available at http://bookreviews.org/pdf/9345_10314.pdf. Eidevall criticises Kratz's thesis that the rise of the so-called "biblical Judaism" should be dated relatively narrowly to a time between two chronological and spatial poles, represented by the Elephantine archive (terminus ca. 400 BCE) on the one side, and the earliest documents from Qumran on the other. In Eidevall's opinion, this scenario is implausible because it creates a number of problems that are not easily solved. He asks why texts and traditions from the monarchic era were mainly preserved and edited by groups that were not linked to the temple in Jerusalem. Moreover, he asks how we can explain the construction of synagogues and the translation of the Torah taking place already during the third century in Alexandria, if biblical Judaism was largely unknown by then. Moreover, according to Eidevall it is unclear how Kratz's thesis can explain how Torah-centered piety suddenly could become a dominant factor during the Maccabean revolt within several competing parties. In Eidevall's view, Kratz's thesis is methodologically flawed and represents a remarkable case of *argumentio e silentio*.

However, in my opinion Eidevall's critique of Kratz's thesis does not seem to take into account the challenges posited by the existence of a fully fledged Yahwism in Africa, an example of Judaean religion that seems to be totally ignorant of the Bible, and what is more, that it is in full swing in a period where Judaeans according to, e.g., Neh 8 were obeying the Torah of YHWH given to Moses. Eidevall's queries regarding how to explain the questions referred to above are relevant. However, as the existence of a fully fledged Yahwism in Elephantine in the (late) Persian period shows, the answer to these questions may be found along the following path: Some of the biblical traditions were existing already, some even before the Persian period. However, they were apparently not *universally* accepted and recognised within all branches of Yahwism. The Judaeans at Elephantine represent proof of this.

of religious practice. The present study has shown that the application of Smart's model of religion to the study of an ancient religion such as Yahwism in Elephantine turns out to be a fruitful one. There are several reasons why. One is the relatively fortunate situation regarding the sources. Taken as a whole, the Aramaic documents pertaining to the Judaean community in Elephantine cover a whole range of the dimensions of religion. In spite of the arbitrary selection of history the surviving documents enable us to see and describe relatively much. However, another reason is the general nature and plasticity of Smart's approach. Any religion will inevitably reflect itself—to a smaller or larger degree—in the dimensions that Smart's model operates with. In my view, the model offers a good combination of sufficient stringency and uniformity at the same time as it has the sufficient inherent "slack" enabling it to handle differences from one case to another.

The Yahwism of the Judaeans in Elephantine reflected itself in the identity and the organisation of the society, that is, in a social dimension. In the material there are glimpses of the formal and informal leadership of the community. Moreover, the religious practice reflected itself in the oath practice. Furthermore, it reflected itself in the fact that there were religious specialists. The highest ranked specialists were *khnyn*, and not *kmryn*. The Yahwism of the Judaeans in Elephantine also had implications for the economy. And, it reflected itself in the organisation of time, even though there are many questions concerning the calendar(s) that remain unanswered.

Moreover, the Judaean religion in Elephantine definitely had a material dimension. On the basis of the textual and archaeological sources, it is safe to state that the most concrete crystallisation of the religious practice was the temple of the deity YHW, "the god dwelling in Elephantine." I have demonstrated that this in fact was a temple, not a house of prayer. In addition, I have attempted to make conjectures about the Judaean temple theology in Elephantine. Although there are uncertainties in our knowledge about the temple (as is to be expected in the light of the material) the Judaeans regarded it neither as a rival nor as a successor to the temple in Jerusalem. On the contrary, they regarded it as a complementary temple. By approaching the Jerusalem priesthood as part of the campaign to rebuild the temple in Elephantine (cf. A4.7:18 – 19 par.), the Judaeans in southern Egypt gave a clear testimony. For them, poly-Yahwism (using a modern term) was, religiously speaking, a valid form of Yahwism.

The Yahwism of the Judaeans in Elephantine also had a ritual dimension, including communal and individual rites. One important type of ritual they performed was represented by the sacrifices. I have conjectured about the Judaean theology of sacrifice, including the changes it underwent as the result of the involvement of (Persian) officials such as the governors of Judah and Samaria, and probably also the Persian satrap of Egypt. Moreover, the sources give glimpses of rites of mourning and prayers. The closest we get to a liturgy in the material is what I (following Lindenberger) regard as a communal prayer of curse. Furthermore, Yahwism in Elephantine may also have reflected itself in rites in connection with festivals such as the Passover and (in want of a better name) the Festival of Unleavened Bread. Finally, the question of the religious status of the Sabbath in Elephantine must in my view remain unsolved. The Judaeans referred to a specific day as the Sabbath (*šbh*). However, it is far from clear whether the day in question referred to the last day of a seven-day week, whether the Judaeans in Elephantine knew the seven-day week at all, and whether it was observed as a day of rest prescribed by divine command.

Yahwism at Elephantine also had a mythic and narrative dimension. The clearest example of that is the temple foundation narrative. On the basis of the documents of the so-called Jedaniah archive it is possible to describe some key aspects of its contents (the *traditum*). However, these documents also shed light on how the narrative was transmitted (the *traditio*) and who took part in the transmission (the *tradentes*) and how it was even slightly altered. Moreover, the Elephantine Judaeans were part of the Achaemenid power structure in Egypt and I have attempted to show how they were exposed to Persian myths about sacral kingship. Furthermore, for several reasons it is likely that the Judaean community were aware of and even recognised both Egyptian and Aramaean pantheons. What is more, we may even speak of a Judaean pantheon. However, the material only allows us to see traces of these pantheons. Unfortunately it does not allow us to flesh out exactly what the myths and narratives connected to these pantheons were, how the gods of the pantheons were organised and if and possibly how the different pantheons were related to each other.

Finally, the Elephantine Yahwism also reflected itself in an ethical dimension. In comparison to other religions of the ancient world, it is not self-evident that worship and ethics were related. In the case of the ethics of the Judaeans in Elephantine, the material is partly the native Elephantine Judaean sources and partly non-native sources (above all *The Words of Aḥiqar* and the Aramaic version of Darius's Bisitun inscription). Together, these sources shed light on both the virtues and the actual, practiced ethics of the Judaeans. I have shown that it is possible ferret out some of the aspects of the anthropology. Moreover, we can also see aspects of how the (male and female) Judaeans conceived of the status of women, slaves, marriage and the authorities of the society, including facets of the norms for these concepts.

An enumeration of the dimensions of religion mentioned above gives the number five, whereas Smart's model has seven. Thus, in the present study, two are missing: the experiential dimension and the doctrinal dimension. Even though aspects of the missing dimensions have certainly been touched upon, in my judgement the contents of the material pertaining to these dimensions does not justify separate chapters devoted entirely to them. Due to the arbitrary nature of the primary sources we only have a limited access to the (religious) emotions and experiences of the Judaeans. The same goes for their more elaborate and systematic doctrinal and philosophical reasoning, if there was such a thing at all. The documents only give us "snapshots" of the practiced religion *in situ*. They were never meant to offer a comprehensive picture of the Elephantine Yahwism in its entire complexity. Moreover, the described limitation is also due to a fundamental methodological limitation every student of an ancient—and extinct—religion faces: in contrast to a religious scholar studying a contemporary religion, a religious historian cannot do fieldwork such as observations and interviews. Thus, from an epistemological point of view the religious experiences and emotions of the Elephantine Judaeans elude us.

7.2.4 Selected Original Particular Findings

A study like the present one will inevitably have to stand on the shoulders of other scholarly contributions, and to this end I hope that I have given adequate credit to others scholars. However, I dare to claim that not only should the present study's contribution to the overall framework be deemed as original, in addition some of its particular, concrete findings are also original.

One of them is my conclusion concerning the physical orientation of the temple of YHW. Even though the axis of the temple structure admittedly was oriented towards the northeast—and when seen on a map: towards Jerusalem—this should most likely *not* be interpreted as reflecting the spiritual orientation of the Elephantine Judaeans, with the implication that in reality, the prayers, the prayers and sacrifices in the temple were made facing Jerusalem. Even though the Judaeans affiliated themselves with the Judaeans of Judah and thus must have regarded the latter as co-religionists, the temple of YHW in Elephantine was self-contained and not a branch of the temple in Jerusalem. Its physical orientation should be interpreted as the result of the general orientation of the streets of the ancient town of Elephantine.

Moreover, another original contribution is my discussion of the Elephantine Judaean temple foundation narrative. The fact that the Judaeans in Elephantine actually had a narrative about the foundation of the temple is intriguing in itself. However, I believe my contribution provides new and original factual as well as methodological insights into how the foundation narrative was modelled on the basis of a general ancient Near Eastern pattern of antiquarianism. Moreover, I believe I can show how the foundation narrative offers an empirically verifiable case of a traditio-historical process.

Finally, I also claim that I contribute new and original factual and methodological insights into the mechanism of the promulgation of the Achaemenid royal ideology and the reception of it in a (garrison) community like the Judaean one. The community, which ultimately was part of the official power structure, may illustrate what kind of propaganda the Achaemenids promulgated, and how this was done.

7.2.5 YHWH, a God Also Dwelling in Africa: Yahwism in Elephantine as a Challenge for Biblical Scholarship

Who has the privilege to define what was true Yahwism in the Persian period? The present study will hopefully challenge the—mostly unarticulated—hegemony of the Hebrew Bible as the source and the norm par excellence of the true worship of YHWH, at least in the last half of the first millennium BCE. In the eyes of the biblical authors, theologians and editors of the Persian or even Hellenistic periods, YHWH was the god dwelling in his chosen place, and the chosen place was Jerusalem. Not seldom modern scholars take on this assumption.

To be sure, the scholarly understanding of YHWH as a—or perhaps even *the* —god of Jerusalem has not come about in a vacuum. Epigraphic sources from Judah suggest that the idea that YHWH was a god whose dwellings were in Jerusalem was anchored in popular religious concepts back in the Assyrian and Neo-Babylonian periods. A good example of this is one of the inscriptions from Khirbet Beit Lei,[4] a place in the Judaean Shephelah about seven kilometres east of Lachish. Due to the uneven surface of the tomb wall it was written on and the fact that the characters of the inscription are difficult to decipher, several, in part quite different readings of the text have been proposed.[5] A possible, and according to Martin Leuenberger almost certain,[6] reading is the following one:

4 Graham I. Davies et al., *Ancient Hebrew Inscriptions: Corpus and Concordance* (Cambridge: Cambridge University Press, 1991), 89 (no. 15.005).

5 For an overview, see Ziony Zevit, *The Religions of Ancient Israel: A Synthesis of Parallactic Approaches* (London: Continuum, 2001), 417–427, and Martin Leuenberger, "Jhwh, »der Gott Jerusalems« (Inschrift aus Ḫirbet Bet Layy 1,2): Konturen der Jerusalemer Tempeltheologie aus religions- und theologiegeschichtlicher Perspektive," *EvT* 74 (2014): 245–260 (252–255). See also Herbert Niehr, "The Rise of YHWH in Judahite and Israelite Religion: Methodological and

yhwh ʾlhy kl hʾrṣ h
ry yhwdh lʾlhy yršlm

A possible translation of the above reading is:

> YHWH is the god of the whole land, the mountains of Judah belong to the god of Jerusalem.

Palaeographic considerations and the archaeological context (a tomb possibly made in the eight or seventh century BCE[7]) suggest a date for the inscription in the eight or seventh century.[8] However, a later, Persian-period date is also possible.[9] In any case, the reading and translation of the inscription offered here suggest that the inscriber venerated YHWH as the patron god of Judah in general and of Jerusalem in particular.[10] Thus, the inscription is a confessional statement about YHWH as a protection deity with a particularly close connection to a certain locus: Judah and Jerusalem in particular. A religious historian obviously has to deal with it in an emphatic way, nevertheless without giving preference to its contents and theological tendency vis-à-vis other comparable statements about YHWH.

So, for the Judaeans of Judah it was probably true that YHWH was the city god of Jerusalem and the national god of Judah. However, for the Judaean community in Elephantine it was equally true that YHW was the god dwelling in Elephantine.

Religio-Historical Aspects," in *Triumph of Elohim: From Yahwisms to Judaisms*, ed. Diana Vikander Edelman, CBET 13 (Kampen: Kok Pharos, 1995): 45 – 72 (55).

6 Leuenberger, "Jhwh, »der Gott Jerusalems«," 245 – 260 (253).

7 See Zevit, *The Religions of Ancient Israel*, 407.

8 For instance, Zevit, *The Religions of Ancient Israel*, 435, hypothesises that the inscriptions were made in connection with Senacherrib's invasion of Judah and siege of Jerusalem in 701 BCE.

9 A linguistic argument for dating the inscription to the Persian period comes from an alternative reading of the second line already suggested by Joseph Naveh who originally published the inscription, cf. Leuenberger, "Jhwh, »der Gott Jerusalems«," 245 – 260 (253 note 22). According to this alternative, the second line reads *hry yhwd lw lʾlhy yrwšlm*, "the mountains of Yehud belong to him, to the god of Jerusalem." If this reading should prove to be correct, the language is in fact Aramaic and not Hebrew (cf. the name *yhwd*) and the date of the inscriptions should be moved correspondingly towards the Persian period.

10 Leuenberger suggests that YHWH functioned as a state god in the Khirbet Beit Lei inscription comparable to how Chemosh functioned as the state god of the Moabites according to the Mesha inscription, cf. Leuenberger, "Jhwh, »der Gott Jerusalems«," 245 – 260 (255).

Thus, the very existence of a Yahwistic community with its own YHW temple in Africa— beyond the boundaries of Judah—challenges biblical theology. It challenges biblical theology regardless of how one understands theology: as a description of the theology of the Bible or in a confessional, normative way as the message of the Bible within the context of one's own faith.[11] The challenge is perhaps most obvious for the believer who holds the Bible to reveal the Word of God, a deity who according to the Bible is especially linked to Jerusalem. How should the believer handle the claim that YHWH also was (or still is, for that matter) a god dwelling in Elephantine? However, the existence of a Yahwistic community with its own temple of YHW in Elephantine also poses a challenge for a descriptive biblical theology. The reason is that the existence of an "African Yahwism" challenges the entire conceptual and spatial framework by means of which the phenomenon Yahwism very often has been and still is being understood. For example, when seen from the perspective of Elephantine, it is meaningless to call an entire period "the Second Temple period." After all, the periodisation takes a Jerusalem perspective on the history and theology of Yahwism.

The Judaeans in Elephantine believed that YHW was accessible in his temple in southern Egypt. Who are we, then—biblical scholars, religious historians, interested readers of various faiths—to raise objections to this fundamental belief?

7.3 Recommendations for Future Research: Elephantine in a Comparative Perspective

As far as the Yahwism that was practiced in Elephantine is concerned, it would no doubt be an exaggeration to state that we have the full picture. Obviously, there are many unfortunate gaps, gaps that are caused by the sources themselves and that will remain open until the discovery of possible additional relevant documents. However, we nevertheless do have the contours of a once thriving form of Yahwism.

In my opinion, the future research on the Judaean community in Elephantine and its religious practice would benefit from being compared to the religious practice of analogous diaspora communities from the same general period. If we loosely understand a diaspora community as an ethnically and/or religiously defined community that actively affiliates and associates itself with another geo-

11 A good discussion of various and differing concepts of biblical theology is offered in Jacob Stromberg, *An Introduction to the Study of Isaiah*, T&T Clark Approaches to Biblical Studies (London: T&T Clark, 2011), 95–98.

graphical home place and the inhabitants there, and moreover, if we delimit the search to assumedly Yahwistic communities, then there are at least two potential candidates.

7.3.1 The Judaean Diaspora in Babylonia in Neo-Babylonian and Achaemenid Periods

The first candidate is at the same time definitely the most famous diaspora community: the so-called Babylonian Captivity of (segments of) the Judaean population from the sixth century BCE and onwards. For millennia the only sources for the exilic community in Babylonia were the texts of the Bible. Again, in spite of centuries of critical research there is still no general consensus with respect to the date of composition of these texts and what exactly their function was. However, since scholars started systematically to dig for cuneiform tablets in the Mesopotamian region in the nineteenth century, epigraphic evidence about the Judaean diaspora in Babylonia has surfaced. For a long time it has been known that the documents of the so-called Murashu archive provide onomastic evidence for the existence of a Judaean population in Babylonia.[12] For better or worse, the existence is dependent upon the interpretation of personal names thought to be either theomorphic with YHWH as the divine element, or other names assumed to reflect a Judaean background. The more than seven hundred documents, found in Nippur, stem from the mid-fifth to the mid-fourth centuries BCE. For a long time, the texts of the Murashu archive have been the most important extra-biblical sources for the Judaean exile in Babylonia in the Achaemenid period. However, even though they shed light on economic and agricultural aspects of the everyday life of the Judaeans in Babylonia, they do not reveal much about how the diaspora Judaeans related themselves to Judah, and, in particular, if and possibly how their religious practice was influenced by the diaspora situation. As Cornelia Wunsch puts it, the documents of the Murashu archive "contain personal names of West Semitic and Hebrew origin (some exhibiting Yahwistic elements) which attest to descendants of Judaeans [*sic*] and other West-Semitic origin. They appear at the margin of transactions:

12 See, e.g., Israel Eph'al, "The Western Minorities in Babylonia in the 6th–5th Centuries B.C.: Maintenance and Cohesion," *Or* 47 (1978): 74–90; Muhammad A. Dandamaev, "The Diaspora: A. Babylonia in the Persian Age," *CHJ* 1: 326–342; and Matthew W. Stolper, "Muraschû, Archive of," *ABD* 4: 927–928.

more as witnesses or people mentioned in passing than as the parties to the transactions."[13]

However, as Wunsch continues, this situation has now has changed, thanks to new evidence from the exilic and early post-exilic times, about one hundred years earlier than the Murashu archive. These documents, in the form of a cluster of cuneiform texts dating to the sixth and fifth centuries BCE, portray Judaeans as the main protagonists and archive holders.[14] The new corpus of some two hundred documents illustrates the administrative, business, and to a certain extent family relations of the inhabitants of three places in particular: "town of Našar" (Ālu-ša-Našar) or "(town of) Našar's house" (Bīt-Našar), "(town of) Abī-râm's house" (Bīt-Abī-râm), and "Judah-town" (Āl-Yāḫūdu) or "town of the Judaeans" (Āl-Yāḫūdāya). Recently, this collection of the earliest extra-biblical evidence for the Judaean diaspora community in Babylonia has been made available to a broader scholarly audience by Laurie E. Pearce and Cornelia Wunsch in their 2014 volume, *Documents of Judean Exiles and West Semites in Babylonia in the Collection of David Sofer.*[15] The recently published edition of Pearce and Wunsch is extremely important for our understanding of (forced or voluntary) migrations and the (re-)settlement policy of the Neo-Babylonian and early Achaemenid periods, and particularly for our understanding of the social and economic everyday life of the exiled Judaeans in Babylonia.

Having that said, as far as I can see, neither the documents of the Murashu archive from the Achaemenid period nor those of the recently published collection of documents of the Āl-Yāḫūdu archive are as illuminating as the Elephantine documents. Admittedly, on the basis of the onomastics of the Āl-Yāḫūdu archive it is evident that YHWH had a special status in the religious life of people in "Judah-town" (Āl-Yāḫūdu). In addition, the name shift of one and the same individual—from Bēl-šar-uṣur ("O Bel, protect the king!") in one document from 552 BCE[16] to Yaḫū-šar-uṣur ("O YHW, protect the king!") in another document dating to 550 BCE[17]—is a telling testimony of how the Judaeans identified two originally separate gods that came from different contexts at the outset. Bel-

13 Cornelia Wunsch, "Glimpses on the Lives of Deportees in Rural Babylonia," in *Arameans, Chaldeans, and Arabs in Babylonia and Palestine in the First Millennium B.C.*, ed. Angelika Berlejung and Michael P. Streck, LAS 3 (Wiesbaden: Harrassowitz, 2013): 247–260 (249).

14 Wunsch, "Glimpses on the Lives of Deportees," 247–260 (249), cf. also Laurie E. Pearce, "New Evidence for Judeans in Babylonia," in *Judah and the Judeans in the Persian Period*, ed. Oded Lipschits and Manfred Oeming (Winona Lake, IN: Eisenbrauns, 2006), 399–411.

15 E. Pearce and Cornelia Wunsch, *Documents of Judean Exiles and West Semites in Babylonia in the Collection of David Sofer*, CUSAS 28 (Bethesda, MD: CDL, 2014).

16 Pearce and Wunsch, *Documents of Judean Exiles*, 102–103 (no. 3:2).

17 Pearce and Wunsch, *Documents of Judean Exiles*, 102–103 (no. 4:2).

Marduk was identified with YHWH, or vice versa. In addition, the fact that an individual belonging to a Judaean diaspora community bore a name that in reality was a prayer to his god to protect the king is by itself a forceful testament of a community that seemed to have attempted to assimilate into a new political reality. Nevertheless, in spite of this neither the Murashu archive nor the Āl-Yāḫūdu archive comes close to the fullness of the Elephantine documents with regard to the many dimensions of religion.

7.3.2 The Israelite ("Samaritan") Diaspora in the Aegean in the Second Century BCE

The second potential candidate for a comparison with the Elephantine community is the group whose worship was directed towards Mount Gerizim. In recent times nearly four hundred Hebrew and Aramaic plus a number of Greek inscriptions have been excavated on the summit.[18] According to Magnar Kartveit, they should be termed dedicatory inscriptions. The Gerizim corpus of inscriptions stem from the Persian and Hellenistic periods or possibly even more narrowly from the first part of the second century BCE. According to Kartveit, the phrase "in this place" (*b'trh dnh*), which is unparalleled in other comparable inscriptions, gives an impression of a community dedicated to its own place of worship, Mount Gerizim. In Kartveit's opinion, "the phrase 'in this place' can be interpreted as an expression of the self-consciousness of the dedicators: they form a community from places around Mount Gerizim, and they emphasize their religious attachment to this place."[19] However, what makes the community in the vicinity of Mount Gerizim an especially intriguing candidate for comparison with the Judaean community in Elephantine are two Greek inscriptions that were found on the island of Delos in the Aegean Sea in 1979. Formally, the Delos inscriptions are honorary inscriptions and it has been suggested to date both of them to the first half of the second century BCE, that is, around the same time as the Gerizim inscriptions.

The group responsible for making the inscriptions refers to itself as "Israelites" and "Israelites [ΙΣΡΑΕΛΕΙΤΑΙ/ΙΣΡΑΗΛΙΤΑΙ] in Delos" who send their "tem-

18 This brief discussion is based entirely upon Kartveit, "Samaritan Self-Consciousness," 449–470, cf. also Magnar Kartveit, "Samaritansk sjølvforståing i innskriftene frå Garisim og Delos," *TeoT* 3 (2014): 271–286.

19 Kartveit, "Samaritan Self-Consciousness," 449–470 (466).

ple tax"[20] to "sacred Argarizein"/"sacred, holy Argarizein."[21] ΑΡΓΑΡΙΖΕΙΝ is a Greek rendering of the Hebrew *har gərizîm*, "Mount Gerizim." Thus, the Delos inscriptions attest to a diaspora community with a religious practice oriented towards a place other than its place of residence. Moreover, according to, for example, Gerizim inscription no. 383 the god worshipped there was YHWH. Therefore, the Delos community that identified itself as Israelites were YHWH-worshippers. It should also be noted that the Delos inscriptions were found less than one hundred metres north of a Jewish synagogue. On the basis of this particular local context, Kartveit argues that the mention of Argarizein/Mount Gerizim carries overtones of identity.[22] Furthermore, one of the inscriptions honours a certain Menippos for having built and maintained a ΠΡΟΣΕΥΧΗ ΤΟΥ ΘΕ[ΟΥ], "a house/place of prayer for Go[d]." According to the honorary inscription in question, the local religious place (the *proseuchē*) clearly cannot have been understood as a rival to or replacement for Argarizein/Mount Gerizim.

How can a comparison between different (Yahwistic) diaspora communities contribute? One answer is that they may function as mirrors for one another. By contrasting the religious practice of one particular group up against that of another, the contours of both may be sharpened. In addition, by letting various diaspora groups function reciprocally as mirrors for one another, we may potentially identify certain aspects of the religious practices in question that turn out to be characteristic. In addition, we may detect features that are present in one group of sources but missing in the other.

7.3.3 Preliminary Outcomes and Prospects of a Comparison

A preliminary comparison between Delos and Mount Gerizim on the one hand, and Elephantine and Jerusalem on the other, may be made by looking at the payment of temple tax. The Israelites of Delos paid temple taxes to a geographically remote temple on Mount Gerizim, even though they themselves were living in the Aegean Sea. Such a practice says something about the (formal or informal) power of commitment the temple on Mount Gerizim exercised on diaspora com-

20 Kartveit indicates that the word ΑΠΑΡΧΟΜΕΝΟΙ (from ἀπάρχομαι, "to make [a first] offering") could refer to the tax (Exod 30:11–16) paid by Jews to the temple in Jerusalem, and, accordingly, by Samaritans to the temple at Gerizim, Kartveit, "Samaritan Self-Consciousness," 449–470 (468).

21 For transcription and a translation of the Greek text, see Kartveit, "Samaritan Self-Consciousness," 449–470 (466–467).

22 Kartveit, "Samaritan Self-Consciousness," 449–470 (467–468).

munities, causing them to pay even though they live far away from the temple. Moreover, it says something about the self-consciousness of the Israelites on Delos, especially in contrast to their assumed YHWH-worshipping Judaean/Jewish neighbours on Delos.

In contrast to the Israelites on Delos in the first half of the second century BCE, the Judaeans of Elephantine in the fifth century BCE did *not* pay any temple tax to Jerusalem, despite the fact that they were clearly aware of the Jerusalem temple. Moreover, the temple of YHW in Elephantine was exactly that: a temple, and not a *proseuchē*. Furthermore, whereas the case of Delos suggests that the Israelites there delimited themselves from other YHWH-worshippers (that is, from the Judaeans/Jews in Delos), no comparable delimitation is reflected in the sources for the Elephantine community. The Judaeans in Elephantine in the fifth century BCE did not delimit themselves from other worshippers of YHW/YHWH. Quite the contrary, the petition to the leaders of Judah *and* Samaria (A4.7 par.) suggests that the Judaeans in Elephantine had an idea of a Yahwistic *oecumene*.

Moreover, the group on Delos that paid temple tax to Argarizein/Mount Gerizim referred to itself as "Israelites." Regardless of what prehistory this particular group had, the self-designation suggests that the group actively affiliated and associated itself with *Israel*. In the second century BCE there was no political or geographical entity with this name. On the contrary, the "home land" of Israelites in this period was in the texts and traditions of the (probably still growing) Bible. Thus, the Israelites on Delos identified both themselves and their co-religionists in the vicinity of Mount Gerizim as (the true) Israel. In addition, by using the self-designation "Israelites," they at the same time identified themselves with the traditions of the Bible. Therefore, the use of the self-designation "Israelites" in the second century BCE was probably a stronger confession of faith and identity than the use of the self-designation "Judaeans" in the fifth century BCE. After all, in the second century BCE the Israel of the biblical traditions had ceased to exist as a geographical and political reality, whereas in the fifth century BCE Judah was a tangible geographical and political reality.

A possible image of the Delos community of the second century BCE is that it was like a satellite circling around its home planet, Argarizein/Mount Gerizim. The Judaean community in Elephantine may also be likened to a satellite. However, in contrast to the Delos community, it seems that the religious orientation of the Judaeans in Elephantine towards the temple of YHW in Elephantine made this community inherently prepared to change its orbit around Judah onto a course away from Judah. However, did such a reorientation of the orbit of the Judaean community in Elephantine actually take place? Unfortunately, because the latest source is a document from 399 BCE its fate has faded into oblivion.

7.4 End: Elephantine As an Archive Challenging the Canon

Again, what was Judaean religion in the Persian period like? Indeed, its centre was the god YHWH/YHW/YHH. However, the Judaean religion had many facets, that is, *it had many dimensions*, above all because it was directed towards multiple places. Thus, from a religio-historical point of view, poly-Yahwism continued to be a characteristic of Judaean religion even in the Persian period.

Thanks to the source for the Judaean community on Elephantine we have the contours of a form of Yahwism that was actually *practiced* and that we can actually link to a concrete place, a concrete environment and a concrete period. The same cannot be said of the texts of the Hebrew Bible that are set in and claim to reflect theological developments, and to narrate events that allegedly took place in the Persian period. Therefore, the Elephantine Yahwism shall not be deemed as an exotic case of a ("pre-deuteronomistic") Yahwism having survived in a remote location in southern Egypt. Rather, it should be counted among the best historically verifiable cases of Persian-period Yahwism there is. This particular case of Yahwism does not seem to have been aware of any kind of sacred texts corresponding to those transmitted in the Hebrew Bible.

The form of Yahwism practiced on Elephantine should not be viewed as an exotic and marginal phenomenon in comparison to the Jerusalem-centred Yahwism emerging from the canon of the Bible and the more or less canonised scholarly writing of the religious history of Judaism pivoting around Jerusalem. Measured up against the Jerusalem-centred and canonised image of Judaean religion, the documents from Elephantine should correct the canonised presuppositions reflected in many discussions on the history of Judaean religion in the Persian period. As touched upon in the introductory chapter, the Judaism of Elephantine is a textbook example illustrating very well the idea that Aleida Assmann once put forward in her seminal essay "Canon and Archive," namely *that an archive can revise the canon.*[23]

The sources for the Elephantine Yahwism can and should be studied on their own, without interpreting them in a framework using theological concepts that are alien to it. Thanks to the Aramaic documents from Egypt it is possible to write sketches of a (descriptive) theology of Persian-period Yahwism. In the present study, this is basically what I have attempted to do. I have described Persian-period Yahwism, using the Aramaic documents from Egypt as windows opening

---

23 Aleida Assmann, "Canon and Archive," in *Cultural Memory Studies: An International and Interdisciplinary Handbook*, ed. Astrid Erll and Ansgar Nünning, MCM 8 (Berlin: de Gruyter, 2008): 97–107.

up to that which we should regard as an ordinary and valid kind of Judaean religion that was typical of that period. Moreover, when describing a kind of Yahwism for which the Hebrew Bible and consequently biblical concepts was alien, the present study has shown that Ninian Smart's multi-dimensional model of religion offers a good approach.

Bibliography

Aharoni, Yohanan, and Anson F. Rainey. *The Land of the Bible: A Historical Geography.* Philadelphia: Westminster, 1979.

Ahn, Gregor. "»Toleranz« und Reglement: Die Signifikanz achaimenidischer Religionspolitik für den jüdisch-persischen Kulturkontakt." Pages 191–209 in *Religion und Religionskontakte im Zeitalter der Achämeniden.* Edited by Reinhard Gregor Kratz. VWGT 22. Gütersloh: Gütersloher Verlaghaus, 2002.

Albertz, Rainer. "Personal Piety." Pages 135–146 in *Religious Diversity in Ancient Israel and Judah.* Edited by Francesca Stavrakopoulou and John Barton. London: T&T Clark, 2010.

Alexander, Philip S. "Remarks on Aramaic Epistolography in the Persian Period." *JSS* 23 (1978): 155–170.

Allen, Lindsay. *The Persian Empire: A History.* London: British Museum, 2005.

Amit, Yairah. *Reading Biblical Narratives: Literary Criticism and the Hebrew Bible.* Minneapolis: Fortress Press, 2001.

Arnold, Dieter. *The Encyclopaedia of Ancient Egyptian Architecture.* Translated by Sabine H. Gardiner and Helen Strudwick. London: Tauris, 2003.

Arnold, William R. "The Passover Papyrus from Elephantine." *JBL* 31 (1912): 1–33.

Arrian, and Peter Astbury Brunt. *Anabasis Alexandri*, vol. 1: Books 1–4. LCL 236. Cambridge, MA: Harvard University Press, 1976.

"Asherah as Tree of Life." *Bible Odyssey* (2015): available online at http://bibleodyssey.org/tools/image-gallery/k/kuntillet-ajrud.aspx. Society of Biblical Literature.

Assmann, Aleida. "Canon and Archive." Pages 97–107 in *Cultural Memory Studies: An International and Interdisciplinary Handbook.* Edited by Astrid Erll and Ansgar Nünning. MCM 8. Berlin: de Gruyter, 2008.

Assmann, Jan. *Ägypten: Theologie und Frömmigkeit einer frühen Hochkultur.* KUT 366. 2nd rev. ed. Stuttgart: Kohlhammer, 1991.

—. "Die Zeugung des Sohnes. Bild, Spiel, Erzählung und das Problem des ägyptischen Mythos." Pages 13–61 in *Funktionen und Leistungen des Mythos: drei altorientalische Beispiele.* Edited by Jan Assmann, Walter Burkert and Fritz Stolz. OBO 48. Freiburg: Universitätsverlag, 1982.

Athas, George. *The Tel Dan Inscription: A Reappraisal and a New Interpretation.* JSOTSup 360. London: JSOT Press, 2003.

Bagnall, Roger S., and Peter Derow. *Greek Historical Documents: The Hellenistic Period.* SBLSBS 16. Missoula, MT: Scholars Press, 1981.

Barag, Dan. "A Silver Coin of Yohanan the High Priest and the Coinage of Judea in the Fourth Century B.C." *INJ* 9 (1988): 4–21 + Plate 1.

—. "Some Notes on a Silver Coin of Johanan the High Priest." *BA* 48 (1985): 166–168.

Barré, Michael L. "An Unrecognized Precative Construction in Phoenician and Hebrew." *Bib* 64 (1983): 411–422.

Beaulieu, Paul-Alain. "Antiquarianism and the Concern for the Past in the Neo-Babylonian Period." *BCSMS* 28 (1994): 37–42.

—. "Mesopotamian Antiquarianism from Sumer to Babylon." Pages 121–139 in *World Antiquarianism: Comparative Perspectives.* Edited by Alain Schnapp. Issues & Debates. Los Angeles: Getty Research Institute, 2013.

Becking, Bob. "Die Gottheiten der Juden in Elephantine." Pages 203–226 in *Der eine Gott und die Götter: Polytheismus und Monotheismus im antiken Israel.* Edited by Manfred Oeming and Konrad Schmid. ATANT 82. Zurich: TVZ, 2003.

—. "Sabbath at Elephantine: A Short Episode in the Construction of Jewish Identity." Pages 177–189 in *Empsychoi logoi—Religious Innovations in Antiquity: Studies in Honour of Pieter Willem van der Horst.* Edited by Alberdina Houtman, Albert de Jong and Magda Misset-van de Weg. AJEC 73. Leiden: Brill, 2008. Reprinted as pp. 118–127 in *Ezra, Nehemiah, and the Construction of Early Jewish Identity.* FAT 80. Tübingen: Mohr Siebeck, 2011.

—. "Temple, *marzēaḥ*, and Power at Elephantine." *Transeu* 29 (2005): 37–47.

—. "Yehudite Identity in Elephantine." Pages 403–419 in *Judah and the Judeans in the Achaemenid Period: Negotiating Identity in an International Context.* Edited by Oded Lipschits, Manfred Oeming and Gary N. Knoppers. Winona Lake, IN: Eisenbrauns, 2011.

Bedford, Peter Ross. "Jews at Elephantine." *AJJS* 13 (1999): 6–23.

—. "The So-Called 'Codification' of Egyptian Law under Darius I." Pages 135–159 in *Persia and Torah: The Theory of Imperial Authorization of the Pentateuch.* Edited by James W. Watts. SymS 17. Atlanta: Society of Biblical Literature, 2001.

Beitzel, Barry J. "Roads and Highways (Pre-Roman)." *ABD* 5: 776–782.

—. "Travel and Communications (OT World)." *ABD* 6: 644–648.

Berenbaum, Michael, and Fred Skolnik. "Mizraḥ." *EncJud* 14: 392–393.

Bivar, A. D. H. "Weights and Measures: i. Pre-Islamic Period." *EIr* (2010): online edition, available at http://www.iranicaonline.org/articles/weights-measures-i.

Blenkinsopp, Joseph. "The Mission of Udjahorresnet and those of Ezra and Nehemiah." *JBL* 106 (1987): 409–421.

Botta, Alejandro F. *The Aramaic and Egyptian Legal Traditions at Elephantine: An Egyptological Approach.* London: T&T Clark, 2009.

—. "Elephantine." *EBR* 7 (2013): 648–651.

—. "Hated by the Gods and your Spouse: Legal Use of *śnʾ* in Elephantine and its Ancient Near Eastern Context." Pages 105–128 in *Law and Religion in the Eastern Mediterranean: From Antiquity to Early Islam.* Edited by Anselm C. Hagedorn and Reinhard Gregor Kratz. Oxford: Oxford University Press, 2013.

Bowman, Raymond A. *Aramaic Ritual Texts from Persepolis.* OIP 91. Chicago: University of Chicago Press, 1970.

Bresciani, Edda. "The Diaspora: C. Egypt, Persian Satrapy." *CHJ* 1: 358–372.

Bresciani, Edda, and Murad Kamil. "Le lettere aramaiche di Hermopoli." Pages 361–428 in *Atti della Accademia Nazionale dei Lincei.* Memorie 12. Rome: L'Accademia, 1966.

Briant, Pierre. "Ethno-classe dominante et populations soumises dans l'Empire achéménide: le cas de l'Égypte." Pages 137–173 in *Method and Theory: Proceedings of the London 1985 Achaemenid History Workshop.* Edited by Amélie Kuhrt and Heleen Sancisi-Weerdenburg. AH 3. Leiden: Nederlands Instituut voor het Nabije Oosten, 1988.

—. *From Cyrus to Alexander: A History of the Persian Empire.* Winona Lake, IN: Eisenbrauns, 2002.

—. "Histoire et archéologie d'un texte. La *Lettre de Darius à Gadatas* entre Perses, Grecs et Romains." Pages 107–144 in *Licia e Lidia prima dell'ellenizzazione: Atti del Convegno internazionale, Roma, 11–12 ottobre 1999.* Edited by Mauro Giorgieri, M. Salvini, M.-C. Trémouille and P. Vannicelli. MSSSUS. Rome: Consiglio Nazionale delle Ricerche, 2003.

Brosius, Maria. *The Persian Empire from Cyrus II to Artaxerxes I*. LACTOR 16. London: London Association of Classical Teachers, 2000.
Brunner, Hellmut. *Die Geburt des Gottkönigs: Studien zur Überlieferung eines altägyptischen Mythos*. Wiesbaden: Harrassowitz, 1964.
Burke, Aaron A. "The Archaeology of Ritual and Religion in Ancient Israel and the Levant, and the Origins of Judaism." Pages 895–907 in *Oxford Handbook of the Archaeology of Ritual and Religion*. Edited by Timothy Insoll. Oxford: Oxford University Press, 2011.
Buttenwieser, Moses. *The Psalms: Chronologically Treated with a New Translation*. Chicago: University of Chicago Press, 1938.
Cameron, George G. *Persepolis Treasury Tablets*. OIP 65. Chicago: University of Chicago Press, 1948.
Chavel, Simeon. "The Second Passover, Pilgrimage, and the Centralized Cult." *HTR* 102 (2009): 1–24.
Clifford, Richard J. *Creation Accounts in the Ancient Near East and in the Bible*. CBQMS 26. Washington, D.C.: Catholic Biblical Association of America, 1994.
Conybeare, F. C., J. Rendel Harris and Agnes Smith Lewis. *The Story of Aḥiḳar from the Aramaic, Syriac, Arabic, Armenian, Ethiopic, Old Turkish, Greek and Slavonic Versions*. Cambridge: University Press, 1913.
Coogan, Michael David. *West Semitic Personal Names in the Murašû Documents*. HSM 7. Missoula, MT: Published by Scholars Press for Harvard Semitic Museum, 1976.
Cowley, Arthur Ernest. *Aramaic Papyri of the Fifth Century B.C.* Oxford: Oxford University Press, 1923.
Cross, Frank Moore. "The Discovery of the Samaria Papyri." *BA* 26, no. 4 (1963): 110–121.
Cussini, Eleonora. "The Career of Some Elephantine and Murašu Scribes." Pages 39–52 in *In the Shadow of Bezalel: Aramaic, Biblical, and Ancient Near Eastern Studies in Honor of Bezalel Porten*. Edited by Alejandro F. Botta. CHANE 60. Leiden: Brill, 2013.
Dalley, Stephanie. *Myths from Mesopotamia: Creation, the Flood, Gilgamesh, and Others*. OWC. 2nd rev. ed. Oxford: Oxford University Press, 2000.
Dandamaev, Muhammad A. "The Diaspora: A. Babylonia in the Persian Age." *CHJ* 1: 326–342.
—. "Slavery (ANE)." *ABD* 6: 58–62.
Davies, Graham I., Markus Bockmuehl, D. R. De Lacey and A. J. Poulter. *Ancient Hebrew Inscriptions: Corpus and Concordance*. Cambridge: Cambridge University Press, 1991.
Dion, Paul-Eugène. "The Aramaic 'Family Letter' and Related Epistolary Forms in Other Oriental Languages and in Hellenistic Greek." *Semeia* 22 (1982): 59–76.
—. "Aramaic Words for 'Letter'." *Semeia* 22 (1981): 77–88.
—. "La religion des papyrus d'Éléphantine: un reflet du Juda d'avant l'exil." Pages 243–254 in *Kein Land für sich allein: Studien zum Kulturkontakt in Kanaan, Israel/Palästina und Ebirnâri für Manfred Weippert zum 65. Geburtstag*. Edited by Ulrich Hübner and Ernst Axel Knauf. OBO 186. Freiburg (Switzerland) and Göttingen: Universitätsverlag Freiburg Schweiz and Vandenhoeck & Ruprecht, 2002.
Dion, Paul-Eugène, Dennis Pardee and James D. Whitehead. "La lettre araméenne passe-partout et ses sous-espèces." *RB* 89 (1982): 528–575.
Dobbs-Allsopp, Frederick William. *Lamentations*. Interpretation, a Bible Commentary for Teaching and Preaching Louisville, KY: John Knox Press, 2002.
Doering, Lutz. *Schabbat: Sabbathalacha und -praxis im antiken Judentum und Urchristentum*. TSAJ 78. Tübingen: Mohr Siebeck, 1999.

Donner, Herbert. *Geschichte des Volkes Israel und seiner Nachbarn in Grundzügen*. ATD Ergänzungsreihe 4/2. 2nd rev. ed., vol. 2: Von der Königszeit bis zur Alexander dem Großen: Mit einem Ausblick auf die Geschichte des Judentums bis Bar Kochba, Göttingen: Vandenhoeck & Ruprecht, 1995.

Drenkhahn, Rosemarie. "Brot." *LÄ* 1: 871.

Driver, Godfrey Rolles. *Aramaic Documents of the Fifth Century B.C.* Oxford: Clarendon, 1954.

Dupont-Sommer, A. "L'ostracon araméen du Sabbat (Collection Clermont-Ganneau No 152)." *Sem* 2 (1949): 29–39.

—. "Sabbat et Parascève à Eléphantine d'après des ostraca araméens inedits." *MémAIBLIF* 15, no. 1 (1960): 67–88.

Eberhart, Christian A. "A Neglected Feature of Sacrifice in the Hebrew Bible: Remarks on the Burning Rite on the Altar." *HTR* 97 (2004): 485–493.

—. "Sacrifice? Holy Smokes! Reflections on Cult Terminology for Understanding Sacrifice in the Hebrew Bible." Pages 3–16 in *Ritual and Metaphor: Sacrifice in the Bible*. Edited by Christian A. Eberhart. RBS 68. Atlanta: Society of Biblical Literature, 2011.

Ehrenberg, Erica. "*Dieu et Mon Droit:* Kingship in Late Babylonian and Early Persian Times." Pages 103–131 in *Religion and Power: Divine Kingship in the Ancient World and Beyond*. Edited by Nicole Brisch. OIS 4. Chicago: Oriental Institute of the University of Chicago, 2008.

Eidevall, Göran. "Review of *Historisches und biblisches Israel: Drei Überblicke zum Alten Testament*, by Reinhard Gregor Kratz." *RBL* 8 (2014): online edition, available at http://bookreviews.org/pdf/9345_10314.pdf.

Ephʿal, Israel. "The Western Minorities in Babylonia in the 6th–5th Centuries B.C.: Maintenance and Cohesion." *Or* 47 (1978): 74–90.

Fales, Frederick Mario. "Aramaic Letters and Neo-Assyrian Letters: Philological and Methodological Notes." *JAOS* 107 (1987): 451–469.

Figueras, Pau. "The Road Linking Palestine and Egypt along the Sinai coast." Pages 121–124 in *The Madaba Map Centenary 1897–1997: Travelling Through the Byzantine Umayyad Period: Proceedings of the International Conference Held in Amman, 7–9 April 1997*. Edited by Michele Piccirillo. SBFCMa 40. Jerusalem: Franciscan Printing Press, 1999.

Fitzmyer, Joseph A. "Aramaic Epistolography." *Semeia* 22 (1981): 25–57.

—. "Aramaic Kephāʾ and Peter's Name in the New Testament." Pages 112–124 in *To Advance the Gospel: New Testament Studies*. Grand Rapids: Eerdmans, 1998.

—. "Some Notes on Aramaic Epistolography." *JBL* 93 (1974): 201–225.

Folmer, Margaretha L. *The Aramaic Language in the Achaemenid Period: A Study in Linguistic Variation*. OLA 68. Leuven: Peeters, 1995.

Frei, Peter. "Persian Imperial Authorization: A Summary." Pages 5–40 in *Persia and Torah: The Theory of Imperial Authorization of the Pentateuch*. Edited by James W. Watts. SymS 17. Atlanta: Society of Biblical Literature, 2001.

Frey, Jörg. "Temple and Rival Temple: The Cases of Elephantine, Mt. Gerizim, and Leontopolis." Pages 171–203 in *Gemeinde ohne Tempel: zur Substituierung und Transformation des Jerusalemer Tempels und seines Kults im Alten Testament, antiken Judentum und frühen Christentum = Community without Temple*. Edited by Beate Ego, Armin Lange, Peter Pilhofer and Kathrin Ehlers. WUNT 118. Tübingen: Mohr Siebeck, 1999.

Fried, Lisbeth S. *The Priest and the Great King: Temple–Palace Relations in the Persian Empire*. BJSUCSD 10. Winona Lake, IN: Eisenbrauns, 2004.

—. "A Silver Coin of Yohanan Hakkôhen (Pls II-V)." *Transeu* 26 (2003): 65–85.
—. "'You Shall Appoint Judges': Ezra's Mission and the Rescript of Artaxerxes." Pages 63–89 in *Persia and Torah: The Theory of Imperial Authorization of the Pentateuch*. Edited by James W. Watts. SymS 17. Atlanta: Society of Biblical Literature, 2001.
Gass, Erasmus. "Der Passa-Papyrus (Cowl 21) – Mythos oder Realität?" *BN* 99 (1999): 55–68.
Geller, M. J. "šapattu." *RlA* 12: 25–27.
German Institute of Archaeology, Cairo. *Elephantine: The Ancient Town: Official Guidebook*. Cairo: German Institute of Archaeology, Cairo, 1998.
Gerstenberger, Erhard S. *Israel in the Persian Period: The Fifth and Fourth Centuries B.C.E.* BibEnc 8. Atlanta: Society of Biblical Literature, 2011.
Gese, Hartmut. "Die Sühne." Pages 85–106 in *Zur biblischen Theologie: alttestamentliche Vorträge*. BEvtThA 78. Munich: Kaiser, 1977.
Gnuse, Robert Karl. *No Other Gods: Emergent Monotheism in Israel*. JSOTSup 241. Sheffield: Sheffield Academic, 1997.
Goodman, William R. "Esdras, First Book of." *ABD* 2: 609–611.
Gordon, Cyrus H. "The Origin of the Jews in Elephantine." *JNES* 14, no. 1 (1955): 56–58.
Görg, Manfred. *Gott-König-Reden in Israel und Ägypten*. BWANT Folge 6 5. Stuttgart: Kohlhammer, 1975.
Grabbe, Lester L. "Elephantine and the Torah." Pages 125–136 in *In the Shadow of Beza'el: Aramaic, Biblical, and Ancient Near Eastern Studies in Honor of Bezalel Porten*. Edited by Alejandro F. Botta. CHANE 60. Leiden: Brill, 2013.
—. *A History of the Jews and Judaism in the Second Temple Period*, vol. 1: Yehud: A History of the Persian Province of Judah. LSTS 47. London: T&T Clark, 2004.
—. *Judaism from Cyrus to Hadrian*. Minneapolis: Fortress Press, 1992.
—. "The Law of Moses in the Ezra Tradition: More Virtual Than Real?" Pages 91–113 in *Persia and Torah: The Theory of Imperial Authorization of the Pentateuch*. Edited by James W. Watts. SymS 17. Atlanta: Society of Biblical Literature, 2001.
Granerød, Gard. *Abraham and Melchizedek: Scribal Activity of Second Temple Times in Genesis 14 and Psalm 110*. BZAW 406. Berlin: de Gruyter, 2010.
—. "Ahuramazdas lojale judeiske soldater: Om Elefantine-judeernes selvbilde." [In Norwegian]. *TeoT* 3 (2014): 288–303.
—. "'By the Favour of Ahuramazda I Am King': On the Promulgation of a Persian Propaganda Text among Babylonians and Judaeans." *JSJ* 44 (2013): 455–480.
—. "A Forgotten Reference to Divine Procreation? Psalm 2:6 in Light of Egyptian Royal Ideology." *VT* 60 (2010): 323–336.
—. "The Former and the Future Temple of YHW in Elephantine: A Traditio-Historical Case Study of Ancient Near Eastern Antiquarianism." *ZAW* 127 (2015): 63–77.
—. "Melchizedek in Hebrews 7." *Bib* 90 (2009): 188–202.
—. "Omnipresent in Narratives, Disputed Among Grammarians: Some Contributions to the Understanding of *wayyiqtol* and their Underlying Paradigms." *ZAW* 121 (2009): 418–434.
—. "The Passover and the Temple of YHW: On the Interaction between the Authorities and the Judaean Community at Elephantine as Reflected in the Jedaniah Archive." Pages in *Arshama and Egypt: The World of an Achaemenid Prince*. Edited by Christopher Tuplin and John Ma. OSAD. Oxford: Oxford University Press, forthcoming.
Gray, John. *I & II Kings: A Commentary*. OTL. London: SCM Press, 1977.

Greenfield, Jonas C., and Bezalel Porten. *The Bisitun Inscription of Darius the Great: Aramaic Version*, vol. V: The Aramaic Versions of the Achaemenian Inscriptions, etc.; Texts I. CII. London: Lund Humphries, 1982.

Grenfell, Bernard P., and Arthur S. Hunt. *The Oxyrhynchus Papyri*, vol. IV: Edited with Translations and Notes. London: Published for The British Academy by The Egypt Exploration Society, 1904.

—. *The Oxyrhynchus Papyri*, vol. III: Edited with Translations and Notes. London: Published for The British Academy by The Egypt Exploration Society, 1903.

Grund, Alexandra. *Die Entstehung des Sabbats: seine Bedeutung für Israels Zeitkonzept und Erinnerungskultur.* FAT 75. Tübingen: Mohr Siebeck, 2011.

Hallock, Richard Treadwell. *Persepolis Fortification Tablets.* OIP 92. Chicago: University of Chicago Press, 1969.

Haran, Menahem. *Temples and Temple-Service in Ancient Israel: An Inquiry into the Character of Cult Phenomena and the Historical Setting of the Priestly School.* Winona Lake, IN: Eisenbrauns, 1985.

Hasel, Gerhard F. "Sabbath." *ABD* 5: 849–856.

Helck, Wolfgang. "Bier." *LÄ* 1: 789–792.

—. "Getränke." *LÄ* 2: 586.

—. "Getreide." *LÄ* 2: 586–589.

—. "Scheidung." *LÄ* 5: 559–560.

Henkelman, Wouter F. M. "Animal Sacrifice and 'External' Exchange in the Persepolis Fortification Tablets." Pages 137–165 in *Approaching the Babylonian Economy: Proceedings of the Start Project Symposium Held in Vienna, 1–3 July 2004.* Edited by H. D. Baker and M. Jursa. AOAT 330. Münster: Ugarit-Verlag, 2005.

—. *The Other Gods Who Are: Studies in Elamite–Iranian Acculturation Based on the Persepolis Fortification Texts.* AH 14. Leiden: Nederlands Instituut voor het Nabije Oosten, 2008.

Herzog, Ze'ev, Miriam Aharoni, Anson F. Rainey and Shmuel Moshkovitz. "The Israelite Fortress at Arad." *BASOR* 254 (1984): 1–34.

Hoehner, Harold W. *Herod Antipas.* Grand Rapids: Zondervan, 1980.

Honroth, W., O. Rubensohn and F. Zucker. "Bericht über die Ausgrabungen auf Elephantine in den Jahren 1906–1908. Mit 9 Tafeln und 27 Abbildungen." *ZÄS* 46 (1909): 14–61.

Horn, Siegfried H. "Foreign Gods in Ancient Egypt." Pages 37–42 in *Studies in Honor of John A. Wilson September 12, 1969.* SAOC 35. Chicago: University of Chicago Press, 1969.

Hundley, Michael B. *Gods in Dwellings: Temples and Divine Presence in the Ancient Near East.* WAWSup 3. Atlanta: Society of Biblical Literature, 2013.

Hutchinson, John, and Anthony D. Smith. "Introduction." Pages 3–14 in *Ethnicity.* Edited by John Hutchinson and Anthony D. Smith Oxford: Oxford University Press, 1996.

Johnson, Janet H. "Ethnic Considerations in Persian Period Egypt." Pages 211–222 in *Gold of Praise: Studies on Ancient Egypt in Honor of Edward F. Wente.* Edited by Emily Teeter and John A. Larson. SAOC 58. Chicago: Oriental Institute of the University of Chicago, 1999.

Joisten-Pruschke, Anke. *Das religiöse Leben der Juden von Elephantine in der Achämenidenzeit.* GOF, 3. Reihe: Iranica, Neue Folge 2. Wiesbaden: Harrassowitz, 2008.

Kamlah, Jens. "Temples of the Levant – Comparative Aspects." Pages 507–534 in *Temple Building and Temple Cult: Architecture and Cultic Paraphernalia of Temples in the Levant (2.–1. Mill. B.C.E.): Proceedings of a Conference on the Occasion of the 50th Anniversary*

of the Institute of Biblical Archaeology at the University of Tübingen (28–30 May 2010). Edited by Jens Kamlah and Henrike Michelau. ADPV 41. Wiesbaden: Harrassowitz, 2012.
Kartveit, Magnar. *The Origin of the Samaritans.* VTSup 128. Leiden: Brill, 2009.
—. "Samaritan Self-Consciousness in the First Half of the Second Century B.C.E. in Light of the Inscriptions from Mount Gerizim and Delos." *JSJ* 45 (2014): 449–470.
—. "Samaritansk sjølvforståing i innskriftene frå Garisim og Delos." [In Norwegian]. *TeoT* 3 (2014): 271–286.
Keel, Othmar. *Die Welt der altorientalischen Bildsymbolik und das Alte Testament: am Beispiel der Psalmen.* 5th ed. Göttingen: Vandenhoeck & Ruprecht, 1996.
Kellermann, Diether, and Mechthild Kellermann. "YHW-Tempel und Sabbatsfeier auf Elephantine?" Pages 433–452 in *Festgabe für Hans-Rudolf Singer zum 65. Geburtstag am 6. April 1990 überreicht von seinen Freunden und Kollegen.* Edited by Martin Forstner. FAS 13. Frankfurt am Main: Peter Lang, 1991.
Kent, Roland G. *Old Persian: Grammar, Texts, Lexicon.* New Haven: American Oriental Society, 1953.
Kitchen, Kenneth A. *Ramesside Inscriptions: Translated and Annotated: Translations*, vol. II: Ramesses II, Royal Inscriptions, Oxford: Blackwell, 1996.
Knauf, Ernst Axel. "Elephantine und das vor-biblische Judentum." Pages 179–188 in *Religion und Religionskontakte im Zeitalter der Achämeniden.* Edited by Reinhard Gregor Kratz. VWGT 22. Gütersloh: Gütersloher Verlagshaus, 2002.
Knoppers, Gary N. "Prayer and Propaganda: Solomon's Dedication of the Temple and the Deuteronomist's Program." *CBQ* 57 (1995): 229–254.
Koch, Heidemarie. "Iranische Religion im achaimenidischen Zeitalter." Pages 11–26 in *Religion und Religionskontakte im Zeitalter der Achämeniden.* Edited by Reinhard Gregor Kratz. VWGT 22. Gütersloh: Gütersloher Verlagshaus, 2002.
Koch, Klaus. "Der König als Sohn Gottes in Ägypten und Israel." Pages 1–32 in *"Mein Sohn bist du" (Ps 2,7): Studien zu den Königspsalmen.* Edited by Eckart Otto and Erich Zenger. SBS 192. Stuttgart: Katholisches Bibelwerk, 2002.
—. *Geschichte der ägyptischen Religion von den Pyramiden bis zu den Mysterien der Isis.* Stuttgart: Kohlhammer, 1993.
—. "Weltordnung und Reichsidee im alten Iran und ihre Auswirkungen auf die Provinz Jehud." Pages 133–338 in *Reichsidee und Reichsorganisation im Perserreich.* Edited by Peter Frei and Klaus Koch. OBO 55. Freiburg (Switzerland) and Göttingen: Universitätsverlag Freiburg Schweiz and Vandenhoeck & Ruprecht, 1996.
Köckert, Matthias. "YHWH in the Northern and Southern Kingdom." Pages 357–394 in *One God – One Cult – One Nation: Archaeological and Biblical Perspectives.* Edited by Reinhard Gregor Kratz, Hermann Spieckermann, Björn Corzilius and Tanja Pilger. BZAW 405. Berlin: de Gruyter, 2010.
Kohler, Josef, and Arthur Ungnad. *Hammurabi's Gesetz*, vol. V: Übersetzte Urkunden, Verwaltungsregister, Inventare, Erläuterungen. Leipzig: Pfeiffer, 1911.
—. *Hammurabi's Gesetz*, vol. III: Übersetzte Urkunden, Erläuterungen. Leipzig: Pfeiffer, 1909.
Kornfeld, Walter. "Aramäische Sarkophage in Assuan." *WZKM* 61 (1967): 9–16.
Korpel, Marjo Christina Annette, and Johannes Cornelis de Moor. *The Silent God.* Leiden: Brill, 2011.
Körting, Corinna. "Sabbat (AT)." *WiBiLex:* available online at http://www.bibelwissenschaft.de/stichwort/25732/.

Kottsieper, Ingo. “Die Religionspolitik der Achämeniden und die Juden von Elephantine.” Pages 150 – 178 in *Religion und Religionskontakte im Zeitalter der Achämeniden*. Edited by Reinhard Gregor Kratz. VWGT 22. Gütersloh: Gütersloher Verlagshaus, 2002.

Kraeling, Emil Gottlieb Heinrich. *The Brooklyn Museum Aramaic Papyri: New Documents of the Fifth Century B.C. from the Jewish Colony at Elephantine*. Publications of the Department of Egyptian Art. New Haven: Yale University Press, 1953.

Kratz, Reinhard Gregor. “Aḥiqar and Bisitun: Literature of the Judaeans at Elephantine?” (forthcoming)

—. *Historisches und biblisches Israel: Drei Überblicke zum Alten Testament*. Tübingen: Mohr Siebeck, 2013.

—. “Judäische Gesandte im Achämenidenreich: Hananja, Esra und Nehemia.” Pages 377 – 395 in *From Daēnā to Dîn: Religion, Kultur und Sprache in der iranischen Welt: Festschrift für Philip Kreyenbroek zum 60. Geburtstag*. Edited by Christine Allison. Wiesbaden: Harrassowitz, 2009.

—. “Judean Ambassadors and the Making of Jewish Identity: The Case of Hananiah, Ezra, and Nehemiah.” Pages 421 – 444 in *Judah and the Judeans in the Achaemenid Period: Negotiating Identity in an International Context*. Edited by Oded Lipschits, Manfred Oeming and Gary N. Knoppers. Winona Lake, IN: Eisenbrauns, 2011.

—. “The Second Temple of Jeb and of Jerusalem.” Pages 247 – 264 in *Judah and the Judeans in the Persian Period*. Edited by Oded Lipschits and Manfred Oeming. Winona Lake, IN: Eisenbrauns, 2006.

—. “Zwischen Elephantine und Qumran: das Alte Testament im Rahmen des antiken Judentums.” Pages 129 – 146 in *Congress Volume Ljubljana 2007*. Edited by André Lemaire. VTSup 133. Leiden: Brill, 2010.

Krauss, Rolf. “Reisegeschwindigkeit.” *LÄ* 5: 222 – 223.

Kuhrt, Amélie. “The Cyrus Cylinder and Achaemenid Imperial Policy.” *JSOT* 25 (1983): 83 – 97.

—. “Making History: Sargon of Agade and Cyrus the Great of Persia.” Pages 347 – 361 in *A Persian Perspective: Essays in Memory of Heleen Sancisi-Weerdenburg*. Edited by Wouter F. M. Henkelman and Amélie Kuhrt. AH 13. Leiden: Nederlands Instituut voor het Nabije Oosten, 2003.

—. *The Persian Empire: A Corpus of Sources from the Achaemenid Period*. London: Routledge, 2007.

Lemaire, André. “Das Achämenidische Juda und seine Nachbarn im Lichte der Epigraphie.” Pages 210 – 230 in *Religion und Religionskontakte im Zeitalter der Achämeniden*. Edited by Reinhard Gregor Kratz. VWGT 22. Gütersloh: Gütersloher Verlagshaus, 2002.

—. “Judean Identity in Elephantine: Everyday Life according to the Ostraca.” Pages 365 – 373 in *Judah and the Judeans in the Achaemenid Period: Negotiating Identity in an International Context*. Edited by Oded Lipschits, Manfred Oeming and Gary N. Knoppers. Winona Lake, IN: Eisenbrauns, 2011.

Leuenberger, Martin. “Jhwh, »der Gott Jerusalems« (Inschrift aus Ḫirbet Bet Layy 1,2): Konturen der Jerusalemer Tempeltheologie aus religions- und theologiegeschichtlicher Perspektive.” *EvT* 74 (2014): 245 – 260.

Lewis, T. J. “Dead.” *DDD*: 223 – 231.

Lincoln, Bruce. “The Role of Religion in Achaemenian Imperialism.” Pages 221 – 241 in *Religion and Power: Divine Kingship in the Ancient World and Beyond*. Edited by Nicole Brisch. OIS 4. Chicago: Oriental Institute of the University of Chicago, 2008.

Lindenberger, James M. "Ahikar: A New Translation and Introduction." Pages 479–507 in *The Old Testament Pseudepigrapha: Expansions of the "Old Testament" and Legends, Wisdom and Philosophical Literature, Prayers, Psalms, and Odes, Fragments of Lost Judeo-Hellenistic Works*. Edited by James H. Charlesworth. Garden City, NY: Doubleday, 1985.

—. *Ancient Aramaic and Hebrew Letters*. WAW 14. 2nd ed. Atlanta: Society of Biblical Literature, 2003.

—. "The Gods of Ahiqar." *UF* 14 (1982): 105–117.

—. "What Ever Happened to Vidranga? A Jewish Liturgy of Cursing from Elephantine." Pages 134–157 in *World of the Aramaeans III: Studies in Language and Literature in Honour of Paul-Eugène Dion*. Edited by P. M. Michèle Daviau, John William Wevers and Michael Weigl. JSOTSup 326. Sheffield: Sheffield Academic, 2001.

Lozachmeur, Hélène. *La collection Clermont-Ganneau: ostraca, épigraphes sur jarre, étiquettes de bois*. MAIBL. Nouvelle série 35. 2 vols. Paris: Boccard, 2006.

MacDonald, Nathan. *Deuteronomy and the Meaning of "Monotheism"*. FAT, 2. Reihe 1. 2nd ed. Tübingen: Mohr Siebeck, 2012.

Malandra, William W. "Zoroastrianism i. Historical Review up to the Arab Conquest." *EIr* (2005): online edition, available at http://www.iranicaonline.org/articles/zoroastrianism-i-historical-review.

Manor, Dale W. "Massabah." *ABD* 4: 602.

Mazar, Amihai. "Temples of the Middle and Late Bronze Ages and the Iron Age." Pages 161–187 in *The Architecture of Ancient Israel: From the Prehistoric to the Persian Periods: In Memory of Immanuel (Munya) Dunayevsky*. Edited by Immanuel Dunayevsky, Aharon Kempinski, Ronny Reich, Hannah Katzenstein and Joseph Aviram. Jerusalem: Israel Exploration Society, 1992.

Meinhold, Arndt. "Scheidungsrecht bei Frauen im Kontext der jüdischen Militärkolonie von Elephantine im 5. Jh. v. Chr." Pages 247–259 in *"Sieben Augen auf einem Stein" (Sach 3,9): Studien zur Literatur des Zweiten Tempels. Festschrift für Ina Willi-Plein zum 65. Geburtstag*. Edited by Friedhelm Hartenstein and Michael Pietsch. Neukirchen-Vluyn: Neukirchener Verlag, 2007.

Meinhold, Johannes. "Die Entstehung des Sabbats." *ZAW* 29 (1909): 81–112.

Mettinger, Tryggve N. D. *No Graven Image? Israelite Aniconism in Its Ancient Near Eastern Context*. ConBOT 42. Lund: Gleerup, 1995.

Monson, John. "The New Ain Dara Temple: Closest Solomonic Parallel." *BAR* 26, no. 3 (2000): 20–35, 67.

Moore, Carey A. "Tobit, Book of." *ABD* 6: 585–594.

Morenz, Siegfried. *Egyptian Religion*. Ithaca: Cornell University Press, 1973.

Muffs, Yochanan. *Studies in the Aramaic Legal Papyri from the Elephantine; with Prolegomenon by Baruch A. Levine*. HdO 66. Leiden: Brill, 2003.

Muraoka, Takamitsu. *An Introduction to Egyptian Aramaic*. LOS III 1. Münster: Ugarit-Verlag, 2012.

Muraoka, Takamitsu, and Bezalel Porten. *A Grammar of Egyptian Aramaic*. HdO 32. 2nd rev. ed. Leiden: Brill, 2003.

Neusner, Jacob. *The Mishnah: A New Translation*. New Haven: Yale University Press, 1988.

Niehr, Herbert. *Aramäischer Aḥiqar*. JSHRZ Neue Folge 2. Gütersloh: Gütersloher Verlagshaus, 2007.

—. "The Rise of YHWH in Judahite and Israelite Religion: Methodological and Religio-Historical Aspects." Pages 45–72 in *Triumph of Elohim: From Yahwisms to Judaisms.* Edited by Diana Vikander Edelman. CBET 13. Kampen: Kok Pharos, 1995.

Nutkowicz, Hélène. "Concerning the Verb *šn'* in Judaeo-Aramaic Contracts from Elephantine." *JSS* 52 (2007): 211–225.

—. "Eléphantine, ultime tragédie." *Transeu* 40 (2011): 185–198.

—. "Note sur une institution juridique à Éléphantine, *'dh*, la « cour »." *Transeu* 27 (2004): 181–185.

Oren, Eliezer. "Sinai." Pages 41–47 in *The Oxford Encyclopedia of Archaeology in the Near East.* Edited by Eric M. Meyers. Oxford: Oxford University Press, 1997.

Pearce, Laurie E. "New Evidence for Judeans in Babylonia." Pages 399–411 in *Judah and the Judeans in the Persian Period.* Edited by Oded Lipschits and Manfred Oeming. Winona Lake, IN: Eisenbrauns, 2006.

Pearce, Laurie E., and Cornelia Wunsch. *Documents of Judean Exiles and West Semites in Babylonia in the Collection of David Sofer.* CUSAS 28. Bethesda, MD: CDL, 2014.

Pilgrim, Cornelius von. "'Anyway, We Should Really Dig on Elephantine Some Time': A Short Tour Through the Research History of the Towns along the First Nile Cataract." Pages 85–96 in *Zwischen den Welten: Grabfunde von Ägyptens Südgrenze = Between Worlds: Finds from Tombs on Egypt's Southern Border.* Edited by Ludwig D. Morenz, Michael Höveler-Müller and Amr El Hawary. Rahden, Westphalia: Leidorf, 2011.

—. "Tempel des Jahu und 'Strasse des Königs': ein Konflikt in der Späten Perserzeit auf Elephantine." Pages 303–317 in *Egypt: Temple of the Whole World: Studies in Honour of Jan Assmann = Ägypten: Tempel der gesamten Welt.* Edited by Sibylle Meyer. SHR 97. Leiden: Brill, 2003.

—. "Textzeugnis und archäologischer Befund: Zur Topographie von Elephantine in der 27. Dynastie." Pages 485–497 in *Stationen: Beiträge zur Kulturgeschichte Ägyptens Rainer Stadelmann gewidmet.* Edited by Heike Guksch and Daniel Polz. Mainz: von Zabern, 1998.

—. "VI. Das Aramäische Quartier im Stadtgebiet der 27. Dynastie." *MDAIK* 58 (2002): 192–197.

—. "XII. Der Tempel des Jahwe." *MDAIK* 55 (1999): 142–145.

Plato, Harold North Fowler, and Walter Rangeley Maitland Lamb. *Plato in Twelve Volumes*, vol. 1: Euthyphro, Apology, Crito, Phaedo, Phaedrus. LCL 36. Cambridge, MA and London: Harvard University Press, 1914.

Porten, Bezalel. "Aramaic Papyri and Parchments: A New Look." *BA* 42, no. 2 (1979): 74–104.

—. *Archives from Elephantine: The Life of an Ancient Jewish Military Colony.* Berkeley: University of California Press, 1968.

—. "Boundary Descriptions in the Bible and in Conveyances from Egypt and the Judean Desert." Pages 852–861 in *Dead Sea Scrolls: Fifty Years After Their Discovery: Proceedings of the Jerusalem Congress, July 20–25, 1997.* Edited by Lawrence H. Schiffman, Emanuel Tov, James C. Vanderkam and Galen Marquis. Jerusalem: Israel Exploration Society in Cooperation with The Shrine of the Book, Israel Museum, 2000.

—. "The Calendar of Aramaic Texts from Achaemenid and Ptolemaic Egypt." Pages 13–32 in *Irano-Judaica II: Studies Relating to Jewish Contacts with Persian Culture Throughout the Ages.* Edited by Shaul Shaked and Amnon Netzer. Jerusalem: Ben-Zvi Institute 1990.

—. "Elephantine Papyri." *ABD* 2: 445–455.

—. "The Jews in Egypt." *CHJ* 1: 372–400.

—. "The Religion of the Jews of Elephantine in Light of the Hermopolis Papyri." *JNES* 28 (1969): 116–121.
—. "Settlement of the Jews at Elephantine and the Arameans at Syene." Pages 451–470 in *Judah and the Judeans in the Neo-Babylonian Period.* Edited by Oded Lipschits and Joseph Blenkinsopp. Winona Lake, IN: Eisenbrauns, 2003.
—. "The Structure and Orientation of the Jewish Temple at Elephantine—A Revised Plan of the Jewish District." *JAOS* 81 (1961): 38–42.
Porten, Bezalel, Joel Farber, Cary J. Martin, Günter Vittmann, Leslie S. B. MacCoull, and Sarah Clackson, eds. *The Elephantine Papyri in English: Three Millennia of Cross-Cultural Continuity and Change.* 2nd rev. ed. DMOA 22. Atlanta: Society of Biblical Literature, 2011.
Porten, Bezalel, and Jerome A. Lund. *Aramaic Documents from Egypt: A Key-Word-in-Context Concordance.* Winona Lake, IN: Eisenbrauns, 2002.
Porten, Bezalel, and Zvi Henri Szubin. "The Status of the Handmaiden Tamet: A New Interpretation of Kraeling 2 (TAD B3.3)." *ILR* 29 (1995): 43–64.
Porten, Bezalel, and Ada Yardeni. *Textbook of Aramaic Documents from Ancient Egypt. Newly Copied, Edited and Translated into Hebrew and English,* vol. I: Letters. Appendix: Aramaic Letters from the Bible. Jerusalem: The Hebrew University of Jerusalem – Department of the History of the Jewish People, 1986.
—. *Textbook of Aramaic Documents from Ancient Egypt. Newly Copied, Edited and Translated into Hebrew and English,* vol. II: Contracts. Jerusalem: The Hebrew University of Jerusalem – Department of the History of the Jewish People, 1989.
—. *Textbook of Aramaic Documents from Ancient Egypt. Newly Copied, Edited and Translated into Hebrew and English,* vol. III: Literature, Accounts, Lists. Jerusalem: The Hebrew University of Jerusalem – Department of the History of the Jewish People, 1993.
—. *Textbook of Aramaic Documents from Ancient Egypt. Newly Copied, Edited and Translated into Hebrew and English,* vol. IV: Ostraca & Assorted Inscriptions. Jerusalem: The Hebrew University of Jerusalem – Department of the History of the Jewish People, 1999.
Preuss, Horst Dietrich. *Einführung in die alttestamentliche Weisheitsliteratur.* Stuttgart: Kohlhammer, 1987.
Provan, Iain W. "Past, Present and Future in Lamentations 3:52–66: The Case for a Precative Perfect Re-Examined." *VT* 41 (1991): 164–175.
Rabinowitz, Louis Isaac, David Davidovitch, Benjamin Zvieli, Karla Goldman, Raphael Posner, and Michael Avi-Yonah. "Synagogue." *EncJud* 19: 352–383.
Rad, Gerhard von. "Das judäische Königsritual." Pages 205–213 in *Gesammelte Studien zum Alten Testament.* Edited by Gerhard von Rad. TB 8. Munich: Kaiser, 1965.
Ray, J. D. "Jew and Other Immigrants in Late Period Egypt." Pages 273 in *Life in a Multi-Cultural Society Egypt from Cambyses to Constantine and Beyond.* Edited by Janet H. Johnson. SAOC 51. Chicago: Oriental Institute of the University of Chicago, 1992.
Reiner, Erica, Robert D. Biggs and Martha T. Roth. "šapattu." *CAD* 17: 449–450.
Rochberg-Halton, Francesca. "Calendars: Ancient Near East." *ABD* 1: 810–814.
Roeder, Günther. *Urkunden zur Religion des alten Ägypten.* Jena: Eugen Diederichs, 1923.
Rohrmoser, Angela. *Götter, Tempel und Kult der Judäo-Aramäer von Elephantine: Archäologische und schriftliche Zeugnisse aus dem perserzeitlichen Ägypten.* AOAT 396. Münster: Ugarit-Verlag, 2014.
Röllig, W. "Baal-Shamem." *DDD:* 149–151.

Römer, Thomas. "Redaction Criticism: 1 Kings 8 and the Deuteronomists." Pages 63–76 in *Method Matters: Essays on the Interpretation of the Hebrew Bible in Honor of David L. Petersen*. Edited by Joel M. LeMon and Kent Harold Richards. RBS 56. Atlanta: Society of Biblical Literature, 2009.

Rosenberg, Stephen G. "The Jewish Temple at Elephantine." *NEA* 67, no. 1 (2004): 4–13.

Rosenthal, Franz. *A Grammar of Biblical Aramaic.* PLO 5. Wiesbaden: Harrassowitz, 1983.

Runesson, Anders. *The Origins of the Synagogue: A Socio-Historical Study.* ConBNT 37. Lund: Gleerup, 2001.

Sachau, Eduard. *Aramäische Papyrus und Ostraka aus einer jüdischen Militär-Kolonie zu Elephantine altorientalische Sprachdenkmäler des 5. Jahrhunderts vor Chr.* Leipzig: Hinrichs, 1911.

Samuel, Alan Edouard. *Ptolemaic Chronology.* MBPF 43. Munich: Beck, 1962.

Schmitt, Rüdiger. *The Bisitun Inscriptions of Darius the Great: Old Persian Text*, vol. I: The Old Persian inscriptions: Texts I. CII. London: School of Oriental and African Studies, 1991.

—. "Bisotun iii. Darius's Inscriptions." *EIr* (2013): online edition, available at http://www.iranicaonline.org/articles/bisotun-iii.

—. "Gab es einen Bildersturm nach dem Exil? – Einige Bemerkungen zur Verwendung von Terrakottafigurinen im nachexilischen Israel." Pages 186–198 in *Yahwism After the Exile: Perspectives on Israelite Religion in the Persian Era: Papers Read at the First Meeting of the European Association for Biblical Studies, Utrecht, 6–9 August 2000.* Edited by Rainer Albertz and Bob Becking. STAR 5. Assen: Van Gorcum, 2003.

—. *The Old Persian Inscriptions of Naqsh-i Rustam and Persepolis*, vol. I: The Old Persian Inscriptions: Texts II. CII. London: School of Oriental and African Studies, 2000.

Schniedewind, William M. "Aramaic, the Death of Written Hebrew, and Language Shift in the Persian Period." Pages 141–151 in *Margins of Writing, Origins of Cultures.* Edited by Seth L. Sanders. OIS 2. Chicago: Oriental Institute of the University of Chicago, 2006.

Schwiderski, Dirk. *Handbuch des nordwestsemitischen Briefformulars: ein Beitrag zur Echtheitsfrage der aramäischen Briefe des Esrabuches.* BZAW 295. Berlin and New York: de Gruyter, 2000.

Scott, Robert B. Y. "Weights and Measures of the Bible." *BA* 22, no. 2 (1959): 22–40.

—. "Wisdom, Wisdom Literature." *EncJud* 21: 95–99.

Seidl, Ursula. "Ein Monument Darius' I. aus Babylon." *ZA* 89 (1999): 101–114.

—. "Eine Triumphstele Darius' I. aus Babylon." Pages 297–306 in *Babylon: Focus mesopotamischer Geschichte, Wiege früher Gelehrsamkeit, Mythos in der Moderne: 2. Internationales Colloquium der Deutschen Orient-Gesellschaft, 24.–26. März 1998 in Berlin.* Edited by Johannes Renger. Saarbrücken: In Kommission bei SDV, Saarbrücker Druckerei und Verlag, 1999.

Shaw, Ian. *Ancient Egypt: A Very Short Introduction.* Oxford: Oxford University Press, 2004.

Silverman, Michael H. *Religious Values in the Jewish Proper Names at Elephantine.* AOAT 217. Neukirchen-Vluyn: Neukirchener Verlag, 1985.

Skjærvø, Prods Oktor. *The Spirit of Zoroastrianism.* New Haven: Yale University Press, 2011.

—. *Zarathustras sanger: de eldste iranske skriftene.* [In Norwegian]. Verdens hellige skrifter 22. Oslo: De norske bokklubbene, 2003.

Smart, Ninian. *Dimensions of the Sacred: An Anatomy of the World's Beliefs.* Berkeley: University of California Press, 1996.

—. *The Religious Experience of Mankind.* New York: Scribner, 1969.

Smith, Jonathan Z. "Here, There, and Anywhere." Pages 21–36 in *Prayer, Magic, and the Stars in the Ancient and Late Antique World*. Edited by Scott Noegel, Joel Walker and Brannon Wheeler. University Park: Pennsylvania State University Press, 2003.

Spiegelberg, Wilhelm. *Die Sogenannte Demotische Chronik des Pap. 215 der Bibliothèque Nationale zu Paris nebst den auf der Rückseite des Papyrus stehenden Texten*. DM 7. Leipzig: Hinrichs, 1914.

Stausberg, Michael. *Contemporary Theories of Religion: A Critical Companion*. London: Routledge, 2009.

Stavrakopoulou, Francesca, and John Barton, eds. *Religious Diversity in Ancient Israel and Judah*. London: T&T Clark, 2010.

Stern, Sacha. "The Babylonian Calendar at Elephantine." *ZPE* 130 (2000): 159–171.

Sternberg-el Hotabi, Heike. "Die persische Herrschaft in Ägypten." Pages 111–149 in *Religion und Religionskontakte im Zeitalter der Achämeniden*. Edited by Reinhard Gregor Kratz. VWGT 22. Gütersloh: Gütersloher Verlagshaus, 2002.

Stolper, Matthew W. "Murašchû, Archive of." *ABD* 4: 927–928.

Stromberg, Jacob. *An Introduction to the Study of Isaiah*. T&T Clark Approaches to Biblical Studies. London: T&T Clark, 2011.

Szubin, Zvi Henri, and Bezalel Porten. "'Ancestral Estates' in Aramaic Contracts: The Legal Significance of the Term *mhḥsn*." *JRAS* (1982): 3–9.

—. "Hereditary Leases in Aramaic Letters." *BO* 42 (1985): 283–288.

Tal, Oren. "On the Identification of the Ships of *kzd/ry* in the Erased Customs Account from Elephantine." *JNES* 68 (2009): 1–8.

Tavernier, Jan. "An Achaemenid Royal Inscription: The Text of Paragraph 13 of the Aramaic Version of the Bisitun Inscription." *JNES* 60 (2001): 161–176.

—. *Iranica in the Achaemenid Period (ca. 550–330 B.C.): Linguistic Study of Old Iranian Proper Names and Loanwords, Attested in Non-Iranian Texts*. OLA 158. Leuven: Peeters, 2007.

Teixidor, Javier. "The Aramaic Text in the Trilingual Stele from Xanthus." *JNES* 37 (1978): 181–185.

Tigay, Jeffrey H. *Deuteronomy*. Philadelphia: Jewish Publication Society, 1996.

Toorn, Karel van der. "Anat-Yahu, Some Other Deities, and the Jews of Elephantine." *Numen* 39 (1992): 80–101.

—. "Herem-Bethel and Elephantine Oath Procedure." *ZAW* 98 (1986): 282–285.

Tuplin, Christopher. "The Administration of the Achaemenid Empire." Pages 109–158 in *Coinage and Administration in the Athenian and Persian Empires: The Ninth Oxford Symposium on Coinage and Monetary History*. Edited by Ian Carradice. BAR International Series 34. Oxford: British Archaeological Reports, 1987.

—. "Arshama: Prince and Satrap." Pages 5–44 in *The Arshama Letters from the Bodleian Library: Volume 1: Introduction*. Edited by John Ma, Christopher Tuplin and Lindsay Allen. OSAD. Oxford, 2013. Available for download at http://arshama.bodleian.ox.ac.uk/publications/.

—. "Persian Garrisons in Xenophon and Other Sources." Pages 67–70 in *Method and Theory: Proceedings of the London 1985 Achaemenid History Workshop*. Edited by Amélie Kuhrt and Heleen Sancisi-Weerdenburg. AH 3. Leiden: Nederlands Instituut voor het Nabije Oosten, 1988.

Ungnad, Arthur. *Aramäische Papyrus aus Elephantine: kleine Ausgabe unter Zugrundelegung von Eduard Sachau's Erstausgabe*. HKAO 4. Leipzig: Hinrichs, 1911.

VanderKam, James C. *An Introduction to Early Judaism*. Grand Rapids: Eerdmans, 2001.
Vincent, Albert. *La religion des judéo-araméens d'Eléphantine*. Paris: Geuthner, 1937.
Vogelstein, Max. "Bakshish for Bagoas?" *JQR* 33 (1942): 89–92.
Voigtlander, Elizabeth N. von. *The Bisitun Inscription of Darius the Great: Babylonian Version*, vol. II: The Babylonian Versions of the Achaemenian Inscriptions: Texts I. CII. London: Lund Humphries, 1978.
Waltke, Bruce K., and Michael Patrick O'Connor. *An Introduction to Biblical Hebrew Syntax*. Winona Lake, IN: Eisenbrauns, 1990.
Watts, James W., ed. *Persia and Torah: The Theory of Imperial Authorization of the Pentateuch*. SymS 17. Atlanta: Society of Biblical Literature, 2001.
—. "The Rhetoric of Sacrifice." Pages 3–16 in *Ritual and Metaphor: Sacrifice in the Bible*. Edited by Christian A. Eberhart. RBS 68. Atlanta: Society of Biblical Literature, 2011.
Weigl, Michael. *Die aramäischen Achikar-Sprüche aus Elephantine und die alttestamentliche Weisheitsliteratur*. BZAW 399. Berlin: de Gruyter, 2010.
Wellhausen, Julius. *Israelitische und jüdische Geschichte*. Berlin: de Gruyter, 1921.
Westenholz, Joan Goodnick. *Legends of the Kings of Akkade: The Texts*. MC 7. Winona Lake, IN: Eisenbrauns, 1997.
Westermann, Claus. *Genesis 1–11: A Continental Commentary*. Minneapolis: Augsburg, 1984.
Weyde, Karl William. "Mazzen/Mazzotfest." *WiBiLex:* available online at http://www.bibelwissenschaft.de/stichwort/25696/.
—. "Passa (AT)." *WiBiLex:* available online at http://www.bibelwissenschaft.de/stichwort/30031/.
Willi, Thomas. *Esra: Der Lehrer Israels*. BG 26. Leipzig: Evangelische Verlagsanstalt, 2012.
—. "'Wie Geschrieben steht' – Schriftbezug und Schrift: Überlegungen zur frühjüdischen Literaturwerdung in perserzeitlichen Kontext." Pages 257–277 in *Religion und Religionskontakte im Zeitalter der Achämeniden*. Edited by Reinhard Gregor Kratz. VWGT 22. Gütersloh: Gütersloher Verlaghaus, 2002.
Wright, Jacob L. "Surviving in an Imperial Context: Foreign Military Service and Judean Identity." Pages 505–528 in *Judah and the Judeans in the Achaemenid Period: Negotiating Identity in an International Context*. Edited by Oded Lipschits, Manfred Oeming and Gary N. Knoppers. Winona Lake, IN: Eisenbrauns, 2011.
Wunsch, Cornelia. "Glimpses on the Lives of Deportees in Rural Babylonia." Pages 247–260 in *Arameans, Chaldeans, and Arabs in Babylonia and Palestine in the First Millennium B.C.* Edited by Angelika Berlejung and Michael P. Streck. LAS 3. Wiesbaden: Harrassowitz, 2013.
Wyatt, Nicolas. "After Death Has Us Parted: Encounters between the Living and the Dead in the Ancient Semitic World." Pages 259–292 in *The Perfumes of Seven Tamarisks: Studies in Honour of Wilfred G. E. Watson*. Edited by Gregorio del Olmo Lete, Jordi Vidal and Nicolas Wyatt. AOAT 394. Münster: Ugarit-Verlag 2012.
—. "Royal Religion in Ancient Israel." Pages 61–81 in *Religious Diversity in Ancient Israel and Judah*. Edited by Francesca Stavrakopoulou and John Barton. London: T&T Clark, 2010.
Yadin, Yigael, and Hannah Cotton. *The Documents from the Bar Kokhba Period in the Cave of Letters: Hebrew, Aramaic and Nabatean-Aramaic Papyri*. JDS 3. Jerusalem: Israel Exploration Society, 2002.
Yardeni, Ada. "Maritime Trade and Royal Accountancy in an Erased Customs Account from 475 B.C.E. on the Aḥiqar Scroll from Elephantine." *BASOR* 293 (1994): 67–78.

Yaron, Reuven. *Introduction to the Law of the Aramaic Papyri*. Oxford: Clarendon, 1961.

Zadok, Ran. *The Jews in Babylonia During the Chaldean and Achaemenian Periods: According to the Babylonian Sources*. SHJPLIMS 3. Haifa: University of Haifa, 1979.

Zangenberg, Jürgen K. "The Sanctuary on Mount Gerizim. Observations on the Results of 20 Years of Excavation." Pages 399–418 in *Temple Building and Temple Cult: Architecture and Cultic Paraphernalia of Temples in the Levant (2.–1. Mill. B.C.E.): Proceedings of a Conference on the Occasion of the 50th Anniversary of the Institute of Biblical Archaeology at the University of Tübingen (28–30 May 2010)*. Edited by Jens Kamlah and Henrike Michelau. ADPV 41. Wiesbaden: Harrassowitz, 2012.

Zevit, Ziony. *The Religions of Ancient Israel: A Synthesis of Parallactic Approaches*. London: Continuum, 2001.

Index of Ancient Sources

Papyri, Ostraca and Tablets

Hebrew Bible/Old Testament

New Testament

Deuterocanonical Works

Old Testament Pseudepigrapha

Mishnah

Babylonian Talmud

Josephus

Classical and Ancient Christian Literature

Ancient Near Eastern and Egyptian Inscriptions and Texts

Index of Aramaic, Hebrew, Old Persian and Greek Words

Old Persian and Elamite

Greek

Index of Ancient Names, Deities and Epithets

Index of Modern Authors